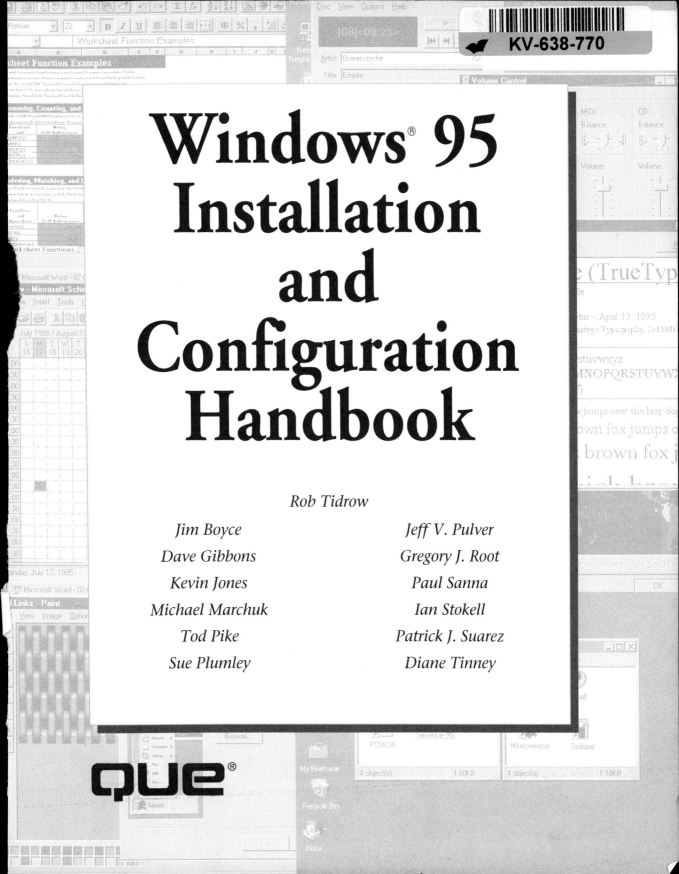

Windows® 95 Installation and Configuration Handbook

Rob Tidrow

Jim Boyce	*Jeff V. Pulver*
Dave Gibbons	*Gregory J. Root*
Kevin Jones	*Paul Sanna*
Michael Marchuk	*Ian Stokell*
Tod Pike	*Patrick J. Suarez*
Sue Plumley	*Diane Tinney*

que®

Windows 95 Installation and Configuration Handbook

Copyright© 1995 by Que® Corporation.

Library of Congress Catalog No.: 95-71470

ISBN: 0-7897-0580-x

97 96 95   6 5 4 3 2 1

Interpretation of the printing code: the rightmost double-digit number is the year of the book's printing; the rightmost single-digit number, the number of the book's printing. For example, a printing code of 95-1 shows that the first printing of the book occurred in 1995.

Screen reproductions in this book were created using Collage Plus from Inner Media, Inc., Hollis, NH.

Composed in *Stone Serif* and *MCPdigital* by Que Corporation.

Credits

President
Roland Elgey

Vice President and Publisher
Marie Butler-Knight

Associate Publisher
Don Roche, Jr.

Editorial Services Director
Elizabeth Keaffaber

Managing Editor
Michael Cunningham

Director of Marketing
Lynn E. Zingraf

Senior Series Editor
Chris Nelson

Acquisitions Editor
Deborah F. Abshier

Product Director
Lisa D. Wagner
Steve Rigney

Production Editor
Lisa M. Gebken

Editors
Geneil Breeze
Silvette Pope
Linda Seifert

Assistant Product Marketing Manager
Kim Margolius

Technical Editor and Graphics Specialist
Cari L. Skaggs

Acquisitions Coordinator
Tracy M. Williams

Operations Coordinator
Patty Brooks

Editorial Assistant
Carmen Phelps

Book Designer
Ruth Harvey

Cover Designer
Dan Armstrong

Production Team
Angela D. Bannan
Claudia Bell
Brian Buschkill
Jason Carr
Maxine Dillingham
Joan Evan
Brian Flores
Amy Gornik
Mike Henry
Darren Jackson
Daryl Kessler
Michelle Lee
Bobbi Satterfield
Andy Stone
Colleen Williams
Jody York

Indexer
Mary Jane Frisby

About the Authors

Rob Tidrow has been using computers for the past six years and has used Windows for the past four years. Tidrow is a technical writer and recently was the Manager of Product Development for New Riders Publishing, a division of Macmillan Computer Publishing. Rob is coauthor of the best-selling *Windows for Non-Nerds*, and has coauthored several other books including *Inside the World Wide Web, New Riders' Official CompuServe Yellow Pages, Inside Microsoft Office Professional, Inside WordPerfect 6 for Windows, Riding the Internet Highway,* Deluxe Edition, and the *AutoCAD Student Workbook*. Tidrow has created technical documentation and instructional programs for use in a variety of industrial settings. He has a degree in English from Indiana University. He resides in Indianapolis with his wife, Tammy, and their two boys, Adam and Wesley. You can reach him on the Internet at **rtidrow@iquest.net**.

Jim Boyce is a contributing editor and columnist for *WINDOWS Magazine*, a columnist for *CADENCE Magazine*, and the author and contributing author of over two dozen books on computers and software. You can reach Boyce at **76516,3403@compuserve.com**.

Dave Gibbons is a former technical trainer and writer for DATASTORM TECHNOLOGIES in Columbia, Mo., and LaserMaster Technologies in Eden Prairie, Minn. He began his professional writing career in chilly Cando, N.D., at age 16. Now a freelance writer and consultant, Gibbons spends much of his free time rock climbing on the Internet (**dgibbons@bigcat.missouri.edu**).

Kevin Jones has worked in the computer industry for 15 years, from large corporations such as IBM and Unisys down to very small startups. He has worked on such flagship products as dBASE III and IV, PC Tools for Windows, and Norton Navigator. Currently, he is a principal software engineer with the Peter Norton Division of Symantec Corp. He has been actively working with Windows 95 since October 1993.

Michael Marchuk has worked in the computer industry since 1979 when he started as a part-time BASIC programming instructor. Along with his bachelor's degree in finance from the University of Illinois, Marchuk has received certification as a Netware CNE and a Compaq Advanced Systems Engineer. He has designed and built an international multi-protocol wide area network for a Fortune 500 company and now serves as an integration engineer and network security chairman for a Forbes 400 corporation.

Tod Pike is a graduate of Carnegie Mellon University, where he first became familiar with the Internet. A system administrator for almost 10 years, he works daily with UNIX, UseNet, and Internet mail. He can be reached on the Internet at **tgp@cmu.edu**.

Sue Plumley owns and operates Humble Opinions, a consulting firm that offers training in popular software programs and network installation and maintenance. She is the author of 12 Que books, including *Crystal Clear DOS*, *Crystal Clear Word 6*, and *Microsoft Office Quick Reference*, and coauthor of 16 additional books, including *Using WordPerfect 6 for DOS*, *Using OS/2 2.1*, and *Using Microsoft Office*, for Que and its sister imprints.

Jeff V. Pulver has been involved in data processing for more than 25 years, with the last 15 years spent as the President of Intercomp Design, Inc., a computer consulting firm. Pulver specializes in the planning and migration of software and operating systems for mainframes and PCs. His other areas of specialty include systems programming, applications programming, documentation, re-engineering of application systems, and beta testing mainframe and PC software, including Windows 95.

Gregory J. Root started his work with computers when TRS-80s were in style and 16K of RAM was equivalent to infinity. Root has worked for Northern Trust Bank and Follett Software Company. He also has made part of his living as a computing consultant for lawyers, churches, and government agencies. Throughout his career, Root has administered and installed peer-to-peer and server-based networks, developed applications using Fortran and Visual Basic, and managed software development projects. He lives in Lake in the Hills, Ill., with his beautiful wife and lifelong companion, Tracy.

Paul Sanna is a project manager in the Development department of Hyperion Software, Inc., in Stamford, Conn. He works on the company's line of client-server financial accounting applications. Sanna has taught, tested, and developed software for the past seven years. He has contributed to *Understanding Windows 95* and *Inside Windows 95* (New Riders Publishing). Paul lives in Bethel, Conn., with his wife Andrea and three daughters: Allison, Rachel, and Victoria.

Ian Stokell is a freelance writer and editor living in the Sierra Foothills of northern California with his wife and three young children. He is also Managing Editor of *Newsbytes News Network*, an international daily newswire covering the computer and telecommunications industries. His writing career began with a 1981 article published in the UK's *New Statesman* and has since encompassed over 1,500 articles in a variety of computing and non-computing publications. He wrote the networking chapter of Que's *Using the Macintosh*, Special Edition, and has also written on assignment for such magazines as *PC World* and *MacWeek*. He is currently seeking representation for two completed novels and a screenplay.

Patrick J. Suarez is an Internet author, software developer, and lecturer. He is most noted for his "The Beginner's Guide to the Internet" series of tutorial software, books, and seminars. Suarez has a B.A. in Constitutional Law and a Master of Science in Administration degree. He is a member of the prestigious Dayton Microcomputer Association and writes a monthly column called "Internet.Talk" for the DMA newsletter, *Databus*. Mr. Suarez is an adjunct professor at Wright State University and Urbana University. He is a proponent of First Amendment cyber-rights and can be reached at **pat@bgi.com**.

Diane Tinney is proprietor of The Software Professional, a business that provides education, development support, and consulting on a variety of Windows 3.x , Windows 95, and Windows NT applications. Tinney specializes in the integration of Windows products, and specifically, database design and implementation. She is the author of Que's *Paradox for Windows Programming By Example,* and is a contributing author to Que's *Killer dBASE 5.0 for Windows, Using Microsoft Office for Windows, Using Paradox for Windows,* and *Using Microsoft Office 95.* You can reach Diane via the Internet at **dtinney@ warwick.net**.

We'd Like to Hear from You!

As part of our continuing effort to produce books of the highest possible quality, Que would like to hear your comments. To stay competitive, we *really* want you, as a computer book reader and user, to let us know what you like or dislike most about this book or other Que products.

You can mail comments, ideas, or suggestions for improving future editions to the address below, or send us a fax at (317) 581-4663. For the online inclined, Macmillan Computer Publishing has a forum on CompuServe (type **GO MACMILLAN** at any prompt) through which our staff and authors are available for questions and comments. The address of our Internet site is **http://www.mcp.com** (World Wide Web). Our Web site has received critical acclaim from many reviewers—be sure to check it out.

In addition to exploring our forum, please feel free to contact me personally to discuss your opinions of this book:

CompuServe: **74404,3307**
America Online: **ldw indy**
Internet: **lwagner@que.mcp.com**

Thanks in advance—your comments will help us to continue publishing the best books available on computer topics in today's market.

Lisa D. Wagner
Product Development Specialist
Que Corporation
201 W. 103rd Street
Indianapolis, Indiana 46290
USA

Note

Although we cannot provide general technical support, we're happy to help you resolve problems you encounter related to our books, disks, or other products. If you need such assistance, please contact our Tech Support department at 800-545-5914 ext. 3833.

To order other Que or Macmillan Computer Publishing books or products, please call our Customer Service department at 800-835-3202 ext. 666.

Contents at a Glance

Appendixes

Appendixes

Contents

6 Configuring the Windows 95 Desktop, Display, and Fonts   147

7 Configuring the Taskbar and Start Button   173

Introduction

What—you didn't have problems installing Windows 95? You only experienced problems when you restarted your computer to *run* Windows 95? Don't worry. You're not alone. Most Windows 95 installation problems occur after you've installed the software, when you reboot your computer. This is when the Windows Setup program configures your computer to work with Windows 95.

Windows 95 is designed to ease installation and configuration burdens. Setting up your Windows environment has never been easier. If you're new to the world of Windows, you'll find installation very easy and simple.

So why is this book needed? In short, because nothing is perfect...including Windows. It's not that Microsoft doesn't want Windows 95 to be perfect and fit every situation perfectly. The problem is that no two computer systems are alike. In fact, chances are if you have two computers in your office or home, they have two different setups and configurations. Even if the two computers are the same make and model, they are unique and have their own idiosyncrasies. What all this means is that Windows 95 must be flexible enough to work on different configurations, yet offer a simple way to customize each individual PC.

That's where this book comes in. *Windows 95 Installation and Configuration Handbook* guides you through the entire Windows 95 installation process. You are shown how to prepare your computer before you install Windows 95, as well as how to add hardware, memory, software, and other devices after Windows 95 is up and running.

For the most part, you can use Windows 95 straight "out of the box" and get most of your work done. If you need to change a setting (called a *property* in Windows 95), you'll need to dig a little deeper into the operating system and become familiar with some of Windows 95's new configuration features. Some of these include the Add/Remove Software and Add New Hardware utilities, the Device Manager, and property sheets. You find out about all these in this book.

Who This Book Is For

This book is designed for users who need to install Windows 95 and who want to customize and reconfigure the way Windows behaves and looks. For beginning Windows users, this book includes step-by-step procedures that guide them through setting up the Windows environment. The new Help utility available in Windows 95 is a much-welcomed addition to Windows. However, not all procedures are covered in Help, and many assumptions are left up to the user to figure out. This book attempts to fill in many of those gaps.

For experienced Windows 3.x users, this book includes customization procedures and techniques to help them configure the Windows 95 environment the way they want it. In many places in this book, comparisons to how a procedure or step was performed in Windows 3.x are included. This helps the experienced user become comfortable with Windows 95 more quickly.

Who This Book Is Not For

Any user of Windows 95 who wants to install new hardware, add software, or reconfigure the Windows 95 environment should appreciate this book. If you need a tutorial of the way in which Windows 95 works, however, you may find this book not meeting your need. Although some chapters give basic overviews of how a feature works, or some of the benefits of using a configuration setting versus another setting, you will need another book to learn how to use Windows 95.

Fortunately, an outstanding book is available that does just this. Que's *Special Edition Using Windows 95* is packed full of instructions, tutorials, and reference materials to help you understand and master Windows 95. If you need to learn how to use Windows 95, you may want to pick up a copy of that book.

Another audience segment that is not addressed specifically is the network administrator. Although many of the procedures and configuration instructions included help administrators troubleshoot common workstation problems, you will not find comprehensive instructions on setting up and configuring Windows 95 across a network. You can find that material in the *Windows 95 Resource Kit* available from Microsoft, or by referencing Que's *Windows 95 Connectivity*.

How to Use This Book

Use this book as you would a reference book. Unless you find your local library or bookstore lacking entertaining novels, you probably don't want to read this book from cover to cover. The best way to use this book is to look over the table of contents at the front of the book and the index in the back to find the topic you want. Turn to that chapter or section and use the instructions and discussions provided. Then close the book and start working with Windows 95.

If you have specific questions, turn to the troubleshooting sections in the book. Troubleshooting sections are provided in almost all chapters to help you solve many of the common problems associated with installing and configuring Windows 95. Appendix B, *Troubleshooting Windows 95*, is a compendium of all the troubleshooting sections from the book, plus additional troubleshooting tips and techniques that help you get up and running and keep Windows 95 functioning properly.

How This Book Is Organized

The following is a quick look at each of the chapters in this book.

Part I: Installing Windows 95

Chapter 1, "Preparing to Install Windows 95," is the place to start if you have not installed Windows 95. It shows you how to prepare your system for Windows 95, and introduces the new Windows 95 installation features.

Chapter 2, "Installing Windows 95 on a Desktop PC," is intended for readers who have prepped their machines and want to install Windows 95 using the Typical installation option during Setup. The Typical install option is designed for users who do not want to monkey around with selecting specific components to install. They just want Windows 95 to install so they can start using it.

Chapter 3, "Installing Windows 95 on a Laptop PC," is for users who have mobile computers and want to install only those files and programs that are necessary for laptop computers. Windows 95 includes some new components that enable mobile users to transfer files back and forth between the mobile computer and the stationary computer. This chapter shows how to configure these options.

Chapter 4, "Using Custom Installation Options," is an overview of the different components you can select during installation. This chapter is intended for users who are comfortable with their computers and know which components they want to install.

Chapter 5, "Installing Windows 95 over a Network," is a primer for setting up Windows 95 in a networked environment. Windows 95 has built-in networking capabilities that make it a powerful operating system for the workgroup environment. This chapter starts you on the path for understanding how to configure these features.

Part II: Configuring Windows 95

Chapter 6, "Configuring the Windows 95 Desktop and Display," picks up after you have Windows 95 installed and running. Now you are ready to customize your Windows 95 environment.

Chapter 7, "Configuring the Taskbar and Start Menu," helps you modify the way the Windows 95 taskbar behaves and looks. You are shown how to add programs and files to the Start menu, which gives you one-button access to them.

Chapter 8, "Configuring Windows 95 Audio," is your guide to setting event sounds in Windows 95, setting sound volumes, and configuring MIDI sounds.

Chapter 9, "Configuring Microsoft Exchange," shows you how to set up Microsoft's new universal "inbox"—Microsoft Exchange. With Microsoft Exchange, you can send, receive, and store Microsoft Mail messages, Microsoft Fax messages, and other documents in one central place.

Chapter 10, "Configuring Microsoft Fax," shows you step-by-step how to set up Microsoft's built-in fax software—Microsoft Fax. In this chapter, you find all the Microsoft Fax options discussed, including those intended for more advanced audiences.

Chapter 11, "Configuring Windows 95 for Online Connections," shows you how to connect to the Microsoft Network, CompuServe, America Online, Prodigy, and local bulletin board systems (BBSes).

Chapter 12, "Configuring a Windows 95 Internet Connection," leads you step-by-step to setting up Windows 95 built-in support for the Internet, as well as how to use the Microsoft Plus! Companion for Windows 95.

Chapter 13, "Configuring Memory, Disks, and Devices," provides information on using system memory, modifying virtual memory, improving hard disk performance, and how to use the Device Manager.

Chapter 14, "Using Norton Desktop Utilities with Windows 95," shows you how to integrate a third-party package—Norton Utilities—to get the most out of your Windows 95 setup.

Part III: Setting Up Windows 95 for Your Software

Chapter 15, "Using DOS Software," is intended for those still using their favorite (or forced to use their least favorite) DOS software under Windows 95.

Chapter 16, "Using Windows 3.x Software," shows how to optimize Windows 95 for Windows 3.x software. Many users will have to rely on Windows 3.x applications for many months after they start using Windows 95 before Windows 95 specific applications hit the market. This chapter shows how to configure your software to perform its best under Windows 95.

Chapter 17, "Using Windows 95 Software," shows some of the Windows 95 applications available on the market and how to use Windows 95 software on the Windows 95 operating system.

Part IV: Setting Up Windows 95 for Your Hardware

Chapter 18, "Configuring Monitors and Video Cards for Windows 95," shows you how to set resolution settings, configure color palettes, and set font sizes for your monitor.

Chapter 19, "Configuring Speakers and Sound Cards," helps you set up your sound card to work with Windows 95.

Chapter 20, "Configuring MIDI Cards," is intended for those users who are adding and configuring a MIDI device to work with Windows 95.

Chapter 21, "Configuring Joysticks and Game Cards," provides information on maximizing your Windows 95 environment for games by showing how to set up joysticks and game adapters.

Chapter 22, "Configuring Mice and Other Pointing Devices," shows how to set mouse properties, troubleshoot common problems with installing pointing devices, and how to configure your pointing device to work with Windows 95.

Chapter 23, "Configuring Keyboards," is just that: how to configure a keyboard for Windows 95.

Chapter 24, "Configuring CD-ROM Drives," may become dog-eared from use if you upgrade or add a CD-ROM to your system. This chapter shows you how to install and set up a CD-ROM to work with Windows 95.

Chapter 25, "Configuring Floppy Disk Drives," leads you through adding a floppy drive to your system, and includes troubleshooting topics that help you configure your floppy drive for Windows 95.

Chapter 26, "Configuring Hard Disk Drives," is similar to Chapter 25, but is written for hard disk drives. You also learn how to partition and prepare a new hard drive to use with Windows 95.

Chapter 27, "Configuring Backup Systems," shows you how to install a backup system to work with Windows 95. Although you may not use a tape backup system, DAT system, or other backup media, you should seriously consider adding one to your system.

Chapter 28, "Configuring Modems," should be used in conjunction with the earlier chapters on setting up online and Internet connections, configuring Microsoft Exchange, and installing Microsoft Fax. You'll need to configure your modem before you start any of those other configurations.

Chapter 29, "Configuring Printers," helps you install a printer for a single computer as well as for a networked PC. The Add Printer Wizard makes installation a breeze, but you may have some problems that this chapter can help you correct.

Chapter 30, "Configuring Scanners and Digital Cameras," shows how to set up scanners to work with Windows 95.

Chapter 31, "Configuring Network Hardware," shows how to configure network adapters, install network cables, configure Microsoft Fax for a workgroup environment, and how to share CD-ROMs on a network using Windows 95.

Part V: Appendixes

Appendix A, "Installing and Using Microsoft Plus! Companion for Windows 95," leads you through installing the Microsoft Plus! Companion software for Windows 95.

Appendix B, "Troubleshooting Windows 95," gathers all the troubleshooting notes from the book and organizes them into one handy reference. This appendix also includes several additional troubleshooting items not included in the rest of the book. Use this appendix to isolate and correct a specific installation or configuration problem you are having.

Using the Bonus Disk

The CD-ROM included in this book contains a variety of software programs developed for Windows 95. The software includes productivity tools, animated cursors and icons, Windows 95 shell replacements, and a few entertainment packages. Appendix C gives a brief explanation of each application and lists the files you need to install or run the application.

Obtaining Additional Windows 95 Information

This book was written during the beta releases of Windows 95 and checked against the final release of Windows 95. Because of changes that occur each time a piece of software appears on the market, software manufacturers sometimes include small changes in their software without announcement. Some changes that appear in release versions after the initial distribution of Windows 95 may not be reflected in this manuscript. For that reason, you should read any text files or directions that come with your Windows 95 disks or CD-ROM. Files named README.DOC, README.TXT, and similar names may contain late-breaking changes in the software that can help answer some of your problems.

Other valuable sources of information include Microsoft's Internet FTP site (**ftp.microsoft.com**) and World Wide Web site (**http://www.microsoft. com**). You can find some technical support documents and updated drivers for some hardware devices at those sites.

Conventions Found in This Book

You find four visual aids that help you on your Windows 95 installation journey: **Notes**, **Tips**, **Cautions**, and **Troubleshootings**.

> **Note**
>
> This paragraph format indicates additional information that may help you avoid problems or that should be considered in using the described features.

> **Tip**
>
> This paragraph format suggests easier or alternative methods of executing a procedure.

> **Caution**
>
> This paragraph format warns the reader of hazardous procedures (for example, activities that delete files).

Troubleshooting

This paragraph format provides guidance on how to find solutions to common problems. Specific problems you may encounter are shown in italic. Possible solutions appear in the paragraph(s) following the problem.

Windows 95 Installation and Configuration Handbook uses margin cross-references to help you access related information in other parts of the book. Right-facing triangles point you to related information in later chapters. Left-facing triangles point you to information in previous chapters.

Windows 95 enables you to use both the keyboard and the mouse to select menu and dialog box items. You can press a letter, or you can select an item by clicking it with the mouse. Letters you press to activate menus, choose commands in menus, and select options in dialog boxes are underlined: File, Open.

Names of dialog boxes and dialog box options are written with initial capital letters. Messages that appear on-screen are printed in a special font: Document 1. New terms are introduced in *italic* type. Text that you are to type appears in **boldface**.

The following example shows typical command sequences:

Open the File menu and choose Copy, or press Ctrl+Ins.

Chapter 1

Preparing to Install Windows 95

by Rob Tidrow

Installing Windows 95 is not tricky, but it can be frustrating at times. You'll notice two things about Windows 95 when you start installing it. First, you need to decide if you want to keep your previous operating system, such as Microsoft Windows 3.11, installed. Second, you need to be patient. The Windows 95 installation process can take some time to install completely. To begin, you should set aside 30 to 60 minutes to install Windows 95. If you need to prepare your hard disk or decide to customize the setup, don't be surprised if you invest two or more hours to ensure everything is properly set up.

This chapter is your guide to preparing for the Windows 95 installation. You don't actually install Windows 95 in this chapter, but you do gain helpful suggestions and pre-install tips that make the installation process go more smoothly. In this chapter, you learn about the following:

- What's new in Windows 95 setup

- Requirements of Windows 95

- Features of Microsoft Plus!

- Preparations for Windows 95 installation

- Installation options

- Boot configuration options

What's New with Windows 95 Setup

Windows 95 is a new operating system, and with it comes a new installation process. Many of the options and customization procedures that users had to perform with older versions of Windows after they installed Windows are now included during setup. Some of these procedures include configuring hardware devices, networking components, and online connections. The following is a list of improved areas over previous versions of Windows setup:

■ Use of installation wizards to guide and interact with users. Novice and beginning users benefit from the easy-to-understand instructions Windows 95 offers them. Advanced users have the capability to select and modify options during setup.

■ Automatic detection of hardware during setup provides users the freedom from configuring all their hardware devices after the setup stage.

■ Introduction of Plug-and-Play technology to help facilitate hardware setup.

■ Use of smart recovery system in case of interrupted setup process. Windows 95 knows when a previous installation has failed and returns to the point of interruption to continue setup.

■ Creation of setup log to verify system is set up properly.

■ Improved network setup, including use of batch installs across local area networks (LANs).

Two of the most obvious changes with Windows 95 are support of Plug-and-Play devices and the use of wizards during installation. These two areas are discussed in the following sections.

Plug and Play Overview

Before preparing your system to install Windows 95, you should learn about one of the most daunting tasks that users have when making system changes and updates—hardware upgrades. Users who decide to add hardware devices to their systems know how difficult it is to reconfigure their operating system and software to work correctly with the new hardware. Updating to a new operating system also requires a great deal of fiddling to get all your hardware devices working in sync. Technical support calls, visits from MIS staff, and working late nights or weekends usually are the only remedies to hardware problems. Sometimes it seems the operating system and hardware are designed NOT to work with one another.

A new specification called Plug and Play hopes to challenge problems associated with hardware upgrades and installations. As you learn in Part IV, "Setting Up Windows 95 for Your Hardware," Plug-and-Play devices soon will dominate the hardware market. Plug and Play is a hardware and software specification supported by Microsoft, Compaq, Intel, and many other manufacturers that free the user from configuring hardware components. The purpose of Plug and Play is to provide a tight integration between the operating system (Windows 95) and the hardware device, such as a sound card, CD-ROM device, or mouse. System settings, memory access, and other configuration settings are now handled by Windows 95 and the device, not by the user.

If you've upgraded your Windows 3.x system or have added hardware to it, you know the frustrations of configuring device drivers, updating INI settings, figuring out the correct IRQ and DMA channels, and determining other details of setup. Each time you upgrade your system, you have to make sure the newest device drivers are on your system to run with your software. Many times the device driver has to be obtained from the manufacturer through a technical support system or bulletin board system, such as CompuServe.

If you are a mobile user, Plug and Play is designed to solve problems associated with linking laptops to desktop computers. A new breed of computers called *docking stations* enables users to detach part of their computers and carry them as portables. When they return to the office, the portable part of the computer can be reattached to the desktop portion. With Plug-and-Play docking stations, users do not have to reboot the computer after they are reattached.

Docking stations without Plug-and-Play specifications require users to reconfigure hardware and software setups when they arrive back at the office to reattach the units. Settings such as network configurations or modem options need to be changed depending on the location or devices to which users connect. One situation, such as docking a PC at a corporate office, may call for a network to be hooked up to an Ethernet connection. Another situation, such as from a home office, may require a dial-up network connection. Plug-and-Play devices search for components to evaluate the environment in which the PC is working and determine how the hardware and software should interact.

Built in to Windows 95 installation is Plug-and-Play support. As it goes through the setup process, Windows 95 hunts down and configures any Plug-and-Play device you have on your system. You are not required to memorize IRQs and DMA settings just to get a piece of hardware working. Plug and Play takes care of all this when Windows 95 is set up.

What if you don't have a Plug-and-Play computer on which to install Windows 95? In an ideal world, you could run out and buy new hardware when you buy a new operating system. Those of us who can't afford such a luxury must rely on current systems to run Windows 95, including 80386 machines built in the early 1990s. Even if you don't have Plug-and-Play hardware—which many PC users do not—Windows 95 still locates many of your devices already set up on your system using Windows' autodetect feature. Known as *legacy hardware*, the hardware you already have installed is automatically set up when you install Windows 95.

> **Note**
>
> As a clarification, Windows 95 snoops out the hardware on your system and attempts to set it up during Setup. If Windows 95 can't figure out what to do with your hardware device and doesn't set it up during install, you can use the Add New Hardware utility in the Windows Control Panel after you have Windows 95 up and running. This utility is examined in more detail in each of the chapters in Part IV, "Setting Up Windows 95 for Your Hardware."

How Plug and Play Works

How does Plug and Play work? For the most part, you don't need to know. You can just rest comfortably knowing that it does work. Sometimes, though, you may have to troubleshoot an installation or configuration concern. For this reason, a basic understanding of the way in which Plug and Play works is in order.

A major component of Windows 95 is the inclusion of the Registry. The *Registry* is a centralized database of your system settings. The Registry is a hierarchical structure that stores text or binary value information to maintain all of the configuration parameters that were stored in INI files in Windows 3.x (see fig. 1.1).

One role of the Registry is to enable the Plug-and-Play system components to access the hardware-specific information. As new hardware devices are added to your system, Windows 95 checks your Registry settings for hardware resource allocations, such as IRQs, I/O addresses, and DMA channels, and determines the settings for the new hardware device. With Plug-and-Play devices, all of these configuration settings are performed at the software level, not the hardware level as before. This (virtually) eliminates the need to adjust settings on the hardware itself prior to installation. You can install the hardware and let Windows 95 do the rest.

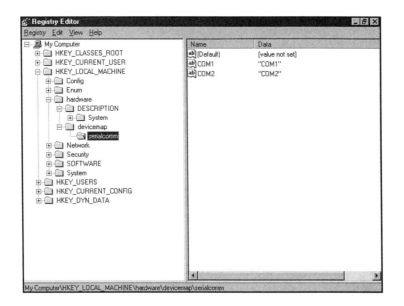

Fig. 1.1
Plug and Play relies on the Windows 95 Registry to determine system information.

> **Note**
>
> After you install Windows 95, you can access the Registry by opening the REGEDIT.EXE application in your Windows 95 main directory.

You activate Plug and Play in one of four ways. The first way is during the Windows 95 installation process. As you learn in Chapter 2, "Installing Windows 95 on a Desktop PC," you are prompted as to whether you want Windows 95 to automatically detect hardware devices during setup, shown in figure 1.2. If you answer Yes, the Plug-and-Play feature sniffs out and attempts to set up your hardware.

The second way in which Plug and Play is activated is when you start the Add New Hardware Wizard in the Windows 95 Control Panel. Again, Windows 95 (see fig. 1.3) asks if you want it to automatically detect your hardware. If you know you have a Plug-and-Play compatible device, your best bet is to answer Yes. Otherwise, you can click No and specify the device type and manufacturer.

▶ See "Analyzing Your Computer," p. 50

The third way is during the normal boot process of Windows 95. As Windows 95 boots, it builds the Registry databases (USER.DAT and SYSTEM.DAT) according to the user information and system information on your computer. If the boot-up process locates a new device—for instance, a sound card— the Plug-and-Play system sets it up. On hardware devices that are not

Plug-and-Play compatible, Windows 95 reports that a new device has been detected and that the Add New Hardware Wizard should be run to configure it.

Fig. 1.2
During installation, Windows 95 asks if you want the Plug-and-Play feature to set up your hardware.

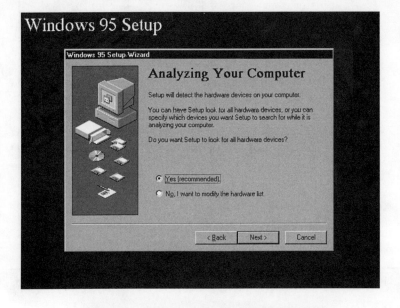

Fig. 1.3
The Add New Hardware Wizard uses Plug-and-Play features to set up hardware.

A fourth way to initiate the Plug-and-Play feature is during a warm or hot docking situation. *Hot docking* refers to inserting a computer in a docking station while the computer is running at full power. (You also can *undock* a computer, or remove a computer from a docking station.) *Warm docking* refers to docking or undocking a computer while it is in *suspended mode*, a state in which the computer is "put to sleep" but not shut off completely. Laptop or portable computers that include a Plug-and-Play BIOS (Basic Input/Output System) and are part of a docking station PC can be hot or warm docked and undocked.

Benefits of Plug and Play

Regardless of your user level, you probably don't like spending large chunks of your time pulling cards out of your system to reset DIP switches or IRQ settings. You probably dread installing SCSI (Small Computer System Interface) devices because of the inevitable software/hardware/operating system incompatibilities that always seem to crop up during hardware installations. In short, you hate adding hardware to your system.

As defined, Plug and Play is intended to let users buy hardware, unwrap it, "plug" it into the system, and begin working. Specifically, Plug and Play addresses the following benefits to users:

■ *Compatibility with older hardware.* As Windows 95's Plug-and-Play system detects hardware on your system, it checks the Registry for device information. Non-Plug-and-Play devices normally cannot be reconfigured through software settings, so they take precedence over Plug-and-Play devices when resources such as IRQ lines and DMA channels are allocated. The purpose of this action is to enable your older hardware to coexist with newer, Plug-and-Play-specific hardware.

Some older hardware devices, including the Microsoft Sound System, are software-configurable, so Windows 95 should not have a difficult time setting them up. Many users have found Windows 95 friendlier than Windows 3.x during the hardware setup stage. Part of this is due to the Registry settings and how it allocates system settings automatically.

■ *Easier PC management and support.* MIS support staff, system administrators, power users, and users with above average computer skills can breathe a sigh of relief. Problems typically associated with installing hardware diminish when Plug and Play manages the system setup. Device driver setup, jumper settings, and IRQ conflicts are not an issue with Plug-and-Play devices. Cost savings for large corporations can be realized when upgrading systems is not a support nightmare requiring hundreds of hours of upgrade and maintenance time.

■ *Universal device driver development.* The number of new device drivers available weekly is impossible to keep track of. As hardware devices are upgraded and improved (and grow older), device drivers are upgraded, making the older ones obsolete. Sometimes, the device drivers that worked fine with one application do not work well or at all with a maintenance release of the software. You are required to find a new and improved device driver to get your system working normally again.

With Plug and Play, this will begin to be a thing of the past with the support of a new proposed standard known as the *universal driver model*. In Windows 3.1, printer drivers were based on this model, but no other hardware components were. Under Windows 95, however, hardware vendors can write device drivers under the universal driver model for the following devices, making device drive updates obsolete:

Communication devices

Display devices

Input devices, such as mice

Disk devices

Availability of Plug-and-Play Devices

Currently, only a handful of Plug-and-Play devices are available on the market. Many OEMs (Original Equipment Manufacturers) are providing Plug-and-Play BIOSs (Basic Input/Output Systems) on new PCs. Over the course of several months after the release of Windows 95, market pressure and user feedback should help drive the need for more Plug-and-Play hardware components on the market. If you don't have a Plug-and-Play device now, chances are you will by this time next year if you upgrade your system or purchase a new one.

Installation Wizards

Probably the most significant new feature to Windows 95's setup process is the use of wizards. If you are a user of Microsoft Word or Access, you probably encounter wizards on a daily or weekly basis. *Wizards* are on-screen guides that walk users through a particular process, such as installing Windows 95 (see fig. 1.4) or adding a modem to your system.

Fig. 1.4
Wizards offer a great deal of help during the installation stage.

Two features of wizards set them apart from normal installation programs:

- They generate questions for the user that are straightforward and intended to be non-intimidating.

- They are designed so that users can press a button and return to the previous screen if necessary. This feature is handy if users are confused or want to change an installation option before Windows 95 installs onto their system.

Wizards are intended to help all users, not just beginners. More advanced users who feel comfortable setting configuration parameters are given opportunities in some wizards to manually set up devices. The Modem Wizard, for instance, enables users to select the modem name and manufacturer from a list (see fig. 1.5). Many users, however, opt for Windows 95 to automatically determine and set up their modem or other hardware device. If Windows 95 cannot detect their modem, then users can manually configure the device by following on-screen instructions that help guide them through the process.

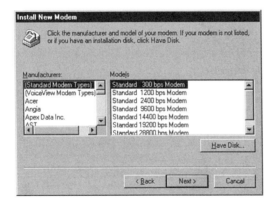

Fig. 1.5
The Modem Wizard enables you to select the name and manufacturer of the modem.

During the Windows 95 installation process, you are presented with numerous wizards that help you get through the installation. Some wizard screens only provide information (see fig. 1.6), while others require you to choose an option or configuration setting (see fig. 1.7).

Wizards have three buttons along the bottom of the screen that provide navigation. They are as follows:

- *Next*. Presents the user with the next step in the wizard. Next is the default button on many wizard screens and can be activated by clicking it or by pressing Enter.

■ *Back*. Sends the user back one screen or step. Use this button if you want to change a setting or reread the previous step. Most wizards let you back up as far as you want in the wizard.

■ *Cancel*. Exits the wizard without performing any actions or making system changes.

Fig. 1.6
Installation wizards can include information screens that simply inform users or warn them against potential hazards.

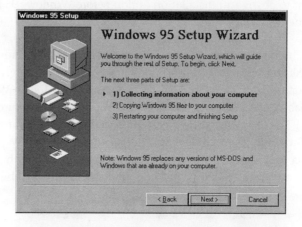

Fig. 1.7
Many wizard screens require users to interact with the wizard and fill in or select specific information as it pertains to their system.

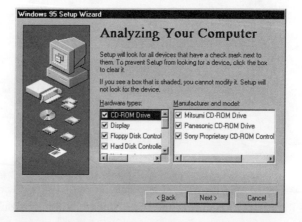

Note

Depending on the wizard and the application you are in, the screen may have a Help button. Use the Help button to obtain online help for that screen or function.

Requirements of Windows 95

One of the primary differences between Windows 95 and previous versions of Windows is its system robustness. Some of the improvements in this area include enhanced resource cleanup after an application has crashed, support of long file names (file names up to 255 characters long), preemptive multitasking for 32-bit applications, and better memory management. With all of these features, plus many more not included here, you need a robust computer that can handle Windows 95.

Specific requirements for installing Windows 95 are addressed in this section. These requirements include the following:

- Operating system
- PC system
- Hard drive setup

Operating System Requirements

First you'll need to make sure your current PC has an operating system to install Windows 95. The recommended choice is to have Windows 3.x or Windows for Workgroups installed. Windows 95 is designed to upgrade these systems.

If you do not have Windows 3.x or Windows for Workgroups, you must have MS-DOS 3.2 or higher installed. If your primary operating system is Windows NT or IBM OS/2, you still are required to have DOS installed in a bootable partition. You cannot install Windows 95 straight from OS/2 or NT.

Note

If your system has a version of DOS but not MS-DOS 3.2 or higher, make sure it can exceed the 32M partition limit, which Windows 95 supports. Some OEM versions of DOS do not meet this standard. Check your system manuals to make sure your version of DOS does. If you do not know what version of DOS you have, type **VER** at the command prompt for this information.

Troubleshooting

Can I set up Windows 95 to dual boot with Windows NT?

Yes, but you must install Windows 95 in a separate directory than Windows NT and have a FAT partition on the hard disk. When you start your PC, select the MS-DOS option from the Windows NT OS Loader menu to boot Windows 95.

System Requirements

A PC that currently runs Windows 3.1 or 3.11 without many performance problems should have few problems running Windows 95. A good way to judge your PC against one that will perform well with Windows 95 is to open three to four applications and check the system resources. You can do this by choosing Help, About Microsoft Windows in the Windows 3.x Program Manager (see fig. 1.8)

Fig. 1.8
Run a few
Windows 3.x
applications to
test your PC's
performance prior
to installing
Windows 95.

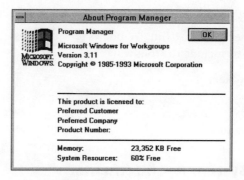

If you can run three to four applications simultaneously and keep the system resources above 50 percent, you should find your system adequate for Windows 95.

Table 1.1 lists the Microsoft minimum system requirements. Table 1.2 lists the recommended requirements.

Table 1.1 Microsoft's Minimum System Requirements	
Component	**Requirement of Windows 95**
Processor	80386 or higher
Hard drive	30M of free disk space for a compact installation; 40M for a typical installation
Memory	4M
Input device	Mouse
Floppy disk	Required for installation from floppy disks
CD-ROM drive	Required for installation from CD
Monitor	VGA
Fax/modem	Required to use Microsoft Network, Remote Access, HyperTerminal (included in Windows 95), Microsoft Fax, and Phone Dialer

Caution

Although Windows 95 is a powerful operating system, it is designed only for Intel x86-based processors. Windows 95 also does not support multiple processors, as does Windows NT.

Another processor limitation you need to be aware of is that Windows 95 cannot install on a 386-based B-step processor. A B-step processor has an ID of 0303, which can be determined from your system documentation or by using a utility such as Microsoft Diagnostics from MD-DOS. Type **MSD** from the DOS command line to start the Microsoft Diagnostics program and check in the CPU settings for the ID of your processor.

Table 1.2   Recommended System Requirements

Component	Recommended for Windows 95
Processor	80486/33 or Pentium
Hard drive	50M of free disk space, particularly if you want to install the Microsoft Plus! pack
Memory	8M minimum; 16M recommended for running four or more applications
Input device	Mouse
CD-ROM drive	Double-speed or quad-speed for multimedia applications
Monitor	Super VGA
Fax/modem	14.4bps; 28.8bps for Internet connectivity

Tip

The recommended hard disk space in table 1.2 does not take into consideration the disk space requirement for installing or reinstalling applications to run under Windows 95. For those requirements, refer to the documentation that comes with the specific application you plan to install.

Also, if you install the Microsoft Exchange client, you need at least 4.6M of hard disk space on top of what Windows uses. If you install Microsoft Fax, The Microsoft Network, and the Microsoft Mail client, you need another 12M of hard disk space. You also need at least 8M of RAM to run Exchange and Microsoft Fax. The Microsoft Network also demands a large amount of memory. You should have at least 8M minimum, and 16M is recommended.

▶ See "The First
Step: Adding a
Network Con-
figuration,"
p. 300

If your budget allows for a system upgrade or replacement, try to settle for nothing less than a Pentium processor, 16M of RAM, 500M+ hard disk, and a quad-speed CD-ROM. You also should look for a system that includes Plug-and-Play devices or a Plug-and-Play BIOS.

You must decide if you want to install Windows 95 on top of your existing Windows 3.x installation. If you choose to install a new directory to preserve your old setup, you must reinstall all your applications to work with Windows 95. (Some applications may run under Windows 95 without reinstalling them, so you might want to try them before reinstalling them.) This means that each must occupy space again on your hard disk if you plan to use the same application under Windows 3.x and Windows 95. For this reason, a hard disk with lots of free space is necessary.

Troubleshooting

What happens to my AUTOEXEC.BAT and CONFIG.SYS files when I install Windows 95 on my system?

Windows 95 creates its own AUTOEXEC.BAT and CONFIG.SYS files and renames your existing ones. When Windows 95 loads, it renames the DOS version of the files to `AUTOEXEC.DOS` and `CONFIG.DOS`. When the regular DOS/Windows 3.x loads, the Windows 95 files are renamed `AUTOEXEC.W40` and `CONFIG.W40`.

Hard Drive Requirements

Aside from sheer volume, your hard drive needs to be prepared to handle Windows 95. "Preparing for Installation" later in this chapter shows you how to optimize your hard disk before you install Windows 95. This section discusses partitioned drives and compressed drives.

Partitioned Drives

Many users use partitioned drives to organize files (to get around the 512-file, single-root directory limitation) or to install another operating system on the same hard disk. To install Windows 95, you must have a file allocation table (FAT) partition on your hard disk. Windows 95 includes new 32-bit, protected-mode enhanced FAT system that enables long file names (file names with more than eight plus three characters) and exclusive access to disk devices, such as ScanDisk. Windows 95 does not support HPFS (High Performance Files System) or NTFS (NT File System) partitions. As you install Windows 95, the setup routine writes information to the master boot record and reads most partitioning schemes, such as those set up by FDISK in MS-DOS.

> **Note**
>
> FAT is the 16-bit standard file system used by MS-DOS, OS/2, and Windows NT and allows only eight plus three character file names.
>
> HPFS is a UNIX-style file system that OS/2 and Windows NT can access. HPFS allows file names to be 256 characters long. DOS applications cannot access HPFS files unless DOS is running under OS/2 or Windows NT.
>
> NTFS is the Windows NT file system that allows 256 character file names and is accessible by Windows NT and OS/2.

Windows 95 installs over existing MS-DOS FAT partitions as long as you have enough space in the partition for Windows 95. You also need at least 5M for the Windows 95 swap file. Partitions set up by third-party schemes, including Disk Manager DMDRVR.BIN and Storage Dimensions SpeedStor SSTOR.SYS are also recognized by Windows 95.

> **Tip**
>
> If you use FDISK to partition removable drives, such as Bernoulli Drives, you shouldn't have a problem with Windows 95 accessing them.

If you have IBM OS/2 installed on your system, you must have MS-DOS installed as well to install Windows 95. Windows 95 must run from MS-DOS if OS/2 is in your primary partition, which usually is the case when running OS/2 to take advantage of the OS/2 dual-boot feature.

As indicated earlier, Windows 95 does not recognize the NTFS system that can be set up for Windows NT. If you are running NTFS, you can install Windows 95 on a FAT partition if enough disk space is present and you use NT's multiple-boot feature to boot into Windows 95. If you do not have a FAT partition established, set up one and then perform the Windows 95 installation.

> **Caution**
>
> If you want to delete disk partitions on your hard disk prior to installing Windows 95, do so with caution. You may want to delete a partition to free up disk space or if you no longer need a particular partition. Make sure you have all critical data backed up and secure before deleting the partition. Keep in mind that during the partitioning stage, you will lose all the data on the hard disk and will need to reload MS-DOS on your hard drive before you can run the Windows 95 Setup.

Troubleshooting

Do I have to be an advanced user to run Windows 95 Setup?

If you are comfortable installing Windows 3.x applications, you should be able to run the Setup program without a problem. You should, however, know the kinds of hardware devices that are installed in your computer and make sure you have prepared your computer for installation, as discussed throughout this entire chapter.

What type of performance hit do I get when I run Windows 95 Setup from MS-DOS?

If you run Setup from MS-DOS and it detects Windows 3.x on your system, it recommends that you quit Setup and run it from within Windows 3.x. If you choose to run Setup from DOS, all your devices may not be detected and Setup may run slower, especially if you are installing from floppy disks.

You can use the DOS-based FDISK command to delete partitions before creating a new primary partition. You must delete partitions in the following order:

- Any non-DOS partitions

- Any logical drives in the extended DOS partition

- Any extended DOS partition

- The existing primary DOS partition

To delete a partition or logical drive, follow these steps:

1. In the FDISK Options screen, type **3**, and then press Enter. The Delete DOS Partition Or Logical DOS Drive screen appears.

▶ See "Partition-ing a Hard Drive," p. 549

2. Press the number as shown on the screen for the kind of partition you want to delete, and then press Enter.

3. Follow the directions on the screen, and repeat the steps for deleting any additional logical drives or partitions.

Tip

If FDISK cannot delete a non-DOS partition, quit FDISK, delete the non-DOS partition by using the software used to create it, and then restart FDISK.

Compressed Drives

Another hard disk situation you may encounter is the use of compression applications to increase the virtual size of your hard disk. Most compression software, such as Microsoft DriveSpace or DoubleSpace, is supported by Windows 95. One point to keep in mind before you start Windows 95 Setup is to make sure you have enough free space on an uncompressed drive for a swap file. Swap files, which Windows 95 uses, can be set up on compressed drives only if you use the DriveSpace utility provided with Microsoft Plus! for Windows. If you do not have this utility, you must set up your swap file on an uncompressed drive.

Note

A Windows *swap file* is a special file on your hard disk that is used by Windows to store files temporarily as you work. Swap files also are known as *virtual memory* because they "virtually" increase the amount of storage area where information can be stored during a Windows operation. The information stored in swap files is lost when you leave Windows.

As a rule of thumb, you need 14M of memory on your system. To figure this amount, add the amount of physical memory you have to the amount of virtual memory you have (this is your swap file size). This gives you your total system memory. If you have 4M of memory in your system, for example, you need a swap file that is at least 10M. Free up that amount of uncompressed disk space before running Windows 95 Setup. Even if you have more than 14M of RAM on your system, you should set aside at least 5M of uncompressed disk space for a swap file in case you ever need it.

Note

For information on freeing up uncompressed disk space, consult your DOS documentation or the documentation that comes with your compression software. You also can pick up a copy of Que's *Special Edition Using MS-DOS 6.2* for coverage of compressed disks.

Windows 95 includes built-in support for Microsoft DriveSpace and is compatible with DoubleSpace, both of which are provided with MS-DOS 6.x. Windows 95 compression uses a 32-bit virtual device driver to give it better performance over the 16-bit product available in MS-DOS 6.x. The 32-bit driver also frees up conventional memory so MS-DOS-based applications can use it. If you currently use DoubleSpace or DriveSpace with DOS 6.x or with

I

Installing Windows 95

Windows 3.x, you do not need to make changes to the compressed volume file (CVF) that these applications are currently using. Except for freeing up enough space for a swap file, as pointed out earlier, you do not have to change any settings or instruct Windows 95 to install over the compressed drive. It does it automatically.

Using Microsoft Plus!

Microsoft Plus! for Windows 95 is a companion software package for Windows 95. Plus! is designed to enhance the look and performance of Windows 95-based computers and also includes an Internet connection application, the Internet Jumpstart Kit. Plus! is a CD-ROM package that users must buy separately from Windows 95. It is not included with the price of Windows 95.

Plus! includes several utilities to help you optimize and customize the look and feel of your Windows 95 configuration. Plus! consists of System Agent technology and disk utilities that help you keep your computer running at peak performance. It also contains Desktop Themes that incorporate sounds, fonts, color schemes, wallpaper, screen savers, photo-realistic icons, and animated cursors to improve the looks of your computer. The Internet Jumpstart Kit provides easy sign-up and one-button access to the Internet. It also includes a version of NCSA Mosaic by Spyglass, Inc. that enables you to use the World Wide Web (see fig. 1.9).

Fig. 1.9
Surf the Web with the Microsoft Plus! Internet Jumpstart Kit.

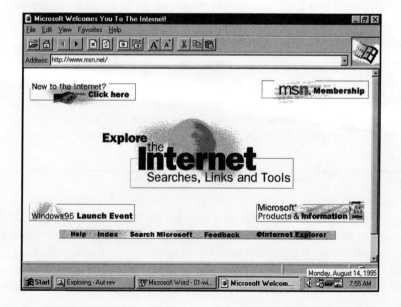

Plus! System Agent and Disk Utilities

The Microsoft Plus! System Agent and disk tools automate PC maintenance, making it faster and easier to keep a computer optimized for performance. Plus! disk utilities are designed to automatically service your computer so that you don't have to think about it. Included with the Plus! software are the following utilities:

■ *DriveSpace 3*. This is an enhanced version of the DriveSpace disk compression that ships with Windows 95. DriveSpace 3 supports large compressed volumes (up to 2G) and greater compression ratios.

■ *Compression Agent*. As a companion application to DriveSpace 3, the Compression Agent is an intelligent offline compression utility that automatically chooses the most appropriate compression algorithm for each file on your system. When used with the System Agent, the Compression Agent enables you to automatically compress data when your computer is not in use but still turned on (such as when you attend a meeting or go to lunch).

■ *System Agent*. This is a "smart" assistant that works in the background to keep your system optimized for top performance (see fig. 1.10). While the system is idle, the System Agent works with the disk utilities to compress data to free up hard disk space and to clean up the hard disk, correcting any disk errors and defragmenting the hard disk. You also can configure the System Agent to automatically back up your files.

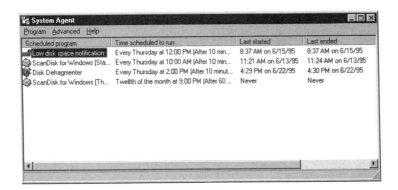

Fig. 1.10
The System Agent in Plus! helps keep your computer running at peak performance.

Microsoft Plus! Desktop Themes

The Desktop Themes bundled with Windows 95 are painfully drab, to say the least. These include themes such as Pumpkin, Eggplant, and Dessert. With the Plus! package, however, you can dress up and animate your desktop with eye-catching and interesting items. The Plus! Desktop Themes provide sounds, fonts, color schemes, wallpaper, screen savers, photo-realistic icons, and animated cursors. To hear the Desktop Theme sounds, you'll need an audio device and speakers in your system.

Each Desktop Theme sets more than 75 different desktop parameters for Windows 95, using a common theme to guide the choice of selections. The following list specifies the Desktop Themes included in Plus!:

Travel	Dangerous Creatures
Nature	Sports
Mystery	The Golden Era
The 60s USA	Inside Your PC
Leonardo da Vinci	More Windows
Science	Windows 95

An example of the background wallpaper for the Mystery Theme is shown in figure 1.11.

Fig. 1.11
The Mystery Desktop Theme is included with Plus!. Notice the bat icon for the mouse pointer in the Preview box.

Additional Plus! Features

Plus! includes Multimedia Pinball, a game that takes advantage of built-in multimedia support in Windows 95 to look, sound, and play like an authentic pinball game. Another feature of Plus! is a full-window drag and font smoothing utility. With full-window drag, windows are dragged as solid blocks rather than outlines. Font smoothing is performed using anti-aliasing techniques and *hinting* of fonts, making them smoother and easier to read.

▶ See "Working with Desktop Themes," p. 665

Internet Jumpstart Kit

The Plus! Internet Jumpstart Kit provides easy sign-up and one-button access to the Internet through The Microsoft Network. The Internet Jumpstart Kit includes a setup wizard to help you sign up with an Internet service provider. The Internet Explorer is Microsoft's Windows 95-based World Wide Web browser, which is a version of NCSA's popular Mosaic software. You also get an Internet mail reader for the Windows 95 Exchange mail client.

System Requirements for Plus!

Microsoft Plus! requires a Windows 95-based PC with a minimum of a 486 processor and 8M of RAM. Depending on which Desktop Themes you install, hard disk requirements vary from 25M to 40M on top of the disk space requirement for Windows 95. You also need a display that can handle at least 256 colors, such as an 8- or 16-bit video card. A sound card is recommended for Desktop Themes and Multimedia Pinball. A modem or LAN-based connection is required to access the Internet using the Internet Jumpstart Kit.

▶ See "Setting up a Microsoft Network Connection," p. 276

> **Tip**
>
> If you use the DriveSpace 3 compression driver, you need approximately 113K of conventional memory, which may affect DOS programs running in real mode. It should not affect applications you run under Windows 95.

Preparing for Installation

You'll find that the Windows 95 installation process goes much smoother if you do a few pre-setup tasks before you launch Windows 95 Setup. You should keep in mind that installing Windows 95 is a major upgrade to your computer. If you decide to do so, you can use Windows 95 to totally replace your existing operating system, such as DOS or Windows 3.x. This section describes many of the preliminary tasks you should do before installing Windows 95 to your system.

▶ See "Installing Microsoft Plus!," p. 658

Back Up System Files

One of the most overlooked areas of computing is backup procedures. You may be one of those lucky users who are connected to a local area network and the system administrator takes care of all your backup needs. Or, you may have been victim to a system crash in the past, so you now regularly run a system-wide backup every day.

If you are like many other users, you don't take the time to back up your data and only think about it when you lose some critical data. Before you run Windows 95 installation, however, back up all the files that you don't want to lose. It is better to assume that you will lose something as opposed to thinking you won't.

> ### Tip
>
> Besides backing up your system, you should also create a boot disk of your current system. A *boot disk* enables you to boot your system from a floppy disk in case you have a major problem during the Windows 95 installation process.
>
> To create a boot disk in Windows 3.x, place a floppy disk in the floppy drive from which your system boots, which usually is drive A. Next, in Windows File Manager choose <u>D</u>isk, <u>M</u>ake System Disk, and select the <u>M</u>ake System Disk check box. Click OK. Store this disk in a safe place and don't copy over it.
>
> In DOS you can make a system disk by using the Format command, such as **FORMAT A:/S**.

As a place to start, you should back up the files shown in the following list. Back up these files onto a tape backup system, recordable CD-ROM, network backup system, floppy disks, or other backup media. Do not back them up to your local hard disk if that's where you are installing Windows 95. You may encounter data loss at some point and may not be able to access your local drive.

- *AUTOEXEC.BAT*. As Windows 95 installs, it modifies your current AUTOEXEC.BAT file to include Windows 95-specific instructions. If a problem occurs during the Windows 95 install process, you may need to reboot into your old configuration. Having a backup of AUTOEXEC.BAT will speed up this process. You can find this file in your root directory.

- *CONFIG.SYS*. As with the AUTOEXEC.BAT file, Windows 95 modifies CONFIG.SYS during installation. A backup copy of it will save you time and headaches if you need to restore your original system. This file is found in your root directory.

- *INI Files*. If you currently run Windows 3.x, you need to make sure all your INI files are backed up. Not all INI files are stored in the same directory, so you'll need to look for them. A quick way to locate all your INI files is to run a search for ***.INI** in Windows File Manager.

- *Personal Documents*. Often overlooked during backup procedures, your personal documents, such as memos, spreadsheets, drawings, and so on, should be backed up. Any templates that you have customized should be backed up as well. In short, anything you don't want to spend time re-creating needs to be backed up.

- *Group Files*. Group files tell Windows 3.x what to display in groups in Program Manager. Group files, denoted as GRP, are in the WINDOWS directory. You can use GRP files to populate the Start menu in Windows 95.

- *Network Files*. Although Windows 95 has built-in networking support, many installations will rely on their existing network setups. Check with your system administrator to find out the files associated with the network that you should back up.

Turn Off TSRs and Time-Out Features

During the Windows 95 installation process, your system may appear at times to pause or stop working. During these times, Windows 95 is preparing system files and checking your existing system configuration. For this reason, if you have power-down features, such as those in laptops, turn off these features so that the installation process is not terminated prematurely.

You also should disable *TSR programs* (terminate-and-stay programs) and screen savers that may turn on during the install process. You need to clear out all but the necessary device drivers and batch files from memory. You can do this by remarking out (using the REMlabel) appropriate lines in your AUTOEXEC.BAT and CONFIG.SYS files (after you've backed them up, of course). Do not, however, delete settings for the following drivers: network drivers, CD-ROMs, video cards, and the mouse. You can remark out lines by starting the DOS EDIT utility, opening the appropriate file, such as AUTOEXEC.BAT, and inserting the word **REM** in front of the line you want to disable. Save the file and restart your machine for these settings to take place.

> **Caution**
>
> Do not turn off TSRs that are used for partitions or hard disk control or you may encounter problems booting your computer into the primary disk partition.

Delete the Windows Swap File

In the "Compressed Drives" section earlier in the chapter, you read that Windows 95 uses a swap file. Windows 3.x uses a temporary or permanent swap file, but Windows 95 uses a dynamic swap file. A *dynamic swap file* changes as needed by the system. Your old permanent swap file is no longer needed by Windows 95, so you can remove it for added hard disk space.

> **Caution**
>
> Before removing your permanent swap file, make sure to read the section "Determining Your Boot Configuration" later in this chapter. Here you learn that Windows 95 enables you to boot into Windows 3.x and Windows 95, if you desire. If you choose to have both operating systems on your computer, DO NOT delete the swap file from your system. You'll still need it for Windows 3.x to run.

Defragment and Check Your Hard Disk

After you back up and delete files from your hard disk, you should run a disk defragment utility to clean up your hard drive. When you run a disk defragment utility, the hard disk reorganizes files so that you get optimal performance from the drive. As you use your computer—copying, deleting, and creating files—your hard disk becomes fragmented, increasing the disk-access time. A disk defragment utility cleans up your disk and eliminates fragmented files.

Microsoft DOS 6.0 and higher includes a disk defragment utility called Defrag. To run it, exit Windows 3.x and type **DEFRAG** at the DOS prompt. Follow the instructions on-screen to optimize your hard drive. Other programs, such as Norton Utilities and PC Tools, include defragment programs as well.

During the Windows 95 installation process, Windows 95 automatically runs ScanDisk to check your drive. ScanDisk is another disk defragment utility included with Windows 95 Setup. The problem with Windows 95 running ScanDisk during installation is that if you have a problem that ScanDisk cannot fix (which occurs many times), you may have trouble cleaning up the problem in DOS. The reason is because during the initial part of the Windows 95 install (even before ScanDisk is executed), long file names are created on your hard drive. If ScanDisk reports a hard disk error it cannot fix, the Windows 95 install stops and you are returned to your old Windows 3.x or DOS setup. Then, when you try to run a disk defragment utility such as DEFRAG, to correct the problem ScanDisk found, you get an error when the software encounters the long file names that Windows 95 placed there. You have to delete those files manually if this occurs. The best solution is to defragment your hard disk before starting the Windows 95 installation process.

Another utility you should run is CHKDSK. Run CHKDSK /F from the DOS prompt to analyze and fix any surface-level problems with your hard disk. If CHKDSK encounters errors or bad files, it prompts you if you want CHKDSK to fix them or leave them for you to fix. You should let CHKDSK fix them in most cases.

Installation Options

Windows 95 provides you with several different installation options from which to choose. Depending on the configuration of your system, you have the following setup options:

- Install Windows 95 from DOS

- Upgrade Windows 3.x to Windows 95

- Choose from Custom, Typical, Portable, or Compact install

- Install Windows 95 from across a local area network

- Create a customized and automated installation

- Maintain or update an installation

The following sections briefly describe the installation options.

Installing from MS-DOS

If you do not have Windows 3.x installed on your system, you can install Windows 95 from DOS. Windows 95 first installs a mini-version of Windows on your system. The Windows 95 Setup program that runs is a 16-bit, Windows-based application, so it needs to use these files to execute. You cannot run install from an MS-DOS prompt from within Windows 3.x.

▶ See "Performing a Server-Based Install," p. 121

▶ See "Starting Windows 95 Setup from Windows 3.x," p. 40

> **Note**
>
> Windows 95 comes in two versions: an upgrade version and a full version. The up-grade version is used when you are upgrading from an existing version of Windows 3.x. If you only have DOS installed, you need to purchase the full version.

In cases where you do not have MS-DOS installed, such as upgrading from OS/2 or NT, you need to install DOS on partition and run the Windows 95 Setup program from the DOS partition.

Upgrading Windows 3.x to Windows 95

The preferred installation method is to install Windows 95 from Windows 3.x. When you do this, Windows 95 migrates your SYSTEM.INI, WIN.INI, and PROTOCOL.INI configuration settings and your Windows 3.x Registry associations into the Windows 95 Registry. The Registry entries in your Windows 3.x configuration are file and program associations. You need to preserve these to make your applications work under Windows 95.

Another conversion that takes place during the Windows 95 setup is that of Windows 3.x Program Manager to Windows 95 *folders*. Folders in Windows 95 have replaced program groups. You access program folders from the Start button in Windows 95.

By default, Windows 95 installs over your existing Windows 3.x. When this occurs, applications installed are automatically updated. If, however, you decide to keep your existing Windows 3.x setup, you need to reinstall all your applications under Windows 95. For more information see the section "Determining Your Boot Configuration" later in this chapter.

Choosing the Install Type

As you read Chapters 2 through 5, you can choose from four installation types: Typical, Custom, Portable, or Compact. Each of these gives you the flexibility you need to configure your computer as you like it to be set up.

The Typical Setup is designed for the average computer user who does not want to interact a great deal with the Setup routine. A Typical install performs most installation steps automatically and only asks the user to confirm the folder where Windows 95 files are installed, provide user identification and computer information, and if the user wants a startup disk created.

Caution

Do not select the Typical Setup option if you want to use the dual-boot feature. The Typical option installs the files over the default directory, which is your old Windows 3.x directory. Use the Custom installation to change the directory in which the files are installed.

Custom Setup enables you to choose many of the installation options offered by Windows 95, such as application settings, network settings, and device configurations. You also can specify the directory in which Windows 95 is installed. If you are an experienced user, use this setting to get more control over the type of utilities and applications that Windows 95 installs. In the Custom Setup, for instance, you can choose the type of applets that Windows 95 installs. In the Typical Setup, you do not have this flexibility.

The Portable Setup is designed particularly for mobile users with laptop computers. Windows 95 installs the Briefcase application and the software for direct cable connections to other computers. Briefcase is a Windows 95 application used to synchronize files that you transfer between your mobile computer and your stationary one. The Direct Cable Connections option enables you to link one computer to another through your parallel or serial ports.

If you have limited disk space on your computer, select the Compact Setup option. This Setup option installs only those files necessary to run Windows 95, which ranges from 10M to 30M of hard disk space.

How do you know which is the best Setup option for you? Table 1.3 lists the files that install during different installation procedures.

Note

You can change many of the options included during the Custom Setup. For instance, if you want to install the Windows Calculator but not the Character Map (both classified as Accessories), you can make these changes during the installation stage.

Table 1.3 Files Installed During Windows 95 Setup				
File Type	**Typical**	**Custom**	**Portable**	**Compact**
Accessories	Yes	Yes	No	No
Backup	Yes	Yes	No	No
Bitmaps	Yes	Yes	Yes	No
Briefcase	No	No	Yes	No
Compression Utilities	Yes	Yes	Yes	Yes
Dial-Up Networking	Yes	Yes	Yes	No
Direct Cable Connection	Yes	Yes	Yes	No
Games	Yes	Yes	No	No
HyperTerminal	Yes	Yes	Yes	No
Multimedia Files	Yes	Yes	Yes	No
Maintenance Tools	Yes	Yes	Yes	Yes
Paint	Yes	Yes	No	No
Screen Savers	Yes	Yes	Yes	No
Windows 95 Tour	Yes	Yes	No	No
WordPad	Yes	Yes	No	No

The following items also are available, but must be selected during the installation process or added after setup:

- Internet Mail Service (you must acquire Microsoft Plus! to obtain this service)
- Microsoft Exchange
- Microsoft Fax
- The Microsoft Network
- Network Administration Tools
- Online User's Guide

Maintain or Update an Installation

If you encounter an error during setup, you can use the Safe Recovery option, which runs automatically if the Setup Wizard detects a previously unsuccessful installation. Safe Recovery skips over the problem that was previously encountered and continues with the installation.

Windows 95 gives you several ways in which to update your installation after it is installed. The applications you use to add, remove, or configure Windows 95 are part of the Control Panel options and are usually wizards. This means users of all levels can feel comfortable adding components such as printers, modems, and other options to their configurations.

This list summarizes these applications and enables you to do the following:

- *Add/Remove Programs*. Install options that you didn't install during the Setup procedure. You also can create a startup disk from this wizard.

- *Add New Hardware*. Install new hardware by starting the application. This wizard walks you through installing hardware device drivers.

- *Display*. Install and configure display drivers.

- *Printer*. Install and configure printers.

- *Modem*. Install and configure modems.

- *Fonts*. Add and remove fonts from your system. You also can view a sample of the font.

- *Mouse*. Configure and set up a new mouse.

- *Network*. Install and configure network components on your system.

Determining Your Boot Configuration

The dual-boot feature of Windows 95 enables you to keep Windows 3.x (actually, the previous version of MS-DOS) intact so you can boot into it. You may want to keep Windows 3.x on your system if a particular application is known not to work under Windows 95, such as Ocean Isle's Reachout for Windows 3.1. Another reason to keep Windows 3.x on your machine is in case you have problems with Windows 95 installing properly. In situations where Windows 95 does not work, you can boot into Windows 3.x and fix the problem or totally remove Windows 95 and restart the installation. This is much easier and quicker than rebuilding your computer system from the ground up.

Installing Windows 95

Dual boots work by displaying a message on your screen during the boot process. When you see the message `Starting Windows`, you can press F4 to bypass the Windows 95 boot-up and boot into your old version of DOS. From DOS, you then can start Windows 3.x.❖

Chapter 2

Installing Windows 95 on a Desktop PC

by Rob Tidrow

You learned in Chapter 1, "Preparing to Install Windows 95," that there are steps you take to prepare your machine for Windows 95. After your machine has gone through these preparations, you are ready to start installing Windows 95. This chapter shows you how to install Windows 95 using the Typical install option you read about in Chapter 1. You are not shown how to customize your setup options in this chapter.

In this chapter, you learn how to

- Start Windows 95 Setup

- Specify the Windows 95 folder

- Create a Windows 95 startup disk

- Select online connection options

- Test your Windows 95 installation

Using Windows 95 Setup

After you prepare your computer for Windows 95, you can start the Windows 95 Setup program. Setup is located on the Windows 95 installation disks or CD-ROM. The Windows 95 Setup program uses a Setup Wizard that displays many dialog boxes and useful prompts to help you install Windows 95 on your system.

> **Note**
>
> You'll find valuable information contained in various text files (such as README.TXT and SETUP.TXT) on the Windows 95 CD-ROM or installation disks. Read these files for information that may pertain to your specific system hardware or software.

Taking Your System's Inventory

Before you start Setup, make a note of the following items on your system:

- Video card and monitor type
- Mouse type
- Network configuration, including network operating system (such as NetWare 3.12), protocol supported (such as TCP/IP), and mapped drive specifications (such as H)
- Printer type and port
- Modem type
- CD-ROM
- SCSI adapter, if installed
- Identification number of your Windows 95 disks or CD
- Other devices, including sound cards, scanners, and joystick

> **Note**
>
> The easiest way to determine your network configuration settings is to ask your system administrator for them.

Starting Windows 95 Setup from Windows 3.x

You are ready to start the Windows 95 Setup program and install Windows 95. If you do not have Windows 3.x installed, you need to install Windows 95 from DOS. For details on running Setup from DOS, see the next section, "Starting Windows 95 Setup from DOS." Use these steps to install Windows 95 from Windows 3.x:

1. Start your computer and run Windows 3.x. Make sure all applications are closed before running Setup.

2. For installation from floppy disk, insert the disk labeled Disk #1 in the floppy drive. If you are installing from CD-ROM, place the CD-ROM in the CD drive.

3. From Program Manager, choose File, Run. In the Run dialog box, type the letter of the drive containing the disk or CD-ROM, a colon, a backslash (\), and the command **SETUP** (see fig. 2.1). The following command, for example, starts Setup from a floppy drive labeled A:

   A:\SETUP

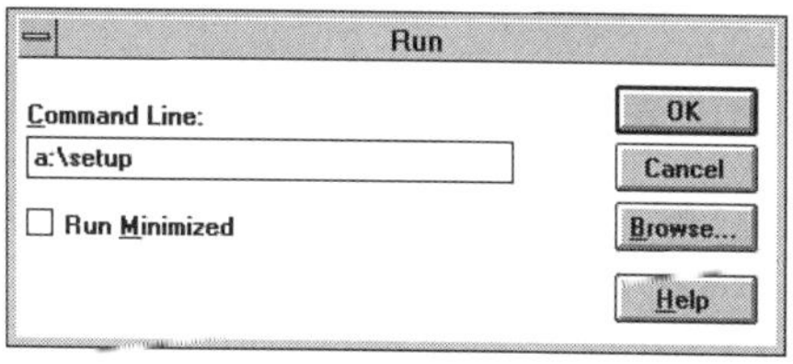

Fig. 2.1
From the Run dialog box in Windows 3.x, you can start the Windows 95 Setup program.

4. Click OK. Setup starts and the Windows 95 Installation Wizard initializes and begins installing Windows 95. See the section "Collecting Setup Information" for the next step in the Windows 95 installation process.

Starting Windows 95 Setup from DOS

To start Windows 95 Setup from DOS, use the following steps:

1. Start your computer.

2. For installation from floppy disk, insert the disk labeled Disk #1 in the floppy drive. If you are installing from CD-ROM, place the CD-ROM in the CD drive.

3. At the DOS command prompt, type the letter of the drive that contains the setup disks, a backslash (\), and the command **SETUP** (see fig. 2.2). The following command, for instance, starts Windows 95 Setup from a floppy disk labeled A:

   C:\A:\SETUP

4. Press Enter. Setup starts and the Windows 95 Installation Wizard initializes and begins installing Windows 95.

Fig. 2.2
You can start
Windows 95 Setup
from the DOS
prompt using the
SETUP command.

Using Special Setup Switches

Windows 95 Setup is designed to be used by any level user. No system, however, can satisfy every user's needs and special configurations. Windows 95
includes command-line switches to control the installation process. To use
these switches, add them to the end of the SETUP command line, such as the
following:

    A:\SETUP /?

The preceding switch tells Windows 95 Setup to display help on using the
command-line switches.

The following describes each of the switches you can type to customize the
Setup procedure:

- **/?**. Displays help on using Setup switches. Shows syntax of each switch.

- **/ih**. Instructs Setup to run ScanDisk in the foreground so that you can
  see the results. Use this switch if the system stalls during the ScanDisk
  check or if an error results.

- **/nostart**. Directs Setup to copy only the required Windows 3.x DLL
  (Dynamic Link Library) used by Windows 95 Setup. After Setup copies
  these files, it exits to DOS without installing Windows 95.

- **/iL**. Instructs Setup to load the Logitech mouse driver, if you have a
  Logitech Series C mouse.

- **/iq**. Directs Setup to bypass the ScanDisk quick check when running
  Setup from DOS. Use this switch if you use compression software other
  than DriveSpace or DoubleSpace.

■ **/is**. Directs Setup to bypass the ScanDisk quick check when running Setup from Windows 3.x. Use this switch if you use compression software other than DriveSpace or DoubleSpace.

■ *script_file*. Directs Setup to use custom script files you create to automatically install Windows 95.

■ **/d**. Directs Setup not to use your existing version of Windows 3.x during the first part of Setup. Use /d when you experience problems with Setup that are due to Windows 3.x files missing or damaged.

■ **/C**. Directs Windows 95 Setup not to load the SmartDrive disk cache.

■ **/id**. Directs Setup to bypass the checking of required minimum disk space to install Windows 95. Use this switch if a previous install of Windows 95 failed but Setup began copying files to your hard disk. This way, you do not get an "Out of Disk Space" error during your next attempt of running Setup.

■ **/t:***tempdir*. Specifies the directory in which Setup is to copy its temporary files. This directory must already exist, but any existing files in the directory are deleted after Setup finishes installing Windows 95.

Collecting Setup Information

After you start Setup, a Welcome screen appears (see fig. 2.3), telling you that Windows 95 is ready to start installing Windows 95 and that the process may take 30 to 60 minutes to complete. Click OK.

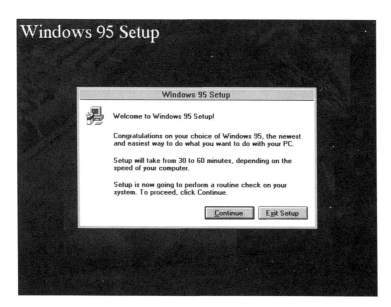

Fig. 2.3
The initial Windows 95 Setup screen tells you how long it typically takes to install Windows 95.

Windows 95 Setup automatically gathers most of the information it needs during the installation process. Some of the items you need to provide manually include the directory name in which to install Windows 95 and the type of Setup you want to perform. Windows 95 by default installs into your current directory of Windows 3.x if it is installed, but you can change this directory if you want to run Windows 95 and your current Windows 3.x installation.

> **Tip**
>
> Press F3 or, if available, the Cancel button to exit Setup anytime.

Use the following steps to continue installing Windows 95:

1. Click Continue on the Setup Welcome screen. Windows 95 checks your system (see fig. 2.4) for available disk space, possible hard disk problems, and other system setting information.

Fig. 2.4

When you first start installing Windows 95, Setup checks your system for hard disk problems and disk space.

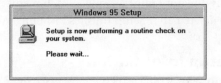

> **Caution**
>
> If Setup detects a problem with your system, such as a hard disk problem, an error message appears. Be sure to read the message and perform the recommended actions. Click OK to leave Windows 95 Setup and return to DOS or Windows 3.x. Setup does not let you continue with the installation process if an error is found.

2. If Setup does not detect a problem during its routine check, it begins the next stage of the installation process automatically. This stage prepares the Setup Wizard, which guides you through the rest of the installation.

3. After the Setup Wizard starts, the Windows 95 Software License Agreement appears, as shown in figure 2.5. Read the license agreement and click Yes if you accept the terms of the agreement. If you do not accept the terms, click No and Setup exits, ending the installation process. You must accept the terms of the agreement to install Windows 95.

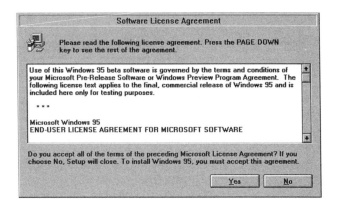

Fig. 2.5
Read and accept
the terms of the
Software License
Agreement to
continue installing
Windows 95.

Installing Windows 95

As mentioned earlier, you should close all applications before running Setup.
If you do not, a warning message appears advising you to do so (see fig. 2.6).

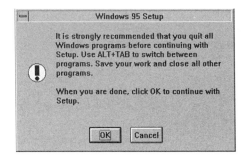

Fig. 2.6
In case you have
another Windows
application
running, Setup
displays a message
telling you to exit
from it before
continuing with
the installation.

To close any application, follow these steps:

1. Press Alt+Tab to task switch to the open application.

2. Use that application's menu to close it.

3. Continue until all applications are closed. Do not close Program Manager.

4. Click OK when you are ready to continue with Setup.

Starting the Windows 95 Setup Wizard

The Windows 95 Setup Wizard appears on-screen. This is your hands-on
guide to installing Windows 95 on your system. The wizard screen (see
fig. 2.7) lists the three major parts of the Windows 95 setup procedure:

■ Collecting information about your computer

■ Copying Windows 95 files to your computer

■ Restarting your computer and finishing setup

Fig. 2.7
The Setup Wizard helps you navigate through the Windows 95 installation process.

Each of these parts is described in the following sections.

Click Next to advance to the next wizard screen. Click Cancel to exit Setup.

Tip

Click Back any time to return to the previous wizard step.

The Choose Directory screen appears (see fig. 2.8). This is where you must decide to keep or install over a previous version of Windows or DOS. To install over your current version of Windows, select the C:\WINDOWS option and click Next. The directory in which your current version of Windows is installed may differ from the one shown in the figure 2.8.

Fig. 2.8
You can tell Windows 95 to install into a new directory, or copy over your previous version.

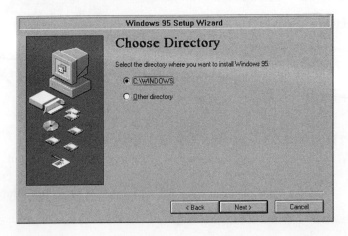

If you want to install Windows 95 into a separate directory and keep your previous version of Windows 3.x, select the Other Directory radio button; click Next.

> **Note**
>
> You need to decide if you want to install Windows 95 over your existing version of Windows. If you decide to keep both versions of Windows on your machine, then you need to reinstall all your applications under Windows 95. The advantage is that you have a fail-safe mechanism if Windows 95 does not work properly on your machine. You can move back to Windows 3.x immediately. Once you test out your new Windows 95 installation, delete your old Windows 3.x files, including the applications installed under Windows 3.x.
>
> On the other hand, if you install over your previous version of Windows, your applications work as soon as you install Windows 95. Also, you do not need as much free disk space to start Windows 95 Setup when upgrading.

If you choose to install Windows 95 to a separate directory, the Change Directory screen appears (see fig. 2.9). This is where you name the directory for Windows 95. Although Setup advises that only advanced users and system administrators modify this directory, you must change the directory name to retain your previous version of Windows.

Fig. 2.9
You must give a new directory name in which to install Windows 95 if you want to keep your previous version of Windows.

In the text box, type the new directory name, such as **C:\WIN95**. The new name must be unique and no more than eight characters. Click Next when this box is filled out. At this point, Setup displays a screen warning you that you must reinstall all your applications.

> **Note**
>
> If you do not choose to install to a new Windows directory, Setup bypasses the preceding step and displays the Preparing Directory screen instead.

Click Yes to continue or No to return to the Change Directory screen. The Preparing Directory screen appears. The Preparing Directory screen informs you Windows 95 is creating your new directory or preparing your existing Windows 3.x directory for Windows 95.

After the directory is prepared, the Setup Options screen appears (see fig. 2.10), in which you select the type of installation you want to perform. To setup Windows 95 on a computer that has adequate hard disk space (35M to 50M), select the Typical option. The Typical install assumes that you do not want to customize the components that Windows 95 installs. As you see in the section called "Selecting Windows Components," you can modify the options that install, although it is not necessary to do so with the Typical install type.

Fig. 2.10
From the Setup Options screen, you can select the type of installation the Windows 95 Setup program performs.

▶ See "Selecting Windows Components," p. 83

▶ See " Selecting Custom Install Options," p. 107

Click Next when you are ready.

When the User Information screen appears (see fig. 2.11), enter your name and company name. Company name is optional, but you must fill in a user name. Click Next.

Caution

As a word of caution, the name and company name you put here are permanent. You cannot change them unless you reinstall Windows 95. Don't use names that you may want to change later. Cute names grow tiresome after awhile.

The next screen, the Product Information screen, is used to input the serial number of your Windows 95 disks (see fig. 2.12). This number is unique to your disks and is used for product support and for registering your software with Microsoft Corporation. You must input this number to successfully install Windows 95.

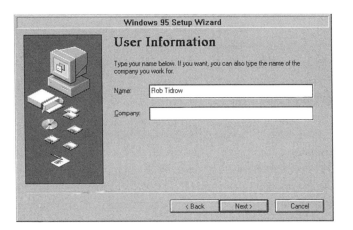

Fig. 2.11
Fill in your name and company name in the User Information screen.

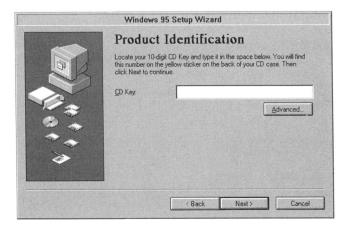

Fig. 2.12
This screen prompts you for the product identification of your Windows 95 disks or CD-ROM discs.

You find this information on your disks or on a yellow sticker on the back of your CD case. It might also be on some paperwork that came with your disks or computer. Click Next after you enter the ID.

Note

Select the Advance button on the Product Information screen if you are installing Windows 95 in a networked environment and have purchased a group license. See Chapter 5, "Installing Windows 95 over a Network," for more information.

Troubleshooting

Do I need to reinstall my programs when I install Windows 95?

Windows 95 picks up program settings when you upgrade an existing version of Windows or Windows for Workgroups. If Windows 95 is installed in a separate directory, all Windows-based programs need to be reinstalled.

Analyzing Your Computer

After you enter your Product ID, the Setup Wizard is ready to check your computer's hardware. In figure 2.13, the Analyzing Your Computer screen appears, displaying the choices from which to select specific hardware devices. Regardless of the choices shown, Windows 95 will autodetect the devices in your computer. In this example, the only choice is Network Adapter. If you have a network interface card in your system and you want Windows 95 to search for and configure it, make sure this option is selected. Depending on your system, other options may appear in this screen. Select the appropriate ones for your system.

Fig. 2.13
The Analyzing Your Computer screen shows some of the devices Windows will detect during Setup.

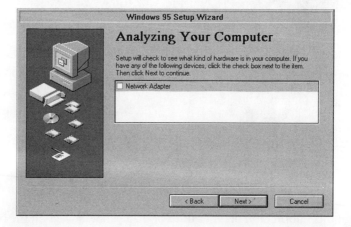

Click Next to have Windows 95 analyze your system. This process may take a few minutes to complete. Often, the on-screen progress bar (which appears at the bottom of your screen) moves rapidly through the first 90 percent of the process and then seems to quit. This is normal and you should not reboot your PC at this point. Give Setup some time to complete this part. It's a good practice to let it sit for 20 minutes before you attempt to recover your computer.

If, after a long time of inactivity (watch your hard drive light on the front of the computer for activity), your system seems to have crashed, reboot the system by turning off your computer, waiting 10 seconds, and restarting it. Start Setup again and use the Smart Recovery program, which starts automatically if Setup can salvage anything from the previous installation attempt. If Smart Recovery does not start automatically, you need to restart Setup by running SETUP.EXE from Windows 3.x or MS-DOS.

Troubleshooting

I was running Setup and my machine crashed. Do I have to run Setup from the beginning again?

The best answer for this is yes, you should restart Setup from the beginning and install all the Windows 95 files again. This is because some files may have become corrupted during the system crash. On the other hand, Windows 95 Setup includes a Smart Recovery mechanism that maintains a log file during Setup. If Setup crashes, the last entry in the Setup log identifies where Windows needs to start from to resume installation.

Getting Connected

Windows 95 provides built-in support for many electronic and online services, including e-mail (using Microsoft Mail), The Microsoft Network, and Microsoft Fax services. After the Setup Wizard analyzes your system, you need to select the types of services you would like Setup to automatically configure. You can select any combination of choices, or pick none. If you are not sure if you want to install one of these choices, you can bypass it now and install it manually after Windows 95 is installed by using Add/Remove Programs in Control Panel.

The Get Connected screen (see fig. 2.14) enables you to select the service or connection you want Setup to install automatically.

If you don't read the Setup Wizard screen for this option closely, you may overlook an important point. If you install one or more of the Get Connected options, Windows 95 automatically installs Microsoft Exchange. Exchange is Microsoft's new electronic mail and communications client that acts as a universal inbox and outbox for your e-mail and faxes.

► See "The First Step: Adding a Network Configuration," p. 300

Exchange requires 4.6M of hard disk space by itself. If you install all three Get Connected options, the total hard disk space required is over 12M. You also need at least 8M of RAM to run Exchange and Microsoft Fax. The Microsoft

Network also demands a large amount of memory. You should have at least 8M minimum and 16M recommended.

Fig. 2.14

If you want Setup to establish your Microsoft Fax, Microsoft Mail, or The Microsoft Network connections, select those choices here.

After you make your choices, click Next.

Selecting Windows Components

The Setup Wizard gives you a choice to modify the list of components to install on your system. The default setting installs the most common Windows 95 components, but you can change the list by selecting the Show Me the List of Components So I Can Choose option (see fig. 2.15).

Fig. 2.15

Although you select the Typical install type, Windows 95 Setup gives you the option of selecting components now.

For most users, the default list of components is recommended, especially if you are a new user and are not familiar with Windows 95 components, many of which are available in previous versions of Windows. If you change your mind later about an option, you can add additional components or remove any by using Add/Remove Programs in Control Panel after Windows 95 is installed. Click Next to continue with Setup. The Startup Disk screen appears.

▶ See " Understanding the Custom Install Process," p. 105

> **Note**
>
> If you're more advanced and want to choose the specific components, click the second choice from the list and click Next. The Select Components screen appears (see fig. 2.16). This screen and its options are discussed in Chapter 4, "Using Custom Installation Options."

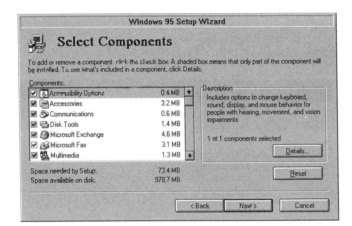

Fig. 2.16
You can select the individual components Setup installs from this screen.

Creating a Startup Disk

Setup lets you create a startup disk. Regardless of how well you think the Windows 95 Setup program is going, *always* choose to make a startup disk. The startup disk is your life preserver in case you experience problems with Windows 95 after it's installed. By taking a few minutes now and using one floppy disk, you insure yourself against potential problems.

You'll need one floppy disk to reformat when the startup disk is created. Because you will lose all the data on this disk, make sure it does not contain anything important. The floppy disk must be one for the floppy drive that your PC can boot from, which is drive A.

> **Note**
>
> Many older PCs have 5 1/4-inch floppy disk drives as drive A. Many users, however, have abandoned the use of 5 1/4-inch floppy disks. If your drive A is the 5 1/4-inch drive, you must use this size floppy disk as your startup disk. You cannot change Setup to create a startup disk on drive B.

The startup disk is a bootable floppy disk that stores several system files (more than 1.2M) on it. In case you need to use the startup disk, place it in your floppy drive and reboot your machine. You are presented with an MS-DOS command line that provides utilities and maintenance instructions to help you recover your installation. Appendix B, "Troubleshooting Windows 95," discusses how to use the startup disk in more detail.

> **Note**
>
> The startup disk has limitations. It cannot, for instance, be used to provide access to a CD-ROM device or to a network connection. You need to fix any problems associated with your installation to recover from these problems.

The files that Setup copies to the startup disk are shown in table 2.1.

Table 2.1   Startup Disk Files

Name	Description of File
ATTRIB.EXE	Sets file attributes, such as hidden and read-only
CHKDSK.EXE	Checks a disk and displays a status report
COMMAND.COM	Starts a new copy of the Windows Command Interpreter, which is the primary operating system file for MS-DOS
DEBUG.EXE	Runs Debug, a testing and editing tool program
DRVSPACE.BIN	DriveSpace disk-compression utility
EBD.SYS	Utility for the startup disk
EDIT.COM	Text editor in MS-DOS
FDISK.EXE	Configures a hard disk for use with MS-DOS
FORMAT.COM	Formats a hard disk or floppy disk for use with MS-DOS
IO.SYS	Core operating system file
MSDOS.SYS	Core operating system file
REGEDIT.EXE	Starts the Registry Editor
SCANDISK.EXE	Starts ScanDisk

Name	Description of File
SCANDISK.INI	Stores system configuration settings for ScanDisk
SYS.COM	Copies MS-DOS system files and command interpreter to a disk you specify
UNINSTAL.EXE	Starts utility for recovering deleted files

A few other files that you may want to copy to the startup disk after Windows 95 is installed include AUTOEXEC.BAT, CONFIG.SYS, WIN.INI, and SYSTEM.INI. Other INI files may also come in handy as well. These files are ones that you should already have backed up in Chapter 1, "Preparing to Install Windows 95."

To instruct Setup to create a startup disk, make sure the Yes, I Want a Startup Disk (Recommended) choice in the Startup Disk screen is selected and click Next.

Troubleshooting

I want to uninstall Windows 95 but I didn't make a startup disk. What do I do now?

You can do one of two things. The suggested choice is to make a startup disk by selecting Start, Control Panel, and double-clicking the Add/Remove Programs icon. Click the Startup Disk tab and click the Create Disk button. You need one floppy disk that works in your A: drive.

The second choice is to use the following steps:

1. Boot from an MS-DOS boot disk.

2. Enter the following at the A: prompt

   C:\WINDOWS\COMMAND\UNINSTALL.EXE

In the preceding syntax, C is the drive letter where Windows 95 is installed, and \WINDOWS is the name of your Windows 95 folder.

Copying Files

Setup has gathered enough information to begin copying files to your hard disk. In figure 2.17, Setup displays a message telling you that it is ready to start copying the files. Click Next to continue.

Fig. 2.17
The moment
you've been
waiting for! Setup
starts copying files
to your system.

Setup begins copying files to your hard disk and displays a meter showing the progress of the action. If you indicated to create a startup disk, Setup instructs you to insert this disk when the progress meter hits about 20 percent. Insert the floppy disk and click OK. After the startup disk is created, Setup displays a message telling you to remove the floppy disk from the drive. Do this now and store it in a safe place.

Tip

To exit from Setup at any time, click the Exit button or press F3. This returns you to Windows 3.x or DOS, depending on where you started Setup. If you exit Setup while Windows 95 copies files to your system, Windows 95 may or may not delete them from your system. In many cases, Windows 95 leaves the files on your system so that if you decide to restart the Setup program later, it does not have to recopy those files.

Setup continues installing Windows 95. As it's copying files, Windows displays screens describing some key features of Windows 95. Some of these are shown in figures 2.18 and 2.19.

Finishing Setup

When the Setup files finish copying onto your system, Setup begins the third and final phase of installation: Finishing Setup. This part restarts your computer and configures your hardware and software to work with Windows 95.

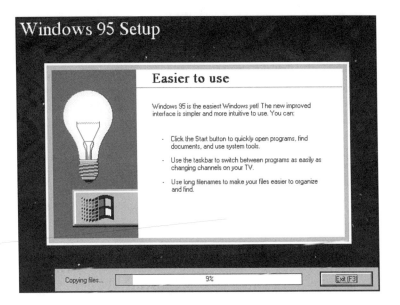

Fig. 2.18
To get a quick idea of what is in store for you with Windows 95, read the messages that flash on-screen during installation.

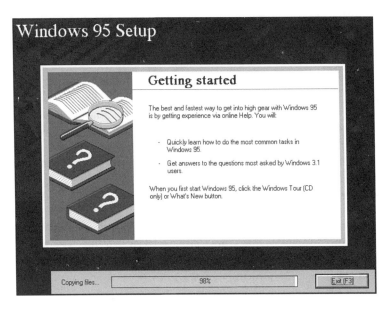

Fig. 2.19
Another helpful screen explains how to get help in Windows.

Some of the tasks that Windows 95 performs during this final stage include the following:

■ Adds a new system file (IO.SYS) to replace the old MS-DOS IO.SYS and MSDOS.SYS. These old files are renamed IO.DOS and MSDOS.DOS.

> **Note**
>
> Even though you've made it to this point in the installation process, you still are not "home free." Many installation errors occur after the Windows 95 Setup restarts your computer and starts configuring your system. One of the primary problems occurs when the Plug and Play configuration part of Windows 95 tries to locate incompatible devices. If you experience any problems during this stage, reference Appendix B, "Troubleshooting Windows 95."

- Copies SYSTEM.DAT to SYSTEM.DA0 and SYSTEM.NEW to SYSTEM.DAT. This is the primary system database that the Registry reads.

- Combines all the virtual device drivers (VxDs) to create VMM32.VXD, which is the 32-bit virtual device driver.

- Renames ARIAL.WIN, USER32.TMP, and LOGO.SYS files used by Setup.

Click Finish to finish setting up Windows 95. This last stage typically takes several minutes to complete.

> **Note**
>
> If your PC does not restart after a reasonable time, such as 20 minutes or more, reboot your system manually. You may be able to boot into Windows 95. If not, you may be able to boot into Windows 95 in Safe Mode, which you select from a menu that automatically displays during the boot process if Windows 95 cannot completely load. See Appendix B, "Troubleshooting Windows 95," if you have problems finishing this stage of Setup.

After your computer restarts and everything functions properly, Windows 95 starts and runs your AUTOEXEC.BAT and CONFIG.SYS files. You'll see the Windows 95 opening screen flash for a few seconds, and then the DOS screen appears. You'll see the following message in DOS:

```
Please wait while Setup updates your configuration files.
This may take a few minutes...
```

Configuring Run-Once Options

After the configuration files are updated, Windows 95 reappears and runs through setting Run-Once options. These options include PCMCIA and MIDI devices, printers, Time Zone, Microsoft Exchange, Windows Help, programs on the Start menu, and the Control Panel setting. Other hardware devices also can be configured at this point. A screen display lists these options as they are being set up.

Troubleshooting

I can't boot into Windows. What can I do?

Reboot your computer and press F8 to start the Startup menu in MS-DOS. Select the Safe Mode option to start Windows 95 in Safe Mode. Now you can boot into Windows and diagnose the problem. In many cases, you may have a device driver conflict. To see if you do, select Start, Settings, Control Panel, and double-click on the System icon. Click on the Device Manager tab and review the device settings listed. If you see a big red X next to a device, select it and click on the Remove button. Click OK. You'll need to reboot your machine to see if this fixes your problem. If this doesn't work, review Appendix B, "Troubleshooting Windows 95."

Many of the items on the list configure automatically, such as the Control Panel and programs on the Start menu. Some, however, require user interaction. When Setup runs the Time Zone option, for instance, you must select the time zone in which you live (see fig. 2.20). Click the list on the Time Zone tab and select your time zone. To modify the time and date, click the Date & Time tab. Click Apply to save these settings, then click Close when you are finished.

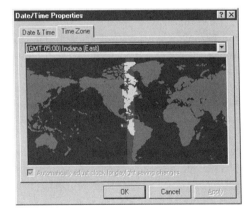

Fig. 2.20
During the Run-Once stage, you can set your time zone and the correct time and date.

Configuring Microsoft Exchange

Next, Setup configures Microsoft Exchange on your system. If you did not select a choice in the Get Connected screen earlier (see "Getting Connected" earlier in this chapter), Setup does not perform this task. You can proceed to the "Starting Windows 95" section.

Setup displays the Inbox Setup Wizard, which guides you through setting up Microsoft Exchange's universal mail inbox. This box is also used to receive e-mail and faxes, and to connect to The Microsoft Network, if you selected this option earlier. Use the following steps to configure Exchange:

1. If you've never used Exchange, choose No when the Setup Wizard asks if you have used Exchange before. Otherwise, click Yes. Click Next.

2. In the next screen, you are prompted to select the services you want to use with Exchange. The services listed include only those you select in the Get Connect screen earlier. These choices include:

   - Microsoft Mail

   - Microsoft Fax

   - Microsoft Online Network

3. By default, the items listed are selected, including the Use the Following Information Services radio button. If you want Setup to automatically configure these services (which is recommended for most users), click Next.

> **Note**
>
> If you are an advanced user, or if you need to modify the configuration of the services, select the Manually Configure Information Services option. This enables you to change, among other settings, the Exchange profile name, which by default is set as MSEXCHANGE. Any configuration setting can be changed later by using the Add/Remove Program option in Control Panel.

▶ See "Adding Exchange After Installing Windows 95," p. 206

4. When you let Setup automatically configure Exchange, the Location Information dialog box appears. This box configures the way in which your phone calls are dialed. In this box, you need to set the country in which you live, area code, any special dialing codes to get an outside number (such as 9), and the type of phone system you use, either tone or pulse. Click OK when you have this dialog box filled out.

5. The next Inbox Setup Wizard screen that appears sets up your Microsoft Fax connection, if this is one of the selections you picked earlier. You are given two choices when installing Microsoft Fax. First, you can set up Fax so that it runs from your local computer. Click the Modem Connected To My Computer option to use Fax only from your computer.

Second, you can set up Microsoft Fax so that others can share it across a network. To do this, you must connect a fax modem to a networked computer and use it as a fax server.

For this chapter, make sure the option that sets up your fax modem on a single computer is selected. Click Next.

▶ See "Setting Up a Fax Server," p. 259

Detecting a New Modem

In the Install New Modem Wizard, you need to configure your modem to work with Windows 95. Before working through the Install New Modem Wizard, make sure your fax modem is attached to your computer and that it is turned on and connected to a phone line. If you need to install an internal modem, skip over this section and finish Setup first. Then install your modem (you'll need to shut down your computer to do this) and start the Add Hardware option in Control Panel to configure the modem. Chapter 28, "Configuring Modems" guides you through setting up and configuring a modem.

If your modem is turned on and ready to be configured now, use the Install New Modem Wizard. Unless you want to select your modem manually, click Next. If you want to specify your modem type, click the Don't Detect My Modem; I Will Select It From a List option and click Next.

Installing Your Printer

After Setup establishes Exchange and other online connections, it configures the printers that are connected to your computer. If you do not want to install a printer now, you can set one up later by selecting the Printers folder after choosing Start, Settings. Double-click the Add Printer icon to start the Add Printer Wizard.

During Setup, you need to specify whether the printer is located locally or on a network. You also need to tell Windows 95 Setup the manufacturer of the printer, such as Hewlett-Packard, and the printer name, such as HP LaserJet IIIP. Click Next to have Setup install the printer drivers on your system. If Setup detects a driver from a previous installation, you can elect to keep it or use an updated one from Windows 95. Select the option and then click Next. Setup next asks if you plan to print from from MS-DOS based programs. Select Yes or No as necessary.

▶ See " Using the Add Printer Wizard," p. 606

The next screen prompts you for the port or connection to which your printer attaches. Select the appropriate connection and click Next. Windows asks you to name the printer, giving you a default name such as HP LaserJet IIIP. Keep or change this name as necessary and click Next.

Note

If you are on a network and will be printing to a network printer, you can instruct Windows 95 to print to a queue name versus a printer port.

Setup then displays a screen that asks if you want to print a test page on your printer. If your printer is set up to your machine or network, it's a good idea to do this. This way Setup can diagnose any problems you may have with your printer now. Click Finish. After your text page prints and you respond that everything is fine, tell Setup that the page printed correctly.

Congratulations! Setup is finished setting up Windows 95.

Starting Windows 95

After Setup installs Windows 95 and configures Exchange, your printer, and other options, Windows 95 starts. Figure 2.21 shows the Windows 95 Welcome screen that includes helpful suggestions for navigating Windows 95.

Tip

If you do not want to see this screen the next time you boot Windows 95, clear the Show This Welcome screen next time you start Windows option on the Welcome dialog box. To show this screen again, double-click the Welcome application in the Windows 95 folder in Windows Explorer.

Fig. 2.21
Welcome to
Windows 95!

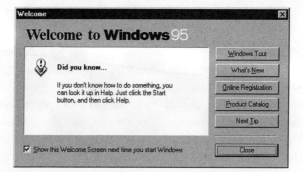

Testing Windows 95 Setup

Before you use Windows 95 for the first item, test to see if it is properly installed. Shut down Windows and restart it by clicking the Start button at the bottom of the screen (this is called the Taskbar) and select Sh<u>u</u>t Down. The Shut Down Windows dialog box appears (see fig. 2.22). Make sure the <u>S</u>hut Down the Computer? option is selected; click Yes. This begins the Windows 95 shut down procedure, which you must do whenever you want to exit Windows 95.

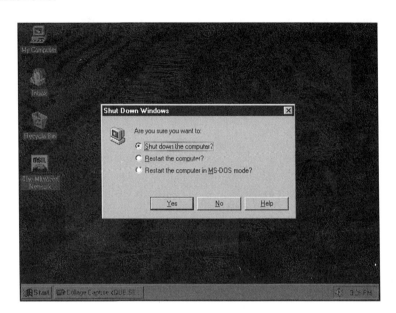

Fig. 2.22
The Shut Down utility is a new feature in Windows 95.

When a message appears on your screen telling you it's OK to turn off your machine, press the reset button on your computer. As your PC reboots, watch the screen to see if you notice any errors. If Windows 95 starts, your system probably works fine and you can start using Windows 95.

If it doesn't start or if you get a DOS screen, your setup has encountered some problems. You can start Windows 95 in Safe Mode and fix the problem.

Using Windows 95 Safe Mode

With luck, your computer starts and you have no problems running your new Windows 95 installation. Many times, however, Windows 95 encounters a problem (such as a Registry setting missing or corrupted) during startup that it cannot fix. When this happens, you need to run Windows in Safe Mode from the Startup menu. You can display the Startup menu by pressing F8 during the boot process. Press F8 when the instructions Starting Windows displays. This usually appears after your system checks the internal RAM on your system. Windows 95 also starts Safe Mode automatically if it detects a problem with the startup files.

The Startup menu has the following options from which to choose. Depending on your specific setup, you may or may not have the same settings.

- *Normal.* Enables you to start Windows 95 in its normal startup manner, loading all device drivers and Registry settings. If Windows 95 automatically displays the Startup menu, choosing this selection will probably just return you to the Startup menu. Choose this option only if you want to watch what happens on-screen during the failed startup.

- *Logged* (\BOOTLOG.TXT). Creates a file called BOOTLOG.TXT in your root directory that contains a record of the current startup process. This file is created during Setup and shows the Windows 95 components and drivers loaded and initialized, and the status of each. You can view this file in Notepad.

- *Safe Mode.* Starts Windows 95 but bypasses startup files and uses only basic system drivers. In Safe Mode, many devices in Windows 95 are not available, such as the Add New Hardware utility in Control Panel. Safe Mode is intended to diagnose and fix problems in the Windows 95 environment. You also can start Safe Mode by pressing F5 during boot-up or typing **WIN /D:M** at the command prompt.

- *Safe Mode with Network Support.* Starts Windows 95, but bypasses startup files and uses only basic system drivers, including basic networking. You can also start this option by pressing F6 or typing **WIN /D:N** at the command prompt.

- *Step-By-Step Confirmation.* Enables you to confirm each line in your startup files, including AUTOEXEC.BAT and CONFIG.SYS. Answer **Y** to lines you want to run; answer **N** to lines you want to bypass. You can also start this option by pressing F8 when the Startup menu displays.

- *Command Prompt Only.* Starts MS-DOS (Windows 95 version) with startup files and Registry settings, displaying only the MS-DOS command prompt.

- *Safe Mode Command Prompt Only.* Starts MS-DOS (Windows 95 version) in Safe Mode and displays only the command prompt, bypassing startup files. Same as pressing Shift+F5.

- *Previous Version of MS-DOS.* Starts your previous version of MS-DOS if you have a multi-boot configuration. You must install Windows 95 into a different directory during Setup for this option to be available. You also can start this option by pressing F4 during startup. This option is only available if BootMulti=1 is in the MSDOS.SYS file.

When Safe Mode is selected from the Startup menu, it bypasses startup files, including the Registry, CONFIG.SYS, AUTOEXEC.BAT, and the [Boot] and [386Enh] sections of SYSTEM.INI. Table 2.2 shows the files that the three most common Safe Mode options bypass and initiate. As the table shows, Safe Mode does not load all the Windows drivers. In fact, during Safe Mode, only the mouse, keyboard, and standard Windows VGA device drivers are loaded. If you are using other drivers, such as a Super VGA video driver, they are not available in Safe Mode.

Table 2.2   Files Loaded During Startup Menu Options

Action	Safe Mode	Safe Mode, Network Support	Command Prompt Only
Process CONFIG.SYS and AUTOEXEC.BAT	No	No	No
Process Registry information	No	Yes	No
Load COMMAND.COM	No	Yes	Yes
Run Windows 95 WIN.COM	Yes	Yes	No
Load HIMEM.SYS and IFSHLP.SYS	Yes	Yes	No
Load DoubleSpace or DriveSpace if present	Yes	Yes	(Loaded if Safe Mode Command Prompt Only option is selected)
Load all Windows drivers	No	No	No
Load network drivers	No	Yes	No
Run NETSTART.BAT	No	Yes	No

After Windows 95 starts in Safe Mode, you can access the configuration files, modify configuration settings, and then restart Windows 95 normally. If you still encounter problems, see Appendix B, "Troubleshooting Windows 95."

Using the Windows 95 Startup Disk

If you instructed Windows 95 to create a startup disk during Setup (see section "Creating a Startup Disk" earlier in this chapter), you can use it to load your previous operating system and display an MS-DOS command prompt.

The startup disk also contains utilities for troubleshooting your Windows 95 operating system. To use the Startup disk, place the disk in drive A and reboot your computer. A command prompt appears, from which you can diagnose and fix problems associated with your installation.

Note

If you did not create a startup disk during Setup, you can create one using a single floppy disk. In the Add/Remove Programs option in Control Panel, click the Startup Disk tab. Then click the Create Disk button, and follow the instructions on-screen. You should do this even if you are not having problems starting Windows 95 now. In the future, you may experience a problem that only the startup disk can remedy.

Troubleshooting

I've changed my mind. Can I uninstall Windows 95?

Yes. You can uninstall Windows 95 and return to a previously installed version of Windows 3.1 by running the Uninstall program. To uninstall Windows 95, you must select the Save System Files during Windows 95 Setup. If Windows 95 is running, use the following steps:

1. Click the Start menu, point to Settings, and then choose Control Panel.

2. Double-click the Add/Remove Programs.

3. In the Add-Remove Programs properties dialog box, click the Install/Uninstall tab.

4. In the list of software that can be removed by Windows, click Windows 95.

5. Click Add/Remove, and then follow the directions on your screen. The Uninstall program removes all long file name entries from your hard disk, and then runs an MS-DOS-based program to remove Windows 95 and restore your previous MS-DOS and Windows 3.x files.

I can't get Windows 95 to start and I want to remove it from my computer. How can I do this?

You will have to boot your computer into MS-DOS and uninstall Windows 95 from there. To uninstall Windows 95 from MS-DOS, use the following steps:

(continues)

(continued)

1. Boot from startup disk you created during setup.

2. Enter **UNINSTAL** at the A prompt.

After I uninstalled Windows 95, I still have some files left on my machine from Windows 95. Why?

These are long file names that Windows 95 installs. If you uninstall Windows 95 using a method other than uninstalling it from Windows 95, you are left with these long file names. You can remove them by running Windows 3.x File Manager and deleting them one at a time.

Chapter 3

Installing Windows 95 on a Laptop PC

by Rob Tidrow

You learned in Chapter 1, "Preparing to Install Windows 95," that you should take steps to prepare your machine for Windows 95. Chapter 2 showed you how to install Windows 95 using the Typical install option. If you have a notebook or portable PC, however, you can set up special options to take advantage of Windows 95's filesharing capabilities. This chapter walks you through installing Windows 95 on a portable computer and shows you how to configure the Briefcase and Direct Cable Connection applications that ship with Windows 95. If you followed Chapter 2's installation instructions, you do not need to read this chapter.

Windows 95 also supports PCMCIA adapters, which are common on portable computers. The end of this chapter discusses the way in which Windows 95 enables you to set up PCMCIA (Personal Computer Memory Card International Association) support for your hardware.

In this chapter, you learn how to

- Start Windows 95 Setup
- Specify the Windows 95 directory
- Instruct Setup to perform a Portable installation
- Test your Windows 95 installation
- Configure Windows 95's Direct Cable Connection feature
- Understand Windows 95's PCMCIA support

Using Windows 95 Setup

After you prepare your computer for Windows 95, you can start the Windows 95 Setup program. Setup is located on the Windows 95 installation disks or CD-ROM. The Windows 95 Setup program uses a Setup Wizard that displays many dialog boxes and useful prompts to help you install Windows 95 on your system.

> **Note**
>
> You'll find valuable information contained in various text files (such as README.TXT and SETUP.TXT) on the Microsoft Windows 95 CD-ROM or installation disks. Read these files for information that may pertain to your specific system hardware or software.

Taking Your System's Inventory

Before you start Setup, make a note of the following items on your system:

- Video card and monitor type
- Mouse type
- Network configuration, including network operating system (such as NetWare 3.12), protocol supported (such as TCP/IP), and mapped drive specifications (such as H:)
- Printer type and port
- PCMCIA adapters
- Modem type
- CD-ROM
- SCSI adapter, if installed
- Identification number of your Windows 95 disks or CD
- PCMCIA card or external network adapter model and their settings

> **Note**
>
> The easiest way to determine your network configuration settings is to ask your system administrator for them.

Starting Windows 95 Setup from Windows 3.x

You are ready to start the Windows 95 Setup program and install Windows 95. If you do not have Windows 3.x installed, you need to install Windows 95 from DOS. For details on running Setup from DOS, see the next section, "Starting Windows 95 Setup from DOS." Use these steps to install Windows 95 from Windows 3.x:

1. Start your computer and run Windows 3.x. Close all applications before running the Windows 95 Setup.

2. For installation from a floppy disk, insert the disk labeled Disk #1 in the floppy drive. If you are installing from CD-ROM, place the CD-ROM in the CD drive.

3. From Program Manager, choose File, Run. In the Run dialog box, type the letter of the drive containing the disk or CD-ROM, a colon, a backslash (\), and the command **SETUP** (see fig. 3.1). The following command, for example, starts Setup from a floppy drive labeled A:

        a:\setup

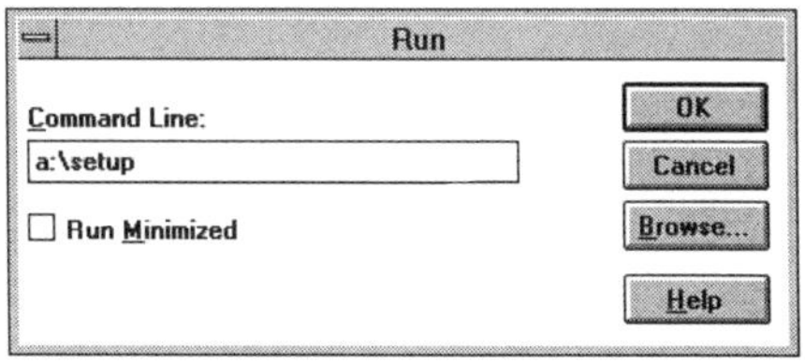

Fig. 3.1
From the Run dialog box in Windows 3.x, you can start the Windows 95 Setup program.

4. Click OK. Setup starts, and the Windows 95 Installation Wizard initializes and begins installing Windows 95. See the section "Collecting Setup Information" for the next step in the Windows 95 installation process.

Starting Windows 95 Setup from DOS

To start Windows 95 Setup from DOS, use the following steps:

1. Start your computer.

2. For installation from a floppy disk, insert the disk labeled Disk #1 in the floppy drive. If you are installing from CD-ROM, place the CD-ROM in the CD drive.

3. At the DOS command prompt, type the letter of the drive that contains the setup disks, a backslash (\), and the command **SETUP** (see fig. 3.2).

The following command, for instance, starts Windows 95 Setup from a floppy disk labeled A:

```
A:\A:\SETUP
```

Fig. 3.2
You can start Windows 95 Setup from the DOS prompt using the SETUP command.

4. Press Enter. Setup starts, and the Windows 95 Installation Wizard initializes and begins installing Windows 95.

Using Special Setup Switches

Windows 95 Setup is designed to be used by any level user, including novice, intermediate, and advanced. No system, however, can satisfy every user's needs and special configurations. Windows 95 includes command-line switches to control the installation process. To use these switches, add them to the end of the SETUP command line, such as the following:

```
A:\SETUP /?
```

The preceding switch tells Windows 95 Setup to display help on using the command-line switches.

The following describes each of the switches you can type to customize the Setup procedure:

- **/?**. Displays help on using Setup switches. Shows syntax of each switch.

- **/ih**. Instructs Setup to run ScanDisk in the foreground so that you can see the results. Use this switch if the system stalls during the ScanDisk check or if an error results.

- **/nostart**. Directs Setup to copy only the required Windows 3.x DLL (Dynamic Link Library) used by Windows 95 Setup. After Setup copies these files, it exits to DOS without installing Windows 95.

- **/iL**. Instructs Setup to load the Logitech mouse driver, if you have a Logitech Series C mouse.

- **/iq**. Directs Setup to bypass the ScanDisk quick check when running Setup from DOS. Use this switch if you use compression software other than DriveSpace or DoubleSpace.

- **/is**. Directs Setup to bypass the ScanDisk quick check when running Setup from Windows 3.x. Use this switch if you use compression software other than DriveSpace or DoubleSpace.

- *script_file*. Directs Setup to use custom script files you create to automatically install Windows 95.

- **/d**. Directs Setup not to use your existing version of Windows 3.x during the first part of Setup. You should use /d when you experience problems with Setup that are due to missing or damaged Windows 3.x files.

- **/C**. Directs Windows 95 Setup not to load the SmartDrive disk cache.

- **/id**. Directs Setup to bypass the checking of required minimum disk space to install Windows 95. Use this switch if a previous install of Windows 95 failed but Setup began copying files to your hard disk. This way, you do not get an Out of disk space error during your next attempt of running Setup.

- **/t:*tempdir***. Specifies the directory in which Setup is to copy its temporary files. This directory must already exist, but any existing files in the directory are deleted after Setup finishes installing Windows 95.

Collecting Setup Information

After you start Setup, a Welcome screen appears (see fig. 3.3), telling you that Windows 95 Setup is ready to start installing Windows 95 and that the process may take 30 to 60 minutes to complete. Click Continue

Windows 95 Setup gathers most of the information it needs automatically during the installation process. Some of the items you need to provide manually include the directory name where you need to install Windows 95 and the type of Setup you want to perform. Windows 95 by default installs into your current directory of Windows 3.x if it is installed, but you can change this directory if you want to run Windows 95 and your current Windows 3.x installation.

Fig. 3.3
The initial
Windows 95 Setup
screen tells you
how long it
typically takes
to install
Windows 95.

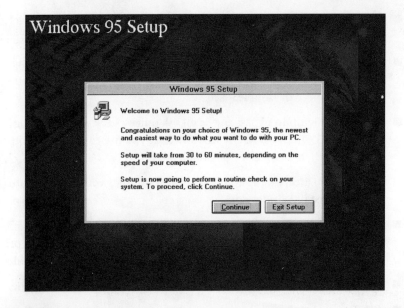

Use the following steps to continue installing Windows 95:

1. Click Continue on the Setup Welcome screen. Windows 95 checks your
   system for available disk space, possible hard disk problems, and other
   system setting information (see fig. 3.4).

Fig. 3.4
When you first
start installing
Windows 95,
Setup checks your
system for hard
disk problems and
disk space.

Note

If Setup detects a problem with your system, such as a hard disk problem, an
error message appears. Be sure to read the message and perform the recommended actions. Click OK to leave Windows 95 Setup and return to DOS or
Windows 3.x. Setup does not let you continue with the installation process if
an error is found.

2. If Setup does not detect a problem during its routine check, it begins the next stage of the installation process automatically. This stage prepares the Setup Wizard, which guides you through the rest of the installation.

3. After the Setup Wizard starts, the Windows 95 Software License Agreement appears, as shown in figure 3.5. Read the license agreement and click <u>Y</u>es if you accept the terms of the agreement. If you do not accept the terms, click <u>N</u>o and Setup exits, ending the installation process. You must accept the terms of the agreement to install Windows 95.

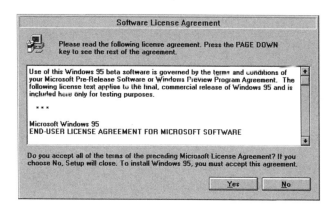

Fig. 3.5
Read and accept the terms of the Software License Agreement to continue installing Windows 95.

As mentioned earlier, you should close all applications before running Setup. If you do not, a warning message appears, advising you to do so (see fig. 3.6).

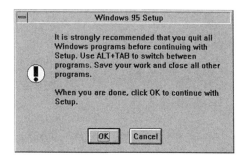

Fig. 3.6
In case you have another Windows application running, Setup displays a message telling you to exit from it before continuing with the installation.

To close any applications you may have running, follow these steps:

1. Press Alt+Tab to task switch to the open application.

2. Use that application's menu to close it.

3. Continue until all applications are closed. Do not close Program Manager.

4. Click OK when you are ready to continue with Setup.

Starting the Windows 95 Setup Wizard

The Windows 95 Setup Wizard appears on-screen (see fig. 3.7). This is your hands-on guide to installing Windows 95 on your system.

Fig. 3.7

The Setup Wizard helps you navigate through the Windows 95 installation process.

The wizard screen lists the three major parts of the Windows 95 setup procedure:

- Collecting information about your computer

- Copying Windows 95 files to your computer

- Restarting your computer and finishing setup

Each of these parts is described in the following sections.

> **Note**
>
> A note at the bottom of the wizard screen informs you that Windows 95 replaces your existing DOS and Windows versions. You can instruct Setup to install Windows 95 in a separate directory from DOS and Windows 3.x, enabling you to keep your previous version installed.

> **Tip**
>
> Click Back at any time to return to the previous wizard step, or Cancel to exit Setup.

Click Next to advance to the next wizard screen.

The Choose Directory screen appears next (see fig. 3.8). This is where you must decide to keep or install over a previous version of Windows or DOS. Make sure the C:\WINDOWS option is selected and click Next to replace Windows 3.x with Windows 95. The directory in which your current version of Windows is installed may differ from the one shown in figure 3.8.

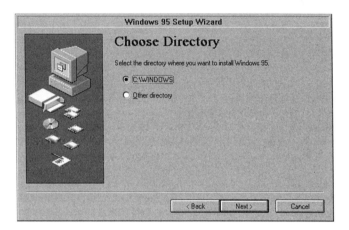

Fig. 3.8
You can tell Windows 95 to install into a new directory or copy over your previous version.

If you want to install Windows 95 into a separate directory and keep your previous version of Windows 3.x, select the Other Directory radio button and click Next.

Should You Replace Windows 3.x?

Should you install Windows 95 over your previous versions of Windows? There are advantages to both sides. If you decide to keep both versions of Windows on your machine, you need to reinstall all your applications under Windows 95. The advantage is that you have a fail-safe mechanism if Windows 95 does not work properly on your machine. You can move back to Windows 3.x immediately. Once you test your new Windows 95 installation, delete your old Windows 3.x files, including the applications installed under Windows 3.x.

On the other hand, if you install over your previous version of Windows, your applications work as soon as you install Windows 95. Also, most laptop PCs have smaller hard disks installed. When you install over your existing Windows 3.x installation, you do not need as much free disk space available to start Windows 95 Setup.

Depending on if you chose to install Windows 95 to a separate directory, the Change Directory screen appears (see fig. 3.9). This is where you name the directory for Windows 95. Although Setup advises that only advanced users and system administrators should modify this directory, you must change the directory name to retain your previous version of Windows.

Fig. 3.9
You must give a new directory name in which to install Windows 95 if you want to keep your previous version of Windows.

In the text box, type the new directory name, such as **C:\WIN95**. The new name must be unique and no more than eight characters. Click Next when this box is filled out. At this point, Setup displays a screen warning you that you must reinstall all your applications. Click Yes to continue or No to return to the Change Directory screen.

> **Note**
>
> If you did not choose to install to a new Windows directory, Setup bypasses the preceding step and displays the Preparing Directory screen instead.

The Preparing Directory screen appears next. This screen informs you that Windows 95 is creating your new directory or preparing your existing Windows 3.x directory for Windows 95.

After the directory is prepped and ready, the Setup Options screen appears (see fig. 3.10), in which you select the type of installation you want to perform. For this chapter, choose Portable. You need between 30M and 45M of hard disk space to install the Portable installation. If you decide to install Microsoft Exchange (necessary when you install Microsoft Mail, Microsoft Fax, or Microsoft Network options), you should add another 6M to your estimated disk requirements.

Fig. 3.10
To install compo-
nents for a laptop
or portable
computer, select
the Portable
option from the
Setup Options
screen.

Note

Two options that install during the Portable installation that are not discussed in
Chapter 2 are the Briefcase and Direct Cable Connection options. See "Configuring
Briefcase and Direct Cable Connection" at the end of this chapter for instructions on
configuring these options.

Click Next when you are ready.

When the User Information screen appears (see fig. 3.11), enter your name
and company name. Company name is optional, but you must fill in a user
name. Click Next.

Fig. 3.11
You must enter
your name in the
User Information
screen. Company
name is optional.

Caution

As a word of caution, the name and company name you put here are permanent. You cannot change them unless you reinstall Windows 95. Don't use names that you may want to change later. Cute names grow tiresome after awhile.

The next screen, the Product Identification screen, is used to input the serial number of your Windows 95 disks (see fig. 3.12). You input the serial number in the CD Key text box (if you are installing from floppy disks, this line will be named Disk Key). This number is unique to your disks and is used for product support and for registering your software with Microsoft Corporation. You must input this number to successfully install Windows 95.

Fig. 3.12
This screen prompts you for the product identification of your Windows 95 disks or CD-ROM discs.

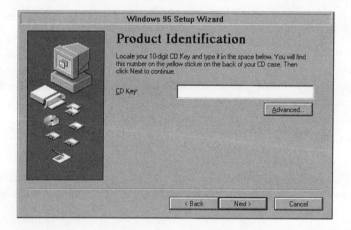

You find this information on your disks or on a yellow sticker on the back of your CD case. It might also be on some paper work that came with your disks or computer. Click Next after you enter the ID.

Note

The Advance button on the Product Identification screen is used if you are installing Windows 95 in a networked environment and have purchased a group license. See Chapter 5, "Installing Windows 95 over a Network," for more information.

Analyzing Your Computer

After you enter your Product ID, the Setup Wizard is ready to check your computer's hardware. In figure 3.13, the Analyzing Your Computer screen appears, showing the choices from which to select specific hardware devices. Regardless of the choices shown, Windows 95 autodetects the devices in your computer. In this example, the only choice is Network Adapter. If you have a network interface card in your system and you want Windows 95 to search for and configure it, make sure this option is selected. Depending on your system, other options may appear in this screen. Select the appropriate ones for your system.

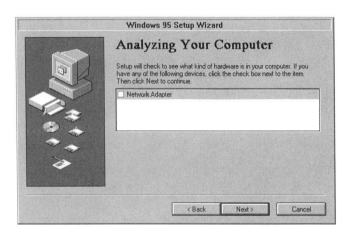

Fig. 3.13
The Analyzing Your Computer screen shows some of the devices Windows detects during Setup.

Click Next to have Windows 95 analyze your system. This process may take a few minutes to complete. You can watch the Progress bar at the bottom of the screen to see Setup's progression through the analyzing stage.

Troubleshooting

I've been watching the Progress bar, but it stopped moving. What happened?

Many times the Progress bar moves rapidly through the first 90 percent of the process and then seems to quit. This is normal, and you should not reboot your PC at this point. Give Setup some time to complete this part. It's a good practice to let it sit for 20 minutes before you attempt to recover your computer.

If, after a long time of inactivity your system seems to have crashed, reboot the system by turning off your computer, waiting 10 seconds, and restarting it. Start Setup again and use the Smart Recovery program, which starts automatically if Setup can salvage anything from the previous installation attempt. If Smart Recovery does not start automatically, you need to restart Setup by running SETUP.EXE from Windows 3.x or MS-DOS.

> **Tip**
>
> You can tell if your hard drive is active or not by watching the hard drive light on your computer. Sometimes this light is labeled HDD and is green or red. You also can put your ear close to the computer to hear whether the hard drive is spinning.

Getting Connected

Windows 95 provides built-in support for many electronic and online services, including e-mail (via Microsoft Mail), The Microsoft Network, and Microsoft Fax services. After the Setup Wizard analyzes your system, you need to select the types of services you would like Setup to automatically configure. You can select any combination of choices or pick none. If you are not sure if you want to install any of these choices, you can bypass it now and install it manually after Windows 95 is installed by using Add/Remove Programs in Control Panel.

The Get Connected screen (see fig. 3.14) enables you to select the service or connection you want Setup to install automatically.

Fig. 3.14
If you want
Setup to set up
your Microsoft
Fax, Microsoft
Mail, or The
Microsoft Network
connections, select
those choices here.

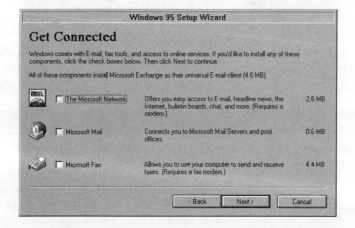

▶ See "Installing
the Exchange
Client," p. 202

If you don't read the Setup Wizard screen for this option closely, you may overlook an important point. If you install one or more of the Get Connected options, Windows 95 automatically installs Microsoft Exchange. Exchange is Microsoft's new electronic mail and communications client that acts as a universal inbox and outbox for your e-mail and faxes.

Exchange requires 4.6M of hard disk space by itself. If you install all three Get Connected options, the total hard disk space required is more than 12M.

You also need at least 8M of RAM to run Exchange and Microsoft Fax. The Microsoft Network also demands a large amount of memory. You should have at least 8M minimum, and 16M is recommended.

After you make your choices, click Next.

Selecting Windows Components

The Setup Wizard now gives you a choice to modify the list of components to install on your system. The default setting installs the most common Windows 95 components, but you can change the list by selecting the Show Me the List of Components So I Can Choose option (see fig. 3.15).

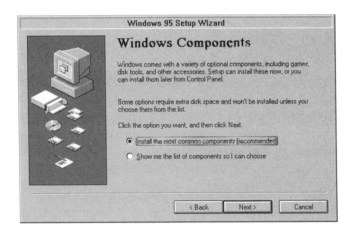

Fig. 3.15
Although you selected the Portable install type earlier, you can modify the list of components Setup installs.

For most users, the default list of components is recommended, especially if you are a new user and are not familiar with Windows 95 components, many of which are available in previous versions of Windows. If you change your mind later about an option, you can add additional components or remove any by using Add/Remove Programs in the Control Panel after Windows 95 is installed. Click Next to continue with Setup. The Startup Disk screen appears.

Note

To select specific Windows components to install, select the Show Me the List of Components So I Can Choose option and click Next. The Select Components screen appears (see fig. 3.16). This screen and its options are discussed in detail in Chapter 4, "Using Custom Installation Options."

Fig. 3.16
You can modify the list of components Setup installs from this screen.

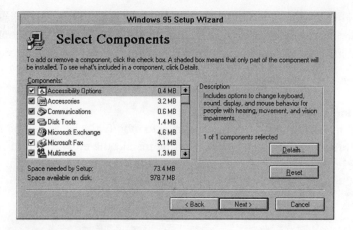

Creating a Startup Disk

Setup now gives you an opportunity to create a startup disk. The *startup disk* is a bootable floppy disk that stores several system files (more than 1.2M) on it. In case you need to use the startup disk, place it in your floppy drive and reboot your machine. You are presented with an MS-DOS command line that provides utilities and maintenance instructions to help you recover your installation. Appendix B, "Troubleshooting Windows 95," discusses how to use the startup disk in more detail.

Regardless of how well you think the Windows 95 Setup program is going, *always* choose to make a startup disk. The startup disk is your life preserver in case you experience problems with Windows 95 after it's installed. By taking a few minutes now and using one floppy disk, you insure yourself against potential problems down the road if you experience problems.

You'll need one floppy disk that can be reformatted when the startup disk is created. Because you will lose all the data on this disk, make sure it does not contain anything important. The floppy disk must be one for the floppy drive from which your PC can boot.

Tip

Add the startup disk to the collection of disks you carry in your laptop case. You never know when you will need it.

Caution

The startup disk does have some limitations. It cannot, for instance, be used to provide access to a CD-ROM device or to a network connection. You need to clean up any problems associated with your installation to recover from these problems.

The files Setup copies to the startup disk are shown in table 3.1.

Table 3.1   Startup Disk Files

Name	Description of File
ATTRIB.EXE	Sets file attributes, such as hidden and read-only
CHKDSK.EXE	Checks a disk and displays a status report of it
COMMAND.COM	Starts a new copy of the Windows Command Interpreter, which is the primary operating system file for MS-DOS
DEBUG.EXE	Runs Debug, a testing and editing tool program
DRVSPACE.BIN	DriveSpace disk-compression utility
EBD.SYS	Utility for the startup disk
EDIT.COM	Text editor in MS-DOS
FDISK.EXE	Configures a hard disk for use with MS-DOS
FORMAT.COM	Formats a hard disk or floppy disk for use with MS-DOS
IO.SYS	Core operating system file
MSDOS.SYS	Core operating system file
REGEDIT.EXE	Starts the Registry Editor
SCANDISK.EXE	Starts ScanDisk
SCANDISK.INI	Stores system configuration settings for ScanDisk
SYS.COM	Copies MS-DOS system files and command interpreter to a disk you specify
UNINSTAL.EXE	Starts utility for recovering deleted files

A few other files that you may want to copy to the startup disk after Windows 95 is installed include AUTOEXEC.BAT, CONFIG.SYS, WIN.INI, and SYSTEM.INI. Other INI files may also come in handy as well. These files are ones that you should already have backed up in Chapter 1, "Preparing to Install Windows 95."

◀ See "BackUp System Files," p. 30

To instruct Setup to create a startup disk, make sure the <u>Y</u>es, I Want a Startup Disk (Recommended) choice in the Startup Disk screen is selected and click Next.

Copying Files

Setup now has gathered enough information to begin copying files to your hard disk. In figure 3.17, Setup displays a message telling you that it is ready to start copying the files. Click Next to continue.

Fig. 3.17
The moment you've been waiting for! Setup starts copying files to your system.

Setup begins copying files to your hard disk and displays a meter showing the progress of the action. If you asked to create a startup disk, Setup instructs you to insert this disk when the progress meter hits about 20 percent. Insert the floppy disk and click OK. After the startup disk is created, Setup displays a message telling you to remove the floppy disk from the drive. Do this now and store it in a safe place.

Tip

To exit from Setup at any time, click the <u>E</u>xit button or press F3. This returns you to Windows 3.x or DOS, depending on where you started Setup. If you exit Setup while Windows 95 copies files to your system, Windows 95 may or may not delete them from your system. In many cases, Windows 95 leaves the files on your system so that if you decide to restart the Setup program later, it does not have to recopy those files.

Setup continues installing Windows 95. As it's copying files, Windows displays screens describing some key features of Windows 95. Two of these are shown in figures 3.18 and 3.19.

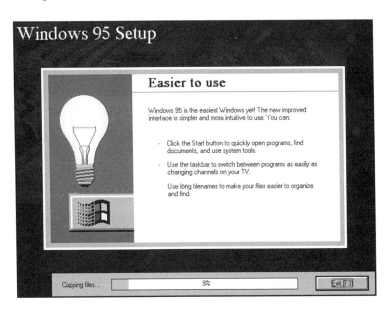

Fig. 3.18
To get a quick idea of what is in store for you with Windows 95, read the messages that flash on-screen during installation.

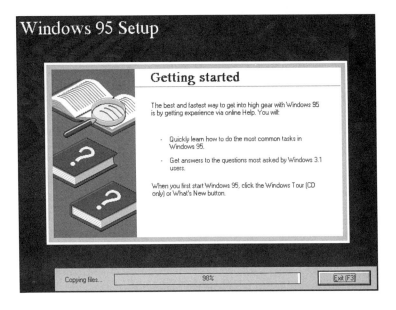

Fig. 3.19
Another helpful screen explains how to get help in Windows.

Finishing Setup

When the Setup files finish copying onto your system, Setup begins the third and final phase of installation: the Finishing Setup phase. This part restarts your computer and configures your hardware and software to work with Windows 95.

Note

Even though you've made it to this point in the installation process, you still are not "home free." Many installation errors occur after the Windows 95 Setup restarts your computer and starts configuring your system. One of the primary problems that occurs is when the Plug and Play configuration part of Windows 95 tries to locate incompatible devices. If you experience any problems during this stage, see Appendix B, "Troubleshooting Windows 95."

Some of the tasks that Windows 95 performs during this final stage include the following:

- Adds a new system file (IO.SYS) to replace the old MS-DOS IO.SYS and MSDOS.SYS. These old files are renamed IO.DOS and MSDOS.DOS.

- Copies SYSTEM.DAT to SYSTEM.DA0 and SYSTEM.NEW to SYSTEM.DAT. This is the primary system database that the Registry reads.

- Combines all the virtual device drivers (VxDs) to create VMM32.VXD, which is the 32-bit virtual device driver.

- Renames ARIAL.WIN, USER32.TMP, and LOGO.SYS files used by Setup.

Click Finish to finish setting up Windows 95. This last stage typically takes several minutes to complete.

Note

If your PC does not restart after a reasonable time, such as 20 minutes or more, reboot your system manually. You may be able to boot into Windows 95. If not, you may be able to boot into Windows 95 in Safe Mode, which you select from a menu that automatically displays during the boot process if Windows 95 cannot completely load. See Appendix B, "Troubleshooting Windows 95," if you have problems finishing this stage of Setup.

After your computer restarts and everything acts as normal, Windows 95 starts and then runs your AUTOEXEC.BAT and CONFIG.SYS files. You'll see the Windows 95 opening screen flash on-screen for a few seconds, and then the DOS screen appears. You'll see the following message in DOS:

```
Please wait while Setup updates your configuration files.
This may take a few minutes...
```

Configuring Run-Once Options

Your PC may appear dormant for several minutes, but be patient. After the configuration files are updated, Windows 95 reappears on-screen and starts to run through setting Run-Once options. These options include PCMCIA and MIDI devices, printers, Time Zone, Microsoft Exchange, Windows Help, programs on the Start menu, and Control Panel setting. Other hardware devices also can be configured at this point. You will see a screen that lists these options as they are being set up.

Many of the items on the list configure automatically, such as the Control Panel and programs on the Start menu. Some, however, require user interaction. When Setup runs the Time Zone option, for instance, you must select the time zone in which you live (see fig. 3.20). Click the list on the Time Zone page and select your time zone. To modify the time and date, click the Date & Time tab. Click Apply to save these settings, and click Close when you are finished.

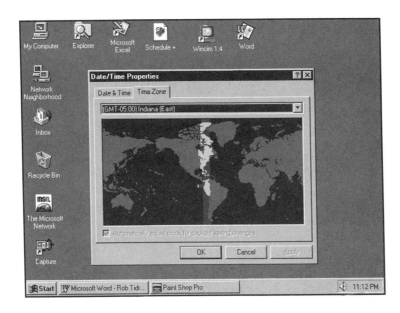

Fig. 3.20
During the Run-Once stage, Setup asks you to select your time zone and set the correct time and date.

Configuring Microsoft Exchange

Next, Setup configures Microsoft Exchange on your system. If you did not select a choice in the Get Connected screen earlier (see "Getting Connected" earlier in this chapter), Setup does not perform this task. You can proceed to the "Starting Windows 95" section.

Setup displays the Inbox Setup Wizard, which guides you through setting up Microsoft Exchange's universal mail inbox. This box is also used to receive e-mail and faxes and to connect to The Microsoft Network, if you selected this option earlier. Use the following steps to configure Exchange:

1. If you've never used Exchange before, make sure No is selected when the Setup wizard asks if you have used Exchange. Otherwise, click Yes. Click Next.

2. In the next screen, you are prompted to select the services you want to use with Exchange. The services listed include only those you selected in the Get Connect screen earlier. These choices include:

   - Microsoft Mail
   - Microsoft Fax
   - Microsoft Online Network

3. By default, the items listed are selected and the Use the Following Information Services radio button is selected. If you want Setup to automatically configure these services (which is recommended for most users), click Next.

> **Note**
>
> If you are an advanced user, or if you need to modify the configuration of the services, select the Manually Configure information Services option. This enables you to change (among other settings) the Exchange profile name, which by default is set as MSEXCHANGE. Any configuration setting can be changed later by using the Add/Remove Program option in the Control Panel.

▶ See "Installing the Exchange Client," p. 202

4. When you choose to let Setup automatically configure Exchange, the Location Information dialog box appears. This box configures the way in which your phone calls are dialed. In this box, you need to set the country in which you live, area code, any special dialing codes to get an outside number (such as 9), and the type of phone system you use, either tone or pulse. Click OK when finished.

5. The next Inbox Setup Wizard screen that appears sets up your Microsoft Fax connection, if this is one of the selections you picked earlier. You are given two choices when installing Microsoft Fax. First, you can set up Fax so that it runs from your local computer. Click the Modem Connected To My Computer option to use Fax only from your computer.

Second, you can set up Microsoft Fax so that others can share it across a network. To do this, you must connect a fax modem to a networked computer and use it as a fax server.

▶ See "Setting Up a Fax Server," p. 259

For this chapter, make sure the first option is selected and click Next.

Detecting a New Modem

In the Install New Modem Wizard, you need to configure your modem to work with Windows 95. Before working through the Install New Modem Wizard, make sure your fax modem is attached to your computer and that it is turned on and hooked to a phone line. If you need to install an internal modem first, skip over this section and finish Setup first. Then install your modem (you'll need to shut down your computer to do this) and start the Add New Hardware program in Control Panel to configure the modem. Chapter 28, "Configuring Modems," guides you through setting up and configuring a modem.

If your modem is turned on and ready to be configured, use the Install New Modem Wizard. Unless you want to select your modem manually, click Next. If you want to specify your modem type, click the Don't Detect My Modem; I Will Select It from a List option and click Next.

▶ See "Installing Your Modem," p. 588

Installing Your Printer

After Setup establishes Exchange and other online connections, it installs the printers connected to your computer. If you do not want to set up a printer now, you can set one up later by selecting the Printers folder after choosing Start, Settings. Double-click the Add Printer icon to start the Add Printer Wizard.

During Setup, you need to specify whether the printer is located locally or on a network. You also need to tell Windows 95 Setup the manufacturer of the printer, such as Hewlett Packard, and the printer name, such as HP LaserJet IIIP. Click Next to have Setup install the printer drivers on your system. If Setup detects a driver from a previous installation, you can elect to keep it or use an updated one from Windows 95. Select the option and then click Next. Setup next asks if you plan to print from MS-DOS based programs. Select Yes or No as necessary.

▶ See "Using the Add Printer Wizard," p. 606

Installing Windows 95

The next screen prompts you for the port or connection to which your printer is connected. Select the appropriate connection and click Next. Windows asks you to name the printer, and gives you a default name such as HP LaserJet IIIP. Keep or change this name as necessary and click Next.

Note

If you are on a network and will be printing to a network printer, you can instruct Windows 95 to print to a queue name versus a printer port.

Setup then displays a screen that asks if you want to print a test page on your printer. If your printer is set up to your machine or network, it's a good idea to do this. This way Setup can diagnose any problems you may have with your printer now. Click Finish. After your text page prints and you respond that everything is fine, tell Setup that the page printed correctly.

Congratulations! Setup is now finished setting up Windows 95.

Starting Windows 95

After Setup finishes installing Windows 95 and configuring Exchange, your printer, and other options, Windows 95 starts. Figure 2.21 shows the initial Windows 95 screen, with a Welcome screen that includes helpful suggestions for navigating Windows 95.

Fig. 3.21
The Welcome to Windows 95 screen displays a different tip each time you start up Windows.

> **Tip**
>
> If you do not want to see this screen the next time you boot Windows 95, clear the Show this Welcome screen next time you start Windows option on the Welcome dialog box. To show this screen again, double-click the Welcome application in the Windows 95 folder in Windows Explorer.

Testing Windows 95 Setup

Before you start using Windows 95 for the first item, you should test to see if it is properly installed. To do this, shut down Windows and restart it by clicking the Start button at the bottom of the screen (this is called the *Taskbar*) and select Shut Down. The Shut Down Windows dialog box appears (see fig. 3.22). Make sure the Shut Down the Computer? option is selected and click Yes. This action begins the Windows 95 shut down procedure, which you must do whenever you want to exit Windows 95.

▶ See "Setting Taskbar Options," p. 173

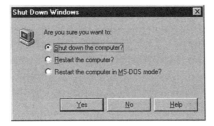

Fig. 3.22
You must use the Shut Down Windows dialog box each time you turn off your computer.

When a message appears on your screen telling you it's OK to turn off your machine, press the Reset button on your computer or flip the power switch off and then on. As your PC reboots, watch the screen to see if you notice any errors. If Windows 95 starts, your system probably is working fine and you can start using Windows 95.

If it doesn't start or if you get a DOS screen, your setup has encountered some problems. You can start Windows 95 in Safe Mode and fix the problem.

Using Windows 95 Safe Mode

With luck, your computer starts and you have no problems running your new Windows 95 installation. Many times, however, Windows 95 encounters a problem during startup that it cannot fix (such as a Registry setting missing or corrupted). When this happens, you need to run Windows in Safe Mode from the Startup menu. You can display the Startup menu by pressing F8 during the boot process. Press F8 when the instructions `Starting Windows` appear on-screen, usually after your system checks the internal RAM on your system. Windows 95 also starts Safe mode automatically if it detects a problem with the startup files.

The Startup menu has the following options from which to choose. Depending on your specific setup, you may or may not have the same settings:

- *Normal*. Enables you to start Windows 95 in its normal startup manner, loading all device drivers and Registry settings. If Windows 95 automatically displays the Startup menu, choosing Normal probably will not do anything except return you to the Startup menu. Choose this option only if you want to watch what happens on-screen during the failed startup.

- *Logged* (\BOOTLOG.TXT). Creates a file called BOOTLOG.TXT in your root directory that contains a record of the current startup process. This file is created during Setup and shows the Windows 95 components and drivers loaded and initialized, and the status of each. You can view this file in Notepad.

- *Safe Mode*. Starts Windows 95 but bypasses startup files and uses only basic system drivers. In Safe mode, many devices in Windows 95 are not available, such as the Add New Hardware utility in the Control Panel. Safe mode is intended to diagnose and fix problems in the Windows 95 environment. You also can start Safe mode by pressing F5 during boot-up or typing `WIN /D:M` at the command prompt.

- *Safe Mode with Network Support*. Starts Windows 95 but bypasses startup files and uses only basic system drivers, including basic networking. You can also start this option by pressing F6 or typing `WIN /D:N` at the command prompt.

- *Step-By-Step Confirmation*. Enables you to confirm each line in your startup files, including AUTOEXEC.BAT and CONFIG.SYS. Answer Y to lines you want to run; answer N to lines you want to bypass. You can also start this option by pressing F8 when the Startup menu is displayed.

- *Command Prompt Only*. Starts MS-DOS (Windows 95 version) with startup files and Registry settings, displaying only the MS-DOS command prompt.

- *Safe Mode Command Prompt Only*. Starts MS-DOS (Windows 95 version) in Safe mode and displays only the command prompt, bypassing startup files. Same as pressing Shift+F5.

■ *Previous Version of MS-DOS.* Starts your previous version of MS-DOS if you have a multi-boot configuration. You must install Windows 95 into a different directory during Setup for this option to be available. You also can start this option by pressing F4 during startup. This option is only available if BootMulti=1 in the MSDOS.SYS file.

When Safe mode is selected from the Startup menu, it bypasses startup files, including the Registry, CONFIG.SYS, AUTOEXEC.BAT, and the [Boot] and [386Enh] sections of SYSTEM.INI. Table 3.2 shows files that the three most common Safe mode options bypass and initiate. As you can see in the table, Safe mode does not load all the Windows drivers. In fact, during Safe mode, only the mouse, keyboard, and standard Windows VGA device drivers are loaded. If you are using other drivers, such as a Super VGA video driver, they are not available in Safe mode.

Table 3.2   Files Loaded During Startup Menu Options

Action	Safe Mode	Safe Mode, Network Support	Command Prompt Only
Process CONFIG.SYS and AUTOEXEC.BAT	No	No	No
Process Registry information	No	Yes	No
Load COMMAND.COM	No	Yes	Yes
Run Windows 95 WIN.COM	Yes	Yes	No
Load HIMEM.SYS and IFSHLP.SYS	Yes	Yes	No
Load DoubleSpace or DriveSpace if present	Yes	Yes	(Loaded if Safe Mode Command Prompt Only option is selected)
Load all Windows drivers	No	No	No
Load network drivers	No	Yes	No
Run NETSTART.BAT	No	Yes	No

After Windows 95 starts in Safe mode, you can access the configuration files, modify configuration settings, and then restart Windows 95 normally. If you still encounter problems, see Appendix B, "Troubleshooting Windows 95."

Using the Windows 95 Startup Disk

If you instructed Windows 95 to create a startup disk during Setup (see the section "Creating a Startup Disk" earlier in this chapter), you can use it to load your previous operating system and display an MS-DOS command prompt. The startup disk also contains utilities for troubleshooting your Windows 95 operating system. To use the Startup disk, place the disk in drive A and reboot your computer. A command prompt appears from which you can diagnose and fix problems associated with your installation.

> **Note**
>
> If you did not create a Startup disk during Setup, you can create one using a single floppy disk. In the Add/Remove Programs option in Control Panel, click the Startup Disk tab. Then click the Create Disk button, and follow the instructions on-screen. You should do this even if you are not having problems starting Windows 95 now. In the future, you may experience a problem that only the Startup disk can remedy.

Configuring Briefcase and Direct Cable Connection

After Setup finishes installing Windows 95 and you have tested it, you can configure Briefcase and the Direct Cable Connection applications. The following sections discuss how to do this.

Briefcase

An option installed during the Portable Setup installation is the Windows 95 Briefcase. Mobile computing users who have both a portable and desktop PC spend several hours a week transferring files from one machine to the other. Part of this time is devoted to ensuring that the most current file is copied and being used each time the file is modified. Briefcase enables users to synchronize files and copy them between their PCs if they have a network or use the Direct Cable Connection (see the next section). Briefcase helps eliminate the possibility of errors and overlooked files that users work on.

To use Briefcase, double-click its icon on the Windows 95 desktop to start it. There are no configuration settings for Briefcase, expect for those related to setting up a network connection or the Direct Cable Connection. After you start Briefcase, drag and drop files and directories from Explorer or your desktop to the Briefcase (see fig. 3.23). This is the same paradigm used for carrying a briefcase or attaché to the office: you stuff your papers and folders into your briefcase to carry them home or on a trip, or back to the office. Windows 95's Briefcase extends this concept to the electronic platform.

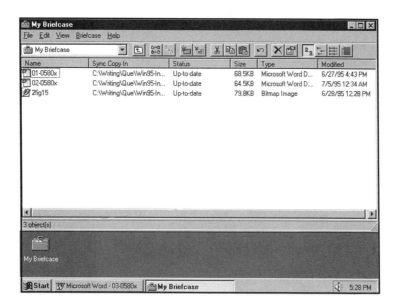

Fig. 3.23

You can use the Windows 95 Briefcase to help you synchronize your files from your portable PC to your desktop PC.

Note

For more information on using Briefcase, see Que's *Special Edition Using Windows 95.*

Direct Cable Connections

Another feature that mobile users can use is Windows 95's Direct Cable Connection. This feature enables users to hook together two PCs using serial or parallel port cables. With Direct Cable Connection, you can share folders, files, or printers with another computer without being on a local area network (LAN). This is handy if you transfer files from a laptop PC to a desktop PC, but your laptop does not have a network adapter. If your other PC is on a network, however, the connected PC (in this case, the laptop PC) can access the network and share files or network printers.

By default, Direct Cable Connection is automatically installed during the Portable Setup (it's also installed by default during Custom and Typical Setups). After Setup installs Windows 95, you need to configure the Direct Cable Connection for each computer you hook together. To do so, use these steps:

1. From Accessories, click Direct Cable Connection. The Direct Cable Connection Wizard starts (see fig. 3.24).

Fig. 3.24
Use the Direct Cable Connection Wizard to let you hook two computers together using a serial or parallel port.

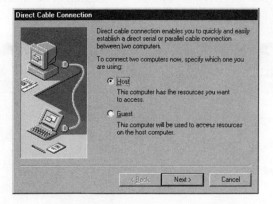

2. On the first Direct Cable Connection screen, you need to specify which computer you are configuring. You have two choices:

   ■ *Host*. This is the PC that contains the files or printer connection you want to copy or share.

   ■ *Guest*. This is the PC that accesses files from the host PC.

   Select Host or Guest.

3. Click Next.

Tip

Host and guest PCs must use the same port connections.

4. Specify the port to which you want to connect. You can use serial (usually COM1 or COM2) or parallel (usually LPT1 or LPT2) ports (see fig. 3.25).

Note

If you need to add a port to your computer, click Install New Port. Windows 95 automatically searches your system for the new port and configures it. If Windows cannot find a new port on your system and you recently installed one, shut down Windows 95, reboot your system, and retry this option. You also can run the Add New Hardware Wizard from the Control Panel and add the new port using that wizard.

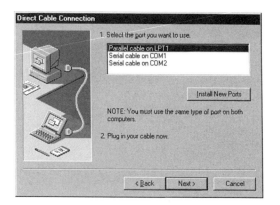

Fig. 3.25
Select the type of
port that each
computer will use.

5. Plug in the cable to the port you specify in step 4.

6. Click Next. If you set up your PC as the guest computer, skip to step 15. Otherwise continue to step 7.

7. You now must specify if you want to enable the guest PC to share printer and file resources on the host machine (see fig. 3.26). To do this, click the File and Print Sharing button to start the Network Control Panel.

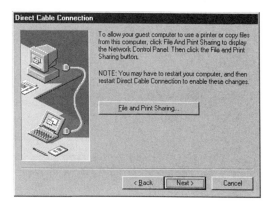

Fig. 3.26
You can configure
the host computer
to enable the guest
computer to use its
printer or files.

8. From the Network dialog box (see fig. 3.27), click File and Print Sharing. Select this option so that your PC can share files and a printer with another PC.

9. In the File and Print Sharing dialog box, you can choose to have the guest computer share only the host's printer, the host's files, or both (see fig. 3.28). Click OK.

10. Click OK in the Network dialog box.

11. Click Next in the Direct Cable Connection Wizard.

Fig. 3.27
The Network dialog box is used to enable File and Print Sharing from one PC to another.

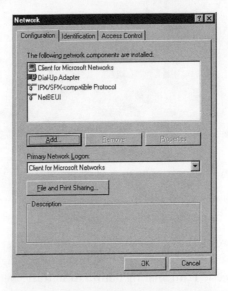

Fig. 3.28
Select the type of file and printer sharing that you want between your connected computers.

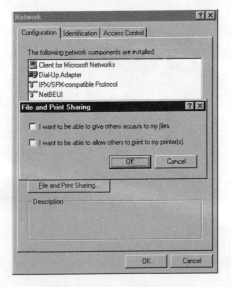

If you do not enable file or printer sharing, the warning screen shown in figure 3.29 appears. Click OK and then click Next again to go to the following wizard screen. If file and print sharing is enabled, this screen is bypassed.

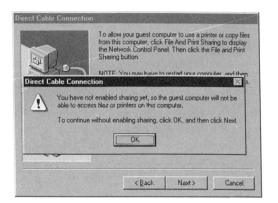

Installing Windows 95

Fig. 3.29
The Direct Cable
Connection
Wizard tells you
that you have not
set up file and
printer sharing
between your two
computers.

12. The host computer is now configured. To add a layer of security to the
connection, you can require that the guest computer input a password
to access the host system. To do this, click Use Password Protection and
then click the Set Password button (see fig. 3.30).

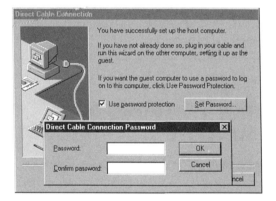

Fig. 3.30
Use a password
to help keep
intruders from
accessing the host
computer from the
guest computer.

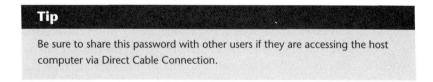

Tip

Be sure to share this password with other users if they are accessing the host
computer via Direct Cable Connection.

13. In the Direct Cable Connection Password dialog box, enter the password and reenter it to confirm the spelling of it. Click OK.

14. If you have not done so already, configure the other computer as the
guest system. Otherwise, click Finish to initialize the host machine.

15. To configure the guest computer, make sure the Direct Cable Connection Wizard is running (see step 1) on the guest machine and click G̲uest. Then click Next.

> **Note**
>
> If your PC has previously been configured as a host computer, click C̲hange after the Direct Cable Connection Wizard starts to change the configuration. You also can change from guest to host by clicking the same C̲hange button.

16. Select the port to which you want to connect. Remember, the port on the guest computer must match the port on the host machine.

17. Plug in the cable and click Next.

18. Click Finish to start using the Direct Cable Connection.

> **Note**
>
> See Que's *Special Edition Using Windows 95* for information on using Windows 95's Direct Cable Connection application.

Configuring Windows 95's PCMCIA Support

Windows 95 supports many PCMCIA cards (also known as *PC cards*) including modems, network adapters, SCSI cards, and others. Windows 95 PCMCIA drivers are 32-bit, dynamically loadable virtual device drivers and consume no conventional memory. Windows 95 enables you to plug in your PCMCIA card in your computer and start using the card immediately. You are not required to shut down and restart your PC for it to recognize the PCMCIA card. (You must have Plug-and-Play compliant drivers for this feature to work properly.) If you have a PCMCIA network card, for instance, you can plug it into your computer and Windows 95 does the rest: it detects the network card, loads the drivers, and connects to the network.

PCMCIA card installation is performed automatically by Plug and Play if Windows 95 includes supporting drivers for your PCMCIA card and socket. If your card is not automatically configured by Windows 95, you'll need to start the PCMCIA Wizard and set up the card manually. When you run the

PCMCIA Wizard, Windows 95 modifies your AUTOEXEC.BAT and
CONFIG.SYS files by removing the lines that start the real-mode driver
and adds a line that enables the PCMCIA socket.

To check if your PCMCIA socket is detected by Windows 95, do the
following:

1. In Control Panel, double-click the System icon. In the System Properties
   dialog box (see fig. 3.31), select the Device Manager tab.

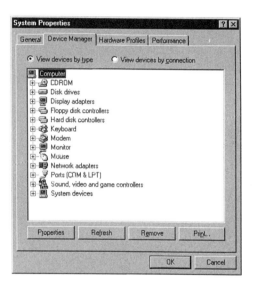

Fig. 3.31
Select the Device
Manager tab to
check for Windows
95 support of your
PCMCIA card.

2. Select View Devices By Type and see if the PCMCIA Socket listing is
   included with the list of devices. If it's not, you must run the Add New
   Hardware Wizard from the Control Panel. If it is, you should be able to
   use your PCMCIA device.

3. In the Control Panel, double-click the Add New Hardware icon.

4. The Add New Hardware Wizard starts. In the first screen, click Next
   and then click No. This tells Windows 95 that you want to select the
   PCMCIA socket from a list, instead of Windows 95 searching for it
   automatically.

5. In the Hardware Types list box, select PCMCIA Socket. Click Next.

6. In the next screen (see fig. 3.32), select the manufacturer and model of
   your PCMCIA device. Click Next to have Windows 95 install the socket.
   If you have a setup disk from the manufacturer, click Have Disk instead.
   This installs the drivers from the floppy disk instead of from the hard
   disk.

Fig. 3.32
Select the
manufacturer and
model of your
PCMCIA device
to set up the
PCMCIA socket on
your computer.

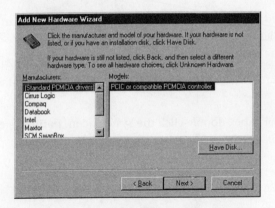

Note

Some legacy PCMCIA cards are not supported "out of the box" with Windows 95. If
your PCMCIA card is not included on the list of supported cards, contact the card's
manufacturer for updated installation disks for Windows 95.

If you have problems installing the PCMCIA socket on your computer,
see Appendix B, "Troubleshooting Windows 95," or contact your specific
PCMCIA manufacturer. They may have updated information and instructions
on using your card with Windows 95.

Troubleshooting

*When Windows 95 Setup runs ScanDisk, it reports errors on my hard disk. I run ScanDisk
from DOS and everything is OK. Can I bypass ScanDisk during Setup?*

Yes. Just use the /IS switch when you run SETUP.EXE from Windows 3.x or MS-DOS.

My drive is compressed using Stacker. Will Windows 95 work?

Yes, but all your drivers will run in real mode instead of protected mode. This goes
for all third-party disk-compression utilities. If you use DriveSpace this is not the case,
however.

My icons in Windows 95 are black. Is this normal?

No, this is not normal and may mean that the SHELLICO file has been corrupted.
This file is a hidden file and is in your Windows folder. Delete this file and reboot your
computer. As Windows 95 restarts, the SHELLICO file rebuilds automatically and your
icons should display correctly. If this doesn't work, reboot the computer and press F8
when your computer boots. At the Startup menu, select Safe Mode and start Windows. Shut down Windows and then reboot your computer again.

Chapter 4

Using Custom Installation Options

by Rob Tidrow

Chapters 2 and 3 walked you through installing Windows 95 using the Typical and Portable installation processes. During both of those installations, you had an opportunity to select the Custom installation type and to choose several options that Windows 95 provides for you to load on your system. This chapter does not walk you through the entire Setup process for the Custom installation type, but it does explain the options from which you can choose to install.

In this chapter, you find out about the following:

- How to start the Custom installation process
- What Windows 95 options are available
- Descriptions of Windows 95 options

Understanding the Custom Install Process

During the Windows 95 Setup Wizard, Windows 95 displays the Setup Options screen, as shown in figure 4.1. (It is assumed that you already have started Setup and have completed the earlier stages of Setup.) The Custom Setup type enables you to pick and choose the way in which Windows 95 is installed on your computer. Custom is designed mainly for those users comfortable setting up their own environment, such as advanced users or system administrators. Even if you don't fall into one of those two categories of users, you still may want to modify the components that Windows 95 installs on your computer.

◀ See "Starting the Windows 95 Setup Wizard," p. 45

Fig. 4.1
Choose the Custom installation type to select the individual components for Windows 95.

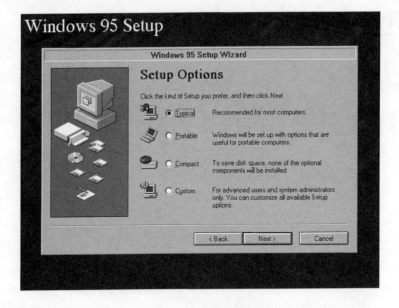

After you click the Custom option and choose Next, you need to fill in your user information and Windows 95 identification data. Next, Windows 95 analyzes your computer and searches for the installed hardware that you may be using. When the Get Connected Wizard screen appears (see fig. 4.2), select those options you want to install, such as The Microsoft Network, Microsoft Mail, and Microsoft Fax. Click Next to continue.

Fig. 4.2
Select the Get Connected options that you want Windows 95 to automatically install. Remember that Microsoft Exchange is installed (4.6M) if any of these options are selected.

◀ See "Getting Connected," p. 51

Setup next displays the Windows Components Wizard screen (see fig. 4.3) from which you can select to have Windows 95 install the most common components or enable you to choose the components. Because you want to modify the list of options to install, click the <u>S</u>how Me the List of Components So I Can Choose option. Click Next.

Fig. 4.3
Click the second choice in this screen to display all the options that Windows 95 can install.

The Select Components screen appears, as shown in figure 4.4. You now can pick the options that are installed on your computer. The next section, "Selecting Custom Install Options," describes all the options in detail.

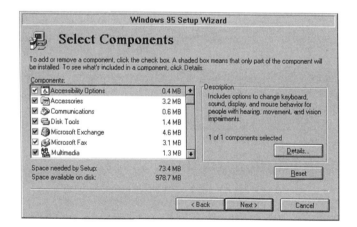

Fig. 4.4
Select the options you want to install on Windows 95 from the Select Components Wizard screen.

Selecting Custom Install Options

In the Select Components screen, you can see that several items are already checked. These are the default settings that Windows 95 installs if you do not change any of the choices manually. Check boxes that are shaded indicate that only part of the options for that component are selected. To see all the options of a component, such as Accessories, highlight that component and click the Details button. A screen appears that enables you to select specific options for the Accessories component.

> **Note**
>
> Depending on the type of hardware and network connections you have, your installation options may differ. If you do not have a sound card installed, for instance, you may not have all the sound schemes available to you in the Multimedia components options.

The component list is broken down into eight categories. The following list also includes the required hard disk space to install the component on your computer:

- Accessibility (0.3M)
- Accessories (space varies)
- Communications (1.5M)
- Disk Tools (space varies)
- Microsoft Exchange (4.3M)
- Microsoft Fax (2.1M)
- Multimedia (0.9M)
- The Microsoft Network (2.1M)

Each of these categories with their hard disk space requirements is explained in detail in the following sections.

> **Note**
>
> You can add any of these options after you install Windows 95 by double-clicking the Add/Remove Programs icon in Control Panel. You must have your Windows 95 Setup disks or CD available when you add these options.

Accessibility Options (0.3M)

Windows 95 includes several utilities that enable users who have hearing, movement, or vision impairments to use Windows 95 easier. These utilities include keyboard, sound, display, and mouse behavior modifications, such as high-contrast color schemes, StickyKeys, and SoundSentry. By default, Windows 95 installs the Accessibility options (see fig. 4.5), which you can access from the Accessibility Options icon in the Control Panel.

Table 4.1 lists and briefly describes the utilities available when you install the Accessibility Options.

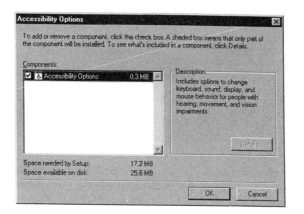

Fig. 4.5
By default, the
Accessibility
Options item is
installed under
the Custom
Setup type.

I

Installing Windows 95

Table 4.1 Accessibility Options

Type	Name	Description
Keyboard		Options that control the way in which the keyboard operates
	StickyKeys	Enables you to use the Ctrl, Shift, and Alt keys by pressing one key at a time, instead of holding down both at the same time
	FilterKeys	Instructs Windows 95 to ignore brief or repeated keystrokes. You also can slow down the repeat rate of keystrokes.
	ToggleKeys	Assigns a sound to beep when you press Caps Lock, Num Lock, and Scroll Lock
Sound		Options that display visual cues when your computer generates a sound
	SoundSentry	Instructs Windows 95 to display visual warnings when your system makes a sound. Some of these actions include flashing the active caption bar or desktop when a sound occurs.
	ShowSounds	Configures your applications to display captions for the speech and sound they make
Display		Option that controls how your monitor displays information
	High Contrast	Directs Windows 95 to use colors and fonts that are easy to read, such as white on black, black on white, or a custom combination that you provide

(continues)

Table 4.1	Continued	
Type	**Name**	**Description**
Mouse		Option that replaces the mouse with keyboard actions
	MouseKeys	Enables you to control the pointer by using the numeric keypad on your keyboard. You also can change the pointer speed and choose to use MouseKeys with Num Lock on or off.
GeneralSettings		Option that Configures Accessibility Options
	Automatic Reset	Turns off Accessibility feature if idle for a specific amount of time. The default is five minutes.
	Notification	Prompts you when an Accessibility feature is turned on or off
	SerialKeys	Enables you to access keyboard and mouse features by using an alternative input device, such as head pointers and eye-gaze systems

If you do not want to install the Accessibility Options, click the check box next to its entry in the Components list to deselect it.

Accessories

If you used Windows 3.x, you are familiar with the Windows Accessories. These include the Calculator, screen savers, and wallpaper. In Windows 95, some of the Accessories are improved and have been replaced by other applications. WordPad, for instance, is a more powerful word processor that replaces Microsoft Write which is available in Windows 3.x. To access these options, click the Define button. The screen in figure 4.6 appears.

Fig. 4.6
You can select
the Accessories
options you want
from this screen.

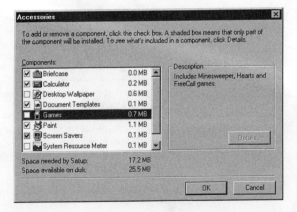

As you can see, only five of nine options are installed by default. You can select all the options or modify the list to your tastes. Each option is described in the following list:

- *Briefcase* (0.6M). Synchronizes files between computers. Installed by default.

- *Character Map* (0.1M). Inserts symbols and characters into your documents.

- *Clipboard Viewer* (0.1M). Displays the Clipboard's contents.

- *Calculator* (0.2M). Enables you to perform calculations. Installed by default.

- *Desktop Wallpaper*. Includes background pictures for your Windows Desktop.

> **Note**
>
> Included on the Microsoft Plus! disk are additional wallpaper files called Desktop Themes. Desktop Themes are full-color bitmaps that also include icons, sounds, and mouse pointers. If you have the Plus! disk from Microsoft, you might want to leave the Desktop Wallpaper option unchecked.

- *Document Templates* (0.1M). Enables you to easily create new documents for your most common programs. You can see these file types after you install Windows 95 and right-click the Windows desktop. On the context-sensitive menu, choose Ne<u>w</u> and the file type you want to create. Installed by default.

- *Mouse Pointers* (1.4M). Installs easy-to-see pointers for your mouse (see fig. 4.7).

- *Net Watcher* (0.2M). On a network, Net Watcher enables you to monitor your network server and connections. Installed by default.

- *Online User's Guide* (7.8M). Installs the online version of the *Windows 95 User's Guide*.

- *Games* (0.7M). Entertainment for your entire family! Includes Minesweeper, Hearts, and FreeCell games.

Fig. 4.7
You can select the types of pointers that your mouse uses by choosing different Schemes in the Mouse Properties sheet.

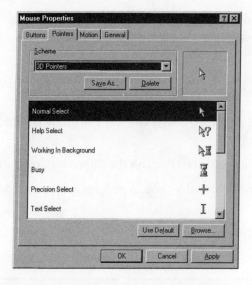

Plus!

Note

On the Microsoft Plus! CD-ROM you can find a copy of a 3-D multimedia pinball game called 3D Pinball.

- *Quick View* (1.8M). Displays a preview of a document without opening it in its native application.

- *Paint* (1.1M). Replaces Windows 3.x's Paintbrush application. Paint is used to create, modify, or view bitmap graphics (see fig. 4.8). Installed by default.

- *System Monitor* (0.2M). Enables you to monitor your system performance. Not to be confused with the System Resource Meter.

- *Screen Savers* (0.1M). By default, Windows 95 installs one of the two screen saver options—Flying Windows. You can select the Additional Screen Savers option and use the following screen savers:

    Flying Through Space

    Mystify Your Mind

    Curves and Colors

    Scrolling Marquee (you provide the message to display)

    Blank Screen

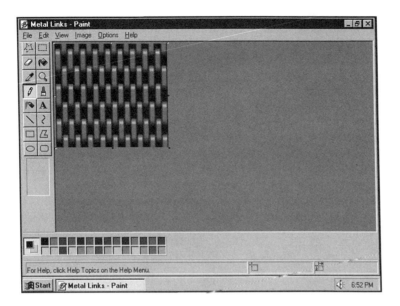

Fig. 4.8
Use Paint if you
don't have a
drawing package
installed on your
system.

- *Windows 95 Tour* (2.5M). Quickly teaches you some basic Windows 95 features and tasks. Only available with the CD-ROM version of Windows 95.

- *WinPopup*. On a network, use this utility to send and receive pop-up messages to other users.

- *System Resource Meter* (0.1M). Although this option is not selected by default, you may want to install it. It's a helpful utility that lets you view system resource levels, including GDI (Graphics Device Interface) and user resources. As you work, the Resource Meter appears on the far left side of the Windows Taskbar. To see the system meter in more detail, double-click the meter to display the screen shown in figure 4.9.

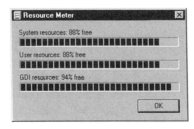

Fig. 4.9
Use the Resource
Meter to see how
your system
resources are being
used by Windows 95.

- *WordPad* (1.2M). An accessory in Windows worth using. WordPad replaces Windows Write that came bundled with Windows 3.x and is a full-featured, OLE 2.0-compliant word processor. You can create and edit documents in WordPad. It reads and saves files in the Microsoft Word DOC format by default. It can read Word 6.x DOC files, Windows Write (WRI), Rich-Text Format (RTF), and text files (TXT). Installed by default.

Communications (1.3M)

The Communications components (see fig. 4.10) include options for connecting to other computers or to online services. By default, all four options are selected, but you can modify these selections if you don't want all the options to install.

Fig. 4.10
The Communications components are helpful if you have a modem installed on your computer.

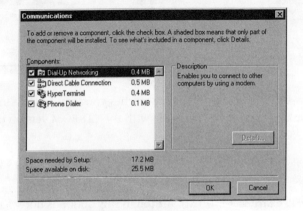

The options available are as follows:

■ *Dial-Up Networking* (0.4M). Enables you to connect to other computers by using your modem.

■ *Direct Cable Connection* (0.5M). Enables you to connect to another computer by using the parallel or serial ports and a cable.

◀ See "Configuring Briefcase and Direct Cable Connection," p. 96

■ *HyperTerminal* (0.4M). Replaces Terminal in Windows 3.x and is a full-featured communications package, which enables you to connect to other computers and online services (see fig. 4.11). HyperTerminal is a superior product if you need a general communications package.

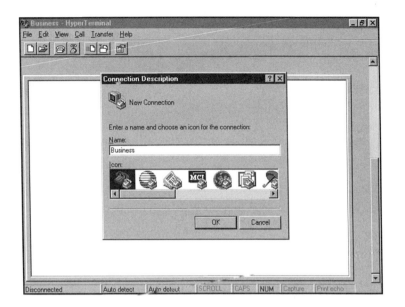

Installing Windows 95

Fig. 4.11
Unless you swear by another communications package, give HyperTerminal a try. It's a very good (and fast) application.

Troubleshooting

I accidentally installed HyperTerminal during the Windows 95 custom setup. I use another communications package instead. How can I get rid of HyperTerminal?

To remove HyperTerminal (or any other application for that matter) from Windows 95, click Start, Settings, Control Panel, and double-click the Add/Remove Programs icon. Click the Windows Setup tab, select Communications, and choose Details. Deselect the HyperTerminal check box and click OK. Click OK again, and Windows uninstalls HyperTerminal from your hard drive.

- *Phone Dialer* (0.1M). Enables you to use your computer to dial a phone number by using your modem. Once dialed, you can pick up the receiver and start talking (assuming someone picks up on the other end). Phone Dialer can be used by itself or with other applications, such as Microsoft Exchange. With Exchange, you can access the Phone Dialer and make calls from Exchange's Address Books.

Disk Tools

The Disk Tools that Windows 95 provides help you maintain and compress your disks. By default, only two of the three options are selected to install. The third option—Backup—is not installed but should be if you plan to back up your hard disk to floppy disks or tape units:

▶ See "Installing the Exchange Client," p. 202

- *Backup* (1.0M). Enables you to back up and restore backed up files from your hard disk to tape or floppy disks. Note that Windows 95 doesn't work with all tape drives, including DAT tape drives.

- *Defrag* (0.3M). Defragments and optimizes your hard disk. Installed by default.

- *Disk compression tools* (1.0M). Compresses your disks using DriveSpace after Windows 95 is installed. Enables you to pack more files onto your hard disk. Installed by default.

Note

Microsoft Plus! includes DriveSpace 3, an improved version of the DriveSpace that is included with Windows 95. Plus! also includes the System Agent, which enables you to schedule when to run other programs, including system maintenance utilities like Disk Defragmenter, ScanDisk, and compression utilities. The System Agent can run other programs as well, and notify you when your hard disk is low on space.

Microsoft Exchange (4.3M)

Microsoft Exchange is a new application that includes e-mail and messaging utilities. Exchange is a universal "in-box" for all the e-mail and fax communications you have. Figure 4.12 shows an example of what Exchange looks like on your desktop. Chapter 9, "Configuring Microsoft Exchange," describes how to set up Exchange on your system.

Fig. 4.12
Exchange can be used as your universal in and out box for most of your electronic correspondence.

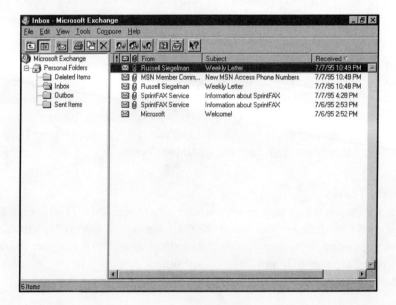

The options that install by default under the Exchange component are as follows:

- *Microsoft Exchange* (3.7M). Includes integrated mail, MAPI (Message Application Programming Interface), and other messaging applications. You must install Exchange if you choose to install Microsoft Mail, The Microsoft Network, or Microsoft Fax.

> **Note**
>
> The *Messaging Application Programming Interface* (MAPI) is a programming API designed by Microsoft that enables software developers to create message-related applications that use a consistent interface. Some of these applications include electronic mail, voice mail, and fax applications.

- *Microsoft Mail Services* (0.6M). Enables you to access Microsoft Mail post offices to which you are connected. You must have a network connection to use this option.

Microsoft Fax (2.1M)

If you selected the Microsoft Fax option in the Get Connected Wizard screen during Setup, this option is selected by default. Microsoft Fax is built-in fax software that enables you to create, send, and receive faxes through Windows 95. The following options are available:

▶ See "Installing Microsoft Fax," p. 241

- *Microsoft Fax Service* (1.8M). Enables you to send and receive faxes.

- *Microsoft Fax Viewer* (0.4M). Enables you to view Microsoft Fax images.

Multilanguage Support

Windows 95 provides support for multilanguages. To write documents in different languages, select the Multilanguage Support component and select from the following options:

- *Central European language support* (2.3M). Includes support for Czech Republic, Hungarian, Polish, and Slovenian languages.

- *Cyrillic language support* (2.3M). Includes support for Bulgarian, Belarussian, and Russian languages.

- *Greek language support* (2.3M). Includes support for the Greek language.

> **Troubleshooting**
>
> *How can I add support for multiple languages on Windows 95?*
>
> During Windows 95 Setup, you can select the Multilanguage Support option in the Select Components screen during the custom installation. If you've already installed Windows 95, click Start, Settings, Control Panel, and double-click the Add/Remove Programs icon. Click the Windows Setup tab and select Multilanguage Support. Click OK, and then click OK again. You'll need to have your Windows 95 Setup disks or CD handy.

Multimedia (0.9M)

By default, Windows 95 installs all seven options for the Multimedia component, which includes programs for playing sound, animation, and video. To use these options, you must have a multimedia-compliant computer, such as one with a CD-ROM and sound card installed.

- *Audio Compression* (0.2M). Utility that compresses audio for playback or recording on your computer. Installed by default.

- *CD Player* (0.2M). Enables you to play audio CDs on your computer's CD-ROM drive.

- *Media Player* (0.2M). Utility to play audio and video clips (see fig. 4.13). Media Player plays the following file formats: Video for Windows (AVI), Wave (WAV), MIDI (MID and RMI), and CD Audio. Installed by default.

Fig. 4.13
In Media Player, you can play back that cool audio clip that you've been dying to hear.

- *Sound schemes*. You can choose from Jungle (3.4M), Musica (0.7M), Robotz (2.0M), and Utopia (1.0M) sound schemes. Sound schemes are sounds associated with different Windows 95 events, such as starting Windows 95 or maximizing a window.

> **Note**
>
> If you have the Microsoft Plus! CD, don't bother installing the sound schemes that come with Windows 95. The ones included on the Plus! CD are much better (plus, if you've paid extra for them, you might as well use them).

- *Sound Recorder* (0.2M). Enables you to record and play sounds on your PC if you have a sound card and microphone. Installed by default.

- *Video Compression* (0.4M). Compresses video for multimedia playback or recording on your computer. Installed by default.

- *Volume Control* (0.1M). Utility to adjust the volume of the sound from your sound card (see fig. 4.14). Installed by default if Windows 95 detects a sound card.

▶ See "Configuring Sound Cards," p. 443

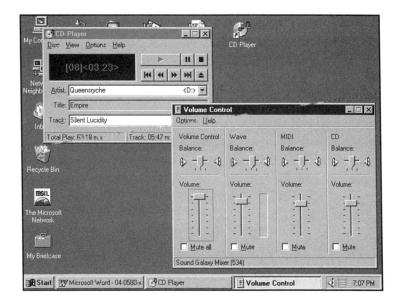

Fig. 4.14
You can adjust the volume of your speakers by using the Volume Control utility.

The Microsoft Network (2.1M)

If you chose to install The Microsoft Network on the Get Connected Wizard screen earlier in the Setup process, this option is automatically selected. The Microsoft Network enables you to connect to Microsoft's new online service. This option requires that you have a modem and that you also install Microsoft Exchange.

Finishing Custom Install

After you select the options that you want to install, click Next to continue the Setup Wizard. As you select components and options, you need to make sure the hard disk requirements do not exceed the space available on your hard disk. Below the Components list, Setup displays the hard disk requirements of your selections, as well as the space you have left on your hard disk.

▶ See "Setting Up a Microsoft Network Connection," p. 276

Keep an eye on this area and make sure the space needed by Setup does not exceed the space available. Even if it does, you will not get a warning until you click Next and want to continue installing Windows 95. Go back over your selections and decrease the number of items you have selected. A good place to do this is in the Accessories or Multimedia area.

Tip

Click Reset to restore the default selections that Custom installs.

Setup continues and starts copying files to your hard disk. Some of the components you install are configured at the end of Setup, such as Microsoft Exchange, Microsoft Fax, and The Microsoft Network. Some options are ready to go once Windows 95 is installed and running correctly.

Troubleshooting

I'm running Setup and I've made a complete mess of things choosing components. I want to go back to what Windows 95 initially had selected when I started the Custom Install option.

If you are still selecting options to install, you can click the Reset button in the Select Components screen.

Chapter 5

Installing Windows 95 over a Network

by Gregory J. Root

Windows 95 offers improved features for installing and running Windows over a network. Windows 95 provides programs and utilities to help you manage the installation of Windows to any number of computers on the network, whether you have 5 or 500 network users. This chapter teaches you how to plan for and take advantage of these new capabilities to successfully deliver Windows 95 to every desktop in your organization.

In this chapter, you learn

- Considerations and requirements for a server-based install
- What to plan for a shared installation
- How to perform the actual installation from a server
- What details remain to finish a server-based install

Performing a Server-Based Install

What is a server-based install? A *server-based install* provides a central storage location of the files necessary to set up Windows 95. Server-based installations provide control over the distribution of Windows 95 to network clients. There are two types of server-based installations you can perform:

- *Shared installation.* Installs the Windows 95 files onto the server. Windows, therefore, is only installed once and then shared with any number of workstations; the Windows 95 files are *not* actually present on the workstation's local drive.

■ *Installation from a network to a workstation.* Performed when the Windows 95 files are copied to a network drive and then installed from the network drive to each individual workstation. In this case, the Windows files do reside on each workstation's hard drive. Installing Windows in this manner is much faster than from floppies or a CD because the network transfers the files quickly.

Tip

Installing from a network to a workstation is an excellent method of installation to use when only the server contains a CD-ROM drive.

Overview of Server-Based Install

It's important to review the major tasks that are part of a server-based install so you know what to expect at each turn as you install. The further you progress in installing Windows, the more decisions you need to make. Planning your task now will help save time and energy later.

The four steps to installing Windows are the following:

1. Planning the server-based install

2. Installing the setup files to the server

3. Installing Windows 95 on the network clients

4. Refining the server-based install

Planning the server-based install and shared-installation is the most important part of installing Windows 95. The decisions you make now affect your network situation in the future. You want to plan for your organization's growth and development as well as prepare for new and improved technologies. This chapter can help you plan for and complete your network installation.

Considerations of Server-Based Install

In conjunction with choosing the method of installation—shared or from the server to each workstation—you must decide how you want to start Windows 95 from the workstations. Preferably all workstations on a network will boot using the same method. The three methods of booting the workstations are as follows:

- The workstation boots from a local hard drive and then runs Windows 95 from the shared installation.

- The workstation boots from a floppy disk and then runs Windows 95 from the shared installation.

- The Windows 95 files are installed and run locally on the hard drive (the server was just a source of setup files).

Note

You also can create remote boot workstations using a disk image created on the server. Since this method of booting the workstation is seldom used with any Windows programs, it is not covered in this chapter; however, for more information about remote booting, see WIN95RK help file in the ADMIN, RESKIT, and HELPFILE folders on the Windows 95 CD.

The first two methods of booting to Windows 95 are used with a shared installation; the last method in the list is used only for workstations containing their own Windows 95 installation.

If you intend to have all the network clients run Windows 95 from a server (the first two items in the preceding list), you'll be able to:

- Control how each type of machine is configured to access the network.

- Give users the ability to move from computer to computer while retaining their desktop, Start menu, and network user ID.

- Reduce the amount of local hard drive space used to install the Windows 95 operating system. A major advantage to setting up Windows with the shared installation is that workstations with low resources can run Windows 95 without upgrading memory and space.

But, be aware that using a shared installation also has its disadvantages, including the following:

- More network traffic is created and thus, the entire system becomes slower, including access to the server's resources.

- Windows will run slower on each workstation than it would if installed to the local drives from the server.

- More hard drive space on the server is used than would be using an installation on a local hard drive.

■ If the workstation has no hard drive or a very small hard drive, the swap files will be stored on the server instead of on the workstation; thus slowing the system even more.

Note

Swap files are temporary files created only when needed and only for the current Windows session. They do not permanently take disk space but they do rely on available disk space temporarily.

One final consideration to your network planning: in past Windows versions, the supervisor control over the program setup was a major reason to perform a shared installation. The supervisor, or network administrator, could control each workstation's files, folders, shared resources, and desktop. With Windows 95, however, a shared installation is no longer necessary for this type of control; a supervisor can easily go into a local setup of Windows and perform these same functions and protect those settings with Windows 95 security features.

Requirements of Server-Based Install

To perform a server-based install, you have to follow some technical requirements. First, the server-based installation programs and scripts are only available on the Windows 95 CD-ROM (in the ADMIN\NETTOOLS\NETSETUP directory). They are not available via online connections or on the Windows 95 floppy disks.

Second, a server-based setup can only be configured from a workstation with Windows 95 already installed. This workstation must also have a compatible network client running. And it must have access to the server on which the setup files are expected to reside and where the shared installation files will be placed.

You need to allocate at least 90M of hard disk space to store the server-based Windows 95 source files. The hard disk space requirements for the server may increase depending on how you have each network workstation start Windows 95. Use table 5.1 to determine how much hard disk space on the server will be used by all the network workstations. First, determine how many of each startup type you'll be using, then multiply the number of configurations of each type by the space required. Total all the startup types to get an estimate for how much space you need.

Table 5.1 Hard Disk Space Requirements for a Server-Based Install by Startup Type		
Windows 95 Network Startup Type	**Workstation Disk Space Required**	**Server Disk Space Required**
Local hard disk startup, running Windows 95 locally	20M	0M
Local hard disk startup, running Windows 95 from server	2M	1.5M
Floppy disk startup, running Windows 95 from server	1.2M on floppy	2M

For each network workstation, you have to plan the amount of memory in each computer. No matter whether your workstation client is protected-mode or real-mode, 16M of RAM is recommended.

Planning Shared Installation

It's important to plan ahead before you define and create the shared installation so you make the most of your time and resources. Incorporate the following topics into your installation strategy:

- Network client components

- Machine directories

- Network card addresses

- Setup scripts

> **Note**
>
> The Windows 95 Resource Kit contains a Deployment Planning Guide that identifies other planning issues a network administrator would want to consider before installation. The Resource Kit help files are located on the Windows CD in the ADMIN, RESKIT, and HELPFILE folders.

Component Issues

Certain technical limitations exist with respect to network access before each workstation installation can begin. Other technical requirements affect which network clients or protocols are available. By considering these issues now, you can avoid hours of frustration.

To create a shared installation environment, you can install the Windows 95 source files on the following networks:

- Banyan VINES 5.52

- Microsoft Windows NT Server

- Novell NetWare 3.x and 4.x

Other types of networks will support a server-based installation to a local hard drive; however, they don't have the technical capabilities to support machine directories and user profiles. A *machine directory* is a directory on the server containing setup information about each workstation, such as memory, disk space, network card, and so on. A *user profile* is a directory that contains setup information about each user's Windows environment, such as desktop, customizations, files, and folders. The administrator uses each of these directories to identify workstations and users on the network.

To execute the installation process on a network workstation, the computer is required to have network access. It must be able to see the location where the server-based installation files are stored. If the workstation doesn't have network access, it won't be able to read the source files to perform the installation.

After you've confirmed all workstations will have network access, you need to consider which components you'll use. Windows supplies the necessary components for the aforementioned networks, including the client, protocol, and service. You can use Microsoft's supplied components or you can supply your own; however, Microsoft's seem to work more smoothly and efficiently than any third-party components. You choose the components in the Network Properties sheet (access through the Control Panel) on the Configuration page.

Note

Windows 95 supports 32-bit components, such as the protocol, network adapter, and File and Printer Sharing services. The Windows IPX/SPX-compatible protocol and TCP/IP (with a DHCP client) are 32-bit versions; Windows also supports a variety of 16-bit clients.

Troubleshooting

I'm using 32-bit protected-mode networking software components instead of the real-mode equivalents, but I'm having trouble with some of my programs. Could the 32-bit components be the problem?

Yes. Although 32-bit protected-mode components ensure speed and stability across the network, you might find compatibility problems with certain programs. Your only choice, at this time, is to stick with the real-mode networking components if you're having trouble, or you can try using different Windows programs.

Some of the workstations on the network use both 32-bit and 16-bit components. Could this cause a problem when I install Windows 95?

Yes. Each workstation must use all 32-bit protected-mode networking components or all 16-bit real-mode components. A workstation cannot use a combination of 16- and 32-bit components.

Client

Client software enables you to use the shared resources, such as files and printers, of other network computers. Microsoft includes the following network clients:

- Client for Microsoft Networks provides the client for a peer-to-peer network between other Windows 95 computers.

- Client for NetWare Networks provides a client that works well with NetWare 3.x and 4.x.

Caution

If you use Microsoft-supplied clients for a shared installation, each workstation *must* use all 32-bit, protected-mode networking components.

You can install other clients, such as Banyan or Novell, using a disk. You *are* able to install more than one network client, if required. However, for the sake of configuration management, you'll want to create as few variations as possible while still fulfilling the needs of the network users. Additionally, more network clients loaded on a computer and accessing data on the server reduce the amount of memory available to other resources and slow down productivity.

Protocol

The *protocol* is the language the computer uses to communicate over a network; and all computers on a network use the same protocol. Microsoft provides the following protocols:

IPX/SPX-compatible

Microsoft DLC

NetBEUI

TCP/IP

Again, you can install another protocol, such as Banyan or Novell, if you have a disk; however, Microsoft's protocols work well as they are.

Service

One type of service enables you to share your files and printers with others on the network. Other services include an automatic backup, network monitor agent, and so on. Microsoft provides file and printer sharing services for Microsoft Networks. You also can install other services, such as Arcada or Cheyenne Backup software, if you have the software disks.

Machine Directories

The concept of a machine directory is new in Windows 95. The *machine directory* contains configuration information specific to a particular computer, called the *hardware profiles*. This information includes video card, mouse type, memory, and so on. Hardware profiles enable Windows to adjust system capabilities to match the hardware. A machine directory can exist anywhere on the network and is required for computers that start from a floppy disk, but optional for a workstation with Windows 95 installed to the local hard drive.

A machine directory is different than a user directory. The *user directory* is where the preferences for the specific person are stored, such as icons on the desktop or screen savers. In cases where someone may move from computer to computer throughout the day, configuration settings like the video card, network card, and monitor type stay with the computer. User profiles, such as Start menu items, desktop items, and font and color preferences, should follow the user when he/she logs onto any workstation on the network.

Machine directories offer several benefits:

■ Each workstation's settings are stored in a central location on the network so that no matter who logs onto that workstation, the correct settings are used.

■ The administrator can use a single boot image from the network to start several computers.

■ The administrator can easily replicate shared installations for new computers without running Setup again.

If you plan to specify machine directories for multiple computers, you can save time by creating a text file that contains the computer names and locations of the machine directories. You can use this file later to specify the machine directories after installation of Windows 95.

To create the text file, use the following format:

computername,\\servername\directory\machinedirectory

where *computername* is the name of the workstation, *servername* is the name of the server, *directory* is the name of the directory and in some cases the drive or volume, and *machinedirectory* is the name of the directory for the workstation.

An example of an entry for the text file is

director,\\humble_41\vol1\winsetup\ibmpc350

In the text file, use only one entry for each machine directory per line. Save the file in text-only format (ASCII), and store it in a shared directory on the server.

Network Card Addresses

For each computer that uses a shared installation machine directory, you need to identify the address of the network card. The network card address is usually a 12-digit alphanumeric field. If any of the addresses are less than 12 digits, zeros must be added to the left side of the field until it is exactly 12.

Tip

The network card address can be found in NetWare environments by typing the command **USERLIST /A** at a command prompt. Each user ID has a network address after it. The address can be found in Windows for Workgroups networks by typing the command **NET DIAG /S** at a command prompt.

In a text editor, compile a list with three columns. The first column should be the computer name. The second column should be the name of the machine directory you create. The third column is the network card address, such as:

```
I.E.Dell   f:\machine\DellPC       00123a5542d3
```

Save the text under any name you can easily recognize later while setting up machine directories and addresses. You can print the file now, or later when you're ready for it. The file you enter this information to is called the MACHINE.INI. The MACHINE.INI file points the computer to the correct machine directory during Windows 95 Setup and thereafter. See the section "Using Network Card Addresses" later in this chapter.

Setup Scripts

Setup scripts are mini-programs that assist in making choices—such as choosing protocols, services, security, clients, and so on—during the Windows setup and installation. Windows offers default scripts that take care of most installation settings; however, you can edit these scripts or create your own as you work with the server-based installation.

The MSBATCH.INF setup script comes on the Windows 95 CD and installs with the other Windows source files to the server. The MSBATCH.INF file contains instructions Windows needs to set up the workstations.

The MSBATCH.INF file contains the following scripts:

[Setup]	WorkstationSetup=1
CCP=0	DisplayWorkstationSetup=0
ProductID=*xxx-xxxxxxx*	Display=1
ProductType=1	Hdboot=1
Uninstall=0	RPLsetup=1
[Network]	

Each line in the script represents a setting for the workstation. Product ID, for example, lists the product's number that you enter when you're installing Windows 95. Uninstall lists whether you choose to enable uninstall (1) or disable uninstall (0). The Network section contains script that affects your remote, floppy, or local drive install of the workstations.

> **Caution**
>
> Creating setup scripts is beyond the scope of this book. Before you choose to write setup scripts, see the MS Windows 95 Resource Kit Help file for clarification.

> **Note**
>
> The Windows 95 CD includes an additional program you can use to create a setup script. The Batch program is located in the Admin, Nettools, Netsetup folder. The Batch file displays a dialog box in which you enter your name, computer's name, workgroup, and so on. Additionally, you can choose network options (protocol, client, and so forth) and installation options (set prompts, search folders for devices, and so on). After you make your choices in the dialog box, you can save the batch file as an INF file and copy it to the Windows directory on the server. Also in the NETSETUP folder is a BATCH help file that you can use if you have problems.

To find out more about creating setup scripts, see the Windows 95 Resource Kit help on Server-Based Setup, located on the Windows 95 CD-ROM. In the ADMIN folder, choose RESKIT, HELPFILE, and the WIN95RK help file.

> **Tip**
>
> The Windows 95 CD-ROM contains some sample scripts with different levels of security. They can be found in ADMIN\RESKIT\SAMPLES\SCRIPTS.

Installing Windows 95 from a Server

After you plan your installation, you're ready to actually install Windows. Installing Windows 95 is a threefold process:

- Copy the installation source files to a server
- Create machine directories
- Install Windows to the workstations

Copy Files to Server

To make the Windows 95 setup files available to everyone on the network, they must be placed in a common area. If you are only creating a common location for everyone on your network to install Windows 95 to their local hard disk, you'll learn everything in this section. If you're creating a shared installation environment, the rest of this chapter will guide you step by step.

For shared installation, you can install the Windows 95 source files on one of the following networks:

- Banyan VINES 5.52

- Microsoft Windows NT Server

- Novell NetWare 3.x and 4.x

For installing from the server to a workstation, you can install on the following networks:

- Artisoft LANtastic 5.x

- DEC PATHWORKS

- IBM OS/2 LAN Server 1.2 or greater

- Microsoft LAN Manager 2.x

- Microsoft Windows 95 peer server (using Client for Microsoft)

- NetWare using Microsoft's Client for NetWare Networks

- SunSoft PC-NFS 5.0

To create a server directory containing the Windows 95 source files, follow these steps:

1. Log onto the network file server with administrator privileges from a machine running Windows 95. Logging on as administrator also guarantees you have the security rights to create new directories and files on the server.

> **Note**
>
> System administrators may want to protect any directories they create (or directories that Windows 95 creates) from the average user so that no one can delete or modify the directories on the server.

> **Note**
>
> The computer you use to install Windows 95 to the server must have a CD-ROM drive. You need your Windows 95 CD as well.

2. Start Windows 95 and open the Explorer.

3. Open the Windows 95 CDI. In the ADMIN\NETTOOLS\NETSETUP\ folder, double-click NETSETUP.EXE. The Server Based Setup dialog box appears, as shown in figure 5.1.

Fig. 5.1
The Server Based Setup dialog box lists the current server where the source files are to be installed.

4. If the path to the server listed in the Set Server Install Path area is not correct or there is no path listed, click the Set Path button (or Change Path if a path has already been set). When you click this button, the Server Path dialog box appears (see fig.5.2). Enter the Universal Naming Convention (UNC) path to hold the source files, and click OK or press Enter.

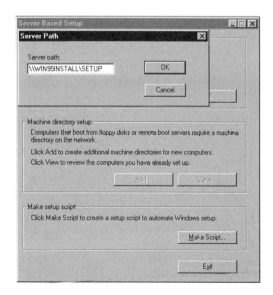

Fig. 5.2
Enter the server and path name in UNC format to specify the destination for the source files.

> ## Tip
>
> The UNC format for a NetWare server directory is
> *servername**volumename**directoryname*

If you enter a directory name that doesn't exist, you are prompted to create it. If you don't remember the exact path for the location, use the Network Neighborhood to browse the network. After you've identified the path, you can click the Server Based Setup icon in the taskbar to bring the application forward.

5. After entering the UNC path of the directory, choose Install. The Source Path dialog box appears (see fig. 5.3). From the following options, choose the Server install policy for installing the Windows 95 files to the server:

- *Server*. Select this option to store the files on the server as a shared installation.

- *Local Hard Drive*. Select this option to install all Windows 95 files to the workstation's hard drive.

- *User's Choice*. Select this option to enable the user to choose where to install the Windows files.

The Path to Install From should already contain the location from which you will be copying. If not, enter the correct path to the CD-ROM drive. Enter the Path to Install To path.

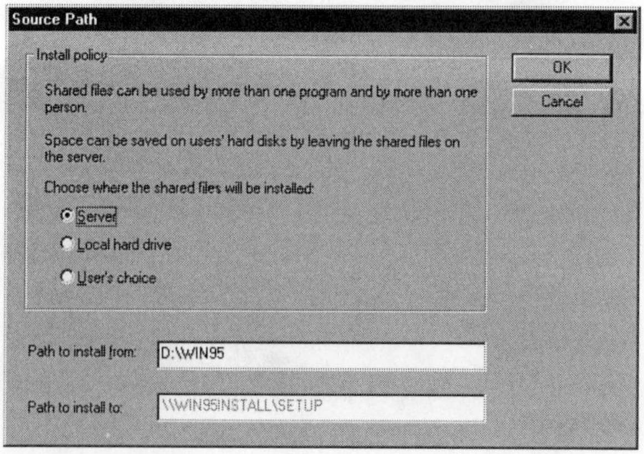

Fig. 5.3
Select the install policy for shared files and enter the directory name from which the Windows 95 source files will be copied.

6. Click OK to confirm your settings. At this point, you are given the option to create a default script. Figure 5.4 shows the Create Default dialog
box. You can choose Don't Create Default to begin installing Windows
95 source files to the server; Windows uses the default MSBATCH.INF
setup script from the server drive.

Alternatively, you can click Create Default to choose specific configuration settings by creating your own setup scripts.

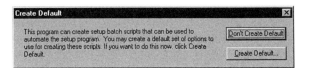

Fig. 5.4
Choose whether
you want Setup to
create the default
script.

7. Next, you are prompted for your CD Key number to identify the product. The 10-digit number is located on the back of the Windows 95 CD
case on an orange sticker. Enter the number in the text box, as shown
in figure 5.5.

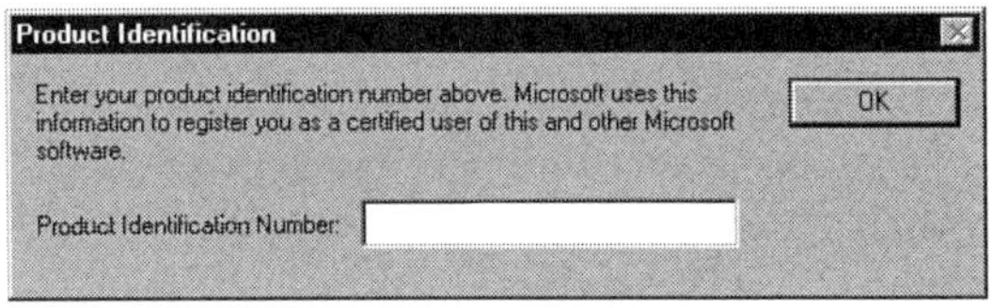

Fig. 5.5
Enter your product
identification
number from the
orange sticker on
the back of the
Windows 95 CD
case.

8. After you confirm your entry in the Product Identification dialog box,
Setup copies all the files into the directory you specified earlier. You are
able to track the progress in the Copying Files dialog box.

If you need to stop the process, click the Cancel button in the Copying
Files dialog box. Notice during the process that Net Setup has marked
all the necessary files and folders as Read Only, just as they would be
marked on the CD. When copying is complete, choose OK.

Note

If you use a special virus scanning-application, a company-wide sales application, or
other such application, be sure to copy the required DLLs and VxDs into the appropriate subdirectories on the server. You should also add these files to the default
MSBATCH.INF file.

Troubleshooting

I get a warning message when I try to enter a UNC path in the Server Path dialog box. Why can't I complete the installation?

You're not logged in as system administrator, or you do not have the access you need to create a directory on this server. You can specify another server, if you have privileges for it, or you can quit Setup and log on using the appropriate account.

Or, perhaps you're not entering the correct path; be sure you include the double backslashes, server name, volume name, and so on.

How do I set sharable attributes in the new Windows 95 folder? Can I use the FLAG command?

You don't need to use the NetWare FLAG or any other command to set sharable attributes; Windows source files are marked read-only automatically so they're ready to be used by the workstations.

If you're creating a shared installation, read the next section to learn how to set up machine directories. If you used Net Setup to copy the files to a central location just for users who will install all of Windows 95 on a local hard drive, you can install those files to the workstation now. Users can double-click the Setup icon in the server's directory to begin the installation.

Create Machine Directories

The machine directories are used by computers that start Windows 95 by booting from a floppy disk. The machine directory is required by the network and contains the WIN.COM, full Registry, and startup configuration files, such as the SYSTEM.INI and WIN.INI, of a workstation on the network. For workstations on which Windows is locally installed, the machine directory is optional.

Tip

For floppy boot disk workstations, the swap files and TEMP directory are also in the machine directory.

Note

If you plan to specify machine directories for multiple computers, you must first create a text file containing the computer names and locations as described in the section, "Machine Directories," earlier in this chapter.

To create the machine directories, follow these steps:

1. In the Server Based Setup dialog box, choose Set Path (or Change Path) and specify the path to the server containing the Windows source files if the path is incorrect or missing. Click OK.

2. In the Machine Directory Setup area, click the Add button. The Set Up Machine dialog box appears.

3. To define a single computer's machine directory, choose the Set Up One Machine option. Enter the computer name and the path to its machine directory (see fig. 5.6).

    To set up multiple machine directories using a batch file, choose the Set Up Mulitiple Machines option. Enter the path and file name of the batch file containing the list of computer names and machine's directories.

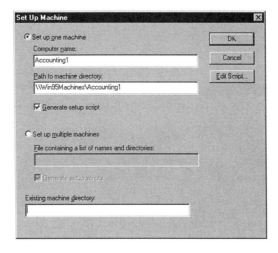

Fig. 5.6
For a single computer, enter its name and the path to the machine directory your creating.

4. To let the Server-based Setup create a default script, select the Generate Setup Script check box.

> **Note**
>
> To edit the default script for the machine directory, click the Edit Script button to display the Default Properties dialog box. This dialog box enables you to create or edit a setup script. For more information about setup scripts, see the Windows 95 Resource Kit help files located on your Windows 95 CD. Click OK when finished editing the script to return to the rest of the steps.

5. If you want to use an existing machine directory instead of creating new machine directories, enter the directory location in the Existing Machine <u>D</u>irectory text box.

> **Note**
>
> If you would like to view the list of computers using this shared installation directory, click the <u>V</u>iew button in the Server Based Setup dialog box. A list of computer names appears. As you highlight each entry in the list, its machine directory is displayed at the bottom of the dialog box.

6. After you've made your choices in the Set Up Machine dialog box, click OK. Setup then creates the machine directories (if you named new directories) and the default installation scripts (if you specified a script should be created). Setup stores the setup script in each machine directory.

> **Note**
>
> You can also click the <u>M</u>ake Script button to create a setup script from the Server Based Setup dialog box.

7. Choose E<u>x</u>it to close the Server Based Setup dialog box.

> **Troubleshooting**
>
> *The Registry for one of the workstations is corrupted. What can I do to fix it?*
>
> The SYSTEM.DAT and USER.DAT files are stored in the machine directory along with other configuration information, such as the SYSTEM.INI and WIN.INI. If the Registry becomes corrupted, you may be able to discern the problem by viewing these files in a text editor. If you cannot restore the Registry in any other way, you need to run the Windows 95 Setup again for that workstation.
>
> If you archive your custom setup scripts, you can save time and energy when running Setup again.

Using Network Card Addresses

Every computer starting Windows 95 from a floppy needs an entry in the MACHINES.INI file. If the computer doesn't have an entry, it can't access Windows 95.

Each entry in this file contains a network card address, the machine directory location, and the drive letters to associate with UNC names required for setup. Using the data you collected in the section Network Card Addresses earlier in this chapter, fill in the data. Format each entry in the MACHINES.INI to look like the example in the file:

```
;[node address]
;SYSDATPATH=drive:\path
;drive=\\server\share specified in sysdatpath
```

;[*node address*] is a 12-character address of the network adapter. In ;SYSDATPATH=*drive*:*path*, the *drive*:*path* is the one mapped to a drive letter in the same MACHINES.INI section.

Installing to the Workstations

Now that you've created a server-based installation, performing the installation on each workstation is your next step. Choose the method you want to use for booting the workstations and create or modify the startup scripting to give you the appropriate results.

The choices for starting Windows 95 Setup on the workstation are

- Starting Setup from a local hard drive
- Starting Setup from a local floppy disk
- Starting Setup on the workstation's hard disk

Booting from a Local Floppy Disk

If computers on your network will be booting from a local floppy disk, you'll run Windows 95 Setup once for each unique network card configuration. A *unique configuration* is defined as the make, model, and hardware settings for the card. The unique configuration has nothing to do with the computer type or model. After Setup creates a boot floppy for each configuration, you can duplicate the disks and distribute them to the corresponding users who have network cards in each configuration.

You need to create a startup disk and install the network client to that disk so you can attach to the network if you're starting Setup from a local floppy disk. Next, you need to edit the MSBATCH.INF, or other scripting file you may have created, to include entries for the appropriate boot type.

To create a startup disk in Windows 95, insert a formatted floppy disk into the floppy drive of the computer from which you run Windows 95. Follow these steps:

1. Click the Start button and choose _S_ettings.

2. Choose _C_ontrol Panel.

3. Double-click the Add/Remove Programs icon.

4. Choose the Startup Disk tab and click _C_reate Disk. Windows creates the disk using the floppy disk.

5. When Windows is finished, choose OK to close the dialog box.

6. From the server or a workstation to which you're logged on as administrator, install the network client to the startup disk to enable you to attach to the network.

To edit the startup script, log on to the network. You can edit the startup script file—whether MSBATCH.INF or another file you created—in a DOS or Windows text editor, such as DOS Edit or Windows Notepad. Edit the [Network] section to include one of the following entries for booting from a floppy drive:

WorkstationSetup=1

Hdboot=0

RPLsetup=0

Save the file under the same name and in the same directory. The name must use an INF extension, and the directory must be the directory to which you copied the Windows source files onto the server.

To install to the workstation, follow these steps:

1. Insert the startup disk into the workstation's floppy drive and reboot the computer. You can press Ctrl+Alt+Delete to warm boot.

2. Attach to the network.

3. You can change to the directory on the server that holds the Windows source files on the server and enter the following command:

   setup msbatch.inf

   SETUP is the Windows setup command, and MSBATCH.INF is the name of the default setup script; you want to substitute another setup script file name if you created the file yourself.

> **Note**
>
> Alternatively, you can enter the UNC paths from the A prompt in this format:
>
> **\\share_dir_server\directory**\SETUP.EXE **machines_server\
> directory\computer**\MSBATCH.INF
>
> Press Enter. *Share_dir_server* is replaced with the name of the server holding
> the server-based Windows 95 source files. *Directory* is the directory name
> containing the source files. *Machines_server* is the name of the server holding
> the machine directories. *Computer* is the name of the machine being set up.
> MSBATCH.INF is the name of the script being used. MSBATCH.INF is the
> default file name, although you may have created your own installation script.

4. Windows performs the ScanDisk system check. Click Continue to continue with the regular setup program.

5. Windows then copies the setup files it needs to complete the workstation installation you specified. As Windows leads the user through the
   process, it prompts for a new startup disk. Do not overwrite the existing
   boot floppy; insert a new formatted disk in the drive.

> **Note**
>
> If you are currently using a real-mode client to access the network, you are
> asked to insert the existing boot disk. Setup retrieves files from your current
> configuration, and then places them on your new startup floppy.

6. Repeat this process for each unique network card configuration. Then,
   duplicate enough copies for the number of users of each type. Don't
   forget to keep one of each type on file in a safe place!

   Each user will restart his/her computer using the new boot disk. Because
   the network card address is entered in the MACHINES.INI file, the correct information is placed in each machine directory.

Troubleshooting

Accessing the swap file takes too long on my workstation. Is this a network problem that can be fixed?

Workstations that boot from a floppy disk are set up so the swap file and TEMP directory are stored in the workstation's machine directory on the server. Since the workstation must go across the network to access the swap file, it will take longer to get through network traffic and back again. If you have sufficient space on your hard drive, you can change the location of the swap file to your hard drive. Add a **pagingfile=** path entry to the [386Enh] section of the SYSTEM.INI file stored in the machine directory.

Booting from a Local Hard Drive

If the computers on your network will be booting from a local hard drive to run the shared copy of Windows 95 on the network, you must change the setup script (INF) file to include the following:

WorkstationSetup=1

Hdboot=1

Each workstation must run Windows 95 Setup by following this process:

1. If you're installing from Windows 3.x or Windows for Workgroups, and a drive letter isn't already mapped to the shared installation directory, choose Disk, Select Drive from the File Manager. Then, choose File, Run in the Program Manager.

Or, from a DOS prompt, change the current working directory to the shared installation directory.

2. You can change to the directory on the server that holds the Windows source files on the server and enter the following command:

setup msbatch.inf

SETUP is the Windows setup command, and MSBATCH.INF is the name of the default setup script; you want to substitute another setup script file name if you created the file yourself.

3. The Windows 95 installation process starts and leads the user through the process. When complete, about 2M of files will reside on the local hard drive. The remaining files will be shared from the shared installation directory.

Installing Windows 95

Note

Alternatively, you can enter the UNC paths in this format:

\\share_dir_server\directory\SETUP.EXE

\\machines_server\ directory\computer\MSBATCH.INF

and press Enter. *Share_dir_server* is replaced with the name of the server holding the server based Windows 95 source files. *Directory* is the directory name containing the source files. *Machines_server* is the name of the server holding the machine directories. *Computer* is the name of the machine being set up. MSBATCH.INF is the name of the script being used. MSBATCH.INF is the default file name, although you may have created your own installation script.

Troubleshooting

While installing to the workstation, Setup asked if I wanted to create a local installation or a shared installation of Windows 95. What should I do?

The setup script file you used to start setup contains the line
DisplayWorkstationSetup=1, which offers the user the choice of how to set up Windows to the workstation. To select a shared installation, you must specify the path for the machine directory. For future installations, remove the DisplayWorkstationSetup=1 statement from the INF setup script file.

Installing Windows to the Workstation's Hard Disk

To install Windows from the server to the Workstation's hard disk, change directories to the directory containing the Windows setup files on the server. Type **setup**. If you have specified a setup script file, enter the name of the file after setup and press Enter. Setup installs the Windows files to the local hard disk.

Finishing Server-Based Install

Now that you've installed Windows to the server and to the workstations, you'll want to make some adjustments to the network configurations.

Networking Support

If you installed Windows 95 on top of a real-mode network client, all network access will be in 16-bit real-mode unless and until you switch to a protected-mode client. The 32-bit protected-mode clients supported by Windows 95 include the Client for Microsoft Networks and the Client for NetWare Networks.

Some advantages to using the protected-mode in Windows include the following:

- Supports multiple network redirectors that access the network file system simultaneously

- The NetWare network adapter driver is installed automatically and improves performance and reliability

- Supports peer resource sharing

- Supports plug and play, client-side caching, and automatic reconnections

- Enables the use of remote administration of the Registry and the use of the Network Monitor

- Supports long file names, if the server supports long file names

- All configurations are stored in the Registry so you don't have to maintain separate configuration files

If you installed Windows 95 to use a local hard drive with a real-mode client, you must install the protected-mode client using the network icon located in the Control Panel.

If you are still using a real-mode client after creating floppy disk-based installation, Windows 95 Setup was not able to locate a protected-mode client in its source files. You have to obtain the protected-mode client from the network vendor and re-create the floppy boot disk.

Setting Configuration Information

When configuring the workstations for shared installations, you may need to modify the AUTOEXEC.BAT of each workstation. If, for example, the AUTOEXEC.BAT previously contained a statement to start the network, such as NET START, Windows Setup places the shared installation commands at the same location. The modification you need to make is to ensure any command lines for DOS-based utilities in the AUTOEXEC.BAT come *after* the comand to start the network:

```
@ECHO OFF
SET PROMPT=$P$G
DOSSHELL
NET START
```

Until the DOSSHELL command is moved after the NET START entry, the DOS utility will never load. The AUTOEXEC.BAT file should be rearranged to look like the following:

```
@ECHO OFF
SET PROMPT=$P$G
NET START
DOSSHELL
```

The following programs reside in the shared installation directory:

CHOICE.COM	FDISK.EXE	SCANDISK.EXE
DISKCOPY.COM	FIND.EXE	SHARE.EXE
DOSKEY.COM	LABEL.EXE	SORT.EXE
EDIT.COM	MEM.EXE	START.EXE
FORMAT.COM	MOVE.EXE	SUBST.EXE
KEYB.COM	MSCDEX.EXE	XCOPY.EXE
FC.EXE	NLSFUNC.EXE	

File and Disk Management

This section offers a few considerations about files and file management when working with shared installations of Windows 95. Windows includes many disk tools you can use to analyze, report, and repair problems with physical disks. Additionally, Windows includes tools you can use to manage and protect the data on the drives.

Consider the following when managing your network workstations:

- *Microsoft Backup or network backup agent.* Back up user data regularly using either MS Backup or one of the two network backup agents included with Windows: Arcada and Cheyenne. Backing up user data safeguards against file loss and corruption.

- *Disk Defragmenter.* Use to organize fragmented files—files stored in noncontiguous sectors on the disk—to improve file access time.

- *DriveSpace.* Use to free space by compressing the drive space and the files on the drive. You can decompress the drive at any time without damaging data on the drive.

- *ScanDisk.* Use periodically to analyze and repair areas on the hard or floppy disks, including file allocation table, long file names, file system structure, directory tree structure, and so on.

You should plan to use the file and disk management utilities at regular intervals. You might, for instance, run ScanDisk every day or two, run Backup every week, and run Disk Defragmenter every third month.❖

Chapter 6

Configuring the Windows 95 Desktop, Display, and Fonts

by Rob Tidrow

By far, the most significant change in the Windows 95 user interface is its Desktop. Instead of limiting the Desktop to open applications or minimized icons, the Windows 95 Desktop can be used to launch applications, store folders, display shortcuts to files or programs, and provide quick access to Windows 95 configuration settings.

You also learn how to install and remove fonts on your system in this chapter. Windows 95 makes it easier than ever to add a font to your system and use that font from any folder on your system or a network folder.

In this chapter, you learn how to

- Create shortcuts

- Set background and wallpaper images

- Change screen savers

- Specify Desktop colors

- Configure the display

- Install and remove fonts

Creating Shortcuts

Windows 95 enables you to create shortcuts. A *shortcut* is a link to an object that enables you to access that object more quickly. Shortcuts are similar to program icons in Windows 3.x, but differ in that shortcuts can be created for any object on your system, including programs, files, documents, or even hardware devices. You might, for instance, provide a shortcut to your word processor application, such as Word for Windows, that you can double-click to start the application. You also might create a shortcut to a specific document, such as an Excel spreadsheet (see fig. 6.1). When you double-click the spreadsheet shortcut, if Excel is not opened, the shortcut opens Excel and loads your linked spreadsheet.

Fig. 6.1

Shortcuts can be created for folders, applications, devices (such as hard drives), files, or other objects.

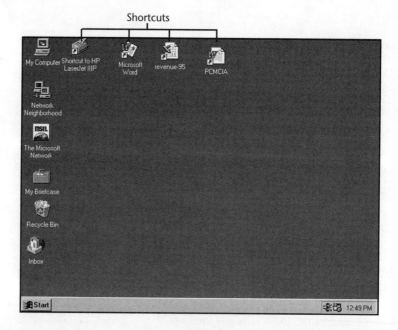

You can distinguish shortcuts from other items on the Desktop, such as folders, by the small arcing arrow on the icon (see fig. 6.2). This denotes that the icon is linked to an object that you can start or open by double-clicking it.

You can add shortcuts to your desktop or place them in a folder so that you can quickly access them as you work. The next two sections show you how to add and delete shortcuts to your desktop.

Arrow ———
Shortcut to HP
LaserJet IIIP

Fig. 6.2
Shortcuts have
tiny arrows on
them.

Troubleshooting

One of my shortcuts lost its link. How can I reestablish it?

For the most part, Windows 95 automatically updates a shortcut when you move the
object's file. If, however, Windows cannot find the file name, you can right-click the
shortcut and click Properties. Display the Shortcuts page on the Shortcuts Properties
sheet. In the Target box, enter the full path of the file name to which the shortcut is
linked.

Adding Shortcuts to Your Desktop

Windows 95 provides a few different ways to add shortcuts to your desktop.
You can stay on the Desktop to create a shortcut, or use the Explorer to drag
and drop objects to the Desktop.

The following steps show you how to create a shortcut using the Desktop
context-sensitive menu:

1. Move the mouse pointer to the Desktop and press the right mouse button. The context-sensitive menu appears (see fig. 6.3).

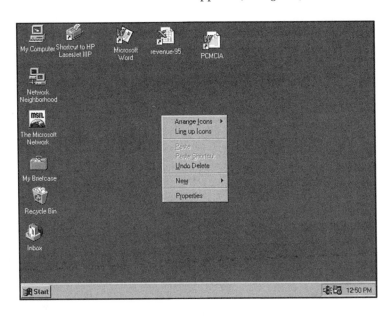

Fig. 6.3
Use the context-
sensitive menu on
the Desktop to
create a shortcut.

II

Configuring Windows 95

2. Choose New, Shortcut. The Create Shortcut dialog box appears, as seen in figure 6.4.

Fig. 6.4
The Create Shortcut dialog box enables you to add shortcuts to your desktop.

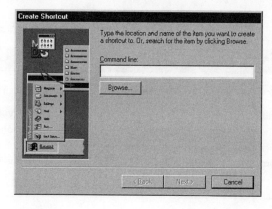

3. In the Command Line box, type the path and file name of the object you want to create a shortcut for.

Tip

Click the Browse button to search your system for a specific object name and location. By default, Windows 95 displays only programs. You can locate any file or object by clicking the Files of Type drop-down button and selecting All Files. Select the object you want, and click the Open button.

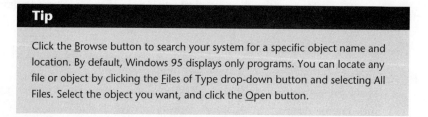

4. Click Next. The Select a Title for the Program dialog box appears (see fig. 6.5).

Fig. 6.5
In the Select a Title for the Program dialog box, you need to specify a name for your new shortcut.

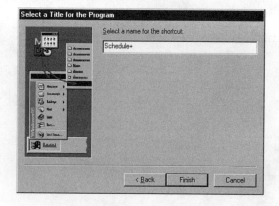

5. In the <u>S</u>elect a Name for the Shortcut box, enter a name for the new shortcut. Windows 95 provides a default name that is the same as the file name of the object. You can use this name or type over it to create your own.

6. Click Finish.

Tip

Changing the shortcut name does not alter the original file name.

Note

When you create a shortcut name, you can use up to 256 characters in it. This is probably overkill. You should, however, name the shortcut using an easy-to-understand name. If you have shortcuts for several documents that use the same application (such as a word processor or spreadsheet), make sure that your shortcut names are distinguishable so you open the appropriate document (see fig. 6.6).

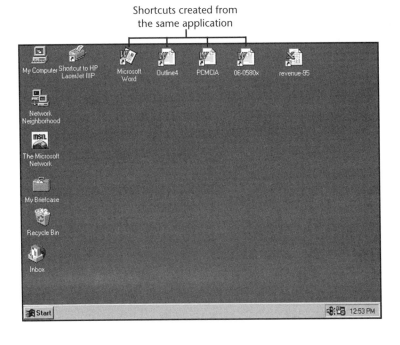

Shortcuts created from the same application

Fig. 6.6
Shortcuts created for different documents within the same application can be difficult to keep straight.

Windows places your new shortcut on the Desktop. You can move it on the Desktop, rename it, or delete it (see "Deleting Shortcuts" later in this chapter).

Another way to create a shortcut is to use the Explorer to drag objects onto the Desktop. This is the quickest way to create several shortcuts at once. Use the following steps to create a shortcut using the Explorer:

1. Open the Explorer to the folder that contains the file or object you want to set up as a shortcut.

2. Press the right mouse button on top of the item you want as a shortcut and drag it to the Desktop. Release the mouse button (see fig. 6.7), and click Create Shortcut Here from the context-sensitive menu.

Fig. 6.7
Click the right mouse button to drag an object to the Desktop so you can create a shortcut for the object.

Dragging a shortcut from the Explorer

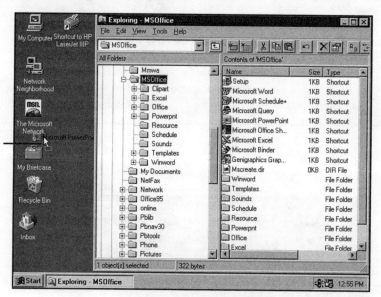

Caution

If you drag an item from the Explorer to the Desktop using the left mouse button, Windows 95 automatically moves that item to the Desktop folder. This occurs for any object except for applications. If you drag an application using the left mouse button, Windows 95 automatically creates a shortcut to that application, without moving the application file.

> **Note**
>
> After a shortcut is created, you can quickly rename it by clicking the shortcut name and typing a new name. Press Enter. You also can right-click the shortcut and select Rename from the context-sensitive menu. Type the new name and press Enter.

As mentioned earlier, you can quickly create several shortcuts at once by dragging several objects from the Explorer. To do this, press Ctrl when clicking objects in the Explorer (see step 2 in the preceding series of steps), and then release both Ctrl and the right mouse button on the Desktop. You then can rename the shortcuts.

> **Note**
>
> To create a shortcut to a printer, choose Start, Settings, Printers. In the Printers folder, click the printer to which you want to create a shortcut and press the right mouse button. Drag the printer icon onto the Desktop and select Create Shortcut(s) Here. Now you can drag files from the Explorer or Desktop on top of the printer shortcut to print your documents.

Changing Shortcut Properties

You can view or change the properties of a shortcut by right-clicking the shortcut and selecting Properties. Click the Shortcut page. Figure 6.8 shows a typical shortcut property sheet. Here you can change the icon, what kind of window it appears in, or the key combinations used to start it.

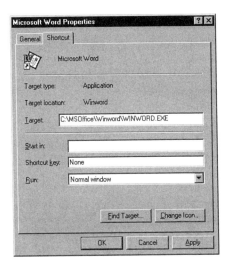

Fig. 6.8

A typical shortcut property sheet enables you to customize your shortcut.

II

Configuring Windows 95

The icon that appears when you create a shortcut may not suit your need. Or, you may have a difficult time seeing it against the Desktop wallpaper. You can change the icon by clicking the Change Icon button and scrolling through the Current Icon list (see fig. 6.9) until you find one you like. Click it and click OK. On the Shortcut Properties sheet, click Apply. The shortcut's icon changes to the one you selected.

Fig. 6.9
Tired of that drabby icon for your shortcut? Change it by modifying the shortcut's properties.

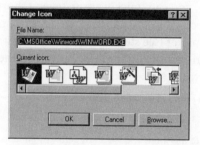

> **Tip**
>
> Click the Browse button to find other icons on your computer.

Another setting that you can change for your shortcuts is the keyboard combination that activates or switches to the shortcut. In the Shortcut Key box on the Shortcut page (refer to fig. 6.8), enter the keyboard shortcut you want to use. This key combination can be used in any Windows application to start or switch to the shortcut's application. For instance, you might want to assign Ctrl+Shift+W to start Word for Windows.

> **Caution**
>
> Any key combination set up using the preceding instruction cannot be used in any other application or feature in Windows 95. The Windows 95 shortcut key combination overrules all other settings you may already have set.

> **Note**
>
> The shortcut property settings also include an option to set the way in which the shortcut item opens. In the Run drop-down list, you can select Normal, Minimized, or Maximized. Normal displays the window sized as you last used it. Minimized opens the object and places it on the taskbar in a minimized state. Maximized displays the object in a maximized window.

Deleting Shortcuts

Shortcuts placed on the Desktop are a handy way to start items that you frequently use. Through the course of a week, if you add a shortcut for each file, application, or device you use, your desktop may start getting cluttered. Even though the resource requirement of shortcuts is minimal, each one adds up after awhile. If you find yourself being hampered by the number of shortcuts set up, delete a few.

You can delete shortcuts in several ways. The quickest way is to click the shortcut and press Delete. Answer Yes to the confirmation dialog box that appears, such as the one in figure 6.10. Another way to delete a shortcut is to right-click on a shortcut and select Delete. Again, answer Yes to confirm the message.

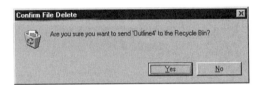

Fig. 6.10
If you are sure that you want to delete a shortcut, answer Yes. Otherwise, select No.

Adding Folders to Your Desktop

Although you can add a shortcut to a folder on the Desktop, you also can create a folder that exists on the Desktop. You might, for instance, want to place a folder on the Desktop that contains all your business-related documents—memos, faxes, spreadsheets, databases—so that you can open one folder to access all of them (see fig. 6.11).

In fact, when you install Windows 95, a few common folders are placed on your desktop automatically (see fig. 6.12), including the following:

- My Computer
- Network Neighborhood, if a network is installed
- Recycle Bin
- Inbox
- The Microsoft Network

Fig. 6.11
Create folders on your desktop to hold all your important—or not so important—documents.

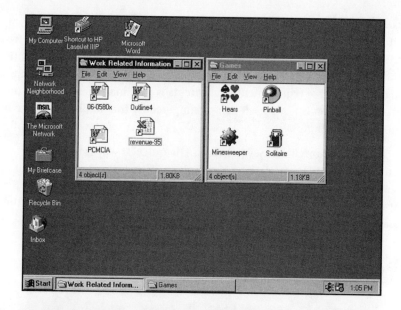

Fig. 6.12
Upon installation, Windows 95 gives you a few folders to start using.

Folders—

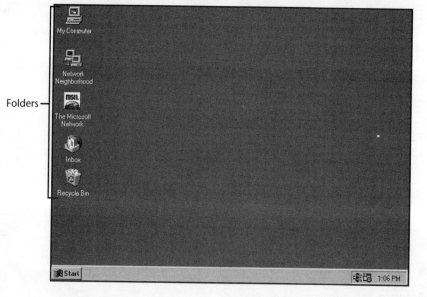

To add a folder to the Desktop, use the following steps:

1. Move the mouse pointer to the Desktop and press the right mouse button.

2. From the context-sensitive menu, choose New, Folder.

3. A new folder appears on the Desktop. Name the folder and double-click it to add items to it.

4. In the new folder, choose File, New, Shortcut to add shortcuts to the folder, or File, New, Folder to add a folder within the folder.

> **Tip**
>
> You also can drag files, folders, and other objects from the Explorer into your new folders to store them. For added convenience, the folder does not have to be open for you to drag an object to it. Just drag and drop the object over the closed folder.

Setting Background and Wallpaper Properties

On your wall or desk in your office, you probably have family pictures, awards, Post-It notes, photographs of the ocean, and other items that help you escape the pressures of the day. Not to be outdone, Windows 95 enables you to jazz up your desktop to add color to it. You can change the background patterns and wallpaper, and even create your own wallpaper. The following sections show you how.

> **Note**
>
> The Microsoft Plus! Companion for Windows 95 gives you more than a dozen different desktop themes to help you dress up your Windows 95 environment.

Changing Patterns and Wallpaper

When Windows 95 installs, it loads a standard Windows Desktop theme and wallpaper. You can experiment with the background patterns and wallpaper to suit your taste. To change the desktop settings, you modify the Desktop properties, which you can access by right-clicking anywhere on the Desktop and selecting Properties from the context-sensitive menu. The Display Properties sheet appears (see fig. 6.13).

Fig. 6.13
You change the
way your desktop
looks using the
Display Properties
sheet.

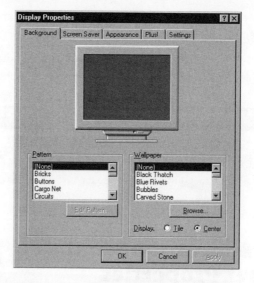

> **Tip**
>
> You also can display the Display Properties sheet by double-clicking the Display icon
> in Control Panel.

In the <u>P</u>attern drop-down list box, you can choose from a number of different
patterns to display on your desktop. These range from Bricks and Buttons to
Triangles and Waffle's Revenge. You also can choose (None), which places no
pattern on the desktop. Scroll through the list of patterns and click one to
view an example of how it looks in the "monitor" on the Background page.
Click <u>A</u>pply to place the pattern on your desktop.

> **Note**
>
> You can change the way the pattern looks, or create your own by choosing a pattern
> in the <u>P</u>attern list and clicking <u>E</u>dit Pattern. In the Pattern Editor (see fig. 6.14), click
> the <u>P</u>attern box to edit or create a new pattern. If it is a new pattern, type in a new
> name in the <u>N</u>ame box. Click <u>D</u>one when you finish and then click OK.
>
> You can remove a pattern when you are in the Pattern Editor by selecting its name
> from the <u>N</u>ame list and clicking <u>R</u>emove.

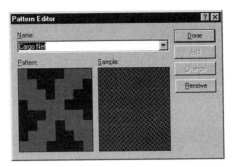

Fig. 6.14
Use the Pattern
Editor to modify
the way your
desktop pattern
looks.

When you select a pattern, it fills the entire background. The color of the
pattern is determined by the color you have set up for your background,
which is set in the Appearance tab of the Display Properties sheet and discussed later in this chapter in "Specifying Desktop Colors."

To change the wallpaper, scroll down the Wallpaper list box. The names of
wallpaper from which you can choose include Black Thatch, Blue Rivets,
Clouds, Metal Links, Setup, and more.

Note

By default, only a few wallpaper files are installed during Windows Setup. To add
additional wallpaper files, double-click the Add/Remove Programs icon in Control
Panel. Then select the Windows Setup page and select the Accessories item in the
Components list. Click the Details button, select Desktop Wallpaper, and click OK
twice. Make sure that you have your Windows 95 installation disks or CD handy
when you do this.

After you select the wallpaper, you can preview it in the preview monitor in
the Display Properties sheet. Click Apply to place the wallpaper on your desktop. You can display the wallpaper in the center of your screen by clicking
the Center radio button, or have it cover the entire screen by clicking the Tile
button.

Tip

When you tile wallpaper, it covers any pattern that you may have selected earlier.

Choose OK when you have the pattern and wallpaper you like. Your desktop
displays your selections, as shown in the example in figure 6.15.

Fig. 6.15
The Forest wallpaper and Buttons patterns is added to the Windows 95 desktop.

Creating Your Own Wallpaper

If you don't like the ready-made images that Windows gives you for wallpaper, you can do one of three things. First, you can elect not to have wallpaper. Second, you can buy the Microsoft Plus! CD and get about a dozen new desktop themes that include colorful wallpaper images. Or third, you can create your own wallpaper image. To do this, all you need is a bitmap image saved as a BMP file. If you have a graphic that you've installed on your computer, such as from an online service like CompuServe or Prodigy, or from a CD loaded with pretty pictures, you can convert it to BMP format using graphic converters. If the file is already in BMP format, you don't need to worry about converting it.

> **Note**
>
> An excellent graphic utility that enables you to convert graphics formats is Paintshop Pro, a shareware utility from JASC, Inc. You can find it on many bulletin boards and online services. It reads several different file formats, including PCX, JPG, TIF, and GIF and then converts them to BMP.

Place the BMP file in any folder on your system and then open the Display Properties sheet. On the Background page, click the Browse button and locate the file on your system. Click OK when you select the file, and then click OK again to place your custom-made wallpaper on the Desktop. Again, you can tile or center the image to your liking.

Changing Screen Savers

Another way to set up the way your desktop behaves is to use a screen saver that starts when your computer is inactive for a specified time. When you set up a screen saver, you need to specify the screen saver name, the time to wait for it to start, and if it will be password-protected. The following sections discuss these items.

Choosing a New Screen Saver

To choose a screen saver, right-click the Desktop and select Properties from the context-sensitive menu. In the Display Properties sheet, click the Screen Saver page (see fig. 6.16). A list of your installed screen savers appears in the Screen Saver drop-down list. Select a screen saver from this list and look at a preview of it in the preview monitor on the Screen Saver page. Click Apply when you locate the screen saver of your choice.

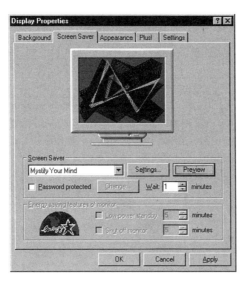

Fig. 6.16
Select a screen saver from the Screen Saver page in the Display Properties sheet.

Tip

Click the Preview button to get a full-screen view of a screen saver. Move the mouse to stop the preview.

You can configure the behavior of the screen saver by clicking the Settings button. This displays a dialog box in which you can adjust specific settings for each screen saver. The name of the dialog box varies depending on the screen saver you select. If you have installed the Microsoft Plus! screen savers, a General Properties sheet appears instead of a dialog box.

Not all screen savers have the same settings in this box. The Marquee screen saver, for instance, has options that enable you to create a message to display on-screen as well as the font, font size, color, and other text characteristics. The Curves and Colors screen saver, for instance, has the following options you can set:

- *Speed and shape*. Set the speed of the screen saver by using the scroll bar. You can set the number of lines that appear in the Lines box, and the number of curves in the Curves box.

- *Density*. Set the thickness of the curves by using the scroll bar. Set the number of colors and the color choices by clicking either the One Color or Multiple Random Colors radio boxes. If you select One Color, you can choose the color by clicking the Choose Color button and selecting the color from the Color dialog box.

- *Clear screen*. Check this option when you want the screen saver to appear against a black background. If this option is not selected, the screen saver runs "on top" of your desktop.

When you set the screen saver's settings, click OK and click Apply in the Display Properties sheet. On the Screen Saver page, you can adjust the time for the screen saver to wait until it starts. Set this time in the Wait box. You can select between 1 and 99 minutes. After your display is inactive for the selected number of minutes, the screen saver starts.

Setting Passwords

You can use your screen saver to ward off sinister snoopers who like to use your computer when you are away from your desk. To do this, set a password that users must type to stop the screen saver. The following steps show you how to set up a password:

1. On the Screen Saver page in the Display Properties sheet, click the Password Protected check box.

2. Click the Change button to set the password. The Change Password dialog box displays.

3. Type in a password in the New Password box. Retype the password in the Confirm New Password box.

4. Click OK to set the password.

To disable the password, deselect the <u>P</u>assword Protected check box on the Screen Saver page.

Specifying Desktop Colors

Earlier you saw how to change the background and wallpaper on your computer. You also can select the colors of your desktop, including the color of the menu bars, dialog boxes, and other elements. Windows 95 provides more than two dozen predefined color schemes that you can choose from, or you can create your own scheme. Another way is to use a predefined scheme and then modify it some to suit your taste.

Using Predefined Color Schemes

In the Display Properties sheet, click the Appearance page (see fig. 6.17) to access the different color schemes available to you. In the <u>S</u>cheme drop-down list, select from the various choices, including Pumpkin, Brick, Storm, and others.

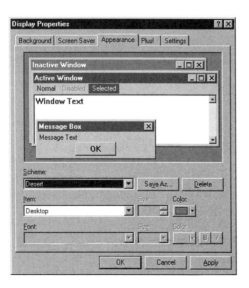

Fig. 6.17
Color schemes are a nice way to add some color to your life.

II

Configuring Windows 95

The best way to decide if you like a scheme is to click it and look at it in the preview window. Some color schemes have interesting names (such as Rainy Day and Marine), but their schemes are somewhat hard on the eyes. Pick the one that's best for you and your display.

After you select one, click OK to change your display to the selected scheme.

Customizing Color Schemes

If you get tired of looking at the built-in schemes that Windows 95 provides, create your own. To do this, return to the Appearance page in the Display Properties sheet. In the Item drop-down box, click the name of an item you want to change, such as Active Title Bar. Depending on the item you choose, you can modify the color, font size, font characteristic (bold or italic), and font.

The following list describes the options you can modify:

- *Size*. Set the size of the selected item. This may be the size of the window and its borders.

- *Color*. Click this button to select the color of the item.

- *Font*. Set the font of the item. You can choose from all the fonts you currently have installed on your system.

- *Size*. Set the font size for the selected item.

- *Color*. Set the color of the font for the selected item.

- *Bold, Italic*. Use these settings to display the selected item's text in bold or italic.

After you create a new color scheme, you can save it and name it. Click the Save As button and type in a name in the Save This Color Scheme As dialog box. Click OK. To delete a color scheme, select the color scheme in the Scheme drop-down list box and click Delete.

Configuring the Display

One of the most-welcomed features of Windows 95 is its capability to change the display resolution on-the-fly. In previous versions of Windows, users had to restart Windows after they reset the resolution. This required that you save your work and shut down all your applications just to get a different resolution. Many users switch between standard VGA resolution (640 × 480) and

Super VGA resolution (1024 × 768) depending on the application and work they are performing.

Windows 95 enables you to change these settings quickly and without restarting Windows. You also can change the font size of elements on your screen as well as the color palette used. The next two sections show you how to modify these settings.

Caution

You can change the resolution of your display without restarting Windows 95 only if the new display uses the same font as the current display. Otherwise, you must restart Windows 95 to change display drivers.

Troubleshooting

When I change the resolution of my display, Windows 95 displays a black screen or has a bunch of wavy lines on it. What happened?

You probably selected a setting that your video adapter and monitor cannot display. To return to your previous setting, reboot your computer and enter Safe Mode by pressing F8 when your system boots and selecting Safe Mode from the Start menu. During Safe Mode, the Windows 95 Standard VGA driver is loaded, enabling you to boot into Windows and change the resolution of your monitor.

Changing the Display Resolution and Palette

In the Display Properties sheet, click the Settings page (see fig. 6.18). From here, you can change how your display looks and behaves. The Color Palette drop-down list shows the number of colors and color palette (high-color or true color) that your monitor supports. For many users, 256 Color is appropriate. For artists or users who work with graphics-intensive software, high color or true color is required to achieve professional results.

The Font Size drop-down list enables you to set the size of the text that appears. You can select either Large Fonts or Small Fonts. If your monitor does not enable you to change the way in which fonts appear, this setting is dimmed.

▶ See "Installing Your New Video Card into Your PC," p. 420

II

Configuring Windows 95

Fig. 6.18
Use the Settings
page to configure
your monitor type
and resolution.

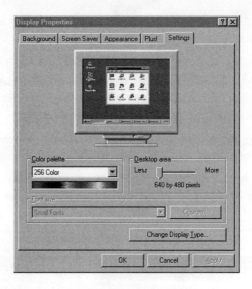

> ### Note
>
> Click the Custom button to create a custom font size for your display. In the Custom Font Size dialog box, set the scale of the font and look at the Sample area for an example of the way the font will look. You also can click on the ruler in the Sample area and drag it to the right or left to increase or decrease its scale. Click OK when you are satisfied with the font size.

Changing the Display Resolution

Now for the *piece d'resistance*. Change the display resolution by clicking the slider in the Desktop Area section. (The slider only appears if your adapter and monitor support higher resolutions.) This changes the amount of information that your monitor displays. A higher setting (such as 1024 × 768), shown in figure 6.19, gives you a lot of room to display windows and icons. A lower setting (such as 640 × 480) yields a much lower area to display information.

> ### Tip
>
> Generally, the higher the resolution, the slower the display refreshes.

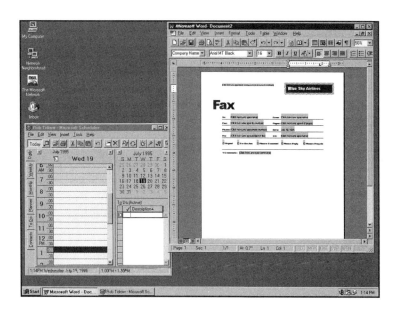

Fig. 6.19
A higher resolu-
tion enables you
to place more on
your desktop, but
it may slow down
your system too
much.

After you set the slider where you want it, click <u>A</u>pply. A warning message appears, telling you that Windows will change your display and that it may take 15 seconds or so. Click OK and then wait a few seconds. Your screen goes black for a moment and then pops, sometimes quite loudly. When it returns, click <u>Y</u>es when Windows 95 prompts you if you would like to keep the setting.

Note

If your display doesn't appear correctly or if you see nothing at all, you need to reboot Windows 95 and start in Safe Mode. In Safe Mode, Windows boots with a standard VGA display driver. After Windows 95 boots, go through the shut-down process and reboot your machine. When it restarts and goes into Windows, it should return to your old display settings.

If you cannot adjust the slider bar, your monitor and video card do not support other display resolutions from the one you have installed. You'll need to get a new driver or upgrade to another video card and/or monitor.

◀ See "Using
Windows 95
Safe Mode,"
p. 63

Troubleshooting

My monitor doesn't work right with the drivers included with Windows 95. Can I use a Windows 3.x driver?

Yes you can, but you should upgrade to Windows 95 drivers to take advantage of the enhanced graphics support in Windows 95. For instance, Windows 3.x drivers do not support changing your monitor resolution on-the-fly. To install Windows 3.1 display drivers, use the following steps:

1. Double-click the Display icon in Control Panel, click the Settings page, and then click Change Display Type.

2. Click the Change button next to Adapter Type, and then click the Have Disk button in the Select Device dialog box.

3. Specify the path to the disk or folder containing the Windows 3.1 drivers you want to use.

4. Select the correct driver to use from the list that appears, and then click OK to install.

Some Windows 3.1 drivers require the screen resolution to be specified in the [boot.description] section of SYSTEM.INI, such as in the following example:

```
display.drv=GD5430 v1.22, 800x600x256
```

Adding Fonts to Your System

Windows 95 includes an enhanced way to manage and view fonts on your system. The Windows 95 FONTS folder stores all the fonts on your system. When you open the FONTS folder, a window similar to the one shown in figure 6.20 appears. You can view a sample of the way in which a font looks by double-clicking the font icon. This displays a window that contains sample text of the font and includes details of other font properties, including font name, file size, version number, and the manufacturer of the font. Figure 6.21 shows the font window for a particular font.

To access the FONTS folder, select the Start button and click Settings, Control Panel. Double-click the FONTS folder in Control Panel. You also can access it by locating the \FONTS folder in your Windows 95 folder, such as \WINDOWS\FONTS. Once the folder appears, you can view, delete, print, and install fonts.

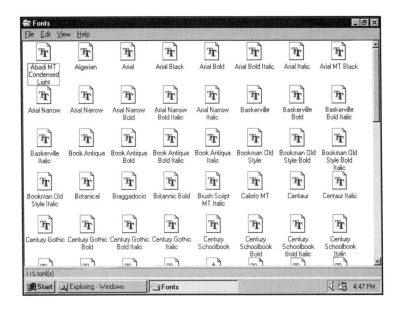

Fig. 6.20
The FONTS folder is used to store and manage all the fonts on your system.

Fig. 6.21
You can see a sample of a font by double-clicking it and viewing the sample in a window.

Configuring Windows 95

You can display a toolbar on the FONTS folder by choosing <u>V</u>iew, <u>T</u>oolbar. On the toolbar, you can reconfigure the way the fonts display in the FONTS folder by clicking the different toolbar buttons. The following list describes how the FONTS folder appears when selecting these buttons:

- *Large icons*. Displays icons of each font. Each icon includes the font name and type of font, such as TrueType (TT), and screen and printer fonts (A).

■ *List*. Displays a list of the icons on your system, with small icons representing the type of font installed.

■ *Similarity*. Sorts each font to show fonts according to their similarity with one another (see fig. 6.22). You can select a font from the List Fonts By Similarity To drop-down list, and Windows sorts the fonts by similarity to the chosen font. You might, for example, want to know how similar other fonts are to the Baskerville family of fonts.

■ *Details*. Displays all the details of the font file, including font name, file name, file size, and last modification date.

Fig. 6.22
You can find fonts that are similar to each other by clicking the Similarity button on the toolbar.

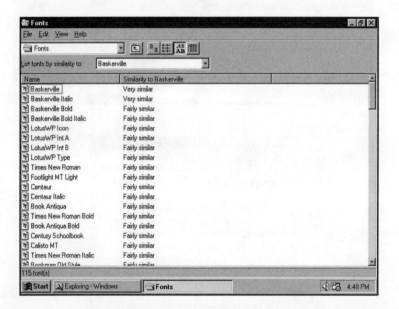

Tip

Use the Details view to obtain the file name of a font that you want to copy or delete from your system.

Installing New Fonts

Simply copying a font file to the \FONTS folder does not install the font for use with your Windows applications. You must install the font by choosing File, Install New Font in the FONTS folder. When you install a new font, Windows 95 places a setting in the Windows Registry to make it available for your applications.

To install a new font, use the following steps:

1. Select File, Install New Font to display the Add Font dialog box
(see fig. 6.23).

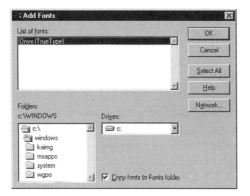

Fig. 6.23
Use the Add Fonts
dialog box to
install new fonts
on your system.

2. Select the font name(s) in the List of Fonts box.

> **Tip**
>
> To select more than one font name in the List of Fonts box, hold the Shift key
> down as you select contiguous fonts, or hold down the Ctrl key to select non-
> contiguous fonts. To select all of the listed fonts, click the Select All button in
> the Add Fonts dialog box.

3. If the font is in another folder, locate the folder in which the font is
stored in the Folders list box. You also can change the drive by clicking
the Drives drop-down list and selecting the appropriate drive.

4. Click the Copy Fonts to Fonts Folder check box to instruct Windows
to copy the selected font(s) to your \WINDOWS\FONTS folder. This
places a copy of the font file in the \FONTS folder on your system,
effectively duplicating the font file on your system. If you leave this
check box clear, the font files remain in the original source location,
but the Windows 95 Registry includes references to these locations.
This enables you to use those fonts in your applications, even when
they are not in your \WINDOWS\FONTS folder.

5. Choose OK to finish the installation steps and to install the fonts on
your system.

II

Configuring Windows 95

Tip

When you operate in a network environment, you may want to leave your font files on the network server to conserve space on your local machine. You can install fonts from the network by clicking the Network button and locating the font file names on your server. Make sure the Copy Fonts to Fonts Folder check box is not checked.

Removing Fonts

You can remove a font from your system by opening the FONTS folder in Control Panel and then clicking the font(s) you want to delete. Next, press Delete or choose File, Delete and click Yes when Windows asks if you are sure you want to delete these fonts. This deletes the font file and places the font file in the Recycle Bin.

Tip

Windows 3.x had a problem of using up a lot of memory when you installed numerous fonts on your system. Windows 95 does not have this same problem, even though you may want to reduce the number of font files on your system if you need to clean up some disk space.

Troubleshooting

How do I view only TrueType fonts in my applications?

If you use only TrueType fonts in your applications, such as Word for Windows, you can instruct Windows 95 to display only TrueType fonts when you are working. In the FONTS folder, choose View, Options and click on the TrueType page. Click the Show Only TrueType Fonts in the Programs on My Computer check box. Click OK.

Chapter 7

Configuring the Taskbar and Start Button

by Rob Tidrow

If you are a Windows 3.x user moving to Windows 95, you'll be in for a big surprise the first time you start Windows 95—Program Manager is gone. For some, this is a big relief. Others may feel a little lost. Microsoft has replaced Program Manager with the Start button. When you want to start a program, change system settings, or do whatever, you can find it using the Start button and its menu.

The taskbar is another fundamental change in Windows 95. The taskbar sits at the bottom of the screen (you can move it, as you'll learn later) and enables you to switch between open applications quickly, shows the time, and displays other system features. It's also where the Start button resides.

This chapter contains useful configuration information about the taskbar and Start button. When you install Windows 95, you don't have to do anything for these two items to work. But you might want to spend a few minutes customizing how they look and function.

In this chapter, you learn how to do the following:

- Set taskbar options
- Hide the taskbar
- Set Start button options

Setting Taskbar Options

You'll first examine the taskbar, which usually is the first item users interact with in Windows 95. By default, it sits at the bottom of the screen, as shown in figure 7.1. The taskbar is intended to make 95 percent of what you want to do in Windows 95 easy to accomplish.

Fig. 7.1
The taskbar is a simple, yet powerful new addition to Windows 95.

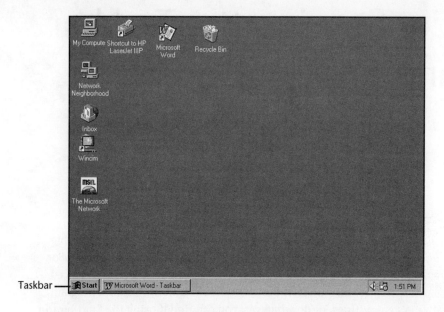

Taskbar ——

Note

The taskbar includes a few items of interest, namely the Start button and task buttons. The Start button is discussed in detail in "Setting Start Button Options" later in this chapter. *Task buttons* (see fig. 7.2) represent all the open applications you are using in Windows 95. Task buttons appear on the taskbar even when an application is not minimized, giving users a quick way to switch between tasks.

Other items that are on the taskbar are shown on the far right side of it. In this area, you can find the clock and applications running in the background, such as the System Agent available in Microsoft Plus!, modems, printers, and sound cards. You can quickly modify the configurations of these items by right-clicking over the tops of their icons. Next, select an item from the context-sensitive menu, such as Adjust Audio Properties if you are want to see the properties for a sound card. This brings up the property sheet of that device, as shown in figure 7.3. After you make adjustments, click OK.

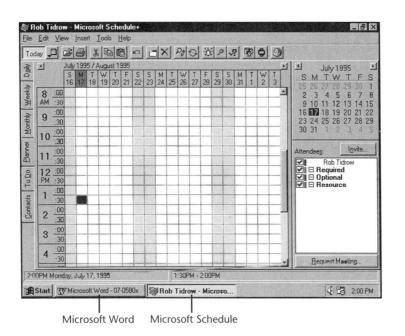

Fig. 7.2
Task buttons make it easy to switch between applications.

Microsoft Word   Microsoft Schedule

Tip

Move the mouse pointer over the time to see the day and the date.

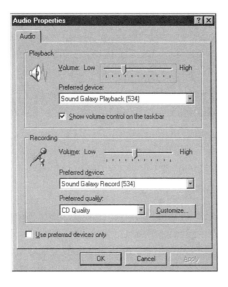

Fig. 7.3
Use the taskbar to access properties of the devices running in the background, such as your sound card.

▶ See "Managing
Utilities with
the System
Agent," p. 670

Some of the ways to customize the taskbar include the following:

■ Reposition and resize the taskbar

■ Set the way in which the taskbar appears

■ Show the clock

These items are discussed in the following sections.

Troubleshooting

I change the time in Windows 95, but my system clock displays a different time. Can you help?

On some systems, you must start your system startup utility during the boot process to change the system time and date on your computer. To do this, refer to the manual that came with your computer to see how you can start the system utility. On some computers, you can press Ctrl+Alt+Esc or press a function key assigned to the utility. Once in the system settings screen, use the navigational commands, such as the arrow keys and Page Up and Page Down, to navigate the screen and to make changes to the system time and date. The way in which you make changes depends on your system.

Repositioning and Resizing the Taskbar

If you don't like the taskbar at the bottom of the screen, grab it with your mouse pointer and drag it to another location on your Desktop. Don't try to put it in the middle of the screen. It only sits on the edges of the Desktop, either on the left or right side, top, or bottom. Figures 7.4 and 7.5 show how the taskbar looks on the top and left sides of the Desktop.

Caution

Depending on the width of the taskbar, you may only see the application icon and its first two letters when the taskbar is moved to the side of the Desktop. This can make it difficult to recognize your open applications.

Another way to customize your taskbar is to resize it. Move your mouse pointer over the taskbar's edge that is exposed. This is the side that is closest to the Desktop, such as the top edge if the taskbar is at the bottom of the screen. When the mouse pointer changes to a double-sided arrow, press and hold your left mouse button and drag the taskbar to the size you want. Figure 7.6 shows a taskbar diagnosed with elephantiasis!

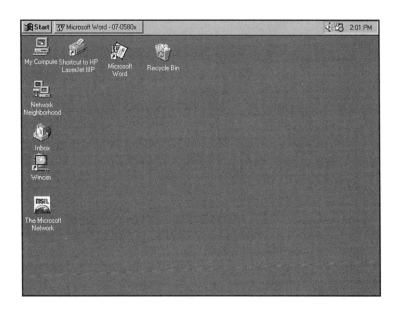

Fig. 7.4
Having the taskbar at the top of the screen is not a bad option.

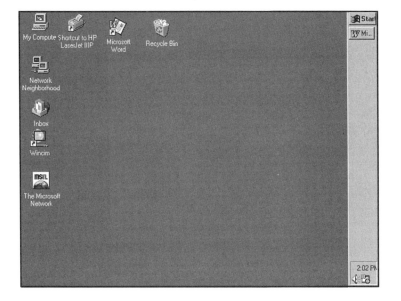

Fig. 7.5
But, having the taskbar on the side requires you to get familiar with your application icons to understand which application is which, because you can't see the words describing what the icon stands for.

Tip

You can resize the taskbar up to the size of your desktop by dragging it with your mouse.

Fig. 7.6
Get frustrated
when you can't
find the taskbar?
Just make it a little
bigger.

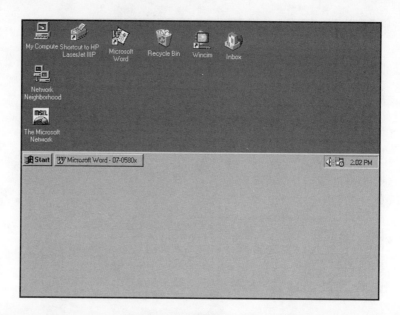

Troubleshooting

How do I remove the Network Neighborhood icon from my desktop?

The Network Neighborhood icon appears on your desktop automatically when you
install network resources under Windows 95. You cannot drag the Network Neighborhood icon to the Recycle Bin, or click on it and select Delete to remove it. You
must use the System Policy Editor to delete it. The System Policy Editor should be
used only by advanced users who feel comfortable making system changes to their
computers. If you are not, you should not try this. Also, before you start the System
Policy Editor, be sure your system is backed up in case you encounter problems and
lose data. The System Policy Editor is available on the Windows 95 installation CD
in the \ADMIN\APPTOOLS\POLEDIT\ folder. Double-click on the Poledit application
to start the System Policy. Chose Open Registry from the File menu, open Local
User (or your user ID), switch to \User\Shell\Restrictions, and check the Hide Network Neighborhood item. Click OK, close the System Policy Editor, and restart
Windows 95.

Setting Display Options

By default, the taskbar always appears. Even when you maximize an application, such as the one shown in figure 7.7, the taskbar is still visible at the
bottom of the screen. Microsoft refers to this state as being *Always on Top* and
is probably the most efficient way to use the taskbar. When the taskbar is on

top, you can quickly see which other applications are open, the time of the day, and the status of your printer or modem, and can readily access any of these items.

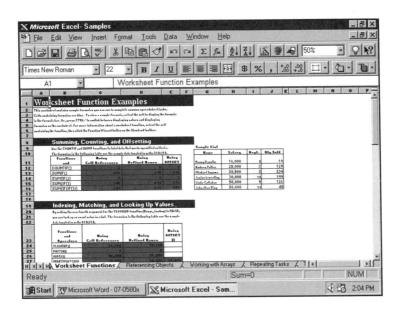

You can make the taskbar disappear when you are not using it. To do so, you need to set the Auto Hide feature, as shown in the following steps:

1. Right-click any exposed part of the taskbar.

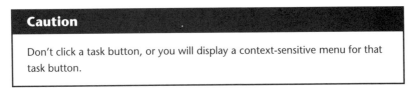

Caution

Don't click a task button, or you will display a context-sensitive menu for that task button.

2. Select Properties to display the Taskbar Properties sheet (see fig. 7.8).

3. On the Taskbar Options page, select Auto Hide and deselect Always on Top.

4. Click OK.

Now when you move the mouse pointer off of the taskbar, the taskbar disappears by sliding below the surface of the screen. To make it reappear, move the mouse down to the bottom of the screen (or wherever you have the taskbar). It automatically "slides" back into view, unless you have an

II

Configuring Windows 95

application covering that part of the screen. If you disabled the Always on Top option in the preceding step 3, the taskbar does not appear on top of the open application. You must move or resize the application's window to see the taskbar. Use this option when your screen real estate is limited and you want to use the entire screen for your applications. Otherwise, leave the default as-is.

Fig. 7.8
You can choose how the taskbar behaves by changing its properties.

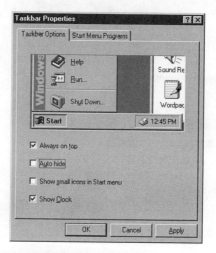

> **Note**
>
> Generally, if you run in 800 × 600 or higher resolution, and you use the taskbar or Start button a great deal, you should have no problem keeping the taskbar visible at all times.

Setting Clock Options

You can change the time that the clock displays by double-clicking it on the taskbar. This displays the Date/Time Properties sheet (see fig. 7.9).

On the Date & Time page, you can adjust the following properties:

- *Date.* Use the drop-down list to select the month, and set the year in the option box next to it. On the calendar, click the correct day of the month. The highlighted day is the current day.

- *Time.* Set the correct time that you want Windows to display in the option box. The large analog clock displays the time. Note that this box does not reset your system clock. You must do this using system utilities that come with your computer.

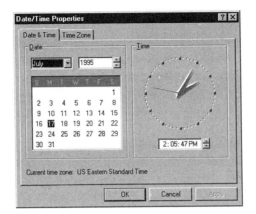

Fig. 7.9
Set the time, date,
and time zone by
double-clicking the
clock on the
taskbar.

On the Time Zone page, you can configure the time zone in which you live
or work. Use the drop-down list box to choose the time zone. If you live in an
area with Daylight Savings Time, click the option at the bottom of the screen
to have Windows automatically update your clock during these time changes.
Click OK when you have these options configured.

If you don't want the clock to show at all, use the following steps:

1. Right-click on any exposed part of the taskbar.

2. Select Properties, to display the Taskbar Properties sheet.

3. Deselect the Show Clock option, and click OK.

Setting Start Button Options

The Start button resides on the far left of the taskbar by default. The Start
button's purpose is to give users a leg up on getting their work done. When
you click the Start button, a menu pops up (see fig. 7.10) that contains several
items. You can use the Start button to launch programs, start Help, shut
down Windows 95, and find files. You also can access Control Panel to configure many of your system settings and devices.

Tip

You can quickly display the Start button on the taskbar by pressing Alt+S.

II

Configuring Windows 95

Fig. 7.10
The Start button's
menu gives you
access to all your
files, applications,
and settings.

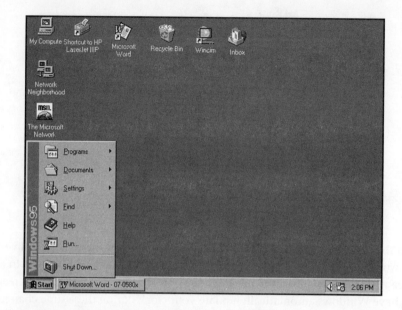

Windows 95 gives you several Start button options to customize according to your tastes. The Start button menu can be set up with the programs or files you use most often to give you one-button access to them. You might, for instance, use WinCIM to dial into the CompuServe Information Service. Place WinCIM on the Start button to quickly start it each time you want to dial CompuServe.

> **Tip**
>
> You also can use shortcuts to programs and applications on your desktop to quickly access them.

Another way to take advantage of the Start button is to add documents or specific files that you use all the time. This may be a daily spreadsheet you fill out, or a document template in Word for Windows.

By default, the Start menu shows large icons and a Windows 95 logo. You can reduce the size of the menu (see fig. 7.11) by using the Show Small Icons options on the Taskbar page, as shown in the following steps:

1. Right-click any exposed part of the taskbar.

2. Select Properties to display the Taskbar Properties sheet. Make sure the Taskbar page is selected.

3. Select the Show Small Icons in the Start menu, and click OK.

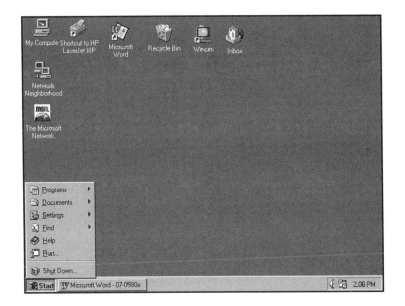

Fig. 7.11
You can configure the Start menu to use small icons to reduce the amount of space the menu takes up.

Add and Remove Items

The Start menu contains programs that are placed there during the Windows 95 installation. If you install Windows 95 over your existing Windows 3.x setup, Windows 95 automatically places all your installed applications on the Start menu. As you use Windows 95 and install new applications, you can add these programs to the Program folder on the Start menu, much as you can add program groups to Program Manager in Windows 3.x.

If you upgrade your system from Windows 3.x to Windows 95, Windows 95 automatically converts your old program groups to folders. You can locate these programs by choosing Start, Programs and looking at the folders that appear, such as those shown in figure 7.12.

Troubleshooting

How can I use my old Windows 3.x Program Manager instead of the new Windows 95 Desktop?

You can use Windows 3.x's version of Program Manager from within Windows 95 if you installed Windows 95 to its own directory (for dual booting). Launch the PROGMAN.EXE file from the Windows 3.x directory to start Program Manager. The only difference you may notice is the groups are not arranged in the same fashion on the desktop as they were when running under your previous Windows 3.x configuration.

Fig. 7.12
On the Start menu,
you can access
program folders in
much the same
way as you can
program groups in
Windows 3.x.

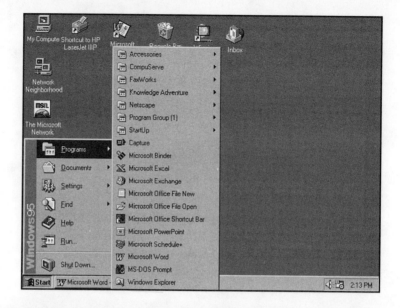

Tip

Another way to see the contents of the Programs folder is to view it in Windows
Explorer. You can view it by opening the folder in which Windows 95 is stored, and
then opening the Start menu and the Programs folder. From here, you can view, and
delete items, and drag and drop other items to the Programs folder.

You can add items to the Start menu by using the following steps:

1. Right-click any exposed part of the taskbar.

2. Select Properties to display the Taskbar Properties sheet.

3. Click the Start Menu Programs tab (see fig. 7.13).

4. Click the Add button to display the Create Shortcut Wizard.

5. In the Command Line text box in the Create Shortcut Wizard, enter the
   full path to the program or file shortcut you want to add to the Start
   menu.

Tip

Use the Browse button to search for the program or file you are looking for.

Fig. 7.13
Use the Start Menu
Program page to
add new programs
and program
folders to the Start
menu.

6. Click Next.

7. In the Select Program Folder dialog box (see fig. 7.14), click the folder
where you want to place the program or file shortcut. Generally, you'll
add the program to the Programs folder or create a new folder by using
the New Folder button and entering a new folder name.

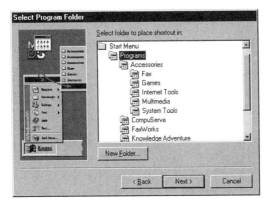

Fig. 7.14
Tell Windows the
folder in which to
place the program
or shortcut.

8. Click Next.

> **Note**
>
> To add a program or shortcut to the Start menu, add the program or shortcut
> to the Start Menu folder in the Select Folder To Place Shortcut In list box (see
> fig. 7.15).

Fig. 7.15
By adding shortcuts to the Start menu, you can decrease the time it takes to start a program.

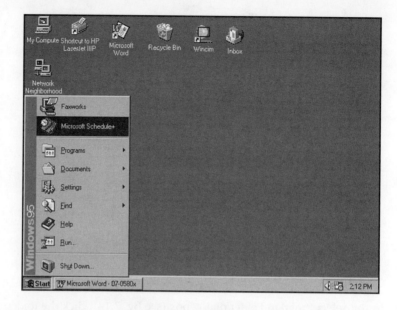

9. In the Select a Title for the Program box, enter a name for the program in the Select a Name for the Shortcut box (see fig. 7.16).

10. Click Finish.

Fig. 7.16
Accept the default name or change it according to your tastes.

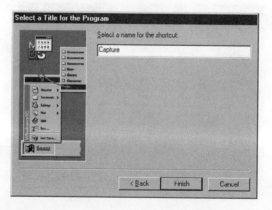

If you want to add more programs or shortcuts, click the Add button on the Start Menu Programs page. If you are finished, click OK to close the Taskbar Properties sheet.

You can remove a program, file, or folder shortcut by clicking the <u>R</u>emove button on the Taskbar Properties sheet and following these steps:

1. Scroll down the list of items in the Remove Shortcuts/Folders dialog box (see fig. 7.17).

Fig. 7.17
You can remove a program or shortcut from the Start menu as quickly as adding one.

II

Configuring Windows 95

2. Click the item to remove.

3. Click the <u>R</u>emove button.

4. Continue selecting and removing items, as needed. When finished, click Close.

5. Click OK.

Note

You can click the A<u>d</u>vanced button on the Taskbar Properties sheet to see your Start menu in Explorer view. You can add items to the Start menu using this view by clicking the Ad<u>v</u>anced button and then opening another session of the Explorer. Next, drag items from the Explorer view that contains all your directories into the Start Menu Explorer view.

You also can remove items from your Start menu using this view. To do so, click the item you want to remove and press Delete. When the Confirm File Delete dialog box appears, click <u>Y</u>es to send the item to the Recycle Bin.

Clear the Documents Menu

On the Start menu is another new feature—the Documents folder. This folder contains shortcuts to the last 15 files that you worked with in Windows 95, giving you quick access to these files for reviewing or editing.

To remove the items from this folder, use the following steps:

1. Right-click any exposed part of the taskbar.

2. Select Properties to display the Taskbar Properties sheet. Click the Start Menu Programs page.

3. In the Documents Menu area, click the Clear button.

Chapter 8

Configuring Windows 95 Audio

by Gregory J. Root

Configuring audio in Windows 95 can be easy. Knowing how to configure your sound can be valuable when you have to adjust your audio quickly. For example, if you are listening to CD audio when the phone rings, it's important to turn down or mute the volume.

Not only do you have control over every sound source, you can adjust and personalize your audio environment to your exact taste. If you've grown tired of the standard "bings" and "beeps" your computer makes, you can create a personalized audio environment no one else has ever heard before.

In this chapter, you learn how to configure your audio environment by learning how to do the following:

- Specify event sounds

- Work with sound schemes

- Use the taskbar volume control

- Use the Volume Control window

- Configure MIDI sounds

Setting System Sounds

When using Windows, you may want to assign sounds to specific events. Or, you may want to use a predefined set of sounds that were placed on your system when you installed Windows 95. If you've made a personalized group of event sounds, you may want to save the configuration or delete an old set of sounds you don't use anymore. In the next few sections, you learn how to do these tasks confidently.

Specifying Event Sounds

Windows knows when certain events occur while you use your computer. For example, it knows when you open or close a program. You can specify sounds to play when these events occur.

To begin configuring event sounds, do the following:

1. From the Start menu, choose Settings, Control Panel. Windows 95 displays the Control Panel window shown in figure 8.1.

Fig. 8.1
The Control Panel is the central location for customizing your Windows environment.

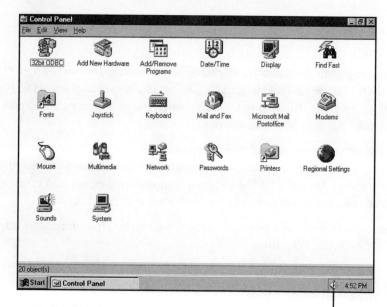

The volume control is located on the taskbar

2. Open the Sounds control panel. The Sounds Properties sheet appears, containing the Sounds page, shown in figure 8.2. In the upper-half of the screen, you see the list of events to which you can assign sounds. You can tell that an event has a sound assigned to it because of the speaker icon to the left of the event name.

> **Note**
>
> When you installed Windows, a default set of sounds and events was chosen for you.

3. Choose an event from the list. For example, choose the Asterisk event. You notice several things happen in the middle of the window shown in figure 8.3. Working from left to right, the name of the sound (Chord in our example) is placed in the Name drop-down list box, the Browse and Details buttons are enabled, the Preview window shows the sound's icon, and the Play button is enabled (it looks like the Play button on a VCR remote control).

The speaker icon indicates the event has an assigned sound

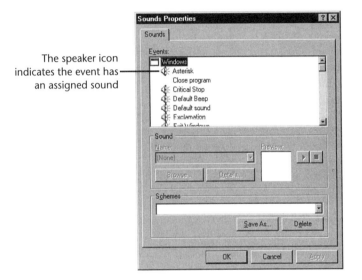

Fig. 8.2
The Sounds Properties sheet allows you to assign sounds to an event.

II

Configuring Windows 95

4. To listen to this sound, press the Play button. If you like the sound, play it again! Then, select other events in the list and listen to their assigned sounds until you find one you want to change.

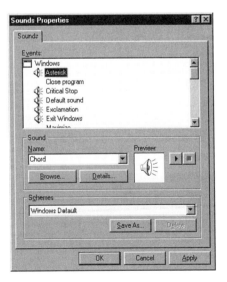

Fig. 8.3
If you've selected an event with a sound, the controls in the middle of the window become enabled.

> **Note**
>
> When you install other programs, more events are listed as those programs make their events known to Windows, giving you an even more personalized audio environment.

▶ See "Configuring Sound Cards," p. 443

> **Note**
>
> If you don't hear sound when you press the Play button, refer to the "Setting Volume" section in this chapter. If you're still having problems, see Chapter 19, "Configuring Speakers and Sound Cards," to verify that your hardware is installed and configured correctly.

> **Tip**
>
> If you know the exact location and file name of the sound you want, you can skip the next step by typing it into the Name drop-down list box.

5. You can assign a WAV file to the selected event in two ways. First, you can click the down arrow at the end of the Name drop-down list box to display a list of available sounds. Scroll through the list and select one of the sounds. To preview what your current selection sounds like, press the Play button again.

> **Note**
>
> The sounds in this drop-down list reside in the WINDOWS/MEDIA folder.

The second method requires using the Browse button to assign a sound. When you click the button, the Browse window appears, as shown in figure 8.4 (the window title matches the name of the event with which you're working). By default, browsing begins in the WINDOWS/MEDIA folder. If you find the name of a sound that piques your interest, highlight it (don't double-click it).

> **Caution**
>
> If you double-click the name of the sound, it is immediately assigned to the event. Since you can't undo this change unless you cancel all the changes you've made so far, just select the name of the sound.

Notice at the bottom edge of the window is another set of preview buttons. These allow you to preview the sounds while you browse. Once you've highlighted the sound you want to use, click the OK button. The name of the sound is placed in the <u>N</u>ame drop-down list box of the Sound Properties sheet.

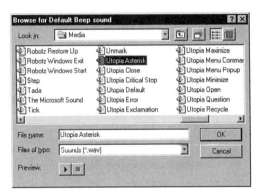

Fig. 8.4
You can preview a sound from the Browse window by using the Preview buttons at the bottom of the window.

6. Sometimes, sounds have extra information which contain useful details. If you like a particular set of sounds and want more, these details sometimes contain the name and address of who to contact to obtain similarly styled sounds. These details can be viewed for the current sound by clicking the <u>D</u>etails button.

   Figure 8.5 shows the Copyright, Media Length, and Audio Format data in the properties sheet. If more detailed information is available, the Other Information group box is also seen in at the bottom of the window. Select an item in the left-hand list of the group box to display its details in the right-hand list.

7. To immediately apply the change you made to the event, click the <u>A</u>pply button in the far lower-right corner of the sheet.

> **Note**
>
> You can repeat these six steps to change other events' sounds without clicking <u>A</u>pply between each change. Windows temporarily remembers all your changes until you're ready to save them.

Configuring Windows 95

II

Fig. 8.5
You can view the
Copyright, Media
Length, Audio
Format, and other
details of a sound.

8. If you decide you like the new combination of sounds, clicking the OK button in figure 8.3 saves them and closes the Sounds control panel. If you aren't sure what changes you've made or didn't like what you created, clicking the Cancel button restores the event sounds to the state they were the last time Apply was selected, and then closes the Sounds control panel.

Working with Sound Schemes

Sometimes, setting individual sounds for each Windows event can take longer than you have time to spend. Or, you may have taken the time to carefully craft a set of event sounds you want to preserve for special occasions or holidays. But right now, you don't want sounds for a national holiday every day of the year. With Windows 95, you can pick a predefined sound scheme.

◀ See "Selecting
Custom Install
Options,"
p. 107

Similarly, you can save that special set of event sounds for the correct time of the year.

To begin working with sound schemes, follow these steps:

1. From the Start menu choose Settings, Control Panel. Windows 95 displays the Control Panel window shown in figure 8.1.

2. Open the Sounds control panel. The Sounds Properties sheet appears containing the Sounds page as seen in figure 8.2. In the upper-half of the screen, you see the list of events to which you can assign sounds

(see the previous section, "Specifying Event Sounds"). At the bottom of the Sounds Properties sheet is the S̲chemes group box. Here you can select, save, and delete sound schemes.

Selecting a Sound Scheme

Choosing a predefined sound scheme is quick and easy. Many of these schemes were placed when you installed Windows. Other schemes are available to be downloaded from online services.

To select one of these schemes, follow these steps:

1. Click the down arrow next to the S̲cheme name.

2. Pick an intriguing, favorite, or personal scheme name.

> **Note**
>
> If you see a dialog box pop up, asking if you want to save the previous scheme, you should choose Y̲es to save your current sound scheme, N̲o to not save your scheme, or Cancel to stop selecting a new sound scheme. If you choose Yes, name the scheme so that it can appear in the S̲chemes drop-down list box.

3. Choose OK at the bottom of the Sounds Properties sheet.

> **Note**
>
> If you've installed Microsoft Plus!, your initial scheme name is blank. The Desktop Themes control panel takes care of your event sound assignments for you. But, feel free to change individual sounds at any time.

Saving a Sound Scheme

If you created your own set of event sound settings or modified an existing one, you should save it for future use. You can do this by following these steps:

1. Click the S̲ave As button in the S̲chemes group box (refer to fig. 8.2). The Save Scheme As dialog box appears, as shown in figure 8.6.

Fig. 8.6
The Save Scheme
As dialog box
allows you to
name your group
of event sounds.

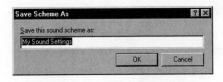

2. Enter a name for the scheme of event sounds defined in the Sounds Properties Events list. If you use the same name as an existing scheme, the dialog box shown in figure 8.7 asks you to confirm your decision to replace the existing scheme.

Fig. 8.7
The Change
Scheme confirma-
tion dialog box
helps prevent you
from accidentally
changing a sound
scheme.

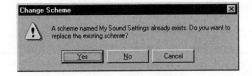

Once you've completed these steps, you can click OK to close the Sounds Properties sheet.

Deleting a Sound Scheme

If you want to delete a configuration of event sounds, you may do so by following these steps:

1. Locate the scheme you want to remove by opening the Schemes drop-down list box (see fig. 8.8).

Fig. 8.8
Select a sound
scheme to delete
from the Schemes
drop-down list
box.

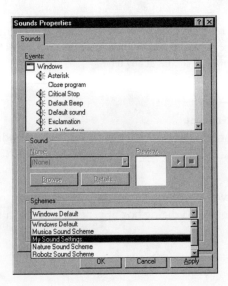

2. Click the D̲elete button in the S̲chemes group box (refer to fig. 8.8). The
   Sounds Properties sheet in figure 8.9 asks you to confirm your decision
   to replace the existing scheme.

Fig. 8.9
The Delete Scheme
confirmation
dialog box helps
prevent you from
accidentally
deleting a sound
scheme.

Note

Deleting the scheme does not delete the actual WAV file, just the connection between the event and which sound to play.

Once you've completed these steps, you can click OK to close the Sounds
Properties sheet.

Setting Volume

While using your computer, you may notice that your volume is too loud or
too soft. Your CD-ROM drive, sound card, and MIDI instrument (usually part
of your sound card) are all sources of the sounds and music. It's not unlikely
that one of them is much louder or softer than the rest. In the next two sections, you learn how to adjust the master volume for Windows audio, and
how to adjust each sound source's volume.

Using the Taskbar Volume Control

If you need to adjust the overall volume of sound coming out of your computer, use the taskbar speaker icon for quick and easy volume changes.

If the yellow sound icon does not appear on your taskbar like it does in the
lower right-hand corner of figure 8.1, use the following steps to enable the
taskbar speaker icon:

1. From the Start menu, choose S̲ettings, C̲ontrol Panel. Windows 95 displays the Control Panel window.

2. Open the Multimedia control panel. The Multimedia Properties sheet
   appears containing the Audio page, as seen in figure 8.10. In the upper-
   half of the screen, you'll see the Playback group box. At the bottom of
   this group box, place a check mark in the S̲how Volume Control on the

II

Configuring Windows 95

Taskbar check box. Selecting this option shows the volume control icon in the taskbar.

Fig. 8.10
The Multimedia Properties sheet allows you to turn on the taskbar volume control.

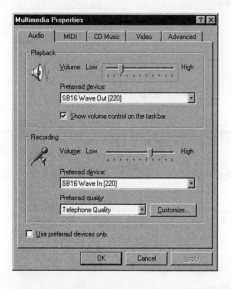

▶ See "Using the Add New Hardware Wizard for Sound Board," p. 438

Troubleshooting

I can't seem to find the Multimedia control panel or the Audio page in the Multimedia Properties sheet. What's wrong?

Either you don't have a sound card installed in your computer or Windows 95 did not recognize it.

3. Click OK to save the new setting and close the Multimedia Properties sheet.

Now that the speaker icon is visible, you'll be able to learn how to adjust the volume or quickly mute the audio level.

To adjust or mute the master volume, use these steps:

1. Position your mouse over the speaker icon and click once. A panel appears with a vertical slider and a check box, shown in figure 8.11.

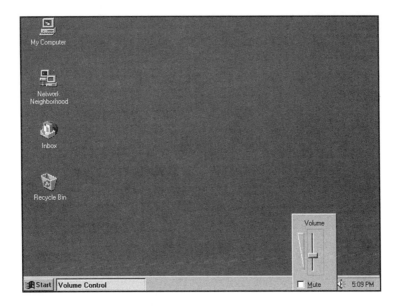

Fig. 8.11
The taskbar's
Volume control
panel appears
when you click the
taskbar speaker
icon.

2. Drag the slider up or down to adjust the master volume accordingly. If you need to mute the volume, check the <u>M</u>ute check box to instantly mute every source of audio on your computer.

> **Note**
>
> If you mute the volume, notice how the speaker icon changes to a speaker icon covered by a red circle with a line through it.

3. To close the Volume control panel, click anywhere else on the screen except on the volume panel.

Using the Volume Control Window

While using Windows 95, you may have noticed that one source of sound is louder or softer than the rest. Or, a particular sound source may not be producing *any* sound. In this section you learn how to access individual sound source volumes and adjust them by following these steps:

1. Verify that the yellow taskbar speaker icon is visible. If it isn't, see the previous section, "Using the Taskbar Volume Control," to enable it.

II

Configuring Windows 95

2. Position your mouse over the speaker icon and double-click. A Volume Control window appears, similar to that in figure 8.12. You may have more or fewer controls and features depending upon the capabilities of your sound card.

Fig. 8.12
The Volume Control window allows access to each sound source.

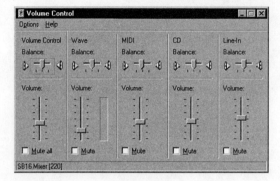

3. The leftmost slider and Mute All check box is the same as the Volume Control panel displayed when you single-click the speaker icon in the taskbar. Each column to the right of this, is a control dedicated to an individual sound source. Each one has a vertical slider and Mute check box. If your sound card supports stereo audio, a left-right balance slider appears above each vertical slider that supports stereo. By causing selected pairs of sound sources to play long segments of sound, you can adjust the vertical sliders correspondingly.

4. Once you have made your adjustments, choose Options, Exit to close the Volume Control window and save your settings.

Chapter 9

Configuring Microsoft Exchange

by Jim Boyce

Windows 95 includes an electronic mail (e-mail) application named Exchange that enables you to combine many, if not all, of your e-mail and faxes into a single inbox. With Exchange, you can send and receive e-mail to a Microsoft Mail post office, the Internet, The Microsoft Network, and CompuServe. Exchange's support for Internet and CompuServe e-mail gives you a gateway to send and receive messages to almost anyone in the world who has an e-mail account on the Internet or on an online service such as CompuServe, America Online, Prodigy, or others.

This chapter helps you install and configure Exchange to enable you to send and receive e-mail and faxes, both locally on your network, and through your modem to remote sites and services. In this chapter, you learn how to

- Install Microsoft Exchange

- Configure Exchange and service providers

- Create and edit an Exchange profile

- Set up your personal message store and address books

- Add other e-mail and fax services to Exchange

- Set up Exchange for remote mail access

- Customize Exchange

Naturally, before you can begin using Exchange, you must install the Exchange software. The following section helps you do just that.

Installing the Exchange Client

Microsoft Exchange is a typical Windows 95 application (see fig. 9.1) that works in conjunction with various *service providers* to enable you to send and receive e-mail and faxes to others. You can think of a service provider as an add-on module that enables the Exchange client to work with specific types of mail and online services. For example, Windows 95 includes service providers that enable it to work with Microsoft Mail, Microsoft Fax, and The Microsoft Network. The Windows 95 CD contains a service provider that enables Exchange to send and receive e-mail to and from CompuServe. Microsoft Plus! for Windows 95 includes a service provider that lets you send and receive mail on the Internet through a network or dial-up connection to the Internet.

Fig. 9.1
Exchange provides a unified inbox for all of your e-mail and faxes.

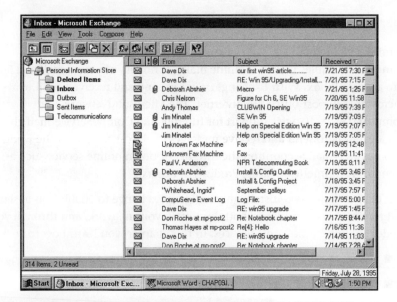

Tip

You can expect other e-mail vendors to offer service providers for Microsoft Exchange that support their e-mail applications. Also look for online services such as America Online and Prodigy to provide Exchange service providers that work with their online services.

Installing and configuring Exchange consists of four phases, which are described in the following list:

- *Install Exchange.* You can install Exchange when you install Windows 95, or you can easily add Exchange to your PC at any time after you install Windows 95.

- *Create at least one profile.* Your Exchange settings and service providers are stored in an Exchange profile. Each profile can contain one or more service providers to support different e-mail and fax systems. A *profile* is a collection of settings you can use to specify which service providers and settings you want to use with Exchange.

- *Add a personal information store and address book.* You need somewhere to store your messages, so the third phase in configuring Exchange is to add a personal information store to your profile, along with an address book to store e-mail and fax addresses.

- *Add service providers.* The final phase of installing Exchange is to add to your profile the service providers you want to use. These could include Microsoft Mail, CompuServe Mail, The Microsoft Network, and Internet e-mail.

Setup doesn't automatically install Exchange when you install Windows 95. Instead, you must specifically select Exchange as an option to install when you run Setup. Or, you can add Exchange after installing Windows 95. The following sections explain how to install the Microsoft Exchange client software. Later sections explain how to create and modify Exchange profiles, add service providers, and set other Exchange options.

Installing Exchange During Windows 95 Installation

If you have not yet installed Windows 95, you can install Exchange at the same time you install Windows 95. To install Exchange, use the following steps:

1. Run Setup from the Windows 95 floppy disk 1 or the \WIN95 folder on the Windows 95 CD.

2. Follow the prompts and windows to choose installation options as explained in Part I of this book.

3. When the Setup Options window appears (see fig. 9.2) and prompts you to select the type of installation you want, choose C̲ustom, then click Next.

4. Follow the prompts and windows to enable Setup to detect your PC's hardware.

II

Configuring Windows 95

5. When the Get Connected window shown in figure 9.3 appears, select the service provider(s) you want to use with Exchange. The listed providers include Microsoft Mail, The Microsoft Network, and Microsoft Fax. You can select one, or more than one. If you want to use only the Internet or CompuServe mail providers (included with Plus! and the Windows 95 CD, respectively) and not use any of the three service providers in the Get Connected window, leave all of the check boxes cleared—you have an option to install only Exchange in step 6. When you've made your selections, choose Next.

Fig. 9.2

Select the Custom option to install Exchange with the rest of the Windows 95 components.

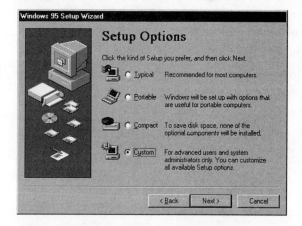

Fig. 9.3

Choose one or more service providers from the Get Connected window.

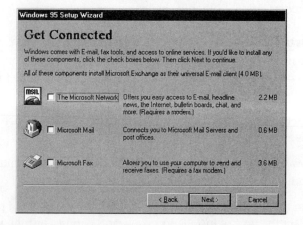

Note

If you forget to add a service provider when you install Windows 95 or add Exchange to your system, you can add the service provider later. Check the section "Creating and Editing User Profiles" later in this chapter to learn how to add a service provider.

6. In the Select Components window (see fig. 9.4), click Microsoft Exchange, then choose <u>D</u>etails to display the Microsoft Exchange dialog box. If the Microsoft Exchange check box does not contain a check mark, enable the check box. If you also want to install the Microsoft Mail provider, enable the Microsoft Mail Services check box. Then, choose OK.

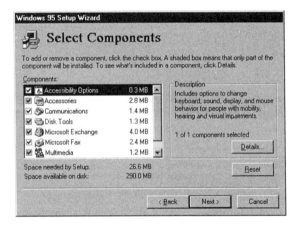

Fig. 9.4
Double-click the Microsoft Exchange item to install Exchange.

II

Configuring Windows 95

7. Choose Next, then follow Setup's remaining prompts to complete the installation process.

After Setup completes the installation process and you start Windows 95, you'll see an Inbox icon on the Desktop. This is the icon you later use to start Exchange. Before using Exchange, however, you need to complete the configuration process. Skip to the section "Creating and Editing User Profiles" later in this chapter to learn how to complete the configuration process for Exchange.

Troubleshooting

When Exchange starts, I receive error messages saying that my Internet Mail server is not available. I don't have an Internet Mail server, and don't use Internet Mail. What's wrong?

You probably installed Plus! for Windows 95, and ran the Internet Wizard, which installed the Internet Mail service provider. Open Control Panel and click the Mail and Fax icon. From the list of installed services, choose Internet Mail, then choose Remove. Windows 95 prompts you to verify that you want to remove the Internet Mail service provider from your profile. Choose Yes to remove the service from your profile.

Adding Exchange After Installing Windows 95

If you didn't install Exchange when you installed Windows 95, don't worry—it's easy to add Exchange. Use the following steps to add Exchange after installing Windows 95:

1. Choose Start, Settings, then Control Panel to open the Control Panel.

2. Double-click the Add/Remove Programs icon to open the Add/Remove Programs Properties sheet.

3. Click the Windows Setup tab and the Windows Setup page shown in figure 9.5 appears.

Fig. 9.5
Use the Windows Setup page anytime you need to add some software to Windows 95.

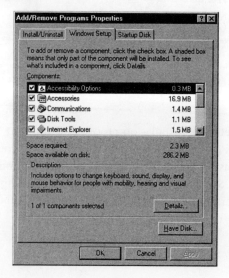

4. Scroll through the Components list to locate and select Microsoft Exchange, then choose Details.

5. In the Microsoft Exchange dialog box, place a check mark beside Microsoft Exchange. If you want to use Exchange to connect to a Microsoft Mail postoffice, place a check mark beside the Microsoft Mail Services item. Then, choose OK.

6. If you want to use Microsoft Fax, place a check mark in the Components list beside the Microsoft Fax item.

7. Choose OK. Windows 95 adds the necessary software to your system, prompting you if necessary to supply one or more of the Windows 95 disks or the Windows 95 CD, if needed.

Tip

If you want to use Microsoft Exchange to send and receive messages on The Microsoft Network, you must first install The Microsoft Network on your system. In the Components dialog box, place a check mark beside The Microsoft Network item. You can add The Microsoft Network to your system at the same time you add Exchange, or you can add it separately.

Creating and Editing User Profiles

Besides installing Exchange, you need to configure at least one user profile. The following section explains user profiles to help you understand how to create and edit them.

Understanding Profiles

A collection of information stores, address books, and service providers is called a *user profile*. For example, you might use a profile that contains your personal information store, one address book, a Microsoft Mail service provider, and a CompuServe service provider. In addition to giving you a means of grouping the service providers and information store you use most often into a named group, Exchange profiles also store the settings for each item in the profile. Figure 9.6 shows items in an Exchange profile.

Fig. 9.6
An Exchange
profile stores your
Exchange settings
by name.

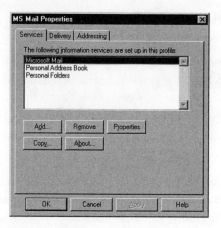

If you're like most people, you will use a single profile. But, you can use multiple profiles. For example, if you use Microsoft Fax very seldom but use Microsoft Mail all the time, you might want to place the Microsoft Fax provider in a separate profile. When you have to use Microsoft Fax, you can make the Microsoft Fax profile active (explained in the next section), then start Exchange to use it.

> **Tip**
>
> Information stores and address books are service providers, just like Microsoft Mail, CompuServe, and other service providers. All of these service providers are often referred to as just *services*.

Configuring Profiles

As with most configuration tasks in Windows 95, you create and edit user profiles from the Control Panel. When you install Exchange, Windows 95 creates a default profile for you named MS Exchange Settings. To view or edit your default profile, open the Control Panel, then double-click the Mail and Fax icon to display the MS Exchange Settings Properties sheet shown in figure 9.7.

From the MS Exchange Settings Properties sheet you can add services to a profile, delete services, set properties for services, and create and view other profiles. You also can set the properties of services in a profile. If you are using the CompuServe Mail provider, for example, you can specify your CompuServe user ID, password, and other properties that control how and when the CompuServe provider logs onto CompuServe to send and receive your CompuServe mail.

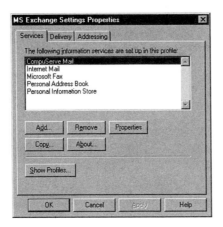

Fig. 9.7
Windows 95
creates a default
profile for you
named MS
Exchange Settings.

Each service is different from another, so the properties that you can set for each service varies from one service to another. Later sections, "Setting Up Personal Information Stores," "Setting Up Address Books," and "Adding Information Services to Exchange," explain how to add services and set their properties. The following section explains how to create and delete profiles.

Creating and Deleting Exchange Profiles

As explained earlier, you might want to use more than one Exchange profile to store different sets of properties and services. You can create a profile in one of two ways—create a completely new profile, or copy an existing profile. Regardless of which method you use, you can edit the profile to add, remove, or edit services after you create the profile.

To copy your existing profile, follow these steps:

1. Open the Control Panel and double-click the Mail and Fax icon to display the MS Exchange Settings Properties sheet.

2. Click the Show Profiles button to display the Microsoft Exchange Profiles property sheet shown in figure 9.8.

3. Select the profile you want to copy, then click the Copy button. A dialog box prompting you to enter a name for your new profile appears (see fig. 9.9).

4. In the New Profile Name text box, enter a unique name for your new Exchange profile, then choose OK. Windows 95 will copy all of the services and settings in the selected profile to your new profile.

5. Use the steps explained in the following sections of this chapter to configure the services in your new profile.

Fig. 9.8
With the Microsoft
Exchange Profiles
property sheet,
you can create a
new profile or
copy an existing
profile.

Fig. 9.9
Enter a unique
name for your
new profile.

Tip

After you create a profile, you need to specify it as your default profile before you can use it with Exchange. Refer to the section "Setting Your Default Profile" to learn how to begin using your new profile.

In addition to copying an existing profile, you also can create an Exchange profile from scratch. Windows 95 provides a wizard to step you through the process. Use the following steps to create a new Exchange profile:

1. Open the Control Panel and double-click the Mail and Fax icon.

2. Click the Show Profiles button to display the Microsoft Exchange Profiles property sheet.

3. Click the Add button and the Inbox Setup Wizard shown in figure 9.10 appears.

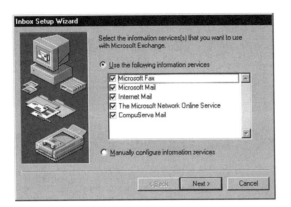

Fig. 9.10
Exchange provides a wizard to help you set up a profile.

4. Click the Use the Following Information Services option button.

5. Place a check mark beside each of the services you want to include in your profile. Deselect any services you don't want included in the profile, then click Next. The wizard displays a new window prompting you for a name for your new profile (see fig. 9.11).

6. Enter a unique name for your profile, then click Next.

7. Depending on which services you selected, the wizard prompts you for information to configure the services. Refer to the sections later in this chapter that describe setup options for services to help you configure the services.

Tip

If you use the previous steps to create a profile and add services to the profile, Windows 95 uses a wizard to step you through the process of configuring the services. If you add services manually as explained later in this chapter, Windows 95 doesn't use a wizard, but instead displays a set of property sheets for the service. Use these sheets to set its properties. If you read through the following sections on configuring services manually, you will have no trouble at all configuring the services using the wizard.

II

Configuring Windows 95

Fig. 9.11
Enter a unique name for your new profile.

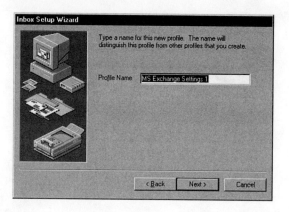

Setting Your Default Profile

Although you can create as many Exchange profiles as you want, you can only use one profile at a time. You have two options for specifying which Exchange profile you use. Each time you want to use a different profile, you must exit Exchange, use the Control Panel to specify which profile to use, then restart Exchange. Or, you can configure Exchange to prompt you to specify which profile to use each time Exchange starts.

To specify a default profile, follow these steps:

1. Open the Control Panel and double-click the Mail and Fax icon.

2. Click the Show Profiles button.

3. From the drop-down list labeled When Starting Microsoft Exchange, Use This Profile, choose the profile you want Exchange to use as a default.

4. Choose Close, then start Exchange to verify that it is using the correct profile.

To have Exchange prompt you to select a profile each time Exchange starts, follow these steps:

1. Start Exchange (double-click the Inbox icon on the Desktop).

2. Choose Tools, Options to display the Options property sheet.

3. From the control group named When Starting Microsoft Exchange, choose the option labeled Prompt for a Profile to be Used. Then, choose OK. The next time you start Exchange, you'll be prompted to select which profile you want to use.

To learn about other general Exchange options you can specify, refer to the section "Setting General Exchange Options" later in this chapter.

Setting Up Personal Information Stores

Without a place to store all of your messages, Exchange wouldn't be much use to you. So, each profile should include at least one information store. An *information store* is a special type of file that Exchange uses to store all of your messages. Whether the message is a fax, an e-mail message from your network mail post office, or other service, incoming messages are placed in the Inbox folder of your default information store. A typical information store contains the following folders:

- *Deleted Items*. This folder contains all of the messages you have deleted from other folders. By default, Exchange will not delete items from your information store unless you select them in the Deleted Items folder and delete them. As explained later in the section "Setting General Exchange Options," you can configure Exchange to immediately delete a message instead of moving it to the Deleted Items folder.

- *Inbox*. Exchange places all of your incoming messages—including error and status messages generated by the various service providers, e-mail, and faxes—in the Inbox.

- *Outbox*. Items that you compose are placed in the Outbox until the appropriate service delivers the message automatically or you manually direct the Exchange to deliver the message(s).

- *Sent Items*. By default, Exchange places in the Sent Items folder a copy of all messages you send. You can configure Exchange not to keep a copy of sent messages (see the section "Setting General Exchange Options" later in this chapter).

In addition to the folders listed previously, you can add your own folders to an information store. And, you're not limited to a single information store— you can add as many information stores to a profile as you like. The folders in each information store show up under a separate tree in the Exchange window. Figure 9.12 shows Exchange with two information stores being used: Personal Folders and Personal Information Store.

Adding multiple message stores to a profile is useful mainly for copying messages between message files. If you are using the latest version of the Microsoft Mail service provider that supports shared folders, however, you can add a shared folder message store to your profile. The shared folder enables you to share messages with other users.

II

Configuring Windows 95

Fig. 9.12

You can use as many information stores in a profile as you like.

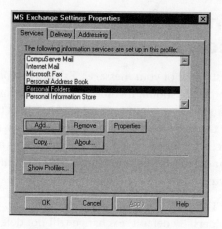

There is one other reason to add a set of personal folders to your profile: you can't use encryption on the Personal Information Store, but you can use encryption on a Personal Folder. The two are identical in function, so if you want to use encryption for your message file for extra security, add a Personal Folders item to your profile, copy your messages from the Personal Information Store to the Personal Folders, then remove the Personal Information Store from your profile. Make sure you configure Exchange to use the Personal Folders to store incoming messages, as explained in the next section.

Troubleshooting

I would like to add a second Personal Information Store to my profile, but Exchange tells me I can only have one in a profile. Is it possible to add another?

You can only have one Personal Information Store in a profile, but you can add as many Personal Folders to a profile as you like. Personal Folders are essentially identical to the Personal Information Store. The only difference is that your incoming mail is directed into the Personal Information Store. If you simply want more places to segregate your incoming mail, create new folders in your Personal Information Store instead of adding Personal Folders to your profile. You can create as many additional folders in the Personal Information Store as you like. To create a new folder, open the folder in which you want the new folder created. Then, choose File, New Folder. Exchange displays a dialog box in which you enter the name for the new folder. Then, you can drag messages to the new folder as you desire.

Configuring Your Personal Information Store

You can change a handful of settings for a Personal Information Store. To change properties for a Personal Information Store, use the following steps:

1. Open the Control Panel and double-click the Mail and Fax icon.

2. If you want to set properties for a Personal Information Store in a profile other than the default profile, choose the Show Profiles button, select the profile you want to change, then choose Properties.

3. Select Personal Information Store from the list of services in the profile, then choose Properties. The Personal Folders property sheet shown in figure 9.13 appears.

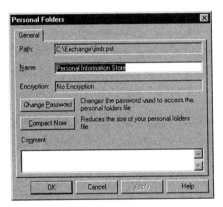

Fig. 9.13
Use the Personal Folders property sheet to set properties for the information store.

4. Set the properties for the Personal Information Store according to the following descriptions and your needs:

   ■ *Name*. If you like, enter a new name for the Personal Information Store. This name will appear in the profile instead of "Personal Information Store."

   ■ *Change Password*. Click this button to change the password for your Personal Information Store. The Create Microsoft Personal Folders dialog box appears. The four properties you can set in the password dialog box are described in table 9.1.

II

Configuring Windows 95

Table 9.1 Password Properties for an Information Store

Property	Purpose
Old Password	Enter in this text box the current password, if any, for the Personal Information Store.
New Password	Enter in this text box the new password you want to assign to the Personal Information Store.
Verify Password	Enter in this text box the new password you want to assign to the Personal Information Store to enable Windows 95 to verify that you have entered the password correctly.
Save This Password in Your Password List	If you want the password stored in your password cache so you don't have to enter the password each time you open Exchange, place a check mark in this check box.

- *Compact Now.* Choose this button to compress (compact) your Personal Information Store. Windows 95 compresses the file, reducing its size. Compressing a Personal Information Store has no effect on your ability to use the file to store messages.

- *Comment.* If you want to add a short comment about the Personal Information Store, enter it in this text box.

After you have specified all of the necessary properties, choose OK, then choose OK again to save the changes.

Adding Other Information Stores

As explained earlier, you can add as many information stores to a profile as you like. These additional stores are called Personal Folders, but they have essentially the same structure and function as your Personal Information Store. You can add a new Personal Folders file to a profile or add an existing file. Adding an existing file enables you to easily import messages from other information stores that you or others have created separately.

To add an information store to a profile, use the following steps:

1. Open the Control Panel and double-click the Mail and Fax icon.

2. If you want to add Personal Folders to a profile other than the default profile, choose the Show Profiles button, select the profile you want to change, then choose Properties.

3. Choose Add, then from the Add Service to Profile dialog box, select Personal Folders and choose OK.

4. The Create/Open Personal Folders File dialog box appears. If you are adding an existing file, locate and select the file in the dialog box, then choose Open. If you want to create a new file, enter a name for the file in the File Name text box, then choose Open.

5. If you are creating a new file, Windows 95 displays a dialog box similar to the one shown in figure 9.14. The Name and Password properties are the same as those explained in the previous section. From the Encryption Setting group, choose one of the following options:

   ■ *No Encryption.* Choose this option if you don't want the file to be encrypted. If the file is not encrypted, other users can open the file and read its contents with another program, such as a word processor.

   ■ *Compressible Encryption.* Choose this option if you want the file to be encrypted for security, but you also want to be able to compress (compact) the file to save disk space.

   ■ *Best Encryption.* Choose this option if you want the most secure encryption. You will not be able to compress the file if you choose this option.

   Or, if you are adding an existing Personal Folders file, the dialog box shown in figure 9.13 appears. Adjust settings as explained.

6. Choose OK, then choose OK again to close the MS Exchange Settings Properties sheet.

Fig. 9.14

The Create Microsoft Personal Folders dialog box enables you to set various properties for your information store.

II

Configuring Windows 95

Setting Delivery Options

Even though you can add multiple information stores to a profile, only one can be assigned to receive incoming messages. You can, however, assign an alternate information store to be used to store incoming messages if the primary store is unavailable for some reason.

To set these delivery options, follow these steps:

1. Open the Control Panel and double-click the Mail and Fax icon.

2. Click the Delivery tab to display the Delivery page (see fig. 9.15).

Fig. 9.15
Specify which store will receive incoming messages.

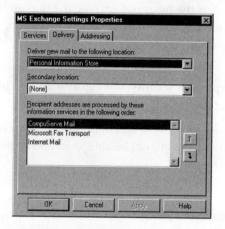

3. Specify settings in the Delivery page based on the following descriptions:

   ■ *Deliver New Mail to the Following Location.* Select from the drop-down list the information store in which you want incoming mail to be placed.

   ■ *Secondary Location.* Select from the drop-down list the information store in which incoming mail should be placed if the primary message store is unavailable.

   ■ *Recipient Addresses Are Processed by These Information Services in the Following Order.* This control lists the order in which mail providers distribute mail when you direct Exchange to deliver mail using all services. To move an item in the list, select it, then click either the up or the down arrow.

4. After specifying the desired settings, choose OK to save the changes.

Setting Up Address Books

Although you can send and receive mail without an address book, adding an address book to your profile makes it possible for you to store addresses and quickly select an address for a message. You can add addresses to the address book yourself, or let Exchange add originating addresses of received mail.

A profile can contain only one Personal Address Book. When you install Exchange, Windows 95 automatically adds a Personal Address Book to your default profile. You can add a new, blank address book, or add an existing address book that already contains address entries.

If you want to add a Personal Address Book to a new profile, or you have accidentally deleted your Personal Address Book from your default profile, follow these steps to add the address book:

1. Open the Control Panel and double-click the Mail and Fax icon.

2. If you want to add a Personal Address Book to a profile other than the default profile, click the Show Profiles button, select the profile you want to change, then click Properties.

3. Click the Add button, then from the Add Service to Profile dialog box, choose Personal Address Book and click OK. The Personal Address Book property sheet shown in figure 9.16 appears.

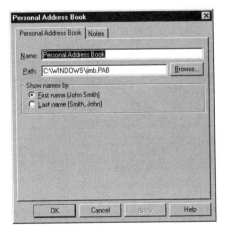

Fig. 9.16
Set properties for your Personal Address Book.

4. In the Name text box, enter a name for the address book (or leave the name as-is, if you prefer).

5. In the Path text box, enter the path and file name for the new address book file, or in the case of an existing address book, enter the path and

file name of the existing file. If you prefer, you can choose the Browse button to browse for the file.

6. From the control group Show Names By, choose how you want names to appear in the address book (sorted by first name or last name).

7. Choose OK, then OK again to save the changes.

Setting Addressing Options

Although you can have only one Personal Address Book in a profile, you can add other types of address books. For example, a CompuServe Address Book is included in the CompuServe Mail provider. Other service providers that you add might also include their own address books. For this reason, you need a way to specify which address book Exchange displays by default, and other addressing options.

To set addressing options, open the Control Panel and double-click the Mail and Fax icon. Then, click the Addressing tab to display the Addressing page shown in figure 9.17.

The properties you can specify on the Addressing page are described in the following list:

■ *Show This Address List First.* Select from this drop-down list the address book you want Exchange to display when you click the To button in the compose window, or choose Tools, Address Book. You'll have the option in Exchange of selecting a different address book if more than one is installed.

Fig. 9.17
Use the Addressing page to specify your default address book.

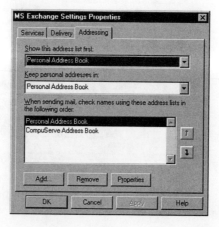

- *Keep Personal Addresses In.* Select from this drop-down list the address book in which you want a new address to be added unless you specifically choose a different address book.

- *When Sending Mail, Check Names Using These Address Lists in the Following Order.* Use this list to set the order in which Exchange checks addresses for validity when you send a message or click the Check Names button in the compose window toolbar.

After you specify the Addressing properties you want to use, choose OK to save the changes.

Tip

For help adding and modifying addresses, see Que's *Special Edition Using Windows 95.*

Setting General Exchange Options

It might sometimes seem to you like Exchange offers an overwhelming number of properties and options that you can set. This section helps you understand and set those properties and options. If you've read through the earlier parts of this chapter, you've already set some general Exchange options, including delivery and addressing options. The following sections explain the other options you can set. To reach the property pages referenced in the following sections, open Exchange, then choose Tools, Options.

Setting General Options

The General page specifies a handful of properties that control how Exchange alerts you to new incoming messages and other common actions, such as deleting messages (see fig. 9.18).

The following list explains the properties you can set on the General page:

- *When New Mail Arrives.* This group contains three options you can enable to control how Exchange notifies you of incoming messages.

- *Deleting Items.* Enable the option Warn Before Permanently Deleting Items if you want Exchange to warn you when you permanently delete a message (rather than deleting it to the Deleted Items folder). Enable the option named Empty the 'Deleted Items' Folder Upon Exiting, if you want Exchange to permanently delete messages from the Deleted Items folder when you exit Exchange.

II

Configuring Windows 95

Fig. 9.18
Use the General
page to set general
Exchange options.

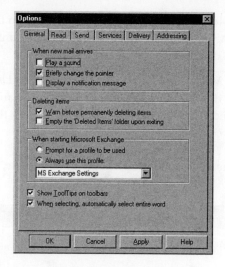

■ *When Starting Microsoft Exchange.* Use the options in this group to either specify a default Exchange profile, or to cause Exchange to prompt you to select a profile each time Exchange starts.

■ *Show ToolTips on Toolbars.* Enable this option if you want Exchange to display a ToolTip for a toolbar button when you rest the pointer on the button for a second.

■ *When Selecting, Automatically Select Entire Word.* Enable this option if you want Exchange to automatically select entire words when you drag over the words with the pointer.

Setting Read Options

The properties on the Read page control the way Exchange handles messages when you read, reply to, or forward the messages (see fig. 9.19).

The properties you can set with the Read page are explained in the following list:

■ *After Moving Or Deleting An Open Item.* The three options in this group control Exchange's actions when you read, move, or delete a message. The options are self-explanatory—select whichever option suits your preferences.

■ *When Replying To or Forwarding An Item.* These properties control how Exchange handles messages when you reply to or forward a message. Enable the option labeled Include the Original Text When Replying if you want Exchange to include the text of the original message in your

reply. If you want the original message text to be indented in the message, with your new text at the left margin, click Indent the Original
Text When Replying. Enable the option labeled Close the Original Item
if you want Exchange to automatically close the original e-mail message
window after you start your reply. Choose the Font button to specify
the font used for your reply text.

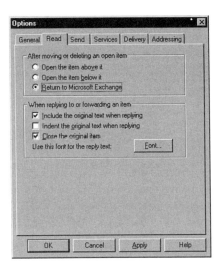

Fig. 9.19
Set options for
reading messages
using the Read
page.

Tip

If you indent original message text or use a special font in a reply or a forwarded
message, the recipient will see those message characteristics only if he or she is using
Microsoft Exchange and a service provider that is capable of sending and receiving
messages in RTF (Rich Text Format). Examples of such providers are the Microsoft
Mail and Microsoft Network services.

Setting Send Options

You also can specify a few properties that control the way Exchange handles
items you are sending. Click the Send tab to display the Send page shown in
figure 9.20.

You can click the Font button to choose the font Exchange will use by default
for your outgoing messages. As with indented text, the recipient must also be
using Exchange and a service provider that supports message transfer in RTF.

Fig. 9.20
Control out-
going message
options with the
Send page.

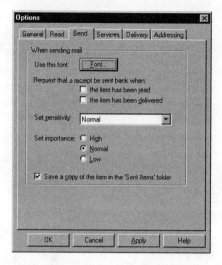

The two options in the group labeled Request That a Receipt Be Sent Back
When control whether you receive a return receipt from the recipient's mail
system. The available options are

- *The Item Has Been Read.* If you choose this option, you'll receive a return
  receipt only after the recipient reads the message, which could happen
  well after he receives the message.

- *The Item Has Been Delivered.* Choose this option to receive a return receipt as soon as the message is delivered, regardless of whether the message has been read.

The Set Sensitivity and Set Importance options are self-explanatory. Choose
the options you want to use by default. Note that you can override either of
these settings when you create a message.

If you enable the option labeled Save a Copy of the Item in the 'Sent Items'
Folder, Exchange automatically places a copy of your outgoing message in
the Sent Items folder. This is helpful if you need to review a message you've
previously sent. Just remember to periodically clean out the Sent Items folder
to avoid having a huge message file filled with old messages.

Configuring Exchange for Microsoft Mail

If you are using Windows 95 on a Microsoft-based network (Windows NT,
Windows for Workgroups, or Windows 95), it's a good bet that you want to

use the Microsoft Mail service provider—all of these Microsoft operating environments include a workgroup version of Microsoft Mail. Or, you might want to connect through Dial-Up Networking to a remote site, such as your district office, that uses Microsoft Mail. In either case, you need to create and configure a workgroup postoffice (WGPO) if your network does not yet include one. The following sections help you do just that.

Tip

A *workgroup postoffice* is a special set of directories that Microsoft Mail clients and Microsoft Mail Exchange clients can use to send and receive e-mail. Before you can begin sending and receiving mail on your LAN using the Microsoft Mail provider, you must have a WGPO on your LAN. Fortunately, Windows 95 makes it easy to create and manage a WGPO, as you learn in the next section.

Setting Up a Workgroup Postoffice

The Control Panel contains an object specifically for creating and managing a workgroup postoffice. Open the Control Panel and double-click the Microsoft Mail Postoffice icon. Windows 95 starts a wizard as shown in figure 9.21. This wizard lets you either create a new WGPO or administer an existing WGPO.

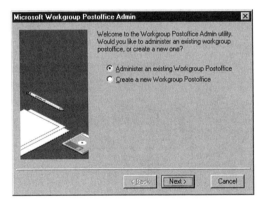

Fig. 9.21
You can create a new WGPO or administer an existing one.

II

Configuring Windows 95

Note

When you create a WGPO, you also create an administrator's account. The administrator is responsible for creating and managing user mail accounts. Before you begin creating the WGPO, decide who will be administering the postoffice. In the following steps, you create an administrator account and should be ready to provide the name of the person who will be administering the postoffice.

To set up a new WGPO, follow these steps:

1. Start the Microsoft Workgroup Postoffice Admin wizard as explained previously.

2. Choose the Create a new Workgroup Postoffice option, then choose Next. Windows 95 then prompts you for the name and location for your new postoffice (see fig. 9.22). Enter the name or choose Browse to browse for a folder for the WGPO.

Fig. 9.22
Enter the path and file name for your new postoffice.

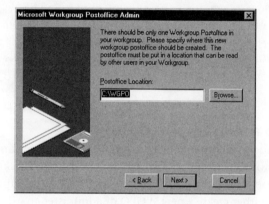

3. After you click Next, the wizard prompts you to verify the path and file name you entered. Choose Next if the path and file name are correct, or choose Back to change the path or file name. After you click Next, the wizard displays the Enter Your Administrator Account Details window shown in figure 9.23.

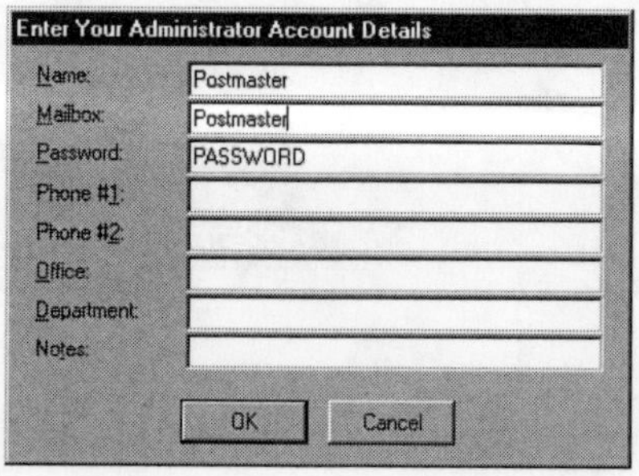

Fig. 9.23
You must specify details for an administrator account for your WGPO.

4. Fill out the fields in the account window. You must provide entries for the following three items:

- *Name*. In this field, enter the first and last name of the person who will be administering the postoffice.

> **Tip**
>
> If you don't want to specify a particular user's name, use Postmaster as the Name and Mailbox entries for the account. When you or anyone else needs to log into the postoffice to administer it, simply log in using the Postmaster account.

- *Mailbox*. Enter in this field the name of the mailbox for the administrator's account. Windows 95 suggests your Windows 95 network name, but you should consider creating a general Postmaster account.

- *Password*. Although you can leave the password blank, it's a bad idea to leave your WGPO administrator's account unprotected. Windows 95 suggests PASSWORD as the account password. You should enter a different password that others won't be able to guess. Just make sure you don't forget the password. If you do, you won't be able to administer the WGPO without re-creating the entire WGPO (and losing all messages contained in it).

The remaining options in the account window are optional, and are self-explanatory. Choose OK after you have specified the information you want included with the account. The general information (not the password) will appear to other users when they browse the postoffice list of accounts.

Administering a Postoffice

After you create the administrator account, you can begin adding, removing, and modifying mail accounts for users. To administer mail accounts, follow these steps:

1. Open the Control Panel and double-click the Microsoft Mail Postoffice icon.

2. Choose Administer an Existing Workgroup Postoffice, then click Next.

3. Enter the path to your WGPO (or click Browse to browse for the WGPO), then click Next.

4. Windows 95 prompts you for the account name and password of the administrator's account. Enter the mailbox name and password, then

choose Next. A Postoffice Manager window similar to the one shown in figure 9.24 appears.

Fig. 9.24
The Postoffice Manager window lets you manage user mail accounts.

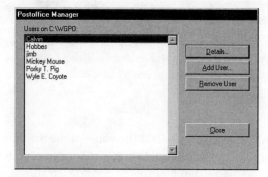

5. To view the account details for a user's account, select the account and choose the Details button. A window similar to the one shown in figure 9.25 appears. Modify any of the properties for the user, then choose OK.

Fig. 9.25
You can modify any mail account property, including the password.

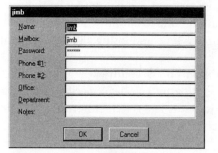

6. To add a user, click the Add User button. Windows 95 displays a dialog box nearly identical to the Details dialog box shown in figure 9.25. Enter the account details for the mail account, then choose OK.

7. To remove a user, select the user and choose Remove User. Windows 95 prompts you to verify that you want to remove the account. Choose Yes to delete the account, or choose No to cancel the deletion.

8. When you are finished administering the WGPO, choose Close.

> ### Troubleshooting
>
> *I created an administrator account for the WGPO, but I've forgotten the password. Can I reassign another account as the WGPO administrator account?*
>
> Unfortunately, there's no way to change the administrator account. Unless you can recall the password, you have no way of gaining access to the account or administering the WGPO. Fortunately, new users can create their own mail accounts in the WGPO, so new and existing users alike can continue to use the WGPO while you attempt to resolve the problem. First, direct all users to back their message folders. A simple way to do this is to make a backup copy of their PST file. Any users who store their messages in the WGPO instead of locally must copy their messages to a local folder. When all users' messages are backed up, delete the WGPO and re-create it, making sure to create an administrator account with a password you can remember. Re-create all of the user accounts in the WGPO.

Adding Information Services to Exchange

Previous sections of this chapter explained how to install Exchange and set a few general options. If you're like most users, you probably want to take advantage of some of the service providers included with Windows 95 and with Microsoft Plus! for Windows 95. This section helps you install and configure the Internet Mail and CompuServe service providers so you can begin using them.

Installing Internet Mail Service

Microsoft Plus! for Windows 95 includes additional Internet features not included in Windows 95. Among these additional features is an Internet Mail service provider for Exchange that enables you to use Exchange to send and receive mail through an Internet mail server.

To install the Internet Mail service for Exchange, you must use the Plus! Setup program. Appendix A, "Installing and Using Microsoft Plus! Companion for Windows 95," explains how to install Plus!, but you can use the following steps as a guide to help you install the Internet Mail service:

▶ See "Configuring Microsoft Fax," p. 237

1. Start Windows 95 and insert the Plus! CD in your CD-ROM drive. The Plus! CD will autoplay, opening a window on the Desktop.

▶ See "Installing Microsoft Plus!," p. 658

2. Click the Install Plus! button.

3. Follow the prompts to start the installation process, and when Setup prompts you to select which Plus! components to install, make sure you select the Internet Jumpstart Kit, then click Next.

4. Follow the prompts to continue the installation process. Eventually, Setup starts an Internet Setup Wizard. When this wizard appears, click Next.

5. Through the next few dialog boxes, the wizard prompts you to specify information about how you connect to the Internet, DNS servers to use, and default gateway. Provide the settings that apply to your connection.

6. The wizard then displays the dialog box shown in figure 9.26, prompting you to specify your e-mail address and mail server. Place a check mark in the Use Internet Mail check box. In the text box labeled Your Email Address, enter your e-mail account name. In the Internet Mail Server text box, enter the domain name of your Internet e-mail server. If you're not sure what to enter for these properties, check with your system administrator or Internet service provider for help. After you enter the necessary information, click Next.

Fig. 9.26
Enter your e-mail address and mail server names.

7. The Internet wizard then displays the window shown in figure 9.27, prompting you to specify in which Exchange profile you want to place the Internet Mail service provider. Select an existing profile from the drop-down list, or choose the New button to create a new profile.

8. After you create or specify a profile to contain your Internet Mail provider, click Next, then follow the prompts and windows to complete the installation process.

Fig. 9.27
Select or create a profile to contain your Internet Mail service.

After you install the Internet Mail provider, you can use the Control Panel to set other Internet Mail properties. To do so, open the Control Panel and double-click the Mail and Fax icon. Select the Internet Mail provider, then click Properties to display the General page shown in figure 9.28.

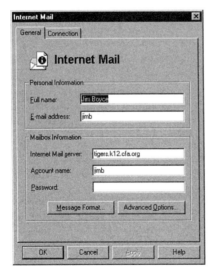

Fig. 9.28
Use the General page to set general Internet Mail properties.

II

Configuring Windows 95

The following list explains the settings on the General page:

- *Full Name.* Enter your first and last names as you want them to appear in message headers.

- *E-mail Address.* Enter your e-mail account name.

- *Internet Mail Server.* Enter the domain name of your Internet mail server.

- *Account Name.* Enter your e-mail account name (generally, the account you use to log onto the Internet server).

- *Password.* Enter the password for your Internet e-mail account.

- *Message Format.* Click this button to specify whether the Internet Mail service uses MIME encoding to send your e-mail messages and attachments.

- *Advanced Options.* Click this button to specify the name of a server to which you want all of your outbound mail forwarded. This is necessary if your default Internet Mail server doesn't process outbound mail.

> **Tip**
>
> Click the Connection tab if you want to change the type of connection you use to connect to the Internet, or to specify a different Dial-Up Networking connection.

Installing the CompuServe Mail Service

If you are a CompuServe member, you'll be happy to know that Windows 95 includes a service provider that enables you to use Exchange to send and receive mail through CompuServe. In addition to exchanging mail with other CompuServe users, the CompuServe Mail provider enables you to exchange e-mail with anyone who has an Internet mail account because CompuServe serves as a mail gateway to the Internet.

The CompuServe Mail provider is included on the Windows 95 CD in the folder \DRIVERS\OTHER\EXCHANGE\COMPUSRV. To install the CompuServe Mail provider, follow these steps:

1. Hold down the Shift key while you insert the Windows 95 CD (this prevents the CD from autoplaying).

2. Open My Computer, right-click the CD icon, then choose Open from the context menu.

3. Open the folder \DRIVERS\OTHER\EXCHANGE\COMPUSRV and double-click the Setup icon. Setup starts and copies the necessary files to your system.

4. Setup asks you if you want to add CompuServe Mail to your default Exchange profile. Choose Yes to add the service to your default profile, or choose No if you want to later add the service to the default profile or a different profile.

Configuring the CompuServe Mail Service

After you add the CompuServe Mail service to your Exchange profile, you need to configure various settings that define how Exchange connects to CompuServe and sends and receives your CompuServe mail. To configure your user account information in the CompuServe Mail service, follow these steps:

1. Open the Control Panel and double-click the Mail and Fax icon.

2. Select CompuServe Mail from the list of installed services, then choose Properties.

3. In the Name text box on the General page (see fig. 9.29), enter the name you want to appear in mail message address headers (not your CompuServe account name).

Fig. 9.29
Use the General page to specify your CompuServe account information.

4. In the CompuServe Id text box, enter your CompuServe account ID.

5. In the Password text box, enter your CompuServe account password.

In addition to configuring your account information, you also need to specify how the service will connect to CompuServe. To do so, use the Connection page and the following steps:

1. Click the Connection tab to display the Connection page (see fig. 9.30).

2. In the Phone Number text box, enter your CompuServe access number.

3. From the Preferred Tapi Line drop-down list, choose the modem you'll be using to connect to CompuServe.

4. From the Network drop-down list, choose the type of network connection provided by your CompuServe access number.

II

Configuring Windows 95

Fig. 9.30
Use the Connection page to specify how the connection to CompuServe is made.

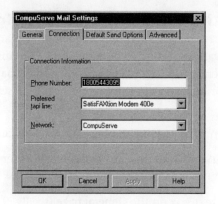

▶ See "Setting Up a CompuServe Connection," p. 278

At this point, you can choose OK, then OK again to begin using your CompuServe Mail service in Exchange. You might, however, want to set a few advanced options. The Default Send Options page contains a selection of properties that define how messages are sent (see fig. 9.31).

Fig. 9.31
The Default Send Options page controls how messages are sent.

The following list explains the properties on the Default Send Options page:

■ *Send Using Microsoft Exchange Rich-Text Format.* Enable this check box if you want Exchange to include character (color, font, etc.) and paragraph formatting in your message. Only recipients who are using Microsoft Exchange will see the special formatting—other recipients receive plain text.

■ *Release Date.* If you enter a date in this field, messages will be held in your Inbox until the date specified, then forwarded on that date to the intended recipients. Leave this field blank if you want the messages to be sent as soon as the service connects to CompuServe.

- *Expiration Date.* If you enter a date in this field, the message will be deleted from the recipient's mail box when the date is reached.

- *Payment Method.* Select one of the three option buttons in this group to specify who pays for surcharged messages.

You can use the Advanced page to schedule automatic connection to CompuServe and other advanced connection options (see fig. 9.32).

Fig. 9.32
Use the Advanced page to control advanced service options.

II

Configuring Windows 95

The following list describes the controls on the Advanced page:

- *Create Event Log.* Enable this check box if you want the CompuServe Mail provider to place in your Inbox log messages describing the results of each connection attempt.

- *Delete Retrieved Messages.* Enable this check box if you want the CompuServe Mail provider to delete mail from your CompuServe mailbox after the mail is retrieved and stored in your Exchange Inbox.

- *Accept Surcharges.* Enable this check box if you are willing to pay for messages that carry a surcharge. Messages such as those from the Internet generally carry a nominal postage-due fee.

- *Change CompuServe Dir.* Click this button to change the folder in which the CompuServe Mail provider stores configuration and address book settings. If you are using another CompuServe product such as WinCIM, the CompuServe Mail provider can use the same address book and connection settings as your other CompuServe product.

- *Schedule Connect Times.* Click this button to display the Connection Times dialog box (see fig. 9.33) and schedule automatic connections to CompuServe. If you want, you can use a selection of different scheduled connection times.

Fig. 9.33

You can schedule the CompuServe Mail provider to connect automatically to CompuServe.

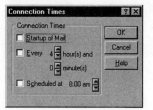

After you have specified all of the settings and properties you want to change for the CompuServe Mail provider, choose OK, then OK again to save the changes. Restart Exchange to begin using the new settings.

Troubleshooting

I configured the CompuServe Mail provider to check for messages at 8 a.m. and every four hours. But, Exchange doesn't check at 8, 12, 4, and so on. It checks for mail at 8 a.m., but the four-hour interval falls at odd times. Why is this?

The CompuServe Mail provider doesn't base its interval connection times on the explicit 8 AM setting you've specified. Instead, the provider checks at four-hour intervals based on the last time it automatically checked for mail. Open Control Panel and click the Mail and Fax icon. Select the CompuServe Mail provider and choose Properties. Choose Advanced, Schedule Connect Times to display the Connection Times dialog box. Clear the Every check box and close the dialog box, then close the Profile property sheets. Shortly before the time when you want one of your hourly interval connections to be made, open the Control Panel, click the Mail and Fax icon, then enable the Every check box in the Connection Times dialog box and specify the interval you want to use. Close the property sheets. Exchange should then connect close to the time you want.

Chapter 10

Configuring Microsoft Fax

by Rob Tidrow

If you run a business today, more than likely you have a dedicated fax machine or you have a fax modem device on your computer. You've come to rely on your fax machine for many of your daily communications needs. In some respects, the fax machine has replaced your phone for the type of critical information that you send and receive with others. Likewise, your computer is a vital piece of equipment in your workplace. By merging the two—the fax and computer—you create a powerful business tool that enables you to communicate by using hard copy faxes or electronic transmissions.

In Chapters 2 and 3, you are shown how to install Microsoft Fax automatically during Windows 95 installation. If you did not install Fax then, this chapter shows you how to set it up manually. This chapter covers the following items:

- Features of Microsoft Fax
- Installing and configuring Microsoft Fax
- Configuring Microsoft Fax for workgroup sharing
- Protecting faxes

Features of Microsoft Fax

Windows 95 includes Microsoft Fax that enables you to send and receive faxes through your fax modem on your computer. You can use Microsoft Fax on a separate computer to service one user, or connect it to a network to use it as a fax server in a workgroup environment. Microsoft Fax has the capability to send a facsimile to another fax modem device or to a dedicated fax machine. If you use Microsoft Fax to send a fax to a fax modem, you can encrypt it with a password to provide a layer of security for the document.

Microsoft Fax is part of Microsoft Exchange and replaces any fax software you may already have installed on your computer. Microsoft Fax enables you to create fax messages, add cover pages, and send the messages to another fax machine or fax modem device. Because Fax is a *MAPI—Messaging Application Programming Interface*—compliant application, you can use other applications, such as Microsoft Word for Windows 95, to send faxes through Windows 95.

Tip

Microsoft Fax includes fax printer drivers so that you can print to a fax modem from within any Windows application.

You also can use Microsoft Fax to receive fax messages. A message can be faxed to you by the sender calling your fax number and delivering the fax. Or, if you use fax-back services to receive technical support information, sales information, or other data, you can dial the service and have it download the document to your fax modem using Microsoft Fax.

Tip

You can store fax messages in the Microsoft Exchange universal inbox.

A Microsoft Fax message can be sent in one of two ways:

- Binary file
- Hard copy fax

The latter option is the traditional way in which fax messages are sent and received via a fax machine, known as a Group 3 fax machine. The limitation of sending faxes this way is that the recipient cannot edit the document or use it as a binary file, unless the document is scanned or keyed into a file. A *binary file* is simply a file created in an application, such as Word for Windows or Lotus 1-2-3 for Windows. Another frustrating aspect of paper faxes is that they may be difficult or impossible to read.

When you use Microsoft Fax to send a binary file to another fax modem, the recipient can view and edit the fax in the application in which it was created and modify it. This feature is handled by Microsoft Fax's *Binary File Transfer* (*BFT*) capability. BFT was originally created for Microsoft's At Work program and is now supported by Microsoft Exchange so that you can create a mail message and attach a binary file to it. Windows for Workgroups 3.11 and other Microsoft At Work enabled platforms also can receive BFT messages.

One way in which you can take advantage of the BFT feature in Microsoft Fax is to use it with other applications, such as Microsoft Word for Windows. You could, for example, create a Word document and send it as a Microsoft Fax message to another user who has Microsoft Fax installed (and Word for Windows). The recipient receives the message and can read it as a Word document.

If the recipient doesn't have a fax modem card and Microsoft Fax, and instead has a Group 3 fax machine, Microsoft Fax automatically prints the Word document as a printed fax image. A problem with sending files this way is the transmission speed and compression feature of the recipient fax machine. Fax machines are much slower than fax modems, so a large binary file (such as a 50-page Word document), may take a long time to transmit and print on the recipient's fax machine. Before you send a large attached document to someone's fax machine, you might want to test this feature first.

Setting Up Microsoft Fax

Microsoft Exchange must be installed on your computer to use Microsoft Fax. If you have not configured Exchange yet, turn to Chapter 9, "Configuring Microsoft Exchange," and install Exchange. You also need to have a fax modem device installed and working on your computer. This topic is covered in Chapter 28, "Configuring Modems." (The type of fax modem required is covered in "Requirements of Microsoft Fax" later in this chapter.)

After you have Exchange set up and a modem working, you need to set up Microsoft Fax to work with Windows 95, Exchange, and your modem. All this is handled by Exchange's profiles.

◀ See "Installing the Exchange Client," p. 202

Fax Modem Requirements of Microsoft Fax

Besides having Windows 95 and Microsoft Exchange installed, your fax modem must meet the following requirements:

- High-speed fax modem, such as a 14.4 kbps fax modem

- Phone line

- Minimum requirements of Windows 95, but an 80486-based computer with 8M of RAM is recommended

◀ See "Requirements of Windows 95," p. 19

When you install Microsoft Fax on a network, your system must meet the following requirements:

- High-speed fax modem, such as a 14.4 kbps fax modem

- Phone line

- At least an 80486-based computer with 8M of RAM

- If the computer will be used as a workstation as well, you'll want to have at least 12M of RAM

Regardless of the way in which you set up Microsoft Fax, either as a stand-alone or networked fax service, you need to make sure that your fax modem is compatible with Microsoft Fax. The technology behind Microsoft Fax is a mature technology that originally was introduced in the Microsoft At Work products and was included as part of Windows for Workgroups 3.11. Because of this, many fax modem manufacturers have ensured that their hardware meets the needs of Microsoft Fax, giving you many choices from which to choose for your hardware.

The following lists and describes the compatible fax modems and fax machines that you can use with Microsoft Fax:

- *Class 1 and Class 2.* You need Class 1 or Class 2 fax modems to send BFT messages with attachments. These classes of fax modems also are required to use security features in Microsoft Fax.

- *ITU T.30 Standard.* This standard is for Group 3 fax machines, which are traditional fax machines common in many business environments. Microsoft Fax converts any BFT fax messages to a T.30 NSF (nonstandard facilities) transmission to enable compatibility with these types of fax machines. (ITU is the International Telecommunications Union.)

- *ITU V.17, V.29, V.27ter standards.* These types are used for high-speed faxes up to 14.4 kpbs.

- *Microsoft At Work platforms.* You need Windows 95, Windows for Workgroups 3.11, or another Microsoft At Work compatible platform to use Microsoft Fax.

Caution

Check the fax modem documentation to ensure that it adheres to the preceding requirements and works with Microsoft Fax. Beware that some fax modems on the market today do not work with Microsoft Fax.

Troubleshooting

My fax modem doesn't work with Windows 95, but I don't know if it is a hardware or software issue.

Many fax modems available on the market today are compatible with Windows 95 and should work fine. For hardware concerns, check with your manufacturer to make sure your fax modem works with Windows 95. It may be one of the few that does not. You also need to make sure your fax modem is a Class 1 or Class 2 fax modem for it to work.

How can I diagnose problems with Microsoft Fax and my modem?

One of the ways is to see if your fax modem is working correctly by selecting Modems from Control Panel. In the Modem Properties sheet, select the Diagnostics page. In the list of ports, select the port to which your fax modem is connected. Click More Info for Windows 95 to run a diagnostics of your fax modem. If everything is okay, you get a report of your modem's properties. If your fax modem is awaiting a call, you receive a message saying that the port is already opened. You need to exit from Microsoft Exchange and rerun the modem diagnostics to get an accurate reading.

If you still experience problems, you need to open the Modem Properties sheet and change some of the advanced settings. It may require you to experiment with these settings before you find one that works for your modem. You also should make sure that you have a Microsoft Fax service set up for Exchange. If not, see the section "Installing Microsoft Fax."

Installing Microsoft Fax

To configure Microsoft Fax, you first need to install the Microsoft Fax software onto your system using the Add/Remove Programs Wizard. You need to have your Windows 95 installation disks or CD-ROM to add these files.

Use the following steps to do this:

1. Double-click the Add/Remove Programs icon in Control Panel.

2. Click the Windows Setup page (see fig. 10.1).

3. Scroll down the Components list box and select Microsoft Fax. Be sure to not click any other component that is already selected, or you will inadvertently remove those programs from your Windows 95 setup.

4. Click OK.

Fig. 10.1
Make sure that the
Windows Setup
page is active.

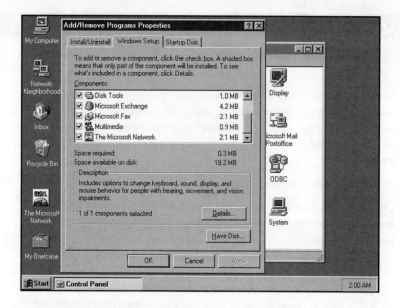

5. When Windows 95 prompts you for a specific Windows 95 Setup disk
or CD-ROM, place it in the disk drive. Windows 95 copies the files onto
your hard disk and returns you to the Desktop when it finishes.

Now that you have Microsoft Fax on your system, you can configure it as a
Microsoft Exchange information service and start sending faxes. You can do
this in one of two ways: by using the Control Panel or by using Microsoft
Exchange. Do the following steps:

1. Double-click the Mail and Fax icon in Control Panel (see fig. 10.2).

The Microsoft Exchange Profiles sheet appears (see fig. 10.3), to which
you can add Fax to a profile.

> **Note**
>
> If you do not see this sheet, click Show Profiles on the General page to reveal
> the Microsoft Exchange Profiles set up on your system.

2. Choose a profile that you want to add Microsoft Fax to, such as MS
Exchange Settings.

3. Click the Properties button to show all the information services set up
for the selected profile (see fig. 10.4). Make sure that the Services page is
displayed.

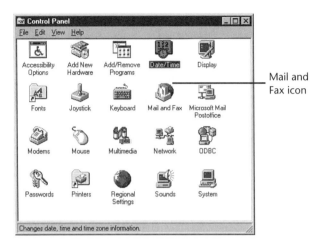

Fig. 10.2
Double-click the
Mail and Fax icon
to configure
Microsoft Fax for
your system.

Mail and
Fax icon

Fig. 10.3
The Microsoft
Exchange Profiles
sheet contains all
the profiles that
you configured
during Windows
95 setup or when
configuring
Exchange.

Fig. 10.4
All the informa-
tion services set up
on your system
appear on the
Services page.

II

Configuring Windows 95

4. Click Add to display the Add Service to Profile dialog box, shown in figure 10.5.

Fig. 10.5
The Add Service to Profile dialog box contains all the available services on your system that you can configure.

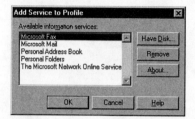

5. In the Available Information Services list, select Microsoft Fax. Click OK.

6. A message appears (see fig. 10.6) asking you to provide the following information:

   ■ Your name

   ■ Your fax number

   ■ Your fax modem type

Fig. 10.6
Enter your user information so that Windows 95 can automatically set up Microsoft Fax now.

If you do not want to provide this information now and let Windows take care of it, you can configure it the first time you use Microsoft Fax. It's best to configure it now so that you do not have to waste time doing it later when you are in a rush to send or receive a fax. Click Yes to continue.

7. The Microsoft Fax Properties sheet appears (see fig. 10.7). Fill out this sheet with the information you are asked for. For the most part, the text boxes are self-explanatory. The only text box that might need some explanation is the Mailbox (optional) item.

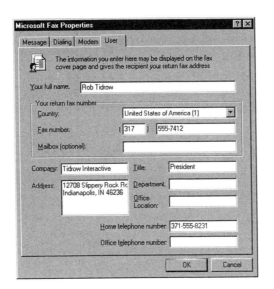

Fig. 10.7
Fill in the information on this sheet so that your fax recipients know who you are.

Note

Believe it or not, according to Federal Communications Commission (FCC) regulation Part 68, Section 68.318(c)(3), you must include the following items on all fax transmissions either on the top or bottom margins of all pages or on a cover page:

■ Date and time fax is sent

■ Identification of the business, "other entity," or the name of the sender

■ Telephone number of the sending fax machine

The Mailbox (optional) item in the Your return fax number section pertains to in-house mailboxes you may have set up to receive fax messages. To fill in this box, type the name your administrator has assigned you, which might be your name, e-mail name, or some other identifier. Otherwise, leave this item blank.

8. After you fill out this page, click the Modem page to set up your fax modem to work with Microsoft Fax (see fig. 10.8). If your fax modem already has been configured for Windows 95 (which it should be if you have an online service set up), your modem should already appear in the Available Fax Modems list.

Fig. 10.8

You need to assign a fax modem to work with Microsoft Fax from this page.

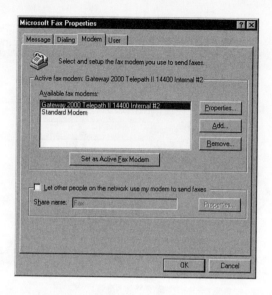

▶ See "Installing Your Modem," p. 588

9. If more than one modem appears in this box, click the modem you want to use as the default fax modem and click the Set as Active Fax Modem button.

Configure Fax Modem Options

Microsoft Fax is a sophisticated application that you can set up to answer your phone automatically after so many rings, let you answer it manually, or not answer your phone at all (if you tend to send instead of receive most of your faxes). As part of the configuration process, you need to tell Microsoft Fax how to behave during a call, and whether it's a received or delivered call. As in most other Windows 95 components, you do all this by configuring Microsoft Fax's properties.

Use the following steps:

1. Click Properties to display the Fax Modem Properties sheet, as shown in figure 10.9.

2. Set up each option, as described in the following list:

   ■ *Answer After.* Set this option to have Microsoft Fax answer a fax call after a certain number of rings. For some reason, you cannot set this value for 1 ring or for more than 10; 2 or 3 are good numbers to set this to.

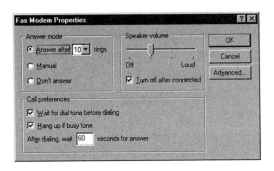

Fig. 10.9
Set the Microsoft
Fax properties for
your fax modem.

- *Manual.* Use this option if you want Microsoft Fax to display a message on-screen when a call comes in. You then answer the call manually. As a recommendation, use this option only if you have one phone line that you use for both voice and fax. Otherwise, select the Answer After option.

- *Don't Answer.* Why have a fax modem if you don't want it to answer incoming faxes? Because you might have to share COM ports with another device. Activate this option if your fax modem shares a port with another device, such as a mouse.

- *Speaker Volume.* It's not a bad idea to set this value to about the middle of the scroll bar so that you can hear when a fax is being received. If it's set too high (such as Loud), your ears may start bleeding when a fax starts transmitting.

- *Turn Off After Connected.* Make sure that a check mark is in this box, unless you enjoy listening to two fax devices talk to each other.

- *Wait For Dial Tone Before Dialing.* For most phone systems, this option needs to be selected to instruct Microsoft Fax to wait until a dial tone is heard before making an outgoing call.

- *Hang Up if Busy Tone.* Leave this option selected so that your fax modem doesn't stay on the line if the number you're calling is busy.

- *After Dialing, Wait x Seconds for Answer.* Many fax machines and fax modems take a few seconds to synchronize after they've been called. This option sets the number of seconds Microsoft Fax waits for the receiving machine to get "in synch" after it answers the call. The default is 60 seconds, which is a good starting number. Increase this number if you notice Microsoft Fax canceling calls too soon.

Tip

Disable the Turn Off After Connection option if you want to hear if your fax transmission is still connected.

After you fill out this screen, click OK to save these configuration settings and to return to the Fax Modem Properties screen.

If you want to configure more advanced fax modem settings, click the Advanced button and read the next section. If not, skip to the "Setting Dialing Properties" section.

Troubleshooting

How do I turn off the fax modem speaker?

Double-click Mail and Fax in Control Panel. Click Microsoft Fax on the MS Exchange Settings Properties sheet and click the Properties button. Select the Modems page and click the Properties button. In the Speaker Volume area, move the slider bar to the Off position.

Configure Advanced Fax Modem Settings

In the Advanced dialog box (see fig. 10.10), you have the option of configuring more sophisticated fax modem settings.

Fig. 10.10
Use the Advanced dialog box to troubleshoot fax modem problems you may be experiencing.

These options are detailed in the following list:

- *Disable High Speed Transmission.* High speed transmissions are anything over 9,600 bps. If your fax modem is rated for higher speeds, such as 14.4 bps, you might experience transmission errors communicating with other devices. Keep this setting disabled (unchecked) unless your outgoing and incoming faxes are not being handled reliably. Select this option to slow down your transmission speeds.

■ *Disable Error Correction Mode.* Fax transmissions demand a great deal of cooperation between the sending fax device and the receiving fax device. You need built-in error-correction procedures to make sure that the fax you send is received properly. This option is used to direct Microsoft Fax to send non-editable faxes, either to a fax machine or as bitmap file, without using error correction. Keep this option disabled unless you cannot send or receive faxes reliably.

■ *Enable MR Compression.* Select this option to compress faxes you send or receive, decreasing the amount of time you're online. This option is disabled by default and is grayed out if your fax modem does not support MR compression.

> **Caution**
>
> Compressed faxes are more susceptible to line noise and interference. If a transmission experiences too much line noise or interference, your fax may become corrupted, or your fax modem connection may be lost.

■ *Use Class 2 if Available.* Select this option if you have problems sending or receiving messages using a fax modem that supports Class 1 and Class 2 fax modems. The default is to leave this option disabled.

■ *Reject Pages Received with Errors.* Most fax transmissions have some sort of problem occur during sending or receiving. You can set Microsoft Fax to have a high tolerance (more errors can occur during transmission), medium tolerance, low tolerance, and very low tolerance (fewer errors can occur during transmission) for errors before rejecting the page being received. The default is to have a high tolerance for errors.

> **Caution**
>
> If you select the Use Class 2 if Available option, you cannot use error-correction, or send or receive editable faxes.

Click OK when these settings are ready. Click OK to return to the Fax Modem Properties sheet.

Setting Dialing Properties

Now that you have Microsoft Fax set up to work with your fax modem, you need to start setting user-specific information, such as how Microsoft Fax should dial your phone. Click the Dialing page in the Microsoft Fax Properties sheet. To begin, click the Dialing Properties button to display the My Locations page (see fig. 10.11).

Fig. 10.11

Set your dialing options, such as area code, calling card numbers, and other user-specific options, in the My Locations page.

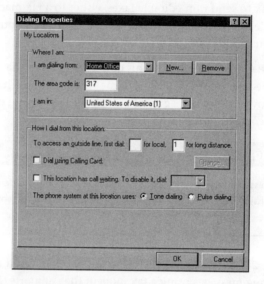

Note

The My Locations information may already be filled in if you set up your modem to make a call out, or if any of your Exchange services previously dialed online services, such as the Microsoft Network.

Microsoft Fax enables you to use several different configurations depending on where you are when you send a fax. If your computer always stays in one place (such as in your office or home), you generally need only one location configured. If, however, you use a portable PC and travel from work to home, or to other places, you can configure several different locations to dial using different configuration settings.

When you are in your office, for instance, you may not need to use a calling card to make a long distance phone call to send a fax. You can set up Microsoft Fax to use a configuration that doesn't require a calling card to be entered first. On the other hand, your office phone system may require you to dial an initial number to get an outside line (such as 9). You can place this in the Microsoft Fax configuration settings that you use from your office.

Another scenario where you use a different dialing procedure is when you stay in hotels. For these calls, you may always place them on a calling card. Set up Microsoft Fax to use your calling card number to place these calls. All your configurations are saved in Windows 95 and can be retrieved each time you use Microsoft Fax.

The following steps show you how to create a new dialing location in Microsoft Fax:

1. Click <u>N</u>ew to display the Create New Location dialog box on the My Locations page (see fig. 10.12).

Fig. 10.12
Set up new locations for each dialing scenario you might use to send faxes, such as home, office, travel, and leisure.

2. Enter a new name for the location, such as **Office** or **On the Road**. Click OK.

3. In The Area <u>C</u>ode Is text box, enter the area code from which you are calling. You may need to change or update this if you are not sure of the area code in which you are staying, such as when you are traveling.

4. Select the country in which you are calling.

5. Enter the number (if any) you need to dial to get an outside line (such as **9**) and to make a long distance call (usually **1**).

> **Note**
>
> Most hotels use their own phone system to get outside lines, so you need to enter those numbers when you know what they are.

6. Click the Dial <u>U</u>sing Calling Card option to enter your calling card information. When you do this, the Change Calling Card dialog box appears (see fig. 10.13).

7. Click the Calling Card to <u>U</u>se drop-down list and select your card name.

8. Enter the card account number in the <u>C</u>alling Card Number text box.

Fig. 10.13
Microsoft Fax can use calling card numbers to place your fax calls.

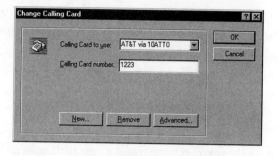

Another powerful feature of Microsoft Fax is one that enables you to write dialing scripts, or *rules*, for each calling card you use. Actually, each calling card you set up has rules set up for it. Microsoft Fax enables you to create your own rules if there are any special considerations that you need to make for a certain dialing situation. To use this feature, follow these steps:

1. Create a new calling card by clicking <u>N</u>ew and entering the name in the <u>C</u>reate a New Calling Card Named text box (see fig. 10.14)

Fig. 10.14
Enter the name of the new calling card in this dialog box.

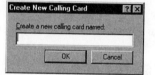

Click OK to enter that name in the Calling Card to <u>U</u>se drop-down list.

2. Click <u>A</u>dvanced. This is where you write the rules for your new card for these dialing scenarios: <u>C</u>alls Within the Same Area Code; Domestic <u>L</u>ong Distance Calls; and <u>I</u>nternational Calls. Table 10.1 shows the characters to use to specify how each dialing rule is processed.

Table 10.1 Dialing Rule Characters

Character	Function
0-9	Specifies number to dial
ABCD	Characters used on some tone dialing units to control certain features
E	Specifies country code
F	Dials area code or city code
G	Dials number as a local number

Character	Function
H	Uses specified calling card number
*, #	Characters used for tone dialing units to control certain features
T	Instructs Microsoft Fax to dial the following numbers using tone dialing
P	Instructs Microsoft Fax to dial the following numbers using pulse dialing
,	Pauses dialing for a fixed time, usually one second per ,
!	Used to send a hookflash (1/2 second on-hook, 1/2 second off-hook), which is like pressing the plunging to hang up the phone
W	Instructs Microsoft Fax to wait for a second dial tone
@	Directs Microsoft Fax to wait for a quiet answer from receiving fax, which is a ringback followed by five seconds of silence
$	Pauses until calling card prompt ("bong") is finished
?	Prompts for user input before continuing dialing

3. Create a rule for a calling card (which is optional) and click Close to save it. Click OK to return to the My Locations page.

Note

To see examples of some rules, or to use a predefined rule, click the Copy From button and select a calling card from which to copy (see fig. 10.15) from the Copy Dialing Rules dialog box. Click OK to enter the rule in the Dialing Rules dialog box.

II

Configuring Windows 95

Fig. 10.15
Review other calling card rules or copy a set of rules from a card by clicking the Copy From button.

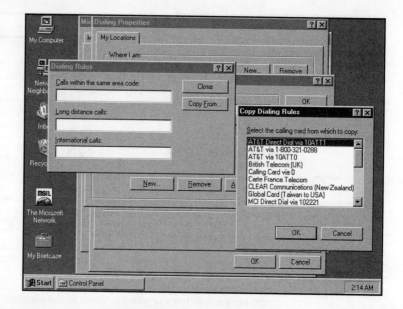

Finishing Setting Dialing Properties

Have you ever been using your modem or fax modem and it crashed for no apparent reason? Although many things can cause this (line noise, interrupt conflicts, port problems, kids pulling out the phone line), if you have call waiting, you probably can blame it first. Many people who use modems and have call waiting do not think to disable call waiting before making an online connection.

Microsoft Fax enables you to add a switch that automatically disables call waiting each time you send a fax (or use your modem for other purposes). Use the following steps to disable call waiting:

1. Click the This Location Has Call Waiting option.

2. Enter the code that disables call waiting. You need to obtain this code from your local phone company, because each system uses a different code. Microsoft Fax provides three common codes in the drop-down list box next to this option: *70, 70#, and 1170. After you finish faxing and your fax modem hangs up, call waiting is turned back on.

3. Next, tell Microsoft Fax the type of phone system—Tone dialing or Pulse dialing—you have. Click OK when you have this location set up. You can create as many locations as you need to.

Setting Toll Prefixes

Now that you have the locations set up, you need to tell Microsoft Fax which numbers in your local calling area require you to dial as a toll call. To do this, click the T<u>o</u>ll Prefixes button. In the Toll Prefixes dialog box (see fig. 10.16), click all the numbers from the <u>L</u>ocal Phone Numbers list to the Dial 1-*xxx* Fir<u>s</u>t list (*xxx* is your area code) that require you to dial your area code first. Click the <u>A</u>dd button to place numbers from the list on the left to the list on the right. Click OK when you finish with this dialog box.

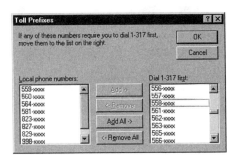

Fig. 10.16
Tell Microsoft Fax which prefixes in your local calling area code are long distance calls.

Every time you call a fax number, you're not going to be lucky enough to get through. You'll hit busy signals. The fax on the other side of the line won't be ready to accept your call. Or, your fax modem and the recipient's fax device won't synchronize properly.

In these cases, you need Microsoft Fax to keep retrying the number you're calling. In the Dialing dialog box, set the <u>N</u>umber of Retries option to the number of times you want Microsoft Fax to dial the number before quitting. The default is three times. You also need to tell Microsoft Fax the amount of time you want it to wait before it tries the number again. In the <u>T</u>ime Between Retries box, set this time in minutes. The default is two minutes.

Now that you've taken care of the dialing options, you now are ready to configure the default settings for your fax messages. Click the Message page.

Configuring Message Options

The Message page (see fig. 10.17) has three main areas:

- Time to Send
- Message Format
- Default Cover Page

Fig. 10.17

Microsoft Fax lets you customize the way your default fax message looks by using settings in the Message page.

Setting Time to Send Options

You may or may not always want to create a fax message and then zip it off to your recipient. You may want to create a message, or several messages, and then send them at specific times, such as when you are going to lunch or when long distance rates are lower. Microsoft Fax enables you to set the time you send fax messages in one of three ways:

- *As Soon As Possible*. This is the default selection; use this option to send faxes immediately after you create one.

- *Discount Rates*. Use this option to send your fax message(s) during pre-defined hours when long distance tolls are lower. Click the Set button to set the discount rates start and end times. The Set Discount Rates dialog box opens and shows the default discounted rate hours—between 5 p.m. and 8 a.m. Click OK when you set the appropriate times for your long distance carrier, or keep the default settings.

- *Specific Time*. Set this option to an exact time to send any fax messages you have in the outbox.

Configuring Fax Message Formats

Microsoft Fax can send fax messages in two primary formats: editable formats (as a binary file) and noneditable formats ("hard copy" faxes). Editable fax messages can be manipulated much the same way a word processing document can be changed. A Microsoft Fax editable fax can be received and edited only by a recipient who also has Microsoft Fax installed. A noneditable fax is a fax that you receive from a "regular" facsimile machine.

In the Message format area, you set the default way in which your messages are sent. Select the Editable, If Possible option when you send faxes to both fax modems and regular fax machines. This is the default selection. If your fax messages always must be edited by the recipient, or if you want to encrypt your fax message with a password, enable the Editable Only option. (See "Setting Up Security" later in this chapter for information on using security options in Microsoft Fax.) This sends all your fax messages as binary faxes. When using this option, if the recipient does not have Microsoft Fax installed, the fax is not sent. Microsoft Fax places a message in your Microsoft Exchange Inbox folder telling you that the message was not sent.

When you're sure that your recipient doesn't have Microsoft Fax installed, or you don't want your fax to be edited, send it as Not Editable. Even if the receiving device is a fax modem, the fax message is sent as a bitmap image, so the recipient cannot directly edit the message. If, however, the user has an OCR (optical character recognition) program, he or she can export the faxed image or text as a file to edit in another application.

With the first and third options, you also can specify the type of paper used to print your fax message. Click the Paper button to display the Message Format dialog box and adjust paper settings, such as size, image quality, and orientation. For most faxes, the default settings are fine. Click OK when your paper settings are configured.

Configuring Default Cover Pages

You can opt to send a cover page with your fax message. Click the Send Cover Page option to send a cover page with all your fax messages. Microsoft Fax includes four standard cover pages that you can use:

- Confidential
- For Your Information!
- Generic
- Urgent

Select a cover page that suits your needs. Generic is the default. As Microsoft Fax creates your fax message and prepares it to be sent, it fills in data fields on the cover page with information, such as recipient name and fax number, your name, and so on.

> **Tip**
>
> Select a cover page name and click Open to see what a cover page looks like.

The New button is used to create new cover pages by using Microsoft Fax's Cover Page Editor. Also, the Browse button can be used to locate cover page files (denoted as CPE) on your computer.

> **Note**
>
> This book does not show you how to modify or create cover pages, or how to use the Microsoft Fax Cover Page Editor. See Que's *Special Edition Using Windows 95* for details on using these features.

Finishing Configuring Message Options

One final option on the Message page is the Let Me Change the Subject Line of New Faxes I Receive option. Use this option to change the subject line of any faxes you receive. Because all incoming faxes are stored in the Microsoft Exchange Inbox, the subject (if it contains a subject) appears in the subject field there. This option gives you control over what appears in the subject field, enabling you to organize your messages as they come in. On the other hand, you must perform one more action as each fax message is received. The default is to leave this option disabled.

Click OK to save all the Microsoft Fax properties and to return to the MS Exchange Setting Properties sheet.

Congratulations! You're ready to send a fax using Microsoft Fax.

Configuring a Shared Fax Modem

To reduce the number of fax devices and dedicated phone lines for fax services, many businesses have one centralized fax machine that everyone shares. Because of their convenience and ease of use, most people do not complain too much about walking to a fax machine to send a message or document to another fax machine. Microsoft Fax enables you to extend this sharing of fax devices by letting users in a network environment share a fax modem.

The computer that contains the shared fax modem is called the *fax server* and is not required to be a dedicated PC. A fax server can be anyone's computer that is set up in a workgroup of other Windows 95 users. When a fax is received on the fax server, it then is routed to the recipient in the workgroup via Microsoft Exchange (or by attaching it as an e-mail message using an e-mail application such as cc:Mail).

> **Tip**
>
> The fax server should have at least 12M of memory and be a 486 or Pentium machine.

> **Caution**
>
> Microsoft Fax cannot automatically route fax messages to workgroup recipients. They must be manually delivered.

Setting Up a Fax Server

Again, make sure that Microsoft Exchange is installed and that a fax modem is installed and working on the fax server before completing these steps.

◄ See "Installing the Exchange Client," p. 202

Start Microsoft Exchange and then perform the following steps:

1. Choose Tools, Microsoft Fax Tools.

2. Click Options.

► See "Installing Your Modem," p. 588

3. In the Microsoft Fax Properties sheet (see fig. 10.18), click the Modem page.

4. Click the Let Other People on the Network Use My Modem to Send Faxes option.

5. If the Select Drive dialog box appears, select the drive the network fax will use from the drop-down list and click OK.

6. Enter the name of the shared directory in the Share Name text box.

7. Click the Properties button to configure the shared modem's properties (see fig. 10.19). The NetFax dialog box appears, in which you tell Microsoft Fax the name of the shared fax modem folder. The NetFax dialog box also enables you to set up passwords for users to connect to the fax server.

II

Configuring Windows 95

Fig. 10.18
Make sure that the
Modem page is
active to begin
setting up a fax
server.

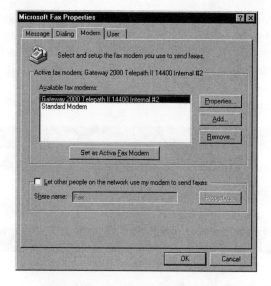

Fig. 10.19
Use the NetFax
dialog box to set
the shared fax
folder and other
settings for
sharing a fax
modem.

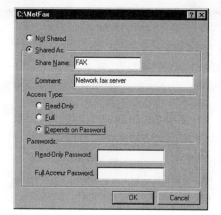

Note

If the Properties button does not work, switch to Control Panel and double-click the Network icon. Click the File and Print Sharing File button on the Configuration page of the Network sheet. Next, select both options in the File and Print Sharing dialog box for the Microsoft network service. You then need to restart Windows 95 for these settings to take affect. These settings enable sharing on your system, so you can share the fax modem with other users in your workgroup.

8. In the Share <u>N</u>ame field, type the name of the shared folder for the fax server. Microsoft Fax displays the name of the network fax shared directory as the default. When a user in your workgroup wants to use this folder, she searches for this folder on your computer on your network.

9. In the Access Type section, select the type of access you want users to have to the shared folder. The default is <u>F</u>ull. Select <u>R</u>ead-Only if you want users to read, but not modify, items in the folder. The <u>D</u>epends on Password option is used if you want to give different people different rights to the shared folder. You can give one password—the R<u>e</u>ad-Only Password—to users who can only have read rights. You then can give another password—the F<u>u</u>ll Access Password—to users who can have full access to the folder.

10. Fill out the Passwords section as necessary, based on your selections in step 9.

For users in the Windows 95 workgroup to access the fax server, they must know the fax server's full network name. The name is formed by joining the server's computer name (defined in the Network option in Control Panel) with the shared folder name, for example, \\RTIDROW\FAX.

Setting Up a Fax Server Client

Not only must you configure a fax server to share a fax modem, but you also must configure the client's access to the server. The clients are those users who want to share the fax server. Start Microsoft Exchange on the client machine and then use the following steps:

1. Choose <u>T</u>ools, Microsoft Fa<u>x</u> Tool.

2. Select <u>O</u>ptions.

3. In the Microsoft Fax Properties sheet, click the Modem page.

4. In Modem properties, click the <u>A</u>dd button to display the Add a Fax Modem dialog box (see fig. 10.20).

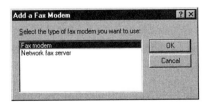

Fig. 10.20
The Add a Fax Modem dialog box includes the types of fax modems to which you can connect.

5. In the Add a Fax Modem dialog box, click Network Fax Server, and then click OK. The Connect To Network Fax Server dialog box appears, as seen in figure 10.21.

Fig. 10.21
To set up a client to use a shared fax server, enter the path of the shared fax server in this dialog box.

6. In the Connect To Network Fax Server dialog box, type the network name of the fax server, such as **\\RTIDROW\FAX**. If you do not know the network name, ask your network administrator. Click OK.

7. In the Microsoft Fax Properties dialog box, click the server name, and then click the Set as Active <u>F</u>ax Modem button.

You may have to reboot your computer for the settings to take effect.

Setting Up Security

One of the most discussed topics in the computer industry is security. You hear about security and the Internet. You hear about LAN security. You hear about voice mail security. Microsoft Fax enables you to securely send fax messages using public key encryption developed by one of the leaders in security, RSA Inc. Microsoft Fax also enables you to password encrypt and use digital signatures on your messages with confidence. The security features, of course, only extend to sending digital messages and files, not to printed or hard copy faxes. These types of faxes are still subject to anyone's eyes who happens to be walking by the fax machine when your transmission comes through.

> **Note**
>
> A *digital signature* is an electronic version of your signature. For most business transactions, such as purchase requests and employee timesheets, a signature is required to process the request. You can use a secure digital signature to "sign" requests, timesheets, and other sensitive documents.

One way to secure your fax messages is to password-protect them as you send them. As you create a fax message and the Send Options for This Message dialog box appears, set the type of security you want to have for your fax message. Click the Security button to display the Message Security Options dialog box (see fig. 10.22).

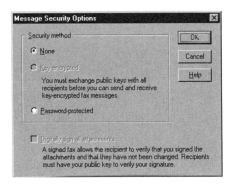

Fig. 10.22
You can set the type of security for your fax message in this dialog box.

Tip

Share your password so that the recipient can open and read your fax message.

If you have not set up public key encryption, you have to before you can use the Key-Encrypted option or use a digital signature on your message. You can, however, secure the fax message with a password by choosing the Password-protected option. Figure 10.23 shows you the Fax Security—Password Protection dialog box that you need to fill out when you want to send a message with a password.

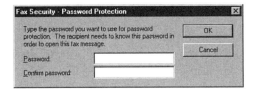

Fig. 10.23
To password-protect your faxes, enter a password in this dialog box.

Setting Up Key Encryption

A *key-encrypted message* uses a public key to unlock the message for viewing. This public key is made available to your fax recipients (who must also have Microsoft Fax installed) so that only they can open your document.

You must create a public key in Exchange. To do this, choose Tools, Microsoft Fax Tools, Advanced Security. The Advanced Fax Security dialog box appears (see fig. 10.24). In this dialog box, if this is first time you have created a public key, the only option you can choose is the last one, New Key Set.

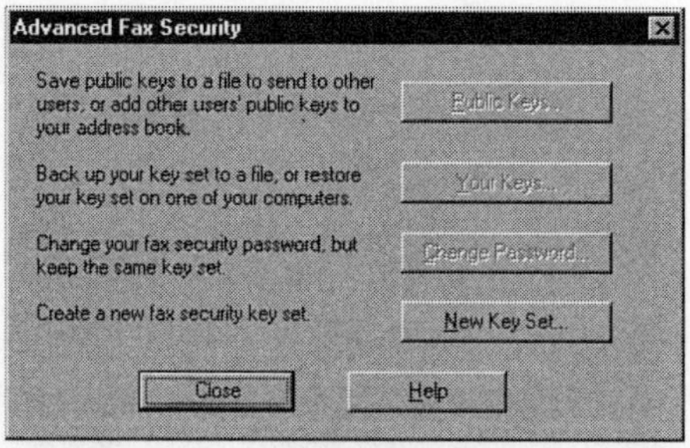

Fig. 10.24
Create a public
key.

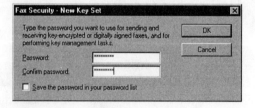

In the Fax Security—New Key Set dialog box, type in a password in the Password field, and then retype it in the Confirm Password field (see fig. 10.25). As you would expect, the password is not displayed; only a string of ***** denotes your password. Don't forget this password; it is now your public key. Click OK to have Exchange create a new public key set on your system. An information box appears, telling you it may take a few moments to create your key set.

Fig. 10.25
You need to enter
a new password to
create a new
public key.

Sharing Public Keys

After you create a public key set, you need to distribute it to your fax recipients in order for them to read your key-encrypted messages. Do this by clicking the Public Keys button in the Advanced Fax Security dialog box (choose Tools, Microsoft Fax Tools, Advanced Security if you've already closed this dialog box). The Fax Security—Managing Public Keys dialog box appears, from which you need to click Save. This saves your public key to a file so that you can send it to other recipients.

In the Fax Security—Save Public Keys dialog box, click the name or names of the public keys you want to share. As a minimum, you should click your name here. Click OK and in the resulting window, select a name and folder in which to store the keys. This file has an AWP extension. To finish, you need to send this file to your recipients either via an attachment to a Microsoft Exchange message or on a floppy disk.

Receiving Public Keys

When you send your public key to a list of recipients, they will need to import the AWP file into Microsoft Fax. Likewise, when you receive a public key from someone, you need to import it into your Microsoft Fax settings and add it to your address book. This enables you to read key-encrypted messages from those users.

After you receive an AWP file from someone, store it on your system and click the Add button in the Fax Security—Managing Public Keys dialog box. Locate the file name that contains the public keys and click Open. Click the key or keys that you want to add. ❖

Chapter 11

Configuring Windows 95 for Online Connections

by Dave Gibbons

The online world offers fun, business, information, and interesting people. But we don't want to waste too much time and effort *getting* there—it's *being* there that's important. Windows 95 takes most of the work out of going online and makes being there an easier experience.

Before Windows 95, setting up a modem with Windows entailed its share of guesswork (and luck). Even if your modem operated in DOS, there was no guarantee Windows 3.x would have any idea the modem existed—or that it wouldn't introduce a new conflict that disabled your modem and more (usually your mouse). Data transfer speed was a problem, too, with Windows 3.x acting as an extra layer of overhead between communications programs and the modem.

Now, Microsoft has addressed the speed and setup issues, removing the Windows-on-top-of-DOS overhead and making Windows 95 much smarter about modems. Many users won't face any obstacles getting their modems to work with Windows 95; if you run into any snags, Windows 95 provides the tools to track down almost any problem, making it an operating system that is more than adequate for modem communications. If you haven't installed your modem, turn to Chapter 28 for step-by-step installation and troubleshooting instructions.

In this chapter, you learn how to

- Use HyperTerminal and other terminal software to connect to a BBS

- Install and use The Microsoft Network

- Set up Windows 95 for Prodigy

- Set up Windows 95 for America Online

- Set up Windows 95 for CompuServe

Using HyperTerminal

Windows 95 includes HyperTerminal, an improved version of the Terminal program from the previous Windows versions. HyperTerminal is a basic *terminal emulation program*, which means it enables Windows 95 to interpret terminal commands from a BBS, online service, or mainframe. It lacks the automation and flash of a high-end terminal program (like its big sibling HyperAccess V), but works well for basic functions. You can use any of these emulations:

- *ANSI.* Used for BBSes.

- *Minitel.* French public terminal program.

- *TTY.* Doesn't interpret any incoming data, just displays it. Useful for machine tools and other simple serial devices like computer-connectable watches.

- *VT52.* Commonly used with mainframes.

- *VT100.* Another terminal commonly used with mainframes.

- *Viewdata.*

The other option in the terminals list is Auto-Detect. When you don't know what kind of system you're calling, this is a pretty good choice. It allows HyperTerminal to analyze the incoming data and guess what the correct terminal type is.

Each BBS or online service you call with HyperTerminal gets a separate icon, called a *connection*, in the HyperTerminal folder. When you select a connection, it tells HyperTerminal to use all the settings you've saved for that connection—not just switch to a different phone number. A connection can contain information about the following:

- Terminal type you want to use

- Speed and settings of the modem

- Which modem or serial port to use if you've installed more than one

- Icon you'll see with the connection's name in the HyperTerminal window

- The phone number (if any) of the connection

- Location you're calling from (very handy for use on a laptop)

Any changes you make in a connection affect only that connection.

Starting HyperTerminal

To start HyperTerminal, follow these steps:

1. Select the Start button.

2. Choose Programs.

3. Choose Accessories.

4. Select the HYPERTERMINAL folder.

> **Tip**
>
> If you use one particular connection in HyperTerminal a lot, you may want to put its shortcut directly on the Start menu so you don't have to open HyperTerminal's folder each time you start it.

5. Double-click the Hypertrm icon (see fig. 11.1) or the icon of the connection you want to use. If you start HyperTerminal with the Hypertrm icon, it assumes you want to create a new connection (see "Creating a New Connection in HyperTerminal" later in the chapter). If you haven't yet installed a modem, Windows 95 prompts you to do so.

Fig. 11.1
HyperTerminal's folder is somewhat reminiscent of Windows 3.x groups, down to its cryptic eight-letter name.

> **Caution**
>
> Don't use the CompuServe icon in the HyperTerminal window. Get WinCIM in-
> stead—it's much more advanced than HyperTerminal, and makes your CompuServe
> use much easier. See "Setting Up a CompuServe Connection" later in the chapter.

If you don't see HyperTerminal's folder in the Accessories menu, it may not be installed. Try using the Start menu's Search function to find the program (HYPERTRM). If that fails, follow these steps to install it from your disk:

1. Click the My Computer icon.

2. Open the Control Panel.

3. Select Add/Remove Programs.

4. Use the Control Panel's easy Add/Remove Programs option to install a Windows 95 program you forgot originally. Don't be tempted to rerun the Setup program (see fig. 11.2) and select Communications.

Fig. 11.2
Don't rerun the Setup program to install a Windows program you forgot originally. Use the Control Panel's easy Add/Remove Programs option.

5. Click the Details button.

6. In the Communications pop-up menu, make sure to put a check in the box beside HyperTerminal. You can choose to install Dial-up Network-ing, Direct Cable Connection, and Phone Dialer if you want, but they're not necessary for HyperTerminal.

7. Make sure the original Windows 95 disk is in your drive. Click OK in the Communications window, then click OK in the Add/Remove Pro-gram Properties sheet. The newly selected HyperTerminal is installed to your computer, and you'll be able to start it using the previous set of steps.

Creating a New Connection in HyperTerminal

When you start with HyperTerminal, you naturally have to build each new connection from scratch. You should know a few things in order to create each one:

- Phone number, if any

- Terminal type (if you don't know, stick with Auto-Detect)

- Port settings (usually 8-N-1 for BBSes, 7-E-1 for mainframes and online services like CompuServe)

To create a connection, follow these steps:

1. If you've just opened HyperTerminal, you see the Connection Description window (see fig. 11.3). If HyperTerminal is already open to the blank terminal screen, you'll have to choose New Connection from the File menu first, but then you'll see the same screen. Enter the name you want to use for the connection and choose an icon. Click OK.

Fig. 11.3
You can choose from 16 different icons for each new HyperTerminal connection.

2. In the Phone Number window (see fig. 11.4), enter the phone number (if any) and choose the connection you want to use. If you're connecting directly to a machine (without a modem), choose the down arrow beside Connect Using. You'll see a `Direct to COMx` for each COM port. Choosing any of those options prevents HyperTerminal from trying to send modem commands through the port. Click OK.

Fig. 11.4
If you put the area code in the Area Code box—not in the Phone Number box— Windows can decide whether or not to dial it based on your current location.

3. The Connect window enables you to make any changes to the phone number or your current location. Most of the time, you'll just click the Dial button and let HyperTerminal complete the connection.

4. When you're finished with the call, choose File, Save to add the connection to the HyperTerminal window.

Viewing the HyperTerminal Screen

While you're online with HyperTerminal, the communication between you and the remote system takes place on the terminal screen, the framed area in the middle of the HyperTerminal window (see fig. 11.5).

Fig. 11.5
If HyperTerminal's terminal screen is too big or small, choose a different font size in the View menu's Font selection.

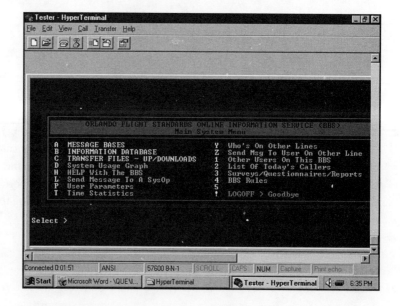

HyperTerminal has a functional (if somewhat sparse) button bar. All the basic functions are covered, from left to right. See table 11.1 for a description of each button.

Table 11.1	HyperTerminal's Button Bar
Button	**Description**
	New Connection
	Open Connection
	Connect (using the currently active connection)
	Disconnect
	Upload (receiving side must be ready to receive before you select the Upload icon)
	Download (sending side must be ready to send before you select the Download icon)
	Properties (used to change any aspect of the current connection's setup)

Along the right side of the terminal window is a scroll bar (the *backscroll* bar—refer to fig. 11.5) which you can use to see any text that has scrolled off the top of the screen.

If you call a BBS with HyperTerminal, you may notice a strange effect in the BBS's graphics. Instead of lines and boxes on the screen, you may see rows of odd letters (see fig. 11.6). This happens because most Windows fonts don't offer the line drawing characters the BBSes expect. To correct the problem, choose View, Font and select the Terminal font. It's not a TrueType font (so it's not scalable on the screen), but it offers the correct characters. You'll probably want to use a video resolution higher than 640 × 480, since the Terminal font makes the terminal screen too big to completely fit on a 640 × 480 screen (refer to fig. 11.5).

Fig. 11.6
This BBS's menu normally has a line-drawn box around it, but not when Courier New is the active font.

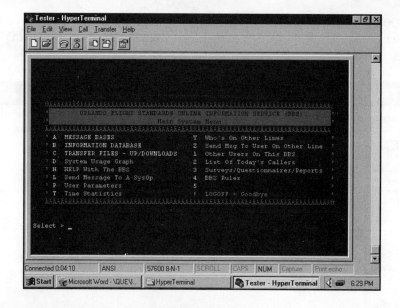

Other Software Options

For more advanced terminal operations, including automating your online sessions, you need something beyond HyperTerminal. Some of the major communications programs on the market are the following:

- PROCOMM PLUS for Windows
- WinCOMM PRO/Delrina Communications Suite
- QModem
- Reflections
- HyperAccess (made by Hilgreave, the company that wrote HyperTerminal)

These programs offer enhanced BBS and mainframe connections, along with their own sets of features to make your online time easier and more productive. You may also decide to get an advanced terminal emulation program for dialing into a UNIX host for an Internet connection. If, however, you only plan to use an online service like Prodigy, America Online, or The Microsoft

Network, an enhanced terminal program won't do you much good—each of these services has its own Windows-based graphical interface. You can use a terminal program with CompuServe, but you'll probably have an easier time with WinCIM, CompuServe's graphical front-end program.

If you decide to get an enhanced terminal emulation program, you shouldn't have much trouble using it with Windows 95. You're able to install it like any other new Windows software (choose Add/Remove Programs in Control Panel and click Install), but you'll need to keep a few things in mind:

■ You may have to tell the program what kind of modem you use and what port it's on, because it might not be able to get that information from Windows 95. Most terminal programs are able to automatically sense your modem during the installation (see fig. 11.7), so this may not be a big issue.

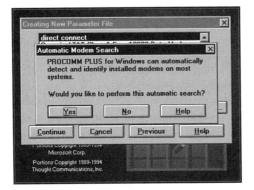

Fig. 11.7

Most big-name terminal programs detect your modem automatically during their installation process.

■ The program may try to install a new communications driver. If so, make sure you have a version that is Windows 95-compatible.

■ If you're using a DOS-based program, you probably won't have trouble with Windows 95's long file names. Most well-written terminal emulation programs are able to deal with transferring files with long file names. Many non-DOS operating systems allow longer names, so communications programs have to know how to deal with them (see fig. 11.8).

Fig. 11.8
Long file names show up as standard eight-and-three names, with a tilde representing the truncated portion.

FILE NAME	SIZE	DATE	TIME
.	<DIR>	7-27-95	09:06
..	<DIR>	7-27-95	09:06
OCTOBE~1.DOC	142	5-03-94	12:37
SEPTEM~1.DOC	62	8-17-94	23:39
NOVEMB~1.DOC	28	1-18-95	08:44
DECEMB~1.DOC	99	9-13-94	17:56
JANUAR~1.DOC	57	1-20-95	03:52

Setting Up a Microsoft Network Connection

The Microsoft Network is one of the most fascinating aspects of Windows 95. It's a full-fledged online service that combines most of the best elements from the other services in this chapter and tosses in a few goodies the others don't have yet. It has standard features like e-mail, Internet access, file libraries, support forums, and games, but the real reasons many people will keep their Microsoft Network accounts (along with or instead of other online services) will probably be twofold:

- The interface is extremely well laid-out and easy to use (see fig. 11.9).

- Microsoft's industry (and financial) position will help it draw major celebrities of all types for online conferences.

Fig. 11.9
The Microsoft Network's interface is straightforward and elegant—a step up from the standard (and confusing) dozens-of-icons approach.

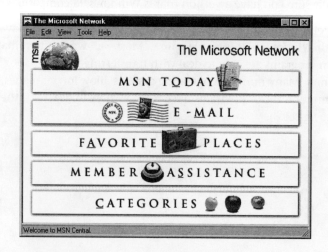

If you choose the default installation of Windows 95, the Microsoft Network software is installed automatically. Its icon should appear on your desktop near the Recycle Bin. If you don't see the Microsoft Network icon, install it from your original disks by following these steps:

1. Choose the My Computer icon on your desktop.

2. Open the Control Panel.

3. Open the Add/Remove Programs icon.

4. Choose the Windows Setup tab of the Add/Remove Program Properties window and select The Microsoft Network.

5. Make sure the original Windows 95 disk is in your drive. Click OK in the Add/Remove Program Properties window. The Microsoft Network is then installed.

To set up The Microsoft Network for the first time, follow these steps:

1. When you first open the Microsoft Network icon, it asks whether you're already a member or if you're a new member. Select New Member.

> **Note**
>
> To become a member, you need a credit card, even though your early use is free.

2. In the next screen (see fig. 11.10), you see the three steps you need to complete to join. The setup is extremely simple. Enter your address (during which you select a local access number to use during all future calls), your credit card number, and read the licensing and fee information for The Microsoft Network.

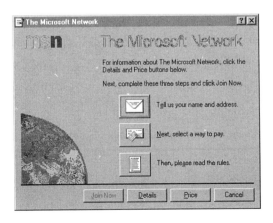

Fig. 11.10
Follow these three simple steps (or at least the first two) to set up your connection.

Signing On

Run The Microsoft Network with its icon, and follow these steps:

1. Enter your name and password (see fig. 11.11).

Fig. 11.11
Select the Remember My Password option if you want the password entered automatically each time. Just make sure no one else has access to your computer.

2. Click Connect.

Signing Off

Click the Close button on the far right of the title bar, just like you'd close any other Windows 95 application. When The Microsoft Network asks if it's all right to hang up, select Yes.

Setting Up a CompuServe Connection

Almost every modem, computer, or software/hardware piece you buy includes a trial offer from CompuServe.

Everyone who joins CompuServe gets a free trial (usually one month of free basic services and a $25 credit for extended services) to try out the service. Even though there are no charges during the trial period, you need one of these to sign up with CompuServe:

- Credit card

- Checking account

To start the free trial period, go through the actual sign-up process. If you decide you don't want to keep CompuServe, remember to cancel your membership within a month of your sign-up—monthly fees are automatically charged to you *even if you don't use the service.*

To get a free copy of CompuServe's WinCIM software (make sure you get version 1.4 or above), call 800-848-8199. You can also find WinCIM at the newsstand bundled with computer-oriented magazines, as well as on many CD-ROMs.

Tip

Make sure you have WinCIM 1.4 or above. Older magazines and CD-ROMs may have version 1.3.1 or earlier.

Installing WinCIM is very straightforward:

1. Choose the My Computer icon on your desktop.

2. Open the Control Panel.

3. Open the Add/Remove Programs icon.

4. Click the Install button.

5. Insert the program disk (or CD-ROM) into your drive.

6. Click Next. Windows 95 searches your drives, starting with A, then goes onto other floppy and CD-ROM drives in sequence until it finds a valid disk. It searches for a SETUP.EXE program (which is correct for WinCIM's installation) or a variation of INSTALL.EXE and displays what it finds (see fig. 11.12). CD-ROMs may have many different SETUP.EXE programs, so you'll probably have to click the Browse button to find the correct one for WinCIM.

Fig. 11.12
If you're installing from a floppy drive, the default SETUP.EXE is a safe bet, but choose Browse on a CD-ROM to find the correct folder first.

> **Tip**
>
> If you're installing from a CD-ROM (drive D for example), make sure you don't have any disks in drives A or B. This saves you a few steps in the Windows 95 Installation Wizard.

7. The Setup program prompts you for a folder name for your WinCIM installation. The default is CSERVE. Select OK to continue. The program then begins copying files from the disk or CD-ROM onto your hard drive, occasionally prompting you for additional information. Make sure you answer Yes to Do you want to copy the signon files? if you don't have a CompuServe membership.

8. After the files are copied, you are prompted to sign up with Compu-Serve (see fig. 11.13). Choose Sign Me Up to answer all the required questions about your home location, billing method, and so on. When you select OK, the WinCIM installation program dials a toll-free number to set up your account. After you're set up, you can start WinCIM by selecting it in the Start menu's Programs menu under CompuServe.

Fig. 11.13
WinCIM's sign-on menu has you answer most of your setup questions before you call the toll-free number.

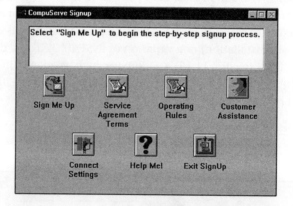

After you get the kit and install the software, you need to get an access number (the local number you use for all your calls to CompuServe):

1. Call 800-848-8199 with a regular phone—not a modem.

2. Press 1.

3. Follow the prompts (which ask you to enter your area code and phone number, then which modem speed you want to use).

4. Write down the access number(s) and the network (for example, CompuServe, Tymnet, or SprintNet).

> **Tip**
>
> If you're in an area that doesn't have a local number, you'll probably save money if you use the closest high-speed access number in the nearest neighboring state. This allows you to avoid the intrastate telephone tax and additional charges some long distance companies add for longer distances.

To set up WinCIM to use the access number, your user ID, and your password, follow these steps:

1. Install WinCIM with the instructions listed earlier in the section.

2. Run WinCIM.

3. At the Connect screen, choose <u>C</u>ontinue.

> **Tip**
>
> If you don't want to go through this extra step each time, deselect the <u>S</u>how at Startup box.

4. Choose Special, Session Settings.

5. Enter all the correct information in the Name, User ID, Password, Phone, Connector, Baud Rate, and Network fields. Remember your password is case-sensitive, so you have to enter it exactly as it appears on your membership. If you don't know some of that information, you may find some help in Chapter 28, "Configuring Modems."

6. Choose OK.

7. Click Basic Services or one of the other icons, or you can choose <u>F</u>ile, <u>C</u>onnect, then click the <u>C</u>onnect button. WinCIM should sign you onto CompuServe at this point.

Signing On with WinCIM

When you use WinCIM, signing on is as simple as clicking the <u>C</u>onnect button in the Connect to CompuServe window that pops up when you start WinCIM. Assuming you've already set WinCIM up with your ID and password, it logs on automatically.

II

Configuring Windows 95

Signing Off

Click the Disconnect button on the far right of the ribbon or just exit the program to sign off.

> **Note**
>
> The buttons on the CIM button bar change around a lot. While you're online, for example, there isn't an Exit button at all—it shows up when you log off, when the Disconnect button disappears.

Setting Up an America Online Connection

America Online (AOL) has made many changes to its interface in recent months, mostly due to its World Wide Web (WWW) integration. The new interface (version 2.5 and above) also takes advantage of Windows 95's multimedia strengths.

Becoming a Member

Everyone who joins America Online gets a free trial—usually 15 hours online. Even though there are no charges during the trial period, you'll need one of these to sign up with America Online:

- Credit card
- Checking account

To start the free trial period, go through the actual sign-up process. If you decide you don't want to keep AOL, remember to cancel your membership within a month of your sign-up—monthly fees are automatically charged to you *even if you don't use the service.*

To get a free copy of AOL's software, call 800-827-3338. You can also find AOL's software at the newsstand bundled with computer-oriented magazines.

Installing AOL is pretty simple:

1. Choose the My Computer icon on your desktop.

2. Open the Control Panel.

3. Open the Add/Remove Programs icon.

4. Select the Install button.

5. Insert the program disk (or CD-ROM) into your drive.

6. Select Next. Windows 95 searches your drives, starting with A, then goes sequentially to other floppy and CD-ROM drives until it finds a valid disk. It searches for a SETUP.EXE program (which is correct for AOL's installation) or a variation of INSTALL.EXE and displays what it finds (refer to fig. 11.12). CD-ROMs may have many different SETUP.EXE programs, so you'll probably have to click the Browse button to find the correct one for AOL. Look for an AOL25 or AOL250 folder.

> **Tip**
>
> If you're installing from a CD-ROM (drive D for example), make sure you don't have any disks in drives A or B. This saves you a few steps in the Windows 95 Installation Wizard.

7. Choose Finish to begin installing AOL.

8. In the America Online-Setup dialog box, choose Install. If you want to change the destination folders for the incoming files (for example, if you have a previous version of AOL which you want to upgrade), select Review.

9. Select Continue to see the folder where files will be copied. You can change this if you like.

10. Click Install to begin copying files. After the files are on your drive, select OK to complete the installation.

After you install the software, you need to get an access number (the local number you use for all your calls to AOL). Run the software (double-click the AOL icon) and choose Sign On. The software dials a toll-free number where it finds a local number—you just enter a little information about your location. Depending on where you live, you may have several choices for local numbers. Always choose the fastest one your modem can handle.

> **Note**
>
> If you are calling from a phone that uses a special prefix to dial long distance (9, for example), click Setup before you try to dial. In the Network Setup dialog box, click the Use The Following Prefix to Reach an Outside Line box and enter the prefix.

When you've got the new local number, choose Sign On again to set up your account. You are prompted for the user ID and password for your trial account (it should be in the documentation that came with the disk). After you click Continue, enter all your acount information: your name and address, credit card number, etc. The service walks you through the process relatively painlessly. After you've set up the account, you are then connected to AOL to start exploring.

Signing On

America Online's interface is very simple to use. To sign on, for example, you need just these four steps:

1. Double-click the AOL icon. If you had already installed AOL before Windows 95, choose the AOL25 icon from the Start menu, Programs, America Online.

2. Select your screen name from the list in the middle of the Welcome window (see fig. 11.14). If you only have one screen name, it automatically appears in the Screen Name box.

Fig. 11.14
AOL allows you to have several screen names for each account.

3. Type your password in the Password box. Don't worry about anyone else seeing it over your shoulder—each letter you type shows up as an asterisk (*) on the screen.

4. Click the Sign On button.

The software then calls the local America Online number, signs you on, and opens two windows: the Main Menu (which has buttons for most major areas) and the Welcome window.

The Welcome window covers up the Main Menu at first, so you can check your mail, read the news, and check out the three featured services (if desired) before diving into AOL's web of other services.

The featured services change at least once a day, giving you a chance to see areas of AOL that you'd probably miss if you had to search through all the menus to get to them. The first few days of each month, one of the featured services is a letter from AOL's CEO Steve Case about new offerings.

When you're done with the Welcome screen, click the Go To Main Menu button at the bottom.

Signing Off

To sign off America Online at any point

1. Select the Go To menu.

2. Select Sign off.

The only time you won't be able to sign off this way is when the AOL software is busy transferring a file or displaying a large amount of text. In both cases, the mouse pointer changes to an hourglass until you're able to sign off normally.

Setting Up a Prodigy Connection

Prodigy is another simple installation, but it is unique because it doesn't matter what version you begin with. Prodigy's network automatically senses which version you're using and gives you the option of upgrading to the current version when you call in.

Configuring Windows 95

Becoming a Member

Call 1-800-PRODIGY to get a free trial offer, including Prodigy's software. Though the first 10 hours of online time are free (maybe more or less, depending on the offer you get), you need a credit card to sign up.

To install Prodigy

1. Choose the My Computer icon on your desktop.

2. Open the Control Panel.

3. Open the Add/Remove Programs icon.

4. Select the Install button.

5. Insert the program disk (or CD-ROM) into your drive.

6. Select Next. Windows 95 searches your drives, starting with A, then goes on to other floppy and CD-ROM drives in sequence until it finds a valid disk. It searches for a SETUP.EXE program (which is correct for Prodigy's installation) or a variation of INSTALL.EXE and displays what it finds (refer to fig. 11.12). CD-ROMs may have many different SETUP.EXE programs, so you probably have to click the Browse button to find the correct one for Prodigy. Because version numbers change so often at Prodigy, you probably won't see a folder with a number (like PRODIGY9.99). It's usually just PRODIGY.

> **Tip**
>
> If you're installing from a CD-ROM (drive D, for example), make sure you don't have any disks in drives A or B. This saves you a few steps in the Windows 95 Installation Wizard.

7. Choose Finish to begin installing Prodigy. The program files are copied to your hard drive. Prodigy prompts you occasionally for additional information about your setup, trial offer, and location.

After you install the software, you sign onto Prodigy with the member ID and password supplied with your trial offer. In the first session, you choose your own password and a local number to use for all future calls to Prodigy.

Signing On

Prodigy's Windows software offers two ways to sign on:

- Manually
- Autologon

To sign on manually

1. Choose the PRODIGY® software for Windows icon in the Start menu.

2. At the Prodigy Network—Sign On screen, type your user ID in the User ID box and your password in the Password box (see fig. 11.15).

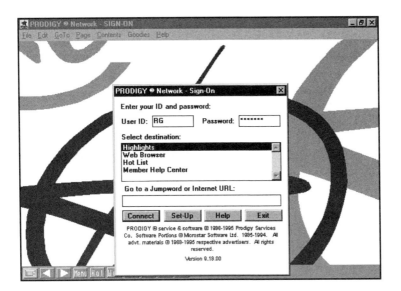

Fig. 11.15
Be careful of typographical errors in the password—you can't see what you're typing.

II

Configuring Windows 95

3. Click one of the buttons in the Select Destination box. For example, if you want to see Prodigy's main screen, select Highlights. If you like to start off in one of Prodigy's other areas, click type one in the Go To a Jumpword or Internet URL box. Whichever option you choose, the software dials the number, logs you on, and shows your selection.

Prodigy's IDs are notoriously tough to remember, so you might want to set up the Autologon feature. Autologon lets you skip typing your ID (and password, if you choose) every time.

To use Autologon

1. Dial Prodigy with the manual procedure, and type **Jump Autologon**.

2. The Autologon screen lets you choose to have your ID *and* password entered automatically (option 1) or just your ID (option 2). Click the option you want.

3. Type your password when asked.

4. Enter a nickname for your account (in case more than one person in your household wants to use Autologon).

Signing Off

When you're done, sign off one of these ways:

- Type **Jump Exit**.

- Click the Close button.

- Choose File, Exit.

You'll see Prodigy's Exit menu, which lets you choose to close Prodigy entirely, hang up and let another member sign on, or stay online.❖

Chapter 12

Configuring a Windows 95 Internet Connection

by Patrick Suarez

The Internet is a global collection consisting of more than 40,000 independent networks and nearly five million computers. These computers, which are sometimes called *hosts*, offer a wealth of information on thousands of subjects and allow millions of people to communicate with one another.

This chapter teaches you how to do the following:

- Obtain a PPP/SLIP account
- Install and configure the Microsoft TCP/IP software stack
- Install and configure the program that dials into your Internet provider
- Troubleshoot your Internet dialup connection

Why You Want an Internet Connection

> **Tip**
>
> Que's *Special Edition Using the Internet*, Second Edition, describes all the Internet tools in detail, and you should acquire a copy of that book as soon as possible if you are new to the Net.

It seems as if the range of resources of Internet hosts is limitless, and more come online every day. With an Internet connection, you can make discoveries well beyond what radio, TV, newspapers, and magazines offer.

Tip

If you purchased Microsoft Plus!, you probably discovered Miscrosoft's World Wide Web browser, the Internet Explorer. When you install the Explorer, it will look for the Internet connection configuration data you learn about in this chapter. If it does not find it, Explorer's Installation Wizard prompts you for it. If you are unfamiliar with configuring Internet connections, you should complete this configuration chapter before installing the Internet Explorer. You may save yourself some potential confusion because the Explorer Installation Wizard will take these steps out of the sequence in this chapter!

▶ See "Setting up the Internet Explorer," p. 662

Note

If you have experience with the Internet and just want to configure Windows 95 for Internet connectivity, skip to "The First Step: Adding a Network Configuration" later in this chapter.

Also, if you have the Microsoft Internet Jumpstart Kit (which is available on the Microsoft Plus! Companion for Windows 95 CD and on some new computers that are pre-installed with Windows 95), see Appendix A, "Installing and Using Microsoft Plus! Companion for Windows 95" for installation and configuration options.

Troubleshooting

What is the Internet Jumpstart Kit and how do I set it up?

The Jumpstart Kit is available in the Microsoft Plus! for Windows 95 CD and from various FTP sites (such as **ftp://ftp.microsoft.com/PerOpSys/Win_News**). If you've purchased a new computer that has Windows 95 pre-installed, the Jumpstart Kit may be installed as well.

Here are the basic tools available to you:

- *Electronic Mail (E-mail)*. Electronic messages created with e-mail software and sent over Internet routers to their destinations, where recipients can read, print, send, save, or forward those messages to other users.

■ *Mailing Lists*. Discussion areas that employ the electronic mail system as the means of transmitting an endless stream of opinions and information on about 7,000 different topics.

■ *Newsgroups*. Electronic versions of cork bulletin boards to which you post and read messages. Newsgroups store the ideas and opinions of millions of users on approximately 12,000 different subjects. You must use a program called a *newsreader*, of which several exist. You can discuss virtually any topic from A to Z within the newsgroup system. Newsgroups are also called *UseNet News*, a reference to the store-and-forward system that carries the postings.

■ *Telnet (remote login)*. The ability to log in from your computer to a network across the street or on another continent and use it as if you were there onsite. Thousands of networks allow *guest* logins, and you can find out almost anything from library holdings, to Vatican paintings, to your local weather forecast.

■ *FTP (file transfer protocol)*. Almost 1,300 host systems exist as computer file storage sites and allow people to log into those sites and transfer copies of the files held there to the users' own computers. These servers hold more than two million files and do not charge for the transfer.

■ *Archie*. A database and search device to locate files stored on FTP host computers.

■ *Gopher*. An ingenious information retrieval program that is menu-based. When you log into a Gopher session, a menu appears on your screen. As you select menu items, you see succeeding menus, layer after layer, until you locate what you want. Gopher incorporates other Internet tools such as file transfer and remote login. Gopher is fast, easy to use, and comprehensive.

■ *Veronica and Jughead*. Two programs found on Gopher menus that search Gopher menus. You enter a keyword, and either program searches all or a selection of Gopher machines for the text string you entered.

■ *WAIS (Wide Area Information Server)*. A database tool that searches the contents of documents, not just the titles of those documents.

■ *Internet Relay Chat (IRC)*. Real-time "chatting" via the computer keyboard. IRC resembles CB radio, except that the "talking" is done by entering text from the keyboard while you are logged into an IRC session.

II

Configuring Windows 95

■ *World Wide Web.* An information retrieval medium that has taken the online world by storm and appears to be doing nothing less than redefining how we might get information in the future. The Web employs the client-server model, in which a Web "client" program, such as Netscape or Mosaic, requests information from a Web *server*, a computer set up to dispense information to the client program. Upon receipt, the client program processes the information and displays it. The retrieved information can take the form of text, photos, sound, and/or video. The Web uses *hypertext linking*, in which text, an icon, or a photo on a Web screen page can link to another Web page or Web computer elsewhere. The links can be endless. More than 10,000 Web servers provide a phenomenal amount of useful and fun information, and more servers go online every week. World Wide Web users also refer to it as *WWW*, *W3*, or simply as the *Web*.

Relating Windows 95's TCP/IP Software to Internet Application Programs

Take a look at what Windows 95's TCP/IP program is, what it does, and how it relates to Internet application programs that enable you to send e-mail, browse the contents of other Internet host computers, and see the technicolor wonders of the World Wide Web. You will also see that the TCP/IP program is not all that you need to make a connection to the Internet.

First, you need to understand two acronyms:

■ *TCP.* Transmission Control Protocol

■ *IP.* Internet Protocol

Basically, Transmission Control Protocol breaks your outgoing message or file into "byte-sized" packets called *datagrams*. Internet Protocol routes the datagrams through the system in search of a target router. When the datagrams find the correct router, they navigate onward to the destination computer, where Transmission Control Protocol reassembles the packets into their original form.

Understanding Routers

A *router* is just one of several pieces of special computer hardware that send Internet messages through the Internet system. Understanding router systems takes some getting used to. But, follow the sequence of events below, then read the handy analogy at the end of the sequence, and the concepts should become clear. The chain of hardware looks something like this:

1. Using Windows 95's Internet tools, your computer and modem dial into an Internet service provider's (or ISP) computer system. Your message goes from your computer and modem to your ISP.

2. The provider's computer system is connected to special communications equipment, one item of which is a router. Your message passes through your ISP's system and out of its router to a high-speed telephone line connected to another "major" Internet provider.

3. Most small- to medium-sized providers connect their routers—via special telephone lines or fiber optic cable—to "major" Internet providers. The systems belonging to the major ISPs also have routers, both incoming (to receive your message) and outgoing (to send your message to one of the many backbones, or high speed fiber optic superhighways, that interlink the major providers). Your message now passes from the major ISP to the backbone system.

4. While riding the backbone, your message passes from router to router, in search of the correct destination router and computer. Simply reverse the preceding steps to get your message to its destination.

5. Your message routes to a target major ISP which hands it off to the correct target mid-sized ISP, which then passes it to the correct target computer.

Here's a nifty analogy: think of the computer, router, backbone system in terms of interstate highways. The backbone cable is the interstate highway road; the router is the highway interchange and exit ramp; the computer is the destination town at the bottom of the interchange ramp.

As you just learned, the TCP/IP program manages the datagrams from and to Internet hosts. But by itself, the TCP/IP stack is useless. It needs a connection to other routers. Windows 95 provides that connection with a program that finds your modem, dials into a provider, locates a PPP connection (which you will learn about later) to the Internet, and matches the Internet addressing information that you gave to Windows 95 with the addressing information

II

Configuring Windows 95

that the provider's system expects to see from Windows 95's configuration. Later sections in this chapter show you how to configure both the TCP/IP stack and the dialer program.

Once you have installed and configured the TCP/IP stack and the dialer, and Windows 95 has made contact with your Internet service provider, you can finally connect to another Internet host and do something! You will need separate application programs to send and receive e-mail, contact Gopher servers, download files, log onto remote networks, view World Wide Web sites, and so on. But where do you find application programs that will do these wonderful things for you?

You get application programs from a number of sources. One is from the CD that accompanies Que's *Special Edition Using the Internet*, Second Edition. Another source is your local computer store. Yet another source is shareware that you download yourself from the Microsoft Network, a commercial service such as America Online, an electronic bulletin board service, or a file transfer protocol site.

Chief among the shareware programs are PC Eudora for e-mail, Trumpet News Reader for UseNet News, WSGopher for Gopher, WSArchie and WS_FTP for file transfer protocol, and Netscape and Mosaic for World Wide Web browsing. These are all available from the sources mentioned in the preceding paragraph.

Understanding Internet Services

There are several ways to obtain an Internet connection. The first is to use standard communication software such as Procomm Plus for Windows. You can use this program to dial into a network or Internet service provider and use its computer system.

This service does not work with Windows 95's TCP/IP program. Instead, it accesses Internet hosts "indirectly" by dialing into your Internet provider's network and turning your computer into a temporary terminal on your provider's network. This access, called *terminal emulation*—usually accomplished through a *shell account*—is not as comprehensive as the kind of connection that Windows 95 offers, but it does work. I won't go into detail on shell accounts in this chapter, but you can learn about them in Que's *Special Edition Using the Internet*, Second Edition.

A second method is to use an online service such as The Microsoft Network or America Online. You need special software provided by the online service to make a successful connection. The Microsoft Network software is included in Windows 95.

A third and more comprehensive way is to use the special Internet software that is included in Windows 95. As you've learned, the software is called TCP/IP, and is easy to set up. If you use Windows 95's TCP/IP software with a dial-up connection called *PPP* or *SLIP* (about which you will learn soon), your computer will be directly linked with the Internet router system and will be an actual Internet host any time it is online. This setup has several positive implications, including the capability to download files from Internet file servers directly onto your hard drive and to navigate the World Wide Web.

◄ See "Setting Up a Microsoft Network Connection," p. 276

Windows 95 offers several ways to configure Internet connections. This chapter focuses on the steps needed to get a direct Internet session using a modem connected to a personal computer. If you access the Internet through a company or school network, some of the settings you will read about may be different. Your organization's network manager or Information Services department should be able to give you the required configuration settings, if not install them for you.

Before you continue, make sure that you have installed and configured a modem for Windows 95.

PPP and SLIP Connections

If you want to enjoy the full glory of the Internet, your computer must have direct access to the Internet system. Direct access to Internet routers and computers is achieved with expensive hardware and a special "dedicated" line wired right to your computer.

► See "Installing Your Modem," p. 588

Most people cannot afford dedicated, leased line access. But most *can* afford the functional equivalents, PPP (Point to Point Protocol) and SLIP (Serial Line Internet Protocol) connections. PPP and SLIP trick the Internet system into thinking that your computer has a dedicated line, even though PPP and SLIP are really dial-up communication protocols that need modems or networks as intermediaries between Internet routers and your computer.

PPP is newer than SLIP. A description of their differences is beyond the scope of this chapter, but most Internet service providers normally issue PPP, not SLIP, accounts. This chapter describes how to establish both PPP and SLIP connections in Windows 95.

PPP and SLIP accounts are associated with the type of Internet addressing that routers understand. This addressing scheme is numeric and has four

II

Configuring Windows 95

positions, separated by periods known as "dots." An example of an IP (Internet Protocol) address is

198.6.245.121

This address identifies a specific host machine among millions of Internet hosts.

Since humans remember strings of letters better than strings of numbers, many numeric IP addresses have text equivalents. If a text equivalent, called a *Fully Qualified Domain Name* (*FQDN*), exists, use it in lieu of the IP address.

FQDNs are constructed like this:

host_computer_name.location.domain_type

An example is **kiwi.wright.edu.** Kiwi is the name of the host machine you are addressing; wright is the location (Wright State University); edu is the *domain type*, or the type of facility that operates the host machine.

Table 12.1 lists the six major domain types.

Table 12.1 Domain Types	
com	Commercial organization
edu	Educational institution
gov	Government facility
mil	A military organization
net	Internet service provider
org	Miscellaneous, usually nonprofit, organization

Countries outside the United States use two-letter identifiers at the end of their fully qualified domain names. A few examples are CA (Canada), UK (United Kingdom), and ES (Spain).

Two Types of IP Addresses

If your computer has a *static* IP address, that IP address is permanently assigned to your computer. Whenever you go online with a PPP or SLIP connection, your computer uses and is identified with that address throughout the system. An advantage of a static IP address is that you can register a specific domain name to that static IP address; you or your business then can be identified all over the world with either the IP address or domain name.

Your computer might also have a *dynamic* IP address which your provider assigns from a pool of IP addresses available whenever you log into a PPP or SLIP session. This is often a less expensive, but very viable, way of getting connected.

The difference between the two is important because Windows 95's TCP/IP configuration will ask you which IP address type, static or dynamic, you have.

Tip

Work closely with your Internet service provider as you configure your TCP/IP setup.

Troubleshooting

My modem connects to my ISP, but my ISP's system doesn't recognize my IP address.

Ensure that your IP address (if you have a static IP address) and your ISP's IP address and DNS are configured properly in Windows 95's TCP/IP configuration. Even a single wrong number or letter can negate a connection.

Why Do I Need a Direct Connection to the Internet?

Millions of Internet users connect to Internet sessions using traditional UNIX *shell accounts*. These accounts are functional and have existed for over a quarter of a century. But UNIX shell accounts cannot display the popular graphical images provided by such World Wide Web browsers as Netscape and Mosaic. Your computer must have the kind of "direct" access to the Internet router system that dedicated leased lines and PPP or SLIP connections provide.

As more and more businesses and information services create Web home pages, you will find yourself needing this enhanced connectivity. Fortunately, the cost of a PPP or SLIP account has dropped dramatically so that many individuals and small business owners can afford this level of service. You might wish to create your own Web page for you or your business. A PPP or SLIP account would be required to view it.

How to Find an Internet Service Provider

You need an ISP in order to establish a PPP or SLIP link. Most large- and medium-sized cities in the U.S. now have providers who sell accounts at a reasonable rate, usually for $20 to $40 per month, depending on whether your PPP connection is static or dynamic. Dynamic IP accounts cost less than static IP accounts. Both function the same way while online. Again, static IP accounts afford you the advantage of establishing your own global identity.

Some ISPs give you a set number of hours for a set price, such as $20 for 15 hours. After you use up the set number of hours, the ISP charges an hourly rate, usually $1 to $3 per hour.

Caution

Do not sign up to this kind of arrangement unless you know beyond any doubt that you will not use more hours than the set price permits. If you find that you will exceed those hours, as many users do, contact your ISP for a revised arrangement.

Most ISPs offer quarterly, semiannual, and annual rates which permit you to stay online as long as you want and not worry about hourly charges.

If your phone book does not list a local ISP, ask someone at your local computer user group or computer store. If there is no local ISP, national ISPs such as UUNET/AlterNet sell accounts. National providers also might have toll-free 800 numbers or use the Tymnet or Sprintlink system to give you a local number. If you contact a national provider, they will explain the options that suit your needs and pocketbook. The last option, a toll call to the nearest dial-up number, is also available, but it is an expensive option.

Selecting an ISP takes some research because there are good ones and bad ones. If you live in a major metropolitan area such as Chicago or Washington, D.C., there are several ISPs from which to choose. If you live in a medium-sized city such as Dayton or Austin, there is still some flexibility. If you live in a small town away from a city or in a rural area, your choices are limited.

Whatever choice you make, your ISP should charge a monthly, quarterly, or annual flat rate instead of charging by the hour, a practice called *metering*. Technical support should be available during business hours and in the early evening. The ISP's connection from the backbone system to its system should be at least a T1 line, and enough incoming lines should exist so that you do not reach a continuous busy signal when you dial in. The ISP should offer all Internet services and should make all UseNet newsgroups available without "filtering" out any of them.

On the other hand, you must be a good customer. Do your own research on Internet basics. There are dozens of books on the subject, including Que's *Special Edition Using the Internet*, Second Edition, previously mentioned. Do not expect miracles. Providing Internet connectivity is a profoundly complex, expensive, and difficult task. If you are having trouble dialing in, make sure that your computer's hardware or software configuration is not the problem. If you have an older computer and a very slow modem (anything under 14,400 baud is too slow), you will probably be underpowered. Invest in new equipment. Of course, if you are running Windows 95, your hardware is probably acceptable. If there is a problem, work with the ISP instead of yelling at him.

Tip

The most important hardware components for a successful Internet session are those that bring data in and draw it to your screen. Ensure that your modem is fast and that you have a UART 16550 chip in your modem's COM port, at least 16M of system RAM, and a fast graphics card.

Troubleshooting

What type of service does my Internet Service Provider (ISP) need to offer to configure Windows 95 for the Internet?

Ask the ISP the following questions:

- Does the access provider offer full Internet access?

- Does the access provider support PPP? SLIP?

- Does the access provider offer technical support?

- What kind of connection speeds does the access provider support?

What kind of information do I need from my ISP?

You must obtain the following data from your access provider to use during configuration:

- Access phone number, preferably local

- Logon name and password

- Your host and domain name (be sure to repeat the numbers to the provider to ensure you have this written down correctly)

- The Domain Name System (DNS) server and IP address

▶ See "Windows 95 Setup and Bootup," p. 680

II

Configuring Windows 95

The First Step: Adding a Network Configuration

Your first task is to create the network tools under the Network icon located in the Windows 95 Control Panel. After you install the network tools, you will be able to install and configure the rest of the tools that are needed for a PPP dial-up.

To add network configuration tools, follow these steps:

1. Click the My Computer folder.

2. Click the Control Panel folder.

3. Double-click the Network icon.

4. The Network sheet opens, with one page, Configuration. If you have not configured a network connection in Windows 95, the Configuration page has no items installed. Otherwise, you may have a few items already installed. Click the Add button.

5. A new sheet called Select Network Component Type opens with four items. Double-click the first item, Client.

6. The Select Network Client window opens with two lists (see fig. 12.1). In the Manufacturers list box, select Microsoft; in the Network Clients list box, select Client for Microsoft Networks. Click OK.

Tip

If you are running under a network such as Novell Network, you need to use the Microsoft's Client for NetWare Networks. You may want to consult your network administrator for more information.

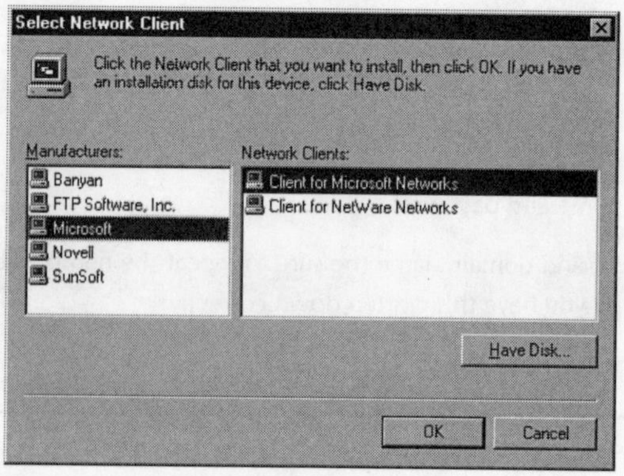

Fig. 12.1
Select the two components highlighted in the Select Network Client window.

Adding the TCP/IP Protocol to Windows 95

You must add the TCP/IP protocol to the new Network Configuration menu you created in the previous section:

1. The four new network menu items appear in the Configuration page, as shown in figure 12.2. Click Add to create the TCP/IP network component.

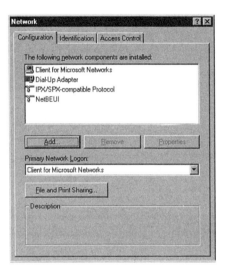

Fig. 12.2
Clicking the Add button will enable you to create the TCP/IP network component.

2. The Select Network Component Type sheet appears. Select Protocol from the list of four items, and then click the Add button.

3. The Select Network Protocol window appears, as shown in figure 12.3. In the Manufacturers list box, select Microsoft; in Network Protocols, select TCP/IP. Click OK.

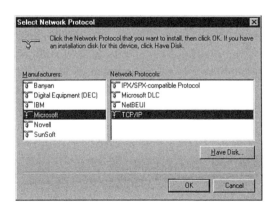

Fig. 12.3
Select Microsoft and TCP/IP as highlighted.

II

Configuring Windows 95

TCP/IP is now added to the list of Network Configuration items, as shown in figure 12.4.

Fig. 12.4
TCP/IP becomes the fifth component in the configuration list.

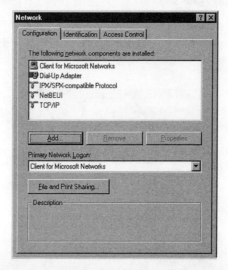

Tip

The TCP/IP program is sometimes referred to as the TCP/IP *stack* because the various functions of TCP/IP occur in vertical layers from the application programs (at the top of the stack) to the network hardware level (at the bottom).

Setting the Dial-Up Adapter Properties

You must next set the properties for Windows 95's dial-up adapter. The Network sheet should still be on-screen, with the Configuration page still selected. (If you use the Client for NetWare Networks, you will not have to set up the Dial-Up adapter.) Follow these steps:

1. Double-click the Dial-Up Adapter item in the Configuration page. The Dial-Up Adapter Properties sheet appears, with the Driver Type page selected. Click the Bindings page.

2. Click the small check box next to TCP/IP to activate it.

3. Click the Advanced page to select it. There are two to four items in a list. To the right of the list, there is a Value box which can read Yes or No. All of the items in the list should be No except for the third one, Use IP header compression, which should be Yes. Select these now. Click OK when finished.

Configuring Your TCP/IP Host

This section configures Windows 95's TCP/IP stack with your specific Internet protocol numbers, or the numbers the Internet router system you will use to interact with other Internet hosts.

Caution

The IP numbers used in the configuration are examples. Do not use them to configure your TCP/IP host! Your Internet service provider will give you the data you need for this section.

As before, the Network Configuration screen should appear. Follow these steps:

1. Double-click the TCP/IP item in the Configuration page.

2. The TCP/IP Properties sheet loads. Note that it has six pages. You will use four of them, beginning with IP Address. If the IP Address page is not selected, select it.

3. If you use a dynamic IP address to dial into your provider, select the Obtain an IP Address Automatically radio button. If you use your own static IP address, select the Specify an IP Address radio button and enter your four-segment numeric IP address in the IP Address box. Note that this is *not* the provider's Domain Name Server (DNS) address, which you will enter elsewhere. This is *your* specific (static) IP address, if you have one.

4. Next, your IP address is probably a Class C address which is what 99 percent of all single-user PPP dial-ups get. Check with your Internet provider to be sure. If your IP address is a Class C, enter **255.255.255.0** in the Subnet Mask field, as shown in figure 12.5.

You have configured your own IP address. You now must configure your provider's Domain Name Server (DNS) information by following these steps:

1. In the TCP/IP Properties sheet, click the DNS Configuration page.

2. Select the Enable DNS radio button.

3. In the Host field, enter the user ID which your provider assigned to you. Some networks require additional information in the Host field. Your provider or network administrator should give you this data if this is the case.

Fig. 12.5
Be sure that the IP
address you use is
your specific IP
address and not
your provider's
DNS address.
Accuracy counts!

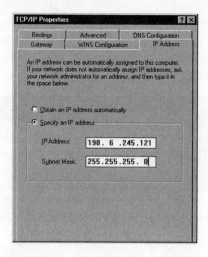

4. Next, enter your provider's domain name in the Domain field.

5. Enter your provider's DNS IP address in the four-segment DNS Server
   Search Order area. After you enter the number, click the Add button
   next to it. Enter as many numbers as your provider gives you. The example in figure 12.6 shows two IP addresses, a primary and secondary.
   Some providers will give you a backup IP address in case there is a problem with the primary one.

Fig. 12.6
The accuracy of
this information
is also very
important!

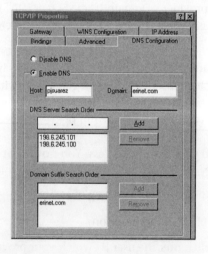

6. In the Domain Suffix Search Order area, type your provider's domain name and click the <u>A</u>dd button.

7. Select the Advanced page in the TCP/IP Properties sheet. The only item that you must set is at the bottom of the page. Click the <u>S</u>et This Protocol to be the Default Protocol check box.

8. Select the Bindings page in the TCP/IP Properties sheet. Click the Client for Microsoft Networks check box. Click OK to complete the TCP/IP Properties configuration.

9. A System Settings Change dialog box appears. Click <u>Y</u>es to reboot your computer. This will cause the changes you have made to take effect.

Adding a Dial-Up Network Folder

After Windows 95 reboots, your system is now able to process the Internet packet sending and receiving protocols. You must now add communications dial-up capability to the TCP/IP configuration so that your host system (Windows 95) can find your provider's host system:

1. Open the Control Panel folder in the My Computer folder. Double-click Add/Remove Programs.

2. The Add/Remove Programs Properties sheet appears. Select the Windows Setup page to find a list of component programs.

3. Double-click the Communications program. The Communications sheet appears. Select Dial-Up Networking. If Dial-Up Networking is already selected, the Dial-Up Networking capability is already installed on your system. Click Cancel and skip to the next section, "Creating a Dial-Up Icon for Your Provider."

4. Windows 95 then asks you to insert either Windows 95 floppy disks or the CD-ROM. At the end of the disk install procedure, click OK. The Dial-Up Networking folder now appears in the My Computer folder, as shown in figure 12.7.

Note

These steps may have been completed during Windows 95's installation.

II

Configuring Windows 95

Fig. 12.7
The new Dial-Up
Networking folder
is installed.

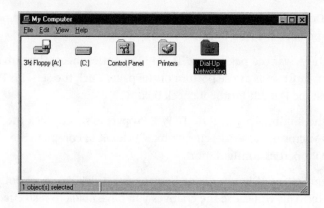

Creating a Dial-Up Icon for Your Provider

Windows 95 allows you to create an icon that launches an Internet session representing a specific source or provider. You can have more than one. Each icon locates information about your Internet account and your provider that you stored earlier into Windows 95. This is handy if you have a single provider or if you must have more than one on-ramp to the Net.

Tip

If you use a third-party TCP/IP stack—such as NetManage's Internet Chameleon—to access the Internet under Windows 95, you still must install the TCP/IP stack using the Control Panel, but you do not have to create a dial-up connection icon. Many third-party TCP/IP programs include their own software for establishing the connection.

You will now create a dial-up icon configured for your Internet service provider's host. Follow these steps:

1. Open the Dial-Up Networking folder you just created. Double-click the Make New Connection icon that appears in the folder.

2. The Make New Connection Wizard opens, into which you enter information about your service provider. In the Type a Name for the Computer You Are Dialing field, enter an identifying name for your provider, such as **Iquest Connection**.

3. Your modem should be identified in the Select a Modem field in the folder. If not, select it from the drop-down list box.

4. Click the Configure button located under the modem name.

5. The Modem Properties sheet appears. Select the Options page.

6. Under Connection control, click the Bring Up Terminal Window After Dialing check box. In the same page, click the Display Modem Status check box under Status Control. Click OK. The Make New Connection dialog box returns to the screen. Click the Next button.

7. In the Make New Connection window, enter your provider's area code and dial-up (not voice) telephone number. Choose United States of America (1) or another country in the Country Code drop-down list box. Click the Next button.

8. Windows 95 announces that you have successfully created a new connection for your provider. Click Finish. An icon for your provider is now in the Dial-Up Networking folder, shown in figure 12.8.

Fig. 12.8

Your new icon for your Internet dial-up appears in the Dial-Up Networking folder.

You're almost ready to dial into your Internet provider and start a PPP or SLIP session! There are a few more configuration steps left to go:

1. The Dial-Up Networking folder should be open, and the icon representing your provider should be highlighted. Using the right mouse button, click *once* on the provider's icon. A small drop-down menu unfolds. Select the last item, Properties.

2. The provider's General configuration screen appears (see fig. 12.9). Enter the Area Code and Telephone Number of your provider's system. If the call to your provider is a local call, you may leave the Area Code blank.

3. If you're calling outside of an internal telephone system, you need to add **8** or **9** in front of the provider's telephone number, as in **9,7654-321**. Add the comma (,) after the 8 or 9 exit code to allow a short pause while Windows 95 gets an outside dial tone.

II

Configuring Windows 95

4. Select the country name you're calling from, such as United States of America (1), in the Country Code drop-down list box.

5. Select the Use Country Code and Area Code check box.

6. Select your modem in the Connect Using area.

Fig. 12.9
Ensure that your modem is properly identified in the Connect Using area.

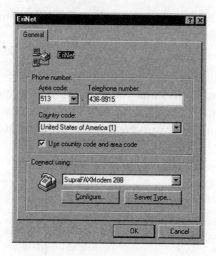

7. Click the modem Configure button. You are now in the Modem Properties sheet's General page (see fig. 12.10). Select your modem's COM Port and Maximum Speed.

Fig. 12.10
Ensure that you select the correct serial (COM) port.

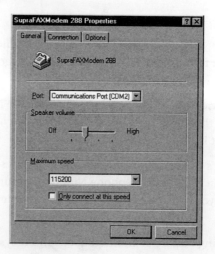

> **Caution**
>
> Do *not* select the Only Connect At This Speed check box. Although you want the connect rate to be as fast as possible, your dial-up might not always achieve that maximum rate. If you select the Only Connect At This Speed check box, Windows 95's dialer will *only* work at the connect rate selected and not at a lower, and probably viable, speed. If your connect rate does not reach the setting you entered, Windows 95 will hang up the connection even though you could have used the lower line speed you encountered.

8. While still in the Modem Properties sheet, select the Connection page, shown in figure 12.11. Ensure that Data Bits is 8, Parity is None, Stop bits is 1; this term is sometimes referred to as *8N1*.

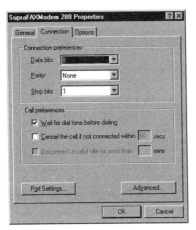

Fig. 12.11
The connection preferences are important. If you set these to anything other than 8N1, your connection will not work.

9. In the Modem Properties sheet, select the Options page (see fig. 12.12). Select the Bring Up Terminal Window After Dialing check box. Select the Display Modem Status check box in the Status Control area. Click OK. The provider's General configuration screen reappears. Click the Server Type button.

10. The Server Types sheet appears (see fig. 12.13). If you have a PPP connection, select `PPP: Windows 95, Windows NT 3.5, Internet` from the Type of Dial-Up Server drop-down list box. If you have a SLIP connection, select `SLIP: Unix Connection`.

Fig. 12.12
This is the last modem configuration screen. You can see the status of your dial-up as it attempts to connect to your provider.

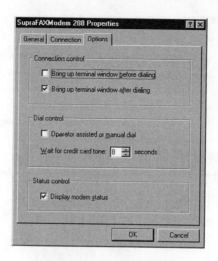

Fig. 12.13
TCP/IP should be selected, not NetBEUI or IPX/SPX Compatible.

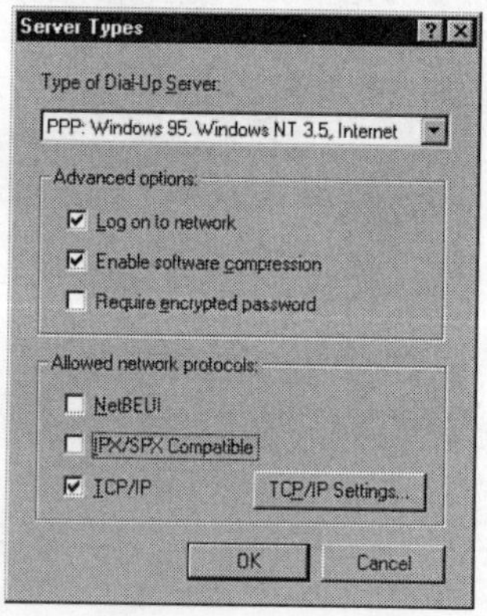

> **Note**
>
> Windows 95 does not automatically install SLIP connection software on your system. You must install it using the Add/Remove Programs icon in Control Panel. See the section "Adding SLIP Connectivity to Windows 95" later in this chapter for more information.

11. In the Advanced Options area, select the Log on to Network and Enable Software Compression check boxes.

12. In the Allowed Network Protocols area, select TCP/IP. Deselect the NetBEUI and IPX/SPX Compatible check boxes. Click the TCP/IP Settings button.

13. You move along to the TCP/IP Settings sheet, shown in figure 12.14. If you use a dynamic PPP account, select the Server Assigned IP Address radio button. If you use a static PPP account, select the Specify an IP Address radio button and enter your specific IP address. Check the Specify Name Server Addresses radio button and enter your provider's Primary DNS number and Secondary DNS number—if there is a secondary number—in the fields provided under the radio buttons. Select the Use IP Header Compression and Use Default Gateway on Remote Network check boxes. Click OK.

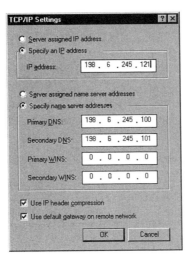

Fig. 12.14

This sheet demonstrates the difference between your specific IP address and your provider's DNS address(es).

14. Click OK in the Server Types dialog box and then click OK in the General connection page.

Tip

If you already have an existing TCP/IP program—for example, Trumpet Winsock or Internet Chameleon—on your hard drive, you can continue to use it if you don't want use Windows 95's TCP/IP stack. If you want to delete your current TCP/IP program, you should install and configure the Windows 95 stack, ensure that it works, then delete the TCP/IP program you want to discard from your hard drive *after* you're sure that the Windows 95 stack functions to your satisfaction.

II

Configuring Windows 95

Troubleshooting

I've connected to my ISP, but each time I use Netscape (or Mosaic), I get the following error message:

```
Netscape is unable to locate the server:
home.netscape.com
The server does not have a DNS entry...
```

What is wrong?

A few things may be wrong. First, double-check the URL that you typed in. Make sure it is exactly right or you will encounter this error. Second, the site may be busy or require specific authorization (such as a password or ID number). Start chopping off the end of the URL and try accessing the site again. Third, the site may have moved locations or shut down. Fourth, you've lost connection to your ISP and you didn't know. Check the Dial-Up Network connection that is opened to see if your connection is still live. If not, reconnect. Fifth, you may not have your IP addresses set up properly in the network connection areas. In the TCP/IP Settings dialog box, make sure the IP addresses are typed in correctly. You may have to call your ISP technical support line to reconfirm your IP address.

How can I increase the speed with which I connect to my ISP using a PPP or SLIP connection?

Right-click the Dial-Up Networking icon for your Internet connection and select Properties. Click the Server Type button. In the Server Type dialog box, make sure the Log On To Network, NetBEUI, and IPX/SPX Compatible options are not checked.

Dialing In

The big moment has arrived! It's time to dial into your PPP session. Follow these steps:

1. Double-click the provider dial-up icon.

2. Enter your the User Name and Password that your provider's system expects to see from you in the Connect To dialog box.

3. Select the Save Password check box. Your provider's data line Phone Number should appear. If it isn't there, type it in the box. Default Location is normally selected in the Dialing From drop-down list box.

4. Click the Connect button. Windows 95 begins the dial-up process (see fig. 12.15).

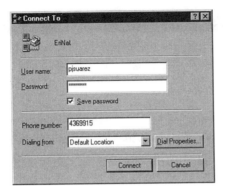

Fig. 12.15
Click the Connect
button to begin
the dial-up
process.

5. Once connected, the Post-Dial Terminal Screen emerges (see fig. 12.16).
   After entering both user ID and password, a string of ASCII characters
   will zoom horizontally across the screen. Click the Continue (F7) button or press the F7 function key. A series of status messages during the
   dial-up process appear.

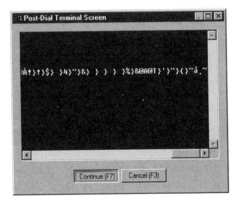

Fig. 12.16
Click the Con-
tinue (F7) button
to complete the
connection
process. Do this as
quickly as you can
so the connection
does not drop.

6. Finally, the system will alert you that you are connected. Minimize the
   Connected sheet by clicking the Minimize icon in the upper right-hand
   corner of the sheet and open an Internet client program such as
   Netscape or Mosaic. Once you open a client program, proceed with
   whatever you want to do online.

Tip

Remember, you can open more than one application at a time while online. That
means you can download weather information from a World Wide Web server at the
same time you check for new e-mail!

Troubleshooting

I have a 28,800 baud modem, but the fastest connection I get is 19,200. Sometimes the connection is choppy and laden with errors when I download files.

Check for any of the following:

- Line noise

- Incorrect modem settings in your communication software

- Modem incompatibilities between your modem and your ISP's modem

- The presence of a UART 16550 in your modem's COM port

If your phone company uses old switches in its central office, there is nothing you can do except get faster, dedicated service.

My modem connects with my ISP's modem, and then it dumps the carrier (hangs up spontaneously).

This is a potential nightmare with many sources. Did you set your parity to 8 bits, No stop bit, 1 parity bit? Is the initialization string in your communication software appropriate to your modem? Does the modem name and other settings in your communication software match your modem? Is there an incompatibility between your modem and your ISP's modem? Carrier dumping requires sleuthing. Be patient and work with your ISP until the problem is solved.

Windows 95 Dial-Up Networking supports SLIP and can connect to any ISP using the SLIP standard. SLIP is available only on the Windows 95 CD-ROM, and you must manually install it after you install Windows 95.

To install SLIP, use the following steps:

1. In the Add/Remove Programs option in Control Panel, click the Windows Setup tab, and then click the Have Disk button.

2. In the Install From Disk dialog box, enter the pathname **D:\ADMIN\APPTOOLS\DSCRIPT\RNAPLUS.INF** and click OK.

3. In the Have Disk dialog box, click the SLIP and Scripting for Dial-Up Networking option (see fig. 12.17). Click the Install button.

Fig. 12.17
The SLIP
connection
software is
available on the
Windows 95 CD
and is set up using
the Add/Remove
Programs icon. It
requires only 0.3M
hard disk space.

4. Click OK when the Add/Remove Programs Properties sheet appears.

The SLIP software is now available on your system, and you can select it in step 10 in the previous section.

> **Note**
>
> Because SLIP servers cannot negotiate TCP/IP addresses, you must configure the Dial-Up Network connection to display a terminal window after you connect to your ISP. In most cases, your ISP displays the IP host address and your IP address. Write down these addresses and place their values in the SLIP Connection IP Address dialog box that appears. Click OK.

Other Windows 95 Internet Configuration Features

The majority of users who have had Internet access for a number years have become familiar with a few standard tools to help them use the Internet's wealth of information. Two of these tools, Telnet and FTP, are included in Windows 95. Windows also includes a TCP/IP configuration utility. The following sections show you how to set up these utilities to use with Windows 95.

Windows 95 FTP Utility

File Transfer Protocol (FTP) is used to transfer files on the Internet from one site to another. Even if you have World Wide Web access, chances are you'll log into an FTP site sooner or later. Windows 95 includes an FTP utility that you can use after you establish an Internet connection. To start an FTP session, click Start on the Windows 95 taskbar and select <u>R</u>un. In the Open field, type **ftp** and click OK. The Ftp window opens (see fig. 12.18).

Fig. 12.18
Windows 95 includes its own FTP utility to access FTP sites on the Internet.

Once you start FTP, you can log onto an FTP site by using the OPEN command, such as

> **open ftp.microsoft.com**

Other FTP commands can be found by typing **?** at the ftp> prompt and pressing Enter.

Windows 95 Telnet Utility

Like FTP, much of the information on the Internet is still available only if you use Telnet. Telnet enables you to log into another computer and use it as if you were there onsite from your own computer. Windows 95 provides a version of Telnet that you can run from the Start menu, as shown in the following steps:

1. Open the Start menu, click <u>R</u>un, and type **telnet** in the <u>O</u>pen field. Click OK. The Telnet window opens.

2. In Telnet, choose <u>C</u>onnect, <u>R</u>emote Session.

3. In the Connect dialog box (see fig. 12.19), type the host name of the Telnet site to which you want to connect in the <u>H</u>ost Name field.

4. In the <u>T</u>erm Type field, select a terminal mode. The default is VT-100, which is a good place to start.

5. In the <u>P</u>ort field, select a port. The default is Telnet.

6. To start the Telnet session, click the <u>C</u>onnect button in the Connect dialog box.

Fig. 12.19
Windows 95's
Telnet utility
enables you to
log onto other
computers
remotely as if you
were sitting in
front of them.

Verify Internet Connections with WINIPCFG

Windows 95 includes an IP Configuration utility called WINIPCFG (see fig. 12.20), which you can use to display all the current TCP/IP network configuration values of your computer. Your computer must be running Microsoft TCP/IP to use WINIPCFG. To run WINIPCFG, select the Start button, click Run, and type **WINIPCFG** in the Open field. Click OK.

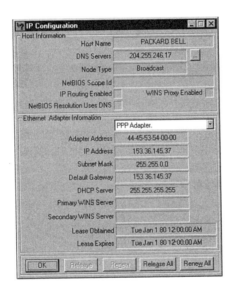

Fig. 12.20
To see current IP settings, use the WINIPCFG utility available with Windows 95.

When you run WINIPCFG, you can see the current IP address allocated to your computer and other useful data about the TCP/IP allocation. The IP Configuration utility does not, however, dynamically update information. If you make any changes, such as disconnecting from your ISP, you must close the IP Configuration utility and restart it.

Microsoft's Internet Explorer

Microsoft Plus! includes a powerful World Wide Web browser called the Internet Explorer (see fig. 12.21), which you can use to display Web sites. Your computer must be connected online to use Internet Explorer. To run Explorer, click the Explorer icon which Plus! installed on your Windows 95

II

Configuring Windows 95

Desktop. Explorer processes information from specially programmed Web servers using its proprietary Blackbird software code. Future Web sites that use the Blackbird system will present vivid pages that, for now, only Explorer will decode and display.

Fig. 12.21
Microsoft's Internet Explorer World Wide Web home page connects you to Microsoft information and the rest of the Web world.

Troubleshooting

How do I know if I'm connected to the Internet?

You can use the PING command to quickly get your answer. To use the PING command, open a DOS window in Windows 95 and type the following, which is the address for the Microsoft FTP server:

> **ping 198.105.232.1**

If this works, then TCP/IP is set up correctly.

You also can start the WINIPCFG utility to see if your IP addresses display. To run WINIPCFG, enter **WINIPCFG** in the Open field after choosing Start, Run.

I'm connected to the Internet through my network at work. I have the same error that I received in the previous question. Can you help?

The best answer is to ask your network administrator to help you configure your Internet connection. He or she is the best qualified to set these settings. You might, however, check to make sure the DNS Configuration tab is set up correctly for your network. You can access this by double-clicking the Networking icon in Control Panel, selecting TCP/IP, and clicking Properties. Click the DNS Configuration page on the TCP/IP Properties sheet and ensure these settings are properly configured.

Chapter 13

Configuring Memory, Disks, and Devices

by Kevin Jones

The Windows 95 installation program does a good job of setting up your computer. It analyzes your hardware and prepares your system for optimal performance. However, as you use your computer, two things may happen. First, you may notice that your system's performance goes down. This is very likely due to your hard disk becoming fragmented. Second, you may add new hardware or software. For example, you may use new programs or perform more complex analysis with your existing programs. You might add a faster CD-ROM or a more powerful video display card. When these types of changes occur, you will require more than the original settings to accommodate your growing needs.

In older versions of Windows, changes of this kind were often very difficult. You'd have to run many different programs to make all the changes. Fortunately, Windows 95 makes performing all of these tasks much simpler than it used to be.

In this chapter, you learn how to

- Modify virtual memory
- Improve hard disk performance
- Set device properties

Modifying Virtual Memory Options

As Windows 95 executes programs—especially when executing several programs at once—it performs better when it possesses more memory. To achieve better performance, Windows 95 uses spare room on your hard disk as additional memory. This is called *virtual memory*. The room on your hard disk that is used by Windows 95 as virtual memory is called the *swap file*. This file grows and shrinks as you use your computer. The more programs you run at once, the larger the swap file grows. As you close programs, the swap file shrinks. Normally, you won't need to adjust the default settings for virtual memory. However, if your hard disk doesn't have much spare room on it, you may want to control how Windows 95 grows and shrinks the swap file.

To change the virtual memory settings, use the Virtual Memory dialog box. To open the Virtual memory dialog box, follow these steps:

1. Click the Start Menu.

2. Choose Settings, Control Panel.

3. Open the System icon by double-clicking it.

4. Select the Performance tab in the System Properties Sheet (see fig. 13.1).

5. Click Virtual Memory.

Fig. 13.1
You can change
System Properties
by using properties
sheets.

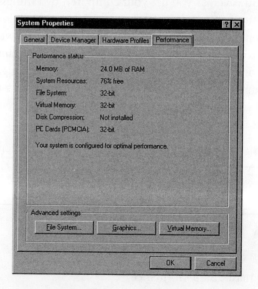

The Virtual Memory dialog box opens.

You only have two main choices when dealing with virtual memory. You can either let Windows decide how to manage the virtual memory, or you can specify your settings. If you need to specify your settings, there are three parameters to set:

- Where (on what disk) should Windows create the swap file

- What's the smallest size the swap file should shrink to

- What's the largest size the swap file can grow to

> **Caution**
>
> If you have 12 or more megabytes of RAM, you will be given the option of turning off virtual memory. Don't do this. If you do turn off virtual memory, you may not be able to run more than a few, small programs simultaneously, or work with large amounts of data. Microsoft (and I) recommend that you don't disable virtual memory.

Hard Disk

Normally, Windows will create the virtual memory swap file on the same disk that Windows 95 is installed. However, you can have Windows 95 create the swap file on a different disk. You may want to use a different disk because it has more free space (allowing you to have more virtual memory) or you may want to use another disk because it is a faster disk drive (improving performance). All of the available disks are listed in the drop-down list box, as well as the amount of free disk space on each disk.

To change the default location for the swap file, follow these steps:

1. Click the Start Menu.

2. Choose Settings, Control Panel.

3. Open the System icon by double-clicking it.

4. Select the Performance tab.

5. Click Virtual Memory.

6. Select the Let Me Specify My Own Virtual Memory Settings option.

7. Show the list of available drives by clicking the down arrow at the far right of the Hard Disk drop-down text box.

8. Click the disk you want to use for the swap file.

9. Choose OK.

Note

Windows 95 is constantly reading and writing to the swap file. Reading and writing to a compressed drive is slower than reading and writing to a non-compressed drive. This is because you have the overhead of compressing and uncompressing data when you read and write it. So, for the best performance, you shouldn't locate the swap file on a compressed drive.

However, if you need more virtual memory than you can fit on any non-compressed drive, you can use a compressed drive. While it works more slowly, you will be able to run more programs simultaneously. For example, if you run large programs, like Word and Excel, and you are using OLE to share data between them, you will need a lot of memory. If you run out of memory using the default swap file, your only option to get everything to work may be to put the virtual memory swap file on a compressed drive.

Set Minimum

You can specify the smallest swap file that Windows 95 will create. If you know you are going to be needing a lot of memory—because you are running several programs or manipulating a large amount of data—you can have Windows 95 pre-allocate the memory. If you don't, you may notice an additional delay as you load new programs or data and Windows 95 has to grow the swap file to increase the amount of virtual memory.

To specify the minimum size for the swap file, follow these steps:

1. Click the Start Menu.

2. Choose Settings, Control Panel.

3. Open the System icon by double-clicking it.

4. Select the Performance tab.

5. Click Virtual Memory.

6. Select the Let Me Specify My Own Virtual Memory Settings option.

7. In the Minimum edit field, type in the size for the smallest swap file (in megabytes).

8. Choose OK.

> **Caution**
>
> Windows 95 will not let you set the minimum memory less than 12M (the total of your physical RAM and virtual memory). However, if you do set your total memory to 12M, you may have problems trying to run additional programs, work with OLE documents, and so on. If you plan to run any large program or work with OLE objects, keep the minimum memory to at least 16M.

Set Maximum

Windows 95 will grow the swap file for virtual memory as large as it needs, unless you set a maximum size. If you don't need a certain amount of space left over, you don't need to set a maximum. However, if you know you need a certain amount of space available for an application to use, you will need to set the maximum value. For example, if you have 20M of room left on your hard disk and know that you will need 5M free for downloading a file, limit the swap file to 15M.

To set the maximum size of the swap file, follow these steps:

1. Select the Let Me Specify My Own Virtual Memory Settings option.

2. In the Maximum edit field, type in the size for the largest swap file (in megabytes).

3. Choose OK.

> **Tip**
>
> You can also get to the System properties sheet page by right-clicking the My Computer icon on the desktop. This will bring up a context menu. Choose Properties, and the System property sheet will open.

Improving Hard Disk Performance

The performance of your hard disk will affect the performance of your system under Windows 95. This happens for several reasons. First, the time it takes to load programs and data files affects performance. Second, since Windows 95 uses the hard disk as virtual memory, maintaining your hard disk's efficiency affects overall performance. Windows 95 provides three tools to help you maintain your hard disk:

II

Configuring Windows 95

- *ScanDisk*. Error checking and correction

- *Disk Defragmenter*. Organizes files into contiguous files

- *Backup*. Make backup copies of files on your hard disk

Given the "object" oriented nature of Windows 95, you can easily keep your hard disk in top condition by working from the properties sheet of the hard disk itself. The individual property pages provide you with information about the drive and ways to easily access the tools you'll use to maintain the drive.

To access the properties of a drive, follow these steps:

1. Open the My Computer folder by double-clicking the My Computer icon on the desktop.

2. Right-click the drive to bring up its context menu.

3. Choose Properties.

The Properties sheet normally contains three pages. These are

- *General*. Displays drive information such as disk label, disk type, and disk usage

- *Tools*. Provides easy access to ScanDisk, Disk Defragmenter, and Backup, as well as informing you of how many days ago you last ran these tools

- *Sharing*. Allows you to control how, and if, you share this drive with other networked users

By selecting the Tools tab, the page shown in figure 13.2 appears. From this page, you can quickly run any of the three disk maintenance tools. The examples in the remainder of this chapter run the disk maintenance tools from the Start menu. But remember, by selecting the "object"—the disk—and choosing its properties, you can access all of the tools from one location.

Perform Error-Checking

While Windows 95 is a much more robust operating system than the DOS–Windows 3.1x combination, the files on your computer are still vulnerable to application errors. When an application crashes—or worse—crashes your entire system, your files and folders may get a bit scrambled. Left unfixed, these scrambled files and folders can produce a domino effect, causing more crashes and further scrambling your disk. Fortunately, Windows 95 comes with ScanDisk, a tool that unscrambles your files and folders.

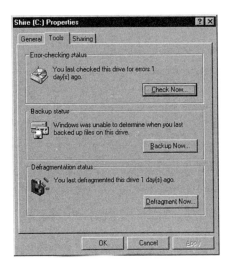

Fig. 13.2
Using the
Properties sheet
box to configure a
drive.

> **Note**
>
> If you did not install ScanDisk, refer to Chapter 4, "Using Custom Installation Options," for information on how to install individual components.

ScanDisk checks your hard drive(s) for any problems. ScanDisk can perform one of two types of tests: *Standard* and *Thorough*. A Standard test checks the file system for errors such as fragments of files or cross-linked files. A Thorough test adds a surface scan test to the Standard test, which helps to detect when a portion of the hard disk is beginning to malfunction.

> **Note**
>
> A Thorough test takes much longer to complete than a Standard test. Depending on the size and speed of your hard disk and your computer's speed, a Thorough test can take a long time to complete. You should either perform a Thorough test on a monthly basis, or if you suspect a problem.

Performing a Standard ScanDisk

To run a Standard ScanDisk on a drive, follow these steps:

1. From the Start Menu, select Programs, Accessories, System Tools, ScanDisk.

2. Select the drive you want ScanDisk to check for errors.

3. Click Stan<u>d</u>ard, or press Alt+D.

4. Choose <u>S</u>tart, or press Alt+S.

Fig. 13.3
You can perform a
Thorough test on
drive C.

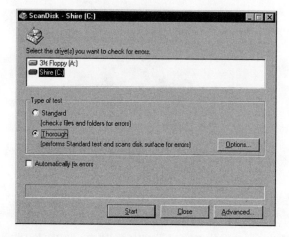

Setting Advanced ScanDisk Options
You can customize the behavior of ScanDisk by choosing the <u>A</u>dvanced button in the ScanDisk main window. The dialog box shown in Figure 13.4 appears.

Fig. 13.4
Set advanced
options for
ScanDisk in the
ScanDisk Ad-
vanced Options
dialog box.

From this dialog box, you can set the following options:

■ If and when to display the results of the ScanDisk test

■ If and how to create a log file of the test

■ How to handle cross-linked files

- How to handle lost file fragments

- What file information to check

- Whether or not to check the host drive of a compressed volume

Select each item by clicking the corresponding radio button or check box. You can also press Alt+the underlined character for each item. For example, to select to always display a summary, you would press Alt+A.

ScanDisk allows you to control six different aspects of its behavior. These are

- *Display Summary*. After ScanDisk finishes testing the drive, it can display a summary of the test. You can choose to always have the results displayed if you wanted to verify any of the hard disk statistics—size, number of files, allocation unit size, and so on. You can choose to never display the results if you automatically run ScanDisk during Start Up. Your third option is to only display the results if an error was detected.

- *Log File*. You can choose to have ScanDisk create a log file. This file contains detailed results of the test. The file is created in the root folder of each drive that is tested and is called, you guessed it— SCANDISK.LOG. You have three choices—always create a new log file (Replace log), add on to the existing log file (Append to log), or never create a log file (No log).

- *Cross-linked Files*. Cross-linked files occur when two (or more) files all use the same part of the disk. When ScanDisk detects a cross-linked file, you can have ScanDisk perform one of three actions. First, ScanDisk can Delete all files containing the cross-link. Second, ScanDisk can Make Copies of the cross-linked information for each file. Third, ScanDisk can simply Ignore the cross-link and continue.

- *Lost File Fragments*. ScanDisk may encounter pieces of data that are no longer contained in any file. You can have ScanDisk either free the data and reclaim that portion of the disk as free space, or you can have ScanDisk convert the data into a file. If you select the latter option, the file will be saved in the root folder of the drive, and given names like `File0000` or `Dir0000` (if the data was part of a folder).

- *Check Files For*. ScanDisk can also check files to make sure that file names, file dates, and file times are all valid. If any invalid information is discovered, ScanDisk will prompt you and ask whether it should fix the problem.

II

Configuring Windows 95

■ *Check <u>H</u>ost Drive First.* If the drive you want ScanDisk to check is compressed with either DoubleSpace or DriveSpace, you can specify whether or not ScanDisk checks the uncompressed host drive for errors first. Only deselect this option if you have already checked the host drive for errors.

Performing a Thorough ScanDisk

To run a Thorough ScanDisk on a drive, follow these steps:

1. From the Start Menu, select <u>P</u>rograms, Accessories, System Tools, ScanDisk.

2. Select the drive you want ScanDisk to check for errors.

3. Select <u>T</u>horough, or press Alt+T.

4. Choose <u>S</u>tart, or press Alt+S.

Setting Thorough ScanDisk Options

If you want ScanDisk to perform a thorough test, you may set several options. These options allow you to customize how ScanDisk will perform the surface scan portion of the test (see fig. 13.5). These options allow you to

■ Select the areas of the disk to scan

■ Restrict ScanDisk to only reading from the disk

■ Restrict the types of files that ScanDisk will repair

Fig. 13.5
Set ScanDisk to scan both the system and data areas of the disk.

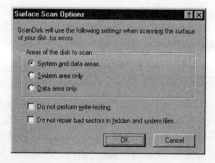

ScanDisk allows you to control three aspects of its Thorough disk test. These are

■ *Areas of the Disk to Scan.* You can specify ScanDisk to scan your entire disk, only the system portion of your disk, or only the data portion of your disk.

- *Do Not Perform Write-Testing.* Normally, to perform the surface test on a disk, ScanDisk will read and write to the drive. You may disable the writing to the disk by selecting this option.

- *Do Not Repair Bad Sectors in Hidden and System Files.* If ScanDisk finds errors, it will move the information to another location on the drive. Normally, you should allow ScanDisk to repair these errors. However, a few older programs require that certain hidden files not be moved. If they are moved, the programs may not work properly. If you run older programs that use this technique as a copy protection scheme, then disable this type of repair.

Automatically Fix Errors

You can have ScanDisk automatically repair errors that it discovers. To set this option, follow these steps:

1. From the Start Menu, select Programs, Accessories, System Tools, ScanDisk.

2. Select the drive you want ScanDisk to check for errors.

3. Select Automatically Fix Errors, or press Alt+F.

4. Choose Start, or press Alt+S.

If you choose to have ScanDisk automatically fix errors, set the advanced options so that

- You make copies of cross-linked files.

- You convert lost fragments into files.

- You append new information to your existing log file.

By setting these options, you will prevent ScanDisk from removing information from your disk without your approval. You need to periodically review the log file to see what ScanDisk has done. At that time, you can delete or recover any files ScanDisk created.

> **Tip**
>
> You can run ScanDisk on several drives at once. To do this, when you select the disk on which to run ScanDisk, press Ctrl and click each drive you want to check for errors.

Tip

You can automate the running of ScanDisk by installing Plus Pack's System Agent. With System Agent, you can schedule when any program—especially the disk maintenance tools—will run.

Troubleshooting

I've tried to run ScanDisk, but it says it can't fix a problem it found.

ScanDisk may be unable to repair errors for files that are in use while ScanDisk runs. Since Windows 95 itself has many files in use, ScanDisk may not be able to completely repair all the errors it finds. To fix these errors, select <u>S</u>hut Down from the Start menu and choose Restart the Computer in MS-DOS mode. Then, run the DOS version of ScanDisk. This file is located in the WINDOWS\COMMAND folder.

Performing Backup

The Backup tool provided with Windows 95 will copy the files on your computer to either floppy disks or supported tape drives. There are two main ways to use Backup. First, the application can be used in a manual mode. In this mode, the Backup program looks and behaves very much like the Explorer. You manually select the folders and files you want to backup. In the second method, you can use the Backup program by creating backup sets. With backup sets, you can back up files using a simple drag-and-drop operation.

Caution

The Windows 95 Backup tool does not support all tape drives. It supports QIC 40, 80, 3010, and 3020 tapes drives connected to the primary floppy disk controller and QIC 40, 80, and 3010 Colorado tape drives connected to the parallel port. It does not support SCSI tape drives. Existing Windows 3.1 backup programs that support SCSI drives should not be used. Because they do not support long file names, backing up and restoring files using one of these programs makes Windows 95 stop working.

Performing a Manual Backup

To perform a manual backup, follow these steps:

1. From the Start Menu, select <u>P</u>rograms, Accessories, System Tools, Backup.

2. Select the folders and files you want to back up by clicking the small rectangle to the right of each folder or file (see fig. 13.6). Drives, folders, or files that are selected for Backup have a check mark in the box. Those files that are not selected for Backup will be empty. If the box for a drive or folder is shaded gray, it means that some items within it are selected for backup, and some are not.

3. Choose Next Step.

4. Select where you back up the folders and files to by clicking the disk drive or tape drive you want. For example, to back up the files to the floppy disks, click one of your floppy drives in the Select a Destination for the Backup window.

5. Start the backup by choosing Start Backup.

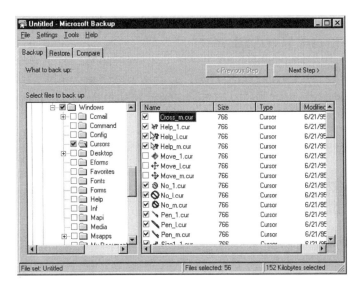

Fig. 13.6
Use Backup to back up the Windows/Cursor folder, except for the "move" cursors.

II

Configuring Windows 95

Using Backup File Sets

Backup file sets make backing up specific sets of files to specific locations easy. After you have created backup sets, you can simply drag-and-drop a set onto the Backup application icon to perform the backup. This icon is located in the Program Files\Accessories folder. To simplify the backup process, you can drag this icon to your desktop so it is always available.

To create a backup set, follow these steps:

1. From the Start Menu, select Programs, Accessories, System Tools, Backup.

2. Select the folders and files you want to back up by clicking the small rectangle to the right of each folder or file.

3. Choose Next Step.

4. Select where you want to back up the folders and files to by clicking the disk drive or tape drive you want to use.

5. Choose File, Save As to save the backup file set definition.

After you have created Backup file sets, you can launch the Backup tool and then choose File, Open File Set to use one of the file sets. Alternately, you can open the folder containing your backup sets and drag-and-drop the Backup file set onto the Backup application icon.

Defragment Hard Disk

Over time, as a hard disk is used—as files are saved, edited and resaved, and deleted—the files become fragmented into pieces scattered on the disk. Then, when a file needs to be loaded, it takes longer to load the file because it is not in one piece. A badly fragmented disk will not perform as well as a disk where all of the files are neatly organized. The Disk Defragmenter tool supplied by Windows 95 helps keep files on your disk organized into contiguous pieces.

◄ See "Using Microsoft Plus!," p. 26

> **Tip**
>
> The System Agent in Microsoft Plus! will schedule and automatically run Disk Defragmenter for you.

To defragment your hard disk, follow these steps:

1. From the Start menu, select Programs, Accessories, System Tools, Disk Defragmenter.

2. Select the drive you want defragmented by choosing the drive from the list in the drop-down list box (see fig. 13.7).

3. Choose OK, or press Enter.

4. Choose Start, or press Alt+S.

Fig. 13.7
The Disk Defragmenter can defragment a drive you choose, such as the C drive.

Fig. 13.8
Set the Disk Defragmenter to perform a full defragmentation.

Setting Advanced Disk Defragmenter Options

You can control how Disk Defragmenter works by setting the Advanced options (see fig. 13.8).

To set advanced options, follow these steps:

1. From the Start menu, select Programs, Accessories, System Tools, Disk Defragmenter.

2. Choose the drive you want defragmented by selecting the drive from the list in the drop-down list box.

3. Choose OK, or press Enter.

4. Click Advanced, or press Alt+A.

5. Select the options you want by clicking the corresponding radio button or check box. These are described in the following section.

Advanced Options

You may select the Defragmentation Method. You have three choices:

- *Full Defragmentation (Both Files and Free Space).* You may choose to have Disk Defragmenter perform both operations. It will rearrange your files so each file is contiguous and so you have one large contiguous free space available. This is the best method of defragmenting your disk; it also takes the most time to complete.

- *Defragment Files Only.* First, you may select to only have Disk Defragmenter rearrange your files, making each existing file contiguous. However, when the Disk Defragmenter tool rearranges your files in this manner, any new files you add to your system will likely be fragmented.

- *Consolidate Free Space Only.* You may select to only have Disk Defragmenter rearrange your files so that you have one large, contiguous, free space on your disk. Any new files you add to your system will not defragment. However, your existing files may actually wind up being more fragmented.

Disk Defragmenter will check a drive for errors before it attempts to defragment the drive. However, you can disable this error-checking by deselecting Check Drive For Errors. Only disable this feature if you are positive that the drive doesn't have any errors. For example, if you have just run ScanDisk on the drive, you could disable the error-checking.

After you have set the advanced disk defragmentation options, you can either save these options to be used whenever Disk Defragmenter is run, or you can use these options for the current session only. Make this selection by choosing either Save These Options and Use Them Every Time or This Time Only Next Time Use the Defaults Again.

Using the Device Manager

While Windows 95 supports Plug-and-Play hardware devices, most of the devices in use are not Plug-and-Play devices. Windows 95 consolidates the management of all of these different devices into one central spot—the Device Manager. With the Device Manager, you can quickly see all the devices in your system and change the setting for any device.

Changing Device Properties

To change the properties of a device using the Device Manager, follow these steps:

1. Right-click My Computer.

2. Choose Properties. The System Properties sheet opens.

3. Select the Device Manager tab in the System Properties sheet. The Device Manager page opens (see fig. 13.9).

4. Click the plus sign in the small rectangle to the left of the type of device you want. This expands the item, showing all of the devices of that type in your system. For example, by clicking the DISK DRIVES folder, the tree expands to show all physical drives in the system.

5. Click the device you want to modify or examine.

6. Choose Properties.

Fig. 13.9
The Device Manager page enables you to change the properties of a device.

While the property sheet for each device is unique, you will see standard pages. All devices have a General page. The General page lists the following information:

■ Device name

■ Device type

■ Manufacturer

■ Hardware version

■ Device status

■ Device usage

Changing Device Resources

Some devices will only have the General page. However, if the device uses system resources, such as IRQ settings, the device will also have a Resources page.

To change the resources for a device, follow these steps:

1. Right-click My Computer.

2. Choose Properties.

3. Select the Device Manager tab in the System Properties dialog box.

4. Click the plus sign in the small rectangle to the left of the type of device you want. This expands the item, showing all of the devices of that type in your system. For example, by selecting the DISK DRIVES folder, the tree expands to show all physical drives in the system.

5. Click the device you want to modify or examine.

6. Choose Properties.

7. Choose the Resources tab. The Resources page opens (see fig. 13.10).

8. If the Use Automatic Settings check box is marked, deselect it; or press Alt+U.

9. Click the resource type you want to change in the Resource Settings list box.

10. Choose Change Settings. A dialog box appears, allowing you to edit the specific resource settings.

Fig. 13.10
You can change the resources used by a modem in this page.

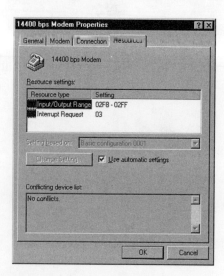

Troubleshooting

I changed the resource for one of my devices and now Windows 95 won't restart.

If you can't restart Windows 95, restart your computer and when the words `Starting Windows 95...` appear on your monitor, press F8. The Windows 95 Startup menu appears. Select Safe mode to restart Windows in a default configuration. You should be able to go back and undo your changes using Device Manager.

Changing Device Drivers

Some devices will have a driver associated with it. If a device does have a device driver, there will be a Driver page. This page displays the following information:

- Device name

- Driver files—the files that are used by the driver

- File details—information about the driver, such as the company that wrote the driver and version of the driver

To change the driver for a device, follow these steps:

1. Right-click My Computer.

2. Choose Properties.

3. Select the Device Manager tab in the System Properties dialog box.

4. Click the plus sign in the small rectangle to the left of the type of device you want. This expands the item, showing all the devices of that type in your system. For example, by clicking the DISK DRIVES folder, the tree expands to show all physical drives in the system.

5. Click the device you want to modify or examine.

6. Choose Properties.

7. Select the Driver tab. The Driver page opens (see fig. 13.11).

8. Choose Change Driver. The Select Device dialog box appears, allowing you to install a new device driver.

II

Configuring Windows 95

Fig. 13.11
You can change a
device driver to a
display device.

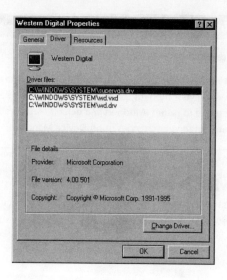

Chapter 14

Using Norton Desktop Utilities with Windows 95

by Kevin Jones

Norton Utilities for Windows 95 is a package of data protection and recovery utility programs designed specifically for Windows 95. These utility programs can be broadly divided into three categories.

First, there are DOS versions of the utility programs. These are used prior to installing Windows 95 to make sure that your computer is top shape. They are also used in the unfortunate event that your system crashes and cannot run Windows 95.

The second category includes the Windows 95 utility programs. These are 32-bit programs designed to fully exploit the power of Windows 95.

The final category contains a single program—System Doctor. Whereas the other programs recover data or analyze your computer for problems, System Doctor continuously monitors your computer and automatically invokes the necessary utilities to correct any problems.

In this chapter, you learn how to

- Tune-up your system prior to installing Windows 95

- Install Norton Utilities for Windows 95

- Configure the behavior of the individual utilities

- Customize the appearance of the individual utilities

- Uninstall Norton Utilities for Windows 95

Note

Although this is the latest release of Norton Utilities, this is not Norton Utilities 9.0. In other words, this is not an upgrade from Norton Utilities 8.0, but rather is designed specifically for Windows 95. Norton Utilities 8.0 will continue to be sold for the Windows 3.1 platform. While there are some components in Norton Utilities 8.0 that are not included in Norton Utilities for Windows 95, there are some totally new components included in Norton Utilities for Windows 95 (for example, System Doctor).

Performing a Pre-Installation TuneUp

The Norton Utilities for Windows 95 contains a collection of DOS-based utilities specifically designed to be run before you install Windows 95. These utilities make sure that your computer is ready to be upgraded to Windows 95. This is called the *Pre-Installation TuneUp* or P.I.T.

The P.I.T. consists of the following three main steps:

- Using Norton Disk Doctor to make sure that your disk is free of errors.

- Using Norton Diagnostics to make sure that you don't have any hardware problems, such as device conflicts.

- Using SpaceWizard to free up as much room as possible on your disk.

Note

A full installation of Windows 95 requires more than 80M. This is substantially more hard disk space than Windows 3.1 required. Because of this and the fact that new 32-bit Windows 95 applications require even more hard disk space, it is very important to clean up your hard disk before you install Windows 95.

To run the Pre-Installation TuneUp, follow these steps:

1. If you are in Windows, exit Windows. The P.I.T. can only be run from DOS.

2. Insert the Norton Emergency Disk.

3. Change to the floppy drive where you inserted the Emergency Disk (for example, A).

4. Type **TUNEUP** and press Enter.

5. Select the drive you want to install Windows 95 onto.

> **Tip**
>
> You can also run the P.I.T. on other drives. Simply rerun TuneUp and select another drive.

6. Click OK.

7. Follow the step-by-step instructions to complete the tune-up. The exact steps vary depending on any problems that may be found.

> **Note**
>
> After you complete the P.I.T. and install Windows 95, you may still find it useful to run the P.I.T. Some of the extensive diagnostic tests available in Norton Diagnostics can only be fully used when executing in MS-DOS mode. To get into MS-DOS mode, select Shut Down from the Start Menu and choose Restart the Computer in <u>M</u>S-DOS Mode. Then follow the preceding steps.

Checking Your Disk with Norton Disk Doctor (DOS)

The DOS version of Norton Disk Doctor analyzes your hard disk for any problems and repairs any problems that it discovers. Although this is a DOS version, it was written for the Windows 95 file system. This means that it can detect and correct problems with long file names (LFN). This is especially important for dealing with serious disk problems that occur after you've installed Windows 95. If the problem is serious enough to prevent Windows 95 from loading and running, you won't be able to use any of the Windows-based applications to fix the problems.

To run Norton Disk Doctor (DOS), follow these steps:

1. Make sure that you run Norton Disk Doctor from MS-DOS mode. If you are running Windows 3.1, exit Windows. If you are running Windows 95, restart the computer in <u>M</u>S-DOS mode.

2. Insert the Norton Emergency Disk or change to the directory where you installed Norton Utilities.

3. Type **NDD** and press Enter.

II

Configuring Windows 95

4. Select Diagnose Disk, or press Alt+D.

5. Select the Drive you want to diagnose.

6. Choose Diagnose, or press Alt+D.

7. If any errors are found, Norton Disk Doctor prompts you before taking any corrective action. NDD walks you through step-by-step to fix the problem.

8. After the test is complete, choose Skip Test (unless you suspect that your drive has physical damage).

9. Select Done, or press Alt+D.

10. You can now diagnose another disk by choosing Diagnose again, or you can choose Quit Disk Doctor if you are finished.

Checking Your Hardware with Norton Diagnostics (DOS)

Norton Diagnostics analyzes your computer to make sure that no problems exist. Although it can be used to test individual components, it can also be used to run the complete set of tests. After each test, you can automatically run the next test. By using this method, you exhaustively test your entire system prior to upgrading to Windows 95.

To run Norton Diagnostics, follow these steps:

1. Make sure that you run Norton Disk Doctor from MS-DOS mode. If you are running Windows 3.1, exit Windows. If you are running Windows 95, restart the computer in MS-DOS mode.

2. Insert the Norton Emergency Disk or change to the directory where you installed Norton Utilities.

3. Type **NDIAGS** and press Enter.

4. Read the Description dialog box.

5. Disconnect all peripherals connected to your computer—printer, modem, and so on—except for your mouse.

6. Choose OK.

7. Let the testing begin!

As Norton Diagnostics takes you step by step through each test, it provides you with a Description of the test and any options you have. After you choose OK (your only choice), the testing begins. After each test is complete, choose Next Test to continue. Norton Diagnostics performs the following tests:

- System Information
- System Board
- Serial Port(s)
- Parallel Port(s)
- CMOS
- IRQ Status
- Base Memory
- Extended Memory
- Hard disk(s)

- Floppy disk(s)
- Video RAM
- Video Mode (Text modes)
- Video Grid (Graphic modes)
- Video Color
- Video Attributes
- Speaker
- Keyboard Press
- Keyboard Lights

II

Troubleshooting

I was running Norton Diagnostics and my system just stopped running. What should I do now?

If your system crashes or freezes during a test, reboot your machine and restart NDIAGS. This time, instead of restarting all the tests, use the menus to restart the test that the computer failed on. Norton Diagnostics tracks where it was at in the testing and attempts to further diagnose what caused the failure.

While the actual time it will take to run the complete set of tests will vary depending on how fast your machine is, how much memory you have installed, how large and fast your hard disk is, and so on, you should expect the testing to take around 15 minutes on a fast machine, or 30 minutes on a slow machine.

Cleaning Up Your Disk with SpaceWizard (DOS)

SpaceWizard checks your hard disk for any files that can be deleted or moved to another volume. SpaceWizard looks for files that are normally temporary in nature (for example, TMP files, files in the Windows TEMP folder), commonly discardable files (for example, BAK files), and very large files. After scanning your disk, you have to explicitly choose to delete the files, so don't worry about accidentally deleting important files.

To run SpaceWizard, follow these steps:

1. Make sure that you run SpaceWizard from MS-DOS mode. If you are running Windows 3.1, exit Windows. If you are running Windows 95, restart the computer in MS-DOS mode.

2. Insert the Norton Emergency Disk or change to the directory where you installed Norton Utilities.

3. Type **SPACEWZD** and press Enter.

4. Select the drive you want to analyze and choose Next, or press Alt+N.

5. Deselect any temporary files you don't want to delete or move, and click Next, or press Alt+N.

6. Deselect any discardable files you don't want to delete or move, and choose Next, or press Alt+N.

7. Select the smallest file to include (the default is 10M). Remember, SpaceWizard is looking for a few really large files that will free up a lot of space, so don't set this value too small.

8. Deselect any large files you don't want to delete or move, and choose Next, or press Alt+N.

9. You can either choose to Delete Files, Move Files, or do nothing.

Troubleshooting

I accidentally deleted some important files using SpaceWizard. What now?

Not to worry; you can run the DOS version of UnErase to recover any files you inadvertently deleted. You must run UnErase before you run any other programs. You can run UnErase by typing **UNERASE** at the DOS prompt.

Installing Norton Utilities for Windows 95

After you have successfully completed the Pre-Installation TuneUp and you have upgraded your computer to Windows 95, you are ready to install Norton Utilities. The Symantec installation program is used by all the Symantec utility packages for Windows 95 (Norton Utilities, Norton Anti-Virus, and Norton Navigator) and follows the guidelines outlined by

Microsoft for installation programs. The installation program allows you to either perform a complete installation of Norton Utilities or a custom installation, installing just the components you want. In either case, the installation program uses a Setup Wizard to walk you step-by-step through the installation process (see fig. 14.1).

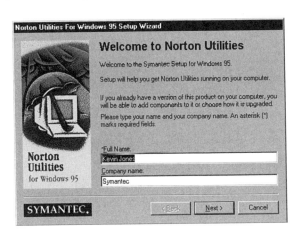

Fig. 14.1
Use the Setup Wizard to install Norton Utilities for Windows 95.

Performing a Complete Installation

A complete installation of Norton Utilities requires about 14M of hard disk space. This installs all the following Windows utilities:

- Image
- Norton Disk Doctor
- Rescue Disk

- Speed Disk
- SpaceWizard
- System Information

And all the DOS utilities:

- Disk Editor
- Norton Diagnostics
- Norton Disk Doctor

- SpaceWizard
- UnErase
- UnFormat

To perform a complete installation of Norton Utilities, follow these steps:

1. Open My Computer by double-clicking the My Computer icon on the Desktop.

2. Open the drive containing the Norton Utilities installation files (floppy, CD, or network drive). If you are on a network drive, you will have to open the folder containing the installation files.

II

Configuring Windows 95

3. Start the installation program by double-clicking SETUP.

4. Type in (or verify) your name and, optionally, your company and choose Next.

5. After reading the License Agreement, choose Next.

6. Select Complete installation and choose Next.

7. After Setup explores your disk for other versions of Norton products, specify where you want to install Norton Utilities.

8. If you want to be able to simply type in the command name when running the DOS versions of the Norton Utilities, you must check Add Program Location to Path.

9. Choose Next.

10. If you want to add Norton file deletion protection to the protection already offered by Windows 95, check Add Norton Protection to the Recycle Bin.

11. Choose Next.

12. If you want to use System Doctor to continuously monitor your computer, check Run Norton System Doctor Every Time Windows Starts.

> **Note**
>
> If you later want to stop System Doctor from automatically running every time you start Windows, open the Windows StartUp folder and delete the shortcut to Norton System Doctor.

13. Choose Next.

14. If you want to create a rescue disk now, check Yes.

15. Choose Next.

16. Review your installation settings and choose Next.

17. Setup now copies the files. If you are installing from floppy disks, you are prompted when you need to switch disks.

18. If you selected to create a rescue disk, Setup runs rescue disk now. Simply insert a floppy disk and choose Save.

19. A series of informative screens appear by the installation program. After reading each one, simply choose Next until you reach the final screen.

20. At this point, choose Finish to complete the installation.

Performing a Custom Installation

If you don't want to install all 14M of Norton Utilities, you can perform a custom installation. You can choose to install only the DOS or only the Windows utilities, or you can select the exact mix of DOS and Windows utilities you want.

To perform a custom installation of Norton Utilities, follow these steps:

1. Open My Computer by double-clicking the My Computer icon on the Desktop.

2. Open the drive containing the Norton Utilities installation files (floppy, CD, or network drive). If you are on a network drive, you have to open the folder containing the installation files.

3. Start the installation program by double-clicking SETUP.

4. Type (or verify) your name and, optionally, your company and choose Next.

5. After reading the License Agreement, choose Next.

6. Select Custom installation, and choose Next.

7. To install all of the Windows utilities, check Norton Windows Utilities (see fig. 14.2). To install only some of the Windows utilities, click Select (across from Norton Windows Utilities). Then select the utilities you want to install.

Tip

While the exact mix of components to install during a custom install depends on many factors, a simple recommendation is to create a rescue disk with all DOS utilities and to install all of the Windows utilities. Since you will almost always be in a Windows environment, and since the Windows utilities help keep your system running smoothly (thereby avoiding problems), these are the best candidates for installing on your computer.

II

Configuring Windows 95

Fig. 14.2
Use the Setup
Wizard to select
components to
install.

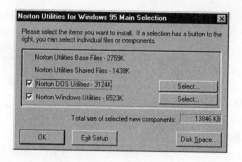

8. To install all of the DOS utilities, select Norton DOS Utilities. To install only some of the DOS utilities, click Select (across from Norton DOS Utilities). Then check the utilities you want to install.

9. Click Next.

10. After Install explores your disk for other versions of Norton products, specify where you want to install Norton Utilities.

11. If you want to be able to simply type in the command name when running the DOS versions of the Norton Utilities, you must select Add Program Location to Path.

12. Click Next.

13. If you want to add Norton file deletion protection to the protection already offered by Windows 95, select Add Norton Protection to the Recycle Bin.

14. Click Next.

15. If you want to use System Doctor to continuously monitor your computer, select Run Norton System Doctor Every Time Windows Starts.

16. Click Next.

17. If you want to create a rescue disk now, select Yes.

18. Click Next.

19. Review your Install settings, support policies, and so on, and click Next after each step.

20. Setup now copies the files. If you are installing from floppy disks, you are prompted when you need to switch disks.

21. If you selected to create a rescue disk, Setup will run Rescue Disk now. Simply insert a floppy disk and choose Save.

22. The installation program displays a series of informative screens. After reading each one, simply click Next until you reach the final screen. At this point, click Finish, and the installation is complete.

Configuring Norton Utilities for Windows 95

The programs in Norton Utilities for Windows 95 are highly configurable. You can change the appearance of the programs. This can be anything from changing colors and fonts to changing the amount of information displayed during execution. You can change advanced options. These include controlling exactly which tests are executed and controlling background operation. You can also configure whether each utility should run during Windows startup.

> **Note**
>
> If you are using System Doctor, you won't need to run any utility during Windows startup. System Doctor continuously runs in the background and monitors your system. If any of the parameters Disk Doctor is monitoring exceed their limits—and Disk Doctor can monitor a lot of stuff—it automatically takes action. Disk Doctor either invokes the needed utilities to fix any problems or alerts you so that you can take care of the problem.

Configuring System Doctor

System Doctor (see fig. 14.3) is like an automobile dashboard. It is a collection of gauges and monitors that show the status of various parameters. System Doctor is capable of tracking and measuring more than 80 different system resources. You can configure System Doctor in several ways. You can alter its appearance, screen colors, fonts, gauge size, and so on. You can also change the resources it is monitoring. You can configure specific gauges, both in appearance and functionality.

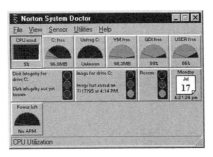

Fig. 14.3
The Norton System Doctor is the program that you will probably interact with the most.

Configuring the System Doctor Window

To change the appearance of the System Doctor, follow these steps:

1. Right-click System Doctor.

2. On the pop-up context menu, choose View, Options.

3. Select the Appearance page.

4. To change the colors of the items of System Doctor, select an Item in the drop-down list box and choose Color.

5. To change the order of the gauges, select a gauge in the Sensor Order list box and then choose Up or Down.

6. Select how you want the window to display.

7. Select if you want System Doctor to automatically load when Windows starts.

8. Choose OK.

To change the size of all the gauges, follow these steps:

1. Right-click System Doctor.

2. On the pop-up context menu, choose File, Options.

3. Select the Dimensions page.

4. To change the size of the gauge, click the horizontal and/or vertical sliders. While holding down your mouse button, drag the sliders to make the gauge larger or smaller.

5. To change the font on the gauge, choose Normal and select the font you want to use.

6. To change the font used in the Date & Time and Up Time sensors, choose Calendar and select the font you want to use.

7. Choose OK.

To change the resources that System Doctor monitors, follow these steps:

1. Right-click System Doctor.

2. On the pop-up context menu, choose View, Options.

3. Select the Active Sensors page.

4. To add more Sensors, click the sensor you want to add in the Available Sensors list box and choose Add.

5. To remove an active sensor, click the sensor you want to remove in the Current Sensors list box and choose Remove.

6. To configure an active sensor, click the sensor you want to configure in the Current Sensors list box and choose Properties.

7. Choose OK.

Configuring a Gauge

To change the appearance of a gauge, follow these steps:

1. Right-click the gauge you want to configure (for example, GDI resource).

2. Choose Properties on the pop-up context menu to bring up the property sheet for the gauge.

3. Select the Style page.

4. To change the type of gauge, select either Bar Gauge, Analog Gauge, or Histogram (see fig. 14.4).

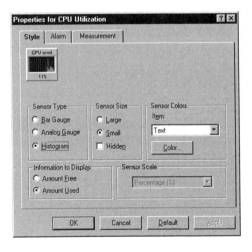

Fig. 14.4
Use the properties sheet to change the style of a gauge in System Doctor.

5. To change the size of the gauge, select either Large or Small.

6. To hide the gauge, select Hidden.

7. To change colors for the gauge, select the colors for each item in the Item drop-down list box and choose Color.

8. To change what type of information to show—how much is free or available, or how much is used or unavailable—select one of the options in the Information to Display group.

9. On some sensors, you can change the scale of the gauge. If you are able to, the drop-down list box in the Sensor Scale group will be active (not grayed out). Select the scale you want. (On some sensors, you can't change the scale. For example, the gauge for the CPU Utilization measures the usage as a percentage. The scale is from 0 to 100 percent and can't be changed.)

10. Choose OK.

To change what happens when a threshold event occurs, follow these steps:

1. Right-click the gauge corresponding to the event (for example, Disk Integrity for drive C:).

2. Choose Properties on the pop-up context menu to bring up the property sheet for the gauge.

3. Select the Alarm page.

4. To turn the alarm on (or off), check (or uncheck) Enabled. If the alarm is enabled, you can set the value at when the alarm will go off.

5. To change what happens when the alarm goes off, select one of the options in the Alarm Action group. You can either decide to do nothing (No Action), have System Doctor make a recommendation to correct the problem (Display Action Recommendation), or have System Doctor automatically try to fix the problem (Take Corrective Action Immediately).

6. To have an audio alarm sound, check Play Sound. To browse for a sound file to use, click the little folder to the right of the edit window. To test the sound, click the little speaker.

7. To change how frequently the alarm goes off after reaching its threshold, type in the number of minutes to wait under Alarm Snooze.

8. Choose OK.

To change how often System Doctor measures each resource, follow these steps:

1. Right-click the gauge corresponding to the resource you want to measure (for example, CPU utilization).

2. Choose Properties on the pop-up context menu to bring up the property sheet for the gauge.

3. Select the Measurement page.

4. To change how often System Doctor checks the resource, change the Time Between Sensor Readings slider.

5. To change the maximum reading to a value you want to specify, click Use Fixed Maximum and type a new maximum. Otherwise, System Doctor sets the maximum to the highest value it has encountered so far.

6. To change the measurement type, click either Actual Value (the number System Doctor has determined) or Decaying Average (an average value that is weighed so that more recent values are more important).

7. Choose OK.

To change the drive that System Doctor is monitoring, follow these steps:

1. Right-click the gauge corresponding to the resource you want to configure (for example, free space on a drive).

2. Choose Properties on the pop-up context menu to bring up the property sheet for the gauge.

3. Select the Drive page.

4. Select the drive in the Drive to Monitor drop-down list box.

5. Choose OK.

Adding a Gauge

To add a gauge to System Doctor, follow these steps:

1. Right-click the background of System Doctor (or on any one of the gauges).

2. Choose Add from the pop-up context menu.

3. Choose the resource or item you want to monitor.

4. You can configure the gauge if you don't like the default settings by following the instructions in the earlier section, "Configuring a Gauge."

Removing a Gauge

To remove a gauge from System Doctor, follow these steps:

1. Right-click the gauge you want to remove.

2. Choose Remove on the pop-up context menu to remove the gauge.

> **Note**
>
> Under most normal conditions, System Doctor will only use 2 to 4 percent of your computer's system resource. You can even use the gauges within System Doctor (GDI Resources and User Resources) to monitor the overhead of using the other gauges.

Configuring Norton Disk Doctor

To make Norton Disk Doctor run each time you start Windows, follow these steps:

1. From the Start menu, choose Programs, Norton Utilities, Norton Disk Doctor.

2. Choose Options.

3. Select the General page.

4. Click Run on Windows Startup.

5. Select the drive(s) you want Disk Doctor to check at startup.

6. Choose OK.

To change what Norton Disk Doctor does when it finds an error, follow these steps:

1. From the Start menu, choose Programs, Norton Utilities, Norton Disk Doctor.

2. Choose Options.

3. Select the General page.

4. Select either to have Disk Doctor ask what you want to do (Ask Me First), to automatically fix the problem (Auto-Repair), or to do nothing (Skip Repairs); or you can customize Disk Doctor to do one of the preceding choices for each different kind of error it finds (Custom and then choose Select).

5. Choose OK.

To change the appearance of Norton Disk Doctor, follow these steps:

1. From the Start menu, choose Programs, Norton Utilities, Norton Disk Doctor.

2. Choose Options.

3. Select the Appearance page (see fig 14.5).

4. To turn on the cartoon animation, choose Enable Animation.

5. To play music while Disk Doctor executes, click Play Music. To browse for a sound file to use, click the little folder to the right of the edit window. To test the sound, click the little speaker.

6. To display a special message if a serious error is encountered, select Show Custom Message. Choose Edit to type the message you want to display.

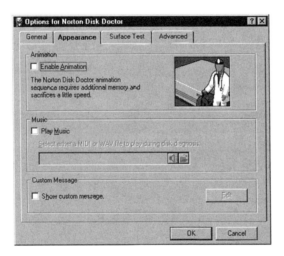

Fig. 14.5

Use the Options sheet to change the appearance of Norton Disk Doctor.

To control how Norton Disk Doctor performs the surface test, follow these steps:

1. From the Start menu, choose Programs, Norton Utilities, Norton Disk Doctor.

2. Choose Options.

3. Select the Surface Test page.

4. To turn on surface testing, choose Enable Surface Testing.

5. To have the test repeat, you can either choose Repetitions and type in the number of times to repeat the test, or you can select Continuous to have the test repeat forever (until you click the Cancel button).

6. To have Disk Doctor perform an in-depth test, check Thorough Test. By default, Disk Doctor performs a quick scan of the disk (Normal Test).

II

Configuring Windows 95

7. To have Disk Doctor only test the area of the disk used by files, select Area Used by Files. By default, Disk Doctor tests the entire disk (Entire Disk Area).

8. To display a map of the disk during the testing, check Show Disk Map During the Surface Test.

9. Choose OK.

To restrict the tests Norton Disk Doctor performs, follow these steps:

1. From the Start menu, choose Programs, Norton Utilities, Norton Disk Doctor.

2. Choose Options.

3. Select the Advanced page.

4. You can restrict the types of tests Disk Doctor performs by checking the items in the Tests to Skip group box.

> **Caution**
>
> You should only need to restrict the types of tests Disk Doctor performs if you have a machine that is not 100 percent compatible and Disk Doctor stops during one of the tests. If this happens, stop Disk Doctor (Ctrl+Alt+Delete) and disable the test that caused the problem.

5. To change how quickly Disk Doctor resumes testing after it has been interrupted, type the number of minutes (Alt+B) and the number of seconds (Alt+D) to wait after Disk Doctor detects idle time.

6. To change what Disk Doctor does when it detects an error, pick one of the four options in the When Errors Are Found drop-down list box—sound a short alarm, flash the taskbar area, sound alarm and flash the taskbar area, or display the report window.

7. Choose OK.

> **Tip**
>
> You can launch all the utilities directly from System Doctor by right-clicking any gauge, choosing Utilities, and then selecting the utility on the pop-up context menu.

Configuring Speed Disk

To configure how Speed Disk optimizes your disk, follow these steps:

1. From the Start menu, choose Programs, Norton Utilities, Speed Disk.

2. Allow Speed Disk to initialize by scanning your drive for errors. If any errors are discovered, Speed Disk exits and suggests you run Norton Disk Doctor.

3. Choose File, Options.

4. Select the Optimization page (see fig. 14.6).

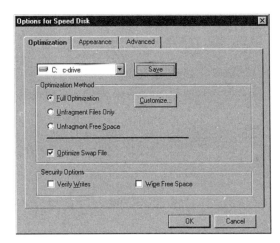

Fig. 14.6
Configure the way Speed Disk optimizes a disk.

5. To change the method used to optimize your disk, select either Full Optimization, Unfragment Files Only, or Unfragment Free Space.

6. To custom a Full Optimization, choose Customize.

7. To have Speed Disk optimize your swap file, check Optimize Swap File.

8. To have Speed Disk erase the data leftover after it moves data around, check Wipe Free Space.

9. To have Speed Disk check to make sure that any data it moves was moved successfully, check Verify Writes.

10. Choose OK.

To configure how Speed Disk looks, follow these steps:

1. From the Start menu, choose Programs, Norton Utilities, Speed Disk.

II

Configuring Windows 95

2. Allow Speed Disk to initialize by scanning your drive for errors. If any errors are discovered, Speed Disk exits and suggests that you run Norton Disk Doctor.

3. Choose File, Options.

4. Select the Appearance page.

5. To change the display Speed Disk uses, select either Block (the default) or Bar.

6. To have Speed Disk play music while it optimizes your disk, select Play Music and enter the name of a sound file. To browse for a sound file to use, click the little folder to the far right of the edit window. To test the sound, click the little speaker to the near right of the edit window.

To configure when Speed Disk runs in the background, follow these steps:

1. From the Start menu, choose Programs, Norton Utilities, Speed Disk.

2. Allow Speed Disk to initialize by scanning your drive for errors. If any errors are discovered, Speed Disk exits and suggests that you run Norton Disk Doctor.

3. Choose File, Options.

4. Select the Advanced page.

5. To change how quickly Speed Disk resumes optimizing your disk after it has been interrupted, type in the number of minutes (Alt+B) and the number of seconds (Alt+D) to wait after Speed Disk detects idle time.

6. To have Speed Disk monitor the communications port for activity, check Watch Communications Port. You should check this if you are using fax software to send and receive faxes. Otherwise, Speed Disk and your communications program may interfere with each other.

7. Choose OK.

Caution

Because Speed Disk was designed for Windows 95, it correctly handles long file names. Also, Speed Disk works with uncompressed drives and drives compressed with DoubleSpace and DriveSpace. However, it does not work with drives compressed with Stacker 4.0, because Stacker 4.0 uses a 16-bit device driver.

Configuring Rescue Disk

To configure Rescue Disk, follow these steps:

1. From the Start menu, choose <u>P</u>rograms, Norton Utilities, Rescue Disk.

2. Select whether you want to include the Emergency Programs by checking or unchecking <u>I</u>nclude Emergency Programs. The Emergency Programs are the DOS versions of the Norton Utilities.

3. Select <u>O</u>ptions.

4. Select the Rescue Items page (see fig 14.7).

Fig. 14.7
Select items to be
placed on the
Rescue Disk.

5. Items with a + are automatically included on the rescue disk(s). Selected items (with a check mark) are included, whereas unselected items (without a check mark) are not. You may change any of these by clicking the item you want to change.

6. Select the Formatting page.

7. Choose how you want to use the floppy disks for rescue disks by clicking one of the three options. Your options are to completely format each disk as you use it, perform only a quick format on each disk, or to use only available disk space on the disk. This last option does not destroy any data already on the floppy disk.

8. Choose OK.

Configuring Norton Protected Recycle Bin

To configure Norton Protected Recycle Bin, follow these steps:

1. Right-click the Norton Protected Recycle Bin icon on the Desktop.

2. Choose P<u>r</u>operties on the pop-up context menu.

3. Select the Norton Protection page on the Property Sheet dialog box.

4. Select the drive you want to change the settings for.

5. Select Enable Protection to turn on the enhanced protection of the Norton Protected Recycle Bin. Deselect Enable protection to turn off this protection.

6. Click Purge Protected Files if you want to purge files after a certain number of days, even if the space is not needed on your disk. If you do choose to purge the files, set the number of days to retain the files before purging them.

7. Click Exclusions if you want to exclude certain file types or folders from being protected. This is useful so you don't save copies of temporary files.

8. Choose OK.

Setting Norton Image Options

To configure Norton Image, follow these steps:

1. From the Start menu, choose Programs, Norton Utilities, Image.

2. Unless you have just run Norton Disk Doctor and are certain that the disk is free of errors, make sure that the Create Image Backup File option is checked.

3. Choose Options.

4. Check Run on Windows Startup to have Norton Image run automatically each time you start your computer. You don't need to do this if you are using System Doctor to monitor your computer.

5. If you are having Norton Image run each time you start Windows 95, you must select the drives you want to image. Select the tries by clicking each drive in the list box (see fig. 14.8). Image creates an image file for those drives with a check mark.

6. Select Create Image Backup File to make a backup copy of IMAGE.DAT when Image is run during Windows startup.

Caution

If you run Image on a damaged drive, don't rerun Image or you will destroy your backup copy. Instead, delete the IMAGE.DAT file (which won't be any good) and rename IMAGE.BAK to IMAGE.DAT.

Fig. 14.8
Use the Options
property sheet to
configure Norton
Image.

Customizing Norton Utilities for Windows 95

While the Norton Utilities are highly configurable—that is, you can control
their behavior—they are also highly customizable. This means that you can
also control the appearance of the applications. This section focuses on
customizing the two programs that you most often have visible on your
screen—System Doctor and the Norton Protected Recycle Bin.

Customizing System Doctor

You can customize System Doctor to appear in three distinct forms. First, you
can have System Doctor appear as a normal window complete with title bar,
menus, and a status bar. To save some screen real estate, you can change
System Doctor into a tool palette (a window without a title bar, frame, menu,
or status bar). Finally, you can turn System Doctor into an application
taskbar. This behaves just like the taskbar in Windows 95, and you can
"dock" it to any of the four edges of the screen.

To make System Doctor appear as a normal window, follow these steps:

1. Right-click any System Doctor gauge.

2. Select <u>V</u>iew from the pop-up context menu.

3. Uncheck <u>D</u>ock.

4. Right-click any System Doctor gauge.

5. Select <u>V</u>iew from the pop-up context menu.

6. Check <u>T</u>itle Bar.

To make System Doctor appear as a tool, follow these steps:

1. Right-click any System Doctor gauge.

2. Select <u>V</u>iew from the pop-up context menu.

3. Uncheck <u>D</u>ock.

4. Right-click any System Doctor gauge.

5. Select <u>V</u>iew from the pop-up context menu.

6. Uncheck <u>T</u>itle Bar.

To make System Doctor appear as a taskbar, follow these steps:

1. Right-click any System Doctor gauge.

2. Select <u>V</u>iew from the pop-up context menu.

3. Select <u>D</u>ock.

Tip

To keep your desktop uncluttered, you can choose to A<u>u</u>to Hide System Doctor. When you do this, system doctor disappears just off the screen, leaving only a single thin line along the edge of the screen. To make System Doctor appear, simply move your mouse to the edge of the screen where you've docked System Doctor. It "pops" back onto the screen.

Customizing Norton Protected Recycle Bin

To customize Norton Protected Recycle Bin, follow these steps:

1. Right-click the Norton Protected Recycle Bin icon on the Desktop.

2. Choose P<u>r</u>operties on the pop-up context menu.

3. Select the Desktop Item page on the Property Sheet dialog box (see fig. 14.9).

4. To change the title, type a new title in the <u>T</u>itle edit window.

5. To enable the icon to change to reflect the status of the Norton Protected Recycle Bin, select <u>S</u>how Norton Protection Status.

6. To set the default action that should happen when you double-click the Norton Protected Recycle Bin icon, select one of the four options in the Double-clicking Item Opens box—Norton UnErase <u>W</u>izard, <u>R</u>ecently Deleted Files, All <u>P</u>rotected files, Standard Recycle <u>B</u>in.

7. Choose OK.

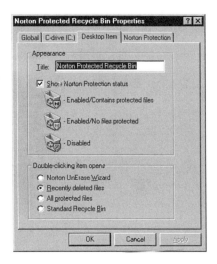

Fig. 14.9
Customize the
look of Norton
Protected Recycle
Bin.

Uninstalling Norton Utilities for Windows 95

To uninstall all the Norton Utilities, follow these steps:

1. From the Start menu, choose Settings, Control Panel.

2. Open the Add/Remove Programs Wizard by double-clicking its icon in the Control Panel folder.

3. Select Norton Utilities and choose Add/Remove.

4. Choose Next.

5. Select Full Uninstall.

6. Answer each question the Uninstall Wizard asks and choose Next.

To uninstall a portion of the Norton Utilities, follow these steps:

1. From the Start menu, choose Settings, Control Panel.

2. Open the Add/Remove Programs Wizard by double-clicking its icon in the Control Panel folder.

3. Select Norton Utilities and choose Add/Remove.

4. Choose Next.

5. Select Partial Uninstall.

6. Check the components you want to remove and choose Next.

7. Answer each question the Uninstall Wizard asks and choose Next.

Chapter 15

Using DOS Software

by Diane Tinney

Operating systems are great, but it's the software that you use every day that makes a difference in your life. Once the operating system is up and running, you should be able to install and use application software without noticing that an operating system is even under the hood. But in reality, we've all wasted hours trying to tweak the operating system to correctly run the application we need, without sacrificing the executability of the other applications we also need.

Windows 95 was designed from the ground up to make the installation, configuration, and execution of application software easier, quicker, and more reliable. DOS software in particular runs better in Windows 95 than in DOS 6.22. In this chapter, we examine how the design of Windows 95 makes this possible and explore the DOS application environment in detail. At the end of the chapter, we explore the most challenging DOS software Windows 95 must run: DOS-based game software.

In this chapter, you learn

- The effect of the Windows 95 architecture on software execution

- How to access and work with the DOS command prompt

- The best way to execute a DOS application

- How to configure and optimize DOS software

- The issues involved in executing DOS game software

III

Setting Up Software

Exploring the Windows 95 Architecture

Before you delve into the nitty gritty of how to install and configure software to work with Windows 95, it is important that you understand a few foundation concepts regarding the Windows 95 architecture. First, Windows 95 is an operating system. *Operating systems* provide the link between hardware and software. When a software application needs to write a file to the hard disk, print a document, or display something on-screen, it is the operating system that provides these services. While Windows 95 and Windows NT are operating systems, keep in mind that Windows 3.x is just an application that runs on top of DOS.

◀ See "What's New with Windows 95 Setup," p. 10

Windows 95 executes software differently, depending on the type of software you are running. Software is divided into three basic categories:

- Applications written for DOS

- Applications written for Windows 3.1 (generally referred to as *16-bit applications*)

- Applications written for Windows 95 and Windows NT (generally referred to as *32-bit applications*)

The Windows 95 application execution environment changes depending on the type of software. The key architectural areas which differ include the Virtual Machine (VM), multitasking, and internal messaging.

Understanding Virtual Machines

To meet the various needs of each type of software application, Windows 95 creates a fictional computer called a virtual machine. A *virtual machine* is an environment created by the operating system and processor that simulates a full computer's resources. To the software application, the virtual machine appears to be a real computer.

The operating system keeps track of the application needs and hardware resources. Windows 95 determines which resources each application will have access to and when it can have access.

All software applications in Windows 95 run in virtual machines (VM). Figure 15.1 illustrates the various VMs and what services run in each VM.

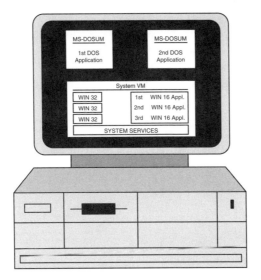

Fig. 15.1
Software applications execute in virtual machines created by Windows 95.

> **Note**
>
> Each DOS application runs in a separate MS-DOS VM. For example, if you ran your DOS-based version of WordPerfect and a DOS-based version of Lotus 1-2-3, Windows 95 would create two separate MS-DOS VMs, one for each DOS-based program.

Providing each DOS application with its own VM is beneficial because most DOS-based programs were created in a single application environment. That is, DOS-based programs usually assume they are the *only* program executing at any particular point in time. This single-mindedness of DOS applications has been known to cause grief (system hang-ups, sudden re-boots and general protection faults) when running DOS applications under Windows 3.x.

Another benefit of the single DOS VM is that each DOS application is shielded from other DOS applications as well as Windows 3.x and Windows 95-type applications. Thus, a misbehaving DOS, Win16, or Win32 application cannot bring down another DOS application. The MS-DOS VM insulates the DOS application from other misbehaving programs.

III

Setting Up Software

> **Note**
>
> As we all know from other software systems, the way a product is designed to work and how it actually performs can be two very different things. The design features of Windows 95 presented here are just that. Time will tell if the design holds up in the real world.

In addition to the MS-DOS VM, Windows 95 creates another virtual machine environment called the System VM. As you can see in figure 15.1, the System VM executes the following:

- System services

- 16-bit applications

- 32-bit applications

The system services such as the *kernel* (core program of the operating system), graphics, and Windows management execute in a separate area (memory address). Each Windows 95 32-bit application executes in its own separate memory address. This design prevents 32-bit applications from interfering with other currently executing 32-bit, 16-bit, or DOS applications.

However, the 16-bit Windows applications all run in the same memory address within the System VM. This design aspect of the Windows 95 architecture was done to maintain downward compatibility with the old Windows 3.x 16-bit Windows-based applications. So, although Windows 95 is compatible with the older Windows 3.x applications, it doesn't offer any better protection against misbehaving 16-bit applications. That is, a misbehaving 16-bit application can still bring down all currently executing 16-bit applications.

> **Note**
>
> DOS applications execute in separate virtual machines (VMs). Windows 3.x (16-bit) applications execute in the System VM, in a single address space. Windows 95 (32-bit) applications run in the System VM, but in separate address spaces.
>
> DOS applications can't bring down the system, other DOS applications, or other Windows (16- or 32-bit) applications. Windows 3.x (16-bit) applications can bring down other 16-bit applications. Windows 95 (32-bit) applications can't bring down other 32-bit, 16-bit, or DOS applications.

Multitasking Your Applications

Running multiple programs at the same time is called *multitasking*. Windows 95 provides a multitasking feature that enables multiple applications to run concurrently by sharing processor cycles. A *processor cycle* is a time slice that the operating system gives a program so that the program can use the CPU, or central processing unit. In Windows 95, this enables you to print a document while sending e-mail and editing a spreadsheet at the same time. Under the PC cover, all three applications are sharing CPU time, one slice at a time.

First, you need to familiarize yourself with some terms:

- A *process* is an executing application.

- A *thread* is a unit of execution within a process, such as one task within a process.

> **Note**
>
> Windows 95 supports multitasking on one microprocessor. Windows 95 doesn't support *Symmetric Multiprocessing* (SMP), which allows the use of multiple microprocessors within one PC. Windows NT and OS/2 Warp do support SMP.

In Windows 95, each executing DOS and Windows application is a single process. For example, if you have Word for Windows 95, Paradox for DOS, and Lotus 1-2-3 for Windows 3.x running, the CPU is handling three processes (in addition to the work of the operating system). Within a process, Windows 95 allows 32-bit applications to schedule individual threads of execution. This is called *multi-threaded processing*.

How an application multitasks depends on the type of application (DOS, 16-bit, or 32-bit). For DOS and 32-bit applications, Windows 95 uses *preemptive multitasking*. In preemptive multitasking, each thread is executed for a preset time period, or until another thread with a higher priority is ready to execute. The Windows 95 Task Scheduler manages multitasking and ensures that no one application monopolizes the processor. At any time, the operating system can *preempt* (take control away from) an application and hand the system resources to another application with a higher priority task.

For Windows 3.x (16-bit) applications, Windows 95 uses a *cooperative multitasking* system. In cooperative multitasking, the program (rather than the operating system) is in control of CPU scheduling. Although programs should yield to the operating system after a reasonable amount of time, we have all encountered the Windows 3.x program which fails to return control of the system resources back to the operating system, and eventually locks up the entire system. Windows 95 uses the less reliable cooperative multitasking model to provide compatibility with existing 16-bit Windows 3.x programs.

For Windows 95 (32-bit) applications that choose to schedule their own threads of execution (multi-threaded processing), Windows 95 again uses the cooperative multitasking method. Up to 32 levels of priority can be assigned.

Note

Windows 95 uses cooperative multitasking for multi-threaded processing, whereas Windows NT uses the more reliable preemptive multitasking method. It remains to be seen how many 32-bit Windows 95 applications lock themselves up by failing to return CPU control after a reasonable time to another thread within their process slot.

How Applications Communicate

Applications communicate with the operating system via the Windows 95 messaging system. The messaging system passes information between the hardware, the applications, and the operating system. For example, when a user moves the mouse, Windows 95 converts the hardware interrupt into a message which is sent to the appropriate message queue.

Caution

Although each DOS and 32-bit application has its own message queue, all the 16-bit applications share one common message queue. Thus, if a 16-bit application hangs, all running 16-bit applications must wait until the hung application is cleared. If the hung application is not cleared, all 16-bit applications may lose their messages.

Summarizing the Application Environment

Table 15.1 summarizes the key architectural features in the Windows 95 application execution environment by application type. Review the table, and refer back to previous text as needed to ensure your understanding of these key concepts before proceeding with Chapters 16 and 17. Once you understand these concepts, it will be easier to understand how to best use DOS, Windows 3.x, and Windows 95 software in the Windows 95 operating environment.

Table 15.1 Application Execution Environment

Feature	DOS Application	16-Bit Application	32-Bit Application
Virtual Machine (VM)	One MS-DOS VM per executing DOS application System VM	All run within a single memory address	All run in System VM executing DOS, but each in a separate memory address
Multitasking	Preemptive scheduling	Cooperative scheduling	Preemptive scheduling
Multi-processing	None	None threaded	Yes, uses cooperative scheduling
Messaging	Each has its own message queue	All share a common message queue	Each has its own message queue

Executing DOS Applications

On a Windows 95 computer, DOS is available in two flavors:

- DOS session (multitasking)
- MS-DOS mode (single task, real mode)

The DOS session starts from within Windows 95. You can switch the DOS session between a windowed view and full-screen view. From a DOS session, you can switch back to Windows 95 and to any other currently running applications. Windows 95 is a multitasking environment, and each DOS session runs in a separate MS-DOS VM. In a windowed DOS session, Windows 95 even provides a toolbar for quick access to cut, copy, paste, property sheets, and fonts. The property sheets are similar to the old Windows 3.x PIF files. The property sheets for DOS sessions allow you to control the MS-DOS VM and what the DOS program sees (you can even hide Windows 95 from the DOS program!).

The MS-DOS mode can start from within Windows 95, or can be accessed during bootup. *MS-DOS mode* (also known as real mode) is a single-task environment. No other programs are in memory, so you can't switch over to another program. Windows 95 leaves a small footprint of itself in memory so that when you close your DOS application (or type **exit** at the DOS prompt),

Windows 95 can load automatically. In MS-DOS mode, you cannot cut, copy, or paste to the Clipboard. The DOS application has complete control of the CPU and all resources. For DOS programs that you start from MS-DOS mode, you can specify certain properties. Properties that require Windows 95, such as fonts, memory management, and screen display are not available. You can, however, specify a custom AUTOEXEC.BAT and CONFIG.SYS to be run for each DOS program running in MS-DOS mode (no more creating separate boot disks for finicky DOS programs that require special treatment!).

In the following sections, you learn how to do the following:

- Display and work with the DOS command prompt

- Start a DOS application from within Windows 95

Displaying the DOS Command Prompt

Although most of the time Windows 95 provides tools for your computing needs via a user-friendly graphical interface, there may be times when you need to or (for us old-timers) want to access DOS. You don't need to exit Windows 95 to access the DOS command prompt or issue a DOS command.

Tip

To start a Windows 95 program from the command prompt, type the new DOS command **START** followed by the program name.

To display the DOS command prompt from within Windows 95, follow these steps:

1. Click the Start button, then choose Programs, MS-DOS Prompt. By default, Windows 95 opens a windowed DOS session (see fig. 15.2).

Note

You can also start a DOS session by clicking the Start button, choosing Run, typing the word **command,** and pressing Enter.

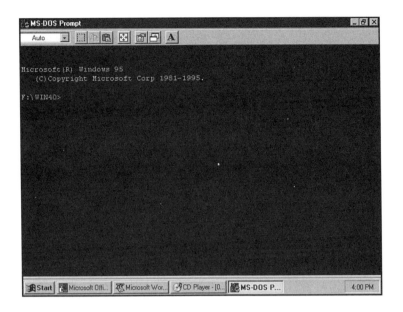

Fig. 15.2
The windowed DOS session provides you with more control over the DOS environment.

2. If you prefer working in a DOS full-screen session, press Alt+Enter (see fig. 15.3).

Fig. 15.3
A full-screen DOS session lets you see more on-screen.

3. If you need to switch between the DOS session and Windows 95, press Alt+Tab.

4. When you finish, type **exit** at the DOS prompt to close the DOS session or, if working in a DOS window, click the (X) close button in the top right-hand corner.

Caution

Be careful when using the X button to close a windowed DOS session. Any open DOS applications with unsaved data or open data files could result in data loss or file corruption. Always close data files and end DOS applications before using the X button.

Tip

Create a shortcut to DOS and place it on the desktop for quick access to DOS.

Note

To display help for a DOS command, type the name of the command you want followed by a space and **/?**. For example, type **md /?** to display help text on the MAKE DIRECTORY (MD) command.

Adding the pipe character | and the word **More** to the end of the statement displays help text one screen at a time. For example:

    md /? | more

To start the computer at the DOS prompt in MS-DOS mode, follow these steps:

1. Choose Start.

2. Choose Shut Down.

3. Choose Restart the Computer in MS-DOS Mode. A full-screen, single application DOS prompt appears.

4. When you finish, type **exit** to start Windows 95.

> **Note**
>
> You can also enter MS-DOS mode when your machine boots up. When the message Starting Windows 95 appears, press F8 and select Command Prompt Only to boot up the computer in the real-mode version of DOS. When you finish, type **exit** to start Windows 95.

Working with DOS Commands

The Windows 95 set of DOS commands are functionally the same as in prior versions of DOS. You can view a list of these commands by opening up the \WINDOWS\COMMANDS folder. File manipulation commands such as COPY, DIR, and RENAME have been enhanced to support long file names. To use a long file name in DOS, enclose the long file name in quotes; for example,

◀ See "Preparing for Installa-tion," p. 29

◀ See "Installa-tion Options," p. 33

◀ See "Determin-ing Your Boot Configuration," p. 37

```
RENAME eastsale.wk1 "Eastcoast Sales.wk1"
```

> **Caution**
>
> Be careful when using long file names. Although the Windows 95 DOS commands support long file names, existing DOS and Windows 3.x programs do not. Further-more, be careful when using a file in Windows 95 with a long file name and then accessing the file in a DOS or Windows 3.x program. Doing so deletes the long file name!

The DIR command has been enhanced to display a seventh column which shows the long file name. DIR also sports a new command line switch called verbose: **/v**. The verbose switch displays additional information such as file attributes and last access date stamp.

Windows 95 DOS also supports the *Universal Naming Convention* (UNC). UNC makes it easier to refer to and use networked resources such as printers and network folders (you no longer need to map folders and remember those cryptic addresses). For example, to copy a file to a shared network folder named "Accounting Sales Data," you would issue the following command line:

```
COPY "Eastcoast Sales.wk1" "\\Accounting Sales Data"
```

III

Setting Up Software

Many of the DOS commands included in prior versions of DOS are not included in Windows 95 because they are no longer needed. In these cases, Windows 95 provides the feature elsewhere. Furthermore, if your computer did not have DOS installed prior to installing Windows 95, you will not have some of the older DOS commands that Windows 95 does not need, but leaves in the old DOS folder.

A powerful new command included in Windows 95 is the START command. You can use START to launch DOS and Windows programs from the DOS command prompt (START is not available in MS-DOS mode). Two syntax forms can be used. The first supplies the program name. The second syntax supplies the document name. For the document name to launch the program and display the document, the file name extension must be properly registered:

```
START [options] program [arg...]
START [options] document.ext
```

The options available include

- **/m**. Run the new program minimized (in the background).

- **/max**. Run the new program maximized (in the foreground).

- **/r**. Run the new program restored (in the foreground). [default]

- **/w**. Does not return until the other program exits.

Suppose that files with the extension DOC are registered as Word for Windows files. Then issuing the following command statement automatically loads Word for Windows and the document SALES.DOC:

```
START sales.doc
```

Using START at the command prompt to load a DOS program actually opens a new MS-DOS VM for that program. If instead you type the name of the DOS program without the command START, the DOS program loads in the current MS-DOS VM.

Note

If you type the DOS command VER at the command prompt, the version information that appears is Windows 95. However, DOS programs which ask internally for the DOS version get the number 7. This could cause conflicts with DOS programs that only work for a specific DOS version number.

Some DOS commands should NOT be used in Windows 95. You should avoid using the following commands in Windows 95:

- CHKDSK /F. You can run this command at the DOS prompt, but not in Windows 95.

- FDISK. Avoid running at the DOS prompt. It can't be used when Windows 95 is running.

- RECOVER. This command exists from an older version of DOS, and doesn't work well with Windows 95 or at the command prompt.

Tip

To configure the DOS command line sessions, set file properties for COMMAND.COM, which is located in the Window's COMMAND folder.

Starting a DOS Program

Starting a DOS program takes a few more steps than you may be used to, but it does have the advantage of being less cryptic than navigating the DOS prompt and cryptic command lines.

To start a DOS program, follow these steps:

1. Open the My Computer folder.

2. Locate the program file.

3. Double-click the program file.

You can also start a DOS program by using any of the following options:

- Choose Run from the Start menu

- Type the START command at a DOS command prompt

- Create a shortcut on the desktop or menu

Working in a DOS Window

When you work in a DOS window, Windows 95 provides you with a very helpful toolbar for easy access to the following features:

- Copy, cut, and paste to and from DOS windows

- Change fonts and font sizes

- Switch between exclusive and foreground processing
- Change property sheets without leaving the DOS window

> **Note**
>
> You cannot paste text into a DOS program when it is running in full-screen mode.

> **Tip**
>
> To select text by dragging the cursor over the selection, open the Properties sheet for the DOS program, select the Misc tab, and click QuickEdit.

To view the toolbar, click the MS-DOS icon in the title bar and click Toolbar (refer to fig. 15.2).

Configuring DOS Applications

In Windows 3.x, DOS applications were configured by editing a *Program Information File* (PIF). The PIF file had to be manually created and maintained by the user via the PIF Editor. This was cumbersome at best. Windows 95 automates the PIF file creation and moves the configuration maintenance into a series of property sheets.

When you first start a DOS application, Windows searches for a PIF file with the same name as the executable file. If Windows finds an existing PIF file, Windows uses the PIF file settings. If no PIF file exists yet, Windows uses default settings to control the DOS application. Windows 95 uses a database of known DOS application settings to create the automatic PIF. The PIF files are viewed and maintained via the property sheets.

> **Note**
>
> Windows 95 stores all PIFs in a hidden PIF folder in the Windows 95 directory. This keeps novice users from inadvertently altering the actual PIF files.

Displaying DOS Property Sheets

You set properties for a DOS program the same way you set properties for any object in Windows 95—by right-clicking the object and choosing Properties.

Windows 95 then displays the property sheet for the DOS application (see fig. 15.4). DOS program properties are organized into six property pages. You'll learn more about each of the property pages in the following sections.

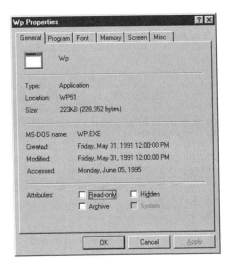

Fig. 15.4

You control how DOS programs execute in Windows 95 by setting program properties.

To display the property sheet, follow these steps:

1. Open the My Computer folder.

2. Locate the DOS file, and right-click it.

3. Choose Properties. Windows 95 displays the property sheet for that DOS file (refer to fig. 15.4).

Tip

To display property sheets while running the DOS program session, press Alt+space bar and choose Properties.

III

Setting Up Software

Setting General Properties

The General property page (refer to fig. 15.4) displays the file name, size, location, file type, and other general information. The only configuration settings that you can change are the file attributes. Changing file attributes here is identical to using the DOS ATTRIB command at a DOS prompt. Table 15.2 describes each file attribute setting.

Table 15.2 File Attribute Settings

Attribute	Description
Read-only	File can be read, moved and copied, but not changed or erased.
Archive	Marks a file as having been changed since it was last backed up.
Hidden	File will not display in directory listings. Most DOS commands such as COPY and DEL won't work on hidden files.
System	Marks a file as belonging to the operating system (Windows 95 or DOS). System files are not shown in directory listings. Currently, Windows 95 does not allow you to set the System attribute here. However, if a file has the system attribute set, it will appear checked although dimmed.

Setting Program Properties

The Program properties page (see fig. 15.5) allows you to control many application settings such as the command line, working directory, shortcut key, and icon. From the Program properties page, you can click the Advanced button to configure how Windows 95 emulates the DOS environment for this program. Clicking the Change Icon button allows you to browse through icon files and select a new icon for the program.

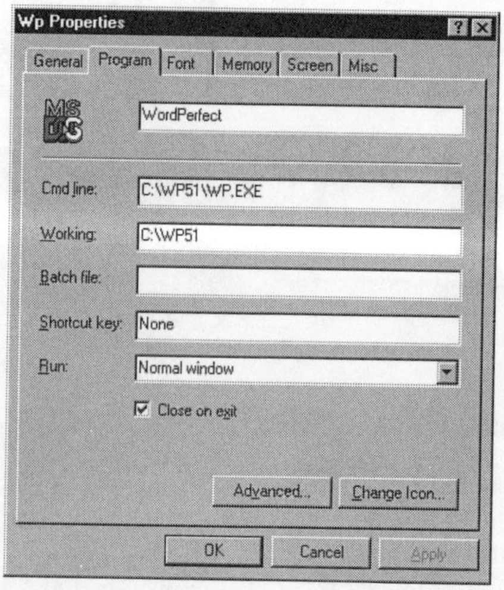

Fig. 15.5
On the Program properties page, you can specify the working folder.

To set Program properties, follow these steps:

1. Open the property folder for the desired DOS program.

2. Edit the name text box as needed.

3. Edit the Cmd Line as needed.

4. Edit the Working folder as needed.

5. If you would like to run a batch file each time this program executes, enter the name of the Batch File.

6. If you would like to assign a Shortcut Key, press Ctrl and/or Alt and the other key.

> **Note**
>
> Assigning a shortcut key to a DOS program gives you quick access to your favorite DOS programs. You can use the shortcut key to start the program or switch back to it once it is running.
>
> Windows 95 contains many shortcut keys (called *access keys*), so you need to be careful when assigning your own shortcut keys. Here is a list of the rules:
>
> - Use Ctrl and/or Alt and another key (for example, Alt+W).
>
> - The other key cannot be Esc, Enter, Tab, space bar, Print Screen, or Backspace.
>
> - No other program can use this key combination.
>
> - If the shortcut key is the same as an access key used by a Windows program, the access key won't work (the shortcut key does work).

7. From the Run drop-down list, select the window size: Normal window, Maximized (full screen window), or Minimized (a button on the taskbar).

8. If you want the MS-DOS window to stay open after you exit the program, deselect the Close On Exit box. Otherwise, Windows 95 will automatically close the MS-DOS window on exit.

9. Click OK to save your changes, or Apply to save the changes without closing the Properties sheet.

Setting Advanced Program Properties

The Advanced Program Settings sheet (see fig. 15.6) allows you to configure the DOS environment in which the DOS program will run. You can hide

III

Setting Up Software

Windows 95 from the DOS program, allow Windows 95 to switch to MS-DOS mode as needed, or require that the DOS program always be run in MS-DOS mode. Table 15.3 describes the Advanced Property settings available.

Fig. 15.6
Use the Advanced Program Settings sheet to control the DOS program execution environment.

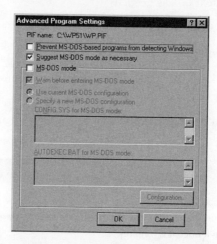

By default, DOS programs run from Windows 95 in a DOS window. Alternatively, DOS programs can be executed in MS-DOS mode (also called *single application mode* and *real mode*). In MS-DOS mode, the DOS program controls all system resources. Before running a program in MS-DOS mode, Windows 95 closes all active Windows and DOS programs. Only a small portion of Windows 95 remains in memory so that Windows 95 can reload itself into memory when you exit the program. Setting a program up to use MS-DOS mode is the same as shutting down Windows 95, restarting in MS-DOS mode, and then re-booting your machine to Windows 95. MS-DOS mode is usually used for DOS programs such as DOS games that won't run under Windows.

Note

Windows 95 property sheets exist for all DOS programs, whether started in MS-DOS mode, from the command prompt, or as a Windows 95 DOS session. For those applications set up to run in MS-DOS mode, many properties do not apply and are therefore not available. When MS-DOS mode is selected, only the following properties are enabled:

■ *General*. File attributes.

■ *Program*. Icon text, command line, close on exit, change icon, and the advanced MS-DOS mode options.

Font, Memory, Screen, and Misc sheets are blank.

Table 15.3 Advanced Program Settings

Setting	Description
Prevent MS-DOS-Based Programs From Detecting Windows	Hides Windows 95 from DOS program. Not enabled if MS-DOS mode is selected.
Suggest MS-DOS Mode As Necessary	Windows 95 automatically detects if DOS program runs better in MS-DOS mode. If so, Windows 95 executes a wizard to set up a custom icon to run the program. Not enabled if MS-DOS mode is selected.
MS-DOS Mode	Runs the program in MS-DOS mode.
Warn Before Entering MS-DOS Mode	Windows 95 displays a warning message that it will close all programs before running MS-DOS mode.
Use Current MS-DOS Configuration	By default, Windows 95 uses the existing AUTOEXEC.BAT and CONFIG.SYS files when it enters MS-DOS mode.
Specify a New MS-DOS Mode	Select to create alternative CONFIG.SYS and AUTOEXEC.BAT files. Enables CONFIG.SYS and AUTOEXEC.BAT text boxes and Configuration button.
CONFIG.SYS for MS-DOS mode	Edit as needed to create custom CONFIG.SYS file for MS-DOS mode.
AUTOEXEC.BAT for MS-DOS mode	Edit as needed to create custom AUTOEXEC.BAT file for MS-DOS mode.
Configuration	Instead of typing in commands, click this button to have Windows 95 create custom configuration files for you.

Tip

If a DOS program detects Windows 95 and won't run properly, select Prevent MS-DOS-based Programs From Detecting Windows from the Advanced Program Settings sheet.

III

Setting Up Software

To allocate all system resources to a DOS program (run in real mode, single application mode), follow these steps:

1. Open the Properties folder for the DOS program.

2. Select the Program tab.

3. Click the Ad_v_anced button.

4. Choose _MS_-DOS Mode.

5. If you do not want the warning message, deselect _W_arn Before Entering MS-DOS Mode.

6. If you do not want to use the current MS-DOS configuration, choose _S_pecify a New MS-DOS Configuration.

7. For manual configuration, type or edit configuration commands in the CO_N_FIG.SYS and _A_UTOEXEC.BAT text boxes.

8. To have Windows 95 generate the configuration commands for you, click the Con_f_iguration button. The Select MS-DOS Configuration Options dialog box appears, as shown in figure 15.7. Select the desired options and click OK to return to the Advanced Program Settings dialog box.

9. Click OK to return to the Program properties page.

10. Click OK to save your changes, or click _A_pply to save the changes without closing the Properties sheet.

Fig. 15.7

For programs starting in MS-DOS mode, you can create custom AUTOEXEC.BAT and CONFIG.SYS files by selecting options.

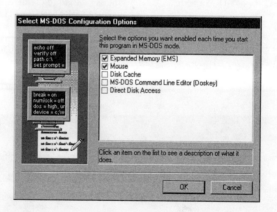

Changing Program Icons

As with every object in Windows 95, DOS-based programs have a graphical picture called an *icon* associated with the program file. By default, the icon can appear in the following places:

- Within file lists

- When you press Alt+Tab to switch between running applications

- On the Start menu

- On the taskbar

If the program file doesn't specify an icon, Windows 95 uses the MS-DOS icon. You can change the icon by displaying the DOS Program property page and clicking the <u>C</u>hange Icon button. Windows 95 displays the Change Icon dialog box, as shown in figure 15.8. To view the contents of another icon file, type in the file name or use the <u>B</u>rowse button to find the file. After selecting the icon, click OK twice to save your changes.

Fig. 15.8
The PIFMGR.DLL file contains many icons to which you can assign a program file.

Note

You can find more icons in the following folders:

\SYSTEM\SHELL32.DLL	\MORICONS.DLL
\SYSTEM\ICONLIB.DLL	\PROGMAN.EXE

Setting Font Properties

A new feature in Windows 95 which is not supported in Windows 3.x is the ability to control the font size and appearance. Windows 95 allows you to use any bitmapped or TrueType font installed on your computer. The font settings work in full-screen and windowed DOS sessions. Figure 15.9 shows the Font property page, which you can use to improve the display of your DOS sessions.

Fig. 15.9
You can reduce eye strain by changing the font type and size.

In addition to giving you control over the font type and size, Windows 95 provides an Auto font size feature (found in the Font Size drop-down list) which automatically adjusts the font size to fit the size of the DOS window. This allows you to see all 80 characters, even when you reduce the size of the DOS window.

Tip

Use the Auto font size setting to automatically scale DOS session windows.

To set font properties for a DOS program, follow these steps:

1. Open the Properties folder for the DOS program.

2. Select the Font page.

3. Select the available types to list in the Font Size scroll box: Bitmap Only, TrueType Only, or Both Font Types.

4. Select the desired font size in the Font Size scroll box. Windows 95 shows you what your selection will look like in the Window Preview and Font Preview boxes.

5. Click OK to save your changes, or click <u>A</u>pply to save the changes without closing the Properties sheet.

Setting Memory Properties

The settings on the Memory page (see fig. 15.10) control the way the DOS application uses the PC's memory. Settings are provided to control conventional, expanded (EMS), and extended (XMS) memory. Note that since each DOS application executes in its own MS-DOS VM, the memory settings apply only to that DOS application. Other executing DOS, Windows 3.x, and Windows 95 applications are unaffected by these memory settings. Table 15.4 describes the Memory property settings.

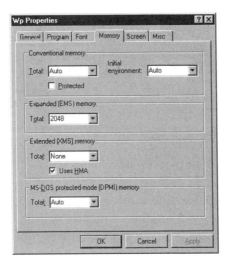

Fig. 15.10

You can customize the memory configuration for each DOS application.

III

Setting Up Software

Table 15.4   Memory Settings

Setting	Description
Conventional Memory	
<u>T</u>otal	Amount of conventional (lower 640K) memory program requires. If unsure, choose Auto.
Initial En<u>v</u>ironment	Number of bytes to reserve for COMMAND.COM. If set to Auto, the size is determined by the SHELL= line in CONFIG.SYS.
<u>P</u>rotected	If selected, system is protected from any problems caused by the program. The program may run slower when this is selected.

(continues)

Table 15.4 Continued	
Setting	**Description**
Expanded (EMS) Memory	
To_tal	Maximum amount of expanded memory allotted to program. The Auto setting sets no limit. If you experience problems, try setting to 8192.
Extended (XMS) Memory	
Tota_l	Maximum amount of extended memory allotted to program. The Auto setting sets no limit. If you experience problems, try setting to 8192.
Uses _HMA	Indicates whether program can use the High Memory Area (HMA).
MS-_DOS Protected Mode (DPMI) Memory	
Total:	Maximum amount of DOS protected mode memory (DPMI) to allocate to the program. The Auto setting lets Windows 95 configure based on your setup.

Setting Screen Properties

The settings on the Screen page (see fig. 15.11) control the way the DOS application appears. You can set up the DOS program to load in a window or full-screen—with or without a toolbar—and determine how many lines of text should appear. In addition, you can set display performance features such as dynamic memory allocation and fast ROM emulation. Table 15.5 describes the screen properties.

Fig. 15.11
By turning on dynamic memory allocation, you can speed up the display performance of a DOS program.

Table 15.5 Display Settings	
Setting	**Description**
Usage	
<u>F</u>ull-Screen	Starts program in a full-screen mode.
<u>W</u>indow	Starts program in a window.
Initial Si<u>z</u>e	Sets the number of screen lines displayed (25, 43, or 50 lines). A setting of `Default` uses the program's number of lines.
Window	
Display <u>T</u>oolbar	If running in a window, checking this box displays the toolbar.
<u>R</u>estore Settings On Startup	If running in a window, restores the font and screen settings when you close the program.
Performance	
Fast ROM <u>E</u>mulation	Controls the read-only video memory usage. Select this to speed up screen display and refresh. If the program has problems writing text to the screen, deselect this setting.
Dynamic <u>M</u>emory Allocation	Controls amount of memory available to switch between text and graphics mode in a DOS program. If you want to maximize the amount of memory available to other programs while this program runs, check this box. If you want to maximize the memory available to this program, clear this setting.

Setting Miscellaneous Properties

The remaining DOS program properties are grouped under the Misc page (see fig. 15.12). On the Misc page, you can control foreground and background settings, the mouse, shortcut keys, and other items. Table 15.6 describes the miscellaneous settings.

III

Setting Up Software

Fig. 15.12
The Misc page
allows you to
resolve conflicts
between Windows
shortcut keys and
DOS programs.

Table 15.6	Misc Settings
Setting	**Description**
Foreground	
Allow Screen Saver	Allows screen saver to work even when this program is active.
Background	
Always Suspend	Prevents program from using system resources when not active.
Idle Sensitivity	Specifies how long Windows allows the program to remain idle before redirecting CPU resources to other programs. Slide toward Low to give the DOS program a longer idle time (more resources). Slide toward High to take resources away from the DOS program sooner.
Mouse	
Quick Edit	Enables the Quick Edit feature which allows you to select text for cut and copy functions with the mouse (otherwise, you must mark text first).
Exclusive Mode	When selected, mouse is controlled exclusively by the DOS program. Mouse is no longer available in Windows.
Termination	
Warn If Still Active	When selected, displays warning message if you try to close a running DOS application.

Setting	Description
Other	
_F_ast Pasting	Enables the fast-paste feature. Could cause problems with older DOS programs.
Windows Shortcut _K_eys	Deselect the desired Windows shortcut key to disable the shortcut key when this program is running.

Configuring DOS Games for Windows 95

DOS games are by far the greatest challenge of Windows 95. By nature, DOS-based games (especially graphically intense multimedia games) want full control of all your computer resources. And, they like to be in charge of CONFIG.SYS and AUTOEXEC.BAT, too. Running a DOS-based game in older versions of DOS often required creating a separate boot disk to properly configure the game (sometimes you even needed a separate boot disk for each game!). But to die-hard gamers, the trade-offs were worth the end result—a realistic, high-quality video and sound experience.

In fact, software vendors who write game software prefer to work in DOS for this simple fact alone. DOS allows the game software engineer to be in complete control of all hardware and the operating system, which allows the gamers to push the hardware to the edge. Often game software bypasses DOS and works directly with the hardware to achieve a higher-quality game. Windows 3.x could not handle this bypassing. The Windows 3.x services and libraries interfere with game software execution. Consequently, game software engineers avoided developing in Windows 3.x, or developed very basic games for Windows 3.x.

When Microsoft began designing Windows 95, they failed to resolve the issues in DOS and Windows 3.x. The first beta of Windows 95 released to the industry in 1994 did not address the needs of game software and hardware. Hardware designers wanted an operating system that would let game developers take advantage of their sound and video board's special features. Soon after that, The PC Games Consortium formed and Microsoft began working closely with it to develop Windows 95 as a solid gaming platform. Microsoft has since created the Game Software Developer Kit for Windows 95. As a result, many DOS-based game vendors such as Origin will port their DOS games to Windows 95, completely bypassing Windows 3.x development.

▶ See "What Windows 95 Software Offers," p. 405

▶ See "Using the Registry," p. 407

▶ See "Optimizing Windows 95," p. 410

III

Setting Up Software

Another vendor, Spectrum HoloByte (makers of STTNG Final Unity), says it will design its long-awaited Falcon 4.0 for Windows 95.

For the existing DOS-based games, Windows 95 offers many benefits. The MS-DOS virtual machine design keeps each DOS game in a separate VM for which you can set properties. If running the DOS game from a Windows 95 session does not work well, you can always run the game in MS-DOS mode. Furthermore, you can create custom AUTOEXEC.BAT and CONFIG.SYS files for each game, rather than shuffling DOS boot disks back and forth. ❖

Chapter 16

Using Windows 3.x Software

by Diane Tinney

Although Windows 95 32-bit software promises to out-perform today's Windows 3.x and DOS software, presently most companies run Windows 3.x software. Its programs are the product of years of performance tuning; businesses and home computer users have invested millions of dollars in Windows 3.x software. In contrast, very few Windows 95 products are available, and when the 32-bit applications are released, they will be brand new and probably need some breaking in.

So, at least for the near future, most of us will be installing, configuring, and using Windows 3.x software in Windows 95. The good news is that Windows 3.x software runs virtually unchanged in Windows 95. With the exception of older Windows 3.0 and perhaps shareware/freeware programs, all third party and custom-developed Windows 3.x software that ran well in Windows 3.x should run well—or better—in Windows 95.

In this chapter, you learn the following:

- How to install Windows 3.x software

- Changes in the user-interface

- How to access the property sheets

- How to view and edit INI files

- Areas that optimize performance

- How to recover from application problems

Setting Up Windows 3.x Software

Windows 3.x applications (also called *Win16 applications*) install and execute in Windows 95 without modification. If you installed Windows 95 to an existing Windows 3.x directory, Windows 95 automatically set up and configured the existing Win16 applications for you. If you installed Windows 95 to a different directory, you need to install (or re-install) the Windows application in Windows 95.

◀ See "Exploring the Windows 95 Architecture," p. 366

◀ See "Multitasking Your Applications," p. 369

◀ See "How Applications Communicate," p. 370

In this section, you learn how to install Windows 95 software and how Windows 95 sets up Windows 3.x software.

Installing Windows 3.x Software

The process for installing Windows 3.x software in Windows 95 is essentially the same as in Windows 3.x. Instead of using the File menu's Run command in Program Manager to install programs, in Windows 95 you use the Start menu's Run command. Alternatively, you could use the Add/Remove Programs feature in the Control Panel. Either way, the installation works the same.

Caution

Be careful when installing or updating Windows 3.x programs that share components (such as MS Graph which is shared by Word and Excel). Setup programs cannot update a component that is being used by a running application. To avoid conflicts, it is best to shut down related programs (and any critical applications/data) before installing or updating software.

To install Windows 3.x software, follow these steps:

1. Start Windows 95.

2. Place the installation disk in the appropriate drive.

3. Choose Start.

4. Choose Run.

5. Enter the full path and name of the installation file (usually SETUP.EXE or INSTALL.EXE), or click Browse to locate the file.

6. Click OK.

7. Follow the Windows 3.x installation instructions and screen prompts.

8. When installation completes, you return to Windows 95.

Figure 16.1 shows a newly installed Windows 3.1 application called Day-Timer Organizer. Notice that instead of a program group, a folder appears with two icons: a shortcut icon that launches the application, and a shortcut icon that uninstalls the application. In addition, Windows 95 added Day-Timer Organizer to the Program group on the Start menu. Within the Day-Timer Organizer menu folder appear the two shortcuts for launching and uninstalling.

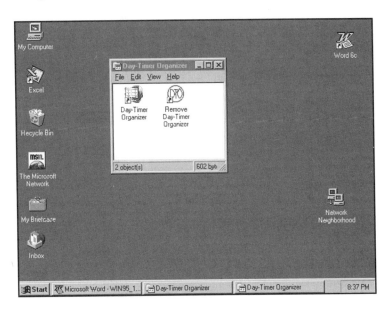

Fig. 16.1
Windows 95 automatically creates shortcut icons for your Windows 3.x programs.

Executing Windows 3.x Programs

When you execute a Windows 3.x program, you notice a few interface changes. First, the window (even in full-screen mode), has the Windows 95 title bar at the top and (by default) the Windows 95 task bar at the bottom (see fig. 16.2). The next interface change that you notice is that menus work like menus in Windows 95—a single mouse click activates the menu. Running the mouse pointer down a menu moves the Select bar. This happens because Windows applications rely on the graphical operating system to display common user interface items such as title bars, drop-down lists, and dialog box controls. As a result, your Windows 3.x programs look and feel like Windows 95 programs.

Although many of the graphical interface features change to a Windows 95 look and feel, the features behave in the same way. For example, the

Windows 3.x control box is replaced by an icon in the top-left corner of the title bar of each window. Clicking this icon displays the familiar menu of window control options (see fig. 16.3).

Fig. 16.2
Windows 3.x programs that are set up in Windows 95 automatically incorporate the Windows 95 GUI look and feel.

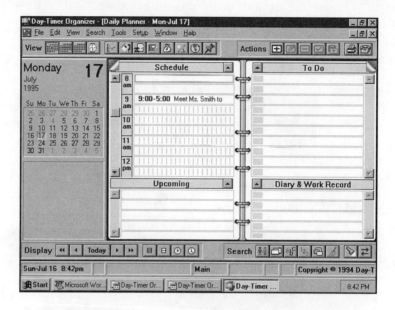

Fig. 16.3
You can still press Alt+F4 to close a program.

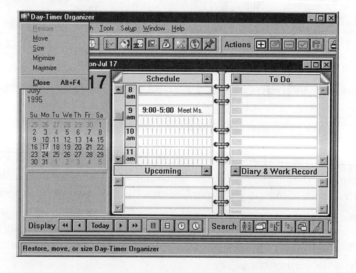

Accessing Windows 3.x Property Sheets

Since Window applications share a common configuration, their property sheets consist of only a General Properties sheet, and possibly a Version sheet. All other properties, such as memory, display, and fonts are managed by Windows 95 in other areas.

To display the property sheets for a Windows 3.x program, right-click the file name and choose Properties. Figure 16.4 shows the General Property sheet for the Day-Timer Organizer program file DTORG.EXE. The only settings you can change here are the file attributes.

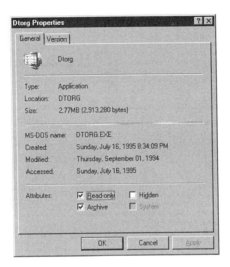

Fig. 16.4
The General Properties sheet for a Windows 3.x program displays the same information as for a DOS program.

Figure 16.5 shows the contents of the Version Properties sheet. Note that you cannot change any settings here; you can only view the program information.

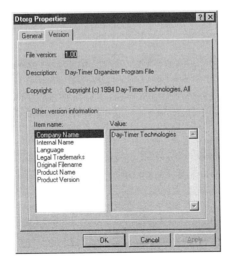

Fig. 16.5
The Version Properties sheet displays information such as the internal Windows 95 program name.

III

Setting Up Software

Uninstalling INI files

Windows 3.x programs relied on *initialization files* (which have the file extension INI) to load real mode and virtual device drivers during the Windows boot process. Windows 3.x applications often created their own initialization files or edited (without backing up or asking for permission) the Windows initialization files (WIN.INI and SYSTEM.INI). Over the years, as you add, update, and delete Windows 3.x applications, the contents and number of INI files increase. Settings and INI files for obsolete or deleted versions of Windows 3.x programs remain unless you invest the time to extract them manually, or spend the money for a Windows uninstall utility. Recently, a few Windows 3.x programs have begun to address this problem by providing their own "uninstall" routines.

In Windows 95, program configuration and initialization data is kept in a database known as the Registry. Ultimately, the Registry will replace not only the INI files but also the AUTOEXEC.BAT and CONFIG.SYS files. Meanwhile, Windows 95 maintains and uses the INI files to provide full compatibility with Windows 3.x programs. For a full description of the Registry and how to edit the Registry, see Chapter 17, "Using Windows 95 Software."

Note

Almost all of the Windows 95 configuration settings can be made interactively through the Control Panel and other settings folders. Although the data is stored in the Registry, you can (and should) view and set these properties via the Windows 95 graphical dialogs. Areas like Control Panel have built-in safeguards that keep you from making critical errors. An incorrect edit to the Registry database could bring your entire system down.

The INI files can be viewed and edited by using any plain ASCII text editor. Windows 95 provides a new version of the Windows 3.x SYSEDIT.EXE program, which allows you to quickly view and edit all of the setup files. You can find SYSEDIT.EXE in the Windows 95 SYSTEM folder. As you can see in figure 16.6, the Day-Timer installation program edited our WIN.INI file and added special initialization settings.

Tip

Before making any changes, you should make a backup copy of the INI files.

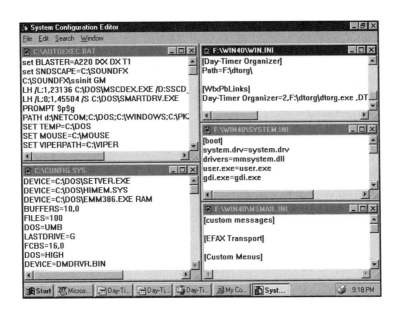

Fig. 16.6
Use the System
Configuration
Editor to check
setup files.

Optimizing for Windows 3.x Software Execution

All of the known tricks on optimizing for Windows 3.x software still apply.
Since Windows 95 runs Windows 3.x software in a Windows 3.x environment, the modifications that worked under Windows 3.x should operate
under Windows 95. So, for example, if your database program worked best
when the INI file contained a special command line, you should continue to
use that command line. For optimization techniques which involve memory
management, swap files, and other AUTOEXEC.BAT and CONFIG.SYS manipulation, you may find that you don't need them. The architecture of Windows 95 enables smoother multitasking, improved memory management,
and better protection for other applications when an application crashes.

You may also find that the Win16 applications perform faster under Windows 95. Although the Win16 applications cannot run at the 32-bit speed,

III

Setting Up Software

they take advantage of the operating system's 32-bit services, such as 32-bit printing and communications. Windows 95 also sports a much improved graphical video handling, which significantly quickens the Windows 3.x applications.

Many factors impact the performance of Windows 3.x programs in Windows 95. The following sections touch upon the areas which yield the greatest improvement.

Work Efficiently

You can optimize performance by working efficiently in Windows 95. Limit the number of applications that you run concurrently. Don't leave open programs that you are not using. Work in a less graphical environment (such as Draft instead of Layout mode). Instead of working in a huge document, break the document down into smaller files.

Use and Configure Hardware Correctly

Choosing the right hardware can make the difference between getting the job done now, or an hour later. Make sure the hardware meets the minimum requirements to run Windows 95. Whenever possible, buy Plug-and-Play components so you won't need to get involved in managing devices and resolving conflicts. For legacy devices (older, non-Plug-and-Play devices), contact the manufacturer for an up-to-date Windows 95 device driver.

Invest In Powerful Hardware

◀ See "Plug and Play Overview," p. 10

If possible, upgrade the PC to a faster processor, with more memory and state-of-the-art communication and multimedia features. The more optimized the hardware is, the more optimized Windows 95 and all your software applications will be.

◀ See "Taking Your System's Inventory," p. 40

Monitor and Maintain Resources

Windows 95 provides many utilities which you can use to periodically check on and improve system resources. The following utility programs can be found under the System Tools folder (Start, Programs, Accessories, System Tools):

- *Disk Defragmentor*. Improves disk access speed.

- *Scan Disk*. Checks disk surface and files for errors.

- *System Monitor*. Reports on performance of system resources.

- *Resource Meter*. Displays percentages of free system, user, and GDI resources.

> **Note**
>
> If your Systems Tools folder does not include all of these tools, you can install them from your Windows 95 Setup disk. Use Add/Remove Programs and select the custom setup option. Select System Tools and click <u>D</u>etails. Select the missing tools to be installed.

Fine-Tune Windows 95

If all else fails, you may need to adjust the Windows 95 system configuration. In the Control Panel folder, the System Properties sheet contains a Performance page. The Performance page allows you to configure file system, graphic, and virtual memory options.

◀ See "Installation Options," p. 33

◀ See "Improving Hard Disk Performance," p. 323

Troubleshooting Application Problems

Typically, the user realizes that an application has a problem when the keyboard or mouse fails to respond, or when Windows 95 displays an error message. Application execution problems are usually caused by one of the following:

- General Protection Fault (GPF)

- Hung application

For assistance in troubleshooting application problems, look in the Help index for the topic "Troubleshooting."

▶ See "Optimizing Windows 95," p. 410

▶ See "Fine-Tuning Virtual Memory," p. 416

Handling a GPF

A *General Protection Fault* (GPF) occurs when an application violates system integrity. The following list provides examples of common GPFs:

- Application tried to use a memory address currently being used by another application.

- Error code returned by a system application programming interface (API).

- A memory fault caused by an invalid reference in memory.

When Windows 95 encounters a GPF, it displays a General Protection Fault message which tells the user which application caused the problem and provides the module name and a reference number. By relaying this information to the application vendor, the problem can be quickly resolved.

III

Setting Up Software

The effect of a GPF on the other applications that are executing depends on whether the offending application is a DOS application, a Windows 16-bit application (Win16), or a Windows 32-bit application (Win32).

GPFs in DOS Applications

Because each DOS application executes in a separate VM, a GPF in one DOS application has no effect on the other DOS, Win16, or Win32 applications currently executing. When the GPF message appears, record the error message information and choose OK to terminate the offending DOS application.

GPFs in Win16 Applications

Because all Win16 applications execute in a single VM, all Win16 application execution ceases until the application which caused the GPF is terminated. When the GPF message appears, record the error message information and choose OK to terminate the offending application. Once the offending application is terminated, the other Win16 applications resume execution.

GPFs in Win32 Applications

Because Win32 applications execute at a separate memory address within the System VM, a GPF in one Win32 application should have no effect on the other DOS, Win16, or Win32 applications currently executing. When the GPF message appears, record the error message information and choose OK to terminate the offending application. Any unsaved data in the offending application will be lost.

When an application is terminated by Windows 95, the normal closing routines are not performed, which could cause problems when you restart the program. For this reason, you may consider contacting the vendor before trying to re-execute the program.

Handling Hung Applications

Applications that are still executing, but fail to respond to system messages, are called *hung applications*. When an application hangs up the computer, the screen may look odd, the mouse may not work, or the keyboard may lock up. As with GPFs, the effect on other applications currently executing depends on whether the offending application is a DOS application, a Windows 16-bit application, or a Windows 32-bit application.

Handling Hung DOS Applications

Because DOS applications execute in a separate VM, a hung DOS application has no effect on the other DOS, Win16, or Win32 applications currently executing.

To end a hung DOS application, follow these steps:

1. Switch back to Windows 95.

2. Display the Properties sheet for the application.

3. Select <u>T</u>erminate the Application.

Handling Hung Win16 Applications

Because all Win16 applications share a common message queue, all running Win16 applications are also hung because they cannot access the message queue. The hung Win16 applications have no effect on any running DOS or Win32 applications.

To end a hung Win16 application, follow these steps:

1. Switch back to the offending Win16 application.

2. Press Ctrl+Alt+Delete. A list of the programs that are not responding to the system appears.

3. Choose <u>E</u>nd Task to terminate the application. Note that data loss is limited to that in the offending application.

Handling Hung Win32 Applications

Because each Win32 application has its own separate message queue, no other DOS, Win16, or Win32 applications are affected.

To terminate a hung Win32 application, follow these steps:

1. Switch back to the offending Win32 application.

2. Press Ctrl+Alt+Delete. A list of the programs that are not responding to the system appears.

3. Choose <u>E</u>nd Task to terminate the application. Note that data loss is limited to that in the offending application.

◀ See "Exploring the Windows 95 Architecture," p. 366

◀ See "Understanding Virtual Machines," p. 366

◀ See "Multitasking Your Applications," p. 369

◀ See "How Applications Communicate," p. 370

> **Note**
>
> Generally, if an application hangs a critical resource, other applications that need that resource are stopped. By terminating the hung application, you free up the resource and allow the stopped applications to resume execution.

III

Setting Up Software

Chapter 17

Using Windows 95 Software

by Diane Tinney

So now you've installed Windows 95. There are many features, particularly the Registry and preemptive multitasking, that you can work with to best optimize the Windows 95 environment for your new 32-bit applications. This chapter starts you down the 32-bit highway.

In this chapter, you learn

- The advantages of using 32-bit Windows 95 software

- How to access and edit the Registry

- How to fine-tune system performance

What Windows 95 Software Offers

The key advantages of Windows 95 software are the following:

- 32-bit processing

- Preemptive multitasking

- Multi-threaded processing

- Easy maintenance

You learn how each feature can save you both time and money.

Fast Processing

The easiest way to understand the difference between 16-bit processing and 32-bit processing is to imagine each as a highway with 16 or 32 lanes.

Imagine your data as buses and cars commuting at rush hour. When the traffic is heavy and the heat is on, 32 lanes provide for more throughput, fewer accidents, and less stress on system resources. In your computer, the Windows 95 operating system is already running at 32-bit speed. The more 32-bit applications that you use, the more work that gets done, fewer GPFs and less stress on the computer resources.

As covered at the beginning of Chapter 15, DOS applications execute in separate virtual machines (VMs). Windows 3.x (16-bit) applications execute in the System VM in a single address space. Windows 95 (32-bit) applications also run in the System VM, but in separate address spaces.

◀ See "Understanding Virtual Machines," p. 366

◀ See "How Applications Communicate," p. 370

DOS applications can't bring down the system, other DOS applications, or other Windows (16- or 32-bit) applications. Windows 3.x (16-bit) applications can bring down other 16-bit applications. Windows 95 (32-bit) applications can't bring down other 32-bit, 16-bit, or DOS applications.

The fastest, best protection exists for the 32-bit applications, which execute within the 32-bit Windows 95 operating system.

Preemptive Multitasking

The 32-bit applications use *preemptive multitasking*, where each thread is executed for a preset time period, or until another thread with a higher priority is ready to execute. The Windows 95 Task Scheduler manages multitasking and ensures that no one application monopolizes the processor. At any time, the operating system can *preempt* (take control away from) an application and hand the CPU to another application with a higher priority task.

This is better than the quirky Windows 3.x (16-bit) applications, which use a *cooperative multitasking system*. In cooperative multitasking, the program (rather than the operating system) is in control of CPU scheduling. Although programs should yield to the operating system after a reasonable amount of time, we have all encountered the Windows 3.x program which fails to return control and eventually locks up the entire system.

Multi-Threaded Processing

Windows 95 32-bit applications can take advantage of *multi-threaded processing* (schedule their own threads of execution). Multi-threaded processing is not available for DOS or Win16 applications. The advantage of multi-threading is that you get to do your work faster. For example, printing a document in Word for Windows 95 is much faster than in Windows 3.1, and you get control of your document back quicker because Word for Windows 95 takes advantage of multi-threaded processing for print jobs.

Easier Maintenance

Consolidation of the system initialization and setup files into a single data-base—which is maintained by the operating system—makes the Win32 plat-form easier to use. Once consumers move to Win32 and no longer need DOS or Win16 applications, the AUTOEXEC.BAT, CONFIG.SYS, WIN.INI, SYSTEM.INI, and other INI files will no longer be needed. This information is kept in the Registry database and automatically modified as software and hardware is installed, removed, and updated. This feature, coupled with the Plug and Play standard, makes Windows 95 a self-configuring system.

Using the Registry

DOS depended on the AUTOEXEC.BAT and CONFIG.SYS configuration files to initialize and set system parameters on what resources were available and how they should be used. Windows 3.x relied on initialization files (which had a file extension of INI) to tell Windows and Windows applications what resources were available and how to work with those resources.

When Microsoft began designing Windows 95, they identified many prob-lems with these resource setting files. These files were difficult to maintain, often contained remnants of old program setups no longer needed, and usu-ally required user intervention to improve performance. To solve these prob-lems, Windows 95 borrowed a good idea from Windows NT: the Registry.

The *Registry* is a single database that contains system and application execu-tion information. Ultimately, the Registry replaces all INI files as well as AUTOEXEC.BAT and CONFIG.SYS. The Windows 95 Registry replaces REG.DAT which was used by Windows 3.1 to store file extension application associations and register OLE applications.

Exploring the Registry

The Windows 95 Registry consists of three data files:

- *USER.DAT*. Stores user preferences such as the Desktop.

- *SYSTEM.DAT*. Stores the computer's hardware configurations such as drives, printers, and sound card settings.

- *POLICY.POL*. Stores administrative policies set up on a network server.

Precautions are taken to protect these data files. First, the Registry data is kept in binary format, so the files cannot be read by a regular text editor. Second, the file attributes are set to read-only, hidden, system files. This prevents accidental deletion.

III

Setting Up Software

When you first install Windows 95, the setup program creates the SYSTEM.DAT file and enters the data regarding installed hardware. If you installed to the Windows 3.x directory, Setup copies the data from REG.DAT into the new SYSTEM.DAT file. From then on, whenever you install new hardware or change a configuration, Windows 95 automatically updates the SYSTEM.DAT data file.

You can view the hardware data stored in SYSTEM.DAT by opening the Control Panel folder and selecting System. Figure 17.1 shows the installed devices, as reported by SYSTEM.DAT.

Fig. 17.1
The Device Manager page displays installed devices by type.

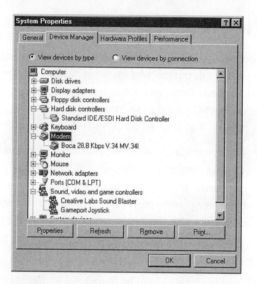

Using REGEDIT

The Registry Editor (REGEDIT) is located in the Windows 95 folder. To run REGEDIT, choose Run from the Start menu, type **REGEDIT**, and press Enter. Figure 17.2 shows the Registry Editor and data for My Computer.

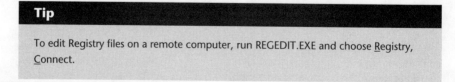

Tip

To edit Registry files on a remote computer, run REGEDIT.EXE and choose Registry, Connect.

Caution

Before you open the Registry Editor and start modifying the settings, be sure you understand what you are changing and why. If the modification desired can be effected by using Control Panel or by setting some other property, make the change there. Avoid using Registry Editor unless it is absolutely necessary.

Microsoft advises that you don't use the REGEDIT utility unless you are on the phone with one of their technicians. That's why they didn't include an icon for it by default—you have to manually create one.

Incorrect edits to the Registry could prevent Windows from working properly and result in a loss of critical data.

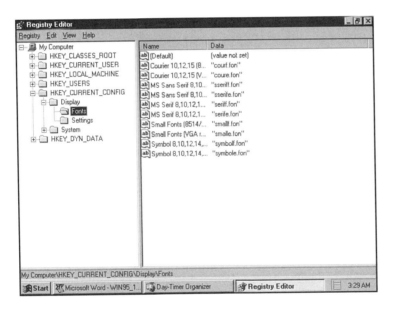

Fig. 17.2
The Registry Editor lists the installed fonts on My Computer.

The Registry is organized into matched keys and values. The keys are listed on the left pane (refer to fig. 17.2) as a hierarchical tree. As you double-click items and drill-down within branches, the values appear in the right pane. To change a key's value, right-click on the value in the right pane. The Registry Editor then displays an object menu: Modify, Delete and Rename. Figure 17.3 shows the Edit String dialog box for a Registry value.

As you change entries, the Registry Editor automatically changes the applicable database file (DAT). However, the changes don't take effect until you restart Windows 95.

III

Setting Up Software

Fig. 17.3
Enter or edit the
Value data in the
Edit String dialog
box.

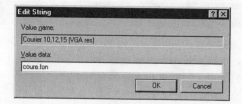

Tip

Double-click a Registry value to modify the value.

Note

Windows 95 maintains backup copies of the Registry data in the Windows 95 folder.
The backup files SYSTEM.DA0 and USER.DA0 are used by Windows 95 in the event
that the actual DAT files become corrupt.

Optimizing Windows 95

In the Control Panel folder, the System Properties sheet contains a Performance page. The Performance page allows you to configure the file system,
graphic, and virtual memory settings.

Exploring File Systems

Before you start fine-tuning the file system, you need to explore the design of
the Windows 95 file system. Operating systems use a file system to organize
files, store files, and control how files are named. Windows 95 continues to
use the DOS File Allocation Table (FAT) file system as its default file system.
However, Windows 95 implements a new approach to file system management, called the *Installable File System* (IFS). IFS is a program that provides an
interface between the application file requests and various supported file
systems.

Windows 95 ships with the following installable file systems:

- Virtual File Allocation Table (VFAT)

- CD-ROM File System (CDFS)

- Network Redirector

In addition to these supported file systems, vendors may create and add their own installable file systems. For example, a vendor may create an installable file system to allow users to access and work with UNIX or Apple files.

The IFS Manager can work with application programming interface (API) calls from Win32 applications and interrupt 21 (INT 21H) calls generated by Win16 or DOS applications. The file system design in Windows 95 supports up to 32 layers from the input/output subsystem (IOS) down to the hardware level. Each layer has defined interfaces with the layers above and below. This enables each component to cooperate with its neighbors.

VFAT

The FAT file system was developed to work with DOS. A clear advantage of FAT is that a disk formatted for FAT can be read by DOS, Windows NT, Windows 95, and OS/2. However, the DOS FAT file system has the following limitations:

- File names are limited to eight characters with a three-character extension.

- Every file access from a Windows-based application requires the system to switch to 8086 mode to execute DOS code, which slows down performance.

- The use of the INT 21H interrupt as the sole interface to every file system function causes conflicts between TSRs, disk caching, disk compression, and network systems.

VFAT is a 32-bit virtualized FAT file system. The VFAT.VXD file system driver (FSD) controls this file system and uses 32-bit code for all file access. VFAT is a protected mode implementation of the FAT file system. The VFAT system supports long file names (up to 255 characters), eliminates the over-reliance on INT 21H, uses 32-bit processing, and allows multiple, concurrent threads to execute file system code.

CDFS

The CDFS file system replaces MSCDEX TRS, which is used to support most CD-ROM devices. CDFS is a 32-bit protected mode ISO 9660 compliant CD-ROM file system. Applications send file requests to the CDFS, which handles the request and passes it to the IOS. The IOS routes the request to the type specific driver (TSD), which converts the logical request to a physical request. From there, a special SCSI translator sends the request to the SCSI port driver and then to the Miniport driver.

Network Redirector

The Network Redirector installable file system is a 32-bit protected mode VXD responsible for implementing the structure of a remote file system. When an application sends or receives data from a remote device, it sends a call to the Redirector. The Redirector communicates with the network via the protocol driver. Windows 95 supports two kinds of redirectors:

- Windows Networking (SMB over NetBEUI protocol)
- Microsoft Client for NetWare (NCP protocol)

Working with Long File Names

◀ See "Networking Support," p. 143

◀ See "Setting Configuration Information," p. 144

▶ See "Installing Network Interface Cards," p. 637

Whereas DOS limited users to file names that were up to eight characters plus a three-character extension (8.3), Windows 95 supports the use of long file names (also known as *LFN*). The long file names follow these filenaming rules:

- File names can be up to 255 characters long, including extensions.
- Uppercase and lowercase are preserved, but are not case-sensitive.
- Filename characters can be any characters (including spaces) except for the following:

    ? / \ " : < > | *

- File size of up to 16 exabytes (16E).

> **Note**
>
> An exabyte is a billion gigabytes. A stack of 3.5-inch disks to equal the capacity of 16E would be 2,300 times the distance from the earth to the moon.

Preserving FAT 8.3 File Names

Windows 95 maintains FAT 8.3 file names for each long file name. For example, the file named "East Coast Sales.EXCEL" would have a FAT name of EASTCOAS.EXC. By doing so, Windows 95 ensures that a program designed for FAT file names can access and work with files created under Windows 95. LFNs also provide additional information about a file, such as the date of the last file modification.

The following rules are used by the Windows 95 file system to convert long file names into the DOS 8.3 format:

■ Remove special characters (such as spaces).

■ If unique, use the first eight characters of LFN.

■ If not unique, use the first six characters, a tilde (~), and a number (for example, EASTCO~2.EXC).

■ For the extension, use the first three characters following the last period.

For example, if you have three files in Windows 95 called East coast budget.xls, East coast expenses.xls, and East coast sales.xls, their 8.3 DOS file names become EASTCO~1.XLS, EASTCO~2.XLS, and EASTCO~3.XLS consecutively.

Note that 8.3 file names do not preserve the case of characters (all uppercase).

Several problems arise when using a file in a Windows 95 application and in a non-LFN aware application:

■ Changing the LFN file name or copying the LFN to a new name, while in a non-LFN application, deletes the long file name.

■ Files created according to the 8.3 file naming rules have an LFN, which is the same as the 8.3 file name.

■ Files created according to the LFN file naming rules have a different 8.3 file name (as outlined in the prior rules).

■ LFNs use a previously reserved area of the File Allocation Table (FAT). DOS utilities that also use this area of FAT may damage this section of FAT.

Note

The Windows NT and Windows 95 long file name schemes are *not* compatible. Also, Windows NT version 3.5 and earlier does not support LFNs in the FAT file system. Windows 95 supports LFNs in FAT.

The OS/2 LFN naming scheme is not compatible with Windows 95 LFNs.

Caution

Do not use disk or backup utilities that are not aware of long file names. If you need to use a backup/restore utility that does not support LFNs, Microsoft supplies a utility called Long File Name Backup (LFNBK) that preserves the LFNs (it comes on the Win95 CD or you can contact Microsoft for this utility).

III

Setting Up Software

Modifying File System Properties

Windows 95 automatically sets file system properties to optimize the performance based on the current configuration. However, there may be times when you need to set a certain property or become aware of a unique need to boost performance. The System object in the Control Panel enables you to view and set disk and CD-ROM file system properties.

To set file system properties, follow these steps:

1. Open the Control Panel folder.

2. Open the System icon.

3. Select the Performance page (see fig. 17.4).

4. Click File System. The File System Properties sheet appears (see fig. 17.5).

Fig. 17.4

The System Performance property page reports on the status of key resources.

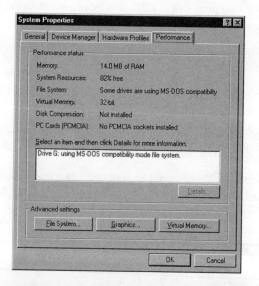

Fig. 17.5

Increase the Read-Ahead Optimization to speed up performance.

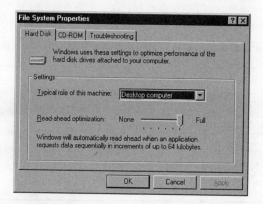

5. Set the desired options.

6. Select the CD-ROM page (see fig. 17.6).

7. Choose OK twice to implement the changes the next time Windows 95 loads.

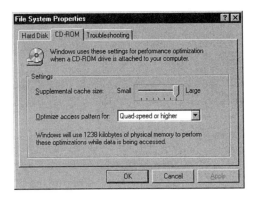

Fig. 17.6
To optimize the CD-ROM performance, select the correct access pattern.

Troubleshooting the File System

If an application does not respond properly to the Windows 95 file system, you can use the File System Troubleshooter to detect the cause of the problem. Using the troubleshooter, you can disable the following Windows 95 file system features:

- File sharing and locking

- Preservation of long file names in non-LFN programs

- Protect-mode hard disk interrupt handler

- 32-bit protect-mode disk drivers

- Write-behind caching for all drives

To start the File System Troubleshooter, follow these steps:

1. Open the Control Panel.

2. Open the System icon.

3. Select the Performance page.

4. Choose File System.

5. Select the Troubleshooting page (see fig. 17.7).

III

Setting Up Software

Fig. 17.7
Use the Trouble-shooting page to disable file system properties when trying to locate a problem.

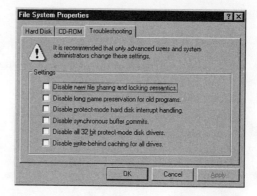

6. Select the setting to be tested.

7. Choose OK to test the setting.

Fine-Tuning Graphics

You can control the graphics accelerator used to control how Windows uses your graphics hardware. To adjust the acceleration rate, open the System Properties Performance page, choose Graphics, and adjust the Hardware Acceleration slide (see fig. 17.8). Click OK twice to save your changes.

Fig. 17.8
The Advanced Graphics Settings dialog box allows you to control the graphics acceleration rate.

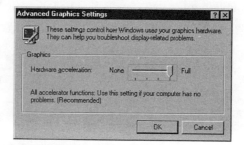

Fine-Tuning Virtual Memory

It is highly recommended that you let Windows manage your virtual memory settings. However, if needed, you can specify your own VM settings and even completely disable virtual memory. To modify Virtual Memory performance, open the System Properties Performance tab, choose Virtual Memory, and select Let Me Specify My Own Virtual Memory Settings. Set the Hard Disk location, and Minimum and Maximum values (see fig. 17.9). Select Yes to continue. Then click OK to save your changes.

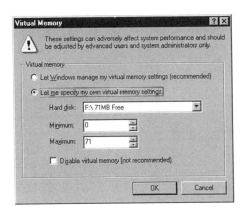

Fig. 17.9
If necessary, you can manually set Virtual Memory options.

Setting Up Software

Chapter 18

Configuring Monitors and Video Cards for Windows 95

by Paul Sanna

The components of your PC that require the least amount of care and feeding most likely are the monitor and video card. With most PCs, when you change your monitor or video card, or when you start your PC for the first time, the correct image usually appears on-screen immediately.

Making changes to your machine's video hardware sometimes spells TROUBLE if you are a Windows 3.x user, however. If you make an inadvertent change to your video configuration from within Windows, there is a chance you won't be able to start Windows again without manually editing an initialization file. Fortunately, Windows 95 makes it easy and safe to configure your video adapter and monitor.

In this chapter, you learn how to

- Install your new video card and tell whether your new device is a Plug and Play device

- Start the Add New Hardware Wizard

- Specify what video card is installed in your PC

- Let Windows 95 detect what video card is installed in your PC

- Configure your screen's resolution, color palette, and font settings

Installing Your New Video Card into Your PC

Before learning how to configure Windows 95 to work with a new video card, you should first know how to get the new piece of equipment installed into your PC, as well as how to run Windows 95 the first time with that new equipment. In fact, after you have installed the card or monitor, you may have very little (or no) work to do to configure Windows 95. For example, if you have a Plug and Play system, Windows 95 will do all the work necessary to configure your new video adapter or monitor.

Tip

What's the most important rule when you are setting up a new appliance? *Have the user's manual or documentation handy.* This rule also applies to setting up new hardware equipment. Before you start to configure a new video card or monitor, be sure you have on hand relevant documentation. You may need to supply information included in the user's manual.

Also, be sure you have any disks (floppy or CD-ROM) supplied with the device; Windows 95 may need software supplied on the disk.

In this section, you learn what happens when you install a new video card or monitor into a PC running Windows 95, including if your system is ready for Plug and Play.

Note

Windows 95 supports PCs with Plug and Play devices. This means that when you install a Plug and Play device such as video adapter, into your PC, or simply plug one in, such as a monitor, Windows 95 automatically detects the presence of the new device and configures it for use in Windows 95. For more information about Plug and Play, refer to Chapter 1, "Preparing to Install Windows 95."

To install a new video adapter into your PC, follow these steps:

1. Shut down Windows 95, turn off the power on your PC, and follow the instructions enclosed with the adapter to install the card into the PC.

2. Turn on your PC. If your PC does not boot Windows 95 automatically, start Windows 95.

3. If the video adapter you installed in step 1 is Plug-and-Play compatible, Windows 95 notifies you that it has detected it. Windows still might ask you for the driver for the video card to complete the setup of the card. If so, enter the location on the hard drive or network where the driver is located. If the driver is on a floppy disk supplied by the manufacturer of the card, insert the disk into the disk drive and then specify the name of the drive (for example, **A**). Refer to the section "Configuring Video Cards and Monitors" for instructions on how to fine-tune your new hardware with Windows 95.

> **Note**
>
> Drivers for video cards are needed so that Windows 95 can properly display images on the screen based on the specifications and capabilities of the video adapter.

4. If the device is not Plug-and-Play compatible, Windows 95 does not prompt you for any information. You should start the Add New Hardware Wizard to configure your new video card and monitor .

Starting the Add New Hardware Wizard

Like all other hardware, new video cards are identified and configured for use in Windows 95 through the Add New Hardware Wizard. The Add New Hardware Wizard automates most of the work you had to complete in Windows 3.1 and DOS to set up a new monitor or video card. The Add New Hardware Wizard can be found in the Control Panel folder, where Windows 95 installs it by default (see fig. 18.1).

> **Tip**
>
> Though the Add New Hardware Wizard is located in the Control Panel folder, you can create a shortcut so you can launch the wizard from wherever you choose. If you plan to do a lot of work with the hardware in Windows 95, you could save some time by creating a shortcut to the wizard right on the Desktop. For instructions on creating a shortcut, refer to Chapter 6, "Configuring the Windows 95 Desktop, Display, and Fonts."

Fig. 18.1

The Add New Hardware Wizard can be found in the Control Panel folder.

Add New Hardware Wizard icon

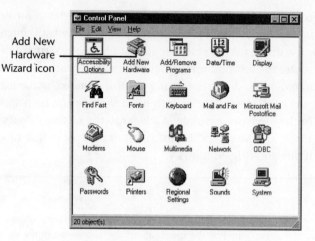

Follow these steps to launch the Add New Hardware Wizard:

1. Start the Add New Hardware Wizard. It is located in the Control Panel folder. The dialog box shown in figure 18.2 appears.

Fig. 18.2

The first dialog box that appears when you start the Add New Hardware Wizard tells you what the wizard does and gives you the opportunity to cancel.

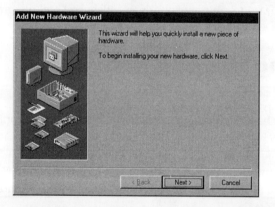

2. The dialog box that appears is part of many wizards in Windows 95. It is used simply to tell you which wizard you started and to give you the opportunity to cancel. To clear this dialog box and continue, click the Next button. To cancel the wizard, click Cancel.

The next step in using the Add New Hardware Wizard to configure a video card or monitor is to decide who will identify which hardware is installed: you or Windows 95.

Deciding Who Specifies the Hardware

There are two different approaches you can use to specify the video adapter and monitor you will use with Windows 95. You can let Windows 95 try to identify your video adapter and monitor automatically, or you can tell Windows 95 explicitly which video adapter and monitor is installed on your PC. The Add New Hardware Wizard gives you the option of choosing which approach to take.

If Windows 95 detects the hardware, the clear advantage is that Windows 95 does all the work. All you do is confirm that Windows 95 properly identified the components on your PC. But, you can also encounter some disadvantages:

■ Windows 95 may make a mistake. It is possible Windows 95 will misidentify your adapter or not be able to identify it at all.

■ It can take up too much time. Windows 95 attempts to identify all of the hardware on your PC, which sometimes can take 30 minutes. You cannot instruct Windows 95 to detect just your new video card or monitor.

You could also tell Windows 95 what hardware you have. One clear advantage is that there is less chance of error. Provided you know what hardware is installed on your PC, you can be sure Windows 95 installs the correct driver by explicitly telling Windows 95 what hardware to configure.

However, this option involves more work for you. You need to know exact manufacturer and model information in order to supply that information to Windows 95.

Lots of work went into the development of Windows 95's ability to recognize your hardware—why not take advantage of it?

Letting Windows 95 Detect the Video Card

The process for letting Windows 95 detect your video card is simple. First, you start the Add New Hardware Wizard. Windows 95 inspects your system and identifies any hardware devices it doesn't recognize since the last time it inspected your system. If Windows 95 finds a video card that it does not recognize, it informs you what model video card it thinks it found. Next, you confirm that information, and then Windows 95 configures itself so it always loads the correct drivers for use with the adapter. Most likely, you won't have to reboot your machine.

To let Windows 95 detect your video card, follow these steps:

1. Follow the instructions to start the Add New Hardware Wizard shown in the earlier section, "Starting the Add New Hardware Wizard."

2. Click the Next button in the first dialog that appears (see fig. 18.3).

Fig. 18.3
Windows 95 lets you specify whether it should detect all new hardware on your PC.

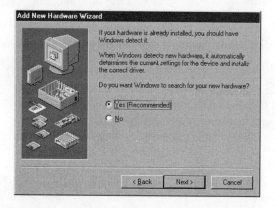

3. Click the Yes (Recommended) option button and then click Next.

4. The dialog box shown in figure 18.4 appears. This dialog box asks you to confirm that you want Windows 95 to detect the hardware on your PC. Click Next. Windows 95 now starts the detection phase when it inspects your PC for installed hardware.

Fig. 18.4
Just before it begins to inspect your system for installed hardware, Windows 95 asks you to verify that you want to continue.

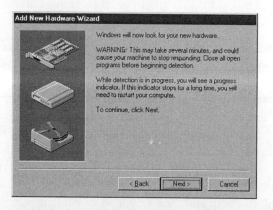

Caution

Windows 95 warns you that your system might freeze while it tries to automatically detect the hardware installed on your system. Don't worry (too much). Be sure you close down any applications you might have running before starting the automatic detection phase. Should your system freeze, reboot the computer and use the manual detection method for configuring your hardware. See "Manually Specifying Your Video Card" later in this chapter.

5. After Windows 95 completes the detection phase, it displays the dialog box shown in figure 18.5. Click the Details button to view the list of new hardware found by the Add New Hardware Wizard.

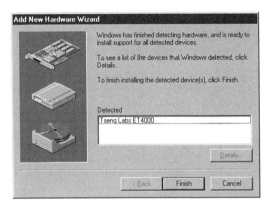

Fig. 18.5
Windows 95 permits you to see the new hardware devices it detected.

6. To configure Windows 95 with the new video adapter, click Finish. Depending upon the capabilities of your video card and monitor, Windows 95 may ask if it can reboot the system for the changes to take effect. If asked, choose Yes to complete installation of the new video card immediately.

Manually Specifying Your Video Card

The process to manually specify your video card has a number of steps, but the process is straightforward and each step is easy to complete: start the Add New Hardware wizard, tell Windows 95 you want to install a display adapter, and pick the adapter from a list provided by Windows 95. Windows 95 configures itself so it always loads the correct driver for use with the card. Most likely, you will not have to reboot your machine.

To manually specify that the video card is installed on your PC, follow these steps:

1. Follow the instructions to start the Add New Hardware wizard shown earlier in the section "Starting the Add New Hardware Wizard."

2. Click the Next button in the first dialog that appears (see fig. 18.6).

Fig. 18.6
You can override the Windows default of inspecting your system for new devices by selecting the No button.

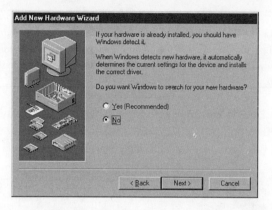

3. Click No to instruct Windows 95 not to automatically detect new hardware, and then choose the Next button. The dialog box shown in figure 18.7 appears.

Fig. 18.7
Windows 95 lets you specify what type of hardware you want to install.

4. Choose Display Adapters in the Hardware Types list box, and then click Next. The dialog box in figure 18.8 appears.

Fig. 18.8
Windows 95 provides a list of supported video card models (and their manufacturers) for you to choose from.

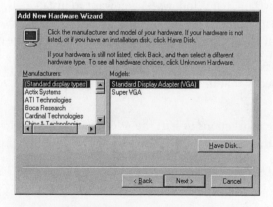

5. Click the manufacturer of your video card in the Manufacturers list box. The list of supported video cards for the manufacturer you chose appears in the Models list box.

6. Click the model of your video adapter in the Models list box.

> **Tip**
>
> You can avoid having to pick the manufacturer and model of your video card from the lists provided with Windows 95 if you have the software installation disk that was shipped with the video card. Insert the disk into a floppy drive and then click the Have Disk button in the dialog box shown in figure 18.8. Follow the prompts to specify the location of OEMSETUP.INF, which should appear on the disk. This file contains all the information needed to configure the video card. This technique also can be useful if you have a late model adapter that is not yet supported by Windows 95. If no software is supplied with the video card, or if you cannot locate the OEMSETUP.INF file, contact the manufacturer of the card.

6. Click the Next button. Windows 95 informs you that it has completed the installation of the video card.

7. Click the Finish button.

> **Troubleshooting**
>
> *I don't recognize (or I don't know) either the manufacturer or the model of my video card in the lists that appear in the Add New Hardware Wizard. Also, I can't find any disks that might be associated with my video card.*
>
> Windows 95 lets you choose a generic driver for use with your adapter if you are not sure what video adapter is installed in your PC. Choose Standard Display Types from the Manufacturers list box and either Standard Display Adapter (VGA) or Super VGA from the Models list box. If you are not sure whether your monitor is Super VGA capable, choose the VGA option.

Configuring Your Monitor and Video Card

Once your video card has been configured for Windows 95, there are a few options you can use to configure your display. For example, you can change the resolution for your display, or you can choose the color palette Windows 95 uses to display image on your screen. Depending on the capabilities of your video card, you may have more or fewer choices to select from for each option. For example, if you have a capable video card, you may have a number of resolution settings to choose from.

You can configure your monitor and video card from the Settings page of the Display Properties sheet (see fig 18.9).

Fig. 18.9
The Display Properties sheet is used to modify the behavior of your monitor and video card.

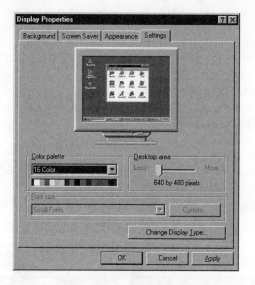

There are a few different methods you can use to view the Display Properties sheet:

- Right-click the Desktop to display the Desktop context menu. The Display Properties sheet appears. Choose the Settings page.

- Open the Control Panel and then click the Display icon. The Display Properties sheet appears. Choose the Settings page.

Specifying Resolution Settings

The Desktop Area slider on the Settings tab in the Display Properties sheet enables you to specify the resolution setting for your monitor and video adapter. This setting determines how much information you see on-screen. By dragging the slider to the right, you are able to see more images on your screen, though the images appear smaller. For comparison purposes, figures 18.10 and 18.11 show the Windows 95 desktop at 640 × 480 resolution and 800 × 600 pixels, respectively.

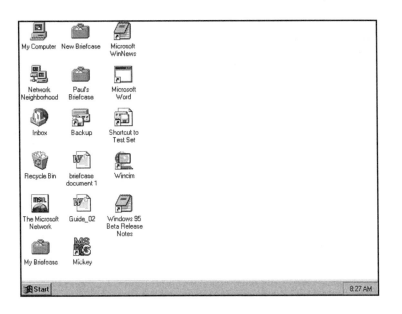

Fig. 18.10
The resolutions
setting for the
system shown
in this picture is
640 × 480 pixels.

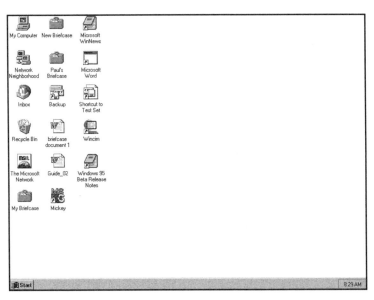

Fig. 18.11
The resolutions
setting for the
system shown in
this picture is
800 × 600 pixels.

Pixels and the Desktop Area Setting

By changing the Desktop Area setting, you change the number of pixels used to
create the images that appear on your screen. Pixels (*picture ele*ments) are the small
units of color that make up the images you see on-screen. The setting that appears

(continues)

(continued)

beneath the slider tells how many pixels will be used to make up the images on the screen. The first number refers to the number of pixels in each row; the second number refers to the number of pixels used in each column. For example, a setting of 640 × 480 pixels means that the images on your screen will be made up of 640 rows of 480 pixels each.

The greater the number of pixels used to create the images on your screen, the more clear the resolution. The smaller the size of the pixels, the greater number of pixels can be used, hence the sharper the resolution is while you see more images on-screen.

To change the resolution, follow these steps:

1. Select the Settings page of the Display Properties sheet.

2. Click the slider in the <u>D</u>esktop Area and drag it to the resolution setting you want; or press Alt+D and then use the left or right cursor keys to move the arrow icon (see fig. 18.12).

   As the slider stops at the different resolution settings permitted by your video adapter, the image of the Desktop that appears in the dialog box changes to show you the relative effect of the resolution setting you have stopped at.

Fig. 18.12
The Desktop Area slider lets you specify the resolution setting for your monitor.

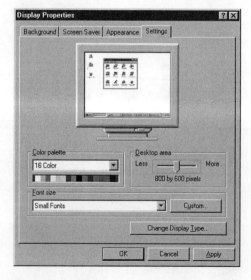

3. Click the Apply button for the resolution setting to take effect immediately and to continue working in the Display Properties dialog box, or choose OK for your changes to take effect and for the Display Properties sheet to close.

Caution

Depending upon the capabilities of your video adapter, Windows 95 might need to shut itself down and then restart in order for the resolution changes to take effect. This is normal and no reason for worry. You will always be warned first, and you have the option of not letting Windows 95 restart itself. If you choose this option, Windows 95 will continue to operate normally, but the changes you've made to your configuration will not take effect until the next time you start Windows 95.

Troubleshooting

I can't seem to move the slider in the Desktop Area in any direction. The Less and More labels appear to be dimmed.

The points along the slider at which you can stop the slider are determined by the capabilities of your video card and monitor. If your video card and monitor are only capable of one setting, you cannot move the slider in the Desktop Area at all. The labels Less and More at each end of the slider appear dimmed if your video adapter and monitor are not capable of multiple resolution settings.

Setting the Color Palette

You can specify the color palette that Windows 95 uses to display colors on-screen. Rather than choose specific colors, you can specify the breadth of the palette Windows uses. For example, you might choose the 16-color palette, or you might choose the 256-color palette.

Caution

While choosing a palette with more colors enhances the images on your screen, more memory is used to display these colors, so overall system performance may suffer.

You choose the color palette from the Color Palette drop-down list box that appears on the Settings page on the Display Properties sheet (see fig. 18.13). The capabilities of your video adapter determines how many choices are shown in the Color Palette drop-down list box.

Fig. 18.13
You can choose
how many colors
are used to paint
the images you see
on your screen.

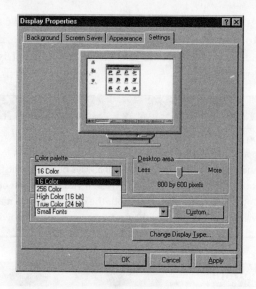

To change the color palette, follow these steps:

1. Display the Settings page of the Display Properties sheet.

2. Choose the palette from the Color Palette drop-down list box. After you make a selection, the rectangular area beneath the drop-down list containing all the colors in the current palette you are using changes to show the palette you chose.

Caution

Depending on your video adapter, Windows 95 might need to shut itself down and then restart in order for the resolution changes to take effect. Windows 95 will always ask for your permission first. Also, you have the option of not letting Windows 95 restart itself. If you choose this option, Windows 95 will continue to operate normally, but the changes you've made to your configuration will not take effect until the next time you start Windows 95.

Setting Font Size

Many users are concerned with screen real estate, that is, having more of it. Users like to see more information on-screen at the expense of the clarity of the on-screen image. You can display more information on your screen by changing the resolution setting, as demonstrated in the Specifying Resolution Settings section. Now, you'll learn how to squeeze more information on the screen by changing the font size of the text used in Windows 95. You could also use the change font size functionality to enlarge the font size in order for text to appear larger in Windows 95.

As an example of changing the font size, figure 18.14 shows the Control Panel with font size enlarged to the Large fonts setting. Notice how the space between the icons has increased and how you can see fewer icons in the folder at one time. Figure 18.15 shows the Control Panel folder with font size decreased to the Small fonts setting. Notice how the space between icons has been decreased so you can see many more at the same time in the folder.

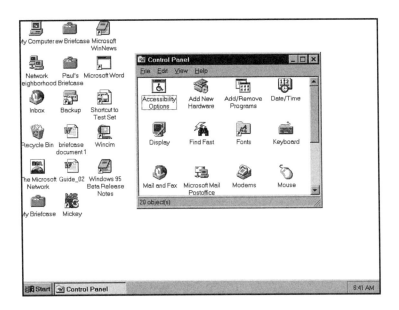

Fig. 18.14
The font size in this figure has been increased to the Large Fonts setting.

Changing the font size in Windows 95 is easy. You can choose from two predefined sizes, small fonts or large fonts, or you can specify a custom size by supplying a percentage size based on the normal size. You may also increase and decrease the size of the font by maneuvering a graphical ruler.

Tip

Your monitor and video card must be capable of multiple resolution settings in order to change the font size. Windows 95 forces users to choose a resolution setting other than 640 × 480 pixels in order to change the font size.

IV

Setting Up Hardware

Fig. 18.15
The font size in this figure has been decreased to 80 percent of its normal size.

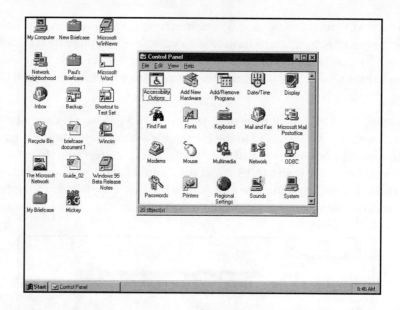

To change the font size by using one of the predefined settings, follow these steps:

1. Select the Settings page of the Display Properties sheet (refer to fig. 18.12).

2. Change the Display Area setting to something other than 640 × 480 pixels (see the earlier section "Specifying Resolution Settings" for help).

3. Choose either Small Fonts or Large Fonts from the Font Size drop-down list.

4. Click the Apply button for the new font size to take effect immediately and to continue working in the Display Propertics sheet.

Or, choose OK for your changes to take effect and for the Display Properties sheet to close. Depending upon the capabilities of your video adapter, Windows 95 might shut itself down and then restart in order for the font size changes to take effect.

To change the font size by specifying a custom size, follow these steps:

1. Display the Settings page of the Display Properties sheet.

2. Change the Display Area setting to something other than 640 × 480 pixels (see the earlier section "Specifying Resolution Settings" for help).

3. Click the Custom button in the Font Size area. The Custom Font Size dialog box shown in figure 18.16 appears.

4. Enter the new percentage size in the <u>S</u>cale Fonts To Be edit box. You can also choose from a predefined percentage by clicking the down arrow

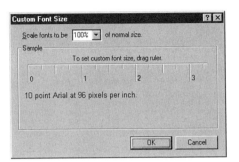

Fig. 18.16
You can specify
a custom size
for the font used
in Windows 95,
expressing the size
as a percentage of
the normal size.

icon; or click anywhere on the ruler and drag to the left to decrease the size or to the right to increase the size.

5. Choose OK.

6. Click the <u>A</u>pply button for the new font size to take effect immediately and to continue working in the Display Properties sheet, or choose OK for your changes to take effect and for the Display Properties sheet to close. Depending upon the capabilities of your video adapter, Windows 95 might shut itself down and then restart in order for the font size changes to take effect.❖

Chapter 19

Configuring Speakers and Sound Cards

by Ian Stokell

Historically, IBM-compatible PCs, unlike the competing Macintosh platform, came with no sound capabilities to speak of, aside from a pathetic beep here and there. Now, most PCs that are shipped into the consumer retail market include built-in multimedia components, such as a CD-ROM drive and sound capabilities in the form of a sound card and speakers. But if you didn't include such multimedia components when you bought your PC, apart from kicking yourself now, you probably realize that a basic PC is severely lacking in terms of entertainment value without a CD-ROM and sound.

This chapter covers how to install and configure a sound board. It also briefly mentions speakers, although there really isn't much to say about them—after you've installed a sound board, you plug them into the card or a suitable port on the PC and *voilà*, they either work or they don't! More about that later. First though, there is the subject of the sound board.

In this chapter you learn how to do the following:

- Use the Add New Hardware Wizard to install a sound board
- Install and configure software drivers for your sound board
- Change multimedia and volume control settings
- Move MIDI instruments between sound cards

Using the Add New Hardware Wizard for Sound Board

Before you can configure sound capabilities under Windows 95, you need to install a suitable audio board in an available expansion slot within your PC. If you are thinking of getting into multimedia when you buy your PC, it's worth paying extra to get one with a sound board and other multimedia components already built-in. This will save you the trouble of configuring the various components when you are ready to start using them.

Under the old DOS/Windows combination, it was quite a hassle to add multimedia components such as a sound board. When adding a new hardware component, you needed to assign it available system resources for it to work properly, such as *input/output* (I/O) and *interrupt request* (IRQ) parameters. Keeping track of such resource allocations was problematic to say the least. However, the good news is that Windows 95 eases the installation pain by providing a central registry where such information is kept and graphically displayed; this place is referred to as the *Device Manager*.

◀ See "Using the Device Manager," p. 334

In addition, the new Plug and Play standard, supported in Windows 95, allows for hardware components manufacturers to ensure their products are instantly compatible with the new operating system. They do this by adhering to the new Plug and Play standard. Then, when you add the new hardware device, Windows 95 can take over installing the necessary software drivers and allocating available system resources. More about that in a moment.

◀ See "Plug and Play Overview," p. 10

The other way Windows 95 helps in the installation of new hardware components—whether they're Plug and Play or not—is through the very useful Add New Hardware Wizard Control Panel. The wizard takes the user through the installation of a hardware device step-by-step. It can take anywhere from 10 to 20 minutes for the manual Add New Hardware Wizard installation procedure to complete.

To show how the Add New Hardware Wizard works in relation to sound cards, you should go through the motions of installing a Sound Blaster 16 AWE-32. Alternatively, if you are installing a new sound card, go ahead and use the manufacturer and model you want to install instead of the Sound Blaster 16 AWE-32.

First, you need to access the Add New Hardware Wizard, which can be accomplished either through the Control Panel or by choosing Sound Cards, Setting Up from the Help Topics option. Follow these steps after selecting the Control Panel option:

1. Click the Start menu.

2. Select Settings, Control Panel.

3. Open the Add New Hardware Control Panel. An introductory screen appears, from which you click the Next button. The real Add New Hardware Wizard appears (see fig. 19.1).

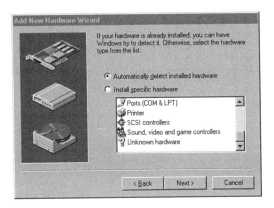

Fig. 19.1
The wizard can automatically detect newly installed hardware, or you can go through the process manually.

4. Select the Automatically Detect Installed Hardware button to let Windows 95 automatically find any new devices that you have added recently. Or, select the Install Specific Hardware option to allow you to select the new hardware to be installed.

5. Choose the type of hardware device you want to add from the wizard list. Select Sound, Video and Game Controllers and then click Next. The hardware manufacturer and model list appears for the device you selected (see fig. 19.2).

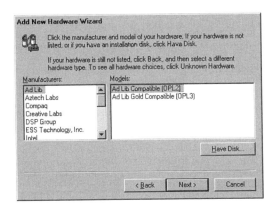

Fig. 19.2
You select the type of device that you want to install.

6. In the left window, click the sound board manufacturer's name. A list of the company's products that Windows 95 supports appears in the right-hand window.

7. Select the board you want to add: Creative Labs Sound Blaster 16/AWE-32. Click the Next button.

> **Note**
>
> At this point you may need to install a software driver from an installation disk if Windows 95 does not support the device. If you do need to install a software driver from a suitable installation disk, just continue along with these steps. If, on the other hand, you do not need to install a driver from a floppy, skip steps 8 through 10 and continue with step 11.

> **Caution**
>
> You might want to use the sound board's own installation program instead, because the wizard can sometimes run into problems identifying the correct interrupts for some components.

8. Click the Have Disk button from the Add New Hardware Wizard panel. The Install From Disk window appears (see fig. 19.3).

Fig. 19.3
Insert the installation disk into the selected drive to install a new device driver from a floppy disk.

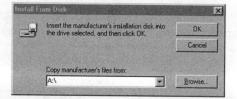

9. Specify the folder and disk that contains the manufacturer's installation files.

10. Click OK. The Install From Disk window disappears, and you are back to the Add New Hardware Wizard. Now you can click the Next button. The wizard window changes to display the settings you should use for the new board (see fig. 19.4).

IV

Setting Up Hardware

Tip

Not all vendors have the correct setup information for Windows 95 on their disks. If this is the case, the disk may not work with Windows 95; call the company and ask them if they have an update.

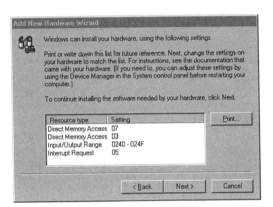

Fig. 19.4
The Add New Hardware Wizard gives you the settings you can use for your new board.

Note

This list of settings is important, and is based on what settings are available as defined in the Windows 95 Device Manager registry.

11. Write down these settings or print them out. These are the settings that the new board should have before you install it.

12. If the wizard asks you for a manufacturer's installation disk, go ahead and install the software direct from the floppy.

13. Shut down your PC.

14. You now need to configure the new sound card according to the settings given by Device Manager during the wizard installation process. However, changing card settings can be a little tricky, so it's important to refer to the documentation that comes with your sound board for how to make changes to I/O, IRQ, and DMA settings.

15. Install the sound card.

A feature in Windows 95 allows for the automatic detection of newly in-stalled hardware devices, such as a sound board. To automatically detect a newly installed sound board, open the Add New Hardware Wizard, as de-scribed in the previous section, and do the following:

1. Check the Automatically Detect Installed Hardware button on the Add New Hardware Wizard (refer to fig. 19.1).

2. Click the Next button. The screen that appears will tell you that Windows 95 will now look for new hardware and that this may take some time (see fig. 19.5).

Fig. 19.5
The first Add New Hardware Wizard screen tells you that the search for new hardware may take some time.

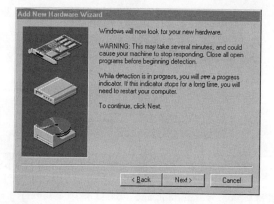

3. Click the Next button. The next thing that appears on the bottom of the screen is a progress bar that tells you how the search is going (see fig. 19.6).

> **Tip**
>
> It is normal for the progress bar to quickly complete about 90 percent of the search and then slow down. The last 10 percent often takes longer than the previous 90 percent altogether!

4. When the search is complete, click the Next button.

The wizard then tells you if it has found any new hardware components. If none are found, it asks if you want to install a new device manually. If so, it will bring you back to the Add New Hardware Wizard screen, from where you can manually install the sound board.

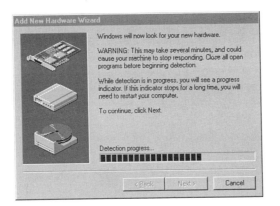

Fig. 19.6
The progress bar
gives you continu-
ous updates
regarding the
hardware search.

Troubleshooting

I hear hissing during the playback of a sound file.

The file may be recording in 8 bits and playing back in 16 bits. The 16-bit board
doesn't realize that the 8-bit file isn't the same high quality as a 16-bit file, so playing
the file with expectations of higher sound quality emphasizes the lower detail.

Configuring Sound Cards

Once you have installed the sound board, there are a number of ways to configure the board. You also may need to change the software driver for a specific board, or add a driver from a floppy disk. This section covers a number
of configuration and driver installation issues.

Adding or Changing Sound Card Drivers

A sound board, as with all hardware devices attached to a PC, requires special
software that communicates with the computer's operating system. This spe-
cialized software, called a *driver*, acts as a sort of intermediary between the
hardware device and the operating system on the PC. Without this special
driver, the two would not be able to communicate properly and the PC
would likely grind to a halt until they are reconciled.

But adding software drivers and communicating their location on the PC to
the operating system has historically been a tedious and—for many non-
technical users—a somewhat challenging operation. However, with Windows
95, much of the complexity revolving around the task has been removed. This
is because you can add or change device drivers using the Device Manager.

> **Note**
>
> Windows 95 doesn't work with all the different sound cards on the market. If you have drivers that come from the component manufacturer, the Device Manager may not properly recognize the board.

As an example, check out the drivers available for MS Windows Sound System Compatible sound:

1. Click the Start menu.

2. Choose Settings, Control Panel.

3. Double-click the System Control Panel. The System Properties sheet appears.

4. Click the Device Manager page (see fig. 19.7).

Fig. 19.7
Device Manager allows you to change the software driver for a sound board.

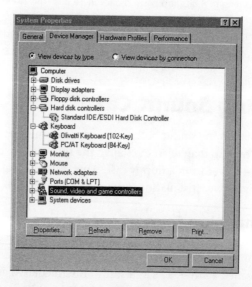

5. Click the plus sign that corresponds to the hardware device you want to change—for example, "Sound, Video and Game Controllers." A list of devices appears under Sound, Video and Game Controllers.

6. Double-click the specific hardware device you are interested in—MS Windows Sound System Compatible, in this case.

7. In the resulting panel, click the Driver page (see fig. 19.8).

8. Click the Change Driver button. The Select Device window appears (see fig. 19.9).

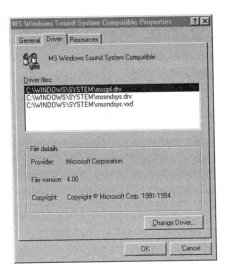

Fig. 19.8
Available software
drivers are listed in
the Driver page.

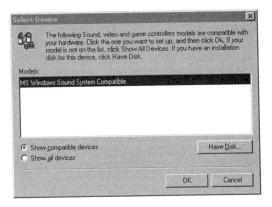

Fig. 19.9
A list of compat-
ible devices allows
you to select a
suitable software
driver.

Note

The Models list shows all compatible sound models available for your PC. The
Show Compatible Devices option needs to be selected. If you are changing
the driver on a sound board and it is not listed, select the Show All Devices
option. The list will change to show all such boards. However, if your board
requires a software driver to be installed from a floppy disk, click the Have Disk
button and refer to the next section, "Installing a Driver from a Floppy Disk."
If no installation disk is required, continue with step 9.

9. Select the device you want to set up and click OK. The Driver tab
showing the driver files and their correct folder path reappears.

10. Select your new driver and click OK. You are now back to the Device Manager hardware type list.

11. Click Close.

Troubleshooting

I try to play video with sound and it isn't synchronized.

You may have a computer that isn't fast enough. You can try improving performance and adding RAM, but if you have an older, slower processor and a relatively slow hard drive, you may need to think about upgrading to a new PC with fast video capabilities built in.

Installing a Driver from a Floppy Disk

At some point you may be required to install a driver from a floppy disk, such as when a newer version is distributed by the manufacturer, for example. To install a software driver from a floppy disk, you need to be in the Select Driver sheet accessed from the Driver page. Here's how:

1. From Driver page in your designated hardware properties sheet, which is accessed by selecting the specific hardware device in Device Manager, click the Change Driver button. The Select Driver window appears (refer to fig 19.9).

2. Click Have Disk. The Install From Disk box appears (see fig. 19.10).

Fig. 19.10
Specify the actual drive and directory where the software drivers can be found.

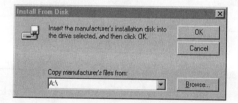

3. Specify the disk and directory where the drivers can be found.

4. Click OK.

5. You return to the Select Device window. Click OK. You are back to the Driver page of System Properties.

6. Click OK. You are now back to the Device Manager sheet.

Volume Setting

You can adjust the volume level of a sound card by using the Volume Control feature. This feature also allows you to adjust speaker balance when playing audio files.

To adjust the volume level, follow these steps:

1. Click the Start menu.

2. Choose Programs, Accessories, Multimedia.

3. Select CD Player (see fig. 19.11).

Fig. 19.11
CD Player allows you to control the audio volume via the View menu.

4. Choose View, Volume Control. The Volume Control dialog box appears (see fig. 19.12).

Fig. 19.12
Volume Control allows for the adjusting of both volume and speaker balance.

5. Select the desired volume by dragging the Volume Control slider.

6. Adjust the balance between speakers by dragging the Balance slider.

7. When the volume and balance are set, exit Volume Control by clicking the close box at the top right of the window.

IV

Setting Up Hardware

Changing Multimedia Settings

There may be occasion for you to change the settings assigned to a multimedia device, such as a sound board. You can change such device settings via the Multimedia Control Panel. Follow these steps:

1. Open the Start menu.

2. Choose Settings, Control Panel.

3. Open the Multimedia Control Panel.

4. In the Multimedia Properties sheet, select the Advanced page (see fig. 19.13).

Fig. 19.13

You can change multimedia device settings by selecting the component from the Multimedia Devices list.

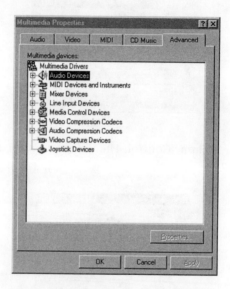

5. Click the plus sign next to the multimedia device category you are interested in.

6. Click the device you want from the resulting list.

7. Click the Properties button at the bottom of the window.

8. Make whatever changes you want using the different pages, and click OK when you are done.

Changing Sound Quality When Recording

You can change the sound quality of your recording reproduction depending on your needs. A presentation will probably require a better quality sound reproduction than something like a short voice file you would attach to an in-house e-mail message to distribute to coworkers. To change the recording sound quality, do the following:

1. Open the Start menu.

2. Choose Settings, Control Panel.

3. Open the Multimedia Control Panel.

4. In the Multimedia Properties sheet click the Audio page (see fig. 19.14).

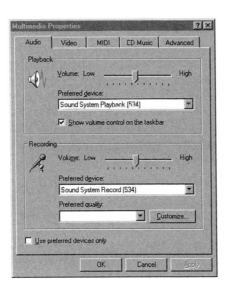

Fig. 19.14
Recording sound quality can be changed according to your needs via the Audio page in Multimedia Properties.

5. Select the quality you want from the Preferred Quality drop-down list box.

6. Click OK.

You may want to create custom recording formats yourself to add to your Preferred Quality list. To do so requires an extra step in addition to those in the previous section. From the Audio tab in Multimedia Properties, do the following:

1. Click the Customize button. The Customize window appears (see fig. 19.15).

2. Name the file in the Name drop-down list box.

3. Select the desired format from the Format drop-down list box.

4. Select the reproduction attributes for the new customized format from the Attributes drop-down list box.

Fig. 19.15
Create your own quality formats using the Customize button on the Audio page in Multimedia Properties.

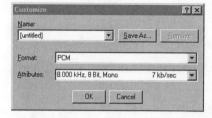

5. Click OK.

Your newly customized recording format now appears in the Preferred Quality list box in the Audio page.

Tip

The higher the quality sound file, the more disk space is required. If you have limited disk storage space, don't select the highest sound quality unless you really need it.

Troubleshooting

My system hangs during a 16-bit digitized sound test, but an 8-bit test works fine.

You may need to switch to a low DMA setting. This result means your system cannot handle high DMA at full speed.

Moving MIDI Instruments Between Sound Cards

There may be an occasion when you want to move a MIDI instrument between sound boards, perhaps if you have both a high-quality 16-bit board and a lower-quality 8-bit board installed at the same time. It's a pretty straightforward operation. Here's how you do it:

1. Open the Start menu.

2. Choose Settings, Control Panel.

3. Open the Multimedia Control Panel.

4. In the Multimedia Properties sheet, click the Advanced page (refer to fig. 19.13).

5. Click the plus sign next to MIDI Devices and Instruments.

6. Click the plus sign next to the sound board your MIDI instrument was connected to from the resulting list.

7. Select the instrument you want to move, and then click the Properties button at the bottom of the window.

8. Click the Details page.

9. From the MIDI Port list box, select the name of the sound board you want to connect the instrument to.

10. Connect your MIDI instrument to the new sound board you just speci-fied using the designated port, according to the instructions that come with your sound board.

Troubleshooting Sound Cards

Because of the complexities involved in getting sound to reproduce properly on PCs, it will be a lucky person indeed who can go through their entire multimedia-use life without running into audio problems. And while Windows 95's Plug and Play and easy-to-use Device Manager Registry help track available IRQs and I/O addresses, things can still go wrong.

Under the old DOS/Windows combination, one of the most intimidating aspects of getting a sound board to work effectively on a PC was figuring out what IRQ, DMA, and I/O settings to use. Getting one of them wrong often meant assigning already-allocated resources to the new sound board, which inevitably resulted in an infamous "hardware conflict." In other words, your sound board wouldn't work.

The Device Manager registry in Windows 95 is designed to track available system resources, such as IRQ and I/O settings. Then, when a new hardware component is added, such as a sound board, you can use the Add New Hard-ware Wizard to take you step-by-step through the installation process. Part of that process is to check the registry for available settings and graphically present them to you so you can configure your board before you install it. The result should be that the new component will work when it is installed, although that isn't always the case.

Hardware conflicts can occur, often at the most inappropriate moments. Fortunately, not only does Windows 95 include a very thorough Help option from the Start menu, but it also features an especially useful step-by-step Hardware Conflict Troubleshooter, which you access by choosing the Hardware, Troubleshooting Conflicts option from the Help Topics Index.

The Troubleshooting Wizard will take you on a step-by-step investigation that should solve the problem.

Getting Speakers to Work

There's not really much to be said about the subject of speakers. Having installed your sound board, you simply take the cable from the speakers and plug it in, either to the card's Speaker Out port or an external speaker socket in the main chassis of a suitably configured PC. Speakers being what they are, they will either work or not work.

Invariably, if they don't work, you need to check a few basic elements to get them working. This may sound pretty obvious to some people, but you'd be surprised at how often the basic things are overlooked in the hysteria of non-working multimedia sound devices.

In the first place, are the speakers switched on? Do they run from a power source such as the mains, and if so, are they plugged in via a mains adapter? If they are battery-driven, are there any batteries installed, and if so, are they fully charged? You might also check to see if the volume on the speakers is turned up! Also, are the speakers plugged into the sound board? If they are plugged into the card and they still don't work, it may not be the speakers at all. In fact, it may be that the board has been misconfigured and the IRQ and DMA settings are wrong. Of course, it may also be a defective set of speakers, but that is extremely rare, especially if they are new.❖

Chapter 20

Configuring MIDI Cards

by Ian Stokell

The MIDI interface card acts as a connection between the MIDI controller, such as a keyboard or guitar, and your PC. Also in that equation is a synthesizer, which actually generates the MIDI sounds. The MIDI interface can be part of a sound card, which is how most users will come to know about MIDI, or as a separate interface card. Either way, without a MIDI interface you can make use of an external controller for your MIDI recordings. If you have a sound board with a MIDI interface in the form of the MIDI/joystick port, you won't need a separate MIDI interface card.

This chapter covers installing and configuring a separate MIDI interface card. The MPU-401 interface protocol is mentioned throughout this chapter. It is actually the MIDI "language" originally invented by Roland and is now virtually the *de facto* standard when it comes to MIDI use on the PC.

In this chapter you learn to do the following:

- Add a MIDI board using the Add New Hardware Wizard

- Install and change MIDI board software drivers

- Set up your MIDI instrument

- Configure your MIDI board—for example, the volume setting

Starting the Add New Hardware Wizard for a MIDI Card

Before you can configure a MIDI card for use with Windows 95, you have to install it. Fortunately, Windows 95 makes it a lot easier to install expansion cards than under the old DOS/Windows combination.

You will see how to install a MIDI board from a hardware vendor such as Music Quest.

The Add New Hardware Wizard can be accessed either through the Control Panel feature or by choosing Sound Cards, Setting Up from the Help Topics option. In this example, we'll go through the control panel option.

1. Click the Start menu.

2. Choose Settings, Control Panel.

3. Open the Add New Hardware Control Panel. The Add New Hardware Wizard appears (see fig. 20.1).

Fig. 20.1

The initial Add New Hardware Wizard screen explains what the wizard does.

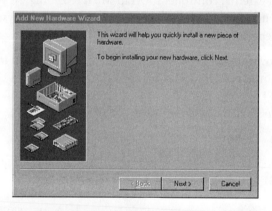

4. Click the Next button. The first screen where the user has to make a choice appears, giving you an automatic detection option (see fig. 20.2).

   You are then asked to answer the question, "Do you want Windows to search for your new hardware?" Answering Yes (Recommended) will let Windows 95 automatically detect new hardware that you have recently installed. Answering No will allow you to manually add the new hardware using the wizard.

5. To learn how to manually add new hardware, click No. The Hardware Types list box appears (see fig. 20.3).

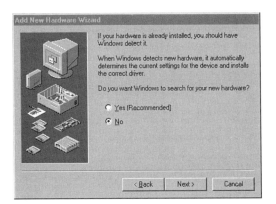

Fig. 20.2
You have the choice to automatically detect new hardware or manually add it.

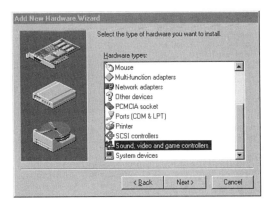

Fig. 20.3
The wizard offers a variety of hardware types from which to choose.

6. Select the type of hardware device you want to add from the wizard list—Sound, Video, and Game Controllers.

7. Click the Next button. A hardware manufacturer and model list appears for the type of device you selected (see fig. 20.4).

8. Click the MIDI board manufacturer's name in the left window. A list of their products that Windows 95 is familiar with appears in the right window. Select the MIDI board you want to add. In this case, it is Music Quest MPU-401 Compatible.

9. Click Next. The window changes to reveal the recommended settings you should use for your new MIDI board (see fig. 20.5).

Fig. 20.4
Choose the manufacturer and hardware model you want to install.

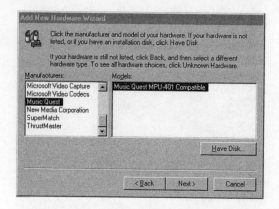

Fig. 20.5
You are provided with the recommended settings for your new MIDI board.

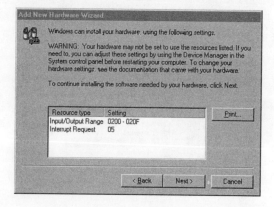

If you need to install a device driver from a manufacturer's floppy disk, refer to the next section, "Installing a Driver from a Floppy Disk."

Note

These settings are very important. They are automatically figured out by Windows 95 based on what resources are available according to the Device Manager registry.

Tip

Because these settings are so important, write them down or print them out. You should configure your new MIDI board according to these settings before you install it.

10. Click the Next button.

11. The wizard screen tells you that the installation of the necessary software for the new board is complete. Click the Finish button (see fig. 20.6).

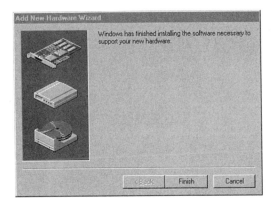

Fig. 20.6
The wizard tells you the software installation is complete.

12. A System Settings Change dialog box appears telling you to shut down your PC and install the necessary hardware (see fig. 20.7).

Answer the question, "Do you want to shut down your computer now?" In this case, click Yes to install the new MIDI card.

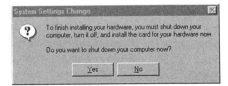

Fig. 20.7
You need to shut down your PC to install the new hardware device.

13. You now need to configure the new MIDI card according to the settings obtained during the wizard process. Read the documentation that accompanies your new MIDI card to learn how to change the interrupt request (IRQ) and input/output (I/O) settings.

14. Install the new MIDI card according to the manufacturer's instructions.

Installing a Driver from a Floppy Disk

You may need to install a driver for a hardware device, such as a MIDI board, from a manufacturer's floppy disk. From the hardware manufacturer and model screen (refer to fig. 20.4), accessed via the steps in the previous section, do the following:

1. Click the <u>H</u>ave Disk button. The Install From Disk box appears (see fig. 20.8).

Fig. 20.8
Insert the manufacturer's installation disk into the selected drive if you need to install a device driver not already supported by Windows 95.

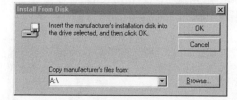

2. Specify the disk drive letter and the directory from where the manufacturer's software files should be copied.

3. Click OK.

Letting Windows 95 Autodetect a MIDI Card

Using the Add New Hardware Wizard, you can automatically have Windows 95 detect hardware components that have been newly installed on your PC. To do this, open the Add New Hardware Wizard, as described in an earlier section "Starting Add New Hardware Wizard for a MIDI Card," and follow these steps:

1. In answer to the question "Do you want Windows to search for your new hardware?" choose <u>Y</u>es (refer to fig. 20.2).

2. Click the Next button. The next screen tells you that the wizard will now locate any new hardware (see fig. 20.9).

Fig. 20.9
The first screen tells you that the automatic search for new hardware may take a few minutes.

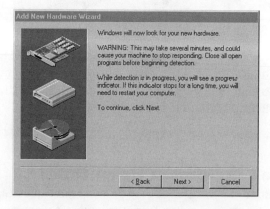

3. Click the Next button. Along the bottom of the screen is a progress indicator informing you of how the search is going (see fig. 20.10).

4. Click the Next button when the search is finished.

Fig. 20.10
The progress indicator tells you how the automatic search for new hardware is going.

The wizard's final screen tells you of any new hardware devices that it has found. If none are found, you have the choice to install a new device manually using the Add New Hardware Wizard.

Troubleshooting

I can't get MIDI files to play back properly.

To start with, check the card's resource settings, such as IRQ settings, to make sure they are configured correctly for your specific MIDI board. Then make sure the MIDI board is correctly identified in Device Manager.

Configuring Your MIDI Card

Having installed your new MIDI card, you can now adjust the sound and also set up a MIDI instrument to use. You may also want to change software drivers at some point, which is the first subject discussed in this section.

Adding or Changing Hardware Drivers

At some point you may need to add or change a driver for a hardware device, such as a MIDI card. For any peripheral hardware component to work with your PC, there must be a software driver installed. The driver acts as a sort of translator. Without that special software driver, the new device and the computer's operating system will not be able to communicate.

Unlike the old DOS/Windows combination, Windows 95 gives you an easy way to change drivers for specific components—using the Device Manager. If you remember, Device Manager is the centralized registry of system properties and configurations.

◀ See "Using the Device Manager," p. 334

You can change a driver for a hardware device by following these steps:

1. Click the Start menu.

2. Choose Settings, Control Panel.

3. Open the System Control Panel.

4. When the System Properties sheet appears, click the Device Manager page (see fig. 20.11).

Fig. 20.11
Device Manager is the central registry of hardware component resource settings.

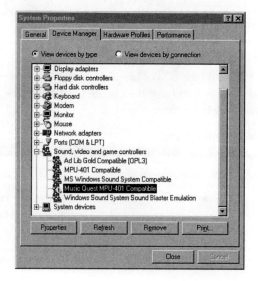

5. Click the plus sign next to Sound, Video and Game Controllers.

6. Double-click the hardware device you are interested in. For this example, choose Music Quest MPU-401 Compatible.

7. The Music Quest MPU-401 Compatible Properties sheet appears. Select the Driver page (see fig. 20.12).

8. Click the Change Driver button. The Select Device window appears (see fig. 20.13).

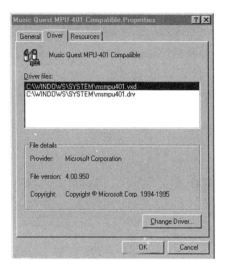

Fig. 20.12
The Driver page shows which drivers are associated with a specific hardware device.

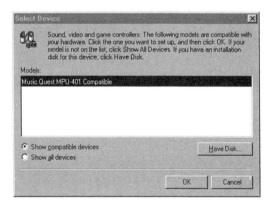

Fig. 20.13
The Select Device window allows you to choose the device that you want to add or change drivers for.

The Models list details the models that are compatible with your PC. Select the Show Compatible Devices option. However, if the hardware model you want is not on the list, you should select the Show All Devices button. The list will then change to show all hardware devices.

9. Click the device for which you want to install the driver and click OK. The Select Device window disappears to reveal the Driver page showing the driver files and their correct directory path.

10. Select the driver you want and click OK. You then return to the Device Manager screen.

11. Click the Close button.

Troubleshooting

There is hissing and distortion when playing MIDI files. How can I get rid of it?

There may be interference coming from either the power source or another card installed in your computer. Turn your PC off and move the MIDI board as far away from both the power supply and other boards as possible. If you can, leave a few empty expansion slots in between the MIDI board and the next card.

Volume Setting

The volume level can be adjusted when using a MIDI card via the Audio page in the Multimedia Properties sheet.

To adjust the playback and recording volume level, do the following:

1. Click the Start menu.

2. Choose <u>S</u>ettings, Control Panel.

3. Select the Multimedia Control Panel. The Multimedia Properties sheet appears (see fig. 20.14).

Fig. 20.14
Multimedia Properties sheet's Audio page lets you set the volume for both playback and recording sound.

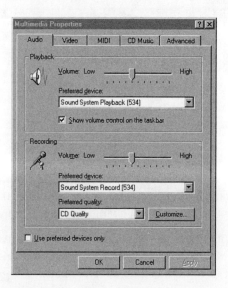

4. You can change both the playback and recording volume levels by dragging the Playback <u>V</u>olume or Recording Volu<u>m</u>e slider.

5. When the desired volume level is obtained, click OK.

Setting Up a MIDI Instrument

Setting up a MIDI instrument to work with a MIDI card is a simple process. Here is a quick overview of setting up such an instrument:

1. Plug the instrument into the MIDI card's MIDI port.

2. Click the Start menu.

3. Choose Settings, Control Panel.

4. Open the Multimedia Control Panel.

5. In the Multimedia Properties sheet, click the MIDI page (see fig. 20.15).

Fig. 20.15
The MIDI page in Multimedia Properties allows you to specify your MIDI output.

6. Click the Add New Instrument button. The MIDI Instrument Installation Wizard appears (see fig. 20.16).

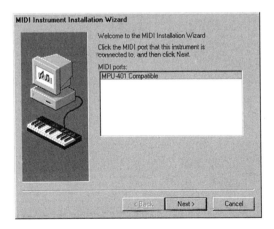

Fig. 20.16
Specify the port that the MIDI instrument is connected to.

7. Click the Next button. The Instrument Definitions screen appears (see fig. 20.17).

Fig. 20.17
For non-general MIDI instruments, you must select their definitions.

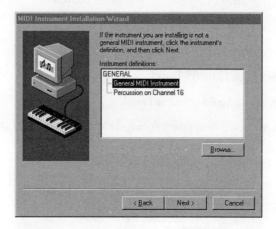

8. Make your selection and click the Next button. The next screen that appears allows you to select a name that identifies the instrument (see fig. 20.18).

Fig. 20.18
Don't use an elaborate title when you name your new MIDI instrument.

9. Name your new instrument and click the Finish button. You return to the MIDI page, which now contains your new instrument (see fig. 20.19).

10. Select Single Instrument on the MIDI page.

11. Select the instrument you just installed, and click OK.

Your new MIDI instrument is now installed.

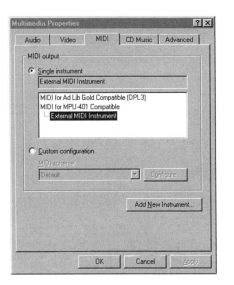

Fig. 20.19
The MIDI page
contains the name
of your new
instrument.

Moving a MIDI Instrument to Another Board

You can move MIDI instruments between boards. There may be an occasion when you have a choice of sound boards for instruments—maybe a high-quality 16-bit board, or a more entry-level 8-bit one. In either case, to move an instrument between boards, follow these steps:

1. Click the Start menu.

2. Choose Settings, Control Panel.

3. Open the Multimedia Control Panel.

4. In the Multimedia Properties sheet, click the Advanced page (see fig. 20.20).

5. Click the plus sign next to MIDI Devices and Instruments.

6. From the ensuing list, click the plus sign next to the board your MIDI instrument was connected to.

7. Click the instrument you want to move, and click the Properties button.

8. From the resulting External MIDI Instrument Properties sheet, select the Detail page (see fig. 20.21).

Fig. 20.20
The Advanced page in Multimedia Properties is where you specify the MIDI instrument you want to move.

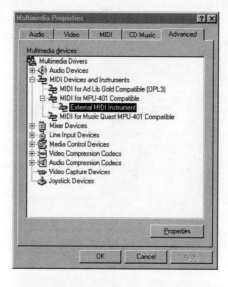

Fig. 20.21
Select the new board from the MIDI port list to where you want to attach the instrument.

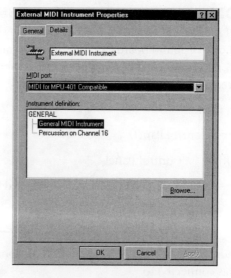

9. Choose the name of the board you want to connect the instrument to from the MIDI port list, and click OK.

10. You return to the Advanced page in Multimedia Properties; click OK.

11. Connect your MIDI instrument into the new board you just specified.

Troubleshooting MIDI Cards

Just as with sound cards, getting sound capabilities to run properly using MIDI interface cards can be problematic at times. While the centralized Device Manager registry and system resources and the highly useful Plug and Play standard both help to alleviate problems, problems can still occur.

By far, the most likely source of problems will involve *hardware conflicts*, or two hardware components trying to use the same system resources at the same time. Device Manager will help in this respect as it will suggest available IRQ and I/O settings when you run the Add New Hardware Wizard. But even this is not foolproof.

Fortunately, when hardware conflicts do occur, Windows 95 provides an excellent Help option (accessed from the Start menu), along with an especially useful step-by-step Hardware Conflict Troubleshooter. The latter is accessed via the Hardware, Troubleshooting Conflicts option from the Help Topics Index.

The Troubleshooting Wizard is a step-by-step investigative process that hopefully will identify the offending problem, and provide at least a suggestion for fixing it.

In addition, your MIDI interface card should also include documentation relating to possible hardware compatibility problems, and a toll-free customer or technical support number that users can call for advice. ❖

Chapter 21

Configuring Joysticks and Game Cards

by Paul Sanna

Don't be embarrassed; go ahead and configure your game card to work with Windows 95! Computer games certainly haven't been limited to the domain of younger folks, and recent action/adventure game titles available on CD-ROM clearly have been marketed towards the adult gamer.

Prior to Windows 95, configuring a PC to run a Windows game was as challenging as the game itself. Most games have extremely high memory requirements, but they also require you have a game card driver loaded into memory as well. A *game card* is an adapter you install in your computer that enables game software to work with a joystick plugged into the game card. Windows 95 makes it much easier to run resource-hungry games, as well as to configure the all-important game controller. This chapter helps you get your game card running with Windows 95.

In this chapter, you learn how to

- Install your new game card into your PC

- Specify what model game card is installed in your PC

- Let Windows 95 detect what game card is installed

> **Tip**
>
> What's the most important rule when you are setting up a new appliance, toaster, VCR, new video game, or whatever? Have the user manual or documentation handy. This rule also applies to setting up new hardware for your PC. Before you start to configure a new game card or monitor, be sure you have any relevant
>
> (continues)

(continued)

documentation by your side. You may need to supply information included in the user manual. Also, be sure you have any disks (floppy or CD-ROM) supplied with the device; Windows 95 may need software supplied on the disk.

Installing Your New Game Card into Your PC

The first task in getting a game card to work with Windows 95 is installing the new piece of equipment in your PC. In fact, after you have installed the card, you may have very little (or no) work to do to configure Windows 95. For example, if you have a Plug-and-Play system and the card is Plug-and-Play compatible, Windows 95 does all the work necessary to configure your new game card. In this section, you learn how to install your game card into your PC and how to recognize if your PC and card are both Plug-and-Play compatible.

> **Note**
>
> Windows 95 supports PCs with Plug-and-Play devices. This means that when you install a Plug-and-Play device into your PC, such as a game card, or simply plug one in, such as a monitor, Windows 95 automatically detects the presence of the new device and configures it for use in Windows 95.
>
> This Plug-and-Play functionality also requires the BIOS on your PC to be Plug-and-Play compatible. Even if you do not have Plug-and-Play BIOS or Plug-and-Play devices, Windows 95 can still detect and configure devices using the Add New Hardware Wizard, as you learn in the next few sections of this chapter. Also, certain devices such as joysticks and game cards can be detected immediately when Windows 95 starts.

Here are the steps necessary to install a new game card into your PC; be sure to check the documentation provided with your game card for specific installation instructions:

1. Shut down Windows 95, turn off the power on your PC, unplug the power cord, and follow the instructions enclosed with the card to install the card into the PC.

2. Turn on your PC and boot Windows 95.

3. If the game card is a Plug-and-Play model, Windows 95 notifies you that it has detected and identified the new card. Windows may prompt you in a dialog box for the location, probably a floppy disk, of the driver of the game card. If so, enter the location of the driver in the dialog box. For example, if the driver is on a floppy disk supplied by the manufacturer of the card, insert the disk into the disk drive and then specify the name of the drive (for example, **A**).

> **Note**
>
> A *driver* is software that helps operating systems and other software communi-
> cate and work with hardware and other systems. For example, a driver is
> required for a printer to work with Windows 3.1. In the case of Windows 95,
> drivers are required to help different hardware devices work with the Windows
> 95 operating systems.

4. If the game card is not a Plug-and-Play model, Windows 95 does not prompt you for any information. You should start the Add New Hardware Wizard to configure your new game card (see next section).

Starting the Add New Hardware Wizard

Game cards are identified and configured for use in Windows 95 through the Add New Hardware Wizard. The Add New Hardware Wizard automates in Windows 95 most of the work you had to complete in Windows 3.x and DOS to set up a new game card. The Add New Hardware Wizard can be found in the Control Panel folder (see fig. 21.1).

Follow these steps to start the Add New Hardware Wizard:

1. Double-click the Add New Hardware Wizard icon; or right-click the icon and then choose Open from the menu that appears; or click once on the icon and choose File, Open. The dialog box shown in figure 21.2 appears.

2. Click the Next button. The next step in using the Add New Hardware Wizard to configure a game card is to decide who will identify which hardware is installed: *you* or *Windows 95*.

Fig. 21.1
The Add New
Hardware Wizard
is stored in the
Control Panel
folder.

Add New
Hardware Wizard

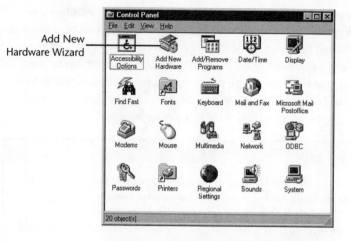

Fig 21.2
The first dialog
box that appears
when you start
most wizards in
Windows 95, such
as the Add New
Hardware Wizard,
tells you what the
wizard does and
gives you the
opportunity to
cancel.

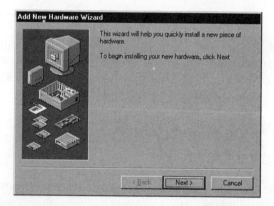

Tip

Though the Add New Hardware Wizard is located in the Control Panel folder, you
can create a shortcut so you can launch the wizard from wherever you choose. If you
plan to do a lot of work with the hardware in Windows 95, you could save some time
by creating a shortcut to the wizard right on the desktop.

Deciding Who Specifies the Hardware

◄ See "Creating
Shortcuts,"
p. 148

You can use one of two different approaches to specify what game card you
have installed in Windows 95. You can let Windows 95 try to identify your
game card automatically, or you can tell Windows 95 explicitly what model
game card is installed on your PC. There are advantages and disadvantages to
both approaches.

Windows Detects the Hardware...

If you let Windows 95 detect the game card, you have little to no work to do. You answer a few prompts, and eventually Windows 95 identifies your game card and configures itself to operate properly with the card. A downside to Windows 95 autodetecting the card, however, is that this is a lengthy process; Windows 95 tries to identify *all* of the hardware in your system. It's impossible to tell Windows 95 to look specifically for a game card. If you are short on time and you know the model of your game card, it may be best for you to tell Windows 95 what hardware you have installed.

I Tell Windows What Hardware I Have...

If you decide to do the legwork and identify for Windows 95 the model of your game card, you have little chance for error. Provided you know what hardware is installed on your PC, you can be sure Windows 95 installs the correct driver by explicitly telling Windows 95 what hardware to configure. However, this approach sidesteps one of the most powerful aspects of Windows 95: its ability to detect hardware. You need to know the exact manufacturer and model information in order to supply that information to Windows 95. Lots of work went into the development of Windows 95's capability to recognize your hardware—why not take advantage of it?

Letting Windows 95 Detect the Game Card

The process for letting Windows 95 detect your game card is simple: start the Add New Hardware Wizard, Windows 95 inspects your system for hardware devices it doesn't recognize, and then you tell Windows 95 you want to configure the game card it found. Next, Windows 95 informs you what model game card it thinks it found, you confirm that information, and then Windows 95 configures itself so it always loads the correct drivers for use with the adapter.

To let Windows 95 detect your game card, follow these steps:

1. Follow the instructions to start the Add New Hardware Wizard shown earlier in the "Starting the Add New Hardware Wizard" section.

2. Click the Next button in the first dialog box that appears. The dialog box shown in figure 21.3 appears.

3. Click the Yes (Recommended) option button and then click Next. The dialog box shown in figure 21.4 appears. This dialog box asks you to confirm that you want Windows 95 to detect the hardware on your PC.

Fig. 21.3
Windows 95 recommends that it detect all of the new hardware installed on your PC.

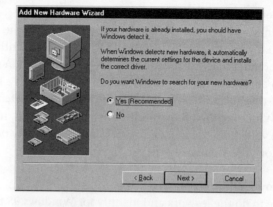

Fig 21.4
Just before Windows 95 begins to inspect your system for installed hardware, Windows 95 verifies that you want to continue.

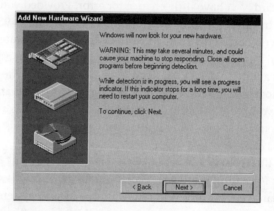

4. Choose the Next button. Windows 95 now starts the detection phase when it inspects your PC for installed hardware.

5. After Windows 95 completes the detection phase, it displays a dialog box from which you can view the list of new hardware the Add New Hardware Wizard found. To configure Windows 95 with the new game card, click the Finish button. Depending upon the capabilities of your game card and monitor, Windows 95 may ask if it can reboot the system for the changes to take effect.

Manually Specifying Your Game Card

The process to manually specify your game card is simple: start the Add New Hardware Wizard; tell Windows 95 you want to install a sound, video, or game controller; pick the game card from a list provided by Windows 95; and then Windows 95 configures itself so it always loads the correct driver for use with the card. Most likely, you won't have to reboot your machine.

To specify the game card that is installed on your PC, follow these steps:

1. Follow the instructions to start the Add New Hardware wizard shown earlier in the "Starting the Add New Hardware Wizard" section.

2. Click the Next button in the first dialog box that appears. The dialog box shown in figure 21.5 appears.

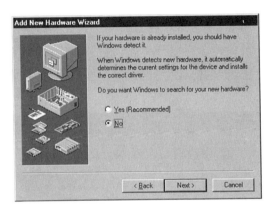

Fig. 21.5
Windows allows you to manually specify what hardware you want to install.

3. Click the No option button and then click Next. The dialog box shown in figure 21.6 appears.

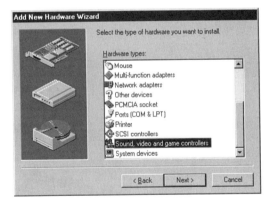

Fig. 21.6
You specify what type of hardware you plan to install.

4. Choose Sound, Video and Game Controllers in the Hardware Types list box and then click Next. The dialog box in figure 21.7 appears.

5. Click the manufacturer of your game card in the Manufacturers list box. The list of supported game cards for the manufacturer you chose appears in the Models list box. Click the model of your game card in the Models list box.

IV

Setting Up Hardware

Fig. 21.7
Windows 95
provides a list of
supported game
card models (and
their manufactur-
ers) for you to
choose from.

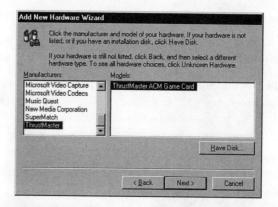

Tip

If you have the software installation disk that was shipped with the game card,
you can avoid having to pick the manufacturer and model of your game card
from the lists provided with Windows 95. Insert the disk into a floppy drive
and click the Have Disk button in the dialog box shown in figure 21.7. Follow
the prompts to specify the location of OEMSETUP.INF, which should appear
on the disk. This file contains all the information needed to configure the
game card.

6. Click the Next button. Windows 95 informs you that it has completed
the installation of the game card.

7. Click the Finish button.

Chapter 22

Configuring Mice and Other Pointing Devices

by Gregory J. Root

Most of the time, when you install Windows 95, the installation process will autodetect your pointing device. Windows can autodetect Kensington, Logitech, Microsoft, and other Microsoft-compatible pointing devices. A pointing device is a hardware peripheral controlling the position and movement of the arrow on your screen. Setting up Windows 95 to receive input from your mouse or other pointing device can be a smooth installation process.

Now, Windows 95 has the capability to accept commands from more than one pointing device. Instead of loading special drivers that devour memory resources, Windows 95 provides simultaneous input from accessibility devices like eye-gazers and head-pointers. If you like using a trackball for specific programs but would prefer to use a mouse for everything else, both can control Windows 95 at the same time.

Within this chapter, you learn how to configure your pointing device by

- Adding your mouse or pointing device
- Manually specifying a pointing device
- Setting pointing device properties

Starting Add New Hardware Wizard for Pointing Devices

The Add New Hardware Wizard provides you the ability to let Windows 95 identify your pointing device. The wizard steps you through the process. It can automatically detect your pointing device, or you may manually specify it. After you've told Windows what pointing device you have, you'll want to customize how your buttons react, how sensitive it is to your motions, or other special features of your device.

Letting Windows 95 Autodetect a Pointing Device

Allowing Windows 95 to automatically detect your pointing device is the easiest way to add a new one to your system. Windows 95 comes with many drivers and should know about your new device.

Before you begin the Add New Hardware Wizard, you should connect your new pointing device to the computer. This allows Windows 95 to query it to determine the type, make, and model. If you don't have the device connected when you run the wizard, you have to manually specify it. Because manually specifying a pointing device is a more complex process, it is highly preferable to use the wizard.

> **Caution**
>
> Make sure your computer power is turned off when adding any new hardware. In this case, you don't want to damage your new pointing device.

To begin detecting your pointing device, use the following steps. A Microsoft PS/2 Port Mouse is used in the example. However, these steps work for any device you might want to configure:

> **Tip**
>
> If you aren't sure if Windows 95 supports your pointing device, let Windows 95 try to identify it anyway. Chances are, it will be able to identify the device.

1. Click the Start button (or press Ctrl+Esc if you don't have any pointing devices currently installed), and choose Settings, Control Panel to open the Control Panel. You'll access the Add New Hardware Wizard here.

2. Double-click the Add New Hardware control panel, as shown in figure 22.1, to start the Add New Hardware Wizard. If you're without a pointing device, use the arrow keys on your keyboard to move to the Add New Hardware icon and press Enter.

Fig. 22.1
The Add New Hardware control panel is accessed via the Control Panel.

3. As shown in figure 22.2, the Add New Hardware Wizard begins to detect your device when you click the Next button. You can also press Enter to continue. At any time during this process, you can click the Cancel button to stop.

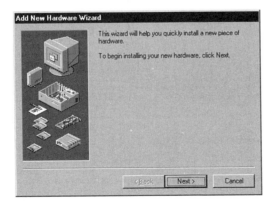

Fig. 22.2
To tell the wizard you're ready for the next step, click the Next button.

4. When the next step of the wizard is shown (see fig. 22.3), make sure the Yes (Recommended) option is chosen when you're asked "Do you want Windows to search for your new hardware?." When using a keyboard to navigate, use the Tab key to select the correct option and press the spacebar. Click the Next button when you're ready to move on.

Fig. 22.3
Choose Yes when asked to let Windows search for your pointing device.

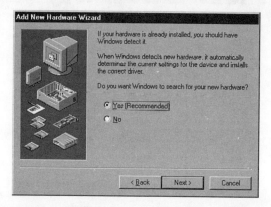

5. The next step of the wizard reminds you that detecting your new device may take a long time. As shown in figure 22.4, click Next (or press Enter) to confirm searching for your pointer.

Fig 22.4
Once you make the final confirmation, a progress bar displays the status of finding your new device.

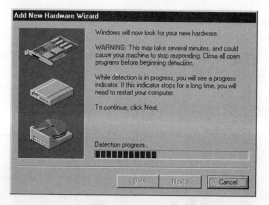

Tip

The progress bar can stop moving for a long time. Before you restart your computer (as instructed on the screen), check to see if the hard drive light is flashing. If you don't have a hard drive activity light, put your ear next to your computer and listen for the clicking of your computer accessing the hard drive. Oftentimes the wizard is still trying to identify a specific device type, even though the progress bar has stopped for a few moments.

Troubleshooting

My computer froze when detecting my new hardware. Shouldn't I just press the Reset button?

If you need to restart your computer because it has stopped responding, don't just use Ctrl+Alt+Delete or press the Reset button on the front of your computer. Turn off the power to your computer, wait three seconds, and then turn it back on. One of the reasons your computer stopped responding was that a piece of hardware became confused. Using Ctrl+Alt+Delete or the Reset button won't initialize your computer hardware to a clean state. Turning the power off and then on is the only way to accomplish this. Once Windows 95 has finished restarting, you need to go back to step 1 in this section.

---

6. The wizard notifies you that it successfully detected your device (see fig. 22.5). If the wizard was not able to detect your pointing device, you have to manually specify it. See "Manually Specifying a Pointing Device" later in this chapter.

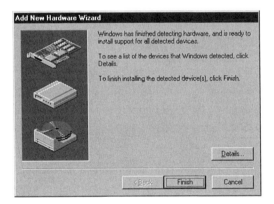

Fig. 22.5
Windows 95 has successfully detected your new pointing device.

7. If you want to see the details of what the wizard found, click the Details button. You see a list of your new hardware.

As shown in figure 22.6, the wizard successfully detected the new Microsoft PS/2 Port Mouse installed in the computer before the power was turned on. If you don't care to see the details or have finished viewing the list of details, click the Finish button to install the drivers that support your device. Your computer is now configured to accept commands from your new pointing device. Congratulations!

Fig. 22.6
You can view the
details of what the
wizard found by
clicking the
Details button.

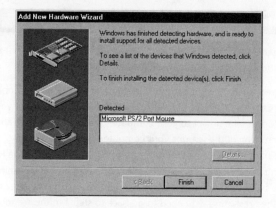

> **Note**
>
> If the device doesn't work at this time or the name of the device in the Detected list
> doesn't seem quite right, choose Cancel instead. Follow the procedures in the next
> section.

Manually Specifying a Pointing Device

You may need to manually specify your pointing device if the Add New Hardware Wizard wasn't able to automatically detect it. Or, you may be installing the driver for the device before you've physically connected it to your computer. Or, you may have a new "designed-for-Windows 95" pointing device that has a setup disk with the correct driver from the manufacturer. You use the Add New Hardware Wizard in any of these cases. Use these steps to let Windows 95 know what type of pointing device you will be using:

1. Click the Start button (or press Ctrl+Esc if you don't have any pointing devices currently installed), and choose Settings, Control Panel to open the Control Panel. You access the Add New Hardware Wizard here.

2. Double-click the Add New Hardware control panel, to start the Add New Hardware Wizard (refer to fig. 22.1). If you don't have a pointing device, use the arrow keys on your keyboard to move to the Add New Hardware icon and press Enter.

3. As shown in figure 22.2, the Add New Hardware Wizard allows you to specify your device when you click the Next button. You can also press Enter to continue. At any time during this process, you can select the Cancel button to stop.

4. When the next step of the Wizard is shown (as in fig. 22.7), make sure the No option is chosen when you're asked "Do you want Windows to search for your new hardware?". When using a keyboard to navigate, press the Tab key to move the focus to the correct option and then press the spacebar. Click the Next button when you're ready to move on.

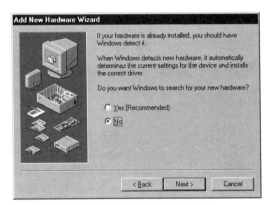

Fig. 22.7
Choose No when asked to let Widows search for your pointing device.

5. From the list of Hardware Types in figure 22.8, choose Mouse if you're adding a mouse, and click the Next button at the bottom of the window.

If using only a keyboard to navigate, use the arrow keys to select Mouse and then press Enter. Windows now knows you want to manually specify a mouse.

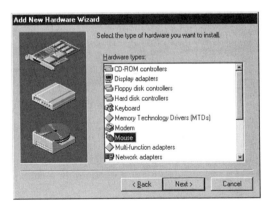

Fig. 22.8
When adding a pointing device, select the Mouse hardware type to manually specify it.

6. From the left-hand side <u>M</u>anufacturers list in figure 22.9, select who made your pointing device. If you don't know who made your pointing device or can't find it in the list, leave the selection on Standard Mouse Types. Then select the specific model you have from the list on the right. If you are using Standard Mouse Types, select the type of input device from the list on the right. In our example, figure 22.9 illustrates a selection of the manufacturer as Microsoft and the model as Microsoft PS/2 Port Mouse.

Fig. 22.9
Select a manufacturer's name in the list on the left, and one of the models from the list on the right. Click <u>H</u>ave Disk if the manufacturer provided one.

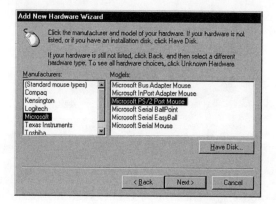

If you have a disk that came with the pointing device from the manufacturer, then click <u>H</u>ave Disk instead. Figure 22.10 shows Windows 95 asking for the manufacturer's disk to be inserted in your floppy drive to be processed. Selecting OK begins loading the driver from the floppy disk. Once this is complete, you're ready for the next step.

Fig. 22.10
Place the manufacturer's driver disk into the floppy drive to load the new driver.

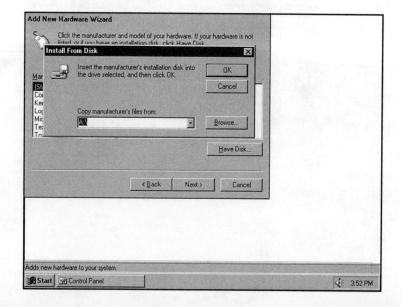

7. Whether you've selected your manufacturer and model from the list or loaded the driver from the manufacturer's disk, you now need to install the correct drivers by clicking Finish, as illustrated in figure 22.11.

Fig. 22.11
Complete the installation of your pointing device by clicking Finish.

You may need to modify some device properties using the Device Manager. This is the case if the wizard tells you that other hardware is conflicting with the pointing device you are trying to install (see the two examples of fig. 22.12). Or, Windows may have found settings usable by the new pointing device, but wasn't able to change the settings on the actual device. First, click the Next button to complete the installation of the device drivers. Then, use the Device Manager in the System control panel to adjust the pointing device resources before you reboot your computer.

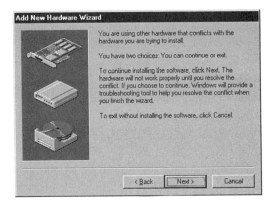

Fig. 22.12
If either of these results appear after you selected your pointing device, you need to modify the device properties using the Device Manager in the System control panel before rebooting your computer.

◀ See "Changing
Device Proper-
ties," p. 334

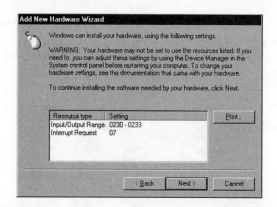

Tip

If Windows was able to allot device settings as shown in the first window shown in fig. 22.12, click the Print button to print a record of what Windows has set aside for your new device. This hard copy comes in handy when you have to use the Device Manager to adjust hardware settings.

8. After completing all these steps, Windows might tell you that the system must be rebooted. You need to reboot the system if your pointing device is not Plug and Play compatible. If you're ready to do so, then go ahead and click Yes to reboot. If you have other devices to set up or need to make modifications to some settings to avoid hardware conflicts, select No.

Caution

Be aware that if Windows is asking to restart the computer, your new pointing device won't work until you do so.

Setting Pointing Device Properties

Your pointing device doesn't have to be a boring little arrow that moves around on the screen. You have a say as to what it looks like. If you're left-handed, you don't have to suffer in a right-handed world—you can reconfigure the buttons. If you don't like to move your pointing device around a lot or think you have to double-click too fast, you can adjust the sensitivity of the device. Also, manufacturers sometimes provide additional features specific to their devices. Read through the next few sections to take advantage of some very nice features.

Every pointing device is adjusted using the Mouse control panel. To get started, access the control panel by following these steps:

1. Click the Start button (or press Ctrl+Esc if you don't have any mice currently installed), and choose Settings, Control Panel to open the Control Panel.

2. Double-click the Mouse control panel, as shown in figure 22.13, to access the properties of your mouse.

Fig. 22.13
The Mouse control panel is accessed via the Control Panel.

From here, you can set buttons, pointer styles, mouse motions, and general properties. Read on to find out how.

Buttons

The Button tab is the default tab displayed when opening the Mouse Properties control sheet. Here you can adjust how fast or slow you double-click. You can also set which button is the primary button if you're left-handed. To adjust the double-click speed:

1. In the Double-Click Speed group box, drag the slider left or right to adjust the speed as seen in figure 22.14. If you drag it to the right, Windows requires you to shorten the amount of time between the first and

second click. If you drag the slider to the left, Windows allows more time between the first and second click.

Fig. 22.14
You can adjust the double-click speed by dragging the slider. Adjust the button configuration at the top by selecting a button configuration.

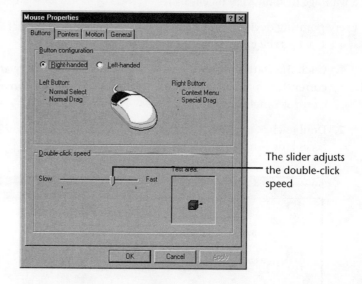

The slider adjusts the double-click speed

2. To test the amount of time between clicks of a double-click, try out your settings by double-clicking the jack-in-the-box in the lower-right Test Area (see fig. 22.15). You can tell if Windows understood the speed of your double-click when the jack-in-the-box jumps out of its box.

Fig. 22.15
The jack-in-the-box jumps out of its box if Windows understood your double-click in the Test Area.

To set the pointing device as a left-handed device, click the Left-handed radio button in the Button Configuration group box shown in figure 22.15. Conversely, to set it as a right-handed device, click the Right-handed radio button in the group box.

Pointers

As you may have noticed when using Windows, when a program is busy working on something or your pointer is positioned over the edges of a window, the pointer changes to a different shape. Now, with Windows 95, you can choose your own pointers. What's even better is that you can choose animated, color pointers.

You can change your pointers individually or as a scheme. To quickly change the set of pointers from the current scheme to another scheme, select the Pointers page at the top of the Mouse Properties sheet. (see fig. 22.16) Open the Scheme drop-down list and pick a new scheme. If no schemes are listed, you haven't created any yet.

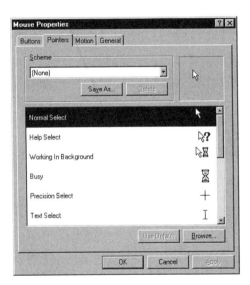

Fig. 22.16
Choose the Pointers page in the Mouse Properties sheet to change the pointers.

> **Note**
>
> If you've installed Microsoft Plus, the Desktop Themes can apply a complete set of mouse pointers appropriate for the theme you've selected. If you want to change a single pointer as part of your current desktop theme, you can do so without permanently changing the desktop theme's regular configuration.

Instead of changing all the pointers at the same time, click the Browse button to change a single pointer to something new and interesting. To learn how to do this, select the Pointers page in the Mouse Properties sheet (refer to fig. 22.16). Then perform these additional actions:

1. Highlight the pointer from the list you want to change and click the Browse button.

> **Tip**
>
> You can double-click the pointer for faster access to the Browse window.

2. From the Browse window, select a new pointer from the CURSORS folder. Only pointers with an ANI or CUR extension are listed. When you highlight a pointer name, the Browse window displays a preview of what the pointer will look like, as seen in figure 22.17. Once you've found the pointer you're looking for, click the Open button. This opens the CURSOR file and associates your choice to the pointer in the Pointer properties list. You can do this with as many pointers as you like.

Fig. 22.17
Select a new look for your pointer by selecting a pointer name in the Browse window.

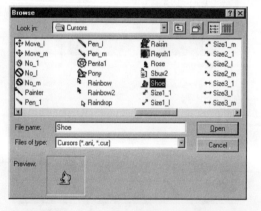

> **Note**
>
> If no pointer names appear in the Browse window, the extra mouse pointers were not installed when Windows 95 was installed. To add them, use the Windows Setup tab of the Add/Remove Software control panel.

◀ See "Selecting Custom Install Options," p. 107

IV

Setting Up Hardware

> **Caution**
>
> Even though it's fun to use color-animated cursors in a pointer scheme, consider using ones that have some relationship to the pointer's original appearance. For example, if you change all your pointers to a set of animals, you'll have a hard time remembering which animal means which type of pointer.

3. If you don't like a change you've made to a particular pointer, you can set it back to the default Windows 95 pointer. Select it in the list and click the Use Default button (refer to fig. 22.16).

> **Tip**
>
> If you want to reset all your pointers to their defaults, use the Scheme drop-down list and set the scheme name to (None).

Now that you've made some changes to the pointers on the property sheet, you may want to save the set of pointers as a scheme. You can do so by performing this step:

4. From the Pointers property sheet, click the Save As button.

5. When the Save Scheme dialog box appears as seen in figure 22.18, give your scheme a name and click OK to save it.

Fig. 22.18
Give your pointer scheme a name in the Save Scheme dialog box.

> **Caution**
>
> Windows does not warn you if you are about to save your new scheme with the same name as an existing scheme. You will replace the existing scheme if it's named the same as the one you use now.

If you would like to delete the current pointer scheme instead, then:

6. Select a pointer scheme name from the list. Then click the Delete button (refer to fig. 22.18). When you delete the pointer scheme, you won't delete the actual pointers. You're just breaking the association of the pointers from the CURSORS folder to the Pointers list.

Lastly, you want to apply all the changes you've made to your pointer settings. To learn how to do this:

7. Click the <u>A</u>pply button at the bottom of the Mouse Properties dialog box (see fig. 22.19). This saves your changes and leaves the dialog open for you to make other adjustments to your mouse. If you are through making changes, click OK to save all of your changes and close the Mouse Properties dialog box.

Caution

If you've added or deleted schemes, choosing Cancel will not undo those actions. Adding or deleting a scheme is permanent.

Motion

While using your pointing device, you might have come to some conclusions. One of them might be that you're moving it too much or too little when compared to the actual pointer movement on-screen. If you use a portable computer, another conclusion might be that it's hard to follow the pointer around on the small screen. In either of these cases, you want to select the Motion page at the top of the Mouse Properties sheet as shown in figure 22.19.

Fig. 22.19
Access the Motion settings in the Mouse Properties sheet by selecting the Motion page.

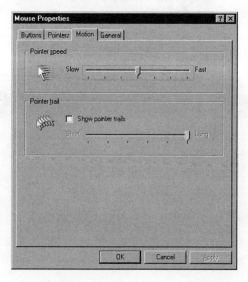

Troubleshooting

My pointer moves erratically.

If, when you shake the cable, it makes the situation better or worse, verify that the connection to your computer is secure. Sometimes, the connector has come loose from the port on your computer.

If that doesn't work, inspect the cable for breaks or cuts. If your cable is broken or pierced, repair or replacement is necessary. If there are no visible breaks, a wire inside the cable may have broken. This may have been caused by severe twisting of the cable, being placed under a heavy object for long periods of time, or a heavy object which dropped on it (for example, a paperweight or stapler).

Also, check the Windows Driver Library (WDL) for an updated driver for your pointing device. The *WDL* is an electronic library of drivers which is updated as new ones become available. You can access the WDL via the Microsoft Network (MSN) in the Windows 95 area; CompuServe via **GO MSL**; the Internet via World Wide Web or Gopher (both at **http://www.microsoft.com**), or FTP (**ftp:/ftp.microsoft.com**); or via the Microsoft Download Service at (206) 936-6735 (you only pay for the phone call).

To learn how to adjust the sensitivity of the pointing device to your taste, follow these steps:

1. Drag the slider left and right to adjust the sensitivity. Dragging the slider towards Slow requires you to move the pointing device more to make the pointer on-screen move in a certain direction. Dragging the slider towards Fast requires less pointing device movement to make the pointer on-screen move in a certain direction.

2. Click the Apply button at the bottom of the Mouse Properties sheet. This saves your changes and leaves the sheet open for you to make other adjustments to your pointing device.

3. If you are through making changes, click OK to save all of your changes and close the Mouse Properties sheet.

Troubleshooting

My pointer movement around the screen seems slow and jerky. What's wrong?

It all boils down to this: your computer is very busy performing a task. Or, if you shared a folder on your hard drive, other users may be heavily reading and writing information in it.

If you find it hard to follow the pointer on your portable computer screen, try turning on pointer trails. *Pointer trails* make it easier to locate your pointer on the screen. To learn how to turn on pointer trails and adjust their length, follow these steps:

1. In the Pointer Trail group box, click the Show Pointer Trails check box, as shown in figure 22.20. Then drag the slider left and right to adjust the trail length. Dragging the slider towards Short displays less of a trail. Dragging the slider towards Long displays a longer trail.

Fig. 22.20

Clicking the Show Pointer Trails check box turns on mouse trails.

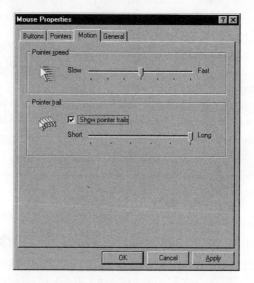

2. Click the Apply button at the bottom of the Mouse Properties sheet. This saves your changes and leaves the sheet open for you to make other adjustments to your pointing device.

3. If you are through making changes, click OK to save all of your changes and close the Mouse Properties sheet.

Troubleshooting

My pointer moves in one direction but not another. Help!

Try cleaning your mouse ball, track ball, and/or any internal motion contacts (usually small plastic wheels). If you're using a mouse, clean the glide pads on the bottom (if you have them). If you use a mouse pad, be sure to clean it regularly to prevent a build-up of dirt. Be sure to follow the cleaning and care instructions provided by your manufacturer. If you don't follow them carefully, you could damage the electronics. Pointing devices are designed to be highly sensitive to small motions.

General

The General page of the Mouse Properties sheet allows you to change the driver for your pointer. Additionally, if your pointing device manufacturer has provided additional capabilities with its driver, you're able to access them here. Click the General page at the top of the Mouse Properties sheet to begin learning about it (see fig. 22.21).

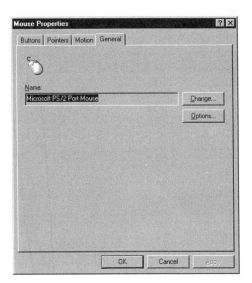

Fig. 22.21
Access the General settings in the Mouse Properties sheet by selecting the General page.

To change the current driver for your pointing device, you can do it via the General properties of the Mouse control panel:

1. Click the Change button on the far right side of the property sheet to display the Select Device window, shown in figure 22.22.

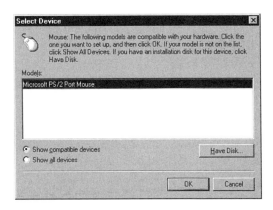

Fig. 22.22
The Select Device window allows you to select a compatible pointing device driver.

2. In most cases, you won't have many choices. Pointing device drivers usually aren't interchangeable. However, if you are presented with other choices, select a compatible driver from the list. You may want to click Show All Devices or Have Disk if you've changed your pointing device since the last time you used your computer.

> **Tip**
>
> If you're configuring a new pointing device, it's best to let Windows 95 try to automatically detect it for you. See "Letting Windows 95 Auto Detect Pointing Device" at the beginning of this chapter.

3. Once you've made your new selection, click the Apply button at the bottom of the Mouse Properties sheet. This saves your changes and leaves the dialog open for you to make other adjustments to your pointing device.

4. If you are through making changes, click OK to save all of your changes and close the Mouse Properties sheet.

If your pointing device manufacturer has provided extra capabilities to control the appearance or actions of your pointer, an Options button appears below the Change button (refer to fig. 22.21). The capabilities vary widely from manufacturer to manufacturer. Some better-known options are to change the size of the pointer or adjust the orientation of the pointing device. To view them, just click the Options button.

Chapter 23

Configuring Keyboards

by Ian Stokell

Despite Windows 95 being a graphical user interface-based operating environment, the keyboard remains a fundamental part of the computer system on which it runs. It does, of course, become essential if you intend to do any word processing or anything that requires more than the point-and-click operation that Windows is known for.

How you set up your keyboard can be a major factor in how efficiently things run. This chapter covers a variety of keyboard-related functions and configurations. In this chapter, you learn how to do the following:

- Install and configure a new keyboard

- Install accompanying keyboard software drivers, which are essential if the hardware device is to communicate properly with the operating system

- Change keyboard properties

- Change resource settings

First, though, you have to install a keyboard before it can be configured, which is the subject of the first section.

Starting the Keyboard Add New Hardware Wizard

Adding a new hardware device, such as a keyboard, is much easier under Windows 95 than under the old DOS/Windows combination because of the new Plug-and-Play standard and the addition of the extremely useful Add

New Hardware Wizard control panel. The wizard is essentially a step-by-step installation guide for any specified hardware device.

You can install a new keyboard by using the Add New Hardware Wizard. The Add New Hardware Wizard can be accessed either through the Control Panel option or by choosing Keyboard, Setting Up from the Help Topics option.

> **Note**
>
> If you turn off your computer and change keyboards, when the computer is switched on again, Windows 95 may be able to automatically detect it if it recognizes the component.

For this exercise you'll go through control panels:

1. Click the Start menu.

2. Choose Settings, Control Panel.

3. Open the Add New Hardware control panel. The Add New Hardware Wizard initial screen appears (see fig. 23.1).

Fig. 23.1
The initial Add New Hardware Wizard screen tells you how it can help you install new hardware.

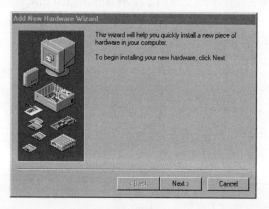

4. Click the Next button. The new Add New Hardware Wizard screen that appears is the first one that allows you to make a choice as to how you want to proceed (see fig. 23.2).

5. If you want Windows 95 to automatically find any new devices that you have added recently, just click the Automatically Detect Installed Hardware option. Or, if you want to select the new hardware to install, click the Install Specific Hardware option.

For this example, select the Install Specific Hardware option.

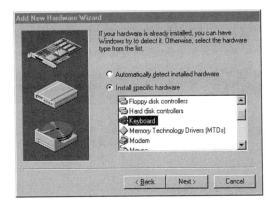

Fig. 23.2
You can use the Add New Hardware Wizard to install a new keyboard.

6. Select the type of hardware device you want to add from the wizard list—for example, select Keyboard.

7. Click the Next button. The hardware models list appears for the type of device you selected—for example, keyboards (see fig. 23.3).

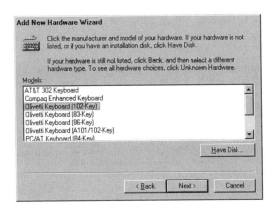

Fig. 23.3
Select the keyboard model you want to add from the wizard's model list.

8. Select the keyboard manufacturer's model type.

9. Click the Next button, or if you have an installation disk for your new keyboard or your keyboard is not listed, follow steps 10 through 12. If you don't need to install from a floppy disk, jump to step 13.

10. From the Add New Hardware Wizard panel, click Have Disk. The Install From Disk dialog box appears (see fig. 23.4).

11. Specify the disk letter and actual folder where the manufacturer's installation files should be copied from.

Fig. 23.4
To install a new device driver, you need to specify the file in the Install From Disk window.

12. Click OK. The Install From Disk window disappears, and you are back to the Add New Hardware Wizard.

> **Caution**
>
> Not all hardware vendors support Windows 95. As a result, sometimes software drivers do not work properly with Windows 95. Check this before buying new hardware. If there is a problem with compatibility, contact the component's manufacturer for advice.

13. Click the Next button. The wizard window changes to display the settings it wants you to use for the keyboard (see fig. 23.5).

Fig. 23.5
The Add New Hardware Wizard gives you the settings to use for your keyboard.

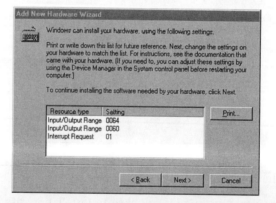

> **Tip**
>
> This list of resource settings is very important. As a result, you should write down these settings or print them out. These are the settings that the new keyboard should use.

14. Click the Next button. You are then asked to restart your PC.

15. Once you have restarted your PC, go into the System Properties control panel and click the Device Manager page. The Keyboard type listing now shows both your old keyboard type and your new keyboard that you just installed.

Not only that, but if you click either of those keyboard types listed and then click the Resources page, that page lists the other keyboard as conflicting with the new keyboard's resource settings—not surprising, as you can only have one keyboard working at once. What you then have to do is make the new keyboard's settings current and remove the old keyboard listed, by following steps 16 through 21.

16. Double-click the new keyboard type in Device Manager.

17. Select the General tab if it is not already selected.

18. Select the Original Configuration (Current) box if it is not already checked.

19. Close the General page by clicking OK.

20. You should now remove the old keyboard type. Click the old keyboard model type in Device Manager, and click Remove.

21. A warning box comes up asking if you are sure you want to remove the keyboard (see fig. 23.6). Click OK.

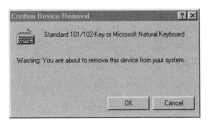

Fig. 23.6
A warning box appears asking you to confirm the keyboard removal.

The box disappears, as does the old keyboard's listing in Device Manager. To make sure, go to the Resources page and you see no conflicts listed for your new keyboard. Conflicts occur when two components, in this case keyboards, are assigned the same system resources.

Windows 95 includes a feature that allows you to automatically detect hardware devices that have been newly attached to the computer on which it is running. To have Windows 95 automatically detect new hardware devices, open the Add New Hardware Wizard and do the following:

1. Select the Automatically Detect Installed Hardware button on the Add New Hardware Wizard in the previous section (refer to fig. 23.2).

2. Click the Next button. A screen appears telling you that Windows 95 will now look for new hardware (see fig. 23.7).

Fig. 23.7
A warning appears telling you the search for new hardware may take some time.

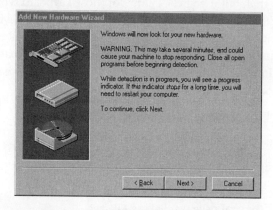

3. Click the Next button. A progress indicator then appears at the bottom of the screen (see fig. 23.8).

Fig. 23.8
A progress indicator tells you how the search for new hardware is going.

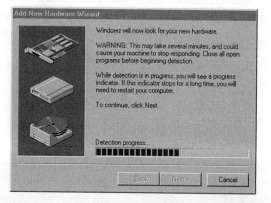

4. When the search is complete, click the Next button.

The screen then notifies you of any new devices it has found. If none are found, it asks if you want to install a new device manually. If you want to manually install a new device, it brings you back to the Add New Hardware Wizard screen in the previous section. You can manually install the keyboard as described.

Adding or Changing Keyboard Drivers

For a hardware device, such as a keyboard, to work with the operating system controlling the computer, you need a sort of intermediary between the two. This is essentially what software drivers do. Every piece of hardware attached to a computer requires some sort of software driver to tell the operating system what the hardware wants to do. Without the correctly installed driver, a hardware device and the operating system will basically be speaking in different languages to each other, not communicating properly, and essentially bringing the system to a standstill.

Adding or changing device drivers has been made substantially easier in Windows 95 than in the previous DOS/Windows combination. With Windows 95, you can add or change device drivers easily using Device Manager, because Device Manager keeps track of assigned system resources.

To change the driver for a standard 101/102-key keyboard, follow these steps:

1. Click the Start menu.

2. Choose Settings, Control Panel.

3. Double-click the System control panel. The System Properties sheet appears.

4. Click the Device Manager page (see fig. 23.9).

Fig. 23.9
You can change a keyboard driver by using the Device Manager page.

5. Along the left edge are plus signs. Click the plus sign that corresponds to the device you want to change—in this case, Keyboard.

6. Double-click the specific hardware device you are interested in.

7. In the resulting System Properties sheet that appears for the specified keyboard, click the Driver page (see fig. 23.10).

Fig. 23.10

The Driver page for the Standard 101/102-Key or Microsoft Natural Keyboard allows you to change drivers.

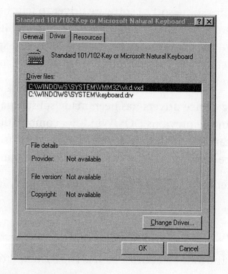

8. Click the Change Driver button. The Select Device window appears (see fig. 23.11).

Fig. 23.11

Select the device you want to set up from the Select Device sheet.

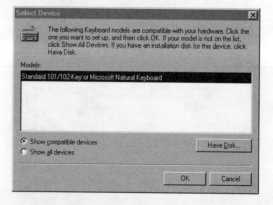

> **Tip**
>
> A Models list details the keyboard models compatible with your hardware. Make sure the Show Compatible Devices button is selected. If the keyboard you want to set up is not on the list, you should select the Show All Devices button. The list changes to show all such keyboards.

9. Click the device you want to set up, and then click OK. The Select Device window disappears, leaving the Driver page showing the driver files and their correct folder path.

10. Exit the Control Panel by clicking the OK button.

You may have a separate installation disk for the device—that is, a floppy disk—which contains the software driver. If this is the case, you need to take an extra step. Follow steps 1 through 8 in the previous list and then do the following:

1. From the Select Device sheet, click Have Disk. The Install From Disk dialog box appears (see fig. 23.12).

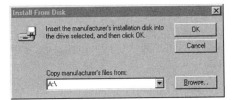

Fig. 23.12
Install manufacturer's software drivers via the Install From Disk dialog box.

2. Specify the directory and disk where the manufacturer's files should be copied from.

3. Click OK.

4. You are now back at the Select Device sheet. Click OK to exit to the Driver page.

5. Click OK on the Driver page to exit.

Changing Your Keyboard Properties

Your keyboard has a variety of properties that dictate how it allows you to interact with the computer. In many cases, they are configurable according to your individual preferences. These include the language used by the keyboard, its layout, and the speed at which keys repeat when pressed. Also, keyboard resource settings can also be viewed and changed, such as I/O and interrupt request settings (IRQs).

You can change the properties associated with a keyboard using the Keyboard Properties control panel. Here's how to open the control panel:

1. Click the Start menu.

2. Choose Settings, Control Panel.

3. Double-click the Keyboard control panel. The Keyboard Properties sheet appears, containing three pages: Speed, Language, and General. Your keyboard layout can be changed using the Language page, detailed in the next section.

Changing a Keyboard Layout

You can change the layout of your keyboard via the Keyboard Properties control panel. After following steps 1 through 3 in the "Changing Your Keyboard Properties" section, do the following:

1. Select the Language page (see fig. 23.13). The top section of the Language page displays the Installed Keyboard Languages and Layout list.

2. Select the language and keyboard layout that you want to change, from the Language and Layout lists.

Fig. 23.13
The Language page in Keyboard Properties is where you can change your keyboard layout.

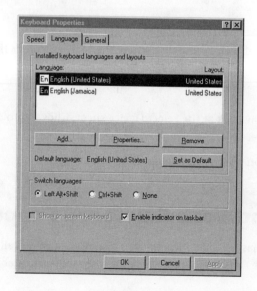

3. Click the Properties button. The Language Properties dialog box appears (see fig. 23.14).

Fig. 23.14
Select the language for your keyboard using Language Properties.

IV

Setting Up Hardware

4. Select the new keyboard layout from the Keyboard Layout drop-down list box.

5. Click OK.

Deleting a Language or Layout

You can also delete a language or layout from the Keyboard Properties control panel. Having opened the Language page, do the following:

1. Select the language and layout you want to delete from the Installed Keyboard Languages and Layouts list.

2. Click the Remove button.

3. Click OK.

Adding Another Language or Layout

You can select a different keyboard layout or language using the Keyboard Properties control panel. Having displayed the Language page, do the following:

1. Click the Add button. The Add Language dialog box appears (see fig. 23.15).

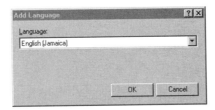

Fig. 23.15
Add another language in Keyboard Properties.

2. Select the language you want from the Language drop-down list box.

3. Click OK. The Add Language dialog box disappears, and the language you just selected now appears on the Installed Keyboard Languages and Layouts area on the Language page.

4. Select the language you want to use as your primary language from the list.

5. Click the Set as Default button.

6. Click OK.

Your new language is now defined as the default language.

> **Tip**
>
> At the bottom of the Language page on the Keyboard Properties sheet is an option box called Enable Indicator On Taskbar. If this is checked, an indicator, called En, appears on the Windows 95 taskbar at the bottom of the main screen. To quickly change between languages, click this indicator and a list of available languages appears. You can instantly switch between available languages by clicking the language you want from that En list.

Changing How the Keys Repeat

You can change the way your keyboard keys repeat using the Keyboard Properties control panel. Follow steps 1 through 3 in the "Changing Your Keyboard Properties" section, then do the following:

1. Click the Speed page (see fig. 23.16).

2. To change the time that elapses before a pressed-down key begins to repeat, drag the Repeat Delay slider to the right for a shorter time, or the left for longer.

3. To change the speed at which characters repeat when you hold down a specific key, adjust the Repeat Rate slider.

4. When you have settled on a suitable repeat setting, click OK.

Changing Your Cursor Blink Rate

You can also change the speed at which your cursor blinks. After accessing the Keyboard Properties control panel, do the following:

1. Click the Speed page (see fig. 23.16).

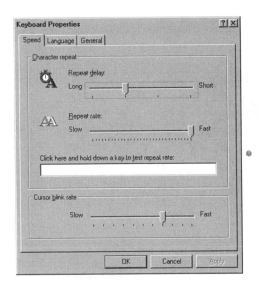

Fig. 23.16
You can change
the repeat rate and
delay using Key-
board Properties.

2. Adjust the cursor blinking speed by dragging the Cursor Blink Rate
   slider to the right to make it faster, or to the left to slow it down.

3. When you have it blinking at the speed you want, click OK.

Changing or Viewing Keyboard Resource Settings

You can change resource settings for your keyboard via the Device Manager
accessed through the System Properties sheet.

You may need to change the settings if another component you're adding
needs to use those same resources, or if you are adding another similar device, such as a keyboard, that wants the same settings.

To make changes to the keyboard resource settings, do the following:

1. Click the Start menu.

2. Choose Settings, Control Panel.

3. Double-click the System control panel. The System Properties sheet
   appears.

4. Click the Device Manager page (see fig. 23.17).

5. Click the plus sign next to the Keyboard device type.

Fig. 23.17
Change keyboard
resource settings
using the Device
Manager page.

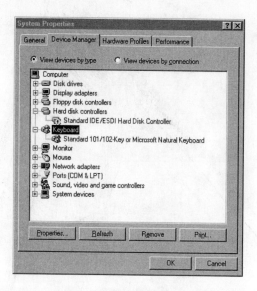

6. Double-click the keyboard you are interested in changing the resource settings for.

7. Select the Resources page (see fig. 23.18).

8. Make the changes to the keyboard resource by double-clicking the resource you want to change.

Fig. 23.18
You can identify
the specific
resources using the
Resources page.

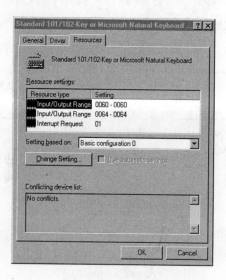

> **Caution**
>
> For a component to work properly, it must have the correct resource settings assigned to it. Do not change resource settings unless you know exactly what you are changing. A new component may need certain resources assigned to it, in which case either the product will specify them, or Windows 95 will tell you what to use when you run the Add New Hardware Wizard.

9. Click OK.

> **Tip**
>
> If the Use Automatic Settings option in the Resources tab is checked, you will not be able to change the resource settings, and the Change Setting button will be grayed out.

Troubleshooting Keyboards

Unfortunately, hardware conflicts and problems are virtually inevitable with the complexities of a modern multimedia personal computer, because of the variety of technologies that are required to work together to provide multimedia capabilities—sound, graphics, text, and even video.

When things do go wrong, though, such as with the keyboard, Windows 95 provides a useful feature called the Hardware Conflict Troubleshooter to help you along the path to solving the problem.

The Hardware Conflict Troubleshooter can be accessed through the Keyboard, Troubleshooting Hardware Conflicts option in the Help Topics Index, accessed via the Start menu.

Once selected, the initial Hardware Conflict Troubleshooter screen offers you a choice of starting the troubleshooter or displaying an overview of the process (see fig. 23.19).

The troubleshooter takes you on a step-by-step investigation of the hardware problems you are experiencing and covers such things as whether the device was installed twice, and what to do if it was; and identifies which resource settings could be causing the conflict (if that is the problem) and how to rectify the situation.

Fig. 23.19
The Hardware
Conflict Trouble-
shooter allows you
to investigate the
problem.

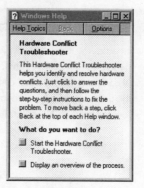

Hardware problems are very often caused by conflicts between hardware resources, such as I/O settings and interrupt requests. When two hardware devices try to use the same resource setting, you have a hardware conflict. The best place to start solving conflicts is to view the keyboard resources in Device Manager, accessed through the System Properties control panel. ❖

Chapter 24

Configuring CD-ROM Drives

by Tod Pike

Most computer systems, whether used at home or at the office, have CD-ROM drives installed in them. Since a large amount of software is distributed in CD-ROM format, and the capability to play audio compact discs is desirable, a CD-ROM drive is a very popular peripheral.

The Windows 95 operating system makes the task of adding and using a CD-ROM drive very easy. This chapter outlines the steps necessary to add a CD-ROM drive to a computer system running Windows 95. In this chapter, you learn how to

- Start the Add New Hardware Wizard for CD-ROM drives

- Set up a CD-ROM drive for network use

Starting Add New Hardware Wizard for CD-ROM Drives

When you install Windows 95 on your computer system for the first time, the Windows 95 installation program automatically runs the Add New Hardware Wizard to detect and install all of the hardware that's in your computer system. After you have installed Windows 95, however, the Add New Hardware Wizard is used if you have added a new device to your computer system, such as a new disk drive, tape drive, CD-ROM, or sound card.

If your computer had a CD-ROM drive installed in it when you installed Windows 95, your system should already support the CD-ROM drive. You can check by opening the Control Panel (from the Start button).

From the Control Panel, you can open the System Properties sheet, which gives you information about the devices connected to your computer system. Figure 24.1 illustrates this sheet.

Fig. 24.1

The System Properties sheet describes the devices connected to your system.

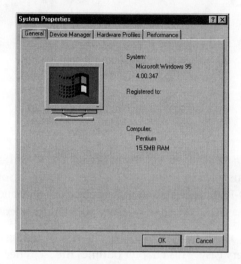

From the System Properties sheet, select the Device Manager tab to display the devices on your system. In figure 24.2, the first item in the list is the CD-ROM device.

Fig. 24.2

The Device Manager displays a list of the devices on your system.

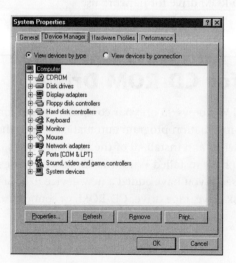

Using the System control panel, you can see that the system as it is currently configured already shows a CD-ROM device as being available. Clicking the CDROM item in the list shows the individual CD-ROM drives that are configured and available for use. Figure 24.3 shows the CD-ROM device exposed in the list.

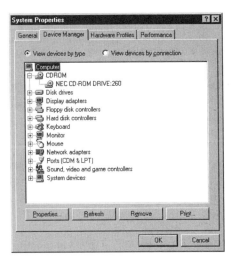

Fig. 24.3
The Device Manager item lists a CD-ROM as being available for use.

If your Device Manager item shows a CD-ROM drive available, but you are unable to use the drive (you cannot access any data on CD-ROM disks, and cannot play audio compact discs), there are several things you can try.

Troubleshooting

I installed the CD-ROM and Windows support, but the CD-ROM still doesn't work.

The most common reason for the CD-ROM not working correctly is a conflict with another device on your system. Open the Control Panel (from the Start menu) and open the System control panel. Select the Device Manager page to display the list of the devices on your system.

Double-click the CDROM entry in the list, and then select your CD-ROM device. Click the Properties button to display the settings for your CD-ROM. The Device Status area tells you if there is a problem with your CD-ROM device. Selecting the Resources page shows you the current settings; this page also tells you if one of the settings for your CD-ROM conflicts with another device in your system.

(continues)

(continued)

If there is a conflict with another device in your system, you have to change one of the hardware settings (such as the Interrupt Request, Input/Output range, or Direct memory access) to another value. You should consult the manual for your CD-ROM drive to determine which values for these settings are legal for your drive.

Once you know which settings you can set your CD-ROM drive to, you have to determine which hardware settings are available on your system. One good way to find out the settings that are in use on your system is to click the Print button on the main Device Manager page. This allows you to print out a summary of all the resources on your system—you can easily find an unused value.

If you have added a new CD-ROM drive to your computer since you installed the Windows 95 operating system, you can run the Add New Hardware Wizard (which is essentially the same routine that Windows 95 runs during installation to detect your hardware configuration).

Before you run the Add New Hardware Wizard, you must install the CD-ROM controller card and any additional hardware that came with your CD-ROM drive. You should follow the manufacturer's instructions to install the drive, including setting any switches or jumpers on the card for the interrupt vector and Input/Output vectors.

Note

If there are default positions for any settings on the CD-ROM device, you should leave the settings at their default. In general, Windows 95 first looks for devices at the default settings for that device. The only time you need to change the settings from their default is if there is a conflict with some other device in your system.

After the CD-ROM hardware has been installed in your computer, you are ready to turn your computer back on and begin the process of telling Windows 95 about the new device.

The Add New Hardware Wizard is run from the Control Panel (choose Start, Settings, Control Panel, Add New Hardware).

When you start the Add New Hardware Wizard, the first screen of the wizard comes up, telling you what the wizard will do. This screen is shown in figure 24.4.

Fig 24.4
The first page of the Add New Hardware Wizard gives general information about the wizard.

Click the Next button to continue to the next page of the Add New Hardware Wizard or click Cancel to stop.

The second page of the wizard (see fig. 24.5) allows you to specify whether the wizard will automatically detect which CD-ROM hardware you have installed.

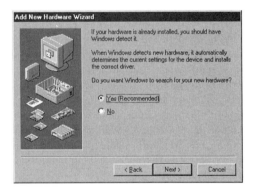

Fig. 24.5
The wizard allows you to specify automatic or manual hardware detection.

Letting Windows 95 Automatically Detect Your CD-ROM

If you are not sure which CD-ROM drive you have installed in your system, or if you just want to let Windows 95 search through your system to detect what hardware you have installed, select Yes (Recommended) on the second page of the Add New Hardware Wizard. This is the first option shown in figure 24.5.

This option is essentially the same process that Windows 95 goes through during the initial installation, and it generally does a good job of locating your installed hardware components. Click Next to proceed to the next page of the wizard.

> **Note**
>
> If you let the wizard automatically detect your installed hardware, it is possible that it may find more than one new hardware component on your system. If all you installed is a CD-ROM drive, you may want to click the Cancel button and restart the wizard, using the option to manually specify the hardware to install.

The next page of the Add New Hardware Wizard is an informational page (see fig. 24.6) telling you what the wizard will do to your system, and how long it will take. It also advises you to close all of your open applications, because the hardware detection process may cause your system to hang. Click Next to proceed to the hardware detection page.

Fig. 24.6
The advisory page in the Add New Hardware Wizard also informs you of the progress indicator.

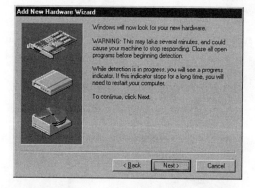

The next page is the actual hardware detection page. As you can see in figure 24.7, this page has a status bar along the bottom that indicates how far the hardware detection phase has run.

Fig. 24.7
Automatic hardware detection is in progress.

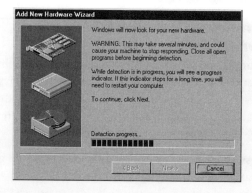

After the Add New Hardware Wizard has completed scanning your system for new hardware, the wizard displays the screen shown in figure 24.8. This screen tells you that the wizard has completed the scan for new hardware and is ready to install support for the new hardware on your system. If you want to see the list of the hardware that was detected, you can click the Details button.

Fig. 24.8
The wizard has finished detecting your new hardware.

When you click the Finish button to install the hardware support, the wizard installs the necessary system drivers and any extra software to support the new CD-ROM drive. Then, the wizard prompts you to restart your system in order for Windows 95 to start supporting your new hardware. If you do not want Windows 95 to restart at this time, just click Cancel.

Note

If the Add New Hardware Wizard couldn't identify your new CD-ROM drive, it tells you that there is no new hardware to install and gives you the option to manually specify the hardware you are installing. This option is discussed in the next section.

Manually Specifying CD-ROM Drives

If you know in advance the type of CD-ROM drive you have installed, or if the Add New Hardware Wizard couldn't identify the type of drive you installed, you can manually tell the wizard the type of drive you have.

After you start the Add New Hardware Wizard, click the Next button to move to the second page. On this page, which asks you whether you want Windows 95 to search for your new hardware, select the No option and click Next. This allows you to manually select the hardware to install.

When you elect to manually install your hardware with the Add New Hardware Wizard, the wizard displays a list of the types of hardware that you can install. This list is shown in figure 24.9.

Fig. 24.9
The list of hardware types available to install appear in this wizard box.

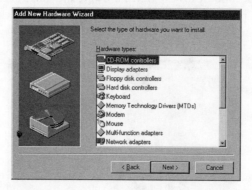

From the Hardware Types list, you should select the item CD-ROM controllers, since this is the type of hardware you are installing. Click the Next button to continue. The wizard now displays a list of the manufacturers (on the left side of the window) and the types of CD-ROM drives (on the right side of the window) that Windows 95 knows about.

> **Note**
>
> Depending on the version of Windows 95 you are running, this list of manufacturers and drives may be different. As Windows 95 matures, more types of hardware will be recognized by the wizard.

If the manufacturer of your CD-ROM drive is listed on the left side of the window, select it in the Manufacturers list box. The wizard displays all of the CD-ROM drives made by that manufacturer (that the system knows about) in Models list (see fig. 24.10).

Fig. 24.10
Select a manufacturer and drive type by clicking its entry in the list.

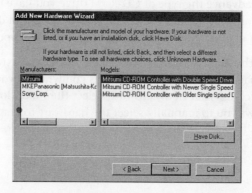

Once you have selected the manufacturer and drive type, click Next to continue with the installation.

Note

If the manufacturer of your CD-ROM drive (or the particular CD-ROM drive you have) is not listed by the wizard, you should check to see if Windows 95 drivers are available for your CD-ROM drive. If so, you can click the Have Disk button instead of specifying the manufacturer and drive type. Windows 95 prompts you for the location of the drivers (generally you load the drivers from your floppy drive) and use those drivers directly to support your CD-ROM drive.

If no Windows 95 drivers are available for your CD-ROM drive, you can use the regular Windows drivers for your drive. See the instructions from your CD-ROM drive and the Windows 95 documentation for help with installing and using Windows/DOS drivers with Windows 95.

On the next page of the wizard (see fig. 24.11), the default settings for the CD-ROM drive are displayed. If these settings do not match the hardware settings on your CD-ROM drive, you either have to change the hardware settings on the drive, or change the Windows 95 configuration using the Device Manager (started from the System control panel). See Chapter 13, "Configuring Memory, Disks, and Devices," for more information about this process.

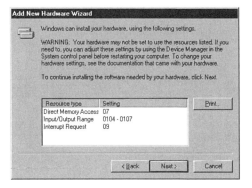

Fig. 24.11
The current hardware settings are displayed for your approval.

Once you have confirmed the current hardware settings, Windows 95 installs the necessary drivers for your CD-ROM drive and prompts you to restart your system (if necessary). After your system has been reset, you are now able to use your CD-ROM drive.

Setting Up Your CD-ROM Drive for Network Use

After you have installed Windows 95 support for your CD-ROM drive, you can easily give people on your network access to the drive. In order to share your CD-ROM drive on the network, you need to make sure that your network hardware is installed and set up and file sharing has been enabled on your system.

To share your CD-ROM on your network, double-click the My Computer icon on your desktop. This brings up the display of all the devices on your local computer disk. Right-click the icon for your CD-ROM drive (generally labeled as D: in the My Computer display) and select Sharing from the options list. This brings up the (currently blank) Sharing page for the CD-ROM drive, as shown in figure 24.12.

Fig. 24.12
The CD-ROM Properties sheet for the CD-ROM drive appears.

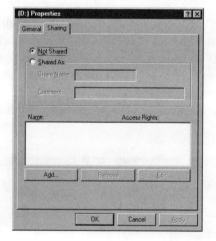

On the Sharing sheet, select the Shared As option. This allows you to fill in the rest of the form. Type a name to share your CD-ROM drive as into the Shared Name box; this is the name that appears when people on your network look at the network resources available on your computer. In the example shown in figure 24.13, the Shared Name is CD-ROM. In addition, you should type a descriptive name into the Comment box; this should be something that describes the contents of the CD-ROM you have mounted. In the example, the Comment is Documentation CD-ROM.

Next, select a list of people who will have access to your shared CD-ROM. The way you set up the access list depends on how you have your access control set up, but you will either set up a password for the CD-ROM (if you have share access control) or a list of users defined on your network server (if you have user access control). You can find out the type of access control you have set up by looking at the properties sheet for your Network Neighborhood, under the Access control page.

In the example shown in figure 24.13, the system is using User Access control, and I have selected the Everyone group (which means all users registered in the NT or Novell server) and allowed those users to only read the contents of our CD-ROM.

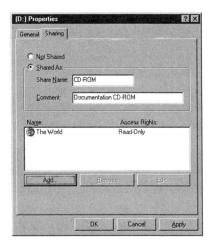

Fig. 24.13
A file sharing window for the CD-ROM is completed.

Once you have filled in the Sharing page, click OK to begin sharing the CD-ROM on your network. The CD-ROM drive appears on the network almost immediately. Other Windows 95 users can access the CD-ROM drive through their Network Neighborhood icon.

New Windows 95 CD-ROM Drive Features

One of the new features of Windows 95 is the capability of the system to automatically recognize and play audio compact disks when they are inserted in the CD-ROM drive. This feature can be controlled from the Properties page for your CD-ROM drive. Double-click the My Computer icon on your desktop and then right-click your CD-ROM drive icon. Select Properties from the list and then click the Settings page from the Properties sheet.

On the Settings page, you see an option called Auto Insert Notification. If this option is checked, the system automatically plays audio compact disks when they are inserted. Deselect this option if you don't want this to happen.

By default, Windows 95 assigns drive letter D to your CD-ROM drive. At times, you may want to change this drive letter assignment, especially if you have more than one CD-ROM drive in your system. You can change this from the Properties sheet for your drive. Bring up the Properties sheet and select the Settings page. You see the setting for Current Drive Letter Assigned; changing this changes the drive letter assigned to your CD-ROM drive.

Caution

If you change the drive letter assigned to your CD-ROM drive, it may force other drives you have mounted (such as network disks) to change to other drive letters, also. This may affect some of your shortcuts or software if they assume that your data was stored on a particular drive letter.

Troubleshooting

My CD-ROM drive seems slow. How can I speed it up?

Windows 95 has several settings for CD-ROM drives, some of which can affect how fast data is transferred from the CD-ROM drive to the system. You can check these settings by opening the System control panel and selecting the Performance tab. Select the File System button and then select the CD-ROM page from the File System Properties sheet.

The two settings on this page affect how much data Windows 95 keeps in memory when reading from your CD-ROM drive. You should keep the Supplemental Cache Size as large as possible (keeping the slider bar as far to the right as possible) unless you are running short of memory.

You should also set the Optimize Access Pattern For option to the type of CD-ROM drive you have (double-speed, for example). When you are finished changing these settings, click OK.

Chapter 25

Configuring Floppy Disk Drives

by Dave Gibbons

One of the most anticipated side effects of Windows 95's introduction was a wave of hardware upgrades. Many people are taking this opportunity to add extra memory, bigger hard drives, and peripherals like sound cards and CD-ROM drives. One of the most basic upgrades is adding a new floppy disk drive. Some upgrade to share disks with others, or convert older 5 1/4-inch archive disks to a more stable format. Others many need a new high-density 3.5-inch drive to install and use new software, much of which is only available in that format. Whatever your reason, installing a new floppy disk drive is an easy process, and Windows 95 doesn't gum up the process too much.

If all the drives in your computer were working before you installed Windows 95, you won't need to do anything to get Windows 95 to recognize them. If you're adding a new drive or having problems, this chapter is for you.

In this chapter, you learn

- What types of floppy disk drives (FDDs) are available

- How to install a new floppy disk drive into your PC

- How to get your PC to recognize the new drive

- How to make sure Windows 95 recognizes the drive

- How to troubleshoot steps if you have problems with the drive

---

Note

For more in-depth coverage of FDDs, read Que's *Upgrading and Repairing PCs*, 5th Edition.

Types of Floppy Disk Drives

The standard list of FDD types (see table 25.1) has just about doubled with the introduction of Plug and Play (PNP) technology. For most types, you now find a PNP version and a non-PNP (or *legacy*) version. With PNP, new devices announce themselves to the computer at powerup, so (in theory) they don't require any manual setup at all. Installing a PNP drive and controller requires the same steps as installing a legacy drive, minus the procedure in the "Getting the PC to Recognize the New FDD" section later in this chapter.

Table 25.1 Floppy Disk Drive Types	
Disk Size	**Capacity**
5.25-inch	360K
5.25-inch	1.2M
3.5-inch	720K
3.5-inch	1.44M
3.5-inch	2.88M

5.25-inch drives are also sometimes distinguished by their height. Half-height drives (about 1 5/8-inch tall) are the most common, but you still occasionally find full-height drives (about 3 1/4-inch tall) and third-height (about an inch tall) drives—sometimes called *slim line drives*. Though physical size is not a good way to guess a drive's capacity, you won't find too many full-height 1.2M drives—most are 360K or the older 180K capacity.

Tip

Check out F. Robert Falbo's "TheRef," an electronic encyclopedia of floppy, removable, and hard disks. It can help you deduce the capacity or settings for a drive if you have no documentation for it. On CompuServe, search for **TREF43**.

Most PC-compatible floppy drives adhere to a common specification, so you won't have to worry about disks from one brand working with another brand. Exceptions to this rule include *floptical* drives, which can use optical disks of 20M or more, as well as regular-capacity floppy disks.

Setting Up the Hardware

To install a new FDD into your computer, follow these steps:

1. If the FDD is still in its box, check to make sure it has the installation screws (usually four to eight or more) and a cable, if necessary (if you've already got an FDD installed, you can use the existing cable). Also make sure you have the right kind of screwdrivers to open your computer's case and to fit the drive's installation screws. Because you'll be working near very sensitive electronic parts, wear an anti-static wristband (available at most computer and electronics stores).

2. Turn off and unplug the computer.

3. Find the location on the front panel where you'll be installing the drive. Note the direction of the opening (vertical or horizontal).

4. Open the computer's case. This usually involves removing or loosening three to six screws in the back and popping off part of the case. You may also have to remove some exterior cables to get the cover off. On some cases, one flat panel comes off. In most, however, the top and sides can be removed as one piece. Set the cover aside.

5. You should see the space in the front of the chassis where the drive will fit. Slide it into place. Lightly attach the installation screws, tightening them only when you're sure the drive's face will be flush with the front of the PC (if possible, use an existing drive as a guide). Some cases require the addition of plastic or metal rails to the sides of the drive before you can slide it in place.

> **Caution**
>
> Most new cases have what looks like a 3.5 inch-wide metal box beside the drive bays. This looks like a perfect place for a 3.5-inch floppy disk drive, but it's made for a *hard* drive. There is no corresponding opening in the front of the computer's case.

> **Tip**
>
> You'll be attaching two cables to the back of the drive. If it looks like you won't be able to get your fingers behind the drive when it's secured, leave the installation screws off until you've attached the cables.

6. The two cables you need to attach are a ribbon cable and a power cable. If you're adding a second FDD or replacing one, you see the ribbon cable running into the back of the original drive. A few inches from the drive end of the cable you should see another connector, which you use for the second drive (the B drive) in the system. The end of the ribbon cable always goes to the A drive. Slide the connector into place on the back of the FDD.

> **Note**
>
> Even though the cables are set up for your A and your B drive respectively, you have to make sure the CMOS is set up the same way.

> **Note**
>
> You may need an adapter to hook the ribbon cable connector to your FDD. For example, if you want to make a 3.5-inch FDD (with a pin connector), you need to get an edge-to-pin adapter because the A drive and the end of the ribbon cable are for a 5.25-inch drive (edge connector).

7. Find a power lead from the computer's power supply for your drive. You should see leads going to the motherboard and any drives you've already got installed, all from the same location. Find one that's not yet connected to a drive. If there aren't any leads available, get a Y connector from a computer supply store to split one of the existing leads. Connect the power lead to the back of the drive.

> **Note**
>
> You may need an adapter for the power supply lead. If the only available leads are the larger type (about 3/4-inch wide in a D shape) and you're installing a drive with a small, square power socket (like most 3.5-inch drives), you need an adapter. Some drives include this adapter with the mounting kit, but if you don't have one, you should be able to get one at a computer supply store.

You shouldn't put the cover back on your computer until you've tested the new drive. Reconnect the computer's power cable and any other cables you disconnected earlier, then turn it back on to complete the next steps in the process.

Getting the PC to Recognize the New FDD

When you turn your computer on after installing a new FDD, it may squawk, beep, and/or display error messages on the screen. This is perfectly normal (unless the drive is PNP-compliant); the PC doesn't know how to handle the new device until you tell it manually.

The PC's device configuration is stored in the Setup or CMOS section of the computer. The information in this section includes what kinds of drives you have, the time of day, the video controller type, and some more arcane settings. The CMOS has its own battery, which is how it retains these settings (and keeps the clock running) when the computer is turned off or unplugged. When you add a new *basic* device (a floppy drive, hard drive, or video card, as opposed to a nonessential device like a sound card or CD-ROM drive), the CMOS needs to find out about the device's settings before it will work.

If the computer halts during startup after you install the new drive, it may give you a message like

```
Press <Enter> to run setup or Press Ctrl+Alt+Insert now.
```

If it just tells you Incorrect CMOS setup and continues to boot up normally, you'll have to turn the computer off and on to get back to the start of the boot sequence. In the early stages of the boot process, you should see a message on your screen telling you what you have to do to start the CMOS setup program. The message might say Press <Delete> to run Setup or F2, F12, or almost any other key or key combination. You usually have to press this key sequence *before* you see the Starting Windows 95 message.

Tip

Some systems don't display any message at all, so you may have to refer to the documentation or manufacturer.

When you've got the Setup program, read its instructions carefully. It may offer you a menu of basic and advanced options. Choosing the floppy drive is usually in the basic section. When you get to the correct screen, you should see a list of drives—usually two FDDs and two hard drives—and some other information about the date, time, and other devices. Instructions on this screen show how to go from section to section. For example, in some Setup programs, you use the arrow keys to move around and the Page Up/Page Down keys to change the settings, while others use Tab or the space bar for these functions. Move to the correct section (usually Floppy A or Floppy B) and change it until it correctly identifies your drive. It should run through a list of standard drive types (both types of 3.5-inch drives, both 5.25-inch drives, and None, which you can use to disable a drive).

After you've selected the correct drive, exit the CMOS Setup program (usually by pressing Esc, Enter, or F10) and make sure you save the settings. You'll probably see a menu with options to ignore the changes or save them, with Ignore as the first option. The computer should start up normally after you exit Setup.

How Windows 95 Affects FDD Installation

The only place Windows 95 really has an effect on FDD installation is in diagnosis. It can't change the drive's settings (at least not in legacy drives); it can only tell you if the drive works properly.

To make sure the drive is properly installed and identified in the CMOS setup, follow these steps:

1. Open the Control Panel.

2. Select the System icon.

3. Select the Device Manager page.

4. Click the plus sign next to the Disk Drives icon (see fig. 25.1). The available drives are displayed under it.

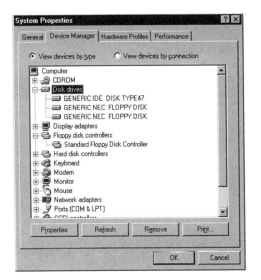

Fig. 25.1
Here you can see the available drives.

Tip

If there is a hardware conflict, Device Manager places an X through the icon meaning that the hardware has been disabled. A circle exclamation point through the icon means the hardware has a problem.

5. Double-click the drive you want to check. The System Properties sheet's General page tells you if the drive is working properly, or if Windows 95 has detected a problem.

Note

If you choose the Settings page and you have a legacy drive, you'll see most of the options grayed out. The current drive letter assignment is one option that looks changeable but isn't. To change the drive assignment, you'd have to switch the cable connections between the floppy drives, then re-run the CMOS setup.

Testing and Troubleshooting FDD Installation

Before you put the cover back on your computer, make sure the FDD works properly. Since the medium (specifically because of its "open air" design) is notoriously susceptible to dust and other contaminants, testing FDDs can be a little taxing. It's all too easy to believe the newly installed drive isn't working when the real problem is a dusty disk—or a strand of hair in the drive. So, before you count out your FDD, test it thoroughly.

The cardinal rule when testing FDDs is to test it on an *entire* disk. Make sure the drive heads can access the entire disk's surface. Viewing a directory of the disk in Windows Explorer, for example, isn't a reliable test because the directory is stored on a very small section of the disk. To verify the drive's operation across the entire disk, try any of these tests:

■ Format a blank floppy disk. (Open the My Computer icon, select the drive, and choose For_mat from the _File menu.)

■ Run ScanDisk from the Start menu's Accessories/System Tools menu (see fig. 25.2). Make sure you choose _Thorough in the Type of Test box before you click the _Start button.

Fig. 25.2
ScanDisk checks
the entire surface
of a disk for errors.

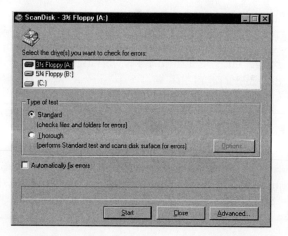

If your drive can successfully complete one or both of these tests, it's a pretty safe bet that it is installed correctly. If it fails these tests, there are several things you can do to track down the problem.

First, find the *general* location of the problem. It could be any of the following:

- Disk
- Drive
- Ribbon cable
- Power cable
- Drive controller

For example, if the drive doesn't appear in the My Computer or ScanDisk windows, the problem is probably not the disk itself. If the drive shows up in these windows, you know the power cable is connected; Windows wouldn't know the drive was there if it didn't have power. This process is often called the *long-knife approach*, because each question eliminates a large chunk of the problem.

When you have shortened the list of suspects enough, eliminate each one until you find the culprit.

Checking for a Faulty Disk

If the disk itself could be the problem, try to read it in another computer. If the disk works in other computers, it's probably not at fault. Verify this by trying other disks in the problem drive. If other disks work, the first disk may be incompatible with the drive (the wrong size, for example).

Tip

If you have access to CompuServe, the Internet, or another online source, look for the freeware program DRIVTY or DRIVTYPS. When you run it from the MS-DOS command line, it tells you whether your disk drive(s) can accept high-density disks or not.

In rare cases, the alignment of a drive's heads allow it to read and write disks that can't be used on other computers. If you need to share disks with other computers and no one else seems to be able to use disks from your computer, try a different drive.

Checking for a Faulty Drive

If all the cables and disks check out, the problem could be in the drive. If you can, try it in another computer with a working disk drive of the same type. If you don't have a spare computer for testing, see if you can try another drive in its place. You may have to take the computer into a computer repair shop for testing.

Before you give up on the drive, try a commercial drive cleaning kit (about $10 to $15 from any computer store), which can help eliminate dust and other contaminants from the drive heads.

Checking for Faulty Cables

When you turn on the computer, watch the light on the drive. It should light up for about one second, and you should hear the drive's motor spinning or "cranking." If it doesn't light up at all (or if it stays lit all the time), you probably have a problem with your cables.

For a drive that does nothing, check the power cable. Disconnect it and reconnect it to make sure it's seated correctly. If that doesn't work, check another of your power supply's leads (refer back to "Installing the Hardware" for information about leads and adapters).

If the drive light is always on, the culprit is probably the ribbon cable. Though most drives only allow you to put the cable on one way, some can be connected upside-down (especially edge connectors). See if you can flip the ribbon cable's connection, either on the drive end or the card end—but not both. If the connectors will only go one way, check pin connectors for folded (bent) or broken pins.

If all the connectors look alright, the problem may be a short in the ribbon cable itself. Try a different one. If possible, try the ribbon cable on a different computer to see if it works. This could point to a faulty drive or controller.

Checking for a Problem in the Controller

If you've eliminated every other possibility, the controller could be at fault. If possible, try a different controller in its place, or try it on a different machine. Even if your disk controller is on the motherboard, you should be able to disable it and try a different controller—but only after you've disabled the onboard controller. To disable it, you'll probably have to reset a jumper on the motherboard. Some motherboards clearly label the jumper you'll need to switch FDD or FD CNTRL (Intel motherboards are a good example), but others have cryptic labels that you'll need a manual or technical support person to decode.

Tip

Some jumper settings for drives and motherboards are available online. Check the manufacturer's forum or Internet site. If you use a major online service, try a software search by typing either the name of the company (like Intel or Sony) or the device (Disk Controller or CD-ROM Drive).

If you've installed a new drive controller on a PC that already has one (either on the motherboard or on another card), you may run into a conflict if the earlier controller isn't properly disabled (see fig. 25.3). Check the jumpers and documentation for the card to make sure.

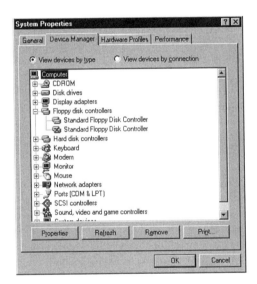

Fig. 25.3
Windows 95 detects most hardware conflicts automatically.

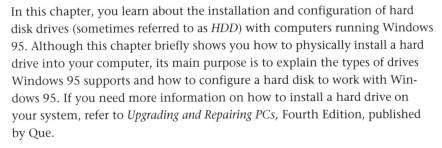

Chapter 26

Configuring Hard Disk Drives

by Rob Tidrow and Jeff Pulver

In this chapter, you learn about the installation and configuration of hard disk drives (sometimes referred to as *HDD*) with computers running Windows 95. Although this chapter briefly shows you how to physically install a hard drive into your computer, its main purpose is to explain the types of drives Windows 95 supports and how to configure a hard disk to work with Windows 95. If you need more information on how to install a hard drive on your system, refer to *Upgrading and Repairing PCs,* Fourth Edition, published by Que.

You've learned throughout this book that one of the main features of Windows 95 is its support of Plug-and-Play devices. Unfortunately, most users do not have hard drives that are Plug and Play-compliant, nor are their systems BIOS (Basic Input/Output Systems) Plug and Play ready. Fortunately, Windows 95 makes it easier than ever to install and configure a hard disk to work with your operating system. With Windows 95's autodetect feature, many hard drives are automatically recognized and configured after you get all the hardware-specific issues ironed out.

In this chapter, you learn how to

- Identify the types of hard drives Windows 95 supports

- Install a new hard drive

- Partition a hard drive

- Configure and prepare your hard drive to work with Windows 95

- Format a hard drive

- Test the performance of a new hard drive

Types of Hard Drives Windows 95 Supports

◀ See "Hard Drive Requirements," p. 22

◀ See "Using Windows 95 Setup," p. 62

The majority of users interested in adding a hard drive to their computer already have Windows 95 installed. If you do not have Windows 95 installed and you want to add a new hard drive to your system, you need to install the new hard drive and then install MS-DOS on it to start the Windows 95 Setup routine. Chapters 1 and 2 should be consulted to install Windows 95 on your system.

> **Note**
>
> A valuable resource you need to have handy when you install a new hard drive is your system documentation. This is the booklet or folder that came with your computer when you purchased it. In this manual you find specific information that relates to your system, such as interrupt settings and CMOS settings.

For this chapter, it is assumed that you are adding another hard drive to your PC to use with your current Windows 95 installation. Some users opt for a second hard disk if their first hard disk becomes full or if they need to separate their data and programs from their operating system. This is the case in many situations when you use a removable hard disk that you carry with you or store in a secure place.

Before you rush in and start installing a hard drive, you first should examine the types of hard drives you can install in Windows 95. The following types of hard disk drives are supported under Windows 95:

ESDI	IDE LBA
Hardcards	MFM
IDE	

Windows 95 supports the following types of bus adapters:

EISA	RLL
ISAMCA	SCSI
PCI	SCSI 2
PCMCIA	VL bus

Windows 95 provides better disk device support than Windows 3.1, but it also ensures compatibility with existing MS-DOS-based and Windows-based disk device drivers. In addition, the disk device drivers in Windows 95 are compatible with Windows NT miniport drivers. Windows 95 also provides enhanced support for large media using logical block addressing, including hard disks with more than 1,024 cylinders.

Although Windows 95 supports other types of drives, the following two sections discuss IDE and SCSI devices in more detail. IDE and SCSI devices are the most prevalent devices available on current computers.

IDE Drives

Windows 95 supports *IDE drives* (*Integrated Drive Electronics*), which are the most popular hard disk interfaces used in computers. If you have a computer that was manufactured in the last several years, it more than likely includes an IDE drive.

One of the improvements Windows 95 has with IDE drives is its support for large IDE disk drives. New IDE drives support the *logical block addressing* (*LBA*) scheme, which enables them to exceed the 528M size limitation. These new drives are sometimes referred to as *Enhanced IDE drives*. Windows 95 can support primary partition sizes of 2G, with support of multiple 2G logical drives in extended partitions. Previous versions of Windows supported large hard disks in real mode, but Windows 95 supports large IDE drives using a protected mode disk driver included with Windows 95.

Troubleshooting

I'm on a network using Windows 95, and I cannot access a hard drive. Windows 95 also reports that a hard drive larger than 2G has only 2G of storage space. What is the problem?

The network client in Windows 95 is designed to be compatible with MS-DOS-based applications that can have a 2G limit. When a network drive has more than 2G of free disk space, Windows 95 reports only that 2G are available and 0 bytes are used. Microsoft recommends against using Windows 95 with a FAT volume larger than 2G created in Windows NT. On a dual-boot computer with both Windows 95 and Windows NT installed, you can read from and write to the drive, but you might experience strange results, such as programs reporting 0 bytes free space on the drive.

> **Note**
>
> A term that you see throughout this chapter is *controller*. A hard disk controller acts as a middleman between the hard disk and your computer. A controller is needed because a PC cannot use a hard disk directly. It needs something to communicate instructions to and from the hard drive. In many cases, the BIOS is used to pass hard disk requests from the PC to the hard disk controller. The controller then accesses the hard disk.

Another feature of Windows 95 is its support of a second IDE controller in your computer, if your computer can support it. You need to refer to your computer's documentation to determine how to set up your CMOS configuration to handle this second IDE controller. If you use a laptop, you can use a combination of an IDE controller and a controller in a docking station, if you use a docking station with your laptop.

> **Note**
>
> Windows 95 also supports CD-ROM drives that are IDE-based. This is good news to the millions of users who don't want to configure a proprietary CD-ROM interface or an SCSI controller. Windows 95 supports Mitsumi, Sony, and Panasonic CD-ROM adapters. If your CD-ROM is not supported automatically, you may need to use a vendor's device driver and load MSCDEX in your CONFIG.SYS file.

SCSI Drives

◀ See "Starting the Add New Hardware Wizard for CD-ROM Drives," p. 513

Unlike Windows 3.x, Windows 95 includes 32-bit disk device drivers for several *SCSI (Small Computer System Interface)* controllers. Some of these controllers include Adaptec, Future Domain, Trantor, and UltraStor. The SCSI interface is a sub-bus to which you can connect up to seven peripherals. The SCSI interface supports up to eight units, but one of the units is used to connect the adapter card to the PC, leaving seven open units. You can attach hard disks, CD-ROM drives, scanners, and other devices to a SCSI adapter.

> **Troubleshooting**
>
> *I have an Adaptec EZ SCSI for Windows drive, but it doesn't work now. Why?*
>
> The Adaptec EZ SCSI Windows version will not run with Windows 95, but the MS-DOS version does work with Windows 95.

In the past, many DOS- and Windows-based users dreaded installing and configuring an SCSI card because of the seemingly endless installation process of trial-and-error to get the device working properly. With Windows 95, many of these installation headaches have gone away. Also, if you already have a SCSI device installed under MS-DOS and it adheres to the ASPI (Advanced SCSI Programming Interface) or CAM (Common Access Method) specifications, you should not have a problem getting your SCSI device to work properly under Windows 95.

Troubleshooting

My SCSI device worked fine under MS-DOS, but it doesn't work with Windows 95. Can you help?

For many SCSI hardware devices, you can specify command-line parameters when the driver is loaded. By default, the Windows 95 miniport driver runs without parameters (in the same way it does for real-mode drivers). If you want to use a command-line parameter, you can add it to the Settings property for the SCSI controller. For real-mode parameters that the controller supports (and if the device has a Windows 95 MPD file), you can enter parameters in the Adapter Settings box in the controller's properties. For information about the switches that can be used for a particular SCSI device, see the documentation from the device manufacturer. There are no additional parameters added by Microsoft.

For example, if your SCSI adapter has full functionality under MS-DOS, but not under Windows 95, you can add any device parameters previously specified in CONFIG.SYS to the Adapter Settings box. As another example, for Adaptec 7700 SCSI devices, you might specify **removable=off** to disable support for removable media if you want to load another ASPI removable disk.

Installing a Hard Disk

When you install a hard disk, you need to be aware of several factors that help lead you to a successful installation. Because each computer, hard disk, and Windows 95 installation is different, this section shows you some of the general steps to help you physically install your hard disk. You should use this section as an overview and reference another resource for hardware-specific questions you might have.

Before you begin ripping open your computer and stuffing a new hard disk inside it, be sure your computer supports the type of hard disk you are installing. You should be able to find this information on the computer specification that you receive with your PC. If you are the type of user who is not comfortable installing hardware, this chapter probably will not make you more comfortable doing so. It will, however, show you how to configure your hard disk after it's installed. You can find out this information in the later section, "Configuring Your Hard Disk for Windows 95."

Tip

Before you turn off your computer to add the new hard disk, you should back up your system in case you lose any data on your existing hard disk.

Plug and Play, and Legacy Hard Drives

In Chapter 1, "Preparing To Install Windows 95," you learned about Plug and Play and how it helps you set up your devices quickly and easily under Windows 95. Another term that you might hear is legacy. *Legacy* refers to devices that do not support the Plug and Play specification. Many of the troubleshooting problems that you run into under Windows 95 are related to legacy devices because they are older devices.

The Plug and Play feature requires the cooperation between BIOS manufacturers, device manufacturers, and the software developers. Therefore, in order to use this feature, you need a BIOS which supports Plug and Play, a hard disk drive which is Plug and Play-compliant, and Windows 95, which has the support to recognize a new Plug and Play-compliant device and perform an automatic installation of it. This makes the addition of new hardware a simple and painless operation. In some cases, you don't even need to turn off the power to the PC to install a Plug and Play device (although it's recommended that you power down your computer anytime you remove its case).

Disk Drive Addressing

To access a hard disk drive, the address of the disk must be specified. The *address* is a single alphabetic character followed by a colon. If the colon is omitted, Windows 95 thinks you are giving it a file name consisting of a single letter, rather than a disk drive address.

> **Note**
>
> The addressing scheme can become very complicated. If you are connected to a network, each disk you want to have on the network will also have an alphabetic character assigned to it. To further complicate the issue, the DOS command **SUBST** can be used to substitute one disk address for another. Schemes such as these are beyond the scope of this book.

In addition, Windows 95 has specific addresses it uses for the disk devices and CD-ROMs. The addresses of the floppy and hard disks are determined by the cables attached to them. To simplify this discussion, you can use a standard form of addressing. You can safely assume the following:

- An installed CD-ROM has an address of K:

- Any network disks have an address starting with L:

- The DOS command SUBST is not be used

When Windows 95 is started, the existing disks are assigned an address based upon the following scheme:

- The first floppy disk drive is A:

- The second floppy disk drive is B:

- The first hard disk drive is C:

- The second hard disk drive is D:

- The third hard disk drive is E:

- The fourth hard disk drive is F:

- The CD-ROM address is specified during installation. If it is not specified, its address is the next alphabetic character after the last hard drive.

> **Tip**
>
> Always assign the address for a CD-ROM drive a few letters after your last hard disk drive. If, for instance, your hard drives are C: and D:, make your CD-ROM F: or G:. That way, if you add more hard disk drives, its address does not change and you do not have to change any links to files on a CD-ROM. See Chapter 24, "Configuring CD-ROM Drives," for information on installing a CD-ROM drive.

Referencing the Windows 95 Device Manager

◀ See "Starting Add New Hardware Wizard for CD-ROM Drives," p. 513

The Windows 95 Device Manager is used to display and change the parameters associated with your system's hardware, including hard disk drives. In most instances, the default settings selected by Windows 95 are the correct ones. Sometimes, however, you may encounter a problem after you install your hard drive, and you need to access the Device Manager to fix the problem. For this reason, you should become familiar with the Device Manager, even before you install a new hard drive. To access the Device Manager, use the following procedure:

1. Choose Start, Settings, Control Panel, and double-click the System icon.

2. When the System Properties sheet appears, click the Device Manager tab (see fig. 26.1).

Fig. 26.1

You can view your system's hardware and properties by using the Device Manager.

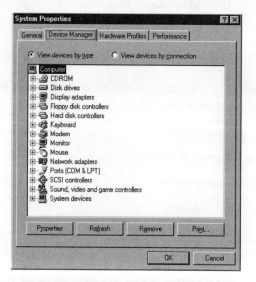

To view your hard drive properties, you need to look at both the Disk Drives setting and the Hard Disk Controller setting. Click the plus sign (+) next to each of these settings to reveal the type of drives and controllers you have installed (see fig. 26.2).

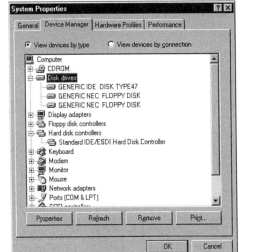

Fig. 26.2
To see the type of hard drive and hard disk controller on your system, click the plus (+) sign next to Disk Drives and Hard Disk Controllers.

In figure 26.2, for instance, three drives are shown under Disk Drives. The drive named GENERIC IDE DISK TYPE47 is the hard disk on the system. The other drive is the floppy disk drive installed. Under the Hard Disk Controllers, one controller is listed, named Standard IDE/ESDI Hard Disk Controller.

Note

If you right-click on any device and select What's This?, Windows 95 explains how you can find out more about that piece of hardware and what the icon looks like when there is a problem with the device.

If there is a hardware conflict on your system, the Device Manager places a circle exclamation point over the icon on the line denoting the conflicting device. Likewise, if a device is disabled but not removed, the Device Manager places a red X over the device. In figure 26.3, for instance, a red X is drawn over the third Standard Hard Disk Controller. In this case, the error occurs because Windows 95 supports only two controllers and the user has attempted to place three on the system.

Fig. 26.3
You can readily
see which device,
if any, is causing a
conflict by using
the Device
Manager.

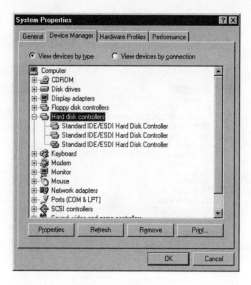

Installing a Hard Drive

As pointed out earlier, this chapter assumes that you already have one hard drive installed on your system. Unless you piece together your own computer, the first hard disk is always installed when you purchase your computer. Today's computers usually can support at least two hard disk drives.

Before you begin disassembling your computer, you want to find a large, uncluttered area to work in, have adequate light, and have the following tools handy:

- 1/4-inch and 3/16-inch nut drivers

- No. 0 and one Phillips screwdrivers

- 3/16-inch and 1/8-inch slotted screwdrivers

- Pen light

- Antistatic strip to reduce static electricity charges

Caution

Static electricity can be discharged from your body and can cause permanent damage to the chips in the computer. If you do not use an antistatic strip, always touch something metal, such as the case, before touching any components inside the computer.

To install new hardware, including your hard disk, the computer case that protects the internal parts of your PC must be removed. Below are the steps required to open your computer:

1. Turn off the power to the computer and remove the power cord.

2. Disconnect all cables from the computer and note their location with a piece of masking tape.

3. Remove the case by unscrewing the six or eight screws holding it to the frame.

You are now ready to install your second hard disk drive. Because each hard disk and computer is different, this is where you need to read and follow the instructions provided by the hard disk manufacturer to install the hard disk drive. Some generalized guidelines follow:

1. Locate an available bay to install the hard disk. Many hard disks come with a drive kit, usually at an additional charge, with all necessary hardware to mount the drive in the bay. You may need an adapter if your bay is for a 5.25-inch hard disk drive and you are installing a 3.5-inch hard disk drive. In addition, rails, which are attached to the side of the hard disk drive, may also be needed. The drive can now be installed with the appropriate screws (usually four $6/32 \times 1/4$-inch screws).

> **Tip**
>
> It may be easier to connect the power connector and hard disk drive cable before sliding the hard disk drive into the bay.

2. Next, locate an available power supply connection. If none are available, you have to purchase a Y-cable. The Y-cable allows you to share an existing power connector with two devices. To install it, you would locate a device near the empty bay which has a power connection plugged into it. You would then disconnect that plug, and then plug the female end of the Y-cable into it. Now, one of the male ends is for the device you just unplugged, and the other male end is for your new hard disk drive. Since a hard disk drive uses more electricity than most other devices, you should use a Y-cable of 18 gauge or heavier.

3. You are now ready to attach the hard disk drive cables between the hard disk controller and the hard disk drive. These are two flat wide ribbon cables, with a red or blue stripe along one edge. This colored edge should be next to pin number one when it is connected to the hard disk drive and the hard disk controller. You can locate the pin number by referring to your computer's documentation and looking at the schematic drawing of the motherboard.

   Most disk drives have a single cable that combines the functions of the data cable and the control cable. Also, to help ensure the cable is connected properly, there may a plastic key that is placed between a row of pins in the connector. With this plastic key, the connector can only be attached to the disk drive.

After the hard disk drive is secured to the bay, and the drive cable and power cable are connected, you are ready to close the computer and begin configuring Windows 95 for your new hard disk drive.

Note

Because Windows 95 supports up to two IDE disk controllers, you can install a second controller if you install a third or fourth hard disk in your system. Again, consult your hardware documentation for the placement of the new controller on your PC's motherboard. Some motherboards include a set of golden pins labeled to identify them for the second controller, such as Secondary IDE.

Closing the Computer

With all of the new hardware installed, you can now close the computer to complete the configuration of the new hardware.

Tip

If you're like me, you like to make sure everything is working before you go through all the trouble of refastening all those screws on your computer. You may want to bypass this section for now and go to the "Configuring Your Hard Disk for Windows 95" section to make sure your hard disk works. Of course, you need to attach all the cables and power cords before booting up your computer, but you may save time if the hard disk doesn't work and you need to check loose cables and the like by keeping the case off for now.

These are the general steps to close your computer:

1. Refasten the case by reversing the procedure used to remove it. Namely, place the case back over the frame of the computer and insert the removed screws to refasten the case to the frame. Ensure all cables and wires are neatly placed inside the computer, in a position where they aren't pinched by other components or trapped between the case and the frame of the computer.

2. All cables can now be plugged into their proper ports, according to the labels on each cable.

3. Attach the power cord and plug it into an electrical outlet.

Note

After you install a new hard drive in your computer, you need to configure it to work properly with your specific computer. To do this, reboot your computer and run your computer's setup program to enable you to make changes to your CMOS settings. On some machines, you can start the setup program by pressing F1 during bootup. With Gateway 2000 computers, you can press Ctrl+Alt+Esc to start it. Refer to your computer's documentation at this point to configure your machine to work with the new hard disk. After you make these changes, be sure to save them and then reboot your computer.

You are now ready to begin configuring Windows 95 for your new hard disk drive.

Partitioning a Hard Drive

Before you use your new hard disk with Windows 95, you need to partition it using the FDISK command. When you *partition* a hard disk, you define the areas of the disk for Windows 95 (or any other operating system for that matter) to recognize as a volume. To Windows 95, a *volume* is part of the disk that is specified as the drive letter, such as C or D.

Partitioning Requirements for Installing Windows 95

Windows 95 Setup cannot install Windows 95 unless a FAT partition exists on the hard disk. It cannot install Windows 95 on a computer that has only

HPFS or Windows NT file system (NTFS) partitions. The following list describes how Windows 95 Setup handles different types of disk partitions:

- *MS-DOS Partition.* Windows 95 Setup recognizes and begins installation over existing MS-DOS FAT partitions. Windows 95 supports MS-DOS FDISK partitions on removable media drives such as the Iomega Bernoulli Box drives.

- *Windows NT.* Windows 95 Setup cannot recognize information on an NTFS (NT File System) partition on the local computer. You can install Windows 95 on a Windows NT multiple-boot system if enough disk space is available on a FAT partition. On a Windows NT multiple-boot system, you must install Windows 95 on an existing FAT partition with MS-DOS or MS-DOS and Windows 3.x. Another way to install Windows 95 is to partition and format free space on the hard disk in a FAT partition, then perform a new installation onto this new FAT partition.

- *OS/2.* Again, a DOS partition must be available from which to install Windows 95. You cannot install Windows 95 straight from OS/2.

Tip

To install a new hard disk as your primary hard drive, you need Windows 95 on a floppy disk instead of CD-ROM. Next, place the Windows 95 Startup disk in drive A: and boot your computer. Upon boot, Windows 95 detects the new drive and asks if you want to allocate all of your unallocated space on your new drive. After you answer Yes. Windows runs FDISK and restarts your computer, then automatically formats the new hard disk's partition.

Using FDISK

When you use FDISK, you can partition your hard drive into one or several partitions. You might want to partition your new hard drive into two partitions if you want to install a different operating system, such as OS/2 Warp, on your computer. This way, you can have both Windows 95 and OS/2 residing on the same computer, but occupying different hard drives.

Caution

Running FDISK destroys all data on the partitions you change or create. Do not use FDISK if you are not comfortable making these changes and if you have not backed up all the data on your drive. If you are in a company, consult your MIS or help desk person before continuing.

Another time when you can partition a hard disk is when you have already set up a hard drive and you want to *repartition* it. If you want to repartition a hard disk that has several logical drives into one drive, you must first use FDISK to delete all existing partitions and logical drives, and then create a new primary partition and make it active. The *active partition* is the partition in which your system boots. For this chapter, your active partition is already set up and is not modified. This is the partition on the hard disk that contains Windows 95. You don't need to worry about partitioning that hard drive. In fact, if you repartitioned that drive, you would lose all the data on it, including Windows 95.

Caution

On hard disks that are already installed, you should not repartition the hard disk by using FDISK if the partition was created using Disk Manager, Storage Dimensions SpeedStor, Priam, or Everex partitioning programs. When these programs are used, they replace the existing PC's BIOS in interactions between MS-DOS and the hard disk controller. For these cases, you must use the same disk-partitioning program that was used to partition the disk in the first place. For example, if you use SpeedStor on a computer that has more than 1,024 cylinders, do not use FDISK to partition your hard drive. Use SpeedStor instead.

You can tell the type of program that created the partition by searching for these files on your system: HARDRIVE.SYS for Priam; SSTOR.SYS for SpeedStor; DMDRVR.BIN for Disk Manager; and EVDISK.SYS for Everex. Usually, you find device= entries for these files in CONFIG.SYS. If you need help repartitioning the hard disk or are unsure whether the BIOS is being replaced, contact the manufacturer of the original disk-partitioning program.

As you just read, when you partition a hard drive, you lose all data on it. When repartitioning an existing hard drive, be sure to back up all your data onto another hard drive or tape backup. You cannot recover the data once you've partitioned the drive.

Note

Although Windows 95 replaces MS-DOS as your primary operating system, the partitions that FDISK creates are still called *DOS partitions*.

FDISK is an MS-DOS-based application that you can run from the DOS command prompt. You also can run it in a DOS window in Windows 95. As you use FDISK, each FDISK screen displays a Current Fixed Disk Drive line, followed by a number. This number is the number of the current drive that is selected. Computers with only one hard disk drive use the label 1. Computers with more than one hard disk drive label the drives as follow: the first hard disk drive on the computer is 1, the second is 2, and so on. The Current Fixed Disk Drive line refers only to physical disk drives, not logical drives.

To configure a hard disk by using FDISK, use the following steps:

1. At the DOS command prompt, type **FDISK**. The FDISK Options screen displays the following:

```
1. Create a partition or logical drive
2. Set the active partition
3. Delete a partition or logical drive
4. Display partition information
5. Change current fixed disk drive
   Enter choice [1]
   Press Esc to exit FDISK
```

> **Tip**
>
> You can press Esc anytime to exit FDISK.

2. In the preceding options list, the fifth option is not available when you have only one hard drive installed on your computer. Because we have two hard drives installed now, select 5 to switch to the second hard disk to partition it and press Enter.

3. Now that your new drive is selected, choose option 1 and press Enter. This creates a partition on your drive. When you are prompted to set the size of the partition, the default is to use the entire drive. Select Yes in most cases.

4. Return to the FDISK menu and be sure to select your primary fixed disk (drive C: usually) by selecting option 5 before you exit FDISK. Otherwise, when you reboot your system, your computer will try to boot from your new drive.

> **Note**
>
> If you installed a disk-compression program from Microsoft or another vendor, FDISK displays the uncompressed size of the drives, not the compressed size. Depending on the software, FDISK may not be able to display information about all the drives used by a disk-compression program from another vendor. You should obtain information from the software vendor if you are having difficulties.

> **Troubleshooting**
>
> *What do I do when I get an error that Windows 95 Setup can't find a valid boot partition?*
>
> This error might be a result of your disk compression software or network components mapping over the boot drive. This can occur if you are mapping a network drive to H, but H is the hidden host drive for your disk compression software. To resolve the invalid partition error, make sure the drive is not mapped over or logically remapped. You should also verify a valid, active partition using the FDISK command. If no active partition exists, use FDISK to mark an appropriate partition as active. Also, make sure the disk compression software's host drive does not conflict with a mapped network drive.

Configuring Your Hard Disk for Windows 95

After your hard drive is installed and the cables reattached to your computer, boot your computer and start Windows 95. During the boot process, Windows 95 looks at your system and, if everything goes as planned, detects your new hard drive. If the hard drive is Plug and Play-compatible, Windows 95 configures it automatically. Windows 95 also automatically configures any Plug-and-Play controller that you may have installed.

One of the problems with Plug and Play is that your computer's BIOS also needs to support Plug-and-Play devices. Most computers being used do not have a BIOS that supports this new specification. For this reason, Windows 95 also includes the auto-detect feature for legacy systems. If Windows 95 finds your new hard drive during bootup, but cannot automatically configure it, you are presented with a screen asking if you want to set up the device now. The best response is to answer <u>Y</u>es to this screen and let Windows 95 try to set it up for you.

Setting Up Plug and Play Controllers

Windows 95 is designed to automatically detect a new Plug and Play-compliant hard disk drive controller. After the physical installation of the hard disk drive controller is complete, and the computer is restarted, the hard disk drive can be configured during the boot process. When that is complete, your new hard disk drive is ready for use.

Follow the procedures for testing your new hard disk drive as outlined later in "Testing the Hard Disk Drive." If the hard disk drive is not operational, you need to install it as a legacy device, as described in the following section.

Configuring a Legacy Hard Disk Drive Controller

Most users need to use the auto-detect or manual detection features of Windows 95 to configure their hard drive for Windows 95. Unless you know that your hard drive will not be detected by Windows 95 during the auto detection phase, you should always try the automatic detection mode first. If that does not work, then use the manual detection mode.

Automatic Detection

To configure a legacy hard disk drive controller, go to the Control Panel and double-click the Add New Hardware icon. The Add New Hardware Wizard displays. Click the Next button to continue. You now are presented with the screen shown in figure 26.4. Make sure the Yes (Recommended) option is marked and click the Next button. The Yes option informs Windows 95 that it should attempt to find the hardware on its own.

Fig. 26.4
You should consider letting Windows 95 try to automatically detect your new hard disk by choosing Yes when the Add New Hardware Wizard displays.

A warning screen then appears, informing you the detection procedure may take a long time to complete. It may take more than 10 minutes depending on your system. While it is running, you hear a lot of noise from the disk and the HDD light flashes. (The HDD light is an optional red or green light on the front of your computer. When on, it indicates the hard disk drive is being accessed.) When this task is completed, you are informed by another display that your device was detected. Click the Finish button to complete the hard disk drive configuration.

If Windows 95 detects your hard drive and displays the correct model and manufacturer, it usually can install the device without any problems. In some cases, if the device driver and other supporting files are not installed on your machine, you need to provide the installation disk that comes bundled with the hard disk. This disk normally is supplied by the manufacturer of the hardware. Windows copies the drivers onto your system and then informs you that it needs to reboot the computer for the new settings to take effect. Click the Yes button when Windows asks if it can restart the computer. After your computer starts and Windows 95 boots, and your new hard disk device doesn't conflict with your system, you're ready to format it and use it.

> **Tip**
>
> If the installation disks do not include up-to-date drivers for Windows 95, you need to contact the vendor to obtain a driver for your hard disk to work with Windows 95. Another place to look for updated drivers is on CompuServe, the Microsoft Download Service (MSDL), or other bulletin board systems that contain hardware support areas. You can contact the MSDL by calling 206-936-6735 with a modem and following the on-screen instructions.

Manual Detection

If, during the auto-detect stage, Windows 95 cannot detect your new hard drive device, the screen shown in figure 26.5 appears. This display informs you that Windows cannot find the hard disk and that you need to manually detect the new hard drive.

To continue with the configuration, click the Next button. The screen shown in figure 26.6 appears. This is the same display you receive if you selected the No option in the wizard screen shown in figure 26.4. In the Hardware Types list box, select the Hard disk controllers item (see fig. 26.6). Click Next.

Fig. 26.5
The Add New
Hardware Wizard
did not find any
new devices,
namely your new
hard disk
controller.

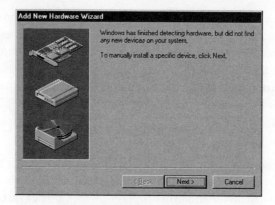

Fig. 26.6
Select the Hard
disk controller
item to tell
Windows to
install that type of
hardware device.

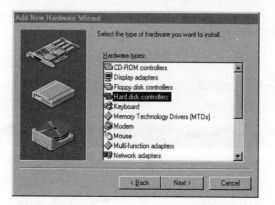

Windows 95 displays a dialog box letting you know that it is building a driver information database. This database contains the listing of all the hard drive controllers that Windows 95 is currently aware of. After the database is created, you are shown models and manufacturers of hard drive controllers in the Add New Hardware Wizard screen (see fig. 26.7).

If you know the name and manufacturer of your device, select it from the two lists. Click Next for Windows 95 to set up your device with the appropriate files. You may need to insert your Windows 95 Setup disks. Windows 95 copies all the necessary files from the disks to your system.

If your device doesn't appear in the list of manufacturers and models, and you have a disk supplied by the manufacturer, click the Have Disk button and enter the path of where these drivers can be located in the Copy Manufacturer's Files From text box in the Install From Disk dialog box. Click OK. Windows 95 copies all the necessary files from the disks to your system.

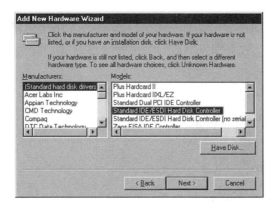

Fig. 26.7
Select the manufacturer and model of the hard disk drive controller installed on your system.

Tip

If you don't have disks from your hard disk vendor and your device doesn't appear in the list of hard disk controllers, select the Standard Hard Disk Drivers selection in the Manufacturer's list. This option uses a generic driver that may work with your device. The problem with this alternative is that the driver may not be optimized for your drive and could limit the performance factors (such as disk access time) of your device.

After all the files are copied to your system, Windows displays the last Add New Hardware Wizard screen. Click the Finish button to complete the hard disk drive controller configuration. Windows 95 prompts you if it can restart your computer so the new device works with Windows 95. Click Yes, sit back and relax, and cross your fingers. When Windows 95 boots up, your hard disk should be ready to be formatted and set up to be used.

If Things Don't Go Right...

If the configuration is unsuccessful, Windows 95 boots with an error message similar to the one in figure 26.8. This message tells you that something is wrong and asks you what to do. In some cases, you may have a conflict with another piece of hardware already installed on your computer. Even though Windows 95 handles the distribution of IRQs and other device settings, your new hard disk drive may not work correctly with the setting Windows is trying to use for it.

Fig. 26.8
If your new hard drive is not set up properly, you receive a hardware conflict message.

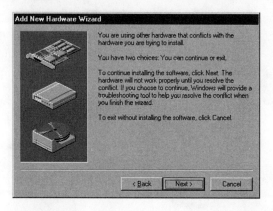

Click the Next button to continue with the hardware configuration, even though something is wrong. This helps you locate the conflict. If you exit at this point, the hardware is not configured and you won't know what is wrong. To continue, follow this procedure:

1. Click Start Conflict Troubleshooter. This displays a Windows Help screen, which you can walk through to troubleshoot and diagnose possible problems with your hard drive.

2. In the Help display, click Start to start the Hardware Conflict Trouble-shooter (see fig. 26.9).

Fig. 26.9
To help you track down possible problems with your hard disk configuration, use the Hardware Conflict Trouble-shooter.

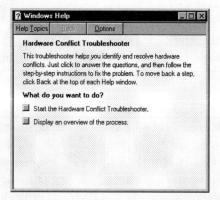

3. Another Help screen appears. Click the shortcut arrow to bring you to the Device Manager (you also can start the Device Manager by double-clicking System in the Control Panel).

4. The Device Manager appears, with the Hard Disk Controllers settings displayed (see fig. 26.10). If you do not see the controller settings, click

the plus sign next to Hard Disk Controllers. In the example shown in figure 26.10, a large red X is placed over one of the controllers telling you that it is not set up correctly, or that the system cannot use the second Standard Hard Disk Controller devices.

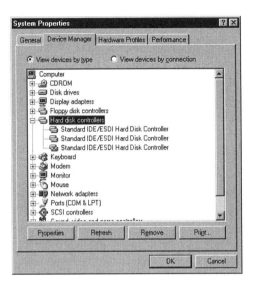

Fig. 26.10
When you troubleshoot a hard drive problem, always check the settings in the Device Manager first.

In this instance, the problem was that a second hard disk controller was defined and only one is allowed. To resolve this problem, highlight the line with the red X in it and click the <u>R</u>emove button. This is one example of how to resolve a hardware conflict. With hard disk drives and hard disk drive controllers, this is usually the only failure.

Troubleshooting

My computer stalls because of hard disk device drivers. What can I do?

The I/O Supervisor requires the hard disk driver files with the extensions PDR, MPD, VXD, and 386 to be located in the SYSTEM\IOSUBSYS subfolder in your Windows 95 folder. The I/O Supervisor is responsible for loading these hard disk device drivers. If your computer locks up during startup or hardware detection, use the following troubleshooting steps to fix the problem:

1. Look for SYS files in the IOSUBSYS folder. These are Windows NT miniport drivers that detect the I/O ports and may cause your computer to stop. Replace the Windows NT driver with either a Windows 95 miniport or a real-mode driver.

(continues)

(continued)

2. Check your IOS.INI file for real mode drivers not replaced by protected-mode drivers.

3. When loading protected mode drivers, the real mode driver generally remains loaded in memory even though the protected mode driver is running. Type **REM** at the beginning of the line in CONFIG.SYS that calls the real mode driver.

4. Some systems may encounter problems with devices that use ASPI drivers, such as tape backup units. Try using only real mode drivers, then try using only protected mode drivers.

Maybe It's a Hardware Problem...

Earlier in the section "Closing the Computer," I suggested that you may not want to replace the computer case just yet. Well, now is when you'll appreciate it. If your device does not work, and it's not because of the preceding failure, the problem might be hardware-related. You need to take a look at the physical connections your new hard disk has inside the computer. Sometimes a loose connection can create huge problems during setup.

Some possible areas to investigate are as follows:

- *Hard disk drive cable is defective.* Replace the cable with another one to see if the problem is resolved.

- *Hard disk drive cable is installed improperly for a single hard disk drive system.* Ensure the hard disk cable has the twist in the center of the cable near the connector to your disk drive. This is how hard disk drive C: is identified. The remaining connector is attached to the hard disk drive controller.

- *Hard disk drive cable is installed improperly for a dual hard disk drive system.* Ensure the hard disk cable has the twist in the center of the cable near the connector to your disk drive. This is how hard disk drive C: is identified. The connector at the center of the cable is for hard disk drive D:. The remaining connector is attached to the hard disk drive controller.

- *Hard disk device is defective.* If the hard disk drive cable is connected properly and the hard disk drive is not working properly, then the fault may be with the hard disk drive itself. Install a different hard disk drive and see if the problem is resolved.

■ *Hard disk controller is defective.* If the hard disk drive cable is connected properly and the hard disk drive is working properly (it was tested on another computer), then the fault may be with the hard disk drive controller. Install a different hard disk drive controller and see if the problem is resolved.

> **Note**
>
> In the following list, the term *hard disk drive cable* is used to mean either the controller cable and/or the data cable, depending on which system you have.

After adjusting the cables and/or replacing the hard drive, reboot the computer and walk through the Add New Hardware Wizard again. If none of these solutions help, call the technical support number that is included with your hard drive. New drivers for Windows 95 may be available that they can send to you.

Formatting a Hard Disk Drive

Now that your hard disk is partitioned, and Windows 95 can recognize it, you need a way for it to be accessed. To do this, you need to perform a high-level format on it. Another reason to format a hard drive is if you want to clean up the hard disk by removing all its files and folders. Of course, you cannot do this on hard disks that currently contain data that you are using, including Windows 95.

▶ See "Memory, Disks, and Devices," p. 689

You can format a hard disk in Windows 95 using a graphical approach with Explorer (see fig. 26.11), or using the FORMAT command at the MS-DOS prompt.

> **Caution**
>
> Before using the FORMAT command or utility on a drive that already contains data, make sure your hard disk does not contain valuable data that is not backed up. When you format a hard drive, all data is erased from the disk and you cannot recover it.

Fig. 26.11
For a more graphical approach to formatting your hard drive, use the Format utility in Explorer.

To format a hard disk drive using Explorer, use the following steps:

1. In Windows Explorer, right-click the drive icon for that disk, and then click Format from the context-sensitive menu.

2. In the Format dialog box, set the appropriate options for the type of format you want to perform. If your hard disk is new, you need to select the Full option in the Format Type section. In the Capacity drop-down list, select the size of your hard disk drive.

3. In the Other options area, type a label for the hard drive in the Label box. The *label* is the name you want to identify this drive with; don't confuse this with drive letter.

4. Click Start. Windows 95 formats the hard drive and, if you selected the Display Summary When Finished option in the Other Options area, a summary sheet appears that shows the amount of space available on the disk and how much space is taken up by system files and bad sectors, if any are found.

5. Click OK when you finish reading the report.

6. Click Close to close the Format dialog box.

Troubleshooting

I've used the Format utility in Explorer and the FORMAT command in MS-DOS, but I still can't format my hard drive.

If the disk was compressed by using DriveSpace, you must use the Format option in DriveSpace to format the compressed drive.

If you need to format a drive at the DOS command line, use the following syntax:

```
FORMAT driveletter
```

The `driveletter` parameter is the letter used to denote the hard drive you are formatting. To include a label for the drive, use the following syntax, with the label name replacing `label`:

```
FORMAT driveletter V:label
```

Your new hard disk is now ready for use.

Troubleshooting

I ran into some major problems with Windows 95 and want to reformat my hard drive. How can I do this?

First, remember that you will lose ALL data on your hard drive, including MS-DOS and Windows 95. If you created a startup disk when you installed Windows 95, you can use that disk to format your hard drive. To do this place the startup disk in drive A and reboot your computer. When the command line appears, type the following:

format driveletter: /s

The driveletter parameter is the letter of the drive you want to format, such as C:. The /s switch copies system files on to the hard disk so that you can reinstall MS-DOS and run the Windows 95 Setup program from DOS. When the warning message appears on-screen, type **Y** to continue with the formatting. Click No to stop. After the hard drive is formatted, you are prompted for a volume label. This is optional. Press Enter, remove the floppy disk, and reboot your computer.

Testing the Hard Disk Drive

Testing the hard disk drive is simple. All you have to do is use it. Before using it, however, you can ask Windows 95 to show you which ones are present. If you have two, they are shown as your C drive and D drives. The third one is the E drive, and the fourth one the F drive. Some possible ways to see it are as follows:

- Double-click My Computer and see which disks are shown.

- From the Explorer, go to the top of the list and see which hard disk drives are listed.

Troubleshooting

My hard disk has become unreadable. How can I repartition it if I can't boot into it?

If you created a startup disk during Windows 95 Setup, a copy of FDISK is on that disk. Place the startup disk in drive A: and reboot your computer. When the A:\ prompt appears on-screen, type **FDISK** and press Enter.

To make sure your new hard drive functions properly, copy a file from your old hard disk to the new hard disk. When finished, compare the two files to see if the file was copied successfully. Likewise, copy the file you just copied to the new hard drive back to the old hard drive and change the name. Now compare the two files on the old hard disk drive to see if they are still identical.

◀ See "Improving Hard Disk Performance," p. 323

Troubleshooting

How do I configure my Sysquest removable IDE drive for Windows 95?

For a Sysquest IDE drive to work properly under Windows 95, be sure to add the entry RemovableIDE=true to the [386enh] section of your SYSTEM.INI file.

Chapter 27

Configuring Backup Systems

by Michael Marchuk

As several-hundred megabyte hard drives become standard on new computers and gigabyte hard drives break the $300 barrier, it is clear that the days of backing up your system to disks are long gone. With that in mind, it is obvious that a tape backup system is needed to perform full system backups.

This chapter discusses tape backup systems and their place as a required peripheral. Additionally, this chapter shows you how to do the following

- Choose a backup system
- Install Microsoft Backup for Windows
- Install tape backup hardware through Windows
- Install unsupported tape backup systems
- Use Microsoft Backup for Windows

Choosing a Backup System

If you already own a tape drive, then you may want to skip this section, since it will cover the basics behind evaluating a tape backup system. If you haven't purchased a tape backup system yet, you'd better read this section quickly and get one soon. Each day you go without a tape backup system you are risking your data against a potential system failure.

When choosing a tape backup system, you have many options to consider. The tape backup market contains several popular tape formats and many new options. You'll look at several of these tape formats and find out the future of tape drives. But first, consider the caveats behind selecting a tape drive that will suit your needs

- Price

- Availability of tape cartridges

- Industry acceptance/standardization

- Capacity

- Support

Price

Pricing affects every decision we make, especially with our computer purchases. When you purchased your computer, you probably shopped around before you spent the couple thousand dollars on the machine you bought. When looking for a tape backup system, the process is similar, but the dollar figures are typically much less.

The average tape backup system will run between $75 and $125. That's not much more than a disk drive or a mouse. Those peripherals are considered "essential" for most every computer, but a tape drive is not. Consider how much time and effort would be lost if your hard drive stopped working today. Wouldn't it be worth $75 to have a backup to be able to restore your system in a few hours?

In addition to the cost of the tape drives, the cost for the tape cartridges cannot be ignored. Most tape cartridges can be purchased for $15 or $20. An average system will need two or three cartridges to complete a full backup. This will be explained more fully in the section "Capacity" later in this chapter.

Availability of Tape Cartridges

When considering a purchase of a tape backup system, flip through a few computer magazines or office supply catalogs. Most tape backup systems will specify a cartridge type that they use. You should be able to find several vendors in the magazines or catalogs who carry tape cartridges for your system. If you cannot find anyone but the manufacturer to sell you tapes, then perhaps you should consider a different tape backup system. The reason for finding alternative sources for tape cartridges is primarily one of standards. If your tape drive manufacturer is the only source for tape cartridges and it goes out of business tomorrow, you may not be able to find secondary sources for your cartridges.

Industry Standards

As with other industries, media formats have certain standards which allow vendors to produce products that consumers can use with their equipment. Audio cassettes, VHS video tapes, and 3 1/2-inch floppy disks all conform to industry standards for each media type. The same holds true for tape backup media.

Several major industry standards exist which are outlined in table 27.1.

Table 27.1 Major Tape Backup Standards		
Tape Standard	**Native Capacity**	**Compressed Capacity**
QIC-40	60M	120M
QIC-80	120M	250M
QIC-3010	350M	700M
QIC-3020	680M	1.4G
Travan	400M	800M
4mm DAT	2G	4G
8mm DAT	4G	8G

As the technology changes, many standards will be added to this list that will undoubtedly have higher capacities. When looking for a tape backup system, try to buy one that conforms to an industry standard.

Capacity

After seeing the various standards, you may be asking yourself, "Which one should I buy?" Your situation will vary from someone else's because your machine may be used differently. However, a good rule of thumb is to buy a tape backup system that can perform a full backup of your system in two tapes or less. That means that if you have a 500M hard drive with 320M of data, then you should not consider a QIC-40 tape drive unless you cannot spend the extra money for any of the higher capacity systems.

> **Note**
>
> The "Two-Tape" rule is not set in stone. This is a good guideline for most people who want to maintain their backups. Think of it this way: if you need to swap five tapes to back up your system, how often will you back up your system? The time and effort it takes to swap all of those tapes will justify purchasing a tape drive that meets your needs.

When estimating your backup capacity requirements, you may use the estimated compressed tape capacity to determine the tape system that fits your needs. Typically a 2:1 compression ratio is average for most types of data.

Support

When choosing a vendor for a tape backup system, you should buy from a manufacturer who has been around for at least a few years. In the computer industry, many companies who have been established for more than 10 years are considered old-timers. Choose a company that has a reputation for building solid tape backup systems. Some companies that come to mind include

- Colorado Memory Systems
- Conner Peripherals
- Iomega
- Mountain Network Solutions

Internal vs. External Tape Drive

You might have to back up more than one computer; for example, you may need to back up both your laptop and workstation. In this case, you may want to consider an external tape drive system. *External tape drives* usually connect to your computer through the parallel port. The transfer rate is limited to the throughput of your parallel port, so backups would take slightly longer with the external drive when compared to the same drive's internal model. External tape drives are somewhat more expensive than internal units; however, the added flexibility of using an external unit will save you from buying additional tape drives.

The benefits of an internal tape drive include the integration with the system as a whole and the increased backup performance. Also, if you don't have to back up laptops or other stand-alone workstations, you don't need the additional hassles of connecting external cables and finding a place to plug in an external tape drive (which tend to have very large power supplies integrated into the plug).

Installing Microsoft Backup for Windows

Microsoft has included a tape backup application along with Windows 95 which allows excellent integration with the operating system. This backup software works with most of the QIC-40, QIC-80, and QIC-3010 compatible tape drives on the market. However, Microsoft Backup for Windows won't work with the high-end tape backup solutions such as QIC-3020 or 4mm and 8mm DAT tape backup systems. Although Microsoft Backup for Windows doesn't support these drives, manufacturers will provide Windows backup software which works with their drives (usually for an additional cost).

After you have installed your internal tape backup drive by following the manufacturer's instructions or connected the external tape drive to the parallel port, you are ready to load the backup software. Windows default installation will not load the Microsoft Backup for Windows. However, you can easily install this accessory using the following steps:

1. Click the Start button.

2. Click Settings.

3. Select Control Panel.

4. Select Add/Remove Programs. You see a dialog box with several property sheets like the one shown in figure 27.1.

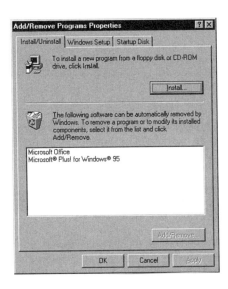

Fig. 27.1
The Add/Remove Programs Wizard enables you to install Microsoft Backup for Windows.

5. Choose the Windows Setup property sheet.

6. Select Disk Tools from the list of components.

7. Click the Details button. This will bring up a list of the default Windows 95 Disk Tools. The tools you have currently installed will be marked with a check, as shown in figure 27.2.

Fig. 27.2
The Disk Tools components currently installed do not include Backup.

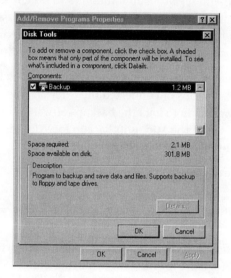

8. Check the box next to Backup to mark it for installation.

9. Click the OK button. Windows will prompt you to insert the appropriate diskette or CD-ROM to load the Microsoft Backup for Windows software.

Once the backup software is loaded, you can proceed to the next step by letting Microsoft Backup auto-detect your tape drive system.

Letting Microsoft Backup Detect Tape Hardware

When you run Microsoft Backup for Windows the first time, it will attempt to automatically detect the type of backup system you have. Microsoft

Backup for Windows only supports one of these types of backup systems connected through the floppy disk controller:

- QIC-40

- QIC-80

- QIC-3010

- Colorado Trakker parallel-port backup drives

If your drive type is not listed here, see the next section, "Installing Unsupported Tape Backup Systems."

Once Microsoft Backup for Windows has detected your drive, you may begin backing up your system. You can skip to the section later in this chapter, "Configuring Windows Backup."

Installing Unsupported Tape Backup Systems

Unsupported tape backup systems are only unsupported in terms of Microsoft Backup for Windows. Many vendors have their own backup software which works with their tape backup systems. Some of the systems listed here will not have Windows backup software while others will. Check with your tape drive manufacturer to see if it currently has a Windows 95 backup solution or if its current DOS or Windows backup software will work with Windows 95.

DAT Tape Systems

Many high-capacity systems will use a Digital Audio Tape (DAT) tape backup drive which uses either 4mm or 8mm tape cartridges to store between 2G and 4G of data. While DAT tape systems tend to be more expensive than QIC-based systems, the DAT systems provide significantly more storage capacity per tape.

Most DAT tape backup systems connect to a SCSI interface board in the computer. Windows 95 will be able to detect and install drivers for many SCSI controllers; however, the manufacturer's Windows tape backup software will still be required to perform the backup.

If you are using DOS-based tape backup software, Windows 95 will prompt you with a warning message like the one shown in figure 27.3.

Fig. 27.3
Windows warns you against using older tape backup software within a Command Prompt box in Windows.

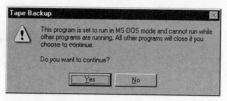

In this case, you will need to restart Windows 95 in a command-prompt only mode. This will allow older DOS programs which may communicate directly with the hardware to work properly. After you have completed a backup using DOS backup software, you can reboot your system back to Windows mode.

Additionally, even if your program does run, you will only be able to back up files and directories which match the DOS format FILENAME.EXT naming convention. While Windows 95 does a good job of shortening long directory names like "Data Files" down to DATAFI[td]1, you will not be able to restore the original directory to "Data Files" once you have backed it up.

Caution

If you ignore the warnings that Windows presents and run your DOS tape backup software in a Command Prompt box, you may cause Windows to lock up. In the worst case, your software may appear to work properly, but you may actually be losing data as it writes to the tape. If you run your software in this way, you will need to verify every tape you write to ensure that no data has been lost. This is not recommended!

QIC-02 Tape Drives

Many companies have older tape backup hardware which is either in its seventh year of active use or is gathering dust on a shelf in the storage room. In either case, you may want to use such a backup system under Windows 95.

QIC-02 tapes run off of an interface board which is provided with the tape drive unit. These units are typically external, because the drive mechanism is about the size of a lunch box. It's unlikely that Windows 95 will recognize the QIC-02 adapter card in your system, so you should take care to verify that the settings of the tape drive adapter do not interfere with the settings of the other cards installed in your system.

Once you have installed your hardware, you need to run the software which was supplied with the tape drive. Since these units are typically pre-Windows, you will most likely be using DOS backup software. In addition to the fact that the programs were written in DOS, you also want to be aware that the backup programs were written for DOS versions that date back 10 years. The programmers did not have to worry about extended memory management or disk compression software like DriveSpace. Your software may or may not run under the Windows running in command prompt mode.

Additionally, even if your program does run, you will only be able to back up files and directories which match the DOS format FILENAME.EXT naming convention. While Windows 95 does a good job of shortening long directory names like Data Files down to DATAFI[td]1, you will not be able to restore the original directory to Data Files once you have backed it up.

> **Caution**
>
> Using tape backup software built before 1990 may not work, or you may get strange or unexpected results.

Other Tape Drives

Many other tape drives exist which may or may not have Windows backup software available. In all cases, you should contact the manufacturer to see if it has a Windows 95 backup solution for your system. This way, you'll know that your system has been tested with Windows 95. If your manufacturer is not working on a Windows 95 version, ask if it has a Windows 3.1 version which has been tested with Windows 95. Often Windows 3.1 software will work the same under Windows 95.

As the earlier sections on DAT and QIC-02 tape systems mentioned, if you have DOS-based software, run it only in Windows command prompt mode. Also, remember that long file names will be shortened to fit DOS file name structures.

Configuring Windows Backup

Microsoft Backup for Windows can be configured with many options to suit your particular needs. This section will cover the options that correspond with the following:

- Backing up your files to the tape
- Restoring your files from the tape

- Comparing the files on the tape with those on the hard drive

- Backing up your local workstation

- Backing up other workstations on your network

Backup Options

Backing up files to the tape system can be done in several ways. Your backup needs will often determine which option you should choose. Look at the Properties page within Microsoft Backup for Windows to see what these options are. To start Backup, follow these steps:

1. Click the Start button.

2. Choose Programs.

3. Select Accessories.

4. Choose System Tools.

5. Select Backup.

You will see a dialog box which looks like the one shown in figure 27.4.

Fig. 27.4

Backup displays a welcome message to instruct you on how to use the program.

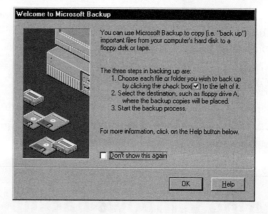

This dialog box explains the steps used to select files to be backed up to the tape. Once you read these directions, you may select the Don't Show This Again check box to prevent Windows from displaying the welcome dialog box each time you start Backup.

After you click the OK button to continue running Backup, Windows displays a second dialog box like the one shown in figure 27.5.

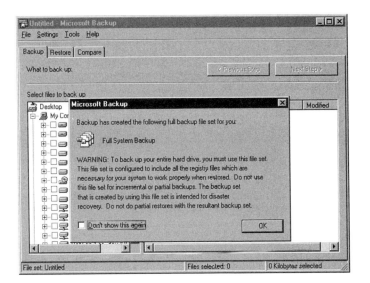

Fig. 27.5
Backup displays a
dialog box
describing the
special backup set
which includes
Windows registry
files.

Registry files include detailed information that holds the configuration data
for running Windows. These special files are automatically included in the
Full System Backup set which Backup creates for you. You'll find out more
about backup sets in "Backup Sets" later in this chapter.

Once Backup has started, you see a screen similar to the one shown in figure
27.6. Notice the three tabs that represent the three operations that Microsoft
Backup for Windows can perform.

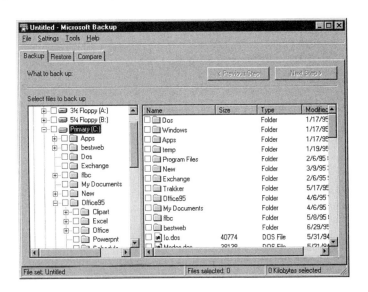

Fig. 27.6
Microsoft Backup
for Windows uses
the Explorer-style
folder display to
allow you to
choose the files to
save to tape.

You'll learn more about the methods for backing up and restoring files later in this chapter in the sections "Backing Up Your Local Workstation," "Backing Up Your Network," and "Restoring Files from Tape." For now, you'll learn about the various options that can affect your backup operations. To view or modify the backup options, follow these steps:

1. Select Settings from the Backup menu bar.

2. Choose Options. You will see a property sheet like the one shown in figure 27.7. The settings on the General property page will not be discussed since these options are straightforward.

Fig. 27.7
All the settings for Backup can be modified through one of the Options property pages.

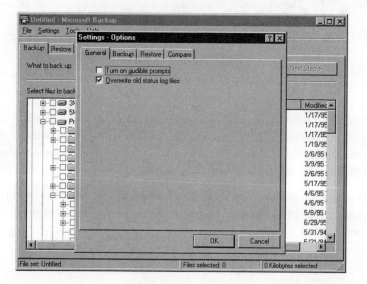

3. Select the Backup property page by clicking the Backup tab. This displays the Backup page shown in figure 27.8.

The first setting on the Backup property page describes what you should do after a successful tape backup operation has occurred. Select the Quit Backup After Operation is Finished option if you intend to be running the backup system in an unattended mode. For instance, if your system has 200M to back up, you may want to wait until you are finished using your machine for the day before starting the backup operation. By running Backup with the Quit option selected, Microsoft Backup for Windows will exit after it has finished backing up your system at night. This is also useful if you have a scheduler application like the one found in Microsoft's Plus Pack for Windows 95 which can initiate a backup operation during the evening. After the scheduled backup is finished, the program will exit and allow your computer to continue processing other scheduled jobs.

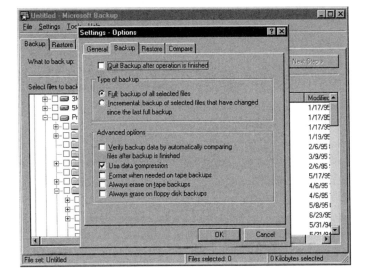

Fig. 27.8
The options listed
on the Backup
property page can
be changed for
each backup or left
the same for all
backups.

The next set of options affect which files will be copied to tape during a
backup operation. The two methods are F<u>u</u>ll and Incremental. A *full backup*
is one in which all files are copied to tape regardless if they have changed or
not since the last time you backed up your system. This option can take a
snapshot of your system as it is right now. An *incremental backup* is one in
which only the files that have changed since the last backup operation are
copied to tape. This makes the backup go much faster, because few files are
changed from week to week under typical circumstances.

Note

Windows keeps track of which files you have modified since the last backup by using
the Archive flag on each file. You can see how Windows stores this by right-clicking a
file in Explorer and choosing Properties. The Ar<u>c</u>hive check box indicates whether or
not the file has been changed since the last backup.

When you perform a full backup, the Archive flag for every file is turned off when it is
copied to tape. When you perform an incremental backup, the backup software
searches your files for the Archive flag and only copies those files with that flag
turned on. After the changed files have been saved on the tape, the Archive flag is
turned off.

The last set of Backup options are usually only modified when you have special reason to do so. You can choose from any of the following options in the Advanced Options area:

■ *Verify Backup Data by Automatically Comparing Fields After Backup is Finished*. This option is commonly used to make sure that the files copied to the tape match the files on the hard drive. Of course, you would think that they always would, because you just finished the backup operation; however, flaws in the tape media may go undetected when you are saving the files. Select this option if you are uncertain about the quality of your tape media or if you are using a tape cartridge for the first time.

> **Tip**
>
> You should always choose to verify your backups after you have completed a full backup of your system. While it will take twice as long to complete the entire operation, you can rely on the integrity of your system backup.

■ *Use Data Compression*. This option enables you to realize the best tape media usage by compressing the files as they are copied to tape. This is how tape manufacturers accomplish the higher storage capacity (usually double the uncompressed capacity) which they advertise for their tape drive systems.

> **Caution**
>
> Data compression can only be estimated over a broad range of file types. For average users, this will approximate the 2:1 compression that most tape system manufacturers advertise. However, you may not get a high compression ratio if you back up these types of files:
>
> ■ Graphics files with the GIF or JPEG formats
>
> ■ Compressed archives like ZIP, LZH, PAK, and ARJ files
>
> ■ Large numbers of EXE files

■ *Format When Needed on Tape Backups*. If Microsoft Backup for Windows detects a new or damaged tape to which you are attempting to copy files, Backup will automatically format the tape before it starts the backup operation if you select this option. This option is useful for unattended or scheduled tape backups; however, a tape format operation could take many hours to perform in addition to the backup process.

■ *Always Erase on Tape Backups.* The default operation for Backup is to append new backup sets to the end of those already on a tape. If you are going to be using a set of tapes regularly for periodic full backups, you may want to select this option to erase the tape before it starts the backup of the new data.

■ *Always Erase on Floppy Disk Backups.* This option is similar to the previous one, but concerns backups to disks rather than to tapes.

Once you have selected the options for your backup, click OK to save your settings.

Restore Options

This section discusses the options that are used for restoring files which have previously been copied to a tape backup set. To access the Restore option settings, follow these steps:

1. Select Settings from the Backup menu bar.

2. Choose Options.

3. Select the Restore page from the Options property sheet by clicking the Restore tab. This will display the Restore property page similar to the one shown in figure 27.9.

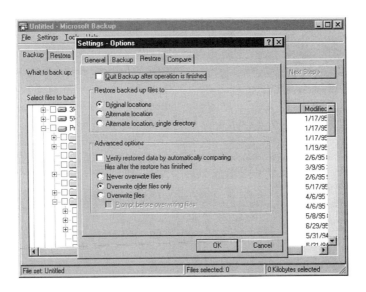

Fig. 27.9
The Restore options affect how your files are copied back to your hard drive from the backup tapes.

The first option is similar to the Quit Backup option explained in the Backup Options section. If you are restoring a large number of files or are running an unattended restore operation, you may want to select the Quit Backup After Operation is Finished option to exit Backup when the files have been restored.

The next set of options configures where restored files will be saved to when they are retrieved from the tape backup. Usually, you will be restoring to the Original Locations because that is where the files came from. However, you may want to choose an Alternate Location if you want to check the differences between a current file on your hard disk and one which was backed up on to tape. Instead of overwriting the current file, you can simply specify that the file be restored somewhere else.

The Alternate Location, Single Directory option will restore all of your files from the backup set into one directory. This will ignore any directory structure that you have saved to tape and only restore the files from those directories. If you have files of the same name in more than one directory, these files will be overwritten as the next file of the same name is restored from tape. Unless you have a specific need to do this, you'll want to stick with the Alternate Location option to avoid overwriting any files that you restore.

The Advanced Options area involves the verification of the restored data. To check that the file which was saved to your hard drive matches the file on the backup tape, select the Verify option. You probably won't need to use this option unless you are uncertain that the hard drive to which you are restoring the files from tape is saving the data properly. The remaining options specify how to handle files that may already exist on the hard drive that the tape backup wants to replace:

- *Never Overwrite Files*. This option allows you to protect any data that you have on your hard drive from being overwritten by the files being restored from tape.

- *Overwrite Older Files Only*. This option overwrites files on your hard drive only if they are older than the files which are being restored from tape.

- *Overwrite Files*. Along with this option, you should also select the Prompt Before Overwriting Files setting. This will prevent you from accidentally losing information if a file on the tape overwrites one you did not want to overwrite.

Compare Options

The options on the Compare property sheet are similar to both the Backup and Restore options previously explained. It's unlikely that you will need to change the Compare options unless you are performing specific tasks, such as unattended tape backup comparisons.

Backup Sets

In most cases, you will perform routine backups on either your entire hard drive or on certain data files. When backing up your data files, it is useful to create a backup set which maintains a list of folders to back up to tape. Instead of choosing several data directories (which may be on multiple drives) every time you want to back them up, you can create a backup set to automate the backup.

> **Tip**
>
> Using backup sets may also help you with your backup routine. By creating a standard backup set for your files, it will be easier to maintain a schedule for saving your files to tape. Running an incremental backup of your files each night could be named "Daily Backup." When you open the Backup application, all you need to do is open your Daily Backup set and let the system do the work.

To create a backup set, follow these steps:

1. Select the folders and files you want to back up.

2. Click the Next Step button.

3. Select the tape drive as the destination for your files.

4. Choose File, Save As.

5. Type a Backup Set name which describes the files which you are backing up.

> **Note**
>
> Be descriptive when naming files. For example, if you have a data folder named "Accounting Data," you may want to name your set **Accounting Data - Full Backup** if you are performing a full backup. Try to avoid set names like "Data," "Tape Backup," "Stuff," or "Files" since these are not very descriptive.

6. Click OK to save your backup set.

Any settings you have changed for the Backup or Restore options will be saved with your backup set.

Backing Up Your Local Workstation

The procedure to back up the files and folders on your workstation is easy. Follow these steps:

1. Select the folders and files you want to back up by placing a check in the box next to the folder or file.

2. Click the Next Step button when you have all of the folders and files selected.

3. Choose a backup media from the drives shown in the Select a Destination for a Backup list. Typically, this will be the tape drive system; however, you can back up to floppy disks, other hard drives, or network drives.

4. Click the Start Backup button.

5. You will be prompted for a backup set label that will identify this set of files on the tape. Type a label for the backup and click OK.

> **Tip**
>
> Use a descriptive title for your individual tape backup sets. Don't simply type Files. Type a title such as Full Accounting Data Backup 8/25/95. The more descriptive you are, the easier it will be for you or someone else to find the right files should they need to be restored.

6. If you want to protect your tape backup set from being restored by someone else, click the Password Protect button, which displays a dialog box in which you can type a password. Choose a password you will remember that is not the name of a family member, the name of your

dog, or some other password which could be easily guessed. A password that includes both numbers and letters is more secure than one which has only letters or only numbers.

Microsoft Backup for Windows now begins to store your selected files to the tape. You see a dialog box similar to the one shown in figure 27.10.

Fig. 27.10
Microsoft Backup for Windows shows the progress of your backup using a graphical display.

When choosing to back up your local workstation, you should set up a rotation of tapes to handle both full system backups as well as incremental file backups. A full system backup might occur only once per month or possibly as frequently as once per week. Incremental file backups can occur either weekly (if you are performing full backups monthly) or daily (if your full backups are performed weekly).

The frequency of your backups will depend on the usage of your machine to store data. If you store most of your data on a network server which is backed up by a computer operations staff, you may find that your backups can occur quarterly. If you store your company's critical data on your computer, you may find that daily backups are essential. In either case, it is important that you actually do the backups when you've planned them.

Tip

You should have at least a full system backup performed twice a year. Even if you don't think your files change much in that time period, you will want to have a backup in case of emergencies.

IV

Setting Up Hardware

You don't need to back up applications as frequently as the data files that you use on a day-to-day basis. Because applications can readily be reinstalled from the original disks or CD-ROMs, you should be most concerned about saving your data files which may be difficult to reconstruct if you lose them. Additionally, backing up your applications will take a long time and a lot of room on your tape.

> **Tip**
>
> If you have not already done so, you should create a special folder called DATA in which you create all of your data files. Not only will this make finding your data easier, but it will also make the job of backing it up all that much easier.

Backing Up Your Network

If your computer is used as a server for other Windows workstations, or if you want to centralize the backup operations for all of the workstations in your workgroup, you will want to set up a procedure for backing up your network. Microsoft Backup for Windows can back up other workstations on the network if the computer with the tape backup drive can access the data on the other systems. You may want to set up some policies (either formally or informally) to ensure that network data can be accessed for backup during the specified times. It could even be as simple as keeping the Read-Only share password on everyone's local hard drive the same so that the person performing the backup can access the data to be saved to the tape.

You should decide on a schedule for when the backups occur. Ideally, it should happen after business hours when network traffic is light and the computers are not being used. If you plan on scheduling an after-hours backup, you may want to invest in the Microsoft Plus! Companion for Windows 95 which includes a scheduling application. This way, your backups can be run unattended.

If your network data does not fit on one tape, however, you may need to switch tapes when they fill up. If you suspect that your network backups will fill up more than one tape, you may want to stagger which workstations are backed up each night or consider purchasing a larger tape backup system to handle the larger volume of data.

Troubleshooting

The tape system I use is supposed to hold 250M on a tape, but sometimes I can only get 150M on one tape. Why?

The tape drive manufacturers often inflate their capacity claims to match an estimated 2:1 compression ratio. Your tape probably can only hold 120M of uncompressed data. If you are experiencing less than a 2:1 compression ratio with the particular files you are backing up, your actual tape capacity is less.

I can't schedule a backup to happen at night using Microsoft Backup for Windows. Why not?

Microsoft Backup for Windows does not directly support a scheduled backup. You may want to purchase another tape backup software package which does, or buy the Microsoft Plus! Companion for Windows 95 which contains a scheduling program.

You will also want to create a backup set that includes the data directories of the computers on your network. A backup set is essential if you are performing unattended backups and are extremely helpful even if you manually start the backup operation before you leave work.

Caution

If someone is using a file on the network or the file is left open during a network backup, that file will not be saved to tape, because the contents of that file are not accessible to another user while the file is open.

You will probably not want to make a full system backup of every computer on the network. It would be much wiser to make individual full system backups which you can easily identify should a problem occur. Your schedule should be a weekly backup of all the data files and a daily backup of only the changed data files. You should at least have one tape for each day of the week and two tapes for alternating full backups. Make sure you buy enough tapes to handle this sort of rotation.

Tip

Try to elect (or appoint) someone to maintain the backup rotation for your network. This person may be you, if your computer hosts the tape backup system.

> **Caution**
>
> Do not store all of your backup tapes near your computers. If you have a fire and all the tapes are destroyed, what good is your backup system? Keep at least the alternating weekly data backups offsite. If that means you bring them home with you, then do it. You may save your company by performing this simple procedure.

Restoring Files from Tape

Once you have successfully backed up your files, there may come a time when you need to restore them from your tape. To restore folders or files from a tape, follow these steps from within the Microsoft Backup for Windows application:

1. Click the Restore tab.

2. Insert the tape containing your files to be restored into your tape drive.

3. Choose the tape drive as the source from which you will be restoring.

4. Choose the backup set which contains the data you want to restore.

5. Click the Next Step button.

6. Select the folders or files you want to restore by placing a check next to the item.

7. Click the Start Restore button to begin restoring the data.

Refer to the section earlier in this chapter, "Restore Options," for more information on settings you may want to alter when restoring data. ❖

Chapter 28

Configuring Modems

by Sue Plumley

A modem converts computer signals to telephone signals and back again so that you can use the telephone lines to communicate with other computers. Use a modem to send and receive e-mail, faxes, and files to any other computer with a modem. Also, you can use your modem to connect to online services like America Online and CompuServe, even the Internet. Windows 95 includes various programs you can use with a modem, including HyperTerminal, Microsoft Fax, Phone Dialer, and The Microsoft Network.

Windows can autodetect and install any of hundreds of modems by use of the Modem Wizard. Alternatively, Windows enables you to install your modem manually by choosing the manufacturer and model from a list.

In this chapter, you learn to do the following:

- Choose a modem
- Use the wizard to configure your modem
- Manually configure your modem
- Modify modem settings
- Troubleshoot modem installation and use

Choosing a Modem

You can choose from numerous modems, and the one you choose governs how fast your computer communicates over the phone lines. You'll really notice the speed of your modem when you're transferring large files to or from another computer. The faster your modem, the more efficiently the data transfers.

> **Note**
>
> A device that converts from digital (computer signals) to analog (telephone signals) is called a *modulator*; a device that converts from analog to digital is called a *demodulator*. *Mo*(dulator)-*dem*(odulator) is how *modem* got its name.

The speed of a modem is measured in bits per second (bps). Make sure that you get the fastest available; today's maximum modem speed is 28,800 bps. Slower modem speeds are 14,400, 9,600, and 2,400 bps. A 14,400 bps modem is also acceptable, but don't use anything slower, or you'll be disappointed with your communications.

The two communicating modems must communicate using the same speeds. If your modem, for example, is 28,800 bps and the modem on the other end of the phone lines is only 14,400 bps, your modem slows down to 14,400 to accommodate the other modem.

> **Tip**
>
> When deciding whether to use an internal or external modem, an internal modem is generally less expensive and takes up less space on the Desktop than the external.

Installing Your Modem

Windows includes a wizard that can detect a modem you've added to your system and identify the port, install the appropriate driver, and identify the modem speed. You can let the wizard configure your modem, or you can manually configure your modem.

Install your modem by first turning off your computer and then attaching the cables to the internal or external modem and attaching the phone line. When you're finished, turn on the modem and restart the computer.

Letting Windows AutoDetect the Modem

When you use the Modem Wizard to identify your modem, Windows queries the attached modem and ascertains the port, speed, and driver needed for the modem. Windows asks you to confirm its findings and then sets up the modem for you.

To use the Windows wizard to set up your modem, follow these steps:

1. Open the Control Panel and double-click the Modems icon. The Install New Modem dialog box appears (see fig. 28.1).

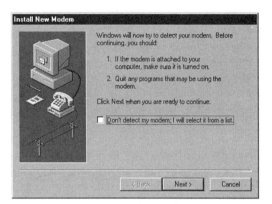

Fig. 28.1
After attaching your modem to your computer, you can use the Modem Wizard to configure the modem for you.

2. Click the Next button to tell Windows to begin checking for your modem. The second wizard dialog box appears (see fig. 28.2).

Fig. 28.2
The wizard searches for your modem and identifies the port to which it's connected.

3. When the wizard finishes querying the modem, it displays the Verify Modem dialog box (see fig. 28.3). If the modem is the correct one, choose Next; if you want to change the modem, choose the Change button and then refer to the next section, "Manually Specifying a Modem."

Fig. 28.3
You can accept or
change the
modem that
Windows
identifies.

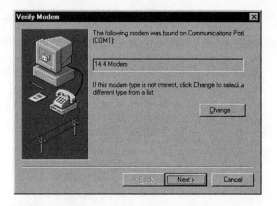

4. Windows sets up your modem and then displays the last wizard dialog
   box (see fig. 28.4). Choose Finish to close the dialog box.

Fig. 28.4
Windows sets up
the modem for
you automatically.

5. When the Modem Wizard dialog box closes, Windows displays the
   Modems Properties dialog box in which you can adjust the modem's
   settings and troubleshoot modem problems. Choose OK to close the
   dialog box.

Manually Specifying a Modem

If you prefer, you can identify your modem instead of letting Windows detect
it. You might for example, want to use the manufacturer's driver with your
modem instead of one supplied by Windows. Windows enables you to
specify both the manufacturer and the modem type, as well as install the
driver from a disk.

To manually specify your modem, follow these steps:

1. Open the Control Panel and double-click the Modems icon. The Install New Modem dialog box appears (refer to fig. 28.1).

2. Choose the option <u>D</u>on't Detect My Modem; I Will Select It from a List and then choose Next. The second wizard dialog box appears (see fig. 28.5).

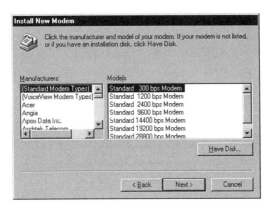

Fig. 28.5
You can choose the manufacturer and model of your modem in this wizard dialog box.

3. In <u>M</u>anufacturers, choose the maker of your modem. In Mode<u>l</u>s, choose the appropriate model of your modem.

    If you do not see the manufacturer or if you want to load the driver from a disk, choose <u>H</u>ave Disk. The Install From Disk dialog box appears. Enter the drive letter in the text box and choose OK. Windows installs the driver from the specified disk.

4. Click Next to continue installing the modem. Windows displays the next wizard dialog box (see fig. 28.6).

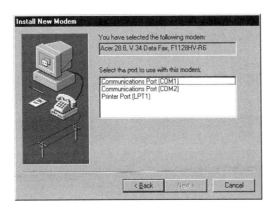

Fig. 28.6
Choose the port the modem is attached to and check to make sure that you've selected the correct modem.

> **Tip**
>
> If you make a mistake in a selection in any wizard dialog box, choose the <u>B</u>ack button and try again.

5. Select the port you want to use with the modem. Click the Next button. Windows installs the modem.

6. When it's done, Windows displays the last wizard dialog box telling you that the installation was successful. Choose Finish to close the dialog box. Windows displays the Modems Properties dialog box in which you can adjust the modem's settings and troubleshoot modem problems. Choose OK to close the dialog box.

> **Caution**
>
> Windows lets you set up any type of modem and assign any port to that modem, regardless of whether it's right. If you assign the wrong port or model, the modem does not work when you're ready to use it. If you are unsure of the port or the modem model, let Windows autodetect the modem for you, as described in the preceding section.

Modifying Modem Properties

You can adjust the modem settings at any time after you install your modem. You might want to change ports, adjust the speaker volume, or change the designated speed. Additionally, you can set the modem for specific dialing preferences, change the location from which you're dialing, set up the modem to use a calling card, and so on.

Finally, you can adjust the advanced connections settings, such as flow control, error control, modulation type, and so on.

> **Note**
>
> You can also configure an installed fax modem to share with others on a network, such as The Microsoft Network or a Novell NetWare network.

Modifying Dialing Properties

Use the Dialing Properties sheet to modify how calls are dialed and to set such options as dialing with a calling card, specifying various locations from which to call, and using tone or pulse dialing.

▶ See "Installing Shared Fax Modems," p. 655

To modify dialing properties, follow these steps:

1. Open the Control Panel and double-click the Modems icon. The Modems Properties sheet appears (see fig. 28.7).

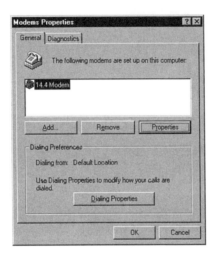

Fig. 28.7
Adjust modem and port settings in the Modems Properties sheet.

2. To set dialing preferences, choose the Dialing Properties button in the General page of the Modems Properties sheet. The Dialing Properties sheet appears (see fig. 28.8).

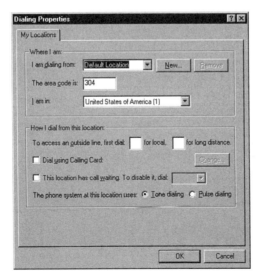

Fig. 28.8
Customize the dialing properties to suit your needs.

3. Enter information and/or choose options as described in table 28.1.

> **Tip**
>
> The dialing properties you define apply to any program from which you dial on the computer.

Table 28.1 Dialing Properties

Option	Description
Where I Am area	
I Am Dialing From	Choose from the list the first location you want to set up. To set up a new location, choose New and enter a location name in the Create New Location dialog box; choose OK. To remove a location, select it from the list and choose Remove.
The Area Code Is	Enter the area code you are dialing from.
I Am In	Choose the country you're in from the drop-down list.
How I Dial From This Location area	
To Access an Outside Line, First Dial	Enter the number for local and/or the number for long distance in the appropriate text boxes; if you do not need to access an outside line, leave these text boxes blank.
Dial Using Calling Card	Select to display the Calling Card dialog box: enter one or more calling card names and numbers. Choose Advanced to enter specific rules for your calling card, such as dialable digits, area code, pauses, second dial tone, and so on.
This Location has Call Waiting	Check if you have call waiting.
To Disable it, Dial	Enter code to disable call waiting.
The Phone System at This Location Uses	Choose either Tone dialing or Pulse dialing.

4. Choose OK to close the Dialing Properties sheet.

> ### Troubleshooting
>
> *I can hear the modem sending tones as it dials but nothing happens afterward.*
>
> Check the telephone cables to be sure that they're properly connected to the modem and to the wall jack. Verify the modem is dialing with pulses or tone by checking the Dialing Properties sheet.

Modifying Your Modem's Properties

You can have more than one modem attached to your computer, and you can choose each modem and modify its specific properties. Each modem's property sheet may contain slightly different options, but the following example gives you an idea of the options you can modify.

To modify a specific modem's properties, follow these steps:

1. In the Modems Properties sheet, select the specific modem you want to modify and choose the Properties button. The modem's Properties sheet appears (see fig. 28.9).

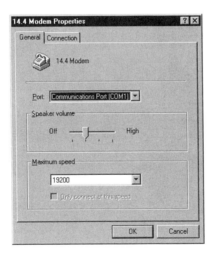

Fig. 28.9

Set the properties of your specific modem in the modem's Properties sheet.

2. On the General page, set your choices for the following options:

   - *Port.* Select the serial port to which your modem is connected.

   - *Speaker Volume.* Adjust the speaker volume for the modem between Off and High.

■ *Maximum Speed*. Set the maximum speed your modem can connect with; your modem will connect at that speed and all speeds less than the set speed.

■ *Only Connect at This Speed*. Choose this option to limit the modem from connecting at any speed other than the specified one.

3. On the Connection page, choose the options you want to modify (see fig. 28.10). Table 28.2 describes the options on the Connection page.

Fig. 28.10
Set preferences for your connection and dialing for your specific modem.

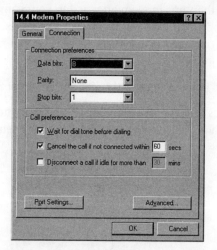

Tip

See the following section for information on port and other advanced settings.

4. Choose OK to close the specific modem's Properties sheet. Choose Close to close the Modem Properties sheet.

Table 28.2 Connection Preferences	
Option	**Description**
Connection Preferences area	
Data Bits	Set the number of data bits—each data character consists of seven or eight bits—specified for your modem.
Parity	Set *parity*—a formula for adding a bit to each byte before sending in data communications—to None, Even, Odd, Mark, or Space.
Stop Bits	Set *stop bits*—the last bit in a set of data—specified for your modem.
Call Preferences area	
Wait for Dial Tone Before Dialing	Choose this option unless you must manually dial the phone for the modem.
Cancel the Call if Not Connected Within _ Secs	Check this option and enter an amount of time for the modem to continue trying to connect before disconnecting.
Disconnect a Call if Idle for More Than _ Mins	Check this option to hang up the phone if there's no activity within the specified amount of time.

Modifying Advanced Settings

Windows enables you to modify specific settings for your modem so that you can control the flow of data between your modem and your computer, and between your modem and the modem with which you're communicating. If you have a question about any advanced settings, refer to your modem's documentation. Not all modems support all the following controls.

Port Settings

If data sent from the computer to the modem is transferred faster than the modem can move it across the line to the other modem, the FIFO data buffers (in conjunction with flow control) keep information from being lost. Adjust buffers in the Advanced Port Settings window.

To change advanced port settings, follow these steps:

1. In the Control Panel, double-click the Modems icon to open the Modems Properties sheet.

2. On the General page, choose the modem from the list and select Properties. The selected modem's Properties sheet appears (refer to fig. 28.9).

3. On the Connection page, select the Port Settings button. The Advanced Port Settings window appears (see fig. 28.11).

Fig. 28.11
Set the FIFO (First In First Out) buffers for the modem's port.

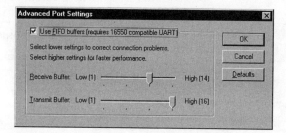

4. Deselect the Use FIFO Buffers option to disable it.

   If the option is enabled, adjust the settings for Receive and Transmit Buffers.

5. Choose OK to close the window and choose OK again to close the modem's Properties sheet.

Troubleshooting

My modem connects with the remote modem but locks up.

Make sure that you are using the proper modem-to-computer flow control and error control for your modem (click the Advanced button on the Connection page of the specific modem's Properties sheet).

My modem disconnects while online.

Check for loose connections between the modem and the computer, and between the modem and the telephone line. Alternatively, line noise or interference may be the problem; try the connection again with a different phone line or at a different time.

Advanced Connection Settings

The Advanced Connection Settings govern the use of error, flow, and modulation control. *Error controls* ensure accurate data transmission; corrupted data sent across the line is automatically detected and retransmitted. If your modem supports error control, you can also choose to compress the transmitted data, which compacts the data before sending it across the lines. The receiving modem then decompresses the data before sending it to the computer. Compressed data travels faster and more efficiently over telephone lines.

Flow control designates the protocol used between your computer and the modem. The flow defines how fast the data can be transferred between your modem and computer. The protocol you choose must be compatible with your modem, the cable, and your computer. Check your modem documentation for more information.

To change advanced connection settings, follow these steps:

1. In the Control Panel, double-click the Modems icon to open the Modems Properties sheet.

2. On the General page, choose the modem from the list and select Properties. The selected modem's Properties sheet appears (refer to fig. 28.9).

3. On the Connection page, click the Advanced button. The Advanced Connection Settings window appears (see fig. 28.12).

Fig. 28.12
Set advanced settings such as flow control and modulation type.

4. Modify the options as described in the following list:

   ■ *Use Error Control.* Choose to activate or deactivate error control of the transmissions. If you deactivate this option, your data may not be reliably transferred.

- *Use Flow Control.* Specifies the protocol used to control the flow of data between the modem and your computer.

- *Modulation Type.* Specifies the modulation type compatible with both your modem and the modem you're connecting with. Standard works in most cases; however, if you're having trouble connecting, try the nonstandard modulation type.

- *Extra Settings.* Enter additional initialization settings necessary for use of your modem.

- *Record a Log File.* Records your calls, errors, and so on in a file named MODEMLOG.TXT in the Windows folder. Use to monitor calls and problems.

Tip

If you're unsure of any of the settings in the Advanced Connection Settings, refer to your modem's documentation.

5. Choose OK to close the Advanced Connection Settings window; choose OK again to close the modem's Properties sheet. To close the Modems Properties sheet, choose OK.

Troubleshooting

I hear the call being answered at the other end, but there's no tone indicating a connection.

The modem on the other end of the line is not working correctly, or there is no modem there.

After connection, I see many data errors on the screen.

Make sure that no one else is using the telephone line. Try calling the other modem again at another time or from a different phone line to get a better connection.

My modem cannot sign on to the remote modem.

Check the communication parameters of the remote station and make sure that your software is configured for the same number of data bits, stop bits, and parity. (See the Connection page of the specific modem's Properties sheet.)

Troubleshooting Modems

You can fix many common modem and connection problems yourself. Additionally, Windows includes a diagnostic tool that can help you identify your modem's connection, driver, speed, and so on.

The first things you should check when you have a modem problem may sound simple, but can save you a lot of time and energy. Check to make sure that the modem is plugged in and connected to the phone line and that the phone line is connected in the wall jack. If the modem is external, make sure that it's turned on.

Make sure that you're using a modem cable—a straight-through cable that connects the computer's pin 1 to the modem's pin 1. Check the phone number and area code you're dialing. Finally, check the dialing properties, port, data bits, parity, stop bits, and so on to make sure that all settings are correct for your modem.

Using Diagnostics

Windows includes a Diagnostics tab in the Modems Properties sheet that you can use to help you identify your modem's connections and to find errors.

To use Windows' Diagnostics, follow these steps:

1. In the Control Panel, double-click the Modems icon. The Modems Properties sheet appears.

2. Choose the Diagnostics page. Figure 28.13 shows the Diagnostics page.

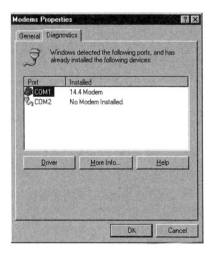

Fig. 28.13
Use Windows' Diagnostics to identify your modem's driver, port, interrupt, address, and so on.

3. Select your modem in the Port list and choose the <u>D</u>river button. Windows displays a dialog box similar to the one in figure 28.14.

Fig. 28.14
The Current Communications Driver dialog box describes the driver you're using for the modem.

4. Note the size, date, and time the driver was loaded. Installing a more recent or updated driver may solve your problem. Choose OK to close the dialog box.

5. Click the <u>M</u>ore Info button. Windows displays a Please Wait message box while it checks your modem. Then it displays the More Info dialog box (see fig. 28.15).

Fig. 28.15
Diagnostics checks your modem and communications port and reports the results in the More Info dialog box.

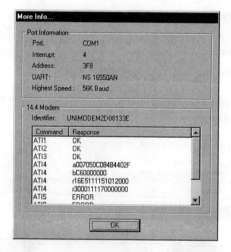

6. The following text describes the options in the More Info dialog box. When you're finished, choose OK to close the dialog box.

Port Information Area

In the Port Information area of the More Info dialog box, the Port lists the port to which your modem is attached (most always a serial port, such as COM1, COM2, and so on). Although PC architecture allows for as many as four COM ports, most systems have only two installed.

When the serial port is installed to the system, it's configured to use specific interrupts and I/O (Input/Output) addresses. An interrupt, or Interrupt Request (IRQ) line, enables access to the device; the I/O address is the port the modem uses to connect to the computer.

The standard IRQs and I/O addresses for the serial (COM) ports are as follows:

Port	Interrupt	Address
COM1	IRQ4	03F8
COM2	IRQ3	02F8
COM3	IRQ4	03E8
COM4	IRQ3	02E8

Because no two devices can use the same COM port, a conflict may arise if, for example, your mouse and your modem are assigned to the same port. Carefully read the documentation before installing any new hardware. You might even keep a list of addresses and IRQs you've already assigned to keep conflicts to a minimum.

If your modem is not working and you suspect there's an IRQ conflict, remove one of the devices, such as the mouse, and see if the modem works. If the modem does work, the two devices were conflicting in interrupt or address.

Tip

You can use Microsoft Diagnostics (MSD), a program supplied with Windows, or purchase other diagnostic software programs that identify available IRQ lines and create a template detailing your communication channels.

The UART (Universal Asynchronous Receiver/Transmitter) chip controls breaking parallel data in the computer into serial format and then converting the data back again. A 16550A UART serial chip or higher is best suited for high-speed communications. If your UART is 8250, 8250A or B, or 16450, your problems could be coming from the slower chip. Lockups, slow communications, or inaccurate data could be caused by the UART chip. Additionally, the 16550 UART had a few bugs in the buffer area; the 16550A UART corrected these problems.

Highest Speed refers to the baud rate of the modem. *Baud rate* is the rate at which a signal between two devices changes in one second. Most modems transmit several bits per baud so the actual baud rate is much slower than the bits per second rate. Use the highest speed listed in the More Info dialog box when your communication between modems is slow. If your modem speed is 14400, for example, and the highest speed listed in the More Info dialog box is 56K, you know your port is fast enough to handle the modem speed, and the problem is more likely with the line connecting the two modems.

Modem Area

The Modem area of the More Info dialog box contains an area specific to your modem. Diagnostics runs AT (ATtention) commands to test the connection to your modem and then lists the response next to the command.

If you see an ERROR code listed in the Response window, something may be wrong with your modem. The command ATI2, for example, performs a checksum on firmware and as a response either returns OK or ERROR. Alternatively, an ERROR code can be returned for a command that is not applicable to your modem. For information about your modem's response to AT commands, see your modem's documentation.

Tip

Commands beginning with a plus sign (+) and an F designate a fax AT command.

Troubleshooting

My modem won't dial.

Check the hardware for loose cables and the communications software for proper configuration. If your modem is hooked to COM2, make sure that your software is looking for it on COM2.

Note

Windows includes a Modem Troubleshooter you can use to help you diagnose a modem problem. To open the troubleshooter, open the Modems Properties sheet and choose the Diagnostics tab. Choose the <u>H</u>elp button, and the Windows Help window appears. Follow the directions on-screen to try to solve your modem problems.

Chapter 29

Configuring Printers

by Sue Plumley

Windows 95 includes several features that enable you to install, configure, share, and use various printers in either a stand-alone computer or a network workstation. A printer wizard helps you install a printer, and Windows supplies the drivers and configuration files for many commonly used printers.

After installing the printer, you can modify printer settings so that you get the most from Windows, your printer, and your applications. You can adjust your printer's properties, such as port, paper size and orientation, fonts, graphics resolution, and so on.

Additionally, Windows makes it easy for you to share printers with others on your network, and you can install someone else's shared printer to your drive. Windows also offers some security features so that you can limit access to shared printers or stop sharing at any time.

In this chapter, you learn to do the following:

- Install a printer to a stand-alone computer

- Configure a printer

- Install a network printer

- Troubleshoot installation and configuration problems

Installing a Printer to a Single PC

Windows makes installing any printer quick and easy with the help of the Add Printer Wizard. The wizard guides you, step-by-step, to configuring the printer and loading the driver. You can use any of Windows' supplied drivers, or you can use your printer manufacturer's disk when installing your printer.

If you have trouble installing your printer, there are a few things you can try to solve the problems. Additionally, Windows supplies a Device Manager that enables you to view printer port settings and see if the problem you're having is with the hardware.

> **Note**
>
> Windows will autodetect your printer when you install the Windows program; use the Add Printer Wizard when you add a printer after Windows is installed.

Using the Add Printer Wizard

Using the Add Printer Wizard, you can quickly and easily add any printer to your system. Before installing the configuration and driver files to your computer, make sure that you attach the printer to your computer and turn on the printer.

To install a printer to your PC, follow these steps:

1. Click the Start button and choose Settings, Printers. The Printers window appears (see fig. 29.1). Alternatively, you can open My Computer and double-click the Printers icon.

Fig. 29.1
The Printers window lists the current printers and enables you to add new printers.

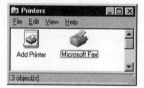

2. Double-click the Add Printer icon. The Add Printer Wizard dialog box appears (see fig. 29.2).

Fig. 29.2
The first Add Printer Wizard dialog box welcomes you; choose Next to continue.

3. Choose the Next button to display the second Add Printer Wizard dialog box (see fig. 29.3).

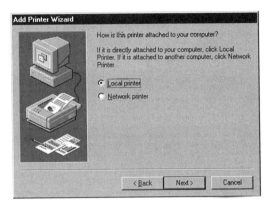

Fig. 29.3
For a stand-alone, or single, computer, choose Local printer.

4. Choose Local printer and choose the Next button. The third wizard dialog box appears (see fig. 29.4).

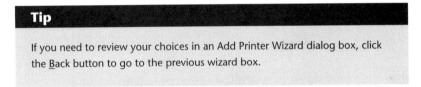

Tip

If you need to review your choices in an Add Printer Wizard dialog box, click the Back button to go to the previous wizard box.

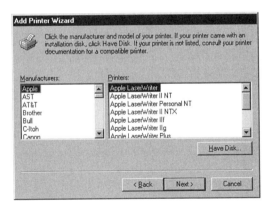

Fig. 29.4
You install the driver and configuration files by choosing the manufacturer and model in this wizard box.

5. In Manufacturer, choose the maker of your printer. The list of Printers changes to reflect those printers made by the selected manufacturer.

6. Select the exact model of your printer in the Printers list.

If your printer is not listed, you can insert the manufacturer's disk that came with your printer and choose the Have Disk button. Windows installs the configuration files and driver from the disk and then returns to this wizard box. Not all printer vendors provide a disk that works with Windows 95; call the printer manufacturer to update the printer drivers.

7. Click the Next button. The fourth Add Printer Wizard box appears, as shown in figure 29.5.

Fig. 29.5
Choose the port your printer is connected to in this wizard box.

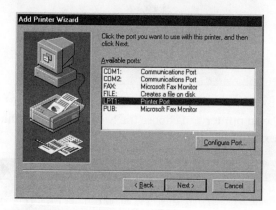

8. Choose the port to which the printer is attached.

Choose Configure Port if you want to change either of the following options:

■ *Spool MS-DOS Print Jobs.* If checked (default setting), spools the documents you print from MS-DOS-based applications. Spooling controls the number of pages sent to the printer at one time so that printing is more efficient.

■ *Check Port State Before Printing.* Runs a check on the connection before sending jobs to the printer.

Choose OK to close the Configure LPT Port dialog box.

9. Choose Next. The fifth Add Printer Wizard box appears, as shown in figure 29.6.

10. In Printer Name, accept the suggested name or enter a new name for the printer.

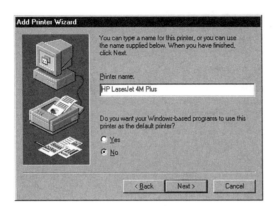

Fig. 29.6
Name the printer
so that you'll
easily recognize it
in your Printers
window.

11. If you want this printer to act as the default printer for your Windows
    applications, choose Yes. If you've already assigned another printer as
    the default printer, choose No.

12. Click Next. The sixth printer wizard dialog box appears asking if you
    want to print a test page. Choose Yes to print a test page or No to skip
    this step. If you choose Yes, Windows displays a dialog box asking if the
    test page printed OK; if you choose No in this dialog box, Windows
    tries to diagnose the problem for you.

13. Click the Finish button. Windows may prompt you for the necessary
    files to set up the printer; insert the Windows CD or disks. The installed
    printer icon appears in the Printers window.

Troubleshooting

The printer won't print my document; what am I doing wrong?

Check that the printer is plugged in, turned on, and online. Often, turning the
printer off and back on clears the memory and makes it start printing again.

Check the cable connections, both to the printer and to the computer, to make sure
that the cable is firmly attached. Also, if the cable is old and tattered, borrow a cable
from another printer and try it. The cable could be bad.

Check that the paper tray is securely in place and that no broken areas are on the
paper tray that would keep it from locking into the printer.

Make sure that all covers on the printer that should be closed are securely closed.

If you're using a print-sharing device or switch box, bypass those devices by cabling
the printer directly to the computer and try printing. If the printer prints, something
may be wrong with the switch box or print-sharing device.

If you're using a network printer, check to make sure your network cable and
connection are good.

Troubleshooting Installation

Following are a few common installation problems you might encounter with your printer. If you need further help with your printer configuration, see the section "Configuring Your Printer" later in this chapter and consult your printer's documentation for more information.

If your printer is not listed in the wizard dialog box, you must use your printer manufacturer's disk to install the configuration files and driver. If you did not receive a disk with your printer, call the dealer who sold you the printer and ask him or her for the disk.

If your selected port is not working with your printer, confirm that you're designating the correct port on your computer. Printer ports are usually the parallel ports LPT1 or LPT2. Next, make sure that your printer cable is appropriate for the port and that the cable is firmly attached to both the computer and the printer.

Confirm that the printer's power cord is plugged into a power outlet and into the printer. Check that the printer is turned on and that the printer's control panel lights are on.

If you're still having trouble with the printer port, follow these steps:

1. Choose the Start, Settings, Control Panel.

2. Double-click the System icon in the Control Panel. The System Properties sheet appears.

3. Choose the Device Manager tab (see fig. 29.7).

Fig. 29.7
Use the Device Manager page to find information about your printer port.

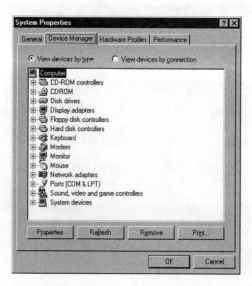

4. Find the Ports (COM & LPT) icon in the list and double-click it. The available ports display below the icon.

5. Select the Printer Port and then click the Properties button. The Printer Port Properties sheet appears (see fig. 29.8).

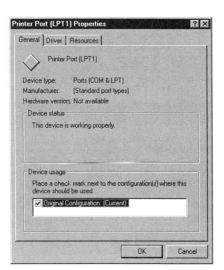

Fig. 29.8
Use the Printer Port Properties sheet to spot problems with the port.

6. On the General page, look in the Device Status area. If the port has a problem, it's listed here with a suggested solution. If there is no problem listed, go on to step 7.

> **Tip**
>
> Note any problem code or number in the Device Status area in case you need to call the printer manufacturer's support line. The number helps identify the problem.

7. In the Device Usage area of the General page, make sure that the Windows-supplied Original Configuration option is checked.

8. To find out about the printer port driver file, choose the Driver tab of the Printer Port Properties sheet (see fig. 29.9).

Fig. 29.9
Windows supplies
the printer port
driver, but you can
change to your
own driver or an
updated driver.

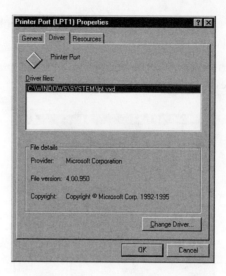

9. The Windows-supplied driver is the C:\WINDOWS\SYSTEM\lpt.vxd driver. If that driver is not selected, select it and try printing to the port again. If the printer port still does not work, go to step 10.

10. Choose the Resources tab on the Printer Port Properties sheet (see fig. 29.10).

Fig. 29.10
Your safest bet is
to use Windows'
automatic settings
unless there's a
device conflict.

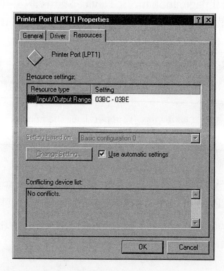

11. In the Conflicting Device List box, check to see if there is a conflict.

The Resource Settings list box specifies the resources in use by the hardware. To change settings, double-click the resource type.

> **Caution**
>
> It's best to not change the resources manually because then the resources become fixed, and Windows is limited when configuring other devices.

12. To change the configuration, click the down arrow beside the Setting Based On option. To change settings of the configuration, click the Change Setting button. These options may not be available, which means the settings for the specific hardware cannot be changed.

> **Caution**
>
> If you change a configuration from the default, your port may not work correctly. It could slow considerably and may also lose some functionality.

13. When you're finished, choose OK to close the Printer Port Properties sheet and then choose OK again to close the System Properties sheet.

Configuring Your Printer

After you install a printer to Windows, you can change its configuration to better suit your working practices. Windows makes it easy for you to change the port, paper size and orientation, graphics mode, font options, and more.

When you configure the printer through the printer's Properties sheet, the changes you make apply to all applications in which you use the printer. If, for example, you set the orientation to landscape, landscape becomes the default orientation when you print a page in your applications. You can, of course, change the printer setup in most applications to override the defaults in that application.

To open the printer's Properties sheet, follow these steps:

1. Choose Start, Settings, Printers. The Printers window appears.

2. Select the icon of the printer you want to configure and choose File, Properties. The specific printer's Properties sheet appears.

> ### Tip
>
> You also can display the Properties command from the pop-up menu by pointing to the printer icon and right-clicking the mouse.

See the following sections for information about each page in the printer's Properties sheet. If you want to set options on more than one page, click the Apply button before changing tabs to make sure that the changes are activated. Options and information on individual pages may vary slightly, depending on your printer. The printer in the following examples is the HP LaserJet 4M Plus.

Using the General Page

▶ See "Installing a Shared Printer," p. 652

The General page of the printer's Properties sheet contains options that are handy if you're sharing your printer on a network. Additionally, you can print a test page from this page to make sure that your printer is working correctly. Figure 29.11 shows the General page of the Properties sheet.

Fig. 29.11
Use the General page to configure the printer for sharing with others on the network.

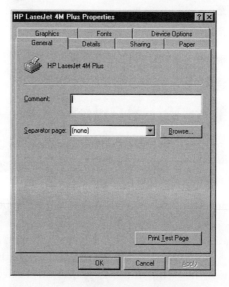

The options you can choose from include the following:

■ *Comment.* The Comment area of the General page enables you to enter a description or comment about your printer, such as what its best use is. When sharing a printer, others on the network who install your printer see the comment.

■ *Separator Page.* Select whether to insert a page between each document that's printed from your printer. You may want to use a separator page if several people are printing documents at once; the separator page makes it easy to divide the jobs. You can choose either a Full or Simple page to use as a separator. Full contains a graphic, and Simple contains only text.

> **Note**
>
> You can also click the Browse button beside the Separator Page option to specify a custom separator page, such as a Windows Metafile.

■ *Print Test Page.* Click the Print Test Page button to send a page to the printer. The page contains various fonts and graphics, depending on your printer. If the test page prints, your printer is attached and working.

Using the Details Page

The Details page of the printer's Properties sheet enables you to set options such as printer port, capture printer port, spool settings, and so on. Figure 29.12 shows the Details page.

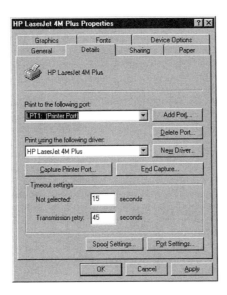

Fig. 29.12
Configure ports and drivers in the Details page of the Properties sheet.

■ *Print to the Following Port.* This box displays the port your printer is connected to. If you're using a network printer, the box displays the path to that printer. If you change the connection to your printer, you'll also need to change the port. Click the down arrow beside this option to display available ports and select one. Alternatively, you can add a port by clicking the Add Port button and typing a path in the Specify Path text box.

When you add a port, the Add Port dialog box appears. Specify whether the port is Network or Other (such as fax modem or local) and enter the path or select the type of port you want to add. Choose OK to close the Add Port dialog box and return to the Properties sheet.

Select a port and choose Delete Port if you want to delete a port.

■ *Print Using the Following Driver.* The driver you're currently using displays in this box, but you can change the driver if your printer supports or emulates the new driver. Click the down arrow for a list of installed drivers or click the New Driver button to change the driver.

▶ See "Installing a Shared Printer," p. 652

■ *Capture Printer Port.* Capturing a printer port is the same as mapping to a network printer. Choose the Capture Printer Port button to display the Capture Printer Port dialog box. If the path is not displayed, enter the path to the network printer in the Path text box, choose the Reconnect at Logon option, and choose OK. The next time you start Windows on the network, the network printer is automatically pathed to your drive and ready for you to use. Note you must have rights to the network queue you are capturing to.

■ *End Capture.* Click the End Capture button to cancel the mapping to the network printer. If you want to use the network printer after canceling the capture, you must either recapture the printer or work your way through numerous folders to get to the printer.

■ *Timeout Settings.* The Not Selected option refers to how many seconds Windows waits for the printer to be online before it reports an error. Enter the amount of time you want Windows to delay.

Transmission Retry specifies the number of seconds Windows waits for the printer to be ready to print before reporting an error.

■ *Spool Settings.* Spool settings govern how your document is sent to the printer. Choose this button to display the Spool Settings dialog box.

The first options specify whether to spool a job or print it directly to the printer. If you spool the job, you can choose to start printing after the first page is sent or after the last page is sent. You spool a print job so that your program can get back to work more quickly while the print queue does all the work. If you choose to print directly to the printer, your computer remains tied up until all the job is sent to the printer.

The Spool Data Format option refers to the way your computer stores the data to be printed. Use EMF (metafile) format to free up your program faster; use RAW format if you have problems with the EMF. RAW format does take longer to print.

Choose the Enable or Disable Bidirectional Support for this Printer to specify whether your printer should communicate with your computer.

Select the Restore Defaults button to change all options in the Spool Settings dialog box back to the default.

■ *Port Settings*. Click the Port Settings button to display the Configure LPT Port dialog box, in which you can choose whether to spool DOS application print jobs and whether to check the port before printing.

Using the Sharing Page

The Sharing page refers to how your printer works with a network, such as the peer-to-peer Microsoft Network. If you choose Not Shared, others on the network cannot access your printer. If you choose Shared As, you can specify a password to limit others' access to your printer. Figure 29.13 illustrates the Sharing page with the Shared As option selected.

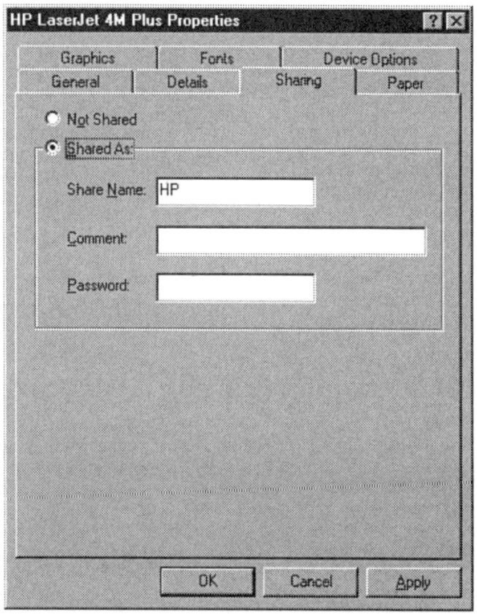

Fig. 29.13
Share your printer with others on the network, but limit access with a password.

▶ See "Installing a Shared Printer," p. 652

In the Shared As area, enter a name to identify your computer on the network in the Share Name text box and enter a Comment if you want. You can also enter a Password to limit those with access to your computer. After you enter the password, Windows displays a confirmation dialog box in which you enter the password again to confirm it.

To stop sharing your printer with the network, click the Not Shared option on the Sharing page.

Using the Paper Page

Use the Paper page of the printer's Properties sheet to set defaults for paper size, orientation, paper source, copies, and so on. The defaults you set on this page are applied to any application using the printer, unless you change printer setup in the specific application. Figure 29.14 illustrates the Paper page.

Fig. 29.14
Set defaults for the printer that apply to all applications that use it.

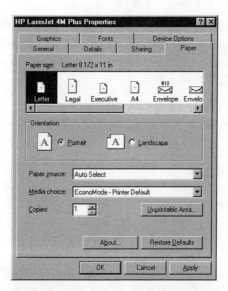

■ *Paper Size*. Select the paper size you want to print from as a default. You might, for example, set up one printer on your network to print only number 10 (commercial-sized) envelopes. Choose the envelope size on this page. To choose a size of paper or envelope, click the icon in the scroll box, and its size description appears above the scroll box.

■ *Orientation*. Choose either Portrait or Landscape as the default paper orientation for this printer.

- *Paper Source*. Specify the paper source for your printer. You can choose, for example, to use the upper tray or lower tray, or manual feed as with an envelope feeder.

- *Media Choice*. If your printer supports a media choice, you can choose to print to paper or to a transparency for overheads.

- *Copies*. Enter the default number of copies to print.

- *Unprintable Area*. Click this button to display the Unprintable Area dialog box. The unprintable area is the margin around the outside of the page that a laser printer, for example, cannot print to. You can change the area not printed to suit your printer or for special print jobs. Enter the amount of unprintable area for the Left, Right, Top, and Bottom of the page. Choose OK to return to the Paper page of the Properties sheet.

- *About*. Click to display the About dialog box, which displays the printer name and driver version. Choose OK to close the dialog box.

- *Restore Details*. Click the Restore Details button to change all options in the Page page back to their defaults.

Troubleshooting

I'm having problems with the paper in my printer; sometimes it jams and sometimes it curls.

If you have trouble with paper jams, check to make sure that you do not have too much paper in the paper tray; too much paper results in unnecessary pressure on the paper and often causes paper jams.

If your paper curls when printed, the heat is causing one side of the paper to dry and shrink faster than the other side. Try turning the paper over in the tray or try using slightly heavier paper. Also, review your paper storage conditions. If the paper is stored in a humid area, curling often occurs because the paper is damp.

Using the Graphics Page

Use the Graphics page to specify graphics resolution, dithering, intensity, and so on. The settings on this page affect only graphics, not text. Figure 29.15 shows the Graphics page of the Properties sheet.

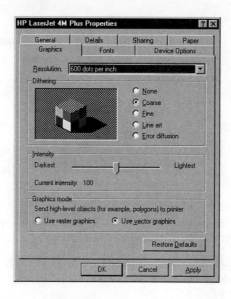

- *Resolution.* Listed in the Resolution box are the available choices with which you can print graphics. Higher resolutions (600 dots per inch, for example) produce high-quality graphics but take longer to print. Lower resolutions (75 dpi) produce coarse and grainy graphics but print quickly.

- *Dithering.* Dithering blends grays in black-and-white printing or colors in color printing to produce smoother transitions. Choose None if you do not want dithering. Choose Coarse for a grainy effect or Fine for a higher quality, smooth effect. If your resolution is low, 150 dpi or less, choose Fine dithering to improve the look of the graphics. Choose Line Art if there are no shades of gray in the graphics; contrast between blacks and whites will be sharper. Choose Error Diffusion for sharpening the edges of photographs.

- *Intensity.* Click and drag the lever to Darkest for darker graphics or to Lightest for lighter graphics. The default intensity is 100. The lowest intensity is 0, which would produce black or nearly black graphics; the highest intensity is 200, which would produce white or nearly white graphics.

- *Graphics Mode.* Choose whether to send objects to the printer in raster or vector format. *Vector images* are formed by outline, and *raster images* are formed by pixels or dots. A vector image is sharper, clearer, and probably faster to print. If, however, you have problems printing vector images, try raster.

Using the Fonts Page

Use the Fonts page to specify how TrueType fonts are printed and to indicate any font cartridges you use with your printer. Figure 29.16 illustrates the Fonts page of the Properties sheet.

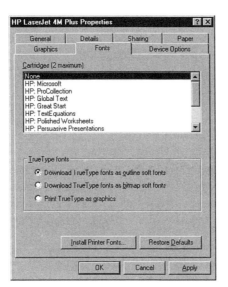

Fig. 29.16
Identify your font cartridges, install printer fonts, and specify TrueType fonts in the Fonts page.

- *Cartridges.* Some printers, mostly Hewlett-Packard printers, enable you to use a font cartridge to add to your list of available fonts. Font cartridges may contain two or twenty fonts and various styles of fonts, such as bold, italic, and so on. If your printer uses a font cartridge, select the cartridge in this list to enable the use of those fonts in your Windows applications.

- *TrueType Fonts.* Choose the Download TrueType Fonts as Outline Soft Fonts option to speed printing and create a high-quality product. Use the Download TrueType Fonts as Bitmap Soft Fonts option for lower-quality output and the Print TrueType as Graphics for artistic effects, such as printing graphics over text so that only part of the character is printed.

- *Install Printer Fonts.* If your font cartridge is not listed in the Cartridges list, choose to install the fonts using the Install Printer Fonts button. From the Font Installer dialog box, click the Add Fonts button. Windows prompts you to insert a disk containing the font files or to enter a directory where the fonts can be found. Choose OK, and the Installer copies the fonts.

■ *Restore Defaults*. Click this button to erase any changes you made and to restore the defaults to the Fonts page.

Troubleshooting

The print quality of my graphics is poor. Is there anything I can do?

If the print quality is poor for graphics, make adjustments to the Graphics page of the printer's Properties sheet. If text quality is poor, adjust the print quality settings in the Device Options page of the printer's Properties sheet.

Using Device Options

Use device options to set the print quality of the text and to control printer memory tracking. Figure 29.17 illustrates the Device Options page of the Properties sheet.

Fig. 29.17
The amount of printer memory, RAM, is listed in the Device Options page of the Properties sheet.

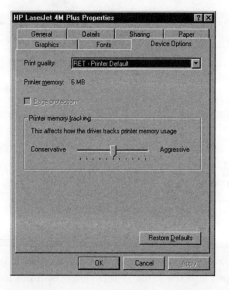

■ *Print Quality*. Select the print quality you want to use for the text in your documents. The selections in this list box depend on the type of printer you're using. In general, use draft quality for proofs and normal or letter quality for finished documents. See your printer's documentation for more information.

- *Printer Memory*. This area lists the amount of RAM in your printer. With some printers, the amount is fixed; with other printers, you can change the amount of memory if you add memory to your printer.

- *Page Protection*. If available with your printer, this option uses some of the printer's memory to apply to complex pages when printing. Although this option makes printing those pages more accurate, it also uses more printer memory.

- *Printer Memory Tracking*. This feature controls printer memory tracking. When printing complex documents, adjust the tracking by dragging the lever to Conservative or Aggressive. The more aggressive the tracking, the more likely the printer driver will attempt to print a complex document; however, the printer's memory may be exceeded, and the print job fails. The more conservative the tracking, the more likely the printer's memory will be available; but the less likely the printer driver will print the complex document.

- *Restore Defaults*. Choose this button to erase any changes you made and to restore the defaults to the Device Options page.

Troubleshooting

I can't get complex pages or graphics to all print on the page; the printer divides it into two pages. What can I do?

Try changing the Printer Memory Tracking in the Device Options page of the printer's Properties sheet. If you still have trouble, consider adding more memory to your printer.

Installing a Network Printer

If you're connected to a peer-to-peer Microsoft Network, you can use other's resources, such as printers, fax modems, files, and so on. If someone else on your network has designated their printer, for example, as a shared resource and designated you as having access to that resource, you can print to that printer from any of your Windows applications.

Note

If you're the one with the network printer connected to your computer, you must first choose to share the printer with the network users through the Network dialog box (File and Printer Sharing) and then through the Sharing page of the printer's Properties sheet.

▶ See "Installing a Shared Printer," p. 652

Installing a network printer is similar to installing a printer connected to your own computer. To install a network printer, follow these steps:

1. In the Printers window, double-click the Add Printer icon.

2. The Add Printer Wizard dialog box appears (refer to fig. 29.2).

3. Choose Next, and the second wizard dialog box appears (see fig. 29.18).

Fig. 29.18
Choose the Network printer if you're attached to a network and have the access rights to share someone else's printer.

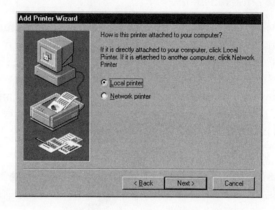

4. Choose the Network Printer option and click Next. The third wizard dialog box appears (see fig. 29.19).

Fig. 29.19
Enter the network path to the printer you want to use.

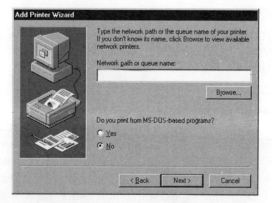

5. Enter the path to the printer in the Network Path text box. Choose whether to use MS-DOS-based programs with the printer. Click the Next button.

6. The next wizard dialog box appears (refer to fig. 29.6). Enter a name to represent the printer on your computer and click Next.

7. The last wizard appears, asking if you want to print a test page. Choose Yes to print a test page or No to skip this step. If you choose Yes, a dialog box appears confirming the test page printed correctly. If you choose No, Windows will try to diagnose the problem.

8. Choose the Finish button. The installed printer icon appears in the Printers window as a network printer. You can print to this printer as you would a printer attached directly to your computer.

Note

If you have problems with printing from Windows, try the Windows troubleshooter in Help. Choose Start, Help. In the Help Topics dialog box, choose the Index tab. Type **Print Troubleshooting** and press Enter; the Print Troubleshooter appears. Follow the directions on-screen.

Chapter 30

Configuring Scanners and Digital Cameras

by Michael Marchuk

While joysticks, mice, tape backup drives, and modems are relatively commonplace among computers running Windows, scanners and digital cameras are not likely to be found attached to an average Windows workstation. There are many reasons for this trend, including the high price tags that were attached to such peripherals. But now that prices for this hardware are dropping, and demand for faxing and document storage is rising, you may be considering the purchase of a scanner or digital camera.

If you are one of the early adopters of scanner or digital camera technology, you may already have one of these devices connected to your computer. This chapter explains how to install scanners and digital cameras to work within Windows 95.

In this chapter, you learn how to

- Install scanner hardware
- Configure scanner drivers and scanning software
- Install digital camera hardware
- Set up drivers and software to download digital camera images
- View scanned images or digital pictures within Windows 95

Installing Scanner Hardware

Most scanner hardware is connected to your computer through a separate interface board; however, some hand-held scanners can connect to your computer's parallel port. If you have to install a scanner adapter in your computer, turn your computer off and follow these steps:

> **Tip**
>
> If your adapter has dip switches or jumpers that are used to configure the adapter, write down the current settings before you install the adapter into your computer.

1. Install the scanner adapter board into your computer. Follow the manufacturer's installation guidelines closely.

2. Restart your computer.

3. Click the Add New Hardware icon within Control Panel. The Add New Hardware Wizard appears, shown in figure 30.1.

Fig. 30.1
The Add New Hardware Wizard assists you with the installation of the correct drivers for your scanner hardware.

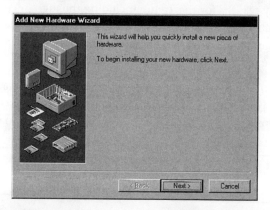

4. Click the Next button to proceed with the installation. The Add New Hardware Wizard displays a dialog box shown in figure 30.2.

5. Select Yes to allow the Add New Hardware Wizard to search for your newly installed adapter. It may take several minutes to detect the hardware that is in your system. If the Add New Hardware Wizard can detect your scanner adapter, you see a list of detected devices that shows which adapter was detected.

Fig. 30.2
The Add New
Hardware Wizard
can automati-
cally detect a
wide range of
hardware.

6. Click the Finish button to complete the installation of the device drivers to your system.

7. Windows displays a dialog box that asks if you want to restart your
   computer. You should allow Windows to reboot your machine in order
   to load the new drivers.

If the Add New Hardware Wizard cannot automatically detect your scanner
board, you have two options:

■ You may run the Add New Hardware Wizard again and select No when
  the wizard asks to automatically detect your new hardware. You can
  then manually install the Windows 95 drivers by selecting from a list of
  manufacturers and their adapter boards. If you cannot find your exact
  adapter board listed, load the driver disk that was shipped with your
  scanner adapter. Select Have Disk, which will search the manufacturer's
  disk for a Windows 95 device driver. If the Add New Hardware Wizard
  can find a Windows 95 driver for your scanner adapter, the wizard will
  display the adapter driver in a list, and the installation procedures may
  continue from step 6 in the preceding installation steps.

■ The Add New Hardware Wizard also may not detect your adapter, and
  the manufacturer disk may not contain a Windows 95 device driver.
  When the driver disk for your adapter only contains DOS and Windows
  3.x device drivers, you need to follow the manufacturer's installation
  instructions for installing the device drivers on your system. Some
  manufacturers may offer a Windows 95 installation section within their
  manuals if their native Windows 95 drivers are not ready yet. Check to

see if the scanner you have or want to purchase will work with Windows 95 or if there are specific installation instructions for Windows 95; otherwise, follow the standard installation procedures outlined in the manuals.

> **Note**
>
> If you are installing a hand-held scanner or a flatbed scanner that connects to your computer's parallel port, you may not need to run any hardware installation procedures. Check your installation manuals regarding this matter.

> **Troubleshooting**
>
> *After installing my scanner, I can't seem to scan anything into my word processor. What's wrong?*
>
> If you are not using the scanning software, you won't be able to scan anything into your word processor. If you are trying to scan text from a document into the word processor, you will need to use special software that uses Optical Character Recognition (OCR) to actually convert the image into text data. This software may have been shipped with your scanner, so you should review the operation of the OCR software and its usage for scanning into word processing documents.

Installing and Configuring Scanner Software

Scanner software communicates with the hardware through a Windows device driver. The device driver controls the way the scanner works when capturing an image. The scanner software is usually written by the manufacturer of the scanning hardware, because each scanner has various capabilities and resolutions.

Some common controls that the scanner software manages include

- Color resolution (if your scanner supports color)
- Image resolution, usually expressed in dots per inch (dpi)
- Image enhancement
- Image cropping, enlargement, and reduction
- File formatting for the captured image

Proprietary Solutions

Because the scanning software is so closely linked to the scanner hardware, you may not have any choice but to use the software that was provided by the manufacturer to perform your scanning. If you have purchased a brand-name scanner with a good reputation, the delivered software will probably be mature and reliable and may even be a 32-bit Windows 95 program. The features included in this software will probably be much of what you are looking for, plus some additional features that may be new to you. However, if you buy an off-brand scanner to save money, the software which you receive may not be what you expected. Oftentimes, to lower the price of a product, the development costs are cut. This could mean that the software which is provided by the manufacturer may only cover the most basic features, may contain serious omissions of functionality, and may not be a 32-bit Windows 95 program. As with every purchase you make, you should evaluate your product options based on more than just price.

To install your scanning software, follow the instructions provided in your scanner's installation manual. This procedure is typically very quick since there are few options to most scanning software. Once your software is installed, you will be able to start scanning images into your computer.

Scanning Software Example

To give you an idea of some of the functions that are available through scanning software, let's take a look at the Hewlett Packard ScanJet software.

Figure 30.3 shows the Hewlett Packard ScanJet software's main screen. On the left-hand side of the screen are the main controls for configuring the operation of the scanner, while the right-hand side of the screen shows a preview image of the scanner.

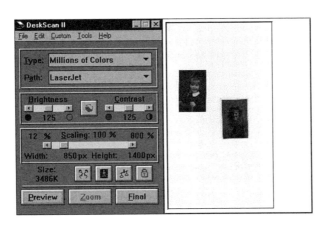

Fig. 30.3
Hewlett Packard's ScanJet software lets you preview the images you are scanning.

When scanning an image, it is common for the scanning software to offer a preview mode for cropping an image. The preview mode will perform a fast scan of the entire scanning bed to allow you to see where your image is positioned in the scanner. Once you can see where the entire image is, you can choose the portion you want to scan at a higher quality. Looking back to figure 30.3, notice that the entire scanning area is represented by the box on the right-hand side of the screen.

Once you have completed the preview scan, you can crop the image to the desired size. This will prevent the scanner from scanning in blank space which not only makes your image look poor, but also requires more hard drive space to store and much longer time to scan.

Take the example of a business card. If you walked up to a photocopy machine and placed the card on the machine, you would end up with an 8 1/2- by 11-inch piece of paper with a business card located somewhere on the page. What you really wanted was a copy of the business card, not a copy of the photocopy machine's cover.

If you placed that same business card on a scanner, you could view the preview scan and crop only the business card by drawing a box around that part of the scanning area. When the scanner digitizes that image, it will only include the part of the scanning area that you cropped. Again, this saves time and disk space while giving you the image that you want.

In addition to the cropping features, another important feature includes the scanning mode in which your image is captured. Since images may be used for many different purposes, you may have to change the scanning mode from time to time. Some images you will only view on the computer screen, so these images should match the number of colors that your video mode can support. Other images will be included in word processing or spreadsheet documents, which will be printed in black and white. Still others may be advertising images which are being sent to a high-quality color printer for proofing. Each of these images has different quality needs that your software should handle.

The ScanJet software provides an image quality selection that allows you to use one of several preset image settings or create your own. Figure 30.4 shows some of these image settings.

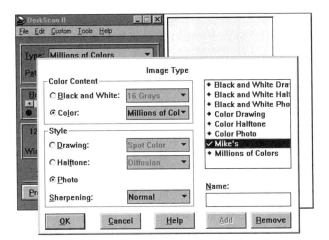

Fig. 30.4
Hewlett Packard's
ScanJet software
provides preset
image quality
settings for various
image types.

There are many other features that the ScanJet software provides, including automatic contrast and brightness correction, multiple file format support, and image scaling. But this is not a review of the ScanJet software, it is simply a benchmark to which you can measure other scanning software.

Troubleshooting

I bought a scanner to do OCR, but I never thought I'd have to do so much re-typing. Why can't the computer do a better job at reading the documents into my word processor?

It sounds like your expectations were a little too high for this technology. While some OCR software can read text with 99.7 percent accuracy, that still means that you could have between 5 to 10 errors on a "good" page and many more on a page with illegible writing or poor text quality. OCR is wonderful technology, but don't expect it to replace your secretaries anytime soon.

Installing Digital Camera Hardware

Digital cameras were once only used by those who could afford a $50,000 camera that took lower-quality images than a Kodak Instamatic camera. The novelty of digital cameras has begun to give way to the reality of high-technology solutions to digital imaging needs.

Newspapers, magazines, and many other industries have needed the digital camera for a long time. Instead of buying film, paying for quick film development, and then spending time and effort scanning the images into the computer to be used in articles or advertisements, the digital camera bypasses all of these steps by directly saving images in a digital format to be downloaded to a computer.

The quality of the newest generation of digital cameras rivals that of high-quality 35mm film cameras. The cost is dropping, too. For around $300 you can buy an entry-level version that will snap average-quality images for use in a variety of settings, while for around $10,000 you can get a top-of-the-line model to replace your 35mm camera.

The installation of digital camera hardware is often a connection to either a serial port or to an SCSI interface in your machine. The low-end digital cameras will typically use the serial port interfaces, while the high-end cameras may use either type of interface.

Check your installation manual to see what type of connection you have. The SCSI connection will be much faster (700 percent) than the serial port interface, but will require an SCSI adapter in your computer. This section assumes that you will be using a serial port interface for the camera, since the $10,000 you might have spent on a high-end digital camera is still locked up in some lottery ticket that you have yet to buy.

With that in mind, you may have one or more serial ports available to you. Most PCs have two serial ports; however, some use one of these ports for a mouse and the other for a modem. You may want to check the availability of your serial ports to see if you'll need to swap cables with your modem before downloading images from the camera.

Installing Digital Camera Software

Like scanners, digital cameras provide their own software that can download the images from your camera. This software is probably in its first or second release because this technology is relatively new. That means that your feature set may be limited when using the digital camera's software. But for most people, the only thing you'll really need the software for is to get the images out of the camera.

The Logitech FotoMan camera is an example of an affordable digital camera. The FotoMan is a black and white camera (actually it uses 256 levels of gray), while the FotoMan II is a color camera. The software that is used has several functions beyond the simple download of images to your computer.

The FotoMan software makes contact with the camera when it loads and automatically downloads small thumbnail images of the pictures within the camera. This feature lets you see which images you want to download from the camera in their full form (496 × 360 pixels). Figure 30.5 shows this thumbnail view of the images.

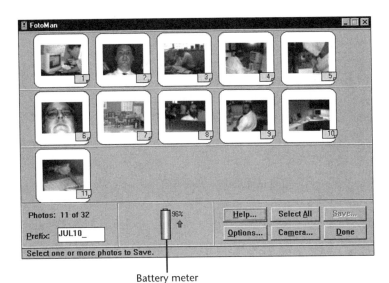

Battery meter

Fig. 30.5
Logitech's FotoMan software lets you preview the images stored in the camera before you download them.

When you have selected the image or images you want to download, you can select one of several popular file formats in which to save them. This allows you to skip a conversion step if you need the images in a particular format.

Another simple feature that makes a lot of sense is the battery strength indicator on the main screen (refer to fig. 30.5). As soon as the FotoMan software makes contact with the camera, the battery meter will read out the current charge level. The FotoMan communication docking base is also the battery charger which lets you see in real-time the charge increasing while you are in the software.

Troubleshooting

I seem to have lost all of my images in my camera that I took only yesterday. What happened? Is my camera or battery bad?

Affordable digital cameras use a flash memory system to store the images. The memory must be refreshed every so often to maintain the images. Logitech estimates that each image consumes 3 percent of the battery life per day. If you have 30 pictures stored in your camera, you may have exhausted the battery just by not retrieving your images sooner.

The last feature shows how the digital camera software can go beyond the simple download feature. The Fotoman software can trigger the camera while it's sitting in the communication docking base. You can set a timer or an instant trigger to take a picture. It may not be practical for many users, but for group shots at the company picnic, it works very well.❖

Chapter 31

Configuring Network Hardware

by Tod Pike

Many computer systems, especially those used at an office, are connected to some kind of computer network. Since Windows 95 has full networking capabilities built in (including the capability to connect to the Internet and use different networking protocols), many users of Windows 95 will be installing networking hardware into their computer systems.

The Windows 95 operating system makes the task of adding and configuring a network interface card (NIC) very easy. This chapter outlines the steps necessary to add an NIC to a computer system running Windows 95 and also how to use resources that may be available on your network. In this chapter, you learn how to do the following:

- Install and configure network interface cards

- Install cables to connect your computer to your network

- Install and configure shared printers from your network

- Install shared fax modems from your network

- Install shared CD-ROM drives from your network

Installing Network Interface Cards (NICs)

When you install Windows 95 on your computer system for the first time, the Windows 95 installation program automatically runs the Add New

Hardware Wizard to detect and install all of the hardware that is in your computer system. After you have installed Windows 95, however, the Add New Hardware Wizard is used if you have added a new device to your computer system, such as a new disk drive, tape drive, NIC, or sound card.

Checking Network Hardware on Your System

If your computer had a network interface card installed when you installed Windows 95, your system should already have support for the card. You can check to see if your system already has support for your NIC by starting the Control Panel (from the Start menu).

From the Control Panel, you can open the System Properties sheet, which gives you information about the devices connected to your computer system.

From the System Properties sheet, select the Device Manager page to display information about the devices on your system (see fig. 31.1).

Fig. 31.1
The Device Manager displays a list of the devices on your system.

Network Adapters

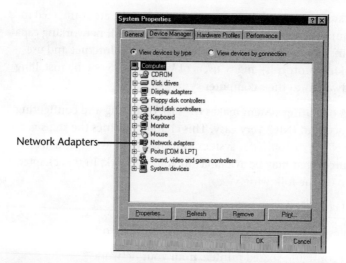

Using the Device Manager page, you can see that the system as it is currently configured already shows a network device as being available (it is listed as Network Adapters). Clicking the Network Adapters item in the list shows the individual NICs that are configured and available for use, as illustrated in figure 31.2.

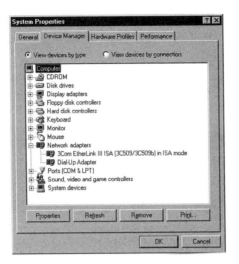

Fig. 31.2
The Device
Manager page lists
the individual
NICs available
for use.

If your Device Manager page shows a network interface as being available, but
you are unable to use the card (you cannot see any other computers in your
Network Neighborhood, for example), there are several things you should
check.

Troubleshooting

I installed the NIC and Windows support, but the card still doesn't work

The most common reason for the network card not working correctly is a conflict
with another device on your system. Open the Control Panel (from the Start menu)
and start the System Properties sheet. Select the Device Manager tab to display the
list of the devices on your system.

Double-click the Network Adapters entry in the list on the Device Manager tab, and
then select your network device. Click the Properties button to display the settings
for your network card. The Device Status area tells you if there is a problem with your
network device. Choosing the Resources page shows you the current settings; this
page also tells you if one of the settings for your NIC conflicts with another device in
your system.

If there is a conflict with another device in your system, you have to change one of
the hardware settings (such as the Interrupt Request, Input/Output Range or Direct
Memory Access) to another value. You should consult the manual for your network
card to determine which values for these settings are legal for your card.

(continues)

(continued)

Once you know which settings you can set your network card to, you have to determine which hardware settings are available on your system. One good way to find out the settings that are in use on your system is to click the Print button on the Device Manager page. This allows you to print out a summary of all the resources on your system—you can easily find an unused value by checking the legal values for your card against the list of interrupts and I/O ports that are used by your system.

If your the Device Manager page does not list any problems with your network card itself, you can look at your network to see if any other computers are shown.

When I browse my network, I don't see the other computers around me.

First, select Entire Network in the Network Neighborhood browser to see if there are any other workgroups available. If there are and computers are in those workgroups, you should make sure that your computer belongs to the correct workgroup.

To set the workgroup for your computer, start the Network control panel and look in the Identification page. Here, you can set your computer's workgroup and computer name. You should check with your network administrator for the workgroups that are available to you.

If you don't see any other workgroups (and you are sure that your network card is working correctly), make sure that you have logged into your network server. If you did not provide a user name and password when you booted your computer system (for example, there was a network login box displayed when your computer booted and you clicked Cancel), you won't see other workgroups in the Network Neighborhood.

Finally, you should check the network cabling that connects your computer to your local network to make sure that you are connected correctly. Your local network administrator can tell you if your connection to the network is active.

Installing a Network Interface Card

If you have added an NIC to your computer since you installed the Windows 95 operating system, you can run the Add New Hardware Wizard (essentially the same routine that Windows 95 runs during installation to detect your hardware configuration) that leads you through the steps necessary for Windows to recognize your new card.

Before you run the Add New Hardware Wizard, you must install the NIC into your computer system. You should follow the manufacturer's instructions for the installation of the card, including setting any switches or jumpers on the card for the interrupt vector and Input/Output vectors.

> **Note**
>
> If there are default positions for any settings on the NIC, you should leave the set-
> tings at their default. In general, Windows 95 first looks for devices at the default
> settings for that card. The only time you need to change the settings from their
> default is if there is a conflict with some other device in your system.

After the network hardware has been installed on your computer, you are
ready to turn your computer back on and begin the process of telling Windows 95 about the new device.

The Add New Hardware Wizard is run from the Control Panel (which can be
started through the Start menu).

When you start the Add New Hardware Wizard, the first screen of the wizard
comes up (as shown in fig. 31.3), telling you what the wizard will do.

Fig. 31.3
The first page of
the Add New
Hardware Wizard
tells you what this
wizard will do.

You should click the Next button to continue to the next page of the Add
New Hardware Wizard. If you don't want to continue, click Cancel.

The second page of the wizard (as shown in fig. 31.4) asks you whether you
want the wizard to search through your system for new hardware. If you
select Yes (the default), the wizard tries to automatically detect the type of
network card you have. If you select No, you have to tell Windows 95 what
type of card you installed.

Fig. 31.4
The wizard lets you request automatic detection of your hardware.

Letting Windows 95 Automatically Detect Your NIC

If you are not sure which NIC you have installed in your system, or if you just want to let Windows 95 search through your system to detect what hardware you have installed, select the Yes option on the second page of the Add New Hardware Wizard (refer to fig. 31.4).

This option is essentially the same process that Windows 95 goes through during the initial installation, and it generally does a good job of locating your installed hardware components (although it can fail to detect some cards). Click Next to proceed to the next page of the wizard.

Note

If you let the wizard automatically detect your installed hardware, it is possible that it may find more than one new hardware component on your system. If all you installed is a network card, you may want to click the Cancel button and restart the wizard, selecting No on the second page to manually specify the network card you have.

The next page of the Add New Hardware Wizard (shown in fig. 31.5) is an informational page telling you what the wizard will do to your system and how long it will take. Click Next to proceed.

The next page is the actual hardware detection page. As you can see in figure 31.6, this page has a status bar along the bottom that indicates how far the hardware detection phase has run.

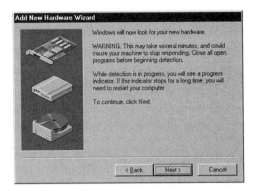

Fig. 31.5
The advisory page in the Add New Hardware Wizard also advises you to close all open applications to prevent your system from hanging.

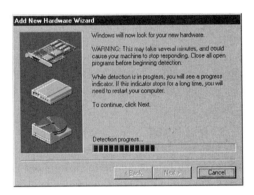

Fig. 31.6
The automatic hardware detection is in progress

After the Add New Hardware Wizard has completed scanning your system for new hardware, the wizard displays the screen shown in figure 31.7. This screen tells you that the wizard has completed the scan for new hardware and is ready to install support for the new hardware on your system. If you want to see the list of the hardware that was detected, you can click the Details button.

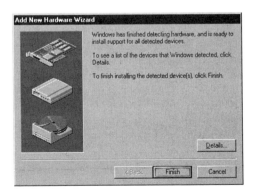

Fig. 31.7
The wizard has finished detecting your new hardware.

IV

Setting Up Hardware

When you click the Finish button to install the hardware support, the wizard installs the necessary system drivers and any extra software to support the new network card. Then, the wizard prompts you to restart your system in order for Windows 95 to start supporting your new hardware. If you do not want Windows 95 to restart at this time, just click Cancel.

Note

If the Add New Hardware Wizard couldn't identify your new NIC, it tells you that there is no new hardware to install and gives you the option to manually specify the hardware you are installing. This option is discussed in the next section.

Manually Specifying Your NIC

If you know in advance the type of network card you have installed, or if the Add New Hardware Wizard couldn't identify the type of card you installed, you can manually tell the wizard the type of drive you have.

After you start the Add New Hardware Wizard, click the Next button to move to the second page. Here, the wizard asks you whether you want Windows 95 to search for your new hardware; select the No option and click Next. This allows you to manually select the hardware to install.

When you elect to manually install your hardware with the Add New Hardware Wizard, the wizard displays a list of the types of hardware that you can install.

Fig. 31.8
The list of hardware types available to install appear in this wizard box.

From the Hardware Types list, you should select Network Adapters, because this is the type of hardware you are installing. Click Next to continue. The wizard now displays the list of the manufacturers (on the left side of the window) and the types of network adapters (in the right side of the window) that Windows 95 knows about.

> **Note**
>
> Depending on the version of Windows 95 you are running, this list of manufacturers and drives may be different. As Windows 95 matures, more types of hardware will be recognized by the wizard.

If the manufacturer of your NIC is listed on the left side of the window, select that manufacturer. The wizard displays all of the NICs made by that manufacturer (that the system knows about) in the right side of the window.

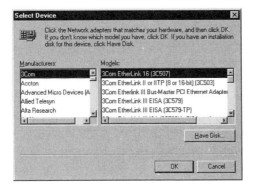

Fig. 31.9
Select a manufacturer and drive type in the Select Device window.

Once you have selected the manufacturer and card type, click Next to continue with the installation.

On the next page of the wizard, the default settings for NIC are displayed. If these settings do not match the hardware settings on your network card, you either have to change the hardware settings on the drive or change the Windows 95 configuration using the Device Manager (started from the System control panel). See the earlier section "Checking Your Network Card" for details on how to do this.

IV

Setting Up Hardware

Fig. 31.10
The current
hardware settings
appear in this
wizard box.

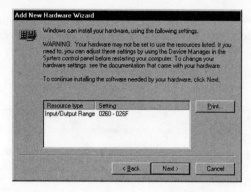

Once you have confirmed the current hardware settings, Windows 95 installs the necessary drivers for your network card and prompts you to restart your system (if necessary). After your system has been reset, you are now able to use your new hardware.

> **Note**
>
> If the manufacturer of your network interface is not listed by the wizard, you should check to see if Windows 95 drivers are available for your card. If so, you can click the Have Disk button instead of specifying the manufacturer and drive type. Windows 95 will prompt you for the location of the drivers (generally you load the drivers from your floppy drive) and use those drivers directly to support your NIC.

If no Windows 95 drivers are available for your NIC, you can use the regular Windows drivers for your drive. See the instructions from your card and the Windows 95 documentation for help with installing and using Windows/ DOS drivers with Windows 95.

Configuring Your Network Interface Card

Once you have installed Windows 95 support for your network interface card, you may have to configure your card in order for it to work correctly. Configuring your NIC is done through the Network sheet, started from the Control Panel.

> **Note**
>
> If Windows 95 had built-in support for your network card, you may not have to configure your card at all. In many cases, Windows 95 will pick the correct settings for your card to work correctly. Checking the properties for your network card tells you if it's already working.

To change or check the settings for your network card, select your NIC from the list of items on the Network control panel (as shown in fig. 31.11).

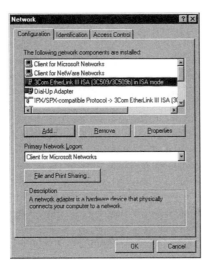

Fig. 31.11
The Network control panel enables you to select your NIC.

Selecting Properties brings up the properties sheet for your network card (as shown in fig. 31.12). The pages on this sheet are the different properties that you can set for your card, and may be slightly different depending on the network card that you have in your system.

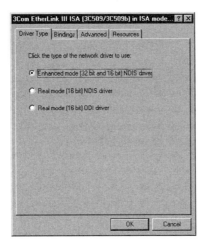

Fig. 31.12
Here's an example properties sheet for a network interface card.

The Driver Type page allows you to select between the different types of drivers that may be available for your card. In general, if there are Windows 95 drivers available, they are listed as Enhanced Mode (32-bit and 16-bit) drivers. You should select this type of driver if possible, as they give the best performance. If Windows 95 drivers are not available, you have to pick one of the DOS drivers listed.

The Bindings page (shown in fig. 31.13) allows you to select which network protocols will use this network adapter. Normally, all of the protocols you have installed are selected on your network adapter, but if you have more than one network adapter (for example, you have an Ethernet card for work and a dial-up adapter for when you are away from work), you may want to have some protocols available only on a particular NIC.

Fig. 31.13

The Bindings page enables you to pick protocols for your adapter.

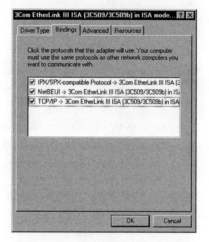

The features on the Advanced page (shown in fig. 31.14) vary depending on the particular card you have installed. You should consult the hardware manual for your NIC for information on these settings.

Depending on the type of network card you have, the Resources page shows different settings that are available (see fig. 31.15). You should know how your hardware is configured before you change any of the settings on this page, so that you can match the Windows 95 settings with the ones on the card.

IV

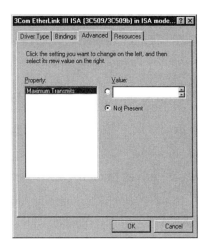

Fig. 31.14
The Advanced
page allows you
to set certain
advanced features
of your network
interface.

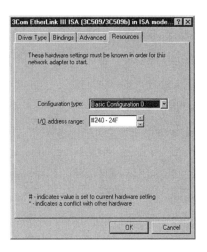

Fig. 31.15
The Resources
page allows you
to set up the
hardware resources
such as the I/O
address range or
Interrupt level.

Caution

Setting one of the resources to a value used by another card can cause the other card
to stop working.

In addition to configuring the NIC on your computer system, you may have
to change some settings for the network software on your computer. These
settings are configured through the Network control panel, on the Identification and Access Control pages.

Configuring the Identification Settings Page

On the Identification page of the Network control panel (as shown in fig. 31.16) are settings which allow you to identify your computer on your local network. The three settings available on this page are:

- *Computer name.* Sets the name that your computer appears under on the network. Often, your computer name is assigned by your local network administrator; it should be unique on your network (no other computer should have the same name as yours).

- *Workgroup.* Sets the default workgroup that your computer belongs to on your network. The workgroup is the group of computers that appear first when you bring up your Network Neighborhood; you should check with either your local network administrator or the people you work with frequently to see which workgroup you should belong to. Also, you can see the workgroups that are available on your network by bringing up Network Neighborhood and selecting Entire Network.

- *Comment.* Sets a comment that appears next to your computer when people browse Network Neighborhood or look up the properties of your computer on the network.

Tip

It is usually a good idea to put the location of the computer and the name of the person who usually uses it in the Comment field so that if there is a problem or question about the computer, it is easy to find.

Configuring the Access Control Settings Page

The Access Control Settings page allows you to select the way that users on your network get access to resources that you make available on your local computer system. The two access control options available are:

- *Share Level Access.* Users on your network must supply a password to connect to a resource on your machine (such as a shared directory or printer). When you make a resource available, you set the password for that resource.

  This type of access is convenient when there is no central control over the resources on your network.

■ *User Level Access*. Users on your network must log into a central server (usually running Windows NT) with an account and password. When you make a resource available, you set up a list of users who can access the resource. The list of users is retrieved from the server; you specify the server on the Resource page.

This type of access is best when everyone on your network logs in through a central server and you want to control exactly who has access to your resources.

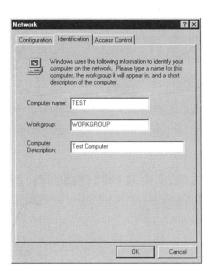

Fig. 31.16
The Identification page shows the name of the computer.

Installing Cables

After your network card is installed on your computer system, you have to attach a cable to connect the network card to your local network. The type of cable you use depends on the type of network hardware that is in use at your site, and also what kind of network card that is installed in your system.

Some network cards support several types of network cabling; the hardware manual included with your card should tell you which cable types are supported. You should also check with your local network administrator to make sure that you are using the right kind of cabling for your site.

Some of the more common types of network cabling include the following:

■ *10 Base-T*. Looks like a normal telephone wire with a modular connector at each end. This type of cable plugs into a socket on your NIC.

■ *Thin-wire Ethernet.* Looks like cable-television cabling. This type of cable has a round connector (called a *BNC connector*) that attaches to a T connector. The T connector then attaches to the connector on your network card. Normally, if the cabling ends at your machine, you must put an Ethernet terminator on the other side of the T connector.

■ *Thick-wire Ethernet.* Looks like large cable-television cabling. This type of cable, which is not used as frequently as the other types, has a connector at the end that has several pins; this connector attaches to the socket on your network card.

Caution

If you are not familiar with the network cabling at your site, check with your network administrator before connecting your computer to your network. An incorrectly connected computer can cause serious network problems!

Installing and Configuring Shared Printers

If you don't have a printer directly connected to your computer, you can use a printer that is connected to another computer on your network, provided that the printer is made available (shared) on the computer it is attached to.

Installing a Shared Printer

The installation process for shared network printers is mostly the same as for installing a printer connected to your computer. The Add Printer Wizard (started from the Printers control panel) leads you through the steps to add a printer to Windows 95.

The first page of the Add Printer Wizard (see fig. 31.17) explains what the wizard will do. Click the Next button to continue.

The second page of the wizard (see fig. 31.18) asks you whether the printer is a local printer (connected directly to your computer) or a printer on the network. Since you are adding a network printer, select the Network Printer option and click Next to continue.

Fig. 31.17
The Add Printer
Wizard first page
appears.

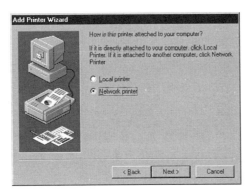

Fig. 31.18
Select a local or
network printer in
this wizard box.

On the third page of the Add Printer Wizard, you specify the network printer
that you are adding. If you are not sure of the exact computer that the printer
is connected to (or the name the printer is shared as) you can click the
Browse button to bring up a browser similar to the Network Neighborhood;
here you can look at the computers on your network to find the printer you
want.

Once you have located the printer (or typed in the name of the printer in the
standard \\COMPUTER\PRINTER_NAME format), you are ready to continue.
If you plan to use the printer to print from a DOS program running under
Windows 95, however, you should select Yes to the question Do you print
from MS-DOS based programs? (see fig. 31.19).

The next page of the wizard (shown in fig. 31.20) asks you to identify the
type of printer you are connecting to. Select the manufacturer of the printer
from the left hand side of the list and the printer type from the right hand
side. If the printer type you want is not listed, you may be able to find a
printer in the list that is compatible with the printer you are attaching; you
can contact the printer manufacturer or look in the printer manual for a list
of compatible printers.

Fig. 31.19
The printer
selection form is
filled in.

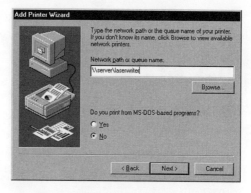

Fig. 31.20
Select a printer
type in this wizard
box.

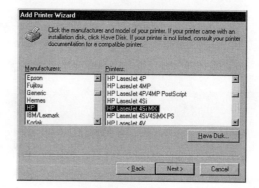

Next, the wizard (as shown in fig. 31.21) asks you to type a name for the printer (the name that appears in print dialogs on your local system) and whether you want this printer to be your default printer. If you want to use this printer as your default printer, select the Yes option below the printer name. Clicking the Next button allows you to continue.

Fig. 31.21
Name the printer
on your local
system.

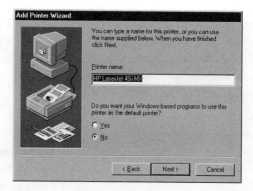

The next page asks you whether you want to print a test page after the printer is installed. This is usually a good idea; it allows you to make sure that the printer is connected correctly.

The wizard now installs the drivers for the printer and prints a test page (if you asked for it). During this process, you may be asked to insert several of your Windows 95 installation disks (or the Windows 95 installation CD-ROM if you have a CD-ROM drive); you should have these available.

After the drivers are installed and the wizard prints the test page (if you asked for one), you are asked whether the test page printed correctly. If you answer No, a troubleshooting wizard is started that leads you through several different procedures to try and resolve the problem.

◀ See "Installing a Printer to a Single PC," p. 605

Configuring Network Printers

You can configure the network printer by right-clicking the printer icon from the Printers control panel and selecting Properties. The printer is configured exactly the same as if it were connected to your local machine.

Installing Shared Fax Modems

Adding a shared fax modem from your network is similar to adding a regular modem (one that is connected to your computer system) to the Microsoft Fax server. The Microsoft Fax configuration program is started from the Control panel Mail and Fax sheet. When you start this control panel (as shown in fig. 31.22), you should select the Microsoft Fax profile and click the Properties button to begin configuring this service.

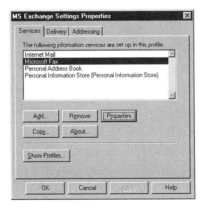

Fig. 31.22
Configure the Microsoft Fax service in this sheet.

On the Microsoft Fax properties sheet, select the Modems page to configure the network modem. Click the Add button to add a new modem to the fax service. This brings up the Add a Fax Modem dialog box, shown in figure 31.23, which asks you to specify the type of modem you are adding. You should select Network Fax Server.

Fig. 31.23

Add a new network modem to the Microsoft Fax service in the Add a Fax Modem dialog box.

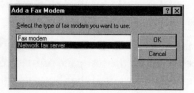

You now need to enter the shared fax folder in the usual \\COMPUTER\ FOLDER form. If you are not sure of the computer or folder name, you should ask your network administrator.

Once you have specified the network fax folder, you should be able to use the Microsoft Fax service.

Installing Shared CD-ROM'S

CD-ROM drives that are shared on the network are mounted just like any other directory that is shared on your network. You can mount a shared CD-ROM drive by choosing Tools, Map Network Drive in the Explorer. The system prompts you for the machine name and share name; if you don't know these, you should open the Network Neighborhood and look for the machine that has the CD-ROM shared on it.

Once you have found the machine and the share name, you can mount the CD-ROM on your system. It appears as a new drive letter and can be accessed from the Explorer or My Computer icon. You can specify the drive letter on the Map Network Drive sheet.❖

Appendix A

Installing and Using Microsoft Plus! Companion for Windows 95

by Rob Tidrow

V

Appendixes

When discussing Windows 95, it's appropriate to give some coverage of the Microsoft Plus! Companion for Windows 95. Plus! is an add-on package to Windows 95 that you must purchase separately from Windows 95. Two of the products included with Plus!—System Agent and the Internet Explorer— are worth the price of Plus!. Other tools and features include Desktop Themes, which add zest to your desktop, ScanDisk 3, an expanded version of ScanDisk that comes with Windows 95, Dial-Up Networking Server, and a 3-D pinball game.

This appendix shows how to install Plus! on your system. You learn the following:

- Install all of Plus! or just the components you want

- Set up your system to connect with the Internet through the Internet Explorer

- Customize your desktop with Plus! Desktop Themes

- Schedule system maintenance with the System Agent

- Configure Dial-Up Networking Server to dial into from another computer

Installing Microsoft Plus!

After you install Windows 95 on your system, you can install the Microsoft Plus! Companion separately. Plus! is available in both the 3.5-inch floppy disk and CD-ROM formats. Before you start the Plus! Setup program, make sure you have the required system resources. Because of the enhanced features of Plus!, your computer must meet higher system requirements than the basic Windows 95 requirements. These requirements are as follows:

- At least a 80486 processor. A Pentium processor is recommended.

- CD-ROM or floppy drive and mouse (or similar pointing device)

- Windows 95 operating system installed

- 50M of hard disk space for a complete installation

- 8M or more of RAM. 12 to 16M recommended.

- Monitor and video card that displays 256 colors or more. Some of the Desktop Themes require a 16-bit display.

- Modem/fax modem to use the Internet and dial-up networking features

- Sound card and speakers are recommended, but required to hear the 3-D pinball sounds and music

- Windows 95 installation disks or CD-ROM

Like the Windows 95 Setup program, the Plus! Setup program enables you to install the complete Plus! package using the Typical installation option or only selected components using the Custom installation option.

Starting the Plus! Setup Program

You can use the Typical Setup option to install all components of Microsoft Plus!, which requires up to 16M of hard disk space. If your system is low on hard disk space, or if you don't want to install all of Plus!'s features, perform a Custom Setup. Both of these options are covered in the following procedures.

Start your computer and wait for the Windows 95 desktop to load. Next use these steps to complete the installation:

1. Insert the Plus! CD-ROM in the CD-ROM drive on your system.

2. If the Windows 95 AutoRun feature is activated, the Microsoft Plus! for Windows 95 screen appears. Click the Install Plus! icon. Skip to step 6.

3. If AutoRun is not activated, start the Add/Remove Programs option in Control Panel and choose the Install/Uninstall page.

4. Click the Install button and click Next on the Install From Floppy Disk or CD-ROM Wizard.

5. Windows automatically searches your floppy and CD-ROM drives for setup programs. When it finds the Plus! setup program, click Finish.

6. The Microsoft Plus! for Windows 95 Setup screen appears.

7. Click Continue. The Name and Organization Information dialog box appears, as shown in figure A.1.

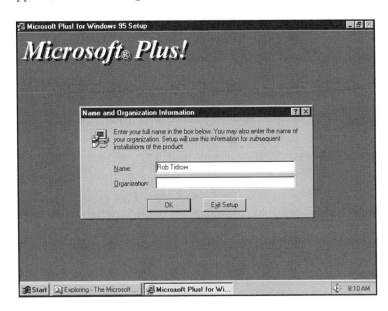

Fig. A.1
Enter your name and business name. Your business name is optional.

8. In the Name and Organization Information dialog box, enter your Name and Organization. Click OK. When the confirmation dialog box appears, click OK to confirm your entries.

9. In the next dialog box, enter the 10-digit CD-key number from your Plus! package in the dialog box that appears. Click OK.

10. The Microsoft Plus! for Windows 95 Setup dialog box appears, which shows you the Plus! product ID number. You should write down this number and store it with your Plus! CD. Click OK to confirm the Product ID number and continue Setup.

11. Next, Setup searches your system and displays a dialog box listing the folder that Setup creates to store the Plus! files (see fig. A.2). In the dialog box asking whether Windows 95 should create the destination

folder, click <u>Y</u>es to continue. Whether you accepted the folder recommended by Setup or specified another one, click OK to accept the Install folder.

Fig. A.2
You need to
confirm if you
want Plus! to be
installed in the
suggested folder.

> **Note**
>
> If you want to install Plus! in a different folder, click the Change <u>F</u>older button.
> In the Change Folder dialog box, specify the drive and folder to use by selecting them from the list or typing a path in the <u>P</u>ath text box. Click OK.

12. You now need to specify which type of installation to perform (see fig. A.3). Select <u>T</u>ypical or <u>C</u>ustom option.

Fig. A.3
If you want to
install everything,
select <u>T</u>ypical. To
choose the
components that
Setup installs,
select <u>C</u>ustom.

> **Note**
>
> When you select the Custom installation option, you can customize how a particular component installs. To do so, click the component name in the Options list, then click the Change Option button. In the dialog box that appears, click to deselect features you don't want to install in the Options list, then click OK to return to the Custom screen. Repeat this step for each of the components you want to customize.
>
> When you've finished specifying which of the components to install in the Custom screen, click the Continue button. After you click Continue, the Setup process progresses the same as for a Typical Setup.

13. If you selected to install the System Agent, Windows prompts you to choose whether to run system maintenance tasks (such as ScanDisk) at night or during your business day. Click Yes to run these utilities at night, but you must keep your computer on at night. Click No to run these utilities during the day, but during times when you normally don't use your PC, such as during the lunch hour.

14. Setup checks your system's video installation. If your display runs in 256 colors, Setup displays the Video Resolution Check dialog box. This dialog box asks whether you want to install the high-color Desktop Themes, even if your monitor currently displays only 256 colors. If your display is capable of displaying more colors (operating in 16-bit color or higher) and you have ample hard disk space, click Yes. Otherwise, click No.

15. Setup checks your system for necessary disk space, then begins copying files to your computer. Setup displays a message that it's updating your system.

> **Note**
>
> After the preceding step, Plus! Setup displays the initial screen for the Internet Setup Wizard, if you selected to install this option. If you don't want to set up the connection now, click Cancel. You can return to it later. If you do want to set up your Internet connection, click the Next button and see "Setting Up the Internet Explorer" later in this chapter. If you click Cancel, the Internet Setup Wizard asks you to confirm that you want to exit the Internet Setup Wizard. Click Yes to do so.

V

Appendixes

◀ See "Setting Background and Wallpaper Properties," p. 157

16. The Set Up a Desktop Theme dialog box appears. Click OK to continue.

17. The Desktop Themes dialog box appears, enabling you to select your first Desktop Theme (see fig. A.4). You can select a theme now, or use the Desktop Themes icon in Control Panel after installation to set up a theme. For now, click OK to continue.

Fig. A.4
You can select a Desktop Theme at this point, or choose one after you have Plus! installed.

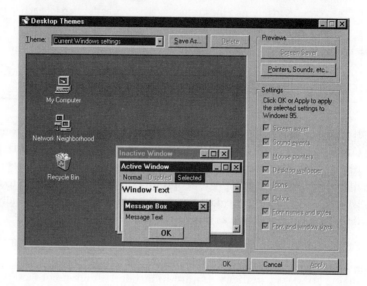

18. Setup displays a dialog box telling you that it needs to restart Windows. To complete the setup, click the Restart Windows button. Your computer and Windows 95 restart. When Windows 95 restarts, you should see the word Plus! on the Windows 95 startup screen to indicate that you've successfully installed Microsoft Plus!.

Tip

Click the Add/Remove Programs icon in Control Panel to remove Plus! items from your computer.

Now you can start using the features of Plus!.

Setting Up the Internet Explorer

The Internet Explorer software enables you to connect to The Microsoft Network or the Internet via a direct network connection or a PPP dial-up account from an Internet service provider. Microsoft Plus! provides the Internet Explorer software, plus the Internet Setup Wizard.

You can use the Internet Setup Wizard to install the Internet Explorer while you're installing the rest of Plus!. Or, if you want to use the Internet Setup Wizard later after Plus! is installed, click the Start button on the Taskbar, point to Programs, Accessories, Internet Tools, and Internet Setup Wizard.

To use the Internet Setup Wizard to install the Internet Explorer, follow these steps:

1. Click the Next button from the Internet Setup Wizard Welcome screen to proceed with the setup. The How to Connect screen appears.

2. Specify whether you want to connect via The Microsoft Network or a PPP account you have with an Internet service provider by clicking the appropriate option button. Click Next to continue.

> **Note**
>
> If you choose the I Already Have an Account with a Different Service Provider, you are presented with the Service Provider Information screen. In this screen, you select your provider. See Chapter 12 for information on setting up a provider under Windows 95.

◀ See "PPP and SLIP Connections," p. 295

3. The Installing Files screen appears, reminding you that you may need your Windows 95 setup CD-ROM or disks. Click Next to continue.

4. The Setup Wizard copies files to your hard disk. When it concludes, it may display a dialog box asking you to insert your Windows 95 setup CD-ROM or disk into the appropriate drive. Do so, then click OK.

5. The Setup Wizard copies additional files to your system. Then, The Microsoft Network dialog box appears.

   You can choose to set up a new Microsoft Network account or connect to an existing Microsoft Network account. Depending on which option you choose, the wizard guides you through the process. Simply respond to each wizard screen, providing information such as user name, password, and dial-up options. Click Next after you provide each item of information the wizard requests.

6. The Setup Wizard displays a dialog box telling you that it needs to restart Windows. To complete the setup, click the Restart Windows button. Your computer and Windows 95 restart.

V

Appendixes

Uninstalling Plus!

If you find that you do not want Plus! on your system any longer, or if you want to remove some Plus! components, you can use the Windows 95 Add/Remove Programs feature. This feature enables you to automatically uninstall a program. To uninstall Plus!:

1. Select Start, Settings, and click Control Panel. The Control Panel window opens.

2. Double-click the Add/Remove Programs icon. The Add/Remove Program Properties sheet appears (see fig. A.5).

Fig. A.5
Use the Add/Remove Programs feature to uninstall part or all of Plus!.

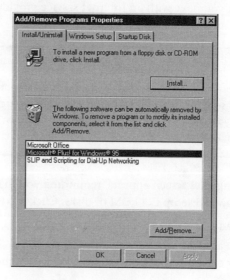

3. In the Install/Uninstall page, a list shows the programs that can be added or removed from your system. Double-click Microsoft Plus! for Windows 95 in the list.

4. The Microsoft Plus! for Windows 95 Setup installation maintenance screen appears.

5. You can choose to remove part of or all of the Plus! program. To uninstall all of Plus!, click the Remove All button. Or, to choose individual components to remove, click the Add/Remove button to display the Maintenance Install screen (see fig. A.6). In the Options list, click to clear the check mark beside each Plus! component to remove from your system, then click Continue.

6. Whether you're removing all or parts of Plus!, a dialog box appears asking you to confirm the removal. Click Yes to continue the uninstall process.

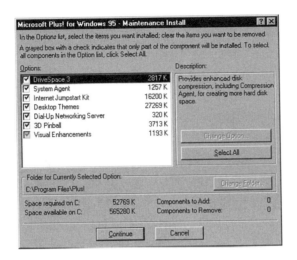

Fig. A.6
You can remove a
Plus! component
by clearing its
check box.

Setup removes the Plus! files from your system.

7. Microsoft Plus! Setup displays a dialog box telling you that it needs to restart Windows. To complete the uninstalling Plus!, click the Restart Windows button. Your computer and Windows 95 restart.

Note

If you uninstall all the Plus! components, the word PLUS! does not appear on the Windows 95 startup screen when Windows 95 reboots.

Working with Desktop Themes

You learned in Chapter 6, "Configuring the Windows 95 Desktop and Display," how to change wallpaper and use different color schemes for your display. With Plus!, you can add even more life to your desktop using Desktop Themes. Desktop Themes combines high-color graphics, sounds, and various icons and mouse pointers to add some zest to your computer.

Tip

Use the Add/Remove Programs icon in Control Panel to add the Desktop Themes if you did not do so during Setup.

Plus! provides Desktop Theme combinations both for computers displaying in 256 colors and computers displaying in 16-bit or higher color. An example of a Desktop Themes screen provided with Plus! is shown in figure A.7.

Fig. A.7
Dangerous
Creatures takes
you on a walk on
the wild side. This
is a 256-color
image.

When you choose a Desktop Theme, you can specify whether to replace Windows screen elements you specify using the Desktop Theme icon in Control Panel. In the Desktop Themes dialog box (see fig. A.8), you can select from the following elements which to use with your system:

Fig. A.8
Select the theme
of your choice
from the Themes
drop-down list, as
well as the
elements to use.

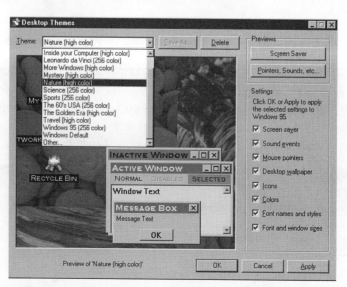

- *Screen Saver.* Displays the Theme screen saver when you leave your computer idle.

- *Sound vents.* Assigns Theme sounds to system events such as starting applications and exiting from Windows.

- *Mouse Pointers.* Applies the Theme pointer styles for different types of pointers. Some of these pointers are interesting; others are clunky looking.

- *Desktop Wallpaper.* Covers the desktop with the decorative background provided by the Theme.

- *Icons.* Assigns custom icons to desktop objects, including the Recycle Bin and My Computer.

- *Colors.* Applies the Theme colors to windows and other screen elements. Unfortunately, many of the color schemes are ugly, but you are the final judge of this.

- *Font Names and Styles.* Assigns Theme fonts for screen elements, including window titles and task buttons.

- *Font and Window Sizes.* Uses the Theme font sizes and default window sizes.

Configuring Windows 95 with a Desktop Theme

Plus Setup! creates an object icon for the Desktop Themes in the Windows 95 Control Panel, which contains other objects for controlling Windows' appearance and operation. Use the following steps to use the Desktop Themes object to select a Theme:

1. Click the Start button on the Taskbar. Point to Settings, then click Control Panel.

2. In the Control Panel window, double-click the Desktop Themes icon. The Desktop Themes dialog box appears. Use this dialog box to select and set up a Theme.

3. Click the down arrow beside the Theme drop-down list to display the available Desktop Themes. Click the name of the theme you want to use. A dialog box tells you that the theme files are being imported. When that dialog box closes, the preview area of the Desktop Themes changes to display the appearance of the Theme you selected, as shown in figure A.9.

V

Appendixes

Fig. A.9

You can see a preview of the Desktop Theme before you decide to use it on your system.

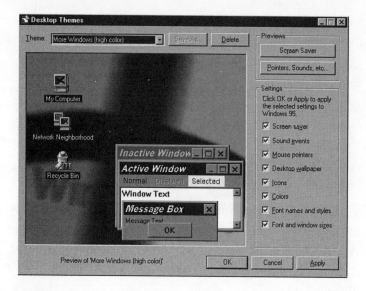

4. At the right side of the dialog box, choose the Settings to use for the Theme you selected. To deselect a setting, click to remove the check from the box beside it.

5. To preview the selected Theme's screen saver, click the Screen Saver button in the Previews area in the upper-right corner of the dialog box. The screen saver appears on-screen. Move the mouse or press a key to conclude the preview.

6. To preview several of the selected Theme's other elements, click the Pointers, Sounds, Etc. button in the Previews area. A Preview dialog box for the Theme appears; the dialog box has three tabs for Pointers, Sounds, and Visuals. Click the tab you want to view. Each tab offers a list box with the elements for the theme. For the Pointers and Visuals tabs, simply click an element in the list to see a preview in the Preview or Picture area at the bottom of the dialog box. For the Sounds tab, click an element in the list, then click the right arrow icon near the bottom of the dialog box to hear the sound. Click the Close button to conclude your preview.

7. After you have selected a theme, chosen settings, and previewed elements to your satisfaction, choose OK to close the Desktop Themes window. The selected Desktop Theme appears on your system.

Adjusting Plus! Visual Settings

Plus! adds new features to the Display settings available in the Windows 95 Control Panel. These visual settings are designed primarily to make your desktop more attractive. Plus! enables you to specify new icons for the My Computer, Network Neighborhood, and Recycle Bin Desktop icons. You can choose to show the contents of a window (rather than just an outline when you drag the window). You can choose whether or not you want to smooth the appearance of large fonts on-screen. You also can choose to show icons with all possible colors or expand the wallpaper (when centered using the Background page of the Display Properties sheet from Control Panel) so it stretches to fill the entire screen.

Note

Most of the Plus! visual settings require more system resources than the normal display settings. In particular, showing window contents while dragging and using all colors in icons consumes more RAM. Consider all your computing requirements before you use up RAM by selecting any of these features. If you notice that Windows 95 runs considerably slower with any of these features enabled, turn off the features.

To work with the Plus! visual settings, click the Start button on the Taskbar. Point to Settings, then click Control Panel. In the Control Panel window, double-click the Display icon. The Display Properties sheet appears. Click the Plus! page to display its options, as shown in figure A.10. To assign a new Desktop icon, click the icon you want to change in the Desktop Icons area near the top of the dialog box. Click Change Icon. In the Change Icon page that appears, scroll to display the icon you want, then click OK to accept the change.

To enable any of the other Plus! display features, select the feature in the Visual Settings area of the Plus! page. When a check appears beside the feature, that feature is selected. If you want more information about a particular feature, right-click the feature, then click What's This?. A brief description of the feature appears. Click or press Esc to clear the description. To accept your visual settings and close the Display Properties sheet, click OK. Close the Control Panel window, if you like.

Fig. A.10
You can make adjustments to the Windows display properties using this dialog box.

Managing Utilities with the System Agent

You learned in Chapter 1, "Preparing To Install Windows 95," that you need to run ScanDisk and other hard disk maintenance programs before you run Setup. After you install and configure Windows 95, you should get into the habit of running these same utilities, plus a backup program, weekly or monthly to keep your hard disk optimized. Most users tend not to perform system maintenance operations until after a disaster strikes. Plus! provides the System Agent, a program that enables you to schedule when to run other programs, such as system maintenance utilities like Disk Defragmenter, ScanDisk, and Compression Agent. The System Agent can run other programs as well, and notify you when your hard disk is low on space.

By default, the System Agent is enabled after you install Plus!. This means that each time you start Windows 95, the System Agent starts automatically and runs in the background, only becoming active when it needs to start a scheduled program or notify you of low disk space. Even though System Agent is active by default, it isn't fully set up. After you install System Agent, it automatically places Low Disk Space Notification, ScanDisk for Windows (Standard Test), Disk Defragmenter, and ScanDisk for Windows (Thorough Test) programs in the System Agent. You need to manually tell the System Agent which other programs to run, when to run them, and which program features to use.

To schedule programs with the System Agent, use the following steps:

1. Click the Start button on the Taskbar. Point to Programs, then to Accessories.

2. Choose System Tools, then click System Agent. The System Agent window opens.

3. Choose Schedule a New Program from the Program menu. The Schedule a New Program dialog box appears (see fig. A.11).

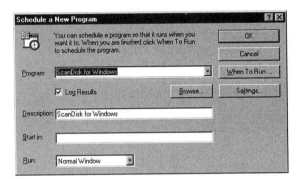

Fig. A.11
The Schedule a New Program dialog box enables you set the schedule for a program to run.

4. Click the drop-down list arrow to open the Program list. Click a program from the list that appears. You can choose ScanDisk for Windows, Disk Defragmenter, Compression Agent, or Low Disk Space Notification. If you want to run a program other than one of these, click the Browse button, select the program to run in the Browse dialog box, then click OK. No matter which method you used, the selected program appears as the Program choice.

5. If needed, you can edit the Description for the program and Start In folder, which specifies the folder containing files to program needs to run.

6. Open the Run drop-down list and specify whether you want the program to run in a Normal Window, Minimized, or Maximized.

7. To specify the schedule for the program, click the When to Run button. The Change Schedule of dialog box appears (see fig. A.12).

8. Click a Run option, such as Weekly or Monthly. Your choice here affects the options available in the Start At area of the dialog box.

Fig. A.12
Use the Change
Schedule dialog
box to set up a
schedule for the
selected program.

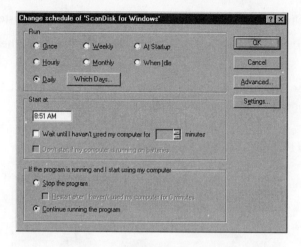

9. Specify the options you want in the Start At area of the dialog box. Although there may be other options depending on your choice in step 8, you'll always need to enter a starting time.

    Also, you can turn on the next check box and specify a number of minutes to tell System Agent to wait if you're using your computer when the scheduled program run time occurs.

10. In the bottom area of the dialog box, choose whether System Agent should Stop the Program or Continue Running the Program should you start using your computer when the scheduled program is running. Stopping the program can protect against data loss while running system utilities.

11. Click the Settings button to control which features the selected program uses when the System Agent runs the program. The Scheduled Settings dialog box that appears varies depending on the selected program.

12. Specify the settings you want for the selected program, then click OK to close the Scheduled Settings dialog box.

13. Click OK again to finish scheduling the program. System Agent adds the program to the list of scheduled programs.

Note

Keep in mind that you can schedule the same program to run at different times with different settings. For example, you can schedule a Standard ScanDisk check once a week, plus a thorough check once per month.

Although you can use the Program menu choices to make changes to the schedule and settings for one of the listed programs, it's faster to simply right-click the program you want to make changes to. A shortcut menu appears, from which you can choose the following:

- *Properties*. Changes things like the program startup folder and settings (click the Settings button in the dialog box that appears).

- *Change Schedule*. Adjusts how often System Agent runs the program.

- *Run Now*. Runs the program immediately, using the settings you've specified.

- *Disable*. Prevents the listed program from running at the designated time but leaves the program on the list; choose Disable again to reinstate the program's schedule.

- *Remove*. Deletes the selected program from the System Agent list; confirm the deletion by clicking Yes at the warning that appears.

The Advanced menu in System Agent offers two commands for controlling System Agent itself. Turn on the Suspend System Agent choice whenever you want to stop all your regularly scheduled programs from running; then toggle this choice back on when you need to. The Stop Using System Agent choice completely stops System Agent operation; after you use this option, System Agent no longer loads when you start Windows, and you have to select System Agent from the System Tools Shortcuts to start using it. To close System Agent after setting it up, select Exit from the Program menu.

Configuring DriveSpace 3

Windows 95 offers DriveSpace disk compression, which enables you to pack more data on your hard and floppy disks. DriveSpace 3, included with Plus!, can handle larger disks—up to 2G—than the Windows 95 DriveSpace, which can only handle hard disks up to 512M in size. To be more efficient, DriveSpace 3 works with smaller units of data on the disk—512-byte sectors as opposed to the 32K-byte cluster size regular DriveSpace works with. This ensures that DriveSpace 3 wastes less space on the disk. Finally, DriveSpace 3 offers two new, more dense compression formats, one of which is particularly suited for Pentium systems.

V

Appendixes

> **Caution**
>
> Although compression provides you with extra disk space, a compressed disk often is slower to use than an uncompressed disk. Also, the greater the compression, the slower your system is likely to perform when working with the compressed disk. Also, compressing your system's primary hard disk can take quite a bit of time, during which you won't be able to work with your system. Some systems may take several hours to compress.

Use the following steps to compress a disk with DriveSpace 3:

1. Click the Start button on the Taskbar. Choose Programs, Accessories.

2. Point to System Tools, then click DriveSpace (after Plus! installation, the icon beside the DriveSpace will include a 3 to indicate DriveSpace 3). The DriveSpace 3 window appears.

3. Click the drive that you want to compress.

> **Note**
>
> You can select a previously compressed disk, then use the Upgrade choice on the Drive menu to convert the disk to DriveSpace 3 format.

4. Open the Advanced menu and choose Settings. The Disk Compression Settings dialog box appears.

5. Click the option button for the compression method you want to use:

    No compression. Does not compress the selected drive.

    No compression unless drive is X% full. Only compresses the disk after it's more full than the percentage you specify.

    Standard compression. Compresses the disk contents by approximately a 1.8:1 ratio.

    HiPack compression. Compresses the disk contents by up to 2.3:1.

6. Click OK to close the Compression Settings dialog box and accept the specified compression method.

7. Open the Drive menu and choose Compress. The Compress a Drive dialog box appears, informing you of the estimated results of the compression operation—that is, how much free space and used space the disk will have after compression.

8. Click the Options button. The Compression Options dialog box appears. Use it to specify a drive letter and free space for the Host drive where DriveSpace 3 will store compressed information about the drive. You should only need to change these first two options if your system is connected to a network that uses drive H for another purpose.

> **Note**
>
> To compress a floppy disk that you use on another computer that doesn't have DriveSpace 3, click to select the Use DoubleSpace-compatible Format check box. Use this option for Windows 95 systems without DriveSpace 3 or for systems using DriveSpace from a DOS 6.x version.

Click OK to accept the compression options you set.

9. Click the Start button in the Compress a Drive dialog box. The Are You Sure? dialog box appears, asking you to confirm the compression operation.

10. Click the Back Up Files button to make a backup copy of the files on the disk before you compress it. Although this is an optional step, you should make a backup of your critical files before compressing your hard disk. If you select the backup option, DriveSpace 3 runs the backup utility installed to work with your system. Follow any on-screen instructions to complete the backup process.

11. When the backup is finished, click Continue to compress the disk. DriveSpace 3 compresses the disk, then redisplays the Compress a Drive dialog box to report on the compression results.

12. Click Close to complete compressing the disk.

Configuring Dial-Up Networking Server

The Dial-Up Networking Server included with Plus! enables you to set up your computer so that others can dial into it from another computer. You can use this option if you travel frequently and use a laptop on the road and want to access files on your stationary PC at your office or home. You also can share files with other people by allowing them to dial into your computer and transfer files back and forth.

V

Appendixes

To set up the Dial-Up Networking Server, you must have a modem configured and the Dial-Up Networking feature installed. Use the following steps to set up your computer so that you can dial into it:

1. Double-click My Computer, and double-click the Dial-Up Networking icon.

2. In the Dial-Up Networking folder menu, select Connections and then Dial-Up Server. The Dial-Up Server dialog box appears (see fig. A.13).

Fig. A.13
You configure the Dial-Up Network Server using the Dial-Up Server sheet.

3. Choose the Allow Caller Access radio button to enable users to dial into your computer.

4. Click the Change Password button to set a password for users to use to gain access to your computer.

> **Caution**
>
> When you use the Dial-Up Network Server feature and do not set a password, you are vulnerable to users hacking into your system. Be sure to set a password and change it periodically.

5. Fill in the Dial-Up Networking Password dialog box and click OK.

6. (Optional) Fill in the Comment field with a description of the connection, such as the phone number needed to access this server.

7. Click the Server Type button to establish the type of server (such as the PPP, Windows 95, Windows NT, Internet server) the Dial-Up Network Server feature uses. The options available are those that are configured for the Dial-Up Adapter for your system.

8. You also can configure the Dial-Up Network Server to use software compression during file transfers and enable the password encryption option. This latter option is used to provide an extra layer of security by encrypting your passwords as you are dialing out. The computer to which you are connected must also support this feature; otherwise, you may encounter problems connecting with it.

> **Tip**
>
> Use the software compression option to speed up the transmission speed between your computer and the connected one.

9. Click OK twice to save your selections and to activate the Dial-Up Network Server.

> **Caution**
>
> When you activate the Dial-Up Network Server feature, your modem port is always open. This means that if you try to use your modem to call out using another communications package (besides those built into Windows 95), you will not be able to initialize the COM port and be unable to dial out. Be sure to deactivate Dial-Up Network Server when you want to use another communications package.

Appendix B

Troubleshooting Windows 95 Installation

by Rob Tidrow

Throughout this book, you've been shown how to install and configure Windows 95 to work with your computer. Many of the chapters include troubleshooting elements to help diagnose and remedy problems you may encounter during setup, whether you're experiencing problems with Windows 95 Setup, installing hardware devices, or configuring your desktop. This appendix gathers all these troubleshooting hints and tips and puts them in one spot for you. In addition, you find many more troubleshooting items that are placed here.

This appendix covers the following topics:

- Windows 95 Setup problems

- Memory, disks, and devices problems

- Windows architecture questions

- Problems associated with applications

- Hardware and printer problems

- Network hardware questions

- Microsoft Fax questions

- Norton Utilities problems

> **Caution**
>
> Windows 95 is a new operating system. With that comes problems supporting every computer and configuration available. The following troubleshooting items are known to work in some situations. We cannot guarantee they work for every computer. Before attempting any of these solutions, make a backup of your entire system. This ensures you against losing critical data if you encounter major problems.

Windows 95 Setup and Bootup

Windows 95 was designed to be easy to install. Although wizards help guide the user through the setup process, the true test comes when you encounter problems during setup or after you boot up Windows 95 for the first time. Use this section to help you troubleshoot some of the most common setup and bootup problems with Windows 95.

> **Tip**
>
> If you are using older hardware device drivers (those not designed for Windows 95), you might encounter problems using some devices. Although this appendix addresses many specific hardware issues, you should contact the device's manufacturer for new Windows 95 device drivers for your component. Another valuable source is to subscribe to the **comp.os.ms-windows.win95.setup** newsgroup on the Internet. You'll find hundreds of messages devoted exclusively to problems with Windows 95.

What are the system requirements for Windows 95?

Windows 95 requires the following components from your system. You may need more or less depending on the installation type you choose:

Component	Requirement of Windows 95
Processor	80386 or higher
Hard Drive	30M of free disk space for a compact installation; 40M for a typical installation
Memory	4M
Input Device	Mouse
Floppy Disk	Required for installation from floppy disks

Component	Requirement of Windows 95
CD-ROM Drive	Required for installation from CD
Monitor	VGA
Fax/Modem	Required to use The Microsoft Network, Remote Access, HyperTerminal (included in Windows 95), Microsoft Fax, and Phone Dialer

I don't have much time. How long does it take to install Windows 95?

Depending on the installation type you choose, Windows 95 requires between 30 minutes and two hours to completely install.

Should I install Windows 95 over my previous versions of Windows?

There are advantages to both options. If you decide to keep both versions of Windows on your machine, then you need to reinstall all your applications under Windows 95. The advantage is that you have a fail-safe mechanism if Windows 95 does not work properly on your machine. You can move back to Windows 3.x immediately. Once you test your new Windows 95 installation, delete your old Windows 3.x files, including the applications installed under Windows 3.x.

On the other hand, if you install over your previous version of Windows, your applications work as soon as you install Windows 95. You also do not need as much free disk space available to start Windows 95 Setup when upgrading a previous version.

What should I do to make this a hassle-free Windows 95 installation?

There are no guarantees for a hassle-free installation, even though most users experience very few installation problems. The best advice is to prepare your system (and yourself) for the installation. Make backup copies of your AUTOEXEC.BAT and CONFIG.SYS files, copy any network files you have, make a DOS boot disk, and back up to floppy or tape *any* file that you cannot live without. These files include documents, graphics, spreadsheets, and the like.

Some other helpful tips include remarking the load= and run= lines in your WIN.INI files (place a semicolon in front of those lines) and turning off any screen savers or TSRs that you may have running. If you have any unnecessary programs starting from AUTOEXEC.BAT and CONFIG.SYS, you should

REM out those lines as well (keep your network and CD-ROM lines in there, however). You might also want to remove any programs from the Startup program group in Windows 3.x before starting Windows 95 Setup.

I have a CMOS (or system BIOS) anti-virus setting. Will this cause a problem during installation?

Yes, Windows 95 will stop and report an error message. You must remove this setting and turn off the virus scan before proceeding with the Windows 95 installation. Consult your system's hardware documentation for information on this.

During Windows 95 Setup, I get an error message that Disk 2 is corrupted. What can I do?

Many users using the floppy disk version of Windows 95 have encountered this problem. Microsoft is aware of it and offers this explanation:

```
We have tracked down a handful of disk sets nationwide from custom-
ers that have reported this problem. In every case the second disk
turned out to have been corrupted by a virus on the customer's
machine that had infected the second disk during install. To be
clear, the virus was on the customer's machine prior to installa-
tion of Windows 95 and not caused by the Windows 95 disks. This
generally happens on disk two because this is the disk where cus-
tomer registration information is stored during install so setup
writes to this disk. The virus, which installs itself undetected
on a typical floppy disk, is exposed because of the unique high-
density format used for Windows 95 distribution diskettes.

Once the virus has infected the diskette, it is bad. The customer
can phone 1-800-207-7766 to receive a new disk one and two. Product
Support will also be able to handle this problem.
```

During Windows 95 Setup, my computer keeps hanging during the information gathering process. What can I do?

First, let it continue working for 20 minutes or so. Sometimes your computer just needs a lot of time to gather the information requested by Windows 95. Second, if you are certain your system has crashed, turn off the computer for 10 seconds and turn it back on. Run Setup again and use the Safe Recovery option if it appears (it may not if your system crashed too soon). Setup by-passes the phase at which it encountered the problem the previous time. If it hangs again, repeat the process a few more times if necessary. If that fails, tell Setup that you want to manually configure the hardware so it doesn't look for it during Setup.

My system hangs on the first boot and I'm installing from a CD-ROM. What happened?

You may have a conflict between real-mode and protected-mode drivers with your CD-ROM. First, remark (REM) out the CD-ROM drivers in your CONFIG.SYS file and reboot. If you still encounter a problem, try to boot into Safe Mode. (Reinstall Windows 95 if you can't boot into Safe Mode.) Also, make sure you have a backup copy of your CD-ROM drivers on a boot disk.

From here, create a BOOTLOG.TXT from the Startup menu to see where Windows failed. Look for a file called DETCRASH.LOG. If you find this, it means that you have a problem with Windows 95 detecting your hardware. In the IOS.INI file, remark out the drivers that are loading in CONFIG.SYS to make sure there isn't a problem with these protected-mode drivers. Also, boot into Windows 95 in Safe Mode and remove any devices from Device Manager that you think may be causing problems. Make a copy of your SYSTEM.INI file (call it SYSTEM.BAK for instance) and copy the SYSTEM.CB file to SYSTEM.INI. Very few drivers load into the SYSTEM.CB file, including the mouse driver. Because of this, you might lose the functionality of your mouse, but that's okay because you are trying to isolate a CD-ROM problem. If this solves your problem, look in your SYSTEM.INI file for any entries made by third-party applications, such as Adobe Type Manager. Remark them out and reboot. After your system reboots, Windows should locate your mouse. If not, add it back to your SYSTEM.INI file and reboot.

Windows 95 has started in Safe Mode. What is this?

In Safe Mode, Windows 95 uses default settings and Windows 95 drivers for your video and mouse, and only the necessary device drivers to run Windows 95. Devices such as network cards and CD-ROMs are not accessible during Safe Mode. Use Safe Mode to diagnose and fix possible problems you may be having with your system.

What can I access during Safe Mode?

When you are at the Setup menu in DOS, you can boot into Windows 95 or boot to a DOS prompt. While in Windows 95, you can open the Settings program in Control Panel to access the Device Manager page. From here, you can disable or remove devices that are causing conflicts with your system.

I'm having too many problems with Windows 95 on my system. Can I uninstall it?

To uninstall Windows 95, you must select the Save System Files option during Setup. This saves a copy of your previous system (such as Windows 3.1) on your computer. Next, while in Windows 95, choose Start, Settings, Control Panel, and double-click the Add/Remove Programs icon. In the Add/Remove Programs Wizard, click the Install/Uninstall page and select the Windows 95 option in the list of software that can be uninstalled by Windows 95. Click the Add/Remove button, and then follow the directions on-screen. The Uninstall program removes all long file names and then runs an MS-DOS program to remove Windows 95 from your computer. Your previous MS-DOS and Windows 3.x files are then restored.

Windows 95 is not running, but I want to uninstall it anyway. How do I do it?

Boot your computer from the startup disk you created during installation (or from a DOS boot disk you created prior to installation) and type **UNINSTAL** at the A:\ prompt. At the A:\ prompt, type the following command:

C:\WINDOWS\COMMAND\UNINSTAL.EXE

The problem with this approach is all long file names are not removed from your system. You may have to delete these manually.

I want to uninstall Windows 95 but I didn't make a startup disk. What do I do now?

You can do one of two things. The suggested choice is to make a startup disk by selecting Start, Control Panel, and double-clicking on the Add/Remove Programs icon. Click the Startup Disk tab and click the Create Disk button. You need one floppy disk that works in your A drive.

The second choice is to use the following steps:

1. Boot from an MS-DOS boot disk you created prior to installation.

2. Enter the following at the A:\ prompt:

C:\WINDOWS\COMMAND\UNINSTALL.EXE

In the preceding syntax, c is the drive letter where Windows 95 is installed, and \WINDOWS is the name of your Windows 95 directory.

After I uninstalled Windows 95, I still have some files left on my machine from Windows 95. Why?

These are long file names that Windows 95 installs. If you uninstall Windows 95 using a method other than uninstalling it from Windows 95, you are left with these long file names. You can remove them by running Windows 3.x File Manager and deleting them one at a time.

I had problems removing Windows 95 using the preceding steps. Is there another way?

Yes, but it requires that you are comfortable making changes to system files and deleting several files at the DOS command prompt. The following steps show this method:

1. Make a backup copy of Windows 95's DELTREE command if you don't have it on your previous MS-DOS.

2. Make a copy of Windows 95's ScanDisk.

3. In SCANDISK.INI, make sure the following lines are there:

    ```
    labelcheck=on
    spacecheck=on
    ```

4. Run ScanDisk to remove all long file names.

5. After ScanDisk finishes, use DELTREE to delete the Windows 95 directory.

6. Use DELTREE to delete WINBOOT.*.

7. If you are using the upgrade to Windows 95, use DELTREE to delete *.w40.

8. From your backup disks, copy the following files back to your root directory: CONFIG.DOS, CONFIG.SYS, AUTOEXEC.DOS, AUTOEXEC.BAT, MSDOS.DOS, MSDOS.SYS, IO.DOS, and IO.SYS.

9. Next use DELTREE to delete the following files: SETUPLOG.*, BOOTLOG.*, and DETLOG.*.

10. You may want to reinstall your old version of MS-DOS to be safe.

During Windows 95 Setup, should I make a startup disk?

Yes, the startup disk is fail-safe in case you run into problems after installation. The startup disk contains utilities that help you diagnose problems with your setup. The startup disk does have some limitations. It cannot, for instance, be used to provide access to a CD-ROM device or to a network connection. You need to clean up any problems associated with your installation to recover from these problems. After you create the startup disk, make copies of other important system files, such as CD-ROM device drivers, password files (PWL files), and any network configuration files on your system.

How do I start my computer without booting into Windows 95?

As your computer boots, watch the screen and when the message Starting Windows 95 appears, press F8. This boots into the Setup menu. You can choose the Step-by-Step Confirmation choice to load the AUTOEXEC.BAT and CONFIG.SYS files one line at a time. This is handy when you want to bypass a configuration instruction that is called during one of these files.

Can I skip my AUTOEXEC.BAT and CONFIG.SYS files during bootup?

Yes. Press F8 during bootup (see previous solution) and choose the Command Prompt Only option. If you want to skip your AUTOEXEC.BAT and CONFIG.SYS files and go to the command prompt without network support, choose Safe Mode Command Prompt Only.

Why do I need an AUTOEXEC.BAT or CONFIG.SYS file? I read that Windows 95 doesn't use them.

In theory, Windows 95 doesn't need to have these files to run. In practice, however, many users still use older devices that need to have drivers loaded (such as CD-ROMs not supported automatically by Windows 95) during bootup. You should, however, look through your AUTOEXEC.BAT and CONFIG.SYS files and remove any lines that you don't need. This will make Windows boot faster and possibly free up additional memory. One way to test whether you need these system files at all is to give them a different name and re-boot your computer. If you notice any problems with certain devices, you need to add these lines back in. If you don't notice any problems, you are probably safe without AUTOEXEC.BAT or CONFIG.SYS.

How do I boot to my previous version of MS-DOS?

If you have MS-DOS version 5.0 or higher, you can boot to it after you install Windows 95. You must modify the MSDOS.SYS file by starting a DOS session in Windows 95 and changing to the root directory of DOS. Next, type the following command:

ATTRIB -R -S -H MSDOS.SYS

Press Enter. Type **EDIT MSDOS.SYS** to start the DOS Editor with MSDOS.SYS loaded.

Place the following line after the [Options] section and save the file:

> **BOOTMULTI=1**

Exit from the DOS window and shut down Windows 95. Reboot your computer and press F8. On the Start menu, select the Previous Version of MS-DOS option.

Desktop and Display

Many of the items in this section discuss problems you may encounter with the Windows 95 Desktop and display options. Overall, Windows 95's Desktop is an environment, but you may run into quirks here and there. If you have problems with your graphics display adapter, consult your manufacturer to obtain any available new device drivers.

How do I create a shortcut to a printer?

To create a shortcut to a printer, select Start, Settings, Printers. In the Printers folder, click the printer to which you want to create a shortcut and click the right mouse button. Drag the printer icon on to the Desktop and select Create Shortcut(s) Here. Now you can drag files from the Explorer or Desktop on top of the printer shortcut to print your documents.

I want to change the name of a shortcut, but I can't change the file name. Will this happen?

No. The shortcut name does not alter the original file name.

Every time I double-click a shortcut, the application starts in a maximized window. How can I start it minimized?

The shortcut property settings also includes an option to set the way the shortcut item opens. In the Run drop-down list, you can select Normal, Minimized, or Maximized. Normal displays the window sized as you last used it.

I've changed my screen resolution, but now Windows 95 hangs. What can I do?

If your display doesn't appear correctly or if you see nothing at all, you need to reboot Windows 95 and start in Safe Mode. In Safe Mode, Windows boots with a standard VGA display driver. After Windows 95 boots, go through the shut-down process and reboot your machine. When it restarts and goes into Windows, it should return to your old display settings.

How can I find out which display driver is loading?

You can check the [boot] section of SYSTEM.INI for an entry as follows:

```
display.drv=pnpdrvr.drv
```

If you see this setting, any display entries you have in SYSTEM.INI are by-passed and the display drivers are loaded from the Registry; otherwise, your drivers are loaded from SYSTEM.INI.

My display driver worked fine in Windows 3.1, but now it won't support the Windows 95 features for changing resolution on-the-fly. Why not?

If your display driver requires the screen resolution to be written in the [boot.description] section SYSTEM.INI, you cannot use the resolution on-the-fly feature.

When I run a multimedia video, my screen is jerky. Can you help?

First, make sure you have the correct display driver loaded by looking in the Device Manager. Next, check your CONFIG.SYS file to determine if the MSCDEX file is installed. If it is, remove it (REM it out temporarily) and use the new Windows 95 built-in CD-ROM file system drivers (if your CD-ROM supports it). When you encounter this problem with DOS applications, increase the amount of XMS memory.

I have a Paradise VLBus3000 accelerator video card. Where can I get Windows 95 video drivers for it?

On the Windows 95 CD-ROM, look in the DRIVERS\DISPLAY\TRIDENT folder for a file called TRID94XX.INF. With this file, you should have no problem using the true color capabilities of the card. You also can receive the drivers from the Microsoft Web server at **http://www.microsoft.com/ Windows**.

I'm using the latest ATI graphics driver (machxw4) but I'm receiving GPFs in various applications, particularly when I'm exiting the program. If I switch to the Windows 95 provided driving, I don't experience this problem.

To correct this problem, you might want to switch from 256 colors to 16 million or high color.

Taskbar and Start Button

The taskbar and Start button features of Windows 95 introduce new ways for users to locate and switch between applications. You probably won't run into too many problems with these items, but you might have some questions about how certain things work with them. This section touches on a few of those concerns.

I moved the taskbar to the left side of my screen, but I can't read the task buttons now. Why?

Depending on the width of the taskbar, you may only see the application icon and its first two letters when the taskbar is moved to the side of the Desktop. This can make it difficult to recognize your open applications. Move the mouse pointer over the right edge of the taskbar until it changes to a two-sided arrow. Hold down the left mouse button and drag the taskbar to the right until it is resized to a point that you can read the task buttons.

I've set Auto Hide in the Taskbar Properties sheet but I can't get the taskbar to reappear when I have maximized windows. Why?

When you set the properties for the taskbar, be sure to click Always on Top to ensure that the taskbar appears on the bottom edge of your application window. You also can press Ctrl+Esc to display the taskbar and open the Start menu.

I had Windows 3.x set up with program groups that I still want to use. How can I quickly add these to the Start menu?

You must have Windows 95 installed in a different folder than your previous version of Windows to do this. Using Explorer, locate all the GRP files for your program groups in the old Windows directory, and double-click them. (They are called Microsoft Program Groups in the Explorer.) This places the old program groups as folders in the Programs folder on the Start menu. (If you haven't re-installed your Windows 3.x applications, you still need to do so to have them work in Windows 95.)

Memory, Disks, and Devices

One of the most significant advances in Windows 95 over the previous DOS and Windows 3.x is the way Windows provides a 32-bit multitasking environment. This section describes some of the changes in this area and offers some troubleshooting advice on running ScanDisk.

In Windows 3.x, I used up a lot of disk space just for virtual memory. Do I need to use virtual memory at all with Windows 95?

You may be able to completely disable virtual memory. Windows won't let you do this if you have less than 12M of physical RAM. This is the minimum amount of memory (RAM plus virtual memory) required by Windows 95. But, if you do have 12M or more of physical RAM, you can completely turn off virtual memory. If you do turn virtual memory off, you may not be able to run more than a few small programs simultaneously or work with large amounts of data. Microsoft (and I) recommend that you don't disable virtual memory.

The Windows 95 box says all I need is 8M of memory. Why won't some of the Object Linking and Embedding (OLE) tasks work?

Windows 95 does not let you set the minimum memory below 12M (the total or your physical RAM and virtual memory). However, if you do set your total memory to 12M, you may have problems trying to run additional programs, working with OLE documents, and so on. If you are planning on running any large program or working with OLE objects, you should keep the minimum memory to at least 16M.

I'm out of disk space (or almost out) and want to compress my entire drive, including the swap file. Can I do this?

For the best performance, you shouldn't locate the swap file on a compressed drive. However, if you need more virtual memory than you can fit on any non-compressed drive, you can use a compressed drive. While performance is not as good, you are able to run more programs simultaneously. For example, if you are running several large programs, like Microsoft Word and Microsoft Excel, and you are using OLE to share data between them, you need a lot of memory. If you run out of memory, use the default swap file. Your only option to get everything to work, however, may be to put the virtual memory swap file on a compressed drive. It works, just slower.

The Recycle Bin eats up a lot of my hard disk space. How can I reduce the percentage of disk space that the Recycle Bin uses?

By default, the Recycle Bin uses 10 percent of drive C's total capacity. That's a lot when you have a large hard drive. For a 1.85G hard disk, for example, you're reserving 121M just for an undelete buffer! To reduce it, right-click the Recycle Bin icon on the Desktop and select Properties. On the Global page, click the Configure Drives Separately option. Click on the C page and move the slider until you are satisfied with the undelete buffer size.

I have several disks that I want to run ScanDisk on, but I don't want to select one at a time. What can I do?

You can run ScanDisk on several drives at once. To do this, when you are selecting the disk to run ScanDisk on, hold down the Ctrl key and click each drive you want to check for errors.

How do I automate disk utilities, such as ScanDisk, to run at specific times?

You can automate the running of ScanDisk by installing the Microsoft Plus! for Windows 95 System Agent. With System Agent, you can schedule when any program, especially the disk maintenance tools, will run.

ScanDisk ran, but it didn't correct all the errors it found. What do I do?

ScanDisk may be unable to repair errors for files that are in use while ScanDisk is running. Since Windows 95 itself has many files in use, ScanDisk may not be able to completely repair all errors it finds. To fix these errors, shut down Windows 95 and choose Restart the Computer in MS-DOS mode and run the DOS version of ScanDisk. This file can be found in the \WINDOWS\COMMAND folder.

Windows 95 does not recognize my tape drive, so I have to run it in DOS mode. Does this affect long file names when I restore the files?

Yes. If you use a DOS tape software to back up long file names and try to restore them later, they all end up truncated to 8.3 convention of DOS. Use the LFNBK utility supplied on the Windows 95 CD-ROM in the \ADMIN\APPTOOLS\LFNBACK folder.

I'm using the Do_cache utility on a Texas Instruments 486. I'm experiencing some performance problems. What can I do?

Most likely, you need to disable this utility and not load it at bootup. One of the symptoms of this problem is crashing while running Explorer or a DOS prompt.

I'm trying to diagnose some memory problems, but I don't know how Windows uses virtual machines.

DOS applications execute in separate virtual machines (VMs). Windows 3.x (16-bit) applications execute in the System VM, in a single address space. Windows 95 (32-bit) applications run in the System VM, but in separate address spaces. DOS applications can't bring down the system, other DOS applications, or other Windows (16 or 32-bit) applications. Windows 3.x (16-bit) applications can bring down other 16-bit applications. Windows 95 (32-bit) applications can't bring down other 32-bit, 16-bit, or DOS applications.

Can Windows 95 handle multitasking on multiple processors?

Windows 95 supports multitasking on one microprocessor. Windows 95 doesn't support Symmetric Multiprocessing (SMP), which allows the use of multiple microprocessors within one PC. Windows NT and OS/2 Warp do support SMP.

Whereas Windows 95 uses cooperative multitasking for multi-threaded processing, Windows NT uses the more reliable preemptive multitasking method. It remains to be seen how many 32-bit Windows 95 applications lock themselves up by failing to return CPU control after a reasonable time to another thread within their process slot.

I still have a lot of DOS- and Windows 3.x-based software. At the architectural level, how does Windows 95 handle these types of applications?

Table B.1 summarizes the key architectural features in the Windows 95 application execution environment by application type. Once you understand these concepts, it will be easier to understand how to best use DOS, Windows 3.x, and Windows 95 software in the Windows 95 operating environment.

Table B.1	Application Execution Environment		
Feature	**DOS App.**	**16-Bit App.**	**32-Bit App.**
Virtual Machine (VM)	One MS-DOS VM per executing DOS application	All run in within a single memory address	All run in System VM executing DOS, but each in a separate memory address
Multi-tasking	Preemptive scheduling	Cooperative scheduling	Preemptive scheduling
Multi-threaded scheduling	None	None	Yes, uses cooperative processing
Messaging	Each has its own message queue	All share a common message queue	Each has its own message queue

DOS Programs

You might have switched to Windows 95 to escape the limitations of MS-DOS, but you still may have plenty of DOS-based applications you want to run. This section provides some troubleshooting items to help you run DOS programs under Windows 95.

I still use the DOS command prompt a great deal, but hate going through the Start menu to start it. What can I do?

Create a shortcut to DOS and place it on the Desktop for quick access to DOS. You can also start a DOS session by choosing Start, Run, typing the word **COMMAND**, and pressing Enter.

I don't want to boot into Windows 95. Can I boot into DOS?

When the message Starting Windows 95 appears, press F8 and select Command Prompt Only to boot up the computer in the real mode version of DOS. When you finish, type **Exit** to start Windows 95.

How do I get help for a DOS command?

To display help for a DOS command, type the name of the command you want followed by /? (make sure you include a space between the command and slash). For example, type **md /?** to display help text on the MAKE DIRECTORY (md) command. Adding the pipe character (|) and the word **more** to the end of the statement displays help text one screen at a time; for example:

```
md /? | more
```

I know Windows 95 supports long file names, but I'm a little hesitant to use them in DOS. Should I be?

A bit of caution is required when it comes to using long file names. Although the Windows 95 DOS commands support long file names, existing DOS and Windows 3.x programs do not support long file names. Furthermore, be careful when using a file in Windows 95 with a long file name and then accessing the file in a DOS or Windows 3.x program. Doing so deletes the long file name!

How do I view long file names in DOS?

The DIR command has been enhanced to display a seventh column which shows the long file name. DIR also sports a new command line switch called verbose: **/v**. The verbose switch displays additional information such as file attributes and last access date stamp.

What version of MS-DOS comes with Windows 95?

If you type the DOS command **VER** at the command prompt, the version information that displays is Windows 95. However, DOS programs that ask internally for the DOS version get the number 7. This could cause conflicts with DOS programs that will only work for a specific DOS version number.

How do I access DOS properties in Windows 95?

To configure the DOS command line sessions, set properties for COMMAND.COM which is located in Windows 95's COMMAND folder.

I used to use PIFs (Program Information Files) all the time in Windows 3.x. I can't find them in Windows 95. Where are they?

Windows 95 stores all PIFs in a hidden PIF folder in the Windows 95 folder. This keeps novice users from inadvertently altering the actual PIF files.

How do I view DOS property sheets?

You set properties for a DOS program the same way you set properties for any object in Windows 95—by right-clicking the object and choosing Properties. Windows 95 then displays the properties folder for the DOS application. DOS program properties are organized into six property sheets.

Windows 95 property sheets exist for all DOS programs, whether started in MS-DOS mode, from the command prompt, or as a Windows 95 DOS session. For those applications set up to run in MS-DOS mode, many properties do not apply and are therefore not available. When MS-DOS mode is selected, only the following properties are enabled:

- *General*. File attributes.

- *Program*. Icon text, command line, close on exit, change icon, and the advanced MS-DOS mode options.

- Font, Memory, Screen, and Misc sheets are blank.

DOS programs that ran fine under Windows 3.x are not working properly under Windows 95. In general, what can I do to fix this?

If a DOS program detects Windows 95 and won't run properly, select Prevent from the Advanced Program Settings sheet for that DOS program.

How can I change the way my DOS program uses memory?

The settings on the Memory property sheet control the way the DOS application uses the PC's memory. Settings are provided to control conventional, expanded (EMS), and extended (XMS) memory. Because each DOS application executes in its own MS-DOS virtual machine (VM), the memory settings apply only to that DOS application. Other applications executing DOS, Windows 3.x, and Windows 95 are unaffected by these memory settings.

What can I do when I get a DOS GPF (General Protection Fault)?

Since each DOS application executes in a separate VM, a GPF (General Protection Fault) in one DOS application has no effect on the other DOS, Win16, or Win32 applications currently executing. When the GPF message appears, record the error message information and choose OK to terminate the offending DOS application.

V

Appendixes

Windows 3.x Software

When Windows 95 hit the market, very few Windows 95-compliant applications were available. Most users had to stay with Windows 3.x-compliant applications until an upgrade became available. If you have general concerns or questions about Windows 3.x software running in Windows 95, you can find some information here.

> **Tip**
>
> Many Windows 3.x applications have quirks when running in Windows 95. You should look through the README.TXT files available on the Windows 95 setup disks to read about any specific problem that you might encounter with your applications.

I want to set up a dual-boot environment with Windows 95, but I need to reinstall all my Windows 3.x software. Will this be a problem?

The process for installing Windows 3.x software in Windows 95 is essentially the same as in Windows 3.x. Instead of choosing File, Run in Program Manager to install programs, in Windows 95 you choose Start, Run. Alternatively, you could use the Add/Remove Programs feature in the Control Panel. Either way, the installation works the same.

Some of my older 3.x programs share components. What should I do to ensure they are all installed properly?

Be careful when installing or updating Windows 3.x programs that share components (such as MS Graph which is shared by Word and Excel). Setup programs cannot update a component which is currently being used by a running application. To avoid conflicts, it is best to shut down related programs (and any critical applications/data) before installing or updating software.

Can I configure Windows applications property sheets, and if so, how?

Since Windows applications share a common configuration, their property sheets consist of only a General Properties sheet and possibly a Version sheet. All other properties such as memory, display, and fonts are managed by Windows 95 in other areas. To display the property sheets for a Windows 3.x program, right-click the file name and choose Properties.

My Windows 3.x programs use INI files for configuration settings. Where are they in Windows 95?

Windows 3.x programs relied on initialization files (which have the file extension INI) to load real mode and virtual device drivers during the Windows boot process. Windows 3.x applications often created their own initialization files or edited (without backing up or asking for permission) the Windows initialization files (WIN.INI and SYSTEM.INI). Over the years as you add, update, and delete Windows 3.x applications, the contents and number of INI files increase. Settings and INI files for obsolete or deleted versions of Windows 3.x programs remain unless you invest the time to extract them manually, or the money for a Windows uninstall utility. Recently, a few Windows 3.x programs have begun to address this problem by providing their own uninstall routines.

How do I modify an INI file for different configuration and setup settings?

The INI files can be viewed and edited by using any plain ASCII text editor. Before making any changes, you should make a backup copy of the INI files. Windows 95 provides a new version of the Windows 3.x SYSEDIT.EXE program which allows you to quickly view and edit all of the setup files. You can find SYSEDIT.EXE in the Windows 95 SYSTEM folder.

What happens when I get a GPF in a Windows 3.x application?

Since all Win16 applications execute in a single VM, all Win16 application execution ceases until the application that caused the GPF is terminated. When the GPF message appears, record the error message information and choose OK to terminate the offending application. Once the offending application is terminated, the other Win16 applications resume execution. Note that a GPF in a Win16 application has no effect on any currently running DOS or Win32 applications.

Problems with Windows 95 Applications

Each week several new Windows 95-compliant applications hit the market. Many of your favorite Windows 3.x programs are being upgraded to take advantage of Windows 95's 32-bit architecture. This section offers some answers to questions you may have about Windows 95 applications.

V

Appendixes

I just got a GPF in Windows 95. I thought I wouldn't have these when I upgraded to Windows 95.

A General Protection Fault (GPF) occurs when an application violates system integrity. The following list provides examples of common GPFs:

- Application tried to use a memory address currently being used by another application

- Error code returned by a system API (application programming interface)

- A memory fault caused by an invalid pointer

I had a GPF in Windows 95. What is the dialog box that appears?

When Windows 95 encounters a GPF, it displays a General Protection Fault message that tells the user which application caused the problem, the module name, and a reference number. By relaying this information to the application vendor, often the problem can be quickly resolved.

Do GPFs affect other applications in Windows 95?

The effect of a GPF on the other applications currently executing depends on whether the offending application is a DOS application, a Windows 16-bit application (Win16), or a Windows 32-bit application (Win32).

What can I do when I get a GPF in a Windows 95 application?

Since Win32 applications execute at a separate memory address within the System VM, a GPF in one Win32 application has no effect on the other DOS, Win16, or Win32 applications currently executing. When the GPF message appears, record the error message information and choose OK to terminate the offending application. Any unsaved data in the offending application will be lost.

What are some of the ways to configure the Windows 95 environment after a GPF occurs?

First, look for any unattended timed backups or termination safety features built into the application.

When an application is terminated by Windows 95, the normal closing routines are not performed. This could cause problems when you restart the program. For this reason, you may consider contacting the vendor before trying to re-execute the program.

To terminate a hung Win32 application, right-click the application's Taskbar button and choose <u>C</u>lose.

Registry Questions

The Windows 95 Registry is the central information database for all the hardware and software you install on your computer. The Registry simplifies the operating system and makes it more adaptable, and in some cases, the Registry can eliminate the need for AUTOEXEC.BAT, CONFIG.SYS, and INI files. This section includes some tips on troubleshooting Registry problems you may have with Windows 95.

Does the Windows 95 Registry replace all my INI files? Can I delete all of them?

No, don't erase these files. If you are using older Windows 3.x applications that require an INI file, keep it on your system. In general, the Windows 95 Registry consists of three data files that manage the way your applications and environment behave:

- USER.DAT. Stores user preferences such as the Desktop.

- SYSTEM.DAT. Stores the computer's hardware configurations such as drives, printers and sound card settings.

- POLICY.POL. Stores administrative policies set up on a network server.

How can I protect the Registry files from becoming erased or tampered with to conserve my configuration settings?

Several precautions are taken to protect these data files. First, the Registry data is kept in binary format, so the files cannot be read by a regular text editor. Second, the file attributes are set to read-only, hidden system files. This prevents accidental deletion.

Also, Windows 95 maintains backup copies of the Registry data in the Windows 95 folder. The backup files SYSTEM.DA0 and USER.DA0 are used by Windows 95 in the event that the actual DAT files become corrupt.

How do I edit the Registry files to change some settings?

Unless you are an experienced Windows user or system administrator, you should not tamper with the Registry file. However, you can locate the

Registry Editor by running REGEDIT.EXE from your Windows 95 folder. To edit Registry files on a remote computer, run REGEDIT.EXE and choose Registry, Connect.

Help! My Registry has become corrupted. How do I restore it?

Reboot your computer. During the Windows 95 boot process, press F8 to display the startup menu. Select the Command Prompt Only option and then change to the Windows 95 folder. Type each of the following commands and press Enter after each one:

```
ATTRIB -H -R -S SYSTEM.DAT
ATTRIB -H -R -S SYSTEM.DA0
ATTRIB -H -R -S USER.DAT
ATTRIB -H -R -S USER.DA0
```

Make a copy of these files (give them an extension of BAK for instance) and then enter the following commands:

```
COPY SYSTEM.DA0 SYSTEM.DAT
COPY USER.DA0 USER.DAT
```

Reboot your system to restore the Registry.

Windows 95 File System

The Windows 95 file system is designed to handle long file names of up to 256 characters, including spaces. Because Windows 95 users still have to communicate with many DOS-based users (such as Windows 3.x users), you may encounter some problems when handling these files between users. This section includes some ways to isolate and determine problems with the Windows 95 file system.

I have an error with the VFAT.VXD file. What does it do?

VFAT is a 32-bit virtualized FAT file system. The VFAT.VXD file system driver (FSD) controls this file system and uses 32-bit code for all file access. VFAT is a protected mode implementation of the FAT file system. The VFAT system supports long file names (up to 255 characters), eliminates the over-reliance on INT 21H, uses 32-bit processing, and allows multiple concurrent threads to execute file system code.

What happens if my system uses long file names, but my disk utilities do not recognize long file names?

Do not use disk or backup utilities that are not aware of long file names. If you do need to use a backup/restore utility that does not support LFNs, Microsoft supplies a utility called LFNBK that preserves the LFNs. You can obtain this utility on the Windows 95 installation CD in the \ADMIN\APPTOOLS\LFNBACK folder.

I'm having problems with the Windows 95 file system. How can I troubleshoot it?

If an application does not respond properly to the Windows 95 file system, you can use the File System Troubleshooter to detect the cause of the problem. Using the Troubleshooter, you can disable the following Windows 95 file system features:

- File sharing and locking

- Preservation of long file names in non-LFN programs

- Protect-mode hard disk interrupt handler

- 32-bit protect-mode disk drivers

- Write-behind caching for all drives

How do I start the file system troubleshooter in Windows 95?

Follow these steps:

1. Open the Control Panel.

2. Open the System icon.

3. Select the Performance page.

4. Choose File System.

5. Select the Troubleshooting page.

6. Select the setting to be tested.

7. Choose OK to test the setting.

Online Communications

Windows 95 promises to make it easier than ever to get online. In some cases, this is true. In others, you may have problems establishing connections or initializing COM ports. One of the biggest concerns is the way Windows 95 enables you to connect to the Internet. This section includes some problems you might have with Windows 95 and its communications support.

The modem won't dial.

Check the hardware for loose cables and the communications software for proper configuration. If your modem is hooked to COM2, be sure that your software is looking for it on COM2.

My modem connects with my ISP's (Internet Service Provider) modem, then it dumps the carrier (hangs up spontaneously).

This is a potential nightmare with many sources. Did you set your parity to 8N1? Is the "initialization string" in your communication software appropriate to your modem? Does the modem name and other settings in your communication software match your modem? Is there an incompatibility between your modem and your ISP's modem? Carrier dumping requires sleuthing. Be patient and work with your ISP until the problem is solved.

I have a 28,800 baud modem, but the fastest connection I get is 19,200. Sometimes the connection is choppy and laden with errors when I download files.

Check for line noise. Check for any incorrect modem settings in your communication software. Check for modem incompatibilities between your modem and your ISP's modem. Check for the presence of a UART 16550 in your modem's COM port. If your phone company uses old switches in its central office, there is nothing you can do except get faster, dedicated service.

My modem connects to my ISP, but my ISP's system doesn't recognize my IP address.

Ensure that your IP address (if you have a static IP address) and your ISP's IP address and DNS are configured properly in Windows 95's TCP/IP configuration. Even a single wrong number or letter here can negate a connection.

I've tried the Windows Dial-Up Networking software to dial into my Internet provider, but I have problems after I connect with it. None of my applications, such as WinVN, Netscaper, and e-mail readers will work. I get a `Can't resolve host name` or a `Sockets error` message.

This indicates a problem with your Host Name Resolution. You need to set appropriate information regarding your Domain Name Server. Right-click the Your Dial Up Network's Icon that you created, and choose Properties. Click Server Type. Select the TCP/IP settings, and enter the DNS host address. You can obtain this from your Internet provider.

I've filled in all the DNS addresses and have confirmed them with my ISP. I still cannot connect to the ISP with a SLIP or PPP connection. What can I do?

If you had no problems connecting with your ISP under Windows 3.x, you should contact them for up-to-date information about new scripts they may have available. Another solution is to ask your provider if it requires two passwords when you connect to it. Sometimes if your ISP creates logon scripts for you, they will create an encrypted password that you may not know about. Ask them for this password, or ask them to change it to match your regular password.

I use CompuServe's WinCIM software to dial into that service. Because I've installed Exchange and the Plus! Companion, my modem won't initialize. Why?

Windows 95 includes built-in TAPI (Telephony Application Programming Interface) support for Exchange clients (such as MS Fax) and the Dial-Up Networking feature. If your port initializes with these clients (test it by running the modem diagnostics explained in the next section), you need to make sure you are not running any of these features in the background. If you have enabled your modem to accept faxes automatically, you see a fax machine icon on the taskbar. Turn this feature off by changing the setting in the Modems properties sheet, or close Exchange.

If you close Exchange and still can't initialize the COM port in WinCIM, you may have set the Dial-Up Networking Server to accept call-ins. You can change this setting by opening My Computer and double-clicking the Dial-Up Networking folder. Choose Connections, Dial-Up Server. Make sure the No Caller Access option is selected.

V

Appendixes

How do I run the modem diagnostics utility?

One way to test your modem's working condition is to double-click Modems in Control Panel and click the Diagnostics page. In the Port list, click one of the ports and select More Info. If your modem is not in use, you are returned with Information about the COM port and modem. Note that you cannot get information on your mouse because it is being used at the time.

How do I get access to commercial online services' software?

To get a free copy of AOL's software, call 800-827-3338. For a free copy of CompuServe's WinCIM software (make sure you get version 1.4 or above), call 800-848-8199. Call 1-800-PRODIGY to get a free trial offer, including Prodigy's software.

You can also frequently find AOL's software at the newsstand, bundled with computer-oriented magazines.

HyperTerminal has an icon for CompuServe. Should I set it up with my user ID and password?

If you already have a CompuServe account and you use CompuServe's WinCIM software, your best bet is to continue with WinCIM. If you haven't set up an account yet, use HyperTerminal to establish an account with CompuServe and then order a copy of WinCIM to use.

I went to configure my CompuServe (or Prodigy or AOL) software to use a local access phone number, but there isn't one for my city. Am I stuck using a long distance number?

Yes, but you'll probably save money if you use a high-speed access number in a neighboring state—but not too far away. This allows you to avoid the intrastate telephone tax and additional charges some long distance companies add for longer distances.

Hardware Problems

One of the most difficult issues to address in Windows 95 is hardware problems. Many users are finding that their older legacy hardware devices do not work properly—or at all—under Windows 95. To cover every known (and unknown) problem with hardware would involve thousands of pages of text. If you experience problems, you should try the procedures listed in this section. You should also contact your hardware manufacturer to get updated drivers for your hardware. Regardless of how many different ways you configure Windows 95, if you have an outdated driver, you will only waste your time.

What does the Windows 95 Device Manager do?

The Device Manager Registry in Windows 95 is designed to track available system resources, such as IRQ and I/O settings. Then, when a new hardware component is added, such as a sound board, you can use the Add New Hardware Wizard, which takes you step-by-step through the installation process.

The start of that process is to check the Registry for available settings and graphically present them to you so you can configure your board before you install it. The result should be that the new component will work when it is installed, although that isn't always the case.

What is the quickest way to resolve hardware problems in Windows 95?

Hardware conflicts can occur, often at the most inappropriate moments. Fortunately, not only does Windows 95 include a very thorough Help option from the Start menu, but it also features an especially useful step-by-step Hardware Conflict Troubleshooter, which you access by choosing the Hardware, Troubleshooting Conflicts option from the Help Topics Index.

The Troubleshooting Wizard takes you on a step-by-step investigation that should result in solving the problem. If it doesn't actually solve it, the wizard suggests possible solutions.

What are some common Plug and Play configuration problems in Windows 95?

Windows 95 supports PCs with Plug and Play devices. This means that when you install a Plug and Play device into your PC, such as a video adapter, or simply plug one in, such as a monitor, Windows 95 automatically detects the presence of the new device and configures it for use in Windows 95. This Plug and Play functionality also requires the BIOS on your PC to be Plug and Play compatible. Even if you do not have Plug and Play BIOS or Plug and Play devices, Windows 95 can still detect and configure devices using the Add New Hardware Wizard. Also, certain devices, such as monitors and video cards, can be detected immediately when Windows 95 starts.

When I add a new video card to my system, how do I configure it for Windows 95?

You can avoid having to pick the manufacturer and model of your video card from the lists provided with Windows 95 if you have the software installation disk that was shipped with the video card. Insert the disk into a floppy drive and click the Have Disk button in the dialog box. Follow the prompts to specify the location of the OEMSETUP.INF, which should appear on the disk. This file contains all the information needed to configure the video card. This technique also can be useful if you have a late model adapter that is not yet supported by Windows 95.

I don't recognize (or I don't know) either the manufacturer or the model of my video card in the lists that appear in the Add New Hardware Wizard. Also, I can't find any disks that might be associated with my video card.

Windows 95 lets you choose a generic driver for use with your adapter if you are not sure what video adapter is installed in your PC. Choose Standard Display Types from the Manufacturers list and either Standard Display Adapter (VGA) or Super VGA from the Models list. If you are not sure whether your monitor is Super VGA capable, choose the VGA option.

Video cards can pose real problems with Windows 95 if you do not have a driver that works with Windows 95. If you have problems with your video card, try using Windows 95's built-in VGA driver. You can change to this by pressing F8 at bootup and selecting the Safe Mode option.

I can't seem to move the slider in the Desktop area frame in any direction. The Less and More labels appear to be dimmed.

The points along the slider at which you can stop it are determined by the capabilities of your video card and monitor. If your video card and monitor are only capable of one setting, you cannot move the slider in the Desktop area frame at all. The labels Less and More at each end of the slider appear dimmed if your video adapter and monitor are not capable of multiple resolution settings.

When I installed my sound card in Windows 95, it automatically configured the interrupts (IRQs) for it, but the wrong settings were established.

You might want to use the sound board's own installation program instead, because the wizard can sometimes run into problems identifying the correct interrupts for some components.

Sound-related problems can be varied and frustrating, as the following random sample of conflicts illustrate:

- Common settings problems, such as an IRQ conflict or a wrong DMA channel selected, can result in no sound coming out at all. A wrong DMA driver setting may also result in distorted WAV file playback.

- If WAV file sounds repeat when you are using a sound card, you may have a defective parallel port card.

- If you hear a hissing during the playback of a sound file, the file may be recording in 8 bits and playing back in 16 bits. The 16-bit board doesn't realize that the 8-bit file isn't the same high quality as a 16-bit file, so playing the file with expectations of higher sound quality emphasizes the lower detail.

- You may need to switch to using a low DMA setting if your system hangs during a 16-bit digitized sound test, but an 8-bit test works fine. This result means your system cannot handle high DMA at full speed.

- Playing sound files on a slow PC can often lead to problems. For example, playing compressed WAV files results in less performance because of the amount of processor-power required to decompress them.

- If you are trying to play video with sound and it isn't synchronized, you may have a computer that isn't fast enough. You can try improving performance and adding RAM. But if you have an older, slower processor and a relatively slow hard drive, you may need to think about upgrading to a new PC with fast video capabilities built in.

How can I change my keyboard's layout in Windows 95?

You can change the layout of your keyboard via the Keyboard Properties sheet from the Control Panel.

V

Appendixes

Use the following steps:

1. Click the Language page.

2. Select the language and keyboard layout that you want to change.

3. Click the Properties button. The Language Properties sheet appears.

4. Select the new keyboard layout from the Keyboard layout list.

5. Click OK.

How do I delete a keyboard language or layout from Windows 95?

You can also delete a language or layout from the Keyboard Properties sheet from Control Panel. Having displayed the Language page, do the following:

1. Select the language and layout you want to delete from the Installed Keyboard Languages and Layouts list.

2. Click the Remove button.

3. Click OK.

How do I add a new keyboard language or layout to Windows 95?

You can select a different keyboard layout or language using the Keyboard Properties sheet in Control Panel. After you display the Language page, do the following:

1. Click the Add button. The Add Language panel appears.

2. Select the language you want from the drop-down Language list.

3. Click OK.

4. Select the language you want to use as your primary language from the list.

5. Click the Set as Default button.

6. Click OK.

I switch between keyboard languages a great deal. Do I have to go through all these steps each time?

At the bottom of the Language page on the Keyboard Properties sheet is an option box called Enable Indicator on Taskbar. If this is checked, an indicator called En appears on the Windows 95 taskbar at the bottom of the main screen. To quickly change between languages, click this indicator and a list of available languages appears. You can instantly switch between available languages by clicking the language you want from that En list.

How do I change the cursor blink rate?

After accessing the Keyboard Properties sheet, click the Speed page. Adjust the cursor blinking speed by dragging the Cursor Blink Rate Slider to the right to make it faster, or to the left to slow it down. Click OK.

I'm left-handed, but my mouse is set up to cater to the right-handed user. Can I change this?

To set the pointing device as a left-handed device, click the Left-Handed radio button in the Button Configuration group box. Conversely, to set it as a right-handed device, click the Right-Handed radio button in the group box.

I set up a pointer scheme but I want to return to my original. How do I do this?

If you want to reset all your pointers to their defaults, use the Scheme drop-down list and set the scheme name to (None).

My pointer seems to move slow or jerky around the screen. What's wrong?

It all boils down to your computer being very busy performing a task. Or, if you have shared a folder on your hard drive using file sharing, they may be heavily reading and writing information in it. Use the Net Watcher application to see who is connected to your computer. You can install the Net Watcher by using the Add/Remove Programs option in Control Panel and clicking the Windows Setup page. Select Accessories and click Details. In the list of components, select Net Watcher. You may need your Windows 95 installation disks or CD-ROM.

My pointer moves in one direction but not another. Help!

Try cleaning your mouse ball, track ball, and/or any internal motion contacts (usually small plastic wheels). If you're using a mouse, clean the glide pads on the bottom (if you have them). If you use a mouse pad, be sure to clean it regularly to prevent a build-up of dirt.

My pointer moves erratically. Why?

If, when you shake the cable, it makes the situation better or worse, verify that the connection to your computer is secure. Sometimes, the connector has come loose from the port on your computer.

Inspect the cable for breaks or cuts. If your cable is broken or pierced, repair or replacement is necessary. If there are no visible breaks, a wire inside the cable may have broken. This may have been caused by severe twisting of the cable, being placed under a heavy object for long periods of time, or a heavy object may have been dropped on it (for example, a paperweight or stapler).

It's not the cable or connection. What else can cause it to move erratically?

Check the Windows Driver Library (WDL) for an updated driver for your pointing device. The WDL is an electronic library of drivers which is updated as new ones become available. You can access the WDL via the Microsoft Network (MSN) in the Windows 95 area; CompuServe via **GO MSL**; the Internet via World Wide Web or Gopher (both at **http://www.microsoft. com**), or FTP (**ftp://ftp.microsoft.com**); or via the Microsoft Download Service at (206) 936-6735 (you only pay for the phone call).

I installed the CD-ROM and Windows support, but the CD-ROM still doesn't work.

The most common reason for the CD-ROM not working correctly is a conflict with another device on your system. Open Control Panel (from the Start menu) and start the System option. Select the Device Manager page to display the list of the devices on your system.

Double-click the CD-ROM entry in the list, and then select your CD-ROM device. Click the Properties button to display the settings for your CD-ROM. The Device Status area generally tells you if there is a problem with your CD-ROM device. Clicking the Resources page shows you the current settings; this page also tells you if one of the settings for your CD-ROM conflicts with another device in your system.

If there is a conflict with another device in your system, you have to change one of the hardware settings (such as the Interrupt Request, Input/Output range, or Direct memory access) to another value. Consult the manual for your CD-ROM drive to determine which values for these settings are legal for your drive.

Once you know which settings you can set your CD-ROM drive to, you have to determine which hardware settings are available on your system. One good way to find out the settings that are in use on your system is to click the Print button on the main Device Manager page. This allows you to print out a summary of all the resources on your system—you can easily find an unused value.

How do I control automatic playing of audio compact discs?

One of the new features of Windows 95 is the capability of the system to automatically recognize and play audio compact discs when they are inserted in the CD-ROM drive. This feature can be controlled from the Properties sheet for your CD-ROM drive. Double-click the My Computer icon on your desktop and then right-click your CD-ROM drive icon. Select Properties from the list and then click the Settings page from the Properties sheet.

On the Settings page, you see an option called Auto Insert Notification. If this option is checked, the system automatically plays audio compact discs when they are inserted. Deselect this option if you don't want this to happen.

How do I change the drive letter that is assigned to my CD-ROM drive?

By default, Windows 95 assigns drive letter D to your CD-ROM drive, unless you have another hard drive installed. You can change this from the Properties sheet for your drive. Bring up the Properties sheet and select the Settings page. You see the setting for Current Drive Letter Assigned; changing this changes the drive letter assigned to your CD-ROM drive.

I've changed the drive letter for my CD-ROM. What problems can occur now?

Note that if you change the drive letter assigned to your CD-ROM drive, it may force other drives you have mounted (such as network disks) to change to other drive letters, also. This may affect some of your shortcuts or software if they assume that your data was stored on a particular drive letter.

My CD-ROM drive seems slow. How can I speed it up?

Windows 95 has several settings that affect how it deals with CD-ROM drives, some of which can affect how fast data is transferred from the CD-ROM drive to the system. You can check these settings by starting the System control panel and selecting the Performance page. Click the File System button and then select the CD-ROM tab from this page.

The two settings on this page affect how much data Windows 95 stores in memory when reading from your CD-ROM drive. You should keep the supplemental cache size as large as possible (keeping the slider bar as far to the right as possible) unless you are running short of memory.

You should also set the Optimize Access Pattern For option to the type of CD-ROM drive you have (double-speed, for example). When you are finished changing these settings, click OK.

I've installed a new hard disk but Windows 95 does not recognize it. Why?

Your hard disk drive cable may be defective. Replace the cable with another one to see if the problem is resolved.

Another problem may be that the hard disk drive cable is installed improperly for a single hard disk drive system. Ensure the hard disk cable has the twist in the center of the cable near the connector to your disk drive. This is how hard disk drive C is identified. The remaining connector is attached to the hard disk drive controller.

If the hard disk drive cable is connected properly and the hard disk drive is not working properly, the fault may be with the hard disk drive. Install a different hard disk drive and see if the problem is resolved. On the other hand, if the hard disk drive cable is connected properly and the hard disk drive is working properly (it was tested on another computer), the fault may be with the hard disk drive controller. Install a different hard disk drive controller and see if the problem is resolved.

I'm looking at the Device Manager and it shows I have two floppy disk drives, but I have only one on my computer. What should I do?

As you set up Windows 95 or when you added a new floppy disk drive, a second floppy disk controller was added but only one is installed. To resolve this problem, highlight the line with the red X in it and click the Remove button on the bottom of the display.

I can't see the tape drive from within Microsoft Backup for Windows. Why not?

You may not be using a supported tape drive unit. Microsoft Backup for Windows only supports QIC-40, QIC-80, QIC-3010, and Trakker parallel-port backup systems. If you have some other tape drive, you need to use the manufacturer's backup software.

The tape system I use is supposed to hold 250M on a tape, but sometimes I can only get 150M on one tape. Why?

The tape drive manufacturers often inflate their capacity claims to match an estimated 2:1 compression ratio. Your tape probably can only hold 120M of uncompressed data. If you are experiencing less than a 2:1 compression ratio with the particular files you are backing up, your actual tape capacity will be less.

I can't schedule a backup to happen at night using Microsoft Backup for Windows. Why not?

Microsoft Backup for Windows does not directly support a scheduled backup. You may want to purchase another tape backup software package which does, or purchase Microsoft Plus! Companion for Windows 95 which contains a scheduling program, System Agent.

After I installed my scanner, I can't seem to scan anything into my word processor. What's wrong?

If you are not using the scanning software, you won't be able to scan anything into your word processor. If you are trying to scan text from a document into the word processor, you need to use special software which uses Optical Character Recognition (OCR) to actually convert the image into text data. This software may have been shipped with your scanner, so you should review the operation of the OCR software and its usage for scanning into word processing documents.

I bought a scanner to do OCR, but I never thought I'd have to do so much re-typing. Why can't the computer do a better job at reading the documents into my word processor?

It sounds like your expectations were a little too high for this technology. While some OCR software can read text with 99.7 percent accuracy, that still means that you could have between 5 to 10 errors on a "good" page and many more on a page with illegible writing or poor text quality. OCR is wonderful technology, but don't expect it to replace your secretary any time soon.

I seem to have lost all of my images in my digital camera that I took only yesterday. What happened? Is my camera or battery bad?

Affordable digital cameras use a flash memory system to store the images. The memory must be refreshed every so often to maintain the images. Logitech estimates that each image consumes 3 percent of the battery life per day. If you have 30 pictures stored in your camera, you may have exhausted the battery just by not retrieving your images sooner.

I can hear the modem sending tones as it dials, but nothing happens afterwards.

Check the telephone cables to be sure they're properly connected to the modem and to the wall jack. Verify the modem is dialing with pulses or tone by checking the Dialing Properties sheet.

I can hear my call being answered at the other end, but there's no tone indicating a connection.

The modem on the other end of the line is not working correctly or there is no modem there. You need to contact the person on the other end of the line to see if there is a problem, or try calling later.

Why do I see data errors on-screen after I've made a connection to another modem?

Make certain no one else is using the telephone line. Try calling the other modem again at another time or from a different phone line to get a better connection.

I can't get my modem to sign on to the remote modem. Why not?

Check the communication parameters of the remote station and make sure your software is configured for the same number of data bits, stop bits, and parity. You can access these settings by using the properties sheet of your modem, selecting the Connection page, and filling in the Connection Preferences area.

My modem connects with the remote modem but locks up.

Make sure you are using the proper modem-to-computer flow control and error control for your modem (click the Advanced button in the Connection page of the specific modem's properties sheet).

My modem disconnects while online. Why?

Check for loose connections between the modem and the computer, and between the modem and the telephone line. Alternatively, line noise or interference may be the problem; try the connection again with a different phone line or at a different time.

How do I start the Windows 95 Modem Troubleshooter?

Windows includes a Modem Troubleshooter you can use to help you diagnose a modem problem. To open the troubleshooter, open the Modems Properties sheet and choose the Diagnostics page. Choose the <u>H</u>elp button and the Windows Help window appears. Follow the directions on-screen to try to solve your modem problems.

Why do I hear sounds when I use Windows 95?

When you installed Windows, a default set of sounds and events was chosen for you. You can change these by selecting the Sounds program in the Windows 95 Control Panel. On the Sounds Properties sheet, click on a sound and assign it to a Windows 95 event. Click OK.

I can't hear sounds when I'm using Windows 95.

Check the volume of your speakers. If you see a speaker icon on the Windows 95 taskbar, double-click it and set the volume controls. Make sure the <u>M</u>ute All check box is cleared. If a speaker icon does not appear, double-click the Multimedia icon in the Control Panel. On the Volume page, adjust the volume controls.

I have the Microsoft Plus! Companion for Windows 95 software. Can I reassign some of the event sounds for Desktop Themes?

If you've installed Microsoft Plus!, your initial scheme name is blank. The Desktop Themes control panel takes care of your event sound assignments for you. But, feel free to change individual sounds at any time.

I've deleted a sound scheme. Is the sound file deleted as well?

No, deleting the scheme does not delete the actual sound file, just the connection between the event and which sound to play. You must use the Explorer or DOS to delete the actual sound file.

I can't get MIDI files to play back properly.

There can be a number of reasons. To start with, check the card's resource settings, such as IRQ settings, to make sure they are configured correctly for your specific MIDI board. Then make sure the MIDI board is correctly identified in Device Manager.

There is hissing and distortion when playing MIDI files. How can I get rid of it?

There may be interference coming from either the power source or another card installed in your computer. Turn your PC off and move the MIDI board as far away from both the power supply and other boards as possible. If you can, leave a few empty expansion slots in between the MIDI board and the next card.

When I print, the quality is low. How can I change this in Windows 95?

If the print quality is poor for graphics, make adjustments to the Graphics page of the printer's properties sheet. If text quality is poor, adjust the print quality settings in the Device Options page of the printer's properties sheet.

My printer does not support complex printing. What can I do?

If your printer does not print a complex page or divides graphics onto two or more pages, try changing the Printer Memory Tracking in the Device Options page of the printer's properties sheet. If you still have trouble, consider adding more memory to your printer.

Why does it take my application so long to print?

You may have the printer spooler turned off. Turn it on by opening the Printers folder in Control Panel. Click the icon for the printer you are using, click the File menu, and then click Properties. Click the Details page, and then click Spool Settings. Try printing your document again.

Why does it take a long time for my document to come out of the printer?

You may need to turn spooling off. If spooling is turned on and Spool Data Format is set to EMF, try changing the setting to RAW. You also can try turning spooling off by clicking Print Directly to the Printer. You might also need to lower the printing resolution of your printer. Open the property sheet for the printer you are using and click on the Graphics page. Select a lower resolution in the Resolution drop-down list.

Should I change the setting on my network card before I try setting up?

If there are default positions for any settings on the NIC, you should leave the settings at their default. In general, Windows 95 will first look for devices at their default settings. The only time you need to change the settings from their default is if there is a conflict with some other device in your system.

Should I let Windows 95 detect my network hardware?

If you let the Windows 95 wizard automatically detect your installed hardware, it is possible that it may find more than one new hardware component on your system. If all you installed is a network card, you may want to click the Cancel button and restart the wizard, using the Install Specific Hardware option.

My network card is not listed in the Network Hardware Wizard. Why not?

Depending on the version of Windows 95 you are running, this list of manufacturers and drives may be different. As Windows 95 matures, more types of hardware will be recognized by the wizard. If no Windows 95 drivers are available for your NIC, you can use the regular Windows drivers for your drive. See the instructions from your card and the Windows 95 documentation for help with installing and using Windows/DOS drivers with Windows 95.

I installed the NIC and Windows support, but the card still doesn't work.

The most common reason for the network card not working correctly is a conflict with another device on your system. Open the Control Panel (from the Start button) and start the System control panel. Select the Device Manager page to display the list of the devices on your system.

Double-click the Network Adapters entry in the list, and then select your network device. Click the Properties button to display the settings for your network card. The Device Status area generally tells you if there is a problem with your network device. Clicking the Resources page shows you the current settings; this page also tells you if one of the settings for your NIC conflicts with another device in your system.

Also, if you are using the Microsoft Network as your network operating system, you can use only 32-bit NICs. If you have a 16-bit card, you need to obtain a new card or install a new network operating system, such as NetWare, to your workgroup.

How can I find out the hardware settings for my network card?

If there is a conflict with another device in your system, you have to change one of the hardware settings (such as the Interrupt Request, Input/Output range or Direct Memory Access) to another value. You should consult the manual for your network card to determine which values for these settings

V

Appendixes

are legal for your card. Once you know which settings you can set your network card to, you have to determine which hardware settings are available on your system. One good way to find out the settings that are in use on your system is to click the Print button on the main Device Manager page. This enables you to print out a summary of all the resources on your system. From this printout, you should be able to find an unused value.

When I browse my network, I don't see the other computers around me.

First, look at the entire network item in the Network Neighborhood browser to see if there are any other workgroups available. If there are, and there are computers in those workgroups, then you should make sure that your computer belongs to the correct workgroup.

Start the Network application in the Windows 95 control panel, and look under the Identification page. On this page, you can set your computer's workgroup and computer name. You should check with your network administrator for the workgroups that are available to you.

If you don't see any other workgroups (and you are sure that your network card is working correctly), you should make sure that you are logged into your network correctly. If you did not log into your computer (for example, there was a network login box displayed when your computer booted and you clicked Cancel), then you don't see other workgroups in the Network Neighborhood.

I use the network, but TCP/IP doesn't work. Why not?

◀ See "Configuring an Internet Connection," p. 289

The TCP/IP support in Windows 95 must be installed separately. The following instructions briefly describe how to set up TCP/IP support.

You need to find out if your network is using a DHCP server to allocate IP addresses automatically. If not, you need to obtain your specific IP address. You can find out this information from your network administrator. Next, in Control Panel, double-click the Network icon and click the Configuration page. Click Add, double-click Protocol, and click Microsoft. Click TCP/IP. After TCP/IP installs, you need to configure it using the settings from your system administrator. Afterwards, you need to reboot your system for these settings to take effect.

Microsoft Exchange and Fax

Microsoft Exchange is destined to revolutionize the way Windows users communicate with each other. Windows 95 includes the Exchange server that consolidates all your e-mail and fax messages. This section describes some of the common problems with Exchange and Windows 95's built-in fax software, Microsoft Fax.

When Exchange starts, I receive error messages saying that my Internet Mail server is not available. I don't have an Internet Mail server, and don't use Internet Mail. What's wrong?

You probably have installed Microsoft Plus! Companion for Windows 95 and ran the Internet Wizard, which installed the Internet Mail service provider. Open Control Panel and click the Mail and Fax icon. From the list of installed services, choose Internet Mail, then choose Remove. Windows 95 prompts you to verify that you want to remove the Internet Mail service provider from your profile. Choose Yes to remove the service from your profile.

I would like to add a second Personal Information Store to my profile, but Exchange tells me I can only have one in a profile. Is it possible to add another?

You can only have one Personal Information Store in a profile, but you can add as many Personal Folders to a profile as you like. Personal Folders are essentially identical to the Personal Information Store. The only difference is that your incoming mail is directed into the Personal Information Store. If you simply want more places to segregate your incoming mail, create new folders in your Personal Information Store instead of adding Personal Folders to your profile. You can create as many additional folders in the PST as you like. To create a new folder, open the folder in which you want the new folder created. Then, choose File, New Folder. Exchange displays a dialog box in which you enter the name for the new folder. Then, you can drag messages to the new folder as you desire.

I created an administrator account for the WGPO, but I've forgotten the password. Can I reassign another account as the WGPO administrator account?

Unfortunately, there's no way to change the administrator account. Unless you can recall the password, you have no way of gaining access to the account or administering the WGPO. Fortunately, new users can create their

V

Appendixes

own mail accounts in the WGPO, so new and existing users alike can continue to use the WGPO while you attempt to resolve the problem. First, direct all users to back up their message folders. A simple way to do this is to make a backup copy of their PST file. Any users who store their messages in the WGPO instead of locally must copy their messages to a local folder. When all users' messages are backed up, delete the WGPO and recreate it, making sure to create an administrator account with a password you can remember. Re-create all of the user accounts in the WGPO.

I configured the CompuServe Mail provider to check for messages at 8 a.m. and every four hours. But, Exchange doesn't check at 8, 12, 4, and so on. It checks for mail at 8 a.m., but the four-hour interval falls at odd times. Why is this?

The CompuServe Mail provider doesn't base its interval connection times on the explicit 8 AM setting you've specified. Instead, the provider checks at four-hour intervals based on the last time it automatically checked for mail. Open Control Panel and click the Mail and Fax icon. Select the CompuServe Mail provider and choose Properties. Choose Advanced, Schedule Connect Times to display the Connection Times dialog box. Clear the Every check box and close the dialog box, then close the Profile property sheets. Shortly before the time when you want one of your hourly-interval connections to be made, open the Control Panel, click the Mail and Fax icon, then enable the Every check box in the Connection Times dialog box and specify the interval you want to use. Close the property sheets. Exchange should then connect close to the time you want.

I can't get Microsoft Fax to install properly. What should I do?

First, make sure you have Microsoft Exchange installed. If you do not, read Chapter 9, "Configuring Microsoft Exchange." If you do, you need to make sure that your fax modem is installed and working. Also, send a test fax to a fax machine that you know is working properly. If it faxes fine, your original phone number may be wrong. Make sure that your phone number is set up to call outside lines, if your phone requires this. Another thing you should do is disable call waiting before you make a call or before you receive an incoming fax.

I want to configure Exchange, but I'm not sure what information stores are.

Information stores and address books are service providers, just like the Microsoft Mail, CompuServe, and other service providers. All of these service providers are often referred to as just *services*.

I'm not near a printer but I need to print out a document. How can I do this?

Microsoft Fax includes fax printer drivers so that you can print to a fax machine from within any Windows application. If you are in a hotel or traveling and have access to a fax machine, send a document to the fax machine to get a hard copy of it.

I received a fax with Microsoft Fax, but I don't know where it is.

The Microsoft Exchange universal Inbox is where fax messages are stored. Double-click the Inbox icon on your desktop to start Exchange.

Norton Utilities

Norton Utilities for Windows 95 is a package of data protection and recovery utility programs designed specifically for Windows 95. Use this section to troubleshoot some of the common problems associated with Norton Utilities.

What if the system hangs while running Norton Diagnostics? Do I have to start all over again?

If your system crashes or freezes during a test, reboot your machine and restart NDIAGS. This time, instead of restarting all the tests, use the menus to restart the test that the computer failed on. Norton Diagnostics tracks where it was at in the testing and attempts to further diagnose what caused the failure.

I accidentally deleted some important files using SpaceWizard. What now?

Not to worry—you can run the DOS version of UNERASE to recover any files you inadvertently deleted.

Can I re-run Image on a damaged drive?

If you run Image on a damaged drive, don't re-run it or you will destroy your backup copy. Instead, delete the IMAGE.DAT file (which won't be any good) and rename IMAGE.BAK to **IMAGE.DAT**.

Tip

If you need a break from troubleshooting, start the Windows 95 Easter egg by using the following steps:

1. Right-click the Desktop, choose New, Folder, and name it **And now, the moment you've been waiting for**.

2. Next, right-click the folder, choose Rename, and enter **We proudly present for your viewing pleasure**.

3. Right-click the folder again and rename it **The Microsoft Windows 95 Product Team!**.

4. Open the folder and watch the credits of the Windows 95 developers. You'll need a sound card to hear the music.

What's on the CD

by Rob Tidrow

The CD-ROM included with this book contains a variety of software programs developed for Windows 95. The software includes productivity tools, animated cursors and icons, Windows 95 shell replacements, and a few entertainment packages. This appendix gives a brief explanation of each application and lists the file you need to install or run the application.

Accessing the Software

Each of the software programs is set up in its own folder on the CD-ROM. To install a package, copy its folder onto your hard drive and then double-click the setup or application executable file listed in this appendix. As an example, to install the Barry Press Utilities, copy the BPUTIL folder to your hard drive and double-click the SETUP.EXE file. Follow the setup instructions on the screen.

> **Tip**
>
> Many of these utilities require the file VBRUN300.DLL to run. Before you install anything from this disk, copy this file from the CD-ROM's root directory to your Windows system folder, then reboot your computer. You only need to install this file once.

What's Included?

The software on the CD is organized alphabetically to help you locate each item quickly. To install all the programs on your system, you will need approximately 40-45M of free disk space, depending on the options you can install for some of the utilities. For additional information for each application, read the README.TXT or similar files included with many of the programs.

The following sections briefly describe each of the programs on the CD.

Accent 3.0

Accent enables you to input special characters that are not normally found on a regular keyboard. These characters include accented characters, called *diacritics*, and other special symbols such as the copyright sign © or the trademark sign ™.

File name: ACCENT\ACCENT.EXE

> pro++ Software
> Gilles Gervais
> 8045 Place Saguenay
> Brossard, Quebec
> Canada, J4X 1N2
> CompuServe: **72571,724**
> Phone: (514) 465-9306

Add Applications v3.1

This is a 32-bit application for Windows 95, Windows NT, and Win32s to help you migrate groups and program icons to new users, move groups from Windows 3.1 to Windows 95 or NT, and more. You can search disks and CD-ROMs to migration applications, icons, and bitmaps to Program Manager or the Windows 95 Desktop.

File name: ADDAPP\ADDAPP.EXE

> Timothy D.A. Cox
> TDAC Software, Inc.
> 12 Miner Circle
> Markham Ontario
> Canada, L3R 1Y2
> CompuServe: **70353,3403**
> Internet: **cox@io.org**
> Phone: (905) 940-1529

Background Noise v1.52

Background Noise is a robust Win32 MCI media player that runs under Windows 95 or Windows NT. Version 1.52 supports Microsoft Video, CD Audio, WAV, and MIDI files. You can create Sound Object Lists of any length and combination, and from more than one device. Hot Keys let you control Background Noise to instantly play predefined selections, skip the current song, or start/stop the playing Sound Object List.

File name: BN\SETUP.EXE

> P&J's Software
> 14150 NE 20th
> Box 277
> Bellevue, WA 98007
> CompuServe: **71303,2375**

The Barry Press Utilities

This is the public release of the shareware Barry Press Utilities for Windows 95 that includes a monthly calendar (CalPop), drag-and-drop ASCII file printer (CodeList), printer-orientation utility (Flipper), ASCII file comparison program (Match), shell extension to add a command line option to Explorer (Runner), digital clock (Time), and multimedia file player (Waver).

File name: BPUTILS\SETUP.EXE

> Barry Press
> 2494 East Cheshire Drive
> Sandy, UT 84093-1849
> CompuServe: **72467,2353**

BmpView 1.0

BmpView 1.0 is a fast 32-bit viewing program that helps you locate BMP files on your system. When you find a BMP file you want to edit, click on it to activate a BMP editor, such as MS Paint. You also can scroll through an entire directory of BMPs to locate the one you need.

File name: BMPVIEW\BMPVIEW.EXE

> Daniel Brum
> 3219 Yonge St., Office 226
> Toronto, Ontario,
> Canada M4N-2L3
> CompuServe: **74762,315**

Capture Professional 2.0

Capture Professional 2.0 is a demo of an advanced screen capture tool for Windows 95 and Windows 3.1. Capture Professional 2.0 features seven capture modes (Window, Client Area, Region, Oval, Rectangle, Desktop, and Icon). You can set up hot keys for each mode to activate them from any Windows application. Capture Professional enables you to save screen captures with 2, 16, 256, and 16.7M colors in the following file formats: BMP, EPS, GIF, ICO, JPG, PCX, RLE, TGA, and TIF. It can import six file formats for viewing, touch-up (more than 20 effects), or conversions to other file formats.

File name: CAPPRO\SETUP.EXE

> Creative Software
> 2003 Lake Park Drive, Suite G
> Smyrna, GA 30080
> CompuServe: **74011,206**
> Phone: (800) 680-9679
> Fax: (800) 430-9679

CD Wizzard CD Player

CD Wizzard is a shareware CD player for Windows 95 that includes a flexible database system and customizable interface. The Disc Database enables you to search for artist, composer, track name, and other search criteria for a particular CD.

File name: CDWIZZRD\CDW.EXE

> BFM Software
> Brett McDonald
> 38602 Lancaster Drive
> Farmington Hills, MI 48331
> CompuServe: **73770,1254**
> America Online: **BrettMc**
> Phone: (810) 661-1797

Collection of 154 Animated Icons

Enhance the look of your Windows desktop with this collection of 154 public domain animated icons collected from various Windows 95 and Windows NT CompuServe forums.

Folder name: 154ICONS

Drag and File

Drag and File v1 For Windows 95 provides powerful Windows File Manager support—it can list files for an entire drive or for multiple drives and directories. It includes a configurable toolbar, built-in DOS command line, and file descriptions in DOS format. You can use context menus and create shortcuts. It even supports network connections.

File name: DRAGFILE\DFSETUP.EXE

> Canyon Software
> 1537 Fourth St., Suite 131
> San Rafael, CA 94901
> CompuServe: **74774,554**
> Phone: (415) 382-7999
> Fax: (415) 382-7998

Drag and Zip

Drag and Zip appears when you run File Manager. You can drag a set of files to the icon on the desktop, specify the ZIP file name, and create a ZIP file or a self-extracting ZIP file that includes all the specified files. You can also drag a ZIP file to the icon or double-click on a ZIP file to display the contents. From the contents window, you can selectively extract (decompress) files, or extract them all. Provided by author, member ASP.

File name: DRAGZIP\DZSETUP.EXE

> Canyon Software
> 1537 Fourth St., Suite 131
> San Rafael, CA 94901
> CompuServe: **74774,554**
> Phone: (415) 382-7999
> Fax: (415) 382-7998

Easy Icons 95

Easy Icons 95 is an Icon Management program that enables you to create icon library files and drag-and-drop files between libraries. With Easy Icons 95, you can open many files at once, as well as extract or view any icon(s) from any file and save it as a separate ICO) or BMP) file. Requires the file VBRUN300.DLL.

File name: EASYICON\EASYICON.EXE

> Paul Traver
> P.O. Box 998
> Bishop, CA 93514
> CompuServe: **72144,422**
> Phone: (619) 873-8754

FaxMail v4.17

FaxMail for Windows enables you to fax from Windows applications (such as Word for Windows) as easily as printing. It does this by adding a Fax button to Windows programs, giving you access to all fax modems or fax machines connected to your computer. Among other features, FaxMail enables you to import up to 1,000 names and phone numbers into each FaxBook phone book using any xBase database. To install FaxMail, you must run INSTALL.EXE from the CD-ROM.

File name: FAXMAIL\INSTALL.EXE

> Jon Krahmer
> Electrasoft
> 3207 Carmel Valley Drive
> Missouri City, TX 77459-3068
> CompuServe: **74464,763**

First Aid 95

First Aid 95 helps you maintain the health of your PC by automatically iden-tifying and fixing more than 10,000 known problems. Exclusive AutoFix technology automatically alerts you when it senses trouble, explains the problem in plain English, and fixes the problem. First Aid fixes GPFs, crashes, multimedia conflicts, Internet access problems, and other performance prob-lems. You also can use First Aid 95 to safely remove features of applications that you never use (or compress them until needed) and help you tweak setup parameters to boost overall system performance. This is a utility that you should install right away.

File name: FIRSTAID\SETUP.EXE

> CyberMedia
> 1800 Century Park East, Suite 1145
> Los Angeles, CA 90067
> Phone: (310) 843-0800
> Fax: (310) 843-0120

FracView 2

FracView 2 v2.01 for Windows 95 plots the Mandelbrot set and enables you to zoom in on a region for closer examination. You can copy the content to the Clipboard to paste into other applications.

File name: FRACVIEW\SETUP.EXE

> Pocket-Sized Software
> 8547 E. Arapahoe Road, Suite J-147
> Greenwood Village, CO 80112
> CompuServe: **73667,3517**

GrabIt Pro 5.0

GrabIt Pro is a Windows 95 application that enables you to capture a screen, a window, a portion of a window, and a menu. You can select user-defined areas, include child windows and mouse cursors, and select the number of colors in which to save the screen capture. You can use the preview feature to view a file before opening it.

File name: GRABIT\GPSETUP.EXE

> Software Excellence by Design, Inc.
> 14801 North 12th Street
> Phoenix, AZ 85022-2515
> CompuServe: **7220,576**

Gravity Well 3.4

Gravity Well is a fast-paced action/strategy game. You must pilot a space ship between planets, leading your empire to expand. Planets orbit stars and exert gravity upon your ship. Three computer opponents compete for the same region of space.

File name: GRAVWELL\GWELL32.EXE

> David Hoeft
> Software Engineering, Inc.
> 8352 S. Sunnyside Place
> Highlands Ranch, CO 80126
> CompuServe: **102330,474**
> Internet: **DaveH@FreeHome.com**
> Phone: (303) 470-7142

Hyper CD

HyperCD is one of the smallest CD audio players for Windows 95 and NT. It's also one of the easiest to use, letting you play, pause, eject, and stop your audio CDs. HyperCD features buttons and controls, and sits on the Windows 95 taskbar when executed.

File name: HYPERCD\HYPERC.EXE

> Lou Schillaci (courtesy of HyperDyne 2000)
> 26/25 Devonshire Street
> Chatswood, Sydney
> N.S.W. 2067
> Australia
> CompuServe: **76702,1774**

IFA v4.00.2

Instant File Access adds many time-saving features to the File dialogs of all Windows applications, such as Previous File History, a Toolbar, File Find, and Floating file lists. Give LONG NAMES to your Windows 3.1 files with Instant File Access. Great for Word and Excel. Now works with 16-bit applications under Windows 95.

File name: IFA400\SETUP.EXE

> Michael Mondry
> Alexoft
> 507 de la Metaire
> Nun's Island, Quebec
> Canada, H3E 1S4
> CompuServe: **72154,15**

Launchpad 95 v1.0

Shift into high gear with Windows 95 by using Launchpad 95. Easily associate folders with the launchpad and use Launchpad 95 to quickly launch applications from the Windows 95 Desktop. You can use this utility to execute the programs of your choice (such as the programs you use most) much faster than the usual process of navigating through nested menus or nested folders.

File name: LAUNCH\SETUP.EXE

> Prasad Thammineni
> CompuServe: **102706,3167**

Microangelo

Windows 95 unleashes the power of icon graphics—Microangelo helps you keep pace. In Windows 95, an icon is a "container" of multiple image formats from 16×16 to 48×48 in size, and up to 256 colors. Microangelo puts them all in your hand, supporting images from 8×8 to 64×64 pixels in depths to 256 colors. Microangelo finds them, copies them, creates them, and edits them.

File name: MICROANG\SETUP.EXE

> Len Gray
> Impact Software
> P.O. Box 457
> Chino, CA 91708
> CompuServe: **71630,1703**
> Phone: (909) 590-8522
> Fax: (909) 590-2202

MIDI Jukebox 2

MIDI Jukebox 2 plays multiple MIDI and WAV files either once or in a continuous loop. You can pause, play, or skip to the next or previous track.

File name: MIDIJB\SETUP.EXE

> Pocket-Sized Software
> 8547 E. Arapahoe Road, Suite J-147
> Greenwood Village, CO 80112
> CompuServe: **73667,3517**

Milestones, Etc. 4.5 (trial version)

There's only one way to keep a project on track: put it on a schedule. But who wants to struggle with complicated project management software? Milestones, Etc. is an easy and flexible project scheduling tool for Windows 95. Just type in each schedule step, drop a starting symbol into place with your mouse, and "click and drag" to the right to add the time span. Create anything from simple Gantt charts and Line-of-Balance charts to milestone schedules and detailed master schedules in minutes with presentation-quality output. Compatible with MS Project (reads and writes Project MPX files). Supports OLE 2.0 as a server, enabling you to link or embed your Milestones, Etc. schedules in other Windows applications.

File name: MILSTONES\DISK1\INSTALL.EXE

> KIDASA Software
> 1114 Lost Creek Blvd, Suite 300
> Austin, TX 78746
> CompuServe: **76702,1305**
> Phone: 800-765-0167/512-328-0167
> Fax: 512-328-0247

Plug-In for Windows v2.60

Plug-In for Windows is an enhancement utility that seamlessly integrates with Windows and works with any Windows Desktop. Major features include Control Center, where you can coordinate all of Plug-In's functions; title bar displays to show date, time, and resource usage; and Power Button, which gives instant access to Plug-In's QuickRun menu. This version works with Windows 95, but does not take full advantage of all of Windows 95's features. A new update is to be released in early 1996.

File name: PLUG_IN\PLUGIN.EXE

> Plannet Crafters
> P.O. Box 450
> Alpharetta, GA 30239-0450
> CompuServe: **73040,334**
> America Online: **DMandell**
> Prodigy: **VSFB48A**
> Microsoft Network: **PlanCraft**

PSA Cards 2.5

PSA Cards is an easy-to-use address program. It looks like a card file and it works like a card file. Just click a divider tab or card to open or close it. PSA Cards is also an OLE 2.0 container application, enabling you to link and embed pictures, maps, documents, sounds, and other objects. You can print Rolodex cards, envelopes, mailing labels, shipping labels, and address booklets from within PSA Cards 2.5. Be sure to read the README.TXT file to see all the features of PSA Cards.

File name: PSACARDS\SETUP.EXE

> William L. Rogers
> PSA Software
> 1319 Silk Oak Drive
> Fort Collins, CO 80525
> CompuServe: **72064,1437**

PolyView 1.8

PolyView is a very fast JPEG, GIF, BMP, and Photo-CD (PCD) viewer, with full 32-bit multithreading and supports of long file names. You can drag and drop graphic files from Explorer, File Manager, and other sources into PolyView. Features include the capability to zoom in and out through a chain of image magnifications, use the entire display screen to view an image, use the entire screen to automatically cycle through all the loaded images, resize an image to better utilize the available display, and more.

File name: POLYVIEW\POLYVIEW.EXE

Polybytes
3427 Bever Avenue S.E.
Cedar Rapids, IA 52403
CompuServe: **70222,300**
America Online: **PolyView**

Programmer's File Editor 6.01

PFE version 6.01 is a freeware programming editor and a replacement for Windows Notepad as a text editor. This version is for Windows 95 and the Intel version of Windows NT 3.5. PFE supports multiple files open at one time, drag and drop (for files and text), multilevel undos, most-recently-used file list, and much more. You also can use PFE to send files as e-mail using MAPI-compliant e-mail programs (such as Microsoft Mail).

File name: PROGEDIT\PFE32.EXE

Alan Phillips
Internet: **A.Phillips@lancaster.ac.uk**

Psychedelic Screen Saver Collection

The Psychedelic Screen Saver Collection v 1.0 is a collection of screen savers that generate hypnotic patterns on your Windows 95 Desktop. Included are 16- and 32-bit versions for Microsoft Windows 3.1, Windows 95, and Windows NT, as well as versions for Berkeley Systems' After Dark v2.0c.

Folder name: PSYCHSAV

Mike Irvine
Northstar Solutions
P.O. Box 25262
Columbia, SC 29224

CompuServe: **73323,2322** or **71561,2751**

Phone: 800-699-6395

Fax: 803-699-5465

QuickTutors 95

QuickTutors 95 consists of 40 minitutorials (five in this demo version) that cover important migration topics ranging from how to use the Windows 95 Explorer to how to activate a new modem. Once installed, QuickTutors 95 is immediately available on the Windows 95 Desktop to assist the user. The program leads you through certain tasks in Windows 95 and actually performs them for the user if desired. You can obtain the full version of QuickTutors 95 at local computer software retail stores via the Internet Shopping Network (**http://www.internet.net**), or via e-mail (**esales@ eticket.com**).

File name: QUICKTUT\SETUP.EXE

E-Ticket, Inc.
Attention: Mail Order Sales
2118 Wilshire Blvd., Suite 1118
Santa Monica, CA 90403-5784
Internet: **rgibson@eticket.com** or **esales@eticket.com**
Phone: (520) 577-2221
Fax: (520) 577-2896

SnapShot/32 Screen Capture

Capture entire desktop, individual window or client area, or draw rectangle to select using SnapShot/32. Print with optional reverse black and white, save to BMP or GIF, or copy to Clipboard. If you want to capture a menu pulled down, you can use the SnapShot/32 hot key support without causing the menu to close. When the capture is finished, you can view the image in the SnapShot/32 window. You then can copy the image to the Clipboard to be pasted into a Windows Device Independent Bitmap-compatible application for processing.

File name: SNAPSHOT\SNAP32.EXE

Greg Kochaniak
3146 Chestnut Street
Murrysville, PA 15668
CompuServe: **71461,631**
Internet: **gregko@kagi.com** (preferred)
Phone: (412) 325-4001 (evenings)

Somar ACTS V1.7

Somar ACTS v1.7 is a Windows 95 and Windows NT program that dials the NIST or USNO time source using a modem, obtains the current time, and uses this time to set the system time on your computer. You should note that similar programs designed for MS-DOS will not work under NT because of security issues.

File name: ACTSNT\ACTSNT.EXE

> Somar Software
> 1 Scott Circle, NW Suite 816
> Washington, DC 20036
> CompuServe: 72202,2574
> Internet: **framos@somar.com**
> Phone: (202) 232-3748

Stereograms 2

Stereograms 2 converts monochrome bitmap files into random-dot stereograms, which can be viewed on-screen or printed. A *stereogram* is a two-dimensional graphic that appears three-dimensional when viewed properly. Stereograms have been recently popularized by *The Magic Eye* and other books. Many newspapers include stereograms in their comics sections.

File name: ST_GRAMS\SETUP.EXE

> Pocket-Sized Software
> 8547 E. Arapahoe Road, Suite J-147
> Greenwood Village, CO 80112
> CompuServe: **73667,3517**

Talking Clock 2

Talking Clock 2 displays the time on your computer and optionally announces the time every 15 minutes, if you have a sound card installed.

File name: TCLOCK\SETUP.EXE

> Pocket-Sized Software
> 8547 E. Arapahoe Road, Suite J-147
> Greenwood Village, CO 80112
> CompuServe: **73667,3517**

V

Appendixes

TaskView V4.0

TaskView is a utility program for Windows 95 and Windows NT 3.51 that provides the capability to view and manage the active tasks currently operating on the computer. It is particularly useful for terminating programs that are no longer cooperative, as well as setting the priorities of operating tasks. If you use the new Windows 95 shell and miss the old Task Manager, this is the utility for you.

File name: TASKVIEW\SETUP.EXE

> Thomas Reed
> Reed Consulting
> 2312 Belvedere
> Toledo, OH 43614
> CompuServe: **76237,516**

TextPad 1.29

TextPad 1.29 is a 32-bit text editor to use with Windows 95. Some of its features include large file support, Universal Naming Convention (UNC) style name support, multiple file edits, automatic word-wrapping, and much more. You also can drag and drop text and files into TextPad.

File name: TEXTPAD\SETUP.EXE

> Helios Software Solutions
> Carr Brook House, Chorley Old Road
> Brindle, Chorley, Lancaster
> England PR6 7Q2
> CompuServe: **100041,235**
> Internet: **textpad@heliosof.demon.co.uk**
> Phone: +44-(0)1772-324353

TILER Image Viewer

TILER is a Windows NT and Windows 95 application that views and manages GIF, JPEG, and Windows BMP image files. Both the "87a" and "89a" versions of GIF are supported. If a GIF file contains more than one image, TILER loads only the first image. TILER can read 1-, 4-, 8-, and 24-bit Windows BMP files; both 4-bit and 8-bit compression is supported.

File name: TILER\TILER.EXE

> David Bowman
> 12050-H Little Patuxent Pkwy.

Columbia, MD 21044
CompuServe: **72057,3253**
Internet: **dbowman@access.digex.net**
America Online: **BowmanDave**

Tessler's Nifty Tools (TNT) v5.0

Tessler's Nifty Tools is a collection of more than 35 high-quality, low-cost Windows 95, NT, 3.1, and DOS programs for both the casual and power user who desires to increase their PC productivity and enjoyment. Some of the utilities available include Cfgcntrl, Grp2ini, Ifwait, Capstat, and others. Review the lengthy PAMPHLET.DOC file included in the TNT folder for more information on all the other utilities included.

Folder names: TNT\PACKAGE1, TNT\PACKAGE2, TNT\PACKAGE3

Gary Tessler
430 Canyon Woods Place, Suite A
San Ramon, CA 94583
CompuServe: **71044,542**

ToolPAL 2.1

ToolPAL 2.1 is a replacement for the Task Manager in Windows 95 and Windows 3.1. With ToolPALs, you can switch between Windows applications, create a launch list of frequently used programs, lock the selected window on the top of the Windows Desktop, set up multiple virtual desktops, move windows between them, and customize the way you use Windows using ToolPAL palettes, file folders, and buttons.

File name: TOOLPAL\SETUP.EXE

Art English
Digital Artistry
3509 Gary Drive
Plano, TX 75023-1266
CompuServe: **74777,1142**
Phone/Fax: (214) 232-3310

Voice Clock 2.02

Voice Clock is a speech clock that can announce the time every 1, 15, 30, or 60 minutes. It has high-quality sound, and includes a title bar clock, desktop clock, and resource clock. The clocks can be set instantly, and feature both male and female voices. Only the male voice is included with the version on the CD-ROM. When you register the product, you are given support for a female voice, too.

File name: VCLOCK\SETUP.EXE

Erwin Koonce
P.O. Box 308
Jacksonville, AR 72078
CompuServe: **72610,1375**

Win Bar Clock 4.1A

Win Bar Clock 4.1A is a utility for the Windows environment that displays information such as the time, date, system resources, or any text message in the title bar of the active window. You also can set it up as a floating bar clock on your system. Win Bar Clock can display date, time, memory, and system resources, display month calendar, and start programs from within any application using the Quick Execute command when you right-click on the clock.

File name: WBCLOCK\WCSETUP.EXE

G.L. Liadis & Associates
5167 1/2 Saling Court
Columbus, OH 43229
CompuServe: **72274,3252**
America Online: **GL Liadis**
BBS: **614-888-4749**

G.L. Liadis Software Inc.
Agali Beach Resort
Kardamyla
83100 Chios, Greece

Win Calculate v4.1+

Win Calculate is a programmer's RPN, a scientific calculator that lets you work with integers ranging from -1 to +2 billion, and includes support of decimal, hexadecimal, octal, and binary modes. You can calculate angles and degrees, logarithmic, trigometric, and hyperbolic values, and determine the cube root, square, and pi of numbers.

File name: WCALC.\WCALC.EXE

G.L. Liadis & Associates
5167 1/2 Saling Court
Columbus, OH 43229
CompuServe: **72274,3252**
America Online: **GL Liadis**
BBS: **614-888-4749**

G.L. Liadis Software Inc.
Agali Beach Resort
Kardamyla
83100 Chios, Greece

Win Calendar v4.1

Win Calendar is a freeware 3-D Windows calendar for Windows 3.11 and
Windows 95. Win Calendar displays in monthly format and lets you view
any month with one mouse click, or click Today to display the current day
and month.

File name: WINCAL\WCALENDR.EXE

G.L. Liadis & Associates   G.L. Liadis Software Inc.
5167 1/2 Saling Court   Agali Beach Resort
Columbus, OH 43229   Kardamyla
CompuServe: **72274,3252**   83100 Chios, Greece
America Online: **GL Liadis**
BBS: **614-888-4749**

Windows 95 and NT Screen Saver Pack

The Windows 95 and NT Screen Saver Pack extends the life of your computer
monitor with the following colorful screen savers: Clock, Dancing Lines,
HyperCycloids, Life, Snakes, Spheres, and Zoom. In addition, a demo of the
Photo Album screen saver is included. See the USERS_GD.WRI file in the
SCRNSAVS folder for more information.

Folder name: SCRNSAVS

Pocket-Sized Software
8547 E. Arapahoe Road, Suite J-147
Greenwood Village, CO 80112
CompuServe: **73667,3517**

Windows 95 Motion Cursors

This is a collection of 43 Motion Cursors to use with Windows 95.

Folder name: MOTION

James Snyder
Shattered Rose Studio
CompuServe: **75141,3544**

Wil DLL Extender Library

This is the latest version of the extender DLL library to add network and
other support to the Windows Interface Language (WIL) for WinBatch 5.x.

V

Appendixes

File name: WILDLL\WSETUP.EXE

Wilson WindowWare
2701 California Ave S.W., #212
Seattle, WA 98116
CompuServe: **76702,1072**

WinBatch 32 5.1c

WinBatch 32 is a 32-bit batch language to create batch files for Windows and replaces dozens of single-purpose utilities. WinBatch has more than 350 functions and includes structured programming features, improved network support, time functions, floating-point calculations, binary file access, registration database functions, child window support, and the capability to access third-party DLLs through DllCall.

File name: WINBATCH\WSETUP.EXE

Wilson WindowWare
2701 California Ave S.W., #212
Seattle, WA 98116
CompuServe: **76702,1072**

Windows Commander 2.0 Preview

Windows Commander is a file manager for Windows 95 similar to the Windows file manager WINFILE.EXE. The main difference between File Manager and Windows Commander is that Windows Commander uses two fixed windows. Windows Commander supports drag-and-drop file and print management; copying, moving, renaming, and deleting of entire trees; and a built-in file viewer to view files of any size in hex, binary, or text format. It also has an internal unzip utility by Info-Zip to quickly unzip files. To install Windows Commander, run the INSTALL.EXE file from the CD-ROM, not your hard disk.

File name: WINCMND\INSTALL.EXE

Christian Ghisler
Lindenmattstr. 60
CH-3065 Bolligen
Switzerland
CompuServe: **100332,1175**

WinImage 2.10a

WinImage 2.10a enables you to make disk images from floppy disks to blank floppy disks. It features a toolbar, status bar, and supports drag-and-drop. WinImage reads the images created by several third-party disk copy utilities, including Wimage (in FdFormat utility) from C.H. Hochstätter, CopyVit from Sébastien Chatard, DrDos 6 and OS/2 2.x diskimage utilities, DCF (Disk Copy Fast) from Chang Ping Lee, DF (Disk Image File Utility) from Mark Vitt, Super-DiskCopy from Super Software, SabDu from S.A. Berman, Disk-RW from K. Hartnegg, DiskDupe from Micro System Design, internal disk Microsoft and Lotus image utilities, and the MFMT sample Windows NT application that comes with Windows NT SDK.

File name: WINIMAGE\WINIMANT.EXE

> Gilles Vollant
> 13, rue Francios Mansart
> 91540 Mennecy
> France
> CompuServe: **100144,2636**

WinPack32 Deluxe v8.0

WinPack 32 is a file compression utility that supports ZIP, GZIP, TAR, ARJ, UUEncode and UUDecode, and BinHex files. WinPack 32 has a Windows 95 Explorer-type interface with Toolhelp bubbles, support for long file names, and a dockable toolbar.

File name: WINPACK\WPACK32D.EXE

> Randy Snow
> Retrospect
> 2115 Industrial Drive
> Altus, OK 73521
> CompuServe: **71540,1240**
> America Online: **RSNOW1**
> Microsoft Network: **RETROSPECT**
> Internet: **snow@retrospect.com**
> Phone: (405) 482-0672
> Fax: (405) 482-0284

WinZip 6.0

Have you ever used the Internet, a BBS, or CompuServe? If so, you've probably encountered ZIP files. Are you a Windows user? If so, WinZip is a great way to handle these archived files. WinZip brings the convenience of Windows to the use of ZIP files without requiring PKZIP and PKUNZIP. It features built-in support for popular Internet file formats, including TAR, GZIP, and UNIX compress. ARJ, LZH, and ARC files are supported by using external programs.WinZip 6.0 for Windows 95 features long file name support and tight integration with the Windows 95 shell, including the capability to zip and unzip without leaving the Explorer.

File name: WINZIP95\SETUP.EXE

> Niko Mak Computing
> P.O. Box 919
> Bristol, CT 06011
> CompuServe: **70056,241**

Zip Tip Demo

Zip Tip provides a tool to add "Tip of the Day" items to any Windows program. To use Zip Tip, software developers create a text file containing a list of tips (up to 2,000 characters long) pertaining to their application. The file can be created using any word processor. Zip Tip is then launched from within the developer's application, similar to the way in which WinHelp is executed when the user requests Help. A dialog box appears with the Tip of the Day showing. Each time the application is started, a new Tip of the Day appears.

File name: ZIPTIP\ZTDEMO.EXE

> Responsive Software
> 1901 Tunnel Road
> Berkeley, CA 94705
> CompuServe: **76367,3673**
> Phone: (510) 843-1034
> Fax: (510) 644-1013

Index

Symbols

\SETUP command
  DOS, 41
  switches, 42-43, 72-73
  Windows 3.x, 41
16-bit applications, 366, 368, 693
  cooperative multitasking, 369
  executing, 395-396
  execution environment, 370-371
  General Protection Faults, 401-402
  hung, 402-403
  INI files, removing, 398-399
  installing, 394-395
  messaging system, 370
  property sheets, 396-397
  Windows 95 performance, 399-401
3.5-inch disk drives, 526-527
32-bit applications, 366, 368, 693
  execution environment, 370-371
  messaging system, 370
  multi-threaded processing, 406
  preemptive multitasking, 369, 406
  Registry, 407
    data files, 407-408
    Registry Editor, 408-410
  speed, 405-406
  system files, 407
  troubleshooting, 697-699
32-bit protected-mode clients, 143-144

32-bit protected-mode components, 127
5.25-inch disk drives, 526-527
80386 processors, 20
80486 processors, 21

A

accessibility options, 108-110
  Automatic Reset option, 110
  High Contrast display option, 109
  keyboard configuration
    FilterKeys option, 109
    StickyKeys option, 109
    ToggleKeys option, 109
  mouse configuration, 110
  notification option, 110
  SerialKeys systems, 110
  sound configuration
    ShowSounds option, 109
    SoundSentry option, 109
Accessories
  Briefcase, 96-97, 111
  Calculator, 111
  Character Map, 111
  Clipboard Viewer, 111
  Document Templates, 111
  games, 111
  mouse pointers, 111
  Net Watcher, 111
  Online User's Guide, 111
  Paint program, 112
  Quick View, installing, 112
  screen savers
    changing, 161-162
    default installation, 112
    turning off, 31-32

  System Monitor
    installing, 112
    Windows 3.x application performance, 400
  System Resource Meter, 113
  wallpaper, 111
    centering, 159
    changing, 157-159
    custom, 160
    previewing, 159
  Windows 95 Tour, 113
  WinPopup, 113
  WordPad, 113-114
Add a Fax Modem dialog box, 261-262
Add Font dialog box, 171
Add Language dialog box, 507-508
Add New Hardware Wizard, 37, 421-422
  CD-ROM drives, 513-517
    autodetection, 517-519
    manual identification, 519-521
  game cards, 471-473
    autodetection, 473-474
    manual identification, 474-476
  hard drives
    autodetection, 554-555
    manual identification, 555-557
  keyboards, 497-502
    autodetection, 498, 501-502
    manual identification, 502
  MIDI interface cards, 454-459

Volume Control feature, 119,
199-200, 447
VT52 emulation, 268
VT100 emulation, 268

W-X-Y-Z

WAIS (Wide Area Information
Server), 291
wallpaper
custom Setup, 111
Desktop Themes, 667
installing additional files,
159
properties, 157
centering, 159
changing, 157-159
custom, 160
previewing, 159
tiling, 159
warm docking, 14
Welcome screen
Setup program, 43-45, 73-76
portable computers,
76-86
Windows 95, 62
portable computers,
92-93
What's This? feature, 545
WIN.INI files, 55, 85-86
WinCIM software
(CompuServe)
installing, 279-280
signing off, 282
signing on, 281
using access numbers,
280-281
WinCOMM PRO
communications program,
274
windows, full-window drag
feature (Microsoft Plus!), 29
Windows 3.x
applications
executing, 395-396
General Protection Faults,
401-402
hung, 402-403
INI files, removing,
398-399
installing, 394-395
property sheets, 396-397
Windows 95
performance, 399-401
boot disks, 30

dual-boot configuration,
37-38
INI files, 12, 398-399
installing Windows 95 over,
46-47
portable computers,
77-78
keeping separate from
Windows 95, 47
portable computers,
77-78
Setup program, starting
from, 40-41
portable computers, 71
swap files, 25
deleting, 32
troubleshooting installation
from, 696-697
upgrading from, 22, 34
utilities, 345
workstation installation, 142
Windows 95
applications
multitasking, 369-370,
406
multi-threaded
processing, 406
Registry, 407-410
speed, 405-406
system files, 407
troubleshooting, 697-699
architecture, 366
execution environment,
370-371
file systems, 410-411
CDFS, 411
long file names, 412-413
Network Redirector, 412
properties, 414-415
troubleshooting, 415-416
VFAT, 411
messaging system, 370
multitasking, 369-370, 406
Norton Disk Doctor checks,
341-342
Pre-Installation TuneUp
(Norton Utilities), 340-341
requirements, 19-22
Safe Mode, 63-65
portable computers,
93-96
Setup Wizard, 45-46
Change Directory screen,
47, 77-78
Choose Directory screen,
46-47, 77

Preparing Directory
screen, 47-48, 78
Product Information
screen, 48-50, 80
Setup Options screen, 48,
78
User Information screen,
48, 79-80
shutting down, 62-63
portable computers, 93
Startup disks
creating, 66
portable computers, 96
using, 65-66
system files, 22
testing Setup, 62-63
portable computers, 93
troubleshooting installation,
679-680
uninstalling, 55, 66-67, 684
from MS-DOS, 66-67
updating installations, 37
virtual machines, 366-368
Welcome screen, 62
portable computers,
92-93
Windows 3.x applications
performance, 399-401
Windows NT dual boot, 19
Windows 95 Resource Kit
Deployment Planning
Guide, 125
setup scripts help, 131
Windows 95 Tour, installing,
113
Windows NT
DOS requirement, 19
dual boot with
Windows 95, 19
hard drive partitions, 550
long file names, 413
multitasking, 370
networks, 126, 132
NTFS system, 23
WINDOWS/MEDIA folder, 192
WINIPCFG configuration
utility, 317
WinPopup, 113
wizards
Add New Hardware Wizard,
421-422
automatic detection of
devices, 442-443
CD-ROM drives, 513-521
game cards, 471-476
hard drives, 554-557

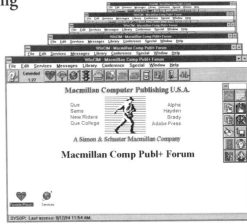

Complete and Return this Card
for a *FREE* Computer Book Catalog

Thank you for purchasing this book! You have purchased a superior computer book written expressly for your needs. To continue to provide the kind of up-to-date, pertinent coverage you've come to expect from us, we need to hear from you. Please take a minute to complete and return this self-addressed, postage-paid form. In return, we'll send you a free catalog of all our computer books on topics ranging from word processing to programming and the internet.

Mr. ☐   Mrs. ☐   Ms. ☐   Dr. ☐

Name (first) ☐☐☐☐☐☐☐☐☐☐☐ (M.I.) ☐ (last) ☐☐☐☐☐☐☐☐☐☐☐☐☐☐☐☐☐

Address ☐☐☐☐☐☐☐☐☐☐☐☐☐☐☐☐☐☐☐☐☐☐☐☐☐☐☐☐☐☐☐☐☐☐☐☐☐

City ☐☐☐☐☐☐☐☐☐☐☐☐☐☐☐☐☐ State ☐☐ Zip ☐☐☐☐☐ ☐☐☐☐

Phone ☐☐☐ ☐☐☐☐ Fax ☐☐☐ ☐☐☐ ☐☐☐☐

Company Name ☐☐☐☐☐☐☐☐☐☐☐☐☐☐☐☐☐☐☐☐☐☐☐☐☐☐☐☐☐

E-mail address ☐☐☐☐☐☐☐☐☐☐☐☐☐☐☐☐☐☐☐☐☐☐☐☐☐☐☐☐☐☐☐

1. Please check at least (3) influencing factors for purchasing this book.

Front or back cover information on book .... ☐
Special approach to the content .... ☐
Completeness of content .... ☐
Author's reputation .... ☐
Publisher's reputation .... ☐
Book cover design or layout .... ☐
Index or table of contents of book .... ☐
Price of book .... ☐
Special effects, graphics, illustrations .... ☐
Other (Please specify): _____ ☐

2. How did you first learn about this book?

Saw in Macmillan Computer Publishing catalog .... ☐
Recommended by store personnel .... ☐
Saw the book on bookshelf at store .... ☐
Recommended by a friend .... ☐
Received advertisement in the mail .... ☐
Saw an advertisement in: _____ ☐
Read book review in: _____ ☐
Other (Please specify): _____ ☐

3. How many computer books have you purchased in the last six months?

This book only .... ☐   3 to 5 books...................... ☐
2 books .... ☐   More than 5 .... ☐

4. Where did you purchase this book?

Bookstore .... ☐
Computer Store .... ☐
Consumer Electronics Store .... ☐
Department Store .... ☐
Office Club .... ☐
Warehouse Club .... ☐
Mail Order .... ☐
Direct from Publisher .... ☐
Internet site .... ☐
Other (Please specify): _____ ☐

5. How long have you been using a computer?

☐ Less than 6 months   ☐ 6 months to a year
☐ 1 to 3 years   ☐ More than 3 years

6. What is your level of experience with personal computers and with the subject of this book?

	With PCs	With subject of book
New	☐	☐
Casual	☐	☐
Accomplished	☐	☐
Expert	☐	☐

Source Code ISBN: 1-7897-0580-X

7. Which of the following best describes your job title?

Administrative Assistant ☐
Coordinator ☐
Manager/Supervisor ☐
Director ☐
Vice President ☐
President/CEO/COO ☐
Lawyer/Doctor/Medical Professional ☐
Teacher/Educator/Trainer ☐
Engineer/Technician ☐
Consultant ☐
Not employed/Student/Retired ☐
Other (Please specify): _____ ☐

8. Which of the following best describes the area of the company your job title falls under?

Accounting ☐
Engineering ☐
Manufacturing ☐
Operations ☐
Marketing ☐
Sales ☐
Other (Please specify): _____ ☐

9. What is your age?

Under 20 ☐
21-29 ☐
30-39 ☐
40-49 ☐
50-59 ☐
60-over ☐

10. Are you:

Male ☐
Female ☐

11. Which computer publications do you read regularly? (Please list)

_____
_____
_____
_____
_____
_____
_____
_____
_____

Comments: _____
_____
_____

Fold here and scotch-tape to mail.

FIRST-CLASS MAIL PERMIT NO. 9918 INDIANAPOLIS IN

POSTAGE WILL BE PAID BY THE ADDRESSEE

ATTN MARKETING
MACMILLAN COMPUTER PUBLISHING
MACMILLAN PUBLISHING USA
201 W 103RD ST
INDIANAPOLIS IN 46209-9042

NO POSTAGE
NECESSARY
IF MAILED
IN THE
UNITED STATES